THE SOUTHWESTERN JOURNALS
OF ADOLPH F. BANDELIER

1885–1888

The Southwestern Journals of Adolph F. Bandelier 1885-1888

EDITED AND ANNOTATED BY

CHARLES H. LANGE,
CARROLL L. RILEY,
AND
ELIZABETH M. LANGE

THE UNIVERSITY OF NEW MEXICO PRESS
Albuquerque
THE SCHOOL OF AMERICAN RESEARCH
Santa Fe

ACKNOWLEDGMENT IS MADE TO

EDGAR L. HEWETT
Founding Director of the School of American Research
and the Museum of New Mexico
who encouraged publication of the Bandelier Journals
and
WAYNE L. MAUZY

Formerly Acting Director of the School of American Research
and Director of the Museum of New Mexico
who initiated editorial and financial arrangements
which brought publication to fruition

Manufactured in the United States of America

Library of Congress Catalog Card No. 65-17862
First edition

CONTENTS

ILLUSTRATIONS

All photographs courtesy of the Museum of New Mexico.

DRAWINGS

From original sketches in Bandelier's journal

PREFACE

THE PRESENT VOLUME is the third in our project to publish the Southwestern portions of the Adolph F. Bandelier journals. These journals were begun in the year 1880 and were continued on a more or less daily basis; they documented Bandelier's adventures in the Southwest, in Mexico, and in South America for almost a quarter century. After his death in 1914, the journals passed to his second wife and fellow scholar, Fanny R. Bandelier, who at one time intended to edit and publish them in three volumes (Hodge 1932: 370; see also Hobbs 1940b: 122). In addition, there was once a plan by Mrs. Bandelier to publish the journals of the years 1886–89, the period in which her husband had served as "Historiographer with the Hemenway Southwestern Archaeological Expedition." There were to be notes by Fanny R. Bandelier and an introduction by Mary Austin. The volume was described as "An Intimate Glimpse into his daily life with its weal and woe." A prospectus of four pages was issued by The Press of the Pioneers, Inc., New York, carrying a date of 1934. The final page contained an "Appreciation" by Warren King Moorehead.

> Adolph Bandelier's Journals should be of great interest to students of Southwest history and archaeology, as well as to the general public. Bandelier was our first Southwest historian and archaeologist, methodical, accurate and one who caught the spirit of the Pueblo–Cliff Dweller country.
>
> Some of those who have since labored in the same field have not accorded Bandelier the praise he deserves. Both Cushing and Bandelier were true pioneers in effective

research. Neither enjoyed the advantages which today accrue to explorers in the Painted Desert Land.

I have felt for many years both history and archaeology are deeply indebted to Bandelier. It is gratifying to know that his intimate record of travels and privations is now to be presented to the American public in an adequate way.

We have benefited, particularly in the preparation of this third volume, from the typescript prepared by Fanny R. Bandelier;[1] all entries were, however, checked against the original journal entries to assure completeness and accuracy. Interestingly, the greatest discrepancies occurred in the omission by Fanny of numerous comments in which Bandelier criticized family members.

The journals were later willed to the Laboratory of Anthropology, School of American Research, Santa Fe, New Mexico. At present, the original journals—mainly handwritten—are among the collections in the Library, Museum of New Mexico, Santa Fe.[2]

A major difficulty in bringing these journals to the public in published form has been the problem of basic editorial policy. Suggestions have ranged from publishing verbatim to extracting only certain data—ethnological, for example—and presenting them with extensive commentary. In editing the Southwestern portions of these journals (1880–92), we have attempted to steer a middle course between these extremes.

The journals contain day-by-day records of Bandelier's activities, having served as both field notebooks and diaries. Their range is amazing; Bandelier was interested in almost everything about him and a particular day's journal may contain information of interest to anthropologists, biographers, botanists, folklorists, geographers, geologists, historians, and zoologists. Some entries have considerable literary quality; others are written in such a cursory manner that phrases or even single words make up the entire record. Often, especially in the early years, Bandelier's Continental European background comes to light in the peculiar wording and complicated structure of his sentences. That he was, himself, aware of these shortcomings is shown by the following excerpt from a letter to Lewis H. Morgan, dated January 29–31, 1876 (White 1940: I, 260):

> There is in my way a great difficulty, which, however, I shall most assuredly overcome; the Spanish idiom is a foreign tongue, although it suits my taste & inclination better than any other,—and the English language, with all my efforts, still remains equally foreign to me. I have, therefore, to translate from one foreign idiom into another.

It is perfectly obvious that Bandelier never intended his journals for publication. Certain parts of them, much modified, later served as the basis for published material (*Final Report, Islands of Lake Titicaca and Koati, Documentary History of Zuñi*, etc.). The most striking feature of the journals, however, is the candid, personal nature of many observations. Not only were field data given with on-the-spot comments, but Bandelier had much to say about the people around him, whether Indian informants, colleagues, friends, or relatives. We see, through Bandelier's eyes, the daily activities, virtues, and faults of a great many people—some famous, others known primarily from the journals themselves. The journals, thus, provide vignettes that are especially valuable to anyone interested in the Southwest. Bandelier's often pungent opinions and criticisms must be taken for what they really were, one man's private comment on, and immediate reaction to, life about him.

In the edited journals, there is considerable annotation. This includes identification of historical figures and places, discussions of ethnographic data, archaeological correlations, etc. If no footnote is given for particular ethnographic information fully accepted by Bandelier, these data, in our opinion, were probably valid for Bandelier's time (in fact, descriptions of everyday life, religious ceremonies, political structure, and social relationships often apply almost equally today). On the other hand, Bandelier's interpretations and reactions often reveal a lack of sophistication, common to his day, in the social sciences.

As a matter of editorial policy, the following modifications in the original Bandelier journal entries have been made.

1. Certain types of entries—incidental information relating to the weather, occasional descriptions of background scenery, and unimportant calculations of elevations and distance—have been deleted entirely with no indication given. Bandelier regularly

started each day's entry with weather data and occasionally interspersed additional comments later in the day.[3] When these serve no practical value, they have been deleted. Where weather conditions were pertinent to the day's activities, the comments have been retained. This policy applies to certain scenic descriptions as well. For example, the skyline of the Sandia Mountains has not changed in the past century, and incidental, out-of-context references to it are not really informative. The deletions are not indicated in the text, in part because such interruptions reduce readability. In addition, the rather haphazard way in which weather and other comments are introduced makes such deletion indicators as ellipses occasionally misleading. For example, Bandelier wrote on March 28, 1882, "Went to Governor Ritch at night. He was exceedingly kind with me. Made some confidential communications" (Lange and Riley 1966: 245). This was followed immediately by a comment on the weather with no subsequent indication ever as to the nature of the confidences. Ellipses at such a point would very likely mislead the reader into thinking that the editors had withheld sensitive material. We stress here that no such censorship has taken place at any point in the journals.

2. A number of sketches found in the original journals are not included in the published version. These are drawings of skylines, plots of fields, ground plans of pueblos, or maps of ruins, some of which were later published in the *Final Report* or elsewhere. We recognize, however, that certain sketches might have particularistic value to specialists, and so we have indicated with an asterisk(*) each point at which a sketch has been deleted. Such sketches, together with various measurements and azimuths, often give the illusion of considerable precision on Bandelier's part. In reality, these data were frequently so incomplete, or lacking in necessary base points, as to make them unusable.[4]

3. Certain types of entries have been deleted in their entirety from the present volume. In such cases, specific notations as to the nature of the content have been inserted. In the first two volumes, such omissions included notations on various archival materials. They were not included on the premise that the originals, having been identified and located, could be consulted or had in the meantime been included in some publication. We have subsequently been made aware that there are instances in

which neither of these premises is true and Bandelier's journal notes constitute the only surviving remnant of such materials. Hence, we have retained enough of these entries, with or without translation, so that the interested reader can determine for himself if the item warrants independent examination of the original typescript or archival collection.

4. A special problem exists in the spelling of certain Indian names. Many spellings used by Bandelier have since been changed—for example, we now use Tewa for Tehua, Keres for Queres, Tiwa for Tihua, Zia for Cia. In these cases, we have shown the modern spelling at the first appearance of the term and subsequently followed Bandelier's usage. In certain cases where Bandelier varied (e.g., Queres, QQueres, Qqueres), we have retained only the most favored spelling.

5. Except for place names and various familiar terms, foreign words and phrases are accompanied by translations in the text, usually at their first appearance only. In addition, a glossary of Spanish terms is included in each volume for the convenience of the reader. Entries in a foreign language of two lines or more are presented only in English, such translations being noted.

6. A few observations, recorded lineally by Bandelier, have been rearranged in chart form for greater convenience.

7. The variable dating styles used by Bandelier have been slightly modified. Such usages as "24 Oct. '80," and other forms, have been standardized, e.g., "October 24."

8. The chaotic punctuation used by Bandelier has been somewhat modified to fit modern usage. Along these same lines, there have been occasional minor changes in sentence structure for purposes of clarity. Paragraph breaks are primarily those of the present editors. The use of italics (for unfamiliar Indian terms and some foreign phrases) is simply an editing policy. Bandelier, himself, was not consistent in handling these terms.

In a number of entries, or in notes concerning them, the mention of an archaeological site may be accompanied by a notation (L.A. ——); this refers to the New Mexico catalogue of archaeological sites maintained by the Laboratory of Anthropology, Museum of New Mexico, Santa Fe. In addition to the designation L.A. and distinctive number, data on the precise location, nature of the remains, analysis of surface potsherds, etc., are included in the catalogue.

In preparation for the editing and annotating of the 1885–88 journals, we have worked in both the Highland, Illinois, and the St. Louis, Missouri, areas. The research on these journals, like those of 1880–82 and 1883–84, has also necessitated much travel in the Southwest. One or more of us worked in Albuquerque, Santa Fe, Phoenix, and Tucson, and traveled through much of the Rio Grande Valley of New Mexico, both sides of the New Mexico–Arizona line, southern Arizona, southwestern New Mexico, and northern Mexico. These travels were of great benefit. In addition, newspaper files and similar materials have been most valuable in elaborating upon the cultural context of Bandelier's work in the last quarter of the nineteenth century. In this regard, we have been gratified to find the extent to which it is possible to recapture Bandelier's time and to supplement significantly his mere mentions of many individuals, frequently the "little people" so often bypassed by the mainstream of history.

Originally, it was the editors' aim to present each volume of *The Southwestern Journals of Adolph F. Bandelier* as a self-contained unit. The first volume included an extended introductory sketch of Bandelier's life (Lange and Riley 1966: 1–67); it was intended that subsequent volumes would have similar, but abbreviated, sketches—each to provide adequate context for the journal entries of the particular volume. However, since the completion of the first manuscript almost ten years ago, publication costs have risen to the point that such extensive duplication of data has become impractical. Accordingly, our initial plan has been modified. In the interest of economy, this volume's Introduction (the biographical sketch), like that of the second volume, has been reduced to a minimum. The reader is alerted to certain corrections that were presented in the Preface and Introduction of the second volume (Lange and Riley 1970: xiii–xv, 1–7); these should be followed rather than the conflicting family data contained in the first volume (Lange and Riley 1966: 1–67).

Rising publication costs have also restricted our use of material from the earlier volumes in notes of the present volume. However, we have adopted a variable policy with the prime purpose of assisting the reader. Some few data have been repeated verbatim; others have been modified or condensed in being integrated with new data; some references have been merely cited; and others, of only limited relevance, have not been used at all. The interested reader is advised to resort to the index of each volume to assure finding as complete data as are available on a particular item.

However, it should be pointed out that in our first two volumes (1966 and 1970), we elected to omit Bandelier's sometimes copious notes on various archival materials on the premise that the originals were otherwise available, either in some archive or in print. Subsequent research and especially discussions with other researchers have convinced us that Bandelier's journal notes, in at least some instances, are the only existing data. Accordingly, we have modified the policy followed in our first two volumes, and we have retained sufficient information to enable the interested reader to locate the item in question so that it may be worked with in toto and verbatim.

Anticipating at least some new data as research progresses relative to the remaining journal entries, we will continue to make corrections or modifications as the evidence dictates, clearly indicating any such changes in the appropriate notes.

ACKNOWLEDGMENTS

AS WE CARRY on with this multivolume project, our indebtedness grows in respect to those who have continued to assist us and also in respect to those who have become newly involved. In numerous cases, acknowledgments expressed in either or both of our first two volumes apply with equal weight to the assistance rendered in the preparation of this third volume.

The following individuals, previously mentioned, deserve further recognition for their significant contributions to the present volume: Dr. A. J. O. Anderson, Mr. George E. Bandelier, Dr. Christa Bausch, Mrs. Kirk Bryan, Father Ernest J. Burrus, S. J., Dr. John M. Corbett, Father Lowrie J. Daly, S. J., Dr. Bertha P. Dutton, Professor Fred Eggan, Mr. Bruce T. Ellis, Mrs. Hulda Hobbs Heidel, Mr. Alden C. Hayes, Susie Henderson, Professor W. W. Hill, Dr. Myra Ellen Jenkins, Professor Harvey Huegy, Professor J. Charles Kelley, Mrs. Marjorie F. Lambert, Mrs. R. L. Ormsbee, the late Miss E. Margaret Patton, Mr. Stewart L. Peckham, and Mrs. J. K. Shishkin.

In addition, we express our deep appreciation to the following persons, whose aid has greatly enriched and strengthened our notes and general perspective: Dr. John C. Abbott and Dr. Theodore R. Frisbie, Southern Illinois University—Edwardsville; Professor James H. Gunnerson, Professor Benjamin Keen, Dr. Dolores A. Gunnerson, and Mr. Matt T. Salo, Northern Illinois University; Professor A. W. Bork and Professor Campbell W. Pennington, Southern Illinois University—Carbondale; Professor Leslie A. White, University of Michigan; Dr. John P. Wilson, Museum of New Mexico; Miss Margaret Currier, Librarian, and Mrs. Katherine B. Edsall, Archivist, Peabody Museum Library,

Harvard University; Mrs. Elizabeth Kirchner, Head Librarian, Mercantile Library, St. Louis; Mrs. Carla Lange, Librarian, Missouri Botanical Garden, St. Louis; Professor Florence Hawley Ellis, University of New Mexico; Mrs. Mary Blumenthal, Librarian, Clinton P. Anderson Library, University of New Mexico; Mr. Martin G. Ruoss and Mr. Rex C. Hopson, Librarians, Special Collections, University of New Mexico; Fray Angelico Chavez, O. F. M., Peña Blanca; the late Dr. Edward P. Dozier, University of Arizona; Dr. Alfonso Ortiz, Princeton University; Mr. Albert H. Schroeder and Mr. Charlie R. Steen, National Park Service, Santa Fe; Mr. Byron Harvey III, Museum of the American Indian, New York; Mrs. Spencer C. Browne, Berkeley, California; Mrs. Rebecca B. Colligan, Laguna Hills, California; Mr. Louis H. Connell, Gulfport, Florida; Mrs. Evelyn C. Frey, Frijoles Canyon Lodge; and Mr. Ernst H. Blumenthal, Jr., Albuquerque.

Special thanks go to Dr. Ignacio Bernal for permission to utilize various of the García Icazbalceta correspondence edited by him and Professor White. Valuable assistance in translations has been cheerfully rendered by Miss Jan Faust, Dr. Benjamin Jegers, and Professor Marvin S. Schindler, Northern Illinois University, and by Miss Marie M. Doenges, Dr. Basil C. Hedrick, Dr. Joan O'-Brien, Miss Luz Maria Pelaez, and Dr. Charles Speck of Southern Illinois University—Carbondale. Glossary items have been improved with the aid of Professor Eleanor B. Adams and Professor Reuben Cobos of the University of New Mexico and Dr. Jon L. Kessel of the National Park Service. Professors John M. Campbell and W. James Judge were most helpful in providing office space for one of us during a stay in Albuquerque in 1971.

From administrators at our respective institutions, we have received encouraging support: Dr. Kenneth L. Beasley and Dr. Ronald G. Hansen, Associate Deans for Research at NIU and SIU —Carbondale, respectively. For arranging crucial financial assistance in publication costs, we thank Dean Paul S. Burtness and Associate Dean Larry R. Sill, College of Liberal Arts and Sciences, and Provost Richard C. Bowers, NIU, and former Executive Vice President and Provost Willis E. Malone, SIU—Carbondale. Finally, additional financial aid was generously provided by the School of American Research, Santa Fe, for which we express our sincere appreciation to Dr. Douglas W. Schwartz, Director.

For typing, proofreading, and other editorial aspects of preparing the manuscript, we are much indebted to the collective efforts of Miss Jan Faust, Mrs. Gail E. Shoemaker, Miss Diane Rothman, Miss Sue DiNardo, Mrs. Christine Welch, Miss Denise Mazer, and Miss Anita Mozga, NIU, and Mrs. D. Kathleen Abbass, Mrs. Jan Chappell, and Miss Theresa Page, SIU—Carbondale.

Our special thanks go the National Endowment for the Humanities, whose grant No. H67–0–62 contributed to the furtherance of this project.

July 1973
Charles H. Lange
Carroll L. Riley
Elizabeth M. Lange

INTRODUCTION

THIS BIOGRAPHICAL SKETCH of Adolph F. Bandelier is intended primarily as background and context for his 1885–88 journals. In the longer account of Bandelier's life presented in our first volume (Lange and Riley 1966: 1–67), we relied rather heavily upon Goad (1939).

Subsequent reexamination of several works and utilization of additional sources, however, as noted in the Introduction of our second volume (1970: 1), provided an appreciable increase in data, gave deeper insights into the life of Bandelier and his relationships with various contemporaries, and also furnished the basis for important corrections detailed in the Preface to our second volume (pp. xiv–xv).

The editorial data, including the Introduction, for this third volume have been prepared with not only these aforementioned sources at hand, but with a number of significant additional materials. Briefly summarized, these materials included items from the Hemenway files at Peabody Museum Archives and Library, Harvard University, the Mercantile Library in St. Louis, the Bandelier Collection and other files at the Museum of New Mexico, the Catron Collection in Special Collections of the University of New Mexico Library, and the Newberry Library (Ayer Collection, especially) in Chicago.

Adolph Francis Alphonse Bandelier was born in Bern, Switzerland, on August 6, 1840. His father, Adolphe Eugene, was a business or professional man with wide scholarly interests, a fact that was to have considerable effect on Bandelier's young life. A few years after Adolph's birth, the elder Bandelier, as political winds shifted, decided to improve family fortunes by establishing a new life abroad. After a brief, disappointing visit in 1847 to Brazil, he settled the following year in the small Swiss community of Highland, Illinois, thirty miles east of St. Louis, Missouri, having been attracted there by the publicity engendered by the writings of the Köpflis (Kaspar Köpfli 1833; Salomon Köpfli 1842; Kaeser 1970).

Later in 1848, Bandelier's father was joined by his wife, Marie Senn Bandelier, his son, and the family maid, Annali Näfiger (Hobbs 1940a), and a new home was established in Highland. According to Brink's *History* (1882: 432), "The Home Government of Switzerland, remembering the sterling qualities of this man [A. E. Bandelier], made him consul of that Republic at an early date; his consulate embraced not only the Mississippi valley to New Orleans, but extended southeast to the Carolinas." A. E. Bandelier, in 1854, joined with two other Swiss immigrants, Frederick C. Ryhiner, a physician, and Moritz Huegy, in the founding of a bank, the F. Ryhiner & Co. They had financial backing from Gruner-Haller and Co. of Bern.

In 1855, Bandelier's mother died, and Annali stayed on to assist the family. Adolph, an only child, probably attended public school, but his education was seemingly more the result of tutoring in languages and a variety of other subjects by his father and others (Brink 1882: 432). The Biographical Publishing Co.'s account (1894: 162) added that Timothy Gruaz, in 1853, "was employed as a private teacher in the home of Adolph [Adolphe E.] Bandelier, . . ." Brink (1882: 436) confirmed Gruaz as a teacher in the Bandelier home. The family spoke German in the home, as did many in the community, and efforts were also made to instruct young Adolph in correct French. Hobbs (1940a) credited the senior Bandelier with stimulating the spirit of scientific inquiry in his son in childhood. Like his father, Adolph F. was active in numerous civic affairs such as the rifle club and the Turnverein, showing particular interest in the intellectual life of Highland.

In his scholarly interests, it is evident that Bandelier was influenced by the scientific work of Baron Alexander von Humboldt; the two were said to have corresponded and may have met in the late 1850s. Earlier biographers, including the present editors (1966: 9) citing Hodge (1932: 353), have stated that Bandelier studied geology in 1857 in Bern under Professor B. Studer and also that he studied law at Bern between 1865 and 1867. However, White (1940: I, 5n3, 5n4) presented data supported by subsequent research by Charles Gallenkamp (personal correspondence) which clearly indicated that the Studer episode was incorrect and that it was another Bandelier, probably a cousin, who had studied law at Bern. (See also Burrus 1969b: 18n34.)

On January 5, 1862, Bandelier married Josephine ("Joe") Huegy, the daughter of one of his father's banking partners. During the 1860s, Bandelier published a number of articles of a climatological nature in the local newspapers and served as a recorder of these data for the Smithsonian Institution in Washington, D. C. He also lectured, locally and in St. Louis, on a wide range of archaeological and historical subjects.

In the early 1870s, Bandelier's life changed significantly. He had been active, for a number of years, in assorted business affairs, a coal mine, a foundry, and other ventures, including some affiliation with the F. Ryhiner & Co. bank. Gradually, however, his interest in the business world declined, probably in part due to his father's domineering and often difficult personality. At this time, Bandelier's scholarly activities and achievements increased.

In 1873, he began to work on Spanish documentary sources for native Mesoamerica, teaching himself Spanish. That same year, he met Lewis Henry Morgan, a leading figure in American anthropology, who, in that period, was developing his famous theories on the evolution of human culture. A concomitant of Morgan's evolutionary reconstruction was the thesis that the American Indians had never progessed beyond the level of tribal social and political organization. Bandelier rapidly became a disciple of Morgan and an advocate of his ideas. In the years after first meeting Morgan, he spent much of his research energies attempting to demonstrate that the Aztecs of Mexico had not attained a level of civilization, as claimed by some, but had achieved only a tribal-based barbarism. The intellectual development of Bandelier under Morgan and their interrelationships have been covered most competently by White (1940).

By the late 1870s, Bandelier had become a respected scholar, having published several monographs on ancient Mexican culture. In these writings and in his reviews of the works of others, he championed thorough and rigid standards of research and revealed a readiness to criticize those who failed to show similar standards in their research. Bandelier was elected to membership in the American Association for the Advancement of Science in August 1876. Parenthetically, in November 1877, he became a naturalized citizen of the United States.

Although he maintained a sincere interest in Mexico, Bandelier's first fieldwork was not in Mexico but in the American Southwest. In the latter half of 1880, thanks largely to Morgan's influence, Bandelier was sent to New Mexico by the newly formed Archaeological Institute of America, Boston; Charles Eliot Norton, the president, and Francis Parkman were prominent and influential members of the Executive Committee. Leaving St. Louis by railroad, Bandelier arrived in Santa Fe on the evening of August 23, 1880.

It is appropriate to comment here that Bandelier embarked upon his fieldwork at an opportune moment in Southwestern history. Mining activities were attracting numbers of individuals into remote areas; military personnel, merchants, ranchers, and others, aided by the gradual expansion of railway and telegraph services, were increasingly active. Many of these people stood ready to facilitate his work, providing local information and then passing Bandelier on to friends or acquaintances elsewhere who could similarly assist him.

Bandelier quickly gained the friendship and interest of the Archbishop, John B. Lamy, and of other churchmen, both archivists and parish priests. He sought out the territorial officials, including Samuel Ellison, librarian, who had formerly been at Peña Blanca, some miles southwest of Santa Fe. Bandelier spent a few days investigating the archaeological remains at the rather recently abandoned pueblo of Pecos, some twenty miles southeast of Santa Fe. Journal entries of that period clearly reflected his great enthusiasm and boundless energy as he entered this initial period of active field investigations.

Perhaps through Ellison, Bandelier had formed the acquaintance of Father José Rómulo Ribera of Peña Blanca prior to his Pecos trip. Upon his return from Pecos, he accepted Ribera's invitation, which, in effect, diverted him from earlier plans and suddenly launched his ethnographic field experience among the Pueblo Indians. He spent a fascinating, but nonetheless nerve-racking, week at the ultraconservative pueblo of Santo Domingo, on the Rio Grande a few miles south of Peña Blanca.

Frustrated in his efforts at Santo Domingo, Bandelier soon shifted a few miles northward to the pueblo of Cochiti, where his reception was much more hospitable, allowing him to begin an ethnographic study. During the autumn of 1880, the Cochiti not only talked with him but guided him to nearby Frijoles Canyon and its prehistoric remains; Bandelier's enchantment with the area was immediate and the Rito de los Frijoles and environs continued to be a favorite area throughout his life. (The area was designated Bandelier National Monument on February 11, 1916, by President Woodrow Wilson.)

Bandelier returned to Highland and his family in time for Christmas, 1880; at the end of that year, his journal entries continued to express his great elation. On the last day of December, he wrote, "Thus the most important year of my entire life draws to a close. Thank God, thank God for every blessing, every sore, for weal and for woe, which He has been pleased to dispense. So far, so good, and there is hope for better. . . . Have no reflections to record. Future action is all that occupies my thoughts" (Lange and Riley 1966: 236–37).

In 1881, Bandelier finally gained his long-desired opportunity to work in Mexico. However, the Lorillard–de Charney Expedition, which he was to join, had disbanded in failure by the time he arrived in Mexico. Nevertheless, Bandelier spent several months doing independent work in Oaxaca and Puebla, aided and advised by his friend, Don Joaquín García Icazbalceta. Professional recognition came to Bandelier, in absentia, when he was elected to membership in the American Antiquarian Society in April 1881. Subsequently, on July 31, an important event for Bandelier occurred in Cholula, Puebla. On that date, Bandelier became a Roman Catholic, García Icazbalceta standing as sponsor and the local priest, Dr. José Vicente Campos, officiating.

The beginning of the year 1882 found Bandelier at home in Highland, Illinois, working over his 1881 Mexican data. In March 1882, he returned to New Mexico under the auspices of the Archaeological Institute of America. During the remainder of that year and in early 1883, he engaged in extensive archaeological and ethnological studies, ranging in his travels from the Salinas region east of the Sandia-Manzano Mountains to Acoma and Zuñi.

While in the Zuñi region, Bandelier formed the acquaintance of Frank Hamilton Cushing, then living at Zuñi Pueblo; Bandelier came to be a great admirer of this unusual man. Leaving Zuñi, Bandelier worked his way west and then south to the deserts of southern Arizona. There he visited the Salado area, Casa Grande, Tucson and Fort Lowell, and Fort Huachuca, traveling through much of the Western Apache country en route.

Concerned about Joe after the false report of his death at the hands of the Apaches, Bandelier left New Mexico on July 10, 1883, and returned to Highland. Reporting on this incident to García Icazbalceta in a letter of August 6, 1883, Bandelier also commented that, "travelling alone and by horse, I have covered 1847 English miles and have traversed successfully the middle of New Mexico and the lands of Arizona" (Lange and Riley 1970: 399n345). Late in 1883, he resumed fieldwork, beginning at Isleta on October 31 and continuing down the Rio Grande Valley to Las Cruces, El Paso del Norte, Senecú, and Isleta del Sur, gathering ethnological data on the Mansos, Piros, Senecus, and Zumas and information about regional Indian ruins. At El Paso del Norte, he also examined archival records.

He returned to Santa Fe on November 10 and was in that area, with visits to San Juan Pueblo and Santa Cruz, until December 11, at which time he returned briefly to Peña Blanca. From there, he went to Socorro, Rincón, Nutt, and Fort Cummings. The beginning of 1884 found Bandelier in the Silver City–Gila Cliff Dwellings area. From there, he continued west to Tucson and Fort Lowell. In February of 1884, Bandelier carried on with the planned program of the Institute, searching for ruins in northern Sonora and crossing the Sierra Madre to extend his archaeological reconnaissance in northern Chihuahua, including the impressive remains at Casas Grandes. In Mexico, he also collected ethnographic data on the Opata and Apaches.

Reaching Deming on June 14, Bandelier went briefly to Tucson, gathering data on the Pima and Papago. He then stopped in Albuquerque and Santa Fe en route to Highland, where he arrived on July 20. With the fieldwork for the Institute completed and the termination of his salary imminent (as of January 1885), and with indications that the affairs of the bank were precarious,

Bandelier went East in September, ostensibly to arrange about his publications but also to see about business matters. He left for Europe in November, this time to arrange for the colored printing of illustrations for his research publications, and also as an agent for his father to negotiate with the Swiss creditors of the F. Ryhiner & Co. bank, the condition of which had continued to deteriorate—as had that of other financial institutions in the country at that time.

In most respects, Bandelier's trip was unsuccessful, as entries in this volume reveal. The spring following his return from Europe brought financial disaster to Highland. Overextended in its investments and refused further aid by the Swiss financiers, the F. Ryhiner & Co. bank faltered and in late April 1885 a run occurred. The elder Bandelier, the only surviving member of the original partnership, fled, first to New Orleans and then to South America, leaving his son and the two junior partners to face the irate townspeople. Bandelier's brother-in-law, Maurice Huegy, committed suicide in late May; the other partner, F. C. Ryhiner, Jr., went to Iowa (though later he offered to return). Bandelier himself was the only principal still on the scene; the fact that he seems to have been no more than an agent for his father became an irrelevant detail in the minds of the townsmen. He was arrested and taken in custody to Edwardsville, the county seat, where he spent the night in jail. Released the next day through the good offices of friends, Bandelier left for New Mexico, leaving Joe with her sister, Bertha (Mrs. Charles Lambelet), in Highland for the next several months. Bandelier never returned to Highland for any appreciable time after that.

Having lost their resources in an attempt to meet at least some of the bank's obligations, the Bandeliers found the next months difficult ones as they adjusted to a new life in Santa Fe. A novel, actually begun by Bandelier in 1883 and written in German as *Die Köshare*, was finished in May 1886; it was not published until 1890 when it appeared serially in a New York German-language newspaper. It appeared also in English the same year as *The Delight Makers;* it was not an immediate success.

Bandelier managed to sell several articles to a number of American and German publications; he also continued to gather archival and other data for his *Final Report*, which he owed the Archaeological Institute of America.

In October 1886, he was commissioned by Archbishop J. B. Salpointe of Santa Fe to write an account of the missions of the Spanish Southwest that was to be sent to Rome for presentation to Pope Leo XIII, who was to commemorate the Golden Jubilee of his priesthood on December 31, 1887, and that of his first Mass on January 1, 1888 (Burrus 1969b: 9).

Also in October 1886 (through a misprint, this date was erroneously given as 1885 in Lange and Riley 1970: 6), the Hemenway Southwestern Archaeological Expedition engaged Bandelier as historiographer, and for several years he worked on Spanish archival materials, both in this country and in Mexico. Bandelier's prime responsibility was to build an accessible archive available to the Hemenway Expedition in the Southwest, which explains his extensive copying of many books already in print and available at libraries in the East and in Mexico City. His bibliography and his scholarly recognition continued to grow in these years. (See bibliography included in this volume.) He made trips to both the living pueblos and the various archaeological sites, though there was some decrease in these activities, in both frequency and duration.

Late in 1887, Bandelier assumed a new responsibility. Father J. A. Stephan, Director of the Bureau of Catholic Indian Missions, hired him as an inspector for the Indian pueblos, primarily concerned with school matters. Bandelier was hired for a twelve-month period, beginning December 1, 1887, at $25 per month and travel expenses. In this period, Bandelier's journals took on a rather different character. Ethnographic data became rare except when he happened to meet an Indian, especially someone from either Cochiti or San Juan. Few remarks on flora, fauna, and geology were made, as he was traveling mostly over familiar ground when he did leave Santa Fe. On these trips, his principal interest shifted to documentary materials, such as the archives he found at Santa Clara Pueblo.

A major event of 1888 was the return of Bandelier's father from Venezuela. Bandelier's closing journal entry for 1888 expressed the somewhat mixed emotions that this unexpected reunion prompted: ". . . another so far fortunate year. We have succeeded in bringing Papa back, but with him we have secured a cloud in our otherwise happy sky. Well, God has so disposed, and we must take it as it comes."

After 1889, Hemenway sponsorship ceased; following an interval of several months in which numerous small projects were undertaken with but little remuneration, Bandelier was offered temporary support from the Archaeological Institute of America. This was expressly for the purpose of enabling him to complete Part II of his *Final Report* which he still owed the Institute.

As noted above, his novel *The Delight Makers,* several years in preparation, was finally published in 1890. Hopeful that it would be successful, Bandelier was disappointed at its failure to gain widespread acclaim during this initial period.

While completing the *Final Report,* Bandelier received an appointment to catalogue and translate the territorial archives. Conceived as a two-year project, the legislature authorized funding for the first year only, and then the monies were exhausted before Bandelier's contract expired. For a brief period, he was actively engaged in business matters, but an anticipated commission from a major land sale, which would have made him virtually independent and would have allowed him to continue his Southwestern research on his own time, did not materialize.

Disappointed that he had received so little recognition and also that further support which would have enabled him to remain in Santa Fe was nowhere apparent, Bandelier decided that future work would be more rewarding if done outside the Southwest. In 1892, after a January-through-April trip to New York City, Baltimore, Washington, Cincinnati, St. Louis, and Highland by Bandelier alone, he rejoined Joe in Santa Fe on May 12. On May 20, Bandelier closed his Southwestern Journals in preparation for a new phase of life and began another journal. Adolph and Joe departed for the west coast the last week in May, bidding the elder Bandelier farewell. On June 6, 1892, the Bandeliers sailed from San Francisco for South America, thus bringing the Southwestern years to a close.

In the autumn of 1892, Joe became ill in Lima, Peru, where she died on December 11. A year later, Bandelier married Fanny Ritter, a young Swiss immigrant. Together, the two did far-reaching studies in Peru and Bolivia. Although he was sent initially to South America on a collecting expedition by Henry Villard, New York financier and philanthropist, Bandelier's support later came from the American Museum of Natural History, New York. A major publication from fieldwork of this period was Bandelier's *The Islands of Titicaca and Koati.*

Returning to the United States in 1903, Bandelier kept his affiliation with the American Museum until 1906, but then, after a publishing disagreement, he moved to the Hispanic Society of America. In his years in New York City, Bandelier also lectured at Columbia University, and between 1909 and 1911 served as a staff member of the Museum of New Mexico and the School of American Archaeology (now the School of American Research) in Santa Fe, although he never returned to the Southwest.

These were active years and yet a period of decline, as Bandelier's eyes failed and his health worsened. Fanny read to him and helped him in many ways. In late 1911, he recovered his sight sufficiently to accept a research appointment with the Carnegie Institution of Washington, going with Fanny to Mexico for several months in 1912–13. In the fall of 1913, the two embarked for yet another research trip, this time to Spain, for archival work in Seville, Madrid, and Simancas.

This was the realization of a long-time aspiration—to examine the archives in Spain for additional sources bearing on New World culture history. He had recognized very early that without these sources his other work would remain incomplete. Unfortunately, Bandelier did not live to achieve his goal.

Seriously ill almost from the time of their arrival in Spain, he worked only briefly in the archives and died in Seville March 18, 1914. Fanny continued their work for several months and extracted an important collection of primary documents on the American Southwest and northern Mexico, which was later published by the Carnegie Institution, Washington (Hackett 1923; 1926; 1937).

Bandelier was first and foremost a research scientist. As the earlier journals revealed, he spent long days on the trail, in good weather and bad, often afoot and sometimes without food or shelter. His amazing stores of energy and determination made him minimize sickness, danger, and privations. Upon his move to Santa Fe in mid-1885 and with his involvement with the *Histoire* in the autumn of 1886, and his appointment as historiographer of the Hemenway Expedition shortly thereafter, Bandelier's activities shifted from field reconnaissance to archival work. Again, the tedious hours of searching for and hand copying voluminous source materials, amidst chaotic and uncatalogued collections and often with inadequate light in uncomfortable buildings, amply testify to his devotion to scholarly research.

THE JOURNALS OF ADOLPH F. BANDELIER

AT THE END of the year 1884, Adolph Bandelier was in Switzerland. Ostensibly, Bandelier's trip to Bern and Geneva was to arrange for the printing of multicolored reproductions to be included in his publications on recent fieldwork. However, the primary purpose of the trip seems to have been an effort, on behalf of the F. Ryhiner & Co. bank of Highland, Illinois, to work out satisfactory financial agreements with Gruner-Haller and Company of Bern. Another important aspect of the trip was the opportunity for Bandelier to examine various archival and museum collections pertaining to his Southwestern researches and to consult with fellow scholars. Finally, the trip gave him a chance to visit relatives and friends in Europe.

1885

JANUARY

JANUARY 1: [At Carouge, five kilometers south of Geneva] Was actually glutted with gifts. Unwell, went to bed early and slept. Card from Alphonse,[5] but no letter from home.

JANUARY 2: Felt better though weak. Called on Mrs. Friedrich and afterwards on N. [?]. Quarrelled and left. Letter from Alphonse. Determined to go to Berne [Bern] at once.

JANUARY 3: Mr. Gavard and Charles Desgranges[6] called after dinner. The latter came with us to the depot. Left at 4:48 P.M. for Berne. It is cold and disagreeable. Snow on the ground after leaving Nyon. At Berne I met Alphonse who speaks favorably on the whole. Prospects better.

JANUARY 4: Went to the Museum of Art, and saw some very handsome things there. Met Mr. Hebler[7] who was very, very friendly. After dinner I went to the "Jura" to meet Mr. Hebler and old Prof. Studer.[8] Then Mr. Hebler and I took a long walk across the "Kirchenfeld." The Alps plainly in sight, and they *are* grand, there is no mistake about it. Evening quietly with Alphonse.

JANUARY 5: Went to Berchthold Haller [of Gruner-Haller and Company] and at 12 A.M. to Mr. de Bùren.[9] The latter is very kind, and we agreed at once. In the afternoon promenaded with Mr. Hebler, then note to A. Guys[10] and a few lines home, so as to give some hope at least.

JANUARY 6: In the morning I wrote cards to Bishop Salpointe,[11] Dr. Eggert,[12] Fathers Grom[13] and Mailluchet,[14] to dear Elliott.[15] In the evening, Alphonse had received a very good letter from Joe.[16] Meeting at Mr. Hebler's; very cordial. Present, Mr. de Bùren, Hebler, Aebi,[17] Burckhard [Burckhardt][18] and Mauderli; also Alphonse, of course. Mr. Burckhard goes to Highland to examine for himself. Thank God!!!

JANUARY 7: Wrote home and Dr. Bastian.[19] In the afternoon at home and night at Mr. Burckhard's. Very cordial and satisfactory.

JANUARY 8: In the morning, called on Mr. Hebler who, after some hesitancy, loaned me *fs.* 15,000. At last, my note can be paid. Returned to Geneva, reaching there at 6:45. Adolphe[20] and Victor Mailtien met me at the depot. Everything all right here.

JANUARY 9: Spent a pleasant day. It is handsome. I mailed some purchases with Adolphe, then spent the rest of the day with him and Joseph Brun.[21] Met C. [?]. Wrote home.

JANUARY 10: At home, and in the afternoon at Mr. Desgranges. Night at home.

JANUARY 11: Rained hard. Took a walk. Returned later and went to bed early.

JANUARY 12: Received good letters from home, and one from Dr. Bastian. Note to Mr. Burckhard. In the afternoon, we went to Geneva. I spent a delicious time with C.—then returned. N. has left. Evening at home and late with Adolphe. He is an excellent and feeling boy.

JANUARY 13: Sent off invitations for the lecture of tomorrow. In the afternoon went to town with Adolphe and returned early. Snow at night. Preparing for lecture.

JANUARY 14: In the morning at home. Mr. Perruy [?] dined with us. Then went with Adolphe to the "Grand Conseil," very interesting. Upon my return, I found a card from Mr. Hassaurck. Lecture beautifully attended. Over 600 persons. Excellent people. Went to bed at midnight.

JANUARY 15: Had a long interview with the Editor of the "Carongeois" who took long notes about the lecture. Then went to the Hotel de la Poste where I met Mr. Hassaurck and Lady, and Mrs. French. Pleasant. In the afternoon I had a long interview with Dr. Gosse.[22] He describes the migration or rather filtration of the Bronze people as starting from the Caucasus in two branches. One passed north of the Black Sea to the Danube, and then up to the Schwarzwald and northern Switzerland to Berne. One, south of the Danube into Asia Minor, thence across to Greece, then up into Illyria, Italy, remaining south of the Alps, into France to the mouth of the Rhone, then up the Rhone to Geneva and southern Switzerland. The third branch followed the Wolga [Volga] to the Baltic Sea, then along it into Germany and the Rhine. Returned early and then went to writing. Wrote to Alphonse. Also home. At night, serenade was given to Brun and Jeanne. Cold.

JANUARY 16: Went to town; saw Mr. Limer[23] and Professor Miltry. Declined positively to speak at Geneva. In the afternoon took a long walk to Lancy and finally to Geneva, where I spent a few pleasant hours with C. Night at home, composing my lecture.

JANUARY 17: Early in the morning, shooting began in honor of [the] marriage. Wrote to Dr. Moore.[24] Also to Mr. Parkman.[25] Wedding began at 1:30 P.M. My lady was Miss Lucile Petitpürre [?]. Charming. Danced and spoke.

JANUARY 18: Considerably "tired"!! Still, I had to get up and go to town in the afternoon. Spent the evening with Moisé [Vautier],[26] afterwards with C. Quarrelled, as usual.

JANUARY 19: Still very tired. Day dull. Retired early and slept soon. Preparing for tomorrow.

FEBRUARY [JANUARY] 20: Ill disposed. Slept very little in the day-time. At 8 P.M., the hall was filled to overflowing. Perfect success in every respect. Moisé made me a little present in behalf of Carouge.

FEBRUARY [JANUARY] 21: Gavard took coffee with us. In the afternoon we went to Mr. Sidler, took leave of him, and of Mr. Révillior at the Museum. Spent the evening at James! Pleasant, but tired.

JANUARY 22: Called around at Hassaurck's. Prof. C. Vogt,[27] Gosse, etc. Afternoon with Adolphe at the Museum; afterwards a few hours at C. Night at home very pleasantly.

JANUARY 23: Left at 1:28 P.M. Sad and dejected, but Adolphe accompanied me to Lausanne. Here I began to cough. The separation from Adolphe was the hardest of all. Reached Neuchatel speechless, in a high fever, and with a dangerous cold. Staid there all day next, very feeble, unable to write and to walk. Coughing, spitting blood, and exceedingly weak in general. Thanks to the kind attentions of Mr. & Mrs. Haller of the Hotel des Alpes at the depot, I recovered gradually. But it was a hard attack.

JANUARY 25 AND 26: Very cold. Went to Couvet, which is covered with deep snow. Fritz is better. Spent a very agreeable time, although the cold is intense. Reached Berne on the 26th, at 6 P.M. Called on Mr. Hebler, Gruner-Haller & Co., and Mr. Aebi. Took leave everywhere at once.

JANUARY 27: Wrote from Berne in the forenoon; then left for Colmar at 1:15 P.M., arriving there at 7:12 P.M. Breisacher in a high glee over my coming. He is a splendid fellow. It is much warmer here than in Switzerland, and I feel very much relieved, although still coughing.

JANUARY 28: Spent day most nicely. Lieutenant Breisacher called at the "Deux Clis" at 10:30 A.M., and proposed a walk and afterwards a trip into the mountains to Münster. So we strolled through the quaint old little city (30,000 souls), and he showed me several very old and very interesting buildings. One church, formally used now as a magazine [store], dates from the 14th century; one house had the date 1538; another, 1648; etc. The promenades, into which the old ramparts have been transformed, are very fine. We left by rail for Münster at 11:30 P.M. What a lovely country Alsace is![28] The plain washes the very foot of the Vosges [Mountains] whose crests and summits are crowned with ruins of former castles. We passed Turkheim, and spent the day, until sunset, charmingly at Münster. Night at home with Breisacher and afterwards with Hartmann. Took leave. Day fine.

JANUARY 29: Wrote home; to Adolphe; and Alphonse. Left Colmar at 11:30 P.M.; traversed Alsace, a beautiful trip, and reached Francfort [Frankfurt a. M.] at 6:48 P.M. Cold & chilly. Was glad to get into the Hotel Landsberg. Everybody kind.

JANUARY 30: All day at the city of Francfort. Weather cloudy and chilly. Wrote home; to Alphonse; to Dr. Eggert; and to Adolphe. Notified Mr. Crujenach of my visit. Went to the Zoological Gardens; then to Mr. Crujenach. Miss Helen Bernays[29] not at home.

JANUARY 31: Left for Stuttgart. Cloudy. Still a very pleasant trip. Passed Heidelberg, Carlsruhe [Karlsruhe], Bruchsal, and finally into Würtemberg [Württemberg]. What a picturesque country! Reached Stuttgart at 1:30 P.M. and stopped at the Hotel Royal. Mr. H. Mohr[30] came immediately. I saw Mr. Koch and Dr. [Karl]

Müller of the *Ausland*.[31] Ratzel is no longer at the head of it. Evening at Mohr's. They are without news of the Dr.[32] since the 9th of December. Astonishing!

FEBRUARY

FEBRUARY 1: Mr. Koch and Mr. Ad. Grimminger called in the morning. Afternoon at Mohr's and dinner also. Very pleasant. Stuttgart is exceedingly attractive.

FEBRUARY 2: Went to A. Grimminger. Spent a very happy evening. Afterwards, with Mr. Mohr, to Mr. Julius Schnon, who criticized my paintings very favorably. Returned and then spent evening with Mr. Mohr and his son, Walther, pleasantly.

FEBRUARY 3:[33] Weather improving. Still the streets are muddy. In the forenoon, I called on Mr. Grimminger again, where I met Professor Beyer. Spent a very pleasant time. Both gentlemen gave me letters to Professor Ebers at Leipzic [Leipzig]. Then I returned. Mr. Mohr went with me to the Museum. Dr. von Krause was not present, his daughter being sick. Evening at Mohr's most pleasantly.

FEBRUARY 4: Last day at Stuttgart. Mr. Mohr came at 10 A.M., after I had written home, to Alphonse, Adolphe, to Dr. Mohr, and to Lieutenant Breisacher. Went to the Library. They have an edition of Oviedo of 1526 (?),[34] but it is only written, not printed. Left at 1:28 P.M. How beautiful is that valley of the Neckar. Past Ulm, Augsburg, reached Munich at 6:25 P.M. and went to the Hotel Maximilian. Wrote to Ratzel, who replied at once, and sent a letter from Adolphe. Strolled about a little.

FEBRUARY 5: Called on Professor Ratzel. Very, very kind. Went to the new Pinakothek.[35] Splendid beyond all description. Wrote home, to Adolphe, Alphonse, and to Lieutenant Breisacher. Munich is magnificent.

FEBRUARY 6: At the R. B. Library,[36] examined all the maps about America, but found nothing of interest, and nothing to change my views at all. De Laet "Descriptionis Indiae occidentalis" 1633. Lib. VI Chap: XXVI, pp. 315–316 has already a very good condensed abstract of Benavides' Report on New Mexico,[37] which abstract is evidently the basis of the description in Jean Blaeu Vol. XII.[38] Prof. Ratzel gave me a certificate for the R. Archives. There is an edition of Oviedo. 1 vol: fol. 20 books, printed at Sevilla in 1535 by Juan Cramburger.[39] [Bandelier then made notes on a series of sources he examined there.][40] Spent the day very pleasantly.

FEBRUARY 7: Yesterday, I had seen Mr. [Baron] von Loher about the Jesuit letters, and he spoke about their presence, but requested me to forward to him a letter of request, as it was urgent to have good reasons for entrusting such rare and valuable documents to a stranger. When, therefore, Professor Ratzel called on me this afternoon, I stated the case to him, and he wrote a form of letter for me. We then went together to Professor Moritz Wagner[41] when [. . .] (this was yesterday, not today, and as I write this on the 25th at Berlin, my Journal is henceforth slightly diffuse and confused). In the morning I had been to the Ethnographic Museum, and Professor Ratzel met me there. The Museum is exceedingly rich in valuable objects from Japan, China, India, and the Indian Archipelago. In regard to America, it is less so; but as far as the Pacific Ocean Islands are concerned, there are some specimens which are of special value, having been brought home by Captain Cook.[42] At Professor Wagner's, spent a very interesting hour, met Mr. Pecht, and spent evening at home.

FEBRUARY 8: Went to the Alte Pinakothek.[43] What an overwhelming collection!! It is simply stupendous!! Those beginnings of German Art, those Albrecht Durer, Memling, Lucas Cranach! and the beginnings of Italian Art also! But there is, at the very inception, a marked difference. While German Art begins with strong details and therefore hardness, Italian Art begins with taste of color but lack of detail, and therefore flatness. As to the Dutch painters, there are marvelous pieces. Pieter de Hooch is simply overwhelming. Teniers and Van Ostade are too brutal; Mieris is too sensual; but Van de Werff is simply splendid! And Murillo, Zurbarán,[44] Pedro de Moya, Ribera, Guido Reni, Cignani, Tizian [Titian?], Tintoretto, Correggio, etc. And the masses of Rubens, Van Dyck. Day at Ratzel's. Charming. Evening at home.

FEBRUARY 9: Went through the Jesuit Letters (MSS) at the Royal Library, but found nothing. At the Pinakothek spent in rapture an hour, then went to the Royal Archive, where Baron von Loher received me most charmingly. Letter[45] of Padre Eusebio Kinus [Kino][46] to Padre Paulus Zignis. . . .[47] In the afternoon I slept, then wrote, and finally took a little stroll.

FEBRUARY 10: Went to the Library again [and made notes on various documents].[48] Spent balance of day quietly at home, occupied with my lecture.

FEBRUARY 11: Rather agitated on account of my lecture. Went out in the morning. Ratzel called for me at 6:45 P.M., the drawings had been carried off before. The lecture began at 7:30 P.M. Prince Louis of Bavaria was present, and was exceedingly kind and pleasant. The drawings appeared splendid. Result of lecture was beyond all description. After the lecture we went to the "Achatz" and spent a pleasant half hour. Captain Forrester, Dr. Simonsfeld,[49] Mr. Raab, Judge Finck, and many others were present. I had to read a chapter of my so-called novel.[50]

FEBRUARY 12: Went to the Library. Met Dr. Simonsfeld, also Professor Michel Bernays. . . .[51] Took dinner with Dr. Simonsfeld. Evening at home. Received and wrote various letters. Met Director Raab at night.

FEBRUARY 13: Went to Dr. Lange, and he gave me a letter to Messrs. Obpacher & Co. They examined the letter and told me to return with drawings. Dined at Professor Michel Bernays, where I met Paul Heyse and Dr. Steub. Evening went to the theatre, with Balener [?]. . . . There met Dr. Bernays again.

FEBRUARY 14: Went to Obpacher & Co. Met Director Raab at 11:30 A.M., with Dr. von Hesling. Left my drawings at Obpacher's. In the afternoon met Mr. E. Sack, who went with me to Burchmann, but they replied by letter that they could not do anything at all. Evening at home. Munich is charming and enchanting in every way.

FEBRUARY 15: At home all morning. Went to take affectionate leave of Ratzel. Afterwards, lay call, to Professor Wagner, and lastly to Dr. Simonsfeld. Met Raab yet.

FEBRUARY 16: Left Munich at 6:48 A.M. Fine view of the Bavarian Alps, rising abruptly over the level plain. Reached Leipsic at 8 P.M.

FEBRUARY 17: Went first to Mr. C. Lane, who received me very politely in appearance, and invited me to supper at 8 P.M. Then to Professor Ebers, who was in bed, but who still gave me the privilege of an interview. He was doubtful about the novel, but still allowed me to send it to him. Then went to Dr. Wenz. Here the reception was magnificent. He and his wife were both lovely. In the evening Lane came to excuse himself and his wife for not having been able to arrange for a supper; she is sick (Seybt)[52] etc. He took me along to a café, and his nephew, Hans Fischer, went with us. They are a mollish, greedy, interested set.

FEBRUARY 18: Went to Meiss & Buch. Kind, but declared inability to guarantee result. Dinner at Wenz'. Evening with Fischer. He is obsolete.

FEBRUARY 19: At home most of the time. Weather very ugly. Leipsic is a poor city. H. Fischer came again. It becomes tedious. They saddle the fellow upon me, and do nothing for me in return.

FEBRUARY 20: At Leipsic. Last calls. At Wenz'—charming. Professor Ebers very encouraging also. Lane overflowing. The false "Seybtish" creature! Fischer again saddled upon me.

FEBRUARY 24: Reached Berlin [on the 21st]. At Bastian's, reception very kind. Evening at the Anthropological Society. Sunday 22, dinner at Virchau's [Virchow].[53] Monday at Dr. [W.] Reiss.[54] Today, went through the Museum, and met Dr. Reiss at Bastian's. Evening at home and with E. Pleasant. Letters. Wrote home, etc.

FEBRUARY 25: [Bandelier began this entry with extended notes on several sources.][55]
    In the morning I went to the Museum of German Art. It is but singular that few of the paintings struck me really as of extraordi-

nary value. There is a picture of an inundation by Schanes, there are two of Calame, there is one by Count Kalkreuth, and the military pictures are good also. But there seems to be a lack of plasticity everywhere, which results apparently from the fact, that *black* is too much discarded. In the attempt to diffuse luminosity everywhere, modern painters forget that *there are* places where absence of light really exists in the most salient parts, and that by acknowledging this darkness in their works, they reach that plasticity which is so striking in the older Masters such as Dürer, Tizian, Van der Werf, Murillo, or in Zurbarán. Rembrandt already is diffuse. Went to Bastian, who showed me many interesting things. He introduced me at the Royal Library. Afterwards went to the "Gesellschaft für Erdkunde" [Geographical Society].

FEBRUARY 26: Put my groundplans in order and carried them to the Gesellschaft für Erdkunde, #191 Friedrichstrasse, and then went to the Royal Library. Selected quite a number of books at once. ...[56] Went to the Geographical Society, and examined their maps. There is one of 1703 with Casas Grandes on it. Evening at the Colloquium of the Geographical Society.

FEBRUARY 27: Meeting last night was very satisfactory. A number of leading men present. Professor Konn, Professor Lange, Dr. Aschersohn,[57] and others. [My] lecture fixed for the 7th of March. This *"Rudo Ensayo"* is certainly a very remarkable work. The knowledge of northeastern Sonora which it betrays is astonishing. Smith surmises that it might have been written by a Curate of Guasavas [Huásabas], in 1761–62, but as the Priest of Guasavas at that time was a Silesian, Father Juan Mentuig [Nentuig, or Nentwig], he thinks he cannot have written such excellent Spanish. This is a great mistake. Germans are far superior to Anglo-Saxons in aptitude for languages. ...[58] Was interrupted by a meeting (informal) of the African Conference, or rather "African Colonization Society." No letters. It is queer, certainly. I have written so many.

FEBRUARY 28: This morning, early, Fritz brought me two letters, or rather a card from Alphonse and a letter from Mr. Mohr. Went to the Royal Library at 10 A.M. . . . At night spent pleasantly with E. I received a letter from Mr. W. Müller.

MARCH

MARCH 1: Spent a very delightful night in every respect! But, Lord, how tired I feel! Card from Breisacher. . . .

It rained hard all day, and was chilly. At night I was invited to Dr. Reiss. Brilliant dinner. Resident Reidel, Professor Lange, Professor Aschersohn, Professor Rothe, etc., were all present. It was exceedingly nice in every respect. But how far this may help me, is another question.

MARCH 2: Wet, but apparently clearing. Chilly. Went to the Library. [Again several pages of notations follow.][59] Received today: letters from Ratzel, card from Lieutenant Breisacher, and sample photographs from Leipzic. Also my drawings back from Asher & Co., with explanatory letter, refusing. I have no chance, certainly, but then, did I ever have any? Before? Ill-luck is nothing new to me, and an early death, without being compelled to seek it myself, my only and last hope. Retired early.

MARCH 3: Dark, cloudy, and gloomy. Went early to Bastian and left my drawings there. Spent the afternoon at Zoological Gardens. Very beautiful. It is chilly and cloudy always. I wrote this A.M., two cards: one to W. Müller, and the other to Breisacher.

MARCH 4: Wrote to Dr. Moore last night yet. Received a card from Alphonse, and one from Mr. Müller. Went to see Dr. Gerlich,[60] but he was not at the Office (No. 2 Wilhelm's Platz), so I just went to the Library. . . . Afterwards went to Dr. Gerlich at the Reichstag, then to Lieutenant Schröter, and finally spent the evening at Mr. W. Müller's. Rainy.

MARCH 5: Dark and raining, not cold. Went to the Library early. . . .[61] It rained hard all day. I received card from Alphonse, from Mr. Müller. Called on Lieutenant Schröter, and at 7 P.M. met him at the "Papago." We spent a few hours very agreeably together, and I afterwards met Resident Reidel.

MARCH 6: It rained hard all day. Went to the Museum and got my drawings. Afterwards to O. Bermann & Co. to buy paper. Then to Mr. Müller's, where [I met] Mr. Lepke. He examined the drawings carefully, but his reply was discouraging. Received letter from Gruner-Haller and Company; card from Alphonse. Sent cards to Salzendel and to Ratzel. Ugly, most ugly, weather. A few hours with E. pleasantly. Home at night.

MARCH 7: Gloomy in the morning, but slowly improved towards the afternoon. Preparing for my lecture. In the forenoon I wrote. Lecture at the "Architectur-Hauss," #92. Very pleasant. Mr. Reidel spoke first, then Dr. Reiss had an altercation with Dr. Kiepert. After the lecture a fine supper. Went home with Dr. Reiss and Professor Virchow. Invited by Dr. H. Lange.

MARCH 8: Fine day, but cold. A.M. at E. Afterwards to Dr. Lange, where I met Signora Ruda. Very pleasant afternoon. It passed away quickly. Night pleasant also. E.

MARCH 9: Gloomy and sprinkling. Went early to Bastian, who gave me a long lecture on Ethnology. He is an excellent old man, but very much exalted and therefore extravagant in his ideas and in his views. Afterwards to Mr. Pechter. At 6 P.M. to Professor Virchow to whom I made a clear statement of everything as far as prudence allowed. I did not want to bore him with private affairs, but still had to tell him enough to explain my position at all events. He would desire me to travel in the cause of American Ethnology, but there is always Highland between me and the future.

MARCH 10: Better weather. Had a long talk with Dr. Reiss and afterwards returned my visit to Dr. Jagor. (Blumeshof #2.) His house is very interesting. Evening at Bilse. Handsome concert.

MARCH 11: Cold and gloomy. Spent nearly the whole day with Bastian, who gave me another long talk and made sundry propositions which I could neither reject nor accept. Got the copies from Berne; they are fair but not very excellent. Afterwards had a long talk with Dr. Reiss again. Shall leave next Friday.

MARCH 12: Gloomy again. Began to write to different parties. Wrote home, to Alphonse, to Vautier, etc. Went to Dr. Gerlich who kindly volunteered to take charge of my drawings for sale.[62] He says that it will take time, but he may succeed. Evening at home.

MARCH 13: Ran about a great deal. Saw everybody yet. Left my drawings at Dr. Gerlich, took leave of Dr. Reiss, and then left at 3:40 P.M. for Hamburg, where I arrived at 8:38 P.M. Country absolutely flat, and partly inundated. Very monotonous.

MARCH 14: Settled my matters at Hamburg, and received the package from Mr. Mohr [Stuttgart] for the Doctor [in Highland or in New York?]. Friederichsen not at home, but Professor Lange had written in my behalf. Strolled about Hamburg the remainder of the day. It is a very interesting city, partly old, crooked and narrow, but striking because it is quaint. The "Alster-Bassin" is beautiful at night, still it is not by far as brilliant as the Quais of Geneva. Cold.

MARCH 15: Foggy and cold. Went on board the little steamer at 8 A.M. Had difficulty to get on board on account of not having a passport. Few passengers. The descent of the Elbe is handsome and recalls somewhat New York bay. At Stade, we met the "Hammenia" [?] and went on board. Are only 11 cabin-passengers, and one of them, Mr. Cuprian, first mate of a sailing vessel, lands at [Le] Havre. He, Mr. Fischer of Heidelberg, and Mr. Diebel of Kimberl[e]y, South Africa, and I formed a little club at once. Had good time soon. At Stade and beyond, the banks of the Elbe became very flat and the river, very broad. At Cuxhaven we at last entered the North Sea, after passing the formidable fortifications; all iron-plated towers. No ships of war in sight. The North Sea is remarkably quiet, and the ship moves beautifully.

MARCH 16: Rather foggy, but very quiet and beautiful. Many ships in sight, presenting a very animated spectacle. About 4 P.M. we came [in] sight of the English coast and had a beautiful view of Dover with its chalky, precipitous cliffs. Fog increased at night.

MARCH 17: Deep fog which compelled us to be still all day at anchor in front of Havre, without seeing land until about 1 P.M. when the fog gradually cleared away, and the French coast came in sight, and in the immediate vicinity a number of steamers and other ships. The remainder of the day grew very beautiful, clear, warm, quiet, and springlike. We amused ourselves nicely. At sunset we danced. Miss Bertha Lemke, Mrs. W. Gebert, and we. The Mate alone did not join. The lights on shore grew magnificent, and we finally went into the harbor. It was a splendid sight, that illumination, and the fine sky. Six more passengers came on board that night yet.

MARCH 18: Rainy and ugly. They have been loading the steamer all night. Cuprian left this morning. Sorry to lose him. Mr. & Mrs. A. Jamens of New York (French), Mr. August Schill of Stuttgart, and two Americans, one of which, a German-American and an exceedingly silly, coarse fellow, came on board last night. Havre has over 104,000 souls, but the port, although very good, and filled with shipping, particularly steamers, is dirty as far as the houses are concerned. A beautiful French steamer, "Amérique," lay in front of us; an Italian, several German, English steamers also, and a magnificent Mexican steamer, manned by a Mexican crew, came gliding in stately. An English steamer caught up with our anchor and took it along. We left port at 11 A.M. and as we got out into the channel, the sky cleared, and we had a very handsome sea for the rest of the day and night.

MARCH 19: Same weather, quiet and handsome. I wrote at my lecture as usual. Began to play "Shuffle-board." I grew very lively, and the company is mixing up, all except the two Americans and one American woman. The latter is sick and so are some others. The steamer made 346 miles till noon.

MARCH 20: A little more lively. People are moving on deck. Mr. C. Reuter, of Hamburg, is a very pleasant old gentleman. So is the physician, Dr. Mitzlaff. Mr. W. Diebel has lived in South Africa for 15 years and, although a young man, is still very nice and not devoid of knowledge of his country. A good deal of playing shuffle-board was done. I wrote again. Day and sea fine.

MARCH 21: Splendid day, almost a perfect calm. Consequently even the ladies went to playing shuffle-board also, and I could do more writing for myself. Wrote at my lecture steadily, although sleepy and with a cold. At night, singing on deck. The French people are very lively and pleasant, and so is Bertha Lemke, who goes to Austin (Texas) to join her bridegroom.

MARCH 22: Ugly weather. Wind southwest and increasing. Birthday of the Emperor of Germany. Playing on deck impossible and also difficult writing. Splendid dinner. I had to give the toast to His Majesty and speech. Night ugly and rainy. Stormy.

MARCH 23: Beautiful, clearing, cold. Northwesterly wind, brisk. Still there is remarkably little motion. Made only 242 miles till noon, on account of contrary winds yesterday. Today are plodding along better. Wrote again as much as possible. Playing on deck, and they also begin to play dice and cards. Begged to be excused.

MARCH 24: Ugly weather. Rain and southwesterly wind, increasing. Hardly any playing on deck possible. Then more writing below, and cards and dice playing in the smoking-rooms. Still we are making headway, 282 miles. We are fast nearing the Banks. Brisk blow from northwest at 4 P.M. Wind unsteady, and gyrating between southeast and west.

MARCH 25: Cold and blustering. Wind westerly increasing in violence to quite a lively breeze. Went along well. Hardly any playing owing to the cold. Are on the Banks now. No fog. A large steamer passed us, but in general but few vessels were seen. Not a fish visible.

MARCH 26: Cold, blustering from northwest. 311 miles till noon. Playing on board, and very noisy. I finished my letters in four envelopes, all directed to Dr. Reiss, 38 pages. Hope it will be accepted. At night wind went back to the south and blew hard for a while, dark and gloomy. Impossible to be out at night, so I sat in the smoking-room with Fischer and Mr. Reuter, and then went to bed. The passengers are now split up. The bulk clusters around the French and play: "Vingt-et-un." Fischer and I, Mr.

Reuter, and little Bertha are quiet and peaceably alone. It is singular how insensible and unfeeling I become. I go home— perhaps,—thoughtless, not resigned, but sullen and indifferent. Poor Joe, if only *She* is not the final victim of all this sad life.

MARCH 27: Finished my Journal. The morning is splendid, but it soon grew squally from south, at which they set sails. It still was very ugly, as the wind blew hard, and it was chilly, the vessel shipping much water. 310 miles till noon. The usual little crowd is gambling on a very small scale at "vingt-et-un." Fischer is asleep, and I write, although the ship rolls quite much. Sky gloomy and cloudy. We are now in the latitude of Halifax but 200 miles off yet, and 470 from New York. It ceased raining in the afternoon, and at 6 P.M., a pilot came on board. He had been out ten days and brought New York papers for the 15th and 16th of March. Night cloudy, breezy and warm. Sultry. Talked all night.

MARCH 28: Fog at night, consequently the ship stopped several times, blowing the whistle (siren) fearfully. Cold; wind westerly. It gradually cleared away, the sky showing brightly. Wrote to Professor F. Ratzel, and to Ad. Grimminger. Also to Professor Ebers. It began to snow at nightfall and we anchored off Sandy-Hook at last. Snowing fast. Cold wind from northwest.

MARCH 29: Cold and snowing while we steamed into the port. Went to the Belvedere Hotel. Afternoon ugly and unwell. The crowd from ship-board called on me, and I went back with them to their Hotel at Hoboken. Returned late and went home with H. Bell, 215 E. 14th Street. Pleasant. Weather cold. Clearing.

MARCH 30: Called at Chemical Bank, and C.B.R. & Co. News at least indifferent, if not absolutely good. In the afternoon went to Hoboken again for arrangements. Staid overnight. Fischer has left.

MARCH 31: Went to Dr. G. H. Moore. Exceedingly kind reception. Nothing very new. Wrote home, and then went to bed, very unwell and ill. My stomach is completely out of order. Diebel left this A.M.

APRIL

APRIL 1: Called on Hans Mohr very early. Also on Ignaz Hosp. Fine day. The latter accompanied me across to Hoboken and to the Hotel. Afterwards Dr. Mohr also came, and Lieutenant Schill. We left at 6:15 P.M., Christ. Asplund and wife, Bertha Lemke and I, by the fast train of the N.Y.,P.,&O. Railroad (O. & M.).

APRIL 2: Asplunds left us at 4 A.M. for Niagara. The country has a dreary aspect, and everything appears very much dilapidated, dirty, and neglected, in comparison with Europe, and Germany in particular. Bertha is a very excellent girl. Besides her, there is but one companion on board who is very palatable, Mr. Sandford of New York; the rest are "coffins." We got to Dayton at 6:10 P.M. and to Cincinnati at 8:30 P.M. Dark & gloomy, everything wet.

APRIL 3: Reached St. Louis at 8:35 A.M., and then, to my Greatest Joy, met dearest Joe at the "Union." All are well at home, and prospects not so very bad. But I must go home. We spent the day very pleasantly together with Cilla,[63] Pauline,[64] and Annie,[65] and I got home safe, with Papa and Morris[66] at the station. Thank God.

APRIL 4: Mr. Burckhardt [of Bern] came. Got a letter from E. A. Allen,[67] Cincinnati. Wrote to Moisé Vautier. Mr. Burckhardt stopped with us until 3:40 train. Pleasant, but Papa has not changed one bit at all. Always suspicious, ill-tempered, and occasionally cross. Called on Fritz [F. C. Ryhiner, Jr.?],[68] Bernays,[69] Müller [Ad. Mueller],[70] and Dr. Schloetzer.[71] Spent evening at Bertha's [Lambelet].[72] Very sleepy and tired.

APRIL 5: Easter Sunday. Cloudy and very warm. Pleasant. Crocus in bloom. Frogs crying since several days. Wrote and mailed letter to Dr. H. Mohr, #201 Clinton Street, N.Y. and also wrote to Mr. Parkman.[73] Cleared fully and grew quite windy, although warm. Hans [Mohr?] called. In the afternoon, we went out on the farm. Called at Mr. Graffenried's.[74] Kind as usual. Spent the afternoon very pleasantly at the farm. On returning, called at Father Meckel's,[75] and spent the night at Morris'. He is lazy and sullen

as usual, but grew more lively after an hour or so. The weather
is warm and pleasant, frogs crying loud. Drying fast.

APRIL 6: Wrote to Alphonse. Mr. Graffenried took dinner with us;
he is perfectly satisfied with the course which I pursued and
hopes for the best. Wrote to F. H. Cushing[76] and to E. A. Allen.
Also to Professor Virchow. Spent the evening at home quietly
and pleasantly.

APRIL 7: Last night I promised to the Turners to speak on the
25th [20th!] anniversary of Lincoln's death (15th of April). Wrote
to S. Eldodt,[77] to Dr. Eggert, and to Garrison.[78] Also to Professor
Lange at Berlin, #44 Ritterstrasse. Mr. Balsiger[79] called; also,
Mrs. Rentschler.[80] Saw Louis Kinne[81] at night. Wrote at
"Cibola."[82] It is a new trial and attempt, which may have no
result, but the intention is to earn some money as soon as possible.
I must have something to live off. All other resources are cut off
for the present, and nothing is left to me but to make money, if
possible, by writing.

APRIL 8: John Wildi[83] called. Wrote to Don Joaquín[84] at Mexico.
Fritz R[yhiner, Jr.] called; he is wild with talk and gab. Evidently
his mind is turning. In the afternoon I called around somewhat,
staid longest at Ad. Müller's. Night at Rentschler's.

APRIL 9: About 1 A.M. was aroused by fire-alarm. The foundry[85]
had burnt down completely. Warehouses saved. The flames must
have caught very rapidly, as none of the neighbors noticed anything until it was all ablaze. Morning chilly with attempts at
snow. Morris, as usual, much dejected, sullen, and whining. I saw
nothing particularly terrible in it. It was an accident, for which
we are not responsible, and which we must therefore take coolly.
I took medicine this morning, and then went out to the ruins.
Everything of the machinery is gone. There is evidence of incendiarism visible, as the fire caught on the southeast side. Called on
John Blattner[86] where I met Mr. Weinheimer[87] who is very pleasant. Got a letter from Bertha Lemke and her husband. Wrote to
Aunt Sauvant,[88] and cards to Ignaz Hosp, W. Diebel, and to Mr.
O. Ottendorfer.[89]

APRIL 10: Left for Edwardsville at 6:30 A.M. with Morris. Took a carriage at Troy and got to Edwardsville in good time. Saw Metcalfe [Metcalf][90] who advised strongly to take a change of venue. Judge Dale,[91] when I explained everything to him, was of the same opinion. He offers to mediate if possible. Saw many acquaintances. Took Henry Lang with us. Reached home well. In the meantime, Mr. Burckhard had been here, but there is nothing new. Letters from E. A. Allen. Saw Blattner yet.

APRIL 11: Papa not well, and I am very unwell. Stomach all to pieces. Spent part of the morning at the office, afternoon partly at Dr. Schloetzer's, and then at the office again. They are better disposed at the office, only Papa is very much dejected and highly discouraged. It is physical weakness rather than anything else.

APRIL 12: Ellison,[92] his son, and Braunschweiler [Brunnschweiler][93] came, with Morris. (It looks again as if they could not do anything without me.) We soon agreed for E[llison] to take an inventory of the remains, including contents of warehouse, and to make a proposal in writing. Morris took dinner with us. I wrote the whole day at "Cibola." Called at Aunt Weber's,[94] and afterwards at Dr. Knoebel's[95] with Joe. Pleasant.

APRIL 13: Note from Garrison. Papa came in and at once set me to work at the R. E. Book. Was interrupted by Dr. Sacconi,[96] who called on me for a recommendation at Washington. Declined temporarily. Afterwards Burckhard came. No news of any importance yet. He left in the afternoon for St. Louis. Now I will have to go to Nashville with him Thursday. Afterwards I had Mr. Stills, and finally I could finish the job at night. Spent the evening with Joe at Dr. Schloetzer's. Pleasant. Friendly letters from Mr. Garrison and from Mr. Parkman today. Uncertainty still.

APRIL 14: Wrote to [G. W.?] Cone at Papa's request. Wrote to H. Mohr's father at Stuttgart, and to E. C. Springer.[97] Lent Bourke's "Snake Dance"[98] to the Lame Bernays[99] at night. Saw J. Scheule, he is very much dejected and discouraged. Old Widmer[100] came; he too is very much depressed and dispirited, has no hope for Highland.

APRIL 15: Letter from Alphonse to Papa; rather favorable prospects. Wrote my skeleton for tonight. Have very little heart for it, the subject, the people, and the times are alike unpropitious for such an occasion. I hate the country and its people, have always hated them, and cannot therefore entertain the slightest enthusiasm on the occasion.[101] Night warm. Hall filled with people, very attentive and quiet. Result good so far. Everybody much elated; got home about 9:30 P.M. Quite satisfied.[102]

APRIL 16: Left for the City at 6:30 A.M. Met Mr. B. [probably Burckhardt]. Hospes[103] not at home. Called at Witter's, and at Ellison's, also on the German Consul. Went, as agreed, to meet Mr. B. at Main Street Depot; he was very pale, and communicated to me the fatal Dispatch.[104] I wandered about the city half-idiotic, notwithstanding a severe thunderstorm.

APRIL 17: Saw Hospes, he also is much stricken. Poked about St. Louis all day, and returned home at night, tired and unwell. Passed a very bad night. Letters from Parkman, Cone, and Dr. Eggert. Friendly, but what does it amount to.

APRIL 19: In bed all night and day yesterday. Very unwell. Better today, but extremely sleepy and dizzy. M[orris] and F. C. R. [F. C. Ryhiner, Jr.] came. Did not talk much. What is the use. Neither is there any use in staying here any longer. In the afternoon went to Mr. Graffenried; he does not give up yet. Wrote to Dr. Eggert about a situation at Santa Fe. Am resolved to leave if possible.

APRIL 20: Letter from Alphonse. Feel better, though weak yet. Wrote the whole day at the controle [audit] for Burckhardt. Hans [Dr. Mohr][105] called. Bertha's [Lambelet] child sick again.

APRIL 21: Very warm. Everything looks greener from day to day; only my hopes are waning hourly. And still, there is a faint hope yet. Everything is not gone yet, but this life! Oh God, it is worse than martyrdom; it is slow burning fire for years and years. Wrote to Burckhard and mailed letter. Election today; much excitement in town. Miserable, to fight and wrangle about poor unimportant Offices. John Wildi is spreading too much entirely. Am weak and dejected. Began to write to James and Hélène [Brun].

APRIL 22: Better news from St. Louis. Papa wants to leave, suddenly. Although there are better indications, he flew into a big passion again against Burckhard, and afterwards against me, and kept bothering me all morning and part of the afternoon. He suspects ill wind everywhere. He thinks now that B. [Burckhardt] wants to take advantage of the situation and cheat the home creditors. Is resolved to go to St. Louis tomorrow. I wrote to Hospes and to Ellison & Son. Quiet, warm, and moist. Wrote all night. Uncle Kinne[106] made a call. No letters.

APRIL 23: Finished copy of controle at 3 P.M. Papa left for St. Louis. Finished my copy. News of death of Ed. Wiggenhausser [Edward B. Wickenhauser][107] and of Mrs. Joseph Speckart.[108] Collated copy with Frank[109] until 9:30 P.M.

APRIL 24: Papa returned from St. Louis, better satisfied. It does not look so bad as before, but it will be a long winded affair. Finished abstract of statements for agents at 11 A.M. Papa wants to go South for awhile. Impatient to finish my controle, but constant delays at the Office; they are desperately sloven, slow, and irresolute. It is an execrable situation in every respect. Got a card from I. Hosp. Finished collating the controle with Frank. Letter from W. Diebel. Telegram from Henry K [Kaune][110] informing us of the death of Willie K's [Kaune's] youngest child.[111] Wrote to Henry about it. Visit by Mrs. Rentschler. Everything looks rather better again, but still it is gloomy yet, and the most of it is that I cannot do anything for myself.

APRIL 25: Got map from H. Hartmann,[112] and letters. Also advice of death of Mrs. Cone. Wrote to Burckhart and to Cone. Card to H. Hartmann. War cloud thickening in Europe.[113] Finished and mailed letter to James and Hélene. Made a short call of condolence to J. Speckart.

APRIL 26: Sunday. Most beautiful day. Serene, cool, and brilliant sky. Wind northwest. Delightful letter from Dr. Eggert. He is a good faithful old friend. Splendid news from Berne. Went out to the farm and to Mr. Wachsmuth's.[114] Sent off the first 11 pages of "Cibola"[115] to New York this A.M. Night beautiful.

APRIL 27: Splendid day again. Warm and quiet. Wrote to Dr. Gerlich, to Dr. Hoffmann[116] about Papa, and to Dr. G. H. Moore. Papa left at 4 P.M.[117] They are all much depressed. Still, there is as yet no immediate danger. Went to old man Widmer and spent a pleasant evening with him and old man Kuhs[?]. Quiet.

APRIL 28: Cloudy, dark. Letters from Don Joaquín[118] and Burckhart. News got here by Hellmuth.[119] Everything quiet so far, but it is well to keep on the lookout. Wrote to Professor Ware,[120] to Burckhart, and to Hospes. Of course, there is a great dejection at the Office. I am much excited myself.

APRIL 29: Clearing. Big run [on the bank!] Great excitement. Impossible to stem the tide. Much depressed. Ruin almost certain. Run kept on, notwithstanding all I said. Sad night. Wildi is firm and friendly, but Louis Kinne and others are mad and ill-disposed.

APRIL 30: Thursday. [Bank] closed today. This is the last of F. Ryhiner & Co., and the last period of my sufferings at Highland begins finally.

M A Y

MAY 1: Wildest rumors afloat; especially about Papa. His departure spoils everything. Dr. Knoebel and George Roth[121] came this morning to the Office and made me a terrible scene, almost an assault. In the afternoon, N. H. Thedinga[122] came. Louis Kinne came up also and made me a terrible scene too. Excitement increasing, especially against me.[123] I am held as the cause of everything. Well, it is a good pretext to get out of this infernal place at last, and become independent.

MAY 2: Excitement still rising. Last night George [Hoffmann][124] came out from St. Louis and brought us some consolation. It is impossible to go out of doors; people are threatening to kill me. All sides warn me to stay indoors. Wrote all day, but little. Henry [Kaune] came at night, and afterwards, Father Meckel. About 9

P.M., a dynamite explosion took place on the west side of the bank. It was fearful; did no damage, however. It is mean, very mean.

MAY 3: Sunday. Mr. Balsiger called. Very kind. In the afternoon, Henry walked in from the farm with Lizzie[125] and the baby. Quiet, and the town is not so very excited, though there is a good deal of talk. Still, towards evening, we were warned about violence, and Garbald[126] came to tell us, that Papa ought to be kept back at St. Louis. We decided upon sending Henry down.

MAY 4: Fine weather. Quiet. Assignment made today. Gloomy. Papa was not on board the train. Henry went down to meet him at St. Louis. Wrote to Mr. Parkman. About 4 P.M. came a letter from Papa stating that he would never return!! This is infamous, and settles him with us. Hereafter, he ceases to exist for us. We have sacrificed ourselves for him in every way, and now he betrays and forsakes us. This is the result of 25 years of slavery! Now I am ready for anything to come. Hermann Thedinga is exceedingly kind. The Assigners are at work again at the office. This was a terrible day all around.

MAY 5: It rained a little last night. Morning splendid. Bertha says the tide is slightly turning in my favor. It appears that Rosalie[127] is crazy. Henry Meyer[128] had a fit of apoplexy this A.M. Henry came. Everything much quieter. Wrote to Dr. G. H. Moore, to Cushing, and to Dr. Eggert. Mrs. Brossard[129] dined with us; she is a Godsend to Joe. Henry and Mali[130] went out to the farm this afternoon. They brought back news of the excitement on the farm, of Henry Todd's[131] villainous conduct (perhaps). The assignment papers were finally completed about at 6 P.M., and Ad. Ruegger[132] took them to Edwardsville. Mr. Bradshaw[133] asserts that neither Morris, nor F. C. R. [F. C. Ryhiner, Jr.] are criminally liable.[134]

MAY 6: Mr. Balsiger is very, very kind. Henry is not well; his feet are sore. Dr. Schloetzer made us a friendly call. In the afternoon, Mrs. Dr. Berg called also. Very Kind. Wrote to Alphonse, Adolphe Vautier,[135] to Garrison, and to Mexico.[136] Wrote to little Bertha [Lemke] and to her husband: B. A. Cornils, Waldrip,

McCulloch Co., Texas. May God be good to them. Henry on the farm.

MAY 7: Morning half-clear, cold; fire needed in the rooms. The "Telephone" is heard,[137] of course, and Mr. Wilandy wrote me a poisonous letter which he sent us through Mr. Balsiger. Poor old man, I pity him. Morris was here twice, downhearted as usual. Colder and colder.

MAY 8: Very cold for the season. Clear. Friendly letters from Mrs. Kyburz [Kieburtz?][138] and Collet.[139] Dr. Knoebel sent a bill of $15—against Papa. Letter from Papa also. Very kind letter from S. Eldodt. There may be a chance there, perhaps. Henry is taking any amount of trouble. Wrote to Eldodt. Huaynopa[140] on the train with Henry.

MAY 9: Quiet in town. Paid account of Ad. Müller. Letters from George Hoffmann and from G. de Luternau. Trial about horse and buggy. Favorable.

MAY 10: Slept fine. Wrote in the morning. At noon got letters. One from Mr. Parkman; one from Mrs. Cushing;[141] and one from Witter, enclosing card from F. B. Perkins, Librarian of Free Public Library, San Francisco, asking price of American Journal of Science & Arts, etc. Replied. In the afternoon, Gustave [Bandelier],[142] Lizzie, and the baby came; also Morris and Emma.[143] Pleasant, although sad yet. Jacob Kleiner[144] called also. Wrote to Mrs. Cushing. She is so very kind to us. Also, to Reverend G. de Luternau, Augusta, St. Charles Co., Missouri.

MAY 11: Letters from Alphonse, Dr. Eggert, and from Mr. Garrison. Kind. Mrs. Brossard called. In the afternoon Lizzie, Wachsmuth, and Mrs. Brossard again, and at night Mr. Balsiger. Pleasant. Henry went out on the farm to stay.

MAY 12: Letter from Dr. H. Mohr. Sent off second part of "Cibola,"[145] with letter of S. Eldodt, to Mr. Ottendorfer. Mr. Balsiger called at night, and I turned over power of attorney to Henry. Widmer was here in the afternoon. Good, kind, noble old man. Father Meckel also made a long, earnest, and friendly call. He, too, is a good friend.

MAY 13: F. C. R. left yesterday evening on the sly,[146] abandoning poor Morris. There is said to be a warrant out against us. Day very bad and exciting. Morris was here most of the time. Mr. Kinne here also.[147]

MAY 14: Another day of suffering. The "Globe-Democrat" [St. Louis][148] has a villainous article about Fritz R., charging it all on to me. It is miserable and mean, low-lived and scandalous. Morris came. He also is affected, but he is powerless to do anything, or at least too apath[et]ic. John Hermann[149] came; the Assigners have no objection against my departure, but I prefer to wait awhile yet. It appears now that Dr. J. B. Knoebel attempted to get a warrant against me, but failed in this. At night, Dr. Schloetzer, and Mrs. Dr. Berg made a friendly call.

MAY 15: The beautiful cactus of Mother's[150] has 8 flowers, and the white one is open also. Wrote to Dr. Eggert. Quiet day. Pleasant evening with Balsiger and with Morris. There seems to be a disposition to quiet down a little, among the people. No letters.

MAY 16: Quiet. Morris was here, also old man Widmer. Am still upset, and have very little heart for any work at all. Dr. Schloetzer called. Night quiet.

MAY 17: Rosalie, Lizzie, etc., Morris and Emma, spent the greatest part of the day [Sunday] with us. Quiet and pleasant.

MAY 18: An infamous libel in the shape of a slanderous, mean circular[151] has been sold publicly and circulated at the Depot. It is an outrageous concern. Wrote to Mr. Parkman and to George Hoffmann. Letter from Alphonse. Afternoon quiet. Joe went out to Graffenried's.

MAY 19: Dr. Schmid [Dr. Werner Schmidt][152] came this morning and challenged me in the name of Dr. Knoebel. I declined; he came back again, and I declined again. It is, of course, exceedingly mean and silly. We are, however, going to prosecute him [Dr. Knoebel] now. How infamous and vile![153]

MAY 20: No new villainy has as yet turned up, but there is no telling. In the afternoon, Mr. Graffenried came. In his eyes, Mr. Burckhart has vindicated me fully and completely. At last, *one* who feels right about it.

MAY 21: Friendly letter from George [Hoffmann]. At 8 P.M., about, Morris and I were arrested and brought before [Justice of the Peace, Henry] Riniker,[154] on a charge by Unterreiner [Unterrainer].[155] Released on Bond, signed by [John] Blattner and by Mr. Balsiger. Horrible night. Dear, poor Joe.

MAY 22: Friendly letter from Bertha Cornils. Hot and sad. Calls from Breese; Hermann & Yager.[156] Letter from Bishop Salpointe. Call from Mrs. Berg. Retired early. They can go so far as —at night, to disfigure and cut our cactus.

MAY 23: Overnight, they dirtied and defaced the house in front. Hot and clear. At night, Mr. Blattner called; also Mr. Balsiger. Determined upon a plan of action. Night clear.

MAY 24: Letter from Professor Ratzel. Very friendly. Wrote to Bishop Salpointe. It grew very sultry in the afternoon. Morris had a specially friendly call from John Kaeser of St. Louis, who went with him to Xavier Suppiger[157] about security on Bond. About 6 P.M. a heavy thundershower from the northwest. Night quiet.

MAY 25: Cooler and partly clearing. Quiet. Warming gradually. Wrote to the "Staats-Zeitung" [*New Yorker Staatszeitung*] and to Dr. Eggert. Mr. Graffenried called. Morris very much disheartened. Dr. Schloetzer came also, and brought me a very friendly letter from Dr. Mohr to A. Müller. In the afternoon, Morris was here again and looked a little better. At night, Mrs. Brossard called. Morris again downhearted. I am now tired of this kind of living and shall try to shift for myself. Joe is rapidly weakening, and I must do something to save poor, dear Joe of this awful condition.

MAY 26: Cloudy, sultry, southerly wind. Preparing for rain. Morris received from Xavier Suppiger a negative reply. Letter from H. Liebler, Schulenburg, Texas. Joe much depressed. At night, call from Mr. Balsiger and from Father Meckel.

MAY 27: Slow rain overnight. Quiet and cloudy. First part of "Cibola" appeared in the "N.Y. Staats-Zeitung" today. Morris unwell. Sultry. Dr. Schloetzer called. Letter from [Father] Meckel. In the evening, Mr. Balsiger called also.

MAY 28: Early in the morning, about 7:20 A.M., the children came over crying. *Morris had committed suicide!!*[158] Terrible! Everything upside down. Day sultry and lowering. Mr. Bradshaw came. State-attorney offered to take a Bond of $1000—, but Mr. Graffenried refused to go it. Rained very hard until noon. At 3:15 P.M., left for the Depot in charge of H. E. Todd. Crowds followed me yelling, hooting, and cursing. At the Depot, a dense crowd. Insults of all kinds.[159] Train was late three hours, so Mr. Todd took a two-horse buggy, and Bradshaw stepped in, and we drove quickly over to Edwardsville and to jail. Treatment kind.

MAY 29: In Jail!! Treatment very kind. Last night, Will Mudge,[160] Hugh Bayle,[161] Athan. Hoffman,[162] Robert Hagnauer,[163] and Henry Todd called. Very friendly. It is different from Highland! Poor, poor, dear Joe! Poor Morris! If only nothing happens at home. About 9 A.M., I was taken out of the cell,[164] and found Will Mudge, two reporters, Athanas Hoffmann, and Bradshaw. They made me sign the Bond for $1000—, and I was free. Afterwards, young Charley Boeschenstein[165] rushed into the Justice's office also and signed the Bond too. Unbounded kindness was shown to me by all. How different from Highland![166] Everybody advised me to leave now. So I went to St. Louis in the afternoon at 3:45, Charley B. going with me as far as East St. Louis. Went to George Hoffmann. Celia is out at Highland, staying with Joe.

MAY 30: At 11 A.M., Henry came. Joe is better, thank God! The hounds at Highland appear quieter, and somewhat surprised through my giving Bond so easily. In the afternoon, went to town. We found Mr. Pretorius [Preetorius],[167] Fritz Suppiger,[168]

Burckhart, and Reverend Streiff. Very kind. Left for the West, 8:45 P.M.[169]

MAY 31: Sunday. Fine day; went all day. Formed pleasant acquaintances on the train. Don Cesar Oliva and wife, from Batopilas, Chihuahua, returning from a trip to Italy, and, principally, Mr. J. D. Warner, Socorro, N.M. Day passed very quickly. In the evening, we took supper at Newton, Kansas, already. The fields look well. Mr. Warner told me that they had an unusually large amount of rain this spring, in New Mexico. Otherwise, the Territory is rather prosperous. All friends are well. Very much excited at the Apaches and against the military.

JUNE

JUNE 1: Splendid day. Breakfasted at La Junta. All the mountains out beautifully. Snow on the Cuerno Verde, on the Huajatoyas, and much snow on the Trinchera, also on the Peak of Taos. Don Cesar Oliva told me a good deal of the Tarahumares.[170] They still sleep in caves in rocks, wear sandals of hide, and a straw-hat. Dined at Raton and met Father Personné [Personnet].[171] Everything green and wet. At Las Vegas, Mr. Warner left us. Formed the acquaintance of Mr. W. E. West, Halifax, Canada, and particularly of Mr. Theo. E. Brown of the City of Mexico. At Lamy,[172] I met Reed[173] and Miller.[174] Reed is at Albuquerque.

JUNE 2: Reached Santa Fe at 1:30 A.M. and went to Herlow's [Hotel][175] at once. Slept well. Quiet. Went to see Dr. Eggert. How kind! How much friendship and care for me. Decided to stay,[176] and to go to San Juan. Called on Archbishop Lamy[177] and Archbishop Salpointe. Kindest of kindness. Kochs[178] are another group of good friends; so is John Pearce.[179] *He* had also prepared a room. But Kochs have got me to stay with them until Saturday A.M. when he, the Dr. [Eggert] and John [Pearce] will drive me up to San Juan. Got a letter from Mr. Ottendorfer. At night, music in the Plaza.

JUNE 3: I went up to Bishop Salpointe and made the catalogue of the collection.[180] While working at it, was called to the church.

Fathers Rolly[181] and Gatignalles [Gatignol][182] were opening the north wall of the choir, very near the floor, and the side of a cyst was discovered, made of brick and coated with a thin film of cement.[183] In this coating, two inscriptions were carved, which I copied. They read as follows:

> Aqui yacen los huesos del V. P. F. Gerónimo de la Llana, Varon apostólico de la horden de S. Francisco que se sacaron de la Mision aruinada de Quarac de las Salinas, en 1 de Abril 1759 por el Señor D. Franc. Anto Marin del Valle, Gobernador y Capitán General de este Reino Quien hizo la Caridad de costear este Sepulcro.[184]
>
> Aqui yacen, los huesos D^1 V. P. F. Asencio Zarate de la Horden de San Francisco, Varon Apostólico que se sacaron en las Ruinas de la Iglesia antigua de San Lorenzo de Pecuries el Dia 8 de Mayo E. 1759 y se trasladaron estos Dos Ven: Varones a esta Parochia de la Villa de Santa Fé Dia 11 de Agosto, D. dicho año.[185]

The church books begin with Santa Fe in 1698, Pecos in 1710, go till 1851.[186] About 3 P.M., I went home and wrote to Joe, to George Hoffmann, and to E. W. Mudge. Afterwards, I called on John Pearce. At night called on Father Defouri.[187] Splendid night, cool, starry, and quiet. The town was most handsome in the twilight. I am still nervous & unsteady, shaken up by the dreadful past. Note to Garrison.

JUNE 4: *Corpus Christi.* Called on Hartmann. Met Lieutenant Fornance,[188] Major Tucker.[189] Got a pitcher from "Pájaro Pinto" to copy. In the afternoon Dr. Meany[190] called. Moved over to Koch's in the forenoon. Wrote out the catalogue for the Church at night. Large procession.

JUNE 5: Early in the morning, I went to the Bishop and turned over the catalogue and copies of epitaphs. They have got three beautiful embroideries (church ornaments) from Santo Domingo. Splendid pieces, also a large, but almost completely faded, St. Francis Xavier, from the same place. Got four letters: Alphonse, Dr. Kranes of Stuttgart, Dr. Simonsfeld, and from dear, good Henry! Joe is better, Thank God! Called at the Brothers,[191] then at Father Defouri, Governor Ritch,[192] and in the afternoon, at Lieutenant Fornance. Copied J. Gold's[193] jar and returned it to him about 3:30 P.M. Met Brother Botulphus.[194] Called at John Pearce's, but he was not at home. Wrote to George Hoffmann, to Mr. Parkman and to Henry. Evening at Koch's with the Doctor.

JUNE 6: Left at 5:30 A.M. for San Juan with the Doctor, Mr. Koch, and John C. Pearce. Trip most splendid.[195] Arrived at San Juan about 3:30 P.M., after having stopped at Bouquet's,[196] at Father Francolon,[197] who is sick since Christmas last.

Kindest possible reception. Captain Simpson[198] here.

JUNE 7: Captain Simpson told me that Gerónimo[199] was now about 40 years old, and the son of one Francisco, of the band of Chi, and of a captive from Socorro. His Indian name is "E-skit-ti-silá." Francisco was, in 1866, when Captain Simpson commanded Fort Goodwin, in Arizona, chief of a rancheria southeast of it, and was killed at the Post in June 1866 having been arrested for the murder of several parties. He told me a great many things about King Woolsey's "Pinole Treaties"[200] and also about Whitlock's fight at the "Ciénega."[201] Eldodt's collection[202] has grown very fine. He doubts the authenticity of the "Pájaro Pinto" find. My friends left before dinner.

JUNE 8: Slept delightfully. Finished my sixth letter to the *Ausland*.[203] Mr. Gutzdorf [Gusdorf][204] came from Taos. The mountains between the Rio Grande and the Tierra Amarilla are the San Antonio, Taoseña, etc. From here to Taos, 45 miles; from Taos to the Costilla, 50 miles. The Costilla is partly in New Mexico, partly in Colorado; the Culebra is all in Colorado.

JUNE 9: Wrote at "Cibola" all day. Rather windy. Had a long talk with Mr. Campbell[205] about the superstitions of the Indians. He says they are much less now than formerly, but still thinks and knows that they keep idols and fetiches. Told me a tale very similar to that of the "Goldenen Kohlen."[206] An Indian informed [him] that, being in the timber one night, he saw a fire and went to light his cigarette at the embers, but as this cigarette did not take fire, he took one of the glowing embers into his hand, and found it was cold. This scared him so, that he dropped it and ran away. Laid carpets in the new parlor tonight.

JUNE 10: Spent a poor night. For abortion they use almagre [red ochre] and rice, mixed, which they drink in cold water. It is very effective. Chiata used it twice, and she miscarried forthwith. [L.] Hughes[207] from Santa Fe came tonight.

JUNE 11: Finished Part III of "Cibola," with page 47 and sent it off. Part IV is to be headed: "Francisco Vasquez Coronado." Finished and sent off six letters for the *Ausland*.[208] Got a friendly letter from Father Mailluchet. Wrote to Joe and to George Hoffmann, enclosing Joe's letter. Wrote to Professor Ratzel. To Padre Mailluchet, and to Eddy.[209]

JUNE 12: Slept splendidly. Mr. Gutzdorf left today for Taos. Fine day; got three letters. One from Miss Anna Reiss,[210] one from Dr. Franzel [Frenzel, probably][211] and one from Ignaz Hosp. Wrote at the article on the Apaches. In the evening, call from Mr. Lowthian. Fine evening. Painted also. Went to bed very late.

JUNE 13: Day of San Antonio de Padua. Mass. They will dance the *"Go-he-ye,"* or "brazo de baylar." Got a letter from Hartmann. The dance began about 1 P.M. It is the usual thing, like the "Ayash-tyu-qotz"[212] of Cochiti, only without the French headdresses. The men wear, each, an eagle's feather on the head. Only one drum. Bodies of the men painted bluish, the faces of women as well as of the men painted red with vermillion. Very windy. The dance lasted until nearly sundown, and afterwards they returned the Saint in procession to the church. Night splendid, although it has been threatening rain all day.

JUNE 14: Painted; finished Pt. 1 of the Apaches, and wrote to Pretorius, sending the article,[213] and enclosing it in a letter to George Hoffmann. Wrote to Dr. Eggert and to Hartmann, as Padre Seux[214] is going to Santa Fe tomorrow. In the afternoon, I went to see Chino,[215] and had a long talk with him. He seems to be a very intelligent Indian and well disposed. Besides, I am positively informed that he is a half-breed (son of a priest, Padre Castro).[216] He says[217] that the present name of San Juan[218] is:

"Ju-o-tyu-te." *"Oj-qué"* is two miles up the river on the same bank and was abandoned probably during the time of the Span- iards. The old church, here, was built about 180 years ago, ac- cording to an inscription found about 20 years ago, when the new roof was put on.[219] San Ildefonso[220] is *"Po-jo-que"* (place where the water is below). The Cañón of Santa Clara is called: northern branch: *"Pu-ye,"* the southern branch, *"Jiu-fin-ne."* The caves there were inhabited by the Tehuas [Tewas] previous to their arrival at their pueblos. *"Pio-ge"* was abandoned probably since the Conquest,[221] and its people went south! Pueblo = *"a-uing";* Pueblos, *"auing-ge."* A ruin above Pioge is called *"Sā-jiu,"*[222] and the one at the Ranchos of Taos, *"Toma-Pooge."* This was also a Tehua pueblo.[223] About two miles west of here, at the junction of the Chama and the Rio Lozo [Oso], there is a small pueblo called *"Te-ouyi."*[224] *"A-bé-chiu"* [Abiquiu][225] (orilla del capulín), an ancient Tehua Pueblo too. About two miles northwest of the Rito Colorado, a very large pueblo, *"Se-pa-ui"* [Sapawe][226] (pájaro azul); three miles beyond it, another one: *"Ponyi-pa- quen."*[227] The Rito de los Frijoles: *"Tu-po-ge."*[228] (*"Tu"* = frijol.) There is a tale that the people of Pioge fled to Mexico, and buried all their stuff across the river. A whole tinaja filled with beads, turquoises, etc. and also their pottery is said to be there.[229]

JUNE 15: Wrote all day at the letter for the "National-Zeitung,"[230] and in the afternoon, painted the yellow tinaja. Got three letters in the evening; one from E. W. Mudge, one from Garrison, and another one from Meysenburg,[231] a very friendly one at that. I replied to Meysenburg, and wrote to Charles Boeschenstein, and sent him a letter to Joe.[232] Louis Baer,[233] of San Marcial, spent the night with us. Padre Seux.

JUNE 16: [San Juan Pueblo expressions] Buenos dias, *"O-sengye- jyam."* Buenas noches, *"O-sengye-jyu."* The question asked any girl for enamorous [*sic*] purposes is *"quinda"* and the affirmative reply to it, *"tyunda."* Sent to Garrison a seven page paper on the Apaches,[234] then painted. Padre Seux returned, with paper, novel,[235] and letter from Dr. Eggert.

JUNE 17: Finished the Apache article for the *Westliche Post*[236] and mailed it to George [Hoffmann]. Letters from Joe, Henry,

Eddy, and Mr. Parkman. Dr. Symington[237] and Mr. Whitney came at dinnertime; then at night, L. Hughes and Don Pedro Sanchez.[238] [Vocabulary items followed.] Don Juan García[239] tells me of a tale, related by Martin Atencio, of seven Spanish soldiers who once entered the old church here and fell asleep and are asleep yet, until war will break out again. What war? Quien Sabe. [More vocabulary here.] They still have their secret dances here. Sun, grandfather of the day. Moon, grandfather of the squash? Wrote to Eddy.

JUNE 18: Last night I still wrote to Mr. Parkman and to Joe. Father Seux told me, previously, of a case of adultery which happened here, in the pueblo. Both, man and woman, were condemned to be *buried alive.* They were saved, but it turned out to be an ancient custom.[240]

Wrote at the Report[241] and at the letter for Berlin. Also painted. Received a good letter from George Hoffmann, and also one from Joe—the first one she wrote, having mailed it to Santa Fe. It was forwarded by the Doctor. Chino called at night and staid until midnight. Very valuable talk. He speaks freely and very plain. *"Ta-nyi"*—parrot or guacamayo. He says that they worshipped and still partly worship: *"T'han-se-ndó"*—the Sun Father, and *"Póquio,"* the moon (or calabash or pumpkin) woman. *"Agoio-soyo"*—the morningstar and *"Zé-jan-quio"*— the eveningstar, the former, male, the latter, female. Besides, they worship (?) the *"Ta-ne"* or fetishes (*ta* like "Tenit" in French) such as *"Quen"* (quin, in French). Puma, the bear, and the Snake (?).

Their belief goes to the effect that the soul, after four days travel, goes to rest in the *"Po-qui"* or lake or lagune, wish [which] is the same as the *Shi-pap*[242] of the Queres [Keres]. This lagune lies in the west or northwest. The little heaps of stones which they erect are votive offerings like altars or stations for to pray there. They call them *"Cai-yi"* and pray there, sacrificing sacred meal *"Cung-qué,"* and plumes. In praying, they address themselves to god, or more properly, to the sun father (which gradually has blended into the Christian God), and to the "Mother," calling her on such occasions *"Caye-quio"* or according to the name of the Pueblo: *"Jyu-o-tyu-te-quio," "Capa-quio," "Nambé-quio,"* etc. It is the same as the *"Po-quio,"* or moonwoman.

To propitiate the affairs of the tribe and stand in relation directly with the gods, there are two religious clusters [moieties][243] whose office it is, on serious occasions, to pray and fast for the Pueblo, and for that purpose they fast always *four* days on great occasions, in their estufa [kiva].[244] Of these estufas, there are two, one for each cluster. One of these clusters is called *"Pay-ojque"* (*"Pay,"* summer) or leaders of summer, also *"Qö-sa-re"* (signification unknown, but they are the *"Qo'share"* [Koshare] of Cochiti), and their time is summer. They are the original medicine men and priests of the tribe. The other cluster is called *"Oyi-que"* (*"Oyi,"* frost), frost people, but also *"Qui-ra-na"* [Kwirena][245] (vide Cochiti).

Membership of these clusters is not hereditary, and obtained through a *votive* offering. If, for instance, a woman is pregnant, or there is danger of miscarriage, or death of mother or child, the father prays, sprinkles meal, sacrifices plumes, and vows that his child, if a boy, shall become either a *"Payojque"* (*Qö-share*) or an *"Oyi-que"* (*Quiranna*). The boy then becomes one in time, or the father himself may vow himself to become one. They are in fact clusters of penitents for the tribe, and stand therefore apart and secret in their performances.[246] At the head of each stands a leader elected for life. For the *"Pay-ojque"* there is the *"Po-a-toyo"* (cacique)[247] also called *"Pay-ojque"* and *"Qösa-se-ndo"* (father of *Qo'share*); at the head of the *"Oyique"* is the *"Oyi-que"* or *"Quirana-se-ndo."* The former is chief-mourner (this is in fact their office) for the tribe from 25 of May (or April) until 25 of November (or October), the *Oyique* for the cold other six months, so that they alternate semi-annually. If anything happens, anybody dies, or falls sick, if there is any important resolution or action pending, they mourn for it, fast four days, and pray and sacrifice; the *"Pay-ojque"* in summer, the *"Oyi-que,"* [in winter].

They alternately regulate the dances, each one in his season or term, but they are not permitted to engage in any strife or quarrel or litigation. Still the governor calls upon them for advice in every important case, and then upon both together. On the first days of the year they meet, alone, for the purpose of electing, or rather appointing, the officers of the Pueblo. (Here there are 12.) It being winter, the *"Oyique"* has the first nomination: that of governor; then the *"Pay-ojque"* appoints the captain of war; the

"Oyique," the lieutenant-governor; the other, the "alguazil" [constable], and so on until all the twelve are appointed.[248]

Then the principals [principales][249] are advised of it, and the new officials are accepted by the people, and installed in office. When the *"Pay-ojque"* dies, the people mourn for him one or two years, and then they go to the *"Oyique,"* begging him to assist them to elect a new head. So if the *"Oyique"* dies, his successor is elected by his cluster assisted by the cacique. No succession in the family. In this way the powers are evenly balanced and even in religion, the democratic cast is preserved. Besides these two esoteric groups (or at least originally esoteric) there are now five gentes or clans, *"Dóa."* These are *"T'han-dóa,"* Sun Clan; *"Po-dóa,"* Moon Clan; *"Qu-dóa,"* Stone Clan; *"Qupi-dóa,"* Coral; *"Ye-dóa,"* Marten (?). They are endogamous now, intermarriage *not* being prohibited.

Four days after the birth of a child, a woman staying with the mother starts with the baby at sunrise to a hillock about the village. There, she sprinkles cornmeal and gets the baby to do the same, prays, and selects the name from the object or phenomenon most striking to her eye (for instance: *"T'hansame,"* solar eclipse), and then brings the child back to her mother with the name. Marriage only through the Church. Courtship made by the boy, and with presents to the parents of girl. The boy asks for the girl. [In cases of] Bastardy, [he] has to marry or care for the child.

The governor has jurisdiction of any offence, except the gravest ones, in which case the principales meet. The *"Pay-ojque"* and the *"Oyique"* are then called, and they are asked for advice. They invariably reply that the meting out of justice does not belong to them, that their office is an occult and humble one, but that it belongs to the governor and his people to judge criminals. This reply constitutes the sanction, given by religion to the judicial functions of the governor and his principales. Then the two "caciques" retire; afterwards, the sentence is pronounced and executed by the capitán de la guerra. Apprehensions are performed by the lieutenant governor if ever resistance is offered; in the other case, it is through the war captain, or his aides.

Of the dances, the *"Paijiare,"* Deer Dance, is danced publicly and also in the estufa. The *"Oque-jiare,"* or Antler Dance, after Christmas (26 December); the *"Sa-qu-jiare,"* Pipe Dance, after

Christmas. The Fruit Dance, *"Ha-qu-jiare,"* was formerly danced in fall and meant to give back to the earth part of the fruit it had produced, in order to propitiate it. All these dances are cachinas [kachinas].[250]

The *"Go-he-ye-jiare,"* or Baile de las Tabletas, and the Baile de los Franceses [?], on San Juan's Day, are not cachinas. At Nambé,[251] they dance, on Christmas, the *"Ta-Jiare,"* or Elk Dance, and at Santa Clara,[252] on September 13, the *"Pingua-jiare,"* or Mountain Sheep Dance. Both cachinas. He also told me of the terrible execution of sorcerers and one witch at Nambé about 25 to 26 years ago.[253] The parties killed were *"Katzire," "Cáyamo," "Fi-ue,"* and one woman. There was a severe epidemic visiting Nambé at the time (fever), and people were dying from it every day. Suspicions of witchcraft arose, and one Matias, upon his return after having gone out to gather wood, prayed at one of the *"Cai-yi"* to God and to the "Madre" that they might enlighten him on the subject. One night, when he had given a rendezvous to a certain woman, outside of the pueblo, and while the "Qö-sare" held a four day fast at their estufa for the epidemic, under surveillance of the "Cacique," he saw a man come down the ladder, and watched him sneaking through the pueblo, stopping successively at the foot of the ladder to a sick man's "Qoye" [home], in the centre of the plaza, at the gate of the cemetery, and at the threshold to the church. At each place he went through the same performance, lifting his hand successively to the north, west, south, and east, praying, and then burying something in the earth. He [Matías] and a friend, who was out after the same woman, went and found that he had buried prayer-plumes of *owls, crows,* and *woodpeckers* feathers! They stopped him at the churchyard gate, accused him with the governor, and he was caught, and sentenced, after having confessed, to be whipped to death. As the war captain was executing the sentence, the culprit denounced his two other companions, *"Ca-tzi-re,"* and *"Cayamo."* They were arrested and suffered the same death as their companion. A great many objects of sorcery were found, such as the feathers above described, obsidian flakes, bands and circles and wreaths of yucca, etc. Their death must have been atrocious. They confessed that it was their plan to kill off the whole Pueblo, seize the lands, and, changing the dead into game, live upon the latter. He also told me a number of tales about the Navajos and their supposed witchcraft.[254]

JUNE 19: Atencio called. He is well informed, but a spy! He assured me that Troomaxiaquince is a Tehua word, but pleads not to know anything about the ruin of that name. Red is the color of mourning, as a woman showed me her wool bracelets, red, which she wears for the death of her children. All this was confirmed afterwards. Got letter from Mr. Henry Dronne.[255] *"Sa-ua-ndé,"* it is good or handsome. Wrote nearly all night. Could not sleep.

JUNE 20: Had an early call. . . . The cacique still has an official manta: black, with white, red, and yellow patterns, and they formerly used to wear a blue garment, like a "Huipil"—sleeveless, and of wool. He told me also that black, and not red, was the color of mourning, and that the red wrist-bands were worn only in order to "gladden the hearts, and to relieve mourning people." At night, Candelario Ortiz came to Mr. Eldodt and brought him a fine old manta, a "faja," and two bands or girdles, turned out of "tule." He said that Santa Cruz[256] was a pueblo, and called *"Tanyi-numbu,"* place of *Opuntia,* but that it was abandoned before the coming of the Spaniards. That the Pueblo of Galisteo was called *"Tage-unye"*[257] and that another of the Tano villages was called *"Pooyé-unge,"* hollow water. That when, during the interregnum,[258] San Felipe was attacked by the Pueblos of Isleta, Sandia, Santa Ana, Cia [Zia], Cochiti, and Santo Domingo, San Juan was also attacked by those of Taos, Picuries [Picurís, or San Lorenzo], Santa Clara, San Ildefonso, Pojuaque [Pojoaque], Nambé, and Tezuque [Tesuque]. All on account of their fidelity to the Spaniards, they fought for four days, and finally defeated the enemy, who afterwards made peace with them in a hollow southeast of the present pueblo, at a place today called *"Pó-a-mū,"* place of speech. Therefore the name: San Juan de los Caballeros![259] *"Quio-tráco"* is a ruin east of Tezuque, near the "Escapulario," in the mountains. He also says that the pueblo of San Juan stood where it stands today, but the houses were other ones. Spent the evening very pleasantly with Mr. E. [Eldodt] at his own house. The people of Taos use snowshoes, in form of a wheel, but he (Candelario) says that the people here wore formerly also sandals of yucca, braided.

JUNE 21: Left for Los Luceros at 8 A.M. It is a beautiful valley, fairly peopled, with groves of álamos, fields, and little groups of houses, and the tall dark mesa on the other side of the river, all frowning, volcanic, and torn up, leaving but a narrow strip of lower plateaux along the stream. I passed "Plaza del Alcalde" about 9 A.M. and reached "Los Luceros."[260] It has its fields like the rest. The ruin stands on the lomas over the fields directly. The side towards the river is abrupt and much worn; the arroyos have eaten up into the center almost of the plaza. Not a trace visible of estufas.* The walls were of adobe, and their width about 0.30 [meter]. The pueblo forms a hollow square, irregular, of course, and is much excavated. The rooms seem to be very small. I succeeded in measuring twelve rooms, and they give an average of 3.1 X 2.0 [meters]. Much pottery about, green and black, cream and black, red and black—glossy.[261] Much obsidian, flint, metates and manos, unfinished axes, etc. Also fragment of a skull.

I then went to the house of Matías Luján, who had been digging in the ruins. They showed me axes, little cups, some bone-trinkets, and ornaments. Much copper ore (probably for paint). An Indian medicine man left a bag there of stuff, which he gathered at the ruins for his purposes.[262] It contains one strangely shaped stone, one large piece of obsidian, and several fragments of petrified wood. Obsidian, they assert, the Indians pulverize and apply on festering wounds and for sore eyes! They told me of a skull, "*muy chiata*" [probably, *muy chata*, i.e., (very small)], artificially deformed, which was found in the ruins. I returned at noon. Very hot and clouding. Dr. Symington and Whitney had arrived. They left soon. In the afternoon I painted the ground-plan of the ruin. A very violent sandstorm from the south, with only a few raindrops, raged from 3 to 5 P.M. No sleep. The Indians are practicing nightly at the estufa.

JUNE 22: The Procession of Señor San Francisco took place today. ... "*Ojua-tza-ue*" is the Tehua name for Maseua, and "*Ojua-pii*," the equivalent of "*Oyo-ya-ua.*"[263] The former comes from the north; the latter, from the south and they pray to them, in August, when the Qoshare have their main dance, also formerly at Easter-time, as at Cochiti. The latter dance is, however, abandoned since some time. I painted, being ill disposed for writing. In the afternoon, the same weather occurred as yesterday. Chino was very emphatic; he says that it is neither sun nor moon which are worshipped but the *gods or person dwelling* there as: "*Nai-*

B.

a to b. 21 steps S.E =

116

17. S to d 18
abt n.

d n.w.w =
18

41. c.
2.5
1.40

0-18
13

0.30
A.

1.8 2D
2.9
4.4 1.5
3.3
1.8

13.
107.S.

A.

a
B.

n.W.
a.s.
12.4
9.

21.steps n.w.

mbi-se-ndo," our father, and *"Nai-mbi-quio,"* our mother. This fully agrees with the other names: *"T'han-se-ndo,"* sun-father, and *"Po-quio,"* pumpkin woman. Letters from Joe, George, and Henry tonight, also MSS from Mr. Dronne. Wrote to Joe and to Mr. Dronne. Handed the MSS to Eldodt for perusal and safe-keeping.

JUNE 23: The *"Pánanas"* are an Indian tribe living near Kansas City (evidently the Pawnees), also the *"Paca-navo."* The *"A-a"* and the *"Zari-tica"* are north, near Cheyenne. The *"Cia-navo"* are with the Comanches. Fathers Courbon[264] and Grom, and Rolly; also Abbé Picard,[265] came here this evening for the fiesta. The whole Pueblo is preparing, cooking, painting, etc. Judge Prince[266] and Mr. Vanderver [Van der Veer][267] arrived late tonight. Adler[268] came.

JUNE 24: Pueblo quiet yet. Mangas Coloradas[269] was killed at Fort West[270] in 1863. After Mass, the dance began, about 120 persons taking part in it. The singers, as usual, with one big drum and 8–10 tambourines.[271] The men wear long crests of eagle-feathers, or fur-caps with eagle-feathers and plumes. They wore gaudy, fancy costumes, buckskin leggings, mostly embroidered with beads, but no manta. Their paint was very diversified and as gaudy and horrible as that of the Qöshare at Cochiti, all colors of the rainbow being represented. They carried pistols, lances, muskets, bows and arrows, also sabres, and wands of various sizes and shapes, all profusely adorned with plumes, and evident "fancy arrangements." The flags were of calico with feathers pending.[272] The girls gaudily dressed with calico skirts, wool, even some with silk, and a few old mantas. Some had white down on their heads. Necklaces, etc., of silver, turquoise, coral, etc. were abundant. Everything looked new and as if just made for the occasion. The dancers remained at the east side of the plaza, and advanced in an irregular double file, then wheeled about, dancing as usual, in a double row, treble, and quadruple row, then in two rows, the woman in the usual [?], the men stamping, and shouting. It was wild and strange. *"Qui-tara-jyare,"* dance of the French. A sprinkle. "Quitara-ué," French people.[273] Got letters from Eddy and *New York Staatszeitung* with $36.00, which I handed to Eldodt to my credit. They kept on singing and dancing, forming a circle, or rather, two circles, with a drum in the center of each one, dancing or rather, stamping around.

JUNE 25: Wrote to Eddy last night. Also to *New York Staatszeitung.* Juan Antonio Cruz was here this morning, and told me the dance of yesterday was also called: *"Sa-rit-yé."*[274] This name is derived from an Indian tribe of the Llanos,[275] near the Comanches, (the Zaritica!) as they met that tribe when they went to trade with the Comanches. They also called the dance, which they borrowed from the wild Indians of the plains, after the French also. He also told me, that according to tradition, the Tehuas came from the north, and settled about the north first; then they drifted southward, on the west side of the Rio Grande, and crossed to the east side, settling and abandoning one pueblo after another, and extending as far south as the Manzano or, perhaps, the Galisteo plain only. Thence they drifted north again, settling at Santa Fe and in the heights east of it, and finally came back north into the sierra of the Jicarrita and Truchas. The plain of Santa Cruz and San Juan was then very wet and muddy, therefore uninhabitable; so they remained on the eastern heights until it dried up, and then finally settled where they are now. This is said to be their tradition. Candelario Ortiz also told me that there was a "Baile de Montezuma" of which he sang me a few passages, and it contains Opata words!![276] Wrote all day at the article for Berlin.

JUNE 26: Got letter from Henry and the *Westliche Post.* At night, had a long and important talk with Chino. The proper name for Montezuma is *"Po-se-ye-mo,"*[277] roçilla or rociada (dew). His sister is called *"Na-vi-tu-a."* He lived at the Pueblo of Ojos Calientes. One day, as the people of Yunque[278] were dancing a cachina, he came in a "carretela" [four-wheeled carriage] drawn by two elks, and in a dress not familiar to them. They did not recognize him and hid themselves. When he saw it, he reprimanded them for not having known him, and then said, "Since you have not known me in disguise, I shall leave you forever, and after me there shall come to rule you, other people." So he went south, and at the Ojo del Lucero, in Chihuahua, he left his tinaja. His sister, *Navi-tua,* followed him on Christmas night. She is said to have rested at the Carrizal, in Chihuahua. The Tehuas themselves came out of a cave up north, called *"Ci-bo-be."* At the time they came out of it, God, or "unos de los Señores" [one of the Saints], divided them into two bands, one of the *"Pay-ojque,"* and one of the *"Oyique."* The former was told to go to the west, and to feed but upon fruit and vegetables, and it was said to them that the land which they were to live in would be perpetual summer. The *"Oyi-que"* was told to go to the east, that on his track there would be perpetual cold, and that he and his people should live off of meat and game alone, and should dress in deerskins, etc., whereas the *Pay-ojque* were barefooted, and wore nothing but the huipil.

The *Ojique* went south by the plains and finally reached this region, where they founded the Pueblo of *"Oj-qué!"* This signifies: the place where there is most strength! Meanwhile, the *Payojque* also were advancing south by the west, but it was very hot and muddy, and many of them grew very tired and staid behind, refusing to go farther on and declaring their intention to return to the cave. At the same time the *"Qö-sa-re"* [Tewa: Kossa; or Keres: Koshare] came out of the cave, fully dressed and painted, and the *"Po-a-toyo"* told him to show himself to the stragglers, and make his pranks before them and thus entice them on.[279] This he did and they indeed followed him. But previous to that, some of them had fallen to making arrowheads of flint, and to killing game, etc. This the *"Poatoyo"* disapproved, telling them it was forbidden to his cluster to kill any living being and to eat it. But they heeded him not and quarrelled among each other, and some were even killed. Thereupon it was decided to cast them off who had thus done wrong, and they became two factions, one of which formed the *Navajos* and the other the *Apaches!*

The *Payojque* then moved on and settled at Yunque, but, the river was so high for twelve years that it could not be forded. Still they wished to join the *Oyique* at Ojqué. So the Poatoyo built a bridge with a parrot's feather, and a feather of the magpie, and they crossed over, but while the last ones were crossing, the bridge was tipped over by some trickery. They fell into the Rio Grande and were changed into fish and trout, and this is the reason why the Navajos, Apaches, and some of the Pueblos, even, do not eat any fish today.[280]

They then settled at Ojqué, the Oyique putting the condition that both bands thereafter should keep separate. From there they spread south in bands, and founded the other pueblos.[281] At Pojuaque was the dividing point, and the large ruined pueblo to the west of the actual houses was called: *"Teje-o-uing-ge-o-ui-ping"*—Pueblo de en el Medio.[282] He thinks that Santa Fe was a Tano village, but does not know whether it was settled at the time of Oñate or not.[283]

The six regions are: *"Tam-pii,"* East; *"Acompii,"* South; *"Tzam-pii,"* West; *"Pein-pii."* North; *"O-pa-ma-con,"* Above; and *"Nan-so-ge-unge,"* Below; and in this order, the smoke is puffed out at the greetings. The symbols are the same as at Zuñi.[284] The colored rainbow is called *"Qua-tembé,"* arco del verano [summer bow]; the white bow with black border is *"Po-tembe,"* arco del invierno [winter bow]. The name of *"Huaja-toya"* he thinks is Cayohua [Kiowa], and he says that the language of the Cayohua does not differ more from the Tehua than the French does from the Spanish!![285] The Cayohuas say *"Po"*—water; *"Qó"*—cibola [buffalo], etc. Cibola is evidently the equivalent of Shi-pap, and the common origin of the Pueblos is thus again indicated. But the Tehuas do not seem to have any recollection of the four successive worlds, nor of the two children of the sun.

JUNE 27: Wrote to Dr. Eggert and sent the letter through Judge Prince, who had come last night later. Letter from Gerdes![286] Don Abelardo Román came. Finished the "San Bernardino Chalchihuapan"[287] and mailed it, in two envelopes, to Dr. Carl Frenzel, #33 Koetheres Strasse, Berlin.

JUNE 28: Wrote to Dr. Reiss and to Miss Reiss, enclosing three views of San Juan. The party of the Oyique is called *"Quäre"* and the party of the Payojque, *"Jai-ye."* Tetilla = *"Qa-téc."* Wrote to Henry also. M [Matías Luján] did not go; Chino and I [went, but Matías] spent a part of the afternoon with me.

It appears that the Oyique and Payojque are hereditary; that is, if the parents are [both] Oyique [or both] Payojque, then the children are the same too. If husband and wife belong to different groups, then the wife may, from Oyique, become Payojque, or the reverse, but she cannot be compelled to do it. If both parents remain in their respective clusters, then the oldest child born belongs to the cluster of the father, the next to that of the mother, the third to the father, fourth to the mother, etc.[288]

It is not the Oyique and Payojque who become thus by a vow of the parents, but only the Qöshare and the Quirana. The latter are not numerous, only about 20 of each in the Pueblo; they lead a very hard life, fasting and praying, and castigating themselves. He hinted at the origin of the gens, stating that it was posterior [subsequent?] to that of the two main clusters, that it was the result of natural increase, & that the names were selected after those natural objects which attracted most attention, like as in giving personal names.

JUNE 29: Catalogued Eldodt's collection in part. Letter from Joe, and papers from the *Staats-zeitung.* His collection is very valuable: The "pregoneros"[289] are chosen by the governor. Chino confirms the statement of Juan José [Montoya, of Cochiti Pueblo], namely, that those who have been governer once, become principales for life afterwards, and they sit as judges in case of trials. In war, both the Po-a-toyo and the Oyique do not carry arms, but they have to watch and cure the wounded; one in the daytime, the other, at night. The yellow and green paint they do not mix with water, but with saliva, and with the calabash-suds, pounded and mixed in a mortar [with a pestle], similar to the so-called chunkey-stones.[290] His name is *"Te-anyi,"* álamo que menía el viento [cottonwood that trembles in the wind], and his wife's name is *"Qua-tzau-ua."* He says that there is a report to the effect that the Qui-ra-na came from the *south,* perhaps. Still it is not impossible that such a tale might exist.

JUNE 30: Wrote to Joe, to Father Eguillon,[291] to Frank E. Robinson,[292] and to E. A. Allen, also. Juan Antonio Cruz came. He told me that, while his father was a young man yet, the Comanches under three "capitanes" appeared at Yunque, and then crossed over and attacked the Pueblo in two bands. The people of San Juan fought them and killed them all, only three men escaping. Afterwards, peace was made with the Comanches at the Huaja-toyas. (It is a name of the Comanche-Idiom.) Letter from Dr. Eggert, which I sent to Henry. Wrote to E. W. Mudge. At night,

Candelario brought a pair of old sandals of yucca, *"A-ji-ue."* They are from Taos, and they used them formerly, previous to having the moccasin‼ This is very important. Name of old pueblo at Ojo Caliente: "Jo-ui-ri" [Howiri].[293]

J U L Y

JULY 1: I wrote to Dr. Eggert, and sent him five numbers of "Cibola" through Louis Baer. [The remainder of this entry was devoted to vocabulary.]

JULY 2: In the afternoon one storm after another on the mountains, the wind blew very heavily here nearly all afternoon, from different quarters. At last, about sunset, a fearful thundershower broke out, at the close of which a beautiful double rainbow spanned the heavens. Arranged Eldodt's pottery. Bishop Salpointe came.

JULY 3: The aboriginal Taos name for the former pueblo of Taos, which they abandoned since the arrival of the Spaniards, is indeed *"Te-gat-ha."* It is about 200 yards from the present pueblo.[294] Their former home is in the mountains to the east, close by a big lagune; it is called *"Mojua-lua."*[295] Picuries is called *"Ui-la-na."* They say *"Ui-ale Ui-la-na,"* let us go up to Picuries.

JULY 4: Wrote all day. Chino was here all evening and gave me the symbols.

JULY 5: North is *blue.* East: *white.* South: *red.* West: *yellow.* Above: *black.* Below: *all colors together.*[296] Staid at home. Hot.

JULY 6: Received letter from [*The*] *Nation* with $20[297] and card from George [Hoffmann]. Painted and finished letter for Ratzel. Sent MSS to him, 31 pp. This is the seventh letter to the *Ausland.*[298]

JULY 7: Painted mostly, finishing the stone arrow-streightener [*sic*]. At sunset, Antonio José and family, and A. Seligman[299] came.

JULY 8: S. Eldodt left for Santa Fe today. Wrote today nearly 12 pp. for the *Westliche Post.* Letter from Joe and from Paris. My eyes are not good; they hurt. I have now got $56.—in all, and $15. —in hands of George.

JULY 9: They still have got the "Madre" here, and it is the "Po-a-toyo" who keeps it. It is of hide, and a painted face.[300] Finished the two first parts of the article for the *Westliche Post,* until page 24.

JULY 10: Wrote and mailed to Pretorius.[301] Painted. Wrote to George Hotz, to H. Hübler, and to James Jackson.[302] Got letter from E. W. Mudge.

JULY 11: Wrote and mailed to Joe and to Eddy. I arranged Mr. Eldodt's collection again, recording such pieces as were not yet entered. Melchiades Ortiz called; he brought me a little stone, a pebble, evidently worked. He promised me also a fetish, of alabaster, but could not get at it. At night two parties came on horseback. Mr. Hauck of Philadelphia, and Kneeland of Tierra Amarilla.

JULY 12: Got up at 5 A.M. Sebastian was ready with the horses and buggy, and so we drove on to Pojuaque. It being Sunday, there were but a few people around, and still sleepy. Old Mr. Bouquet received us with the customary kindness. He directed me to Alonzo Aguilar at San Ildefonso. The valley of the Rio Pojuaque is wide and sandy, and all peopled; there are even two little villages on the road. The Tezuque River joins the other about one-and-a-half miles below Pojuaque. Drove to Pojuaque with Sebastian Magsanen [?]. Reached Pojuaque at 8 P.M.

They deny that the Caves of Santa Clara were ever inhabited by the Tehuas, but say that they were the abodes of a people who were like them and went south long ago. The Tanos claimed Santa Fe; the Cieneguilla, *"Tzi-mu-o,"* and the Bajada, up to the Alamo [Canyon]. There, was the division line.[303] The people of Cochiti [call] the Tanos, *"Puy-at-ye."* The information about Tehua is from Alonzo Aguilar; about the Tanos, from Juan Pacheco of Santo Domingo; about the Queres, from Juan José [of Cochiti]. Cacique, *"Ho-tshañi;"* second [assistant] *"T'shay-qa-*

tze;" third [assistant], *"uisht-yaqqa."* He attended to the cacique, cooked and attended to the house, when there are three. *"Yaya,"* mother. *"Chayana,"* medicine men, [or] *"shyay-yaq."*

For the warriors he does not recall the word, but I think that he belongs to them, and therefore does not want to tell.[304] The Tehuas call the people of Cochiti, *"Tema."* The Queres call the Rito de los Frijoles, *"Tyu-onyi,"*[305] that is the place where the Pueblos had their last separation or treaty, the place where they divided into branches. Juan José thinks that the Piros have indeed been Queres once.[306] He says that, if they want something (of their idolatries) they have to come up here to get it, and if they do not get it here, they have to go to Taos, even, this being the most northerly place where they can obtain it.[307] (I write this on the 15th.)

From Pojuaque there is a somewhat sandy, but fertile, narrow valley down to San Ildefonso. The ruined pueblos are on the south side of the Rio Pojuaque, and the Tezuque River empties into it about a mile west of Pojuaque. On the promontory, lies the pueblo of *"Te-je"* (the one "en el medio").[308] Farther down is *"T'ham-ba,"*[309] and between the latter and San Ildefonso is *"Sa-co-na"* (Jacona).[310] San Ildefonso lies three miles south of the high mesa of *"Tu-Yo,"* a very conspicuous object.[311] On its top [are] permanent tanks of water, and ruins of houses erected after 1680. I reached San Ildefonso at 4 P.M., distance six miles. The pueblo forms about a square, there being four "cuarteles" around the plaza.* Stopped at the house of Alonzo Aguilar. Very friendly. Many people are going to Cochiti, and I arranged to go with them very early.

JULY 13: Left at 2 A.M. with Juan Rey and his son. Until sunrise we trudged along, up and down hills covered with sabinos [junipers] and small piñones, sandy arroyos, past the dark mesa of *"Jyuma,"* which is called "los Gigantes," whereas the northern mesa is called "el Huérfano." At sunrise, we were in the sandy flat of the Arroyo del Caja del Rio. It empties into the Rio Grande south of the mesa of *"Jyuma,"* and north of another volcanic mesa[312] which we ascended. It is partly covered with sabino and piñón but there are also open spaces. From its top a wide view is had to the east, to the mountains of Taos and of Colorado. This mesa is absolutely waterless, and we traversed it to the south. It took us from 5 to 8 A.M., one hour's rest till 9 A.M., then again till 11:30 A.M., to reach the first terrace. *"O-ma"* [grandfather, in Keresan; here applied to a small mesa] was on the right hand, and towards the southern half, it became very broken, high volcanic hills towering up on all sides, and higher timber, but no water. Exceedingly hot. Sky clear, hardly a breeze.

About 10 A.M., the western chain appeared, and close to the river, the ruins of *"Tzi-re-ge"* (Pajarito) [Tshirege], *"Sa-quéui,"* and of *"Po-tzu-yé"* [Potsu'ui] on low mesas, were visible.[313] Also the Rito [de los Frijoles]. The pueblo of *"Pe-ra-ge"*[314] is too near the Rio Grande (*"P'oo-so-ge"* in Tehua!) to be seen. When we reached the brink [of Mesa Chino], an immense view spread out of the south. The Sierra Ladrona was plainly visible, the Sierra del Oso, and on the far west-southwest, the Sierra de Zuñi. In the south-southeast, a mountain chain parallel to the Sandia which I could not identify; it can hardly be the Gallina. The descent of the three terraces is rocky and steep, and very high. I should judge about 1500 feet. Clouds rising northwest with thunder. Terribly hot. At the foot, in the plain, I struck for Peña Blanca, and reached it at 2 P.M., half dead of thirst and fatigue. Father A. Navet[315] received me in the kindest manner possible. Evening very stormy, but hardly a sprinkle. Zashua[316] came. All right at Cochiti. Night quiet and cool.

JULY 14: [San Buenaventura's Day, Cochiti major feast] Fine day, but very hot. Left for Cochiti early. Reception kindest imaginable. Everybody flocked to embrace the newcomer.[317] People of Santo Domingo, San Felipe, Jemez, and Cia, and from above [the Tewas]. Had a talk with Juan Pacheco of Santo Domingo. He is a *Tano.*[318] He says that the Tanos extended to the north beyond Santa Fe, which was a Pueblo of the Tanos. (He speaks the Tehua language perfectly well.) The Bajada is yet doubtful. The Cieneguilla was a Tano Pueblo, also *"Tzi-muc-o"* [Tzi-guma?]. To the east, was San Cristóbal, *"Yam-p'am-ba."* South was San Pedro, *"Pá-qa"* [Paa-ko]. To the south of the *"Tunque"* (which was a Tano village), was *"Qui-pa-na,"* on the hill above the Tejón, *"O-ja-na."* The Pueblo of Valverde, *"Cem-po-a-pi;"* that of the Tuerto, *"Ca-p'oo."* The Pueblo Largo, *"Hi-shi,"* Pueblo Colorado, *"Tzé-man-tu-o."* Pueblo Blanco, *"Ca-ye-pu."* I afterwards got some *Navajo names.* . . .

Juan José assured me that they had the four orders: priests, *"Yaya"* ("los madres"); warriors (did not recollect name); hunters, *"Shyay-yac,"* medicine men, *"Chayana."* There were formerly three caciques: *"Hó-tshan-yi";* the second cacique, *"Shay-qa-tze,"* and the last one, *"Uisht-yaqqá."*

José Hilario [Montoya][319] was mad all right, and therefore washed himself only after he got consoled. [?] They danced as usual. One kind (Shyuamo [Turquoise Kiva group]), the men wear brown [paint]; the Tanyi [Pumpkin] wear blue. Women vermillion, in both [groups]. Hot. Night cooler. Slept at the pueblo.

JULY 15: Fine day. A little more wind. Crossed the river on horseback with Victoriano [Cordero?][320] behind me. There are three currents now, the main channel reaching to above the knee on horseback. The river is constantly encroaching upon the right hand side. At Santo Domingo, it is very near the church, and will wash it away unless it is protected very solidly.[321] Reached Peña Blanca again at 8 A.M. Hot. Father Navet came from Zile [Sile] about 10 A.M. The name of Zile is said to be an Indian personal name, from an Indian who lived there formerly and who was called thus. The foundations of his house are still visible.

Thermometer, 102° F., the same on the 13th. In the afternoon, very stormy again, mostly from the west. Hardly a sprinkle even. Severe blows of sand.

There seems to exist a tradition about giants around San Ildefonso, for the deep caverns in the Black Mesa are said to have been the home of giants. Juan José stated that, in former times, when there were three caciques, the *"Hotshanyi"* appointed the [war] captain, and the *"Shayqatze,"* the governor, the captain being the chief officer. He is evidently inclined towards the warriors. The *"Uisht-yaqqa"* attended to the personal wants of the cacique, cooked for him, etc., as often as the three were together. This would indicate that there were times when they had to live together alone![322]

At San Ildefonso, I saw pottery—painting in three colors. They mix even the almagre [red ochre] with guaco [Rocky Mountain bee weed], as the almagre would not burn fast alone. By mixing some guaco with it, however, it becomes indelible after burning. They take the plant (not the root) of the guaco, boil it in water, sift [strain?] it, and then let it cool. It is always soluble in water except after having been burnt, when it becomes absolutely fast![323] The evening pleasant and cool. It has been raining all around on the mountains in streaks today, but here we have had almost nothing.

JULY 16: José Hilario came. He cannot go with us, on account of his wheat harvest which begins. The warriors, "cuando peléan" [when they fight]; *"qu-uanyi;"* "Cuando van á pelear" [when they are going to fight]: *"Na-uanyi qo-sa."* This may be the guild or secret order, although it is not quite certain, still, as he treated it rather mysteriously. It may be that he indeed gave me the desired information.

Wrote to S. Eldodt and sent letter to Wallace.[324] Jesús Sena[325] not at home yet. Called on his wife yesterday and today. The old pueblo of Santo Domingo is again stated as having been on the west bank of the river. This is the very old one, and it was probably not on the banks but on the potreros west. ("Potrero de la Cañada quemada.") Probable, but not certain.[326]

Libro de Entierros [Burial Book] de N. P. Santo Domingo, 1770 (MSS). In the year 1816 (p. 115, Fray Gerónimo de Riega being Curate). Great epidemic. 29 were buried without the priest in August; three by the priest. In September (pp. 116–118), 47; on the 5th, four; on the 9th, four; 13th, five; 17th, six. In October: 43; on the 3rd, five; 6th, five; 7th, eight; 9th, six; 11th, six; 12th, seven.

Father Navet saw, in Cochiti, in January, the "Venado" [Deer Dance]; they danced it for his reception. Two solo dancers with antlers. No headdresses, neither male nor female. The "Cibolo" [Buffalo Dance], with only one woman in the center [between two men] and the ear of corn, which she holds out to the men who wear buffalo heads, and who surround her as if attracted by the corn.

At San Felipe, they have many ancient customs preserved yet, dances, etc. Change of plan. Clouding over at noon, though not as densely as yesterday. Thermometer, 97° F. at noon.

[Here Bandelier devoted two pages of his journal to excerpts from the "Germania" of Tacitus and "Ad Romanos" of Horace, along with translation excerpts from León Halevy in French.]

We left Peña Blanca at 3 P.M. and reached the Bajada (*"Tze-na-*

ta") at 5 P.M. The usual heat, the usual blow. Visited the old pueblo and collected pottery. Night with sprinkle.

JULY 17: The pueblo of the Bajada is said to have been called *"Cinnicú."* It is doubtful, although the woman (Francisca Gonzalez)[327] is said to have been raised at Santo Domingo. This was confirmed afterwards by an Indian of that Pueblo, who positively stated that the Bajada,[328] as well as the Cieneguilla were Tano.

At night, about 3 A.M., it rained, but at sunrise it was clear again. We started at 8 A.M. for Wallace, reaching it at 9:30 A.M. Met McIlvain[329] [of Wallace]. Left again at 11 A.M. and began to rise gradually to the southeast, making directly for the Sierra de los Nuevos Placeres [Ortiz Mountains]. We first rose to the top of the lomas, and then a level plateau, absolutely arid, with few sabinos, *Opuntia* in bloom. Towards the southern end of the Sierra, higher timber appeared, and it grew cooler. We then turned due south towards the Sierra Francisco and reached Golden about 3:30 P.M. Distance travelled: Bajada to Wallace, six miles; Wallace to Golden, 25 miles. Total 31 miles.

We crossed the Arroyo Tuerto over the Ojos de Valverde. The ruin is right there, and another one on Arroyo Tuerto, right close to Golden, north. That of Valverde[330] is in the fields of Juan Sanchez. Wrote to Joe, a long letter.

There is a captive of the Apaches here, that is, a boy from Socorro, who was captured about five to six years ago near the Padillas, and went with Victorio to the Mexican frontier, then escaped. His father was shot, his little sister brained on a stone. He is very deaf, but appears a good boy, quiet, and gentle. The Apaches ill-treated him fearfully.

Golden has decreased rather than increased since 1882.[331] Wallace is about gone. The people with whom we stay are very good. Heavy thunderstorm over the Rio Grande Valley, and slow rain at night. Cool and pleasant.

JULY 18: Did not rain long last night, but much water fell. Morning quiet and cool. Clouded, but clearing from the northwest gradually. Mailed letter. Started at 8:30 A.M., about, for the Tuerto, and found the ruins easily.*[332] They are immediately west of the mill, on the banks of the arroyo. Not a bit of pottery, but many fragments of basalt and volcanic rock. No obsidian. The ruins are so indistinct that no measurements are possible without long excavations. They are on the right bank of the arroyo. I then descended the arroyo about three-and-a-half miles to where the other arroyo joins it. The cañada is narrow and affords little room for fields. The banks are hills of drift alternating with red and white rock. Abandoned mine-works along the road. Not finding anything at all, I turned up the Arroyo de Valverde and followed it to the field of Juan Sanchez where there are a few indistinct signs of ruins. But no pottery; nothing but fragments of stones and basalt or lava. It became very hot; summerclouds rising all around, but as yet no signs of rain for today. The Cerro Cabezon [Cabezon Peak, 8,300 feet] shows up splendidly in the northwest. Wrote to S. Eldodt. There is a small pueblo between the Pueblo Largo and San Lázaro [important Galisteo ruins].[333] The mountains which I saw from the top of the mesa coming from San Ildefonso are the Sierra de Gallegos above Chililí, being in front of the Pass of Carnoé. The Arroyo of Valverde runs through the town, and almost parallel with the Tuerto.*

JULY 19: My informants [for a considerable body of vocabulary items deleted here] are, in regard to the Queres idiom, Manuel Trujillo, who has lived all his youth at Santo Domingo; in regard to the Tigua [Tiwa] idiom, Maria Panda, raised at Isleta. All these data I got last night. The name for governor and war captain are the same [at Santo Domingo] as at Cochiti, but he claims that the cacique is called "Ca-sic"—which is evidently but a Spanish corruption. Shall go to the Tejón directly from here, and not stay nor pass by the Madera. I am only wasting my time here if I remain longer. From here they have carried away stone hatchets and axes, pottery, etc. to Albuquerque. It appears that Maseua and Shiuana are the same, and they invoke them whenever the corn is raising [sic] and the rain is needed.[334]

From Golden to the Tejón, the distance is 11 miles, east-northeast, in the spur running north out of the Sandia Mountains; to San Felipe, ten miles. This will be a hot day. The "Madera" is 11 miles south of here. San Pedro, two-and-a-half miles; the ruins [Paa-ko],[335] eight miles; San Antonio, 13 miles; the Tijera, 18 miles.

I left for the Tejón at 9 A.M. with Romualdo Montoya in a wagon. We followed the Arroyo Tuerto, all the cañada downwards, to the opening of the cañada. A broad view opened to the northwest and north, with the Cabezon in full view. At the Uña de Gato, the Arroyo (or Rio) San Pedro joins the Arroyo del Tuerto; the country is broken with high peaks rising. The Sandia looms up to the south, and the cuchillo of the Tejón appears broken and steep, extending three miles north of the Tejón. Then at the northeast corner, at the foot of the heights, lies the Pueblo of Tunque.[336] Reached Tejón at 2 P.M. and went to the house of Juan Antonio Gallego y Barreras. Nice reception, pleasant and open. It is a good, cheerful house and small family. There is a pueblo at the "Chi-mal,"[337] three miles northwest of San Pedro and about eight miles south-southeast of the Tejón, on the height. There are many small houses around.* They are scattered on the banks of the dry Arroyo de la Yuta, which was from south to north to the Arroyo at the Tunque. The pottery is of the modern pattern, painted and glossy, and I found no corrugated or indented pieces. They are evidently watch-houses, and some of them summer houses. The soil is very fertile, and although there is no permanent water about, the people raise excellent crops. Small houses are scattered everywhere, on the creston in the west, on the many crags which dot and surround the plain. It is a very picturesque spot, this Tejón. Situated on the brink of the creston, or rather on the slope, it overlooks, not only the valley, but also the whole [area] to the Sierra de San Francisco, Sierra de San Pedro, the Sierra de Santa Fé, and the long, inclined slope of the Sandia.

Founded in 1843 (the Uña de Gato in 1838), its people suffered greatly from wolves, Navajos, and Apaches. In the beginning there was only one single horse, which the wolves ate. Then they had one burro, and the wolves killed him also. The Mescaleros killed a boy near the Uña de Gato, and another at the Tunque. It was dangerous to go out [even] within one mile of the settlement. Barreras was the first settler.[338] I found no obsidian with the ruins, hardly any flint, and little basalt. The Pueblo of Ojana was evidently on one of the hills or peaks south of this place. There is another ruin between the Tunque and the river [Rio Grande].

JULY 20: The ruins are about two-and-a-half miles north of the Tejón, on the right bank of the Rio San Pedro, which here is called also Arroyo del Tunque. They are on a slope, descending to the west and northwest, and they have, in their lower portions, evidently been somewhat eaten by the river or creek.* Could find no trace of estufas. In many places, there are only foundations left, which are of stone, that is, rubble, but often the foundations are destroyed or scattered about. Long rows of debris, however, show the lines in the same manner as at Puaray and at the Parida in the soil.* The soil is light yellowish, and the adobe walls show darker brown. The walls appear to have been all of adobe and about a foot wide. Size of adobe undeterminable.

In several places the whole of the first story seems to be preserved,* and the rooms are probably little disturbed, and perhaps empty; fragments of the roof are visible through cracks and openings, showing that it was made with splinters resting on beams, and covered with earth. Consequently, there must have been at least two stories in places. The rubbish hardly warrants more than two, although three stories in places are not impossible. The northern and principally the eastern parts are more destroyed. In regard to the eastern sections it is evident that the drainage has had a good deal to do with it, as it is all in this direction, and the slope, though not steep, still very much abraded. As for the northern rows, it is also possible that they were abandoned at an earlier time than the others and that consequently the pueblo was not simultaneously occupied in all its parts, and that thus its size and great extent do not give the measure of its former population. It is singular that no traces are found of any circular estufa. At all events it was a pueblo of the many-house, scattered form, common to the villages around Galisteo. This may be the result of the more open country and of greater abundance of room for spreading.

The fields were evidently scattered up the Arroyo de la Yuta and towards the Tejón, whose arroyo, with its permanent flow, may have allowed irrigation, whereas along the other, it was only rain that could water the crops, as the bottom has no room, no soil, and its banks are nearly everywhere precipitous, and from ten to fifteen feet high and red clay. Watch-houses are scattered everywhere—on both sides of the creston (this ridge is not continuous, but forms a series of little crested peaks, with dykes of yellow rock protruding at the top), and on the tops of the higher southern peaks, and of the western creston also. They are scattered everywhere.*

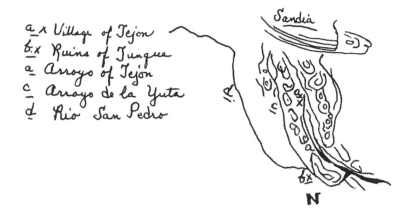

a. x Village of Tejon
b. x Ruins of Junque
a. Arroyo of Tejon
c. Arroyo de la Yuta
d. Rio San Pedro

Sandia

N

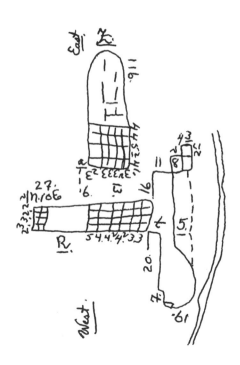

Much pottery is scattered everywhere, but not a single corrugated or indented piece is found, only glossy ware, plain red, and plain black, smoked. I found a piece with three colors. A good deal of obsidian, less flint, but particularly basalt, are at the ruins. Of obsidian, I found a fragmentary arrowhead; of basalt, broken axes, knives, several chisels, and at last, a spade. All these I took home, after having completed the survey about noon.

It grew hot. After my return I painted pottery.[339] Everybody complaining terribly about the heat. It is certainly not oppressive, although I should think it to be above 100° F. in the shade. Clouds are looming up in the distance, but do not reach us. It grew cooler towards the night.

The people here are plain and simple; the man, Antonio José Gallego y Barreras, is a good fellow, but his wife, who appears to be of Navajo descent, is a perfect ogress and a fool at that, a real coarse, ugly, clumsy wench. The slope is steep on the west side of north so that its western branches are much lower than the upper or eastern part. The night was delightfully cool.

JULY 21: Painted all day. To the northeast of this place, the lomas are all carboniferous, seams of coal from one to five feet thick are either cropping out at the surface, or at a depth not exceeding six feet. The creston to the west is volcanic. The little valleys are exceedingly fertile; the soil is deep and loose, and easily worked. Today, even, it needs no irrigation, so abundant are the rains, and as there are several arroyos which meet here and which run almost parallel, there is an ample supply of water. It clouded more and more towards evening, and after Father Navet had come, a bountiful rain set in, slow and beneficial. He is full of joy over the "Madera," seven miles south-southeast of here, and says there is beautiful timber, and the cañón is magnificent. There are two pueblos at the "Chimal," a deserted rancho, south of here, on the San Pedro River. I am through here, and well satisfied.

JULY 22: Left the Tejón on foot at 5 A.M. and passed along the beautiful little cañada down the arroyo, leaving the Tunque behind the last heights of the creston to the right. There are no fields in the cañada, but beautiful small grass. The cañada empties into the Arroyo of the Tunque about four miles northwest of Tejón, and then the broad and arid cañada, emptying almost in front of San Felipe, opens. The lomas on both sides present the aspect of great aridity, a sign that we are approaching the Rio Grande.

Reached the summer ranches opposite the Pueblo [of San Felipe] at 8 A.M. They are almost surrounded by trees, or rather shrubbery, of fruit; peaches, abricots [apricots], apples, pears, but the quality of all this fruit is coarse and they are of little taste. The ranchos are well built adobe houses, and present the appearance of neatness and of comfort. Father Navet followed me soon, and I crossed over to the pueblo in the canoe. It is made of two trunks of trees, well joined so as to afford a thinner partition. They use wooden paddles like shovels. Their mode of crossing consists in using the current, as this diagram shows: The canoe rests at *a*. Thence, it is dragged up to *b* along the shore. From *b*, it drifts to *c*, across with the current and little help of paddles. Sometimes, it has to be hauled in then with the rope, and from *c* it shoots across back to *a* in the same manner. Sometimes it moves very swiftly, according to the force of the current.

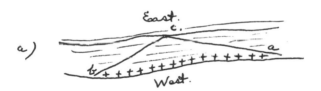

I was received in the most pleasant manner by the family of the sacristan (he was not at home), and the fiscal told me the old story of the priest who escaped from Cochiti, leaving a candle to burn in his room in order to deceive the Cochiteños who were discussing his death in their "junta" (The sacristan had previously warned the priest). It is singular, however, that the deed was to be committed at night! The priest, however, fled, crossing the river, and it so happened that on the morning after his escape, the people of San Felipe had sent out scouts to the mesas to examine the country, as they were preparing a hunt for the cacique! These scouts on the mesa near the "Cangelón"[340] saw the form of the priest, but could not distinguish what it was.

When the people met for the chase, the runners reported, the tracks were found, and the priest was captured near Algodones.

He told the Indians to kill him, but they assured him of their
protection, dressed and painted him like themselves, and were
carrying him thus to the pueblo when people of Cochiti and
Santo Domingo who had come in pursuit met them. Those of San
Felipe refused to give him up, and a fight ensued; the pursuers
were beaten back to near Cubero with the loss of several
wounded (none killed).[341]

The old Pueblo of San Felipe was then on the east bank of the
river, on the north of the present ranchos, and at the foot of the
small black Mesa of *"Ta-mi-ta,"* on the Arroyo of Tunque. There
was a church there; San Felipe, or *"Q'a-tish-tye,"* is a clean and
well-built pueblo, built around a large and clean plaza, perfectly
square. All the houses around the plaza are uniformly of two
stories, only the outlying houses towards the river are sometimes
one-story high, and present a less dilapidated appearance. The
church is on the south end. One estufa (*"Shyu-amo"* [Turquoise])
is near the river; the other (*"Ta-nyi"* [Pumpkin]), on the upper
side near the mesa. This mesa frowns directly over the pueblo.
They have only one cacique here, as at Cochiti; the other two
they had, but abandoned or lost the offices. They weave wonderful zarapes [serapes] here, but do not sell any. Make no pottery
themselves.[342]

JULY 23: [Spent] the whole day painting pottery. Very few men
in the pueblo, all out on the acequias and in the fields. Got no
information. At night a fine shower from the west with wind and
thunder. Cooled off a great deal. People are pleasant, but only a
few speak Spanish, and their dialect is different somewhat.

JULY 24: Beautiful day, and not hot at all in the morning. Ascended the mesa (*"Titi-tza-tua"*), and reached the ruins. The
walls are well preserved, and of large blocks of lava, fairly filled,
like well-laid rubble; the church is of adobe. It stands on the brink
of the precipice, which here is about 150 feet, but only the first
ten to twenty feet are vertical; the rest is a very steep slope,
covered with volcanic debris. *A.* Church. *B.* Convent. *a.* and *b.*
Small houses, purpose unknown. Pottery glossy, also yellow.
None corrugated. Obsidian and basalt flakes.

Although covered with a volcanic ledge, whose debris have
rolled down the sides, and thus have given it the black appear-

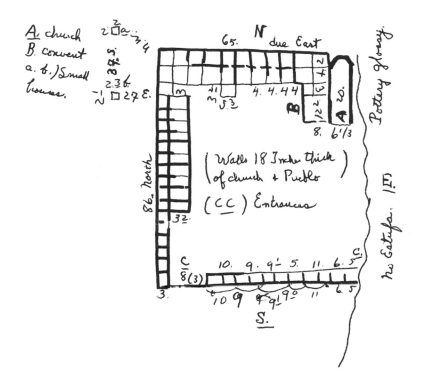

ance, the mesa is formed by friable red and yellow shale, merging into red clay. It is absolutely treeless, but in parts the soil is so soft that although rocks large and small cover the whole surface, crops might be raised with the summer rains only. This character of grassy barrenness and ledges of dark lava is carried on up to the heights of the Mesa of Santa Ana, which stands west, very prominent, closing the outlook in that direction, and about eight miles off.

On the top of it stand the ruins of the old Pueblo of *"Ta-ma-ya,"* the present village at its southern foot, invisible from here. The view from the top of this mesa is fine, but not as extensive as it might be, as the rise of it is on the west and southwest and bars the view. In the south, the Sierra de Sandía (*"Qô-na"*) is plain and majestic, and even the "Ladrona" appears faintly. The whole distance from the ruin to above the pueblo is about a mile.

We descended by the road to Santa Ana, and here the boy pointed out to me a bank or seam of red paint clay. They call this rock *"Shqora-Shqora."* ("Cubero," they call *"Tyi-ti-ha."*) A hill opposite San Felipe is called *"Shyuama-Qo-tye."* The view on the pueblo from directly above is surprisingly fine and distinct.

Upon returning home, I called on an old man who talked pretty freely. He told me that their tradition is that all the Queres together lived at *"Cua-pa"* [Kuapa][343] and while there were attacked by a people of Pygmies called *"Pi-ni-ni"* who, while small, were very strong and slew them all except one woman who hid behind a metate-frame with a guacamayo [macaw, or parrot], and a boy who concealed himself in a storeroom. When the Pygmies had gone, the three came forth and started the new generation of Queres. Those of San Felipe settled first near Cubero on the west bank, thence they crossed over to the foot of the Mesa of *"Ta-mi-ta"* where the Spaniards met them first, and where their first church was built. It would seem that no priest dwelt with them in 1680, for when they saved the priest of Cochiti, and the intertribal wars began, they were attacked and fled to the mesa and built the present ruined church and village, holding out there, the priest being with them. This ruin and church, therefore, dated from between 1680 and 1692, like the pueblos on the top of the Mesa of Zuñi,[344] the Potrero Viejo,[345] and others. They were besieged up there, and cut off from water, when the priest, opening one of his veins, procured water through a miracle in the church, and the enemy had to withdraw. He [the old informant] indistinctly mentioned a document relating these occurrences.

In regard to the Pygmies, the analogy between the name *"Pinini"* and "Pygmies" looks a little suspicious; still it is possible that while the name may indeed be a Spanish corruption, the fact of the destruction of "Cua-pa" by a foreign tribe, attributed at Cochiti to the Tehuas, appears to be indeed embodied in an aboriginal historical tradition. The Pygmies came from the east also! It is noteworthy that, while the Cochiteños state that the division of the Queres into their present tribes took place at the *Tyu-o-nyi* (Rito de los Frijoles), here the most southerly Rio Grande tribe of that [linguistic] stock places the locality where they separated correspondingly farther south, to the "Cañada de Cochiti."

This old man states also, that all the other pueblos, like the "Bajada" and "Tunque," were of the *"Tanos,"* and that the old Pueblo of Santo Domingo (*"Gui-puy"*) was at the foot of the loma, on the north bank of Galisteo Creek, and that the latter caused its destruction and abandonment. The same old man told me that there were only five clans left at San Felipe: *"Jay-shatze," "Ha-me," "Tyame," "Tzitz,"* and *"Shu-tzu-na"* (that *"O-shatsh"* and *"Yssi"* had only men left and therefore were dying out).[346] He also stated that the cacique had two *"Shay-qatze"* with him, but no *"Uishtyaqqa"* anymore. The governor has eight alguazils and fiscales, and the [war] captain, six "capitancitos," besides the lieutenants of each one of these two officers. It is the cacique who chooses the officers, selecting the [war] captain first. The boy who lived after the destruction of *"Cua-pa"* was fed by the parrot until he was grown and then the parrot told him and the woman to go south [and also to take] a certain object placed in a bowl inside of the storeroom. So they went south all together, the boy carrying the parrot and the "object" ("la cosa!!"). The pursuit by the *"Pi-nini"* stopped at a place above Santo Domingo called *"Ish-tue-ye-ne"* (*"Ish-tua,"* arrow) where many arrows are found.

They went to Sandia [Pueblo] but were not well received, turned north, and went and lived among the Tanos. But there was a famine for two years, and the woman had given birth to five children, one girl and four boys. The boys, quarrelling with the other boys of the village, were often taunted as being outlanders, strangers, etc. They asked their mother about it, and she said that it was true, and that their country was where the mesa of *"Ta-mi-ta"* is, or near Cubero, giving a description.

The four boys went and descended the Cañada of Tunque to opposite the Mesa of San Felipe, found fertile lands, and raised good crops. These they brought home to their mother, and brought about an emigration to the old Pueblo of San Felipe, near Cubero, a place called *"Qa-tish-tyam"* (Qatishtyam), whence the present name of San Felipe is derived.

Afterwards the other side was settled, and finally, after 1680, they fled to the top of the mesa, and after 1692, changed to the present location. This gives, for San Felipe, five different locations successively occupied. There are here three principal

"Tshay-anyi" [Chai-añi, medicine men], but these do not cut and streak and punch their bodies as the medicine men of the Tanos did, for which reason the Tanos are called *"Puy-atye"* or *"Pu-yua-que."* He says that the customs of the Rio Grande Pueblos are different from those east and west. Afternoon fine. Quiet and warm. The priest came about with José Hilario [Montoya, of Cochiti Pueblo]. [Father Navet] told me, among other things, that he had the governor of this pueblo [San Felipe] deposed once and a new one chosen.[347] This was done in his presence by the three officers "Qui ont a'les nomener" [Who did the naming]. (The three Caciques.) It plainly confirms what the Chino and what Juan José and Estévan told me.[348]

JULY 25: Early in the morning, went with Father Navet to the church and looked up the archives. Nothing prior to 1726. Took along various documents.

Afterwards there was a junta in the house of Santiago, the sacristan; all the principals appeared, among them the two *"Shay-qatze,"* but the *"Ho-tshan-yi"* [cacique] was not present. The case was curious. A young man of the tribe, who had been to Carlisle School,[349] and wore American dress, had not only grossly insulted his uncle (one of the principals), but also the other principals, given out false reports about the priest and other matters. He was accused and the investigation took place with great passion. José Hilario spoke with great vehemence, and the discussion was earnest and violent.[350] At the suggestion of the priest, two alternatives were left to the boy: either to beg pardon of each, or to be expelled from the Pueblo. He finally, though with bad grace, took choice of the former, pulled off his shirt, knelt down with only his pants on and begged off. Then he was pardoned, and the three principals most offended, the governor, lieutenant governor, and his own uncle, stood up and embraced him one after another. Then he went around and shook hands with the rest; finally, the padre forgave him also. At last the question of taxation came up shortly.

We left at 12:30 A.M., I on foot; I walked to Santo Domingo in two-and-a-half hours. (In the Tigua idiom of Isleta, the Pueblo of Sandia is also called *"Ua-¢lapa."* Ruined pueblos they call, in general terms, *"Na-ta-¢o-¢lé,"* but it is not a local name at all.) The arroyo, which is crossed before reaching Santo Domingo, is called: "Arroyuelo de los Vasquez," and is a dark, gloomy furrough [furrow] deep and broad also. I presume that the old Pueblo of Santo Domingo stood on its northern banks, about a mile south of the [present] pueblo. At Santo Domingo, "Gallazos," but no Mexicans, and therefore no "Cuartazos."[351]

Went to Juan Domingo Pacheco, who gave me the following names of ruined pueblos: "Cieneguilla," *"Tzi-gu-mo"*; "Arroyo Hondo," *"Cua-qaa"*; "Bajada," *"Tzé-nat-a"*; pueblo at the mouth of the Rio de Santa Fé, opposite Cochiti, *"Tzu-yu-na."* Called on Antonio Tenorio and on the sacristan: Santiago Crispín.[352] The latter said that Santo Domingo was also called *"Pu-a-ge"* by the Tanos. Hot afternoon, thunderstorm east and southeast. At 4 P.M., a violent wind blast, and sandblow which lasted about an hour. Reached Peña Blanca[353] at 6 P.M.

JULY 26: Santiago Crispín was here from Santo Domingo. He assured me that the old pueblo of *"Guipuy"* was on the banks of the Galisteo Creek, northeast of the present village, and that then it was moved to west of the present church, when the river obliged them to move to the present location. Painted nearly all day. From the Archives of San Felipe: Father José Benito Pereyro. *"Noticia de la Misión de Sr. San José de la Laguna,"* 20th June 1801: In 1800, the Pueblo of Laguna contained 702 Indians, and 129 Spaniards. In 1801, 692 Indians, and 132 Spaniards. *Father José de la Prada, "Carta Cordillera á los R. R. P. P. de las Missiones de Cochiti etc."* mentions a campaign against the Navajos and ordains that public prayers be said for it. 22 June 1804. *"Breve noticia de la Provincia del Nuevo Mexico y su custodia de la conversión de San Pablo"* (fragment, author therefore not named, written in 1831). Mentions the Rio Grande as taking its source in the "Sierra de la Gruya" (Grulla) and speaks of highly disastrous inundations in 1780, 1823, 1830. In that last-named year, the river destroyed two churches, and two convents. In 1813, the population was about 22,000. Mentions among the former missions, then abandoned: San Pedro,[354] Tabira, Manzano, also San Lázaro. The Jemez call their own pueblo, *"Ua-la-na."* So I was told by Estévan at San Felipe. He understands, somewhat, the Jemez language.

JULY 27: Took medicine. Rather ill. Last night Don Amado Baca[355] told me that the "Alamo" was one-and-a-half miles east of the Cieneguilla, and that there were vestiges of ruins near by.

JULY 28: Painted. In the afternoon, went to Wallace with Father Navet! On the whole my visit has been profitable, but the trouble consists now in returning to San Juan. It rains almost daily in the mountains, and I do not want to wet my papers. Night pleasant and cool.

JULY 29: Ran after José Hilario all morning, unsuccessfully. Wheat is splendid. Finished the San Felipe plate. The boy José, which Father Navet has brought from Golden, is showing Apache tricks in his behavior. He is not to be trusted, and may finally turn out to be an Apache, and not a captive at all [see entry of July 17, 1885]. These fellows can never be relied upon. Spent the evening with Don Nicolás Lucero.[356] Killed a Pichicuate [Pichicuata];[357] happily, a young one.

JULY 30: Arranged with José Hilario. Cusick[358] came from Wallace. Wrote to Joe and gave him letter to mail. Hot, but hardly any wind at all, distant thunder. Fixed the well-house tolerably well; José is very handy at everything, but there are no tools at all, so that it is almost impossible to do anything. One good-for-nothing axe, one blunt hatchet, and a still worse butcher-knife, and rusty nails, are all what is here. Still the work looks tolerably fair, but it is all due to the skill of the boy.[359]

[At this point, Bandelier devoted a half-page to a quotation from Tacitus, *Julii Agricolae Vita S. X.*]

A quite lively thundershower occurred about 3 P.M. with strong rain, and very refreshing. Navajo personal names: *"Na-cay-tzu-se"* (Delgadito, the name given to Román Baca[360] when he was young). *"Te-ja-na-ua-da-né"* and *"Na-qué-e."* Several Navajos with horses for sale came tonight. They live in the Sierra de Chusca [Chuska Mountains, between Gallup and Shiprock]. Wear very beautiful turquoises. José Hilario came late at night to tell me that it was impossible for him to go tomorrow, on account of his wheat. So we arranged for Saturday. Another delay again. It is hard to leave here; all the Indians are very busy.

JULY 31: Beautiful morning, almost cloudless. Quiet and hot. [Here, Bandelier copied almost a page of Virgil's *Aeneidos*, Lib IV, 480–491.]

Don Nicolás Lucero says that, at the fight of the "Arroyo Seco" (1837) only 50 dragoons participated. They lost four killed, the Indians two killed and some wounded. After the dragoons had been repulsed, the whole rest fled; mostly to Santa Fe.[361] The afternoon was stormy. I painted, not knowing what else to do. Father Navet left at 3 P.M. for Albuquerque, and it soon afterwards sprinkled somewhat. At 6 P.M., a fine but short rain, with lightning and thunder, set [in]. I hope to be able to leave tomorrow at last, for it is high time to go. I hope also that the project of staying here will turn out well. It would afford quietness to poor, dear Joe, at last, and much needed rest.

AUGUST

AUGUST 1: At last, José Hilario came to tell me [he was ready] to leave. So I went down to the meadow to see him and Juan José. We left for Cochiti at 10 A.M.; it became very hot.

The river has fallen considerably, and yet it is very difficult to cross. We attempted to cross it below, but it was impossible on account of the quicksand. José Hilario and his horse came very near perishing in it. At last we succeeded in crossing above, at the former old crossing, but the current was so fierce that we had to put the horses' heads downstream to stem it, and the water rose almost to the seat of the saddle. Another delay of an hour, which I spent at the cacique's, very pleasantly. He told me that there was an old pueblo of the Tanos (probably Galisteo) which they called *"Shu-mo-te,"* but it might also be *"Shyu-amo-te,"* in which case it would indicate a ruin at the Cerrillos; possibly the *"Cua-qaa"* of the Tanos?

At 12 A.M., we left at last, in a blazing sun, thunderclouds rising north and northwest. We crossed the lower part of the Arroyo de la Cañada in a deep gorge of basalt with frowning crags at least two to 300 feet high, very picturesque. The Cañada winds through it to the northwest and empties into the Rio Grande almost at the foot of the Mesa Prieta. It is only a cleft. The "Cueva Pintada" is called: *"Tzi-quiat-a-tanye."*[362] José Hilario's name is *"Shte-ranyi"* but, properly, he was baptized *"Tzi-uati-ra."* *"Hai-go-tzosh"* adonde vas. [Where are you going?] *"Ha-te-shaq,"* de adonde vienes. [Where did you come from?] The ruin on the top of the Potrero de San Miguel was Cochiteño [Ha-atze, San Miguel, L.A. 370].

Reached the Rito without rain at 5 P.M. and were well received by Pacífico Vaca [Baca],[363] who has a rancho there. His crops are very fine. What a beautiful spot, this Rito! But the large estufa-like structure southeast of the open-air buildings is probably a tank and may be Spanish. There are two old acequias still visible; one on the south side of the brook, and the other on the north side, passing along the south wall of the pueblo.

My description of the Rito in the novel [*Die Köshare*] is so far correct, only the southern declivity is steeper, more craggy, and more wooded than I had remembered. The rancho of Pacífico is near the ruin which I measured [sketched] on the other side [of this page]. There are consequently three pueblos in the valley, and one estufa less than I had expected or counted upon in my first measurements and in my novel. The last building has but one estufa. The steps are about 0.85 centimeters. During the day, thundershowers, drifting from northwest to southeast, passed around us, rain falling on the Sierra de San Miguel. The evening was cloudy, the night cool, almost chilly, with a sprinkle. Pacífico found a black olla, entire, in one of the caves; also two stone axes. Many arrowheads. Much glossy pottery about, and also obsidian and basalt, flint, moss agate, etc.

AUGUST 2: Scattered clouds early in the morning, and the day announcing itself very hot. We ascended the north side of the Rito, a steep cleft in the otherwise vertical crags, very difficult for the poor horses, and found ourselves on the top of the Mesa, or Potrero, del Pajarito, *"ciro-qa-uash."* It is like the others, wooded, or rather densely sprinkled with piñón and sabino. Here I found this ruin.[364] It recalls those on the [nearby] Potrero Chiato, and the pottery is identical, black-and-white, nicely corrugated and indented, some black and some of it also red. Much obsidian and basalt, also flint. Metates as usual. There is no water near, but there are indications of stone walls like those in the Sierra Madre for terracing.*

We descended into another cañón, for which José Hilario had no name; it is similar to the Rito and contains also caves, the same rock, only darker red. There we crossed another cañón exactly similar. They all run nearly west and east. Finally we descended

into the "Cañada Ancha" [Ancho Canyon], a beautiful broad valley, lined with red and very picturesque rocks of pumice and
volcanic ash, much eroded and perforated, with large artificial
caves. Very similar to the Rito, beautiful timber, but not a drop
of water.

We descended into it, and rode up to its northern head and
then climbed to the top of the potrero. Terrible descents and
climbs. The Cañada Ancha is as follows:* There we crossed a hilly
potrero, to the northwards, and finally came to a deep gorge with
frowning walls of brown and black trap. Fine timber, but no
water, except perhaps higher up. This descent was awful. The
gorge we followed to the east. It has no caves, but at its termination, yellow ash and pumice reappear, and caves also, sparingly
scattered. We followed a trail leading north, out of the cañón,
through the broken, low elevations terminating its sides, and
struck the ruin of *"Tzi-re-ge."* It was a large pueblo, and may
have been the one called *"Troomaxiaquino"* by Oñate.[365] At
least Tzirege means: "Pajarito"! It is on a long slope with rocky
sides, not very high (perhaps 30 feet), but filled with caves, so that
here the pueblo rests on the caves. There are permanent water
holes here.

Then comes an open, treeless and waterless plain, bordered on
the east by small mesitas of light-colored pumice with occasional
caves in them. We wended our trail through there and finally
came in sight of the river, which was 1500 feet beneath us, while
yellow and light red crags towered over us yet several hundred
feet. The river rushes and boils here in a cañón about 2000 feet
deep. A long steep and horrible descent brought us to the bottom
which is about a quarter-of-a-mile wide. We were about five miles
south of San Ildefonso, in front of the Mesa of *"Shyu-ma."*
Crossed the Rio Grande about a mile above the pueblo. Then I
walked up to Pojuaque. Very tired and heated. Night clear.

AUGUST 3: The gorge below San Ildefonso is gloomy and frowning; the rocks rise about 2000 feet on both sides, but on the east,
while *"S[h]yu-ma"* has a perfectly vertical wall to the west, the
section is still very different. The following represents both
sides.* The western plateaux are consequently about 2500 to
3000 feet higher than the river, which gives them an altitude of
8 to 9000 feet.

Left Pojuaque at 10 A.M., reached Santa Cruz at 12 A.M. and saw Father Medina.[366] Exceedingly hot. Left Santa Cruz at 1 P.M. and got to San Juan at 2:15 P.M. Soon after, thundershowers all around. Archbishop Salpointe and Padre Courbon are here. Many good letters. At nightfall, a terrible storm on the Sierra de Nambé. Night sultry and hot, cloudy.

AUGUST 4: Quiet but hot, calm, few clouds. Wrote to Mr. Wilborn,[367] to Henry, to Ad. Ruegger; card to [The] Nation. To Joe, Eddy, Mr. Balsiger, and to Mr. Graffenried. Had a visit from John Pearce, friendly. Very hot and the usual thunderstorms.

AUGUST 5: Clear and hot. Wrote to Father Meckel and to Dr. Schloetzer. Opened my books; they are somewhat damaged by rain (probably at St. Louis) but not much, and although they got mouldy, it will not be of much consequence. Wrote at "Cibola." Letter from Dr. Reiss, very friendly. Rainy afternoon, though only sprinkles.

AUGUST 6: Hot early in the morning. Last night, Don Francisco Chavez came and staid in my room. Wrote the whole day at "Cibola." Afternoon cloudying, very hot. At sunset, severe blow and a few drops of rain with brisk thunder. Night cool. [It is interesting that Bandelier failed to mention his birthday, his forty-fifth, in this entry.]

AUGUST 7: Day cooler and partly cloudy. Quiet. Wrote 13 pages, nearly, at "Cibola." Letters from Joe and from Henry. Replied at night to both. Joe is coming to Peña Blanca. Mr. Seligman came from Ojo Caliente.[368] Handed the papers from Doña Béatriz for Francisco Salazar to Don José Salazar y Ortiz, this evening. Wrote to Father A. Navet.

AUGUST 8: S. Eldodt left for Santa Fe this A.M. with A. Seligman. I finished the fifth part of "Cibola"[369] tonight. Hot in the afternoon and the usual storm of wind at nightfall. Night cool. Am unwell and cannot sleep; intestines don't work well. Stomach spoiled.

AUGUST 9: I sent off my MSS to the *Staatszeitung* (p. 48 to p. 78 incl.) with a letter. Also a letter to Alphonse. The Chino is back again. He told me that the masks of the *"Shi-ua-na,"* a dance of the Queres, were the black faces which are on the rock-paintings near Acoma, and that the black and white fellow at Abó is a *"Qo-sha-re"* handling a snake, as they said that the *"Qo-sha-re"* formerly used to handle and charm snakes. (See Moqui Dance of Capt. [John G.] Bourke.)[370] This is very important, and an evidence that the snake dance existed here also.

AUGUST 10: It appears that the old Pueblo of Abiquiu was the one near the "Puente." It stormed and sprinkled in the afternoon, and I wrote at the paper on "Cibola." Letter from Joe. Painted also at the arrow-straightener of horn.

AUGUST 11: Weather similar; finished the arrow-straightener. Letter from Eddy. Colonel Wyncoop[371] and Mr. Swope[372] came from Santa Fe. A long and confidential talk with two young men from Taos. They have seven estufas, and in each estufa, there are two sets of people, except in the first and second, which have a third set in common. Sun and moon are both male; moon is the older, sun, the younger brother.[373] The sun, in summer, sets in a house in the west. The gens or clan is called: *"Day-na-ma,"* and there must be 13 of them at Taos. They know nothing of Montezuma. The *Qoshare* are called by them *"Chi-u-wuina,"* and they belong to the third estufa. The Pueblo itself is called *"Tegat-ha,"* Picuries [Picuris], *"Uilat-ha,"* and the latter has only two estufas owing to its small population.[374] Of course they claim that Taos is the principal Pueblo of all.

When the *man who is the sun* started from the estufa, he told the Pueblos that since he had given them everything, animals, birds, flowers, herbs, and fruits, etc., for their use, they should also do all things, dancing, singing, racing, etc., make offerings, to and for him also, and that from the moment they would cease to do so, they would be obliterated. (This is the reason why they cling with such tenacity to the Cachinas and their customs.) They claim to have originated at the headwaters of the Rio Colorado, where there are still the ruins of a pueblo called *"Tu-siu-ba."*

This would place it into the Sierra Sangre de Cristo, or there-abouts.

When there is a solar eclipse, they must pray, fast, and dance, and race, for five days, in order that the sun should not perish, and not go back in its course, as else it would go down to the earth and the Pueblos would perish by some inundation or otherwise.

They at once recognized the symbols of Zuñi and of the Tehuas, except the two suns, as they have no green sun, but only one figure for it. The seven estufas are: 1) the principal one. *"Pia-lu-¢a-day-ba"* (cuenta de gente, or bead people) with the second cluster which is called: *"Tia-day-qua-¢la-una."* (Created at *"Tu-siu-ba."*) 2) *"Paa-day-ba"* (agua de gente, water people) and #2 *"Upe-la-go-day-na."* (To these two estufas, belongs a third cluster, the *"Qua-day-na."*) 3) *"Cua-¢la-una."* (Hacha hombres grandes?) and *"A-¢lul-day-na."* Here belong the Qoshare. 4) *"Tia-day-na"* (pluma de gente, feather people) and *"Ha-n'l-day-na."* 5) *"Tul-tu-day-na."* (Sol de gente—sun people) and *"Tu-shul-mo-baa-day-na."* 6) *"Chia-day-ba"* (cuchillo de gente —knife people). Only one cluster. 7) *"Ma-jo-u-na-ma-na."* 2d cluster: *"Sa-ma-no."*

The house of the Sun in the west is called *"T-ul-di-naga,"* and this is properly in the northwest, "la casa del Sol en el Verano." Father Seux came home, bringing news of the resignation of Archbishop Lamy. Also of Denver matters and of the troubles at Mora.[375] My Taos boys came at night and staid till midnight. They were much afraid lest through their telling me of their tribal affairs they might become liable to punishment from heaven, and also that I might betray them perhaps. I quieted them at last.

AUGUST 12: Feast of Santa Clara, and the whole town [San Juan Pueblo] gone there [to Santa Clara Pueblo]. They danced the tablet [Tablita, or Corn, Dance], raced, drank, and fighted, hurting one boy from San Juan badly. I painted today, got a letter from Eddy, and wrote to Joe, to Eddy, to George Hoffmann, to E. W. Mudge, and to Meysenburg.

AUGUST 13: Got a letter from Dr. Eggert through Mr. Eldodt, and sent the Deed to A. Ruegger. Candelario tonight gave me the names of more clans: *"Nan-doa,"* Earth. *"Quña-doa,"* Turquoise. *"Tze-doa,"* Eagle. *"Pe-din-doa,"* "gente de palo de monte." "*Ojua-doa,*" Cloud people. "*Tze-pin-doa,*" "águila pinta." "*Ta-doa,*" Zacate. "*Po-doa,*" calabash. "*Jung-doa*"— Corn people. Thus there are fourteen clans in all. [See entry of June 18, 1885.] "*Ojua*" are the clouds. But they are at the same time also people, male and female, who fell from the clouds and are enchanted, living in the water, in the sea, the lakes.

Thus when I showed to Francisco Chavez this afternoon, and to Candelario this evening, the picture of "*Mait-zalaima,*"[376] they both exclaimed: "*Ojua,*" and when I showed them the black masks of Acoma, they exclaimed: "*Shi-ua-na,*" which is the same among the Queres, but those of Santo Domingo call it "*Je-ro-ta.*"[377] All signifies the clouds, but also deified beings, originating from the clouds in some way. The moon is both male and female, "*Po-se-ndo*" and "*Po-quio,*" but it is also the real mother, "la Madre," "*Ya-quio.*" The sun has an "assistiente" called "*T-an-y-Ojua*" and the twin brothers of the Zuñi are known by the name of "*Tay-Ojua*" and "*U-u-yu-ta.*" Thus the same features appear here also.

AUGUST 14: Hot all day. Painted. Eldodt went to see Candelario's sanctum. He has got the picture of the Water God painted on the wall. He brought back a splendid piece of jade or nephrite, used for medicine-purpose.[378] Whenever drouth sets in, they have to fast four days, or until it rains. During that time, they are allowed to eat but once a day. The matter of dancing balls and feathers is a mere trick made with the aid of a boy assistant. It looks as if Candelario was the medicine man of the water medicine. Got a letter from H. Liebler, and wrote to Dr. Reiss at Berlin. At night it began to cloud. Rather quiet. Several drummers came this evening.

AUGUST 15: Quiet day, hot, but undisturbed. Finished "Cibola" tonight, and sent off. Got a letter from Dr. Eggert enclosing one from the Secretary of the Geographical Society of Paris about some publications which remunerate, at Paris. At night, Dr. Theodore Williams came with his wife; they are from Boston, although at present living at New York.

AUGUST 16: Splendid day. Almost always cloudless. Spent the day agreeably with Dr. Williams and with his wife. They are good and intelligent people, exceedingly curious to know everything, mild in their appreciations and in their views. They went to Mass in the morning; Father Seux preached very well. His organ is beautiful, and the whole ceremony was very impressive. The little choir did not sing so very badly. It is composed of Doña Gregoria, of the daughter of Luis M. Ortiz,[379] of the Chinita, the China,[380] Don Tomás Trujillo, and Alejandro. In the afternoon, they drove out towards Plaza del Alcalde with Eldodt. The night was particularly serene, beautiful, and cool.

AUGUST 17: Began to write in French on the Discovery of New Mexico by Fray Marcos Nizza [Niza].[381] Vicar-General Eguillon came. He is hale and hearty, although his shoulder hurts him a little yet; therefore, he goes up to the Ojo Caliente near Taos. Got letters from Mr. Balsiger, from Henry, and from Father Navet. The one from Henry pains me much. His propositon is well intended but I cannot, from a standpoint of honor and of morality, accept it. I cannot withhold my property from those to whom it justly belongs. My creditors! Let them have it all, and if then I am unable to support myself and dear Joe out here, may I be justly and duly punished for it.

At nightfall, my two boys from Taos, José Loreto Mondragón and Leandro Romero, came back from Santa Fe. They gave [a series of vocabulary items]. After calling on Father Eguillon, and writing a little, I tried to go to bed. To my full dismay, I noticed that while I was gone, somebody had taken out the beautiful Navajo tilma on my bed and another red blanket. I at once started for Eldodt. The robbery had been committed through the open window. We stumbled around the whole night, looking for a clue, but in vain. Simpson, Warren,[382] and Aaron Adler came tonight.

AUGUST 18: Cloudy. Continued to investigate about the blankets, but without avail. Walked up to the Plaza del Alcalde to inform José Salazar and Prudencio Borrego. Warm. In the afternoon, dust storm from the east. Went to the house of Candelario Ortiz and in his inner room, on a wall facing the east, found the picture of *"Tan-yi-ojua"* with the two marine monsters, *"Poo-va-nyu,"*[383] crosswise at its feet. It is the water god, and the others are "Compañeros del mar y del agua." I copied it at once, and then we began talking with the old man. He is evidently the equivalent of the "Water doctor" (*"Tzitz-cha-yan"*) of the Queres.

He claims his God to be [among] the principal ones. He, the *"Po-a-tu-yu,"* the *"Ojique,"* and three others, form the highest order, that of the *"Pa-tu-abu,"* equivalent to the *Yaya*. Besides these, there are the medicine men, *"Uo-ca-ne,"* the hunters, *"Ping-Pang,"* and the warriors, *"Te-tu-yo."* The hunters have disappeared here. The green jade is used at present for invocations; they strike it with a large knife of basalt, and use it as a bell. The jade is called, *"Cua-co,"* and the other, *"Qu-qung."* They have another set besides.[384] They are fixing their plume-sticks now. He also gave to Eldodt an instrument to whirl around by means of which they produce a terrible roaring noise, like thunder.[385]

Wrote to Henry a positive refusal.

AUGUST 23: In the past four days I wrote at the French paper, wrote to Dr. Frenzel, and to Mr. Jackson, and arranged Eldodt's collection. It is handsome. We had visitors. Mr. Springer,[386] Honorable A. Joséf[387] came. It was very pleasant. Other visitors. Mr. Reid and daughter came from Cincinatti [*sic*]. (Tenderfeet of the worst kind.) Weather hot, but not unpleasant. Got letters from Joe, from Eddy, from Padre Navet, and from Mr. Balsiger. Mr. J. E. Evans of Pueblo, Colorado, came. It rained hard on Saturday. Candelario told me that the Americans, and all people from the East were called *"Tan-doa"* since they came from the east, or rising sun, and all the Mexicans were called *"Messi-cu-ge,"* or *"Misa-qu-ge,"* people of the altar stone ("ara"). He says that they fast now four days; all the six medicine men. Their longest fast is 12 days, with nothing but a shell full of meal and some water once in 24 hours. This is very hard. Wrote to Joe and to Dr. Eggert. Had a confidential call from old Francisco Chavez. He is a suspicious old fellow. He wanted me to paint Montezuma for him. I made one copy after the Codex of 1607, and one copy after the Codex Mendoza.[388] He evidently wanted to see whether I had the *"Po-se-ye-mo."* There is a great festival approaching, the marriage of Francisco Chavez with the daughter of Louis Ortiz. Father Defouri came tonight. Evening splendid.

AUGUST 24: Dark, and cool. Kept writing, but with many interruptions. Ramos Ortiz[389] told me that the four pueblos in the mountains to which the people fled in 1542 may have been *"Te-e-ouinge," "Fessere,"* and two even higher up near the Ciénega.[390] I doubt it. Francisco came after his pictures. He was disappointed greatly. It was not *"Po-se-ye-mo,"* for the latter wore mocassins [*sic*] with beads, leather breeches, and leather jacket, with long fringes, and a tall crest of eagle's feathers.[391]

There is a split in the tribe, the *Oyique* and Candelario are accused of having intrigued with Eldodt for the sale of land. Francisco and others against them. Candelario told me that while he had the department of rain, Francisco Chavez had the hunt. Miguel the *Qosare;* the last one, the *Quirana;* the caciques, the earth; and the *Oyique,* light, fire, cold and frost and the snow. Francisco Chavez told me as much as that there was one central pueblo for their religious performances, one common head and centre for all the Pueblos combined. He was quite inquisitive, but I cannot well find out what he really wants. His hints are mysterious; he is evidently suspicious, but knows not why and wherefore. Mr. Springer and the Honorable A. Joseph came tonight, but they went to the wedding with Eldodt. Candelario is fasting until next Wednesday.

AUGUST 25: Eldodt and the two others came home at 4 A.M. well pleased. The "Chino" woke me up. He had been there and was slightly touched. It began to rain at 9 A.M. from the south, but we started nevertheless for the Ojo Caliente in a covered buggy. The opportunity for going is too good to be lost, as it may never return again. It rained hard. We crossed over to Chamita,[392] and drove up the beautiful green valley. It is one of the most fertile and most handsome spots in New Mexico. Outline of mesa.*

As Don Antonio [José] justly remarked, "it has twice as much resources as Sante Fe." The rain became very heavy. We were following the west foot of a high mesa, stratified below, and capped with lava above. Its height is varied, from 300 to 800 feet. It was formerly called the "Mesa de la Canoa," now only the "Mesa," and runs from northwest along the Chama for about ten miles, then it deflects to the north. Its whole length is about 20 miles, and it skirts the Rio Grande on the west. There was formerly a very small settlement at its foot, called the "Canoa." The valley is narrow, but fertile, the bed of the river wide and much quicksand, but the water channel proper is not much.* There are trees, and much grass, and many former ranches of Mexicans, abandoned, also a round watchtower, called "el Torrejón de José Vaca."

At the confluence of the Chama with the Rio del Ojo Caliente, we turned northwest and finally into the bed of that little river. It is exceedingly sandy on the hills. The bed is about narrow, but the valley is one to one-and-a-half miles wide and exceedingly fertile. Rather abrupt mesas, continuous, confine it. The one on the east is a level grassy treeless plateau; on the west, narrow hills, surmounted behind by bold porphyritic crests. Three miles to the east of the springs is the "Cerrito de la Vívora" not unlike the "[Picacho] de Bernal" but capped with lava. North of the springs is what they call the "Cueva," a double-peaked mountain, and northwest, the "Cerro Colorado." There are many springs, issuing from the mere porphyry.* The water colors red and orange, and one spring colors *green*. The buildings are only too spacious. The water is warm, but not too hot. Their medicinal powers are beyond all doubt. Mr. Joseph told me that turquoise beads had been found, also shoes made of *rock!* Probably gneiss, showing the holes for the bands to fasten them with. [?] Rain ceased.

We got there at 3 P.M. Cloudy and chilly. Kind reception. About 4:30 P.M., I went to the ruins with young Mr. S. [Springer]. They stand on a mesa, about 100 feet above the valley. Its banks are abrupt, though not vertical, but still naked. To the south-south-west is the ravine, dry and steep. To the north are hillocks and ravines, and to the west, high crests of porphyry and small grassy patches, lower than the pueblo. Much pottery, white-and-black, *glossy,* and corrugated black, corrugated covered with a coating of mica (compare Coronado or Castañeda),[393] and indented after the manner of the jar from Abiquiu in Eldodt's collection. Glossy has red, black, white, greenish, cream color, and orange just as at the Tunque.[394] Very little obsidian, much basalt, flint flakes, chalcedony, quartz, moss agate. Plates of mica-schist, or gneiss. Metates (one of gneiss), manos of lava, porphyry, gneiss. Stone axes have been found, also arrowheads. Jars filled with corn, and charred corn. The walls are exposed in several places; they are from 10 to 12 inches [wide], mostly of adobe without straw, but sometimes flat slabs are interlaid in rows.

The doorways (I saw only the tops.) are low and narrow as at the Rito de los Frijoles. The beams were round; over them there was brush, or probably splinters laid crosswise, *flat*, and then little round sticks. Jars filled with *wheat* are said to have been found. Also, many skeletons in every imaginable position, and in the rooms the greatest portion of them, sitting, lying down in the middle of the rooms, with skulls broken and crushed. Mr. Josef says over one hundred. This whole thing is doubtful. One grave, according to Mr. Josef, was found with a skeleton seven feet, six inches long; in flesh about 8 feet. (Doubtful too.) In 1811, there was an earthquake, and smoke arose from the top of the "Cerro Colorado." (Perhaps.) This pueblo is surrounded with the usual traditions and lore. The people assert that the valley was, in the past century, covered with dense wood and timber to the river, and that the river ran along the west mesa.

AUGUST 26: Went to the ruins at 9 A.M. with Mr. S. J.[395] Day beautiful. The pueblo is magnificently situated. The view to the east and south is splendid. The whole of the Santa Fe Range is visible and plainly divided into three groups. The Santa Fe and Nambé group, south; the "Truchas," in the center, and the Jicarrita in the north. The Taos Range is plainly visible beyond it, and finally the "Culebra," or "Sangre de Cristo," in the distant northwest. As a lookout, it commands the whole valley. Arable ground there is none around it of any extent[!]. This place is like a watchpost, where the trail comes up to the mesa of the ruins. The structure* at the verge of the path appears very much like a watch place. The stones are set on edge; the whole forms nearly a square; and the smaller squares are like rude watchtowers.*

For agriculture, it may have been but it is not likely at all. Still there was certainly not an elevated structure on it! Got through about 1 P.M., went to dinner, and at 4:30 P.M., set out for the little mesa north of the springs. The ascent is over a declivity of porphyritic and syenitic rock tumbled down and projecting. Whereas there is a well-worn and very clear trail, old, leading up to the ruins, here the trails are hardly perceptible. The crests of bare rock, much splintered and with many fissures, traversed with more or less vertical small dykes of granite, quartz, and

feldspar, covered with steep slopes, very near to the edge of the
mesa, and having only little "ancones" [bays, or pockets] of
ground. Along the slopes, little dykes are built parallel, mostly of
upright stones set in the ground. They are surprisingly like the
little "banquitos" and "trincheras" of Sonora, only not in the
arroyo, but on the slope; the terraces are only two to three-and-a-
half feet wide. [They] resemble the "gardenbeds" of Arizona.[396]
Soda-springs, now disappeared, have once filtered and sickened
out through them. They approach the brink of the mesa considerably. Along the brink of the mesa there are hollows, mostly
round, and they are surrounded by heaps of pebbles, like dug-
outs [quarries] from which the stones have been removed. They
seem to stand in some relation to the lines of stones. This is about
the plan and sketch of the place.*

From the top, an extensive view is had. The Sierra de Sandía
appearing in the south very distinctly. It hardly ever snows here,
and the snow never covers all the ground. [There] is a complete
set of typical "banquitos" or "audenes [shelves]." They run close
to the edge of the mesa, and are from two to three-and-a-half feet
apart with the terraces plainly visible and formed. Beneath the
terraces, the mesa falls abruptly. To the north, the lines of rocks
are continuous along the trail.* No pottery found. On the top of
the crestón to the west, there is a quartz vein and innumerable
splinters and chips of that material are scattered about. The hollows are evidently scooped out for purposes of living, but they
may have been Apache, or some other, temporary abodes.[397] The
fact that the valley was densely wooded prior to its settlement,
explains the necessity of cultivating the high mesas.

AUGUST 27: Beautiful morning, cloudless and cool and quiet. Got
shaved. Started at 8:30 A.M. and tramped across the little river
and the bottom which is sandy but rises to a terrace, about ten
feet high, before reaching the broken and low border of the mesa
on the east. I do not think the bottom is, in all, over three-fourths-
of-a-mile wide. On that terrace, north of the little village, I found
some old pottery, and it looked as if there had been an old settlement, but no traces of houses.

The bluffs are much less abrupt here than on the west side,
showing that the river has always been hugging that shore and
bluff. On the east they are broken, and the long mesa is not as

high. A few Mexican ranches are in the bottom. We travelled north about one-and-a-half miles and then the road turned to the northeast and we ascended a hill about 50 feet high, and stood on a promontory of the mesa, at where the "Cañada de los Comanches" empties into the bottom of the Rio del Ojo Caliente.

Here are the ruins. They are low and flat mounds, but very long, and are older in ruin than those at the springs. Considerable washing has taken place in some of the mounds. Pottery, etc. identical with that at the springs.* Little obsidian. Saw some axes which had been commenced. Metates of lava and of gneiss; manos, etc. I was informed by Tomás Lucero that large "tina-jones" containing flour or meal had been excavated 30 years ago, also skeletons. He also is of the opinion that the valley was for-merly wooded, but knows of no ancient acequias in the bottom. The ruin has eight estufas clearly distinguishable;* there may be more, but I am not sure of it. We then crossed over to the rancho of Tomás Lucero, which is on the east side of the river and near where the latter comes out of the gorge beneath the "Cueva." There we crossed the river at the foot of the high bluff, very steep, of gravel capping sandrock, on which the third pueblo stands. It is built almost on the brink and in its southern parts on the brink of the slope which is nearly vertical. The mounds are old; still the rooms are often visible. Remains absolutely identical with those of the two others. One estufa is very deep and very well preserved. Its top is made of slabs standing on edge. It may have been a tank!! The walls are mostly of adobe, like those of the others, and have the same thickness, that is, 12 inches about. It is almost perfectly closed in, for the west is barred by a high mountain which stands about 250 feet off, right on a plain 20–25 feet lower than the top of the mounds, and on the other two sides, the edge of the mesa crowds in, whereas on the south there is an arroyo with a deep rocky cleft down to the river. On every side the access to it is very difficult, and that is why I believe that the estufa is a tank, used in case of necessity.

We then crossed over to the little mesa south of it, and found [the second and third structures], all separated by deep gashes of narrow arroyos, and literally covered with the "Gardenbeds."* The little compartments are found on the slopes, the large inclo-sures on level ground. On the third mesita stood a ring of boul-ders, 14 feet wide, and two feet high, enclosing, without

entrance, a level space, 25 X 27 feet. They are just thrown together without clay or earth between. What is it? It may be
Apache, or it may have been made for defence by the little
colony of Sonoreños who mined here 50 years, and who flew at
the approach of the American troops in 1846.[398] Descending to
the river bottom, we found "banquitos" not three feet wide, in
numbers on the lowest slope or terrace, not 20 feet above the
river bottom. They are all on the mesa on the west side, between
the third pueblo and the springs. Returned at 12:30 [P.M.] well
satisfied.

Wrote and painted all afternoon. Day fine and warm. Mr. Joseph says that there are, in all, eight pueblos around the Ojos, but
Hernandez says there are only five. Night very fine. It is so quiet
here, so peaceable and still.

AUGUST 28: Ojo Caliente is about 55 miles south of the Colorado
line. Day fine, but white clouds scattered over it with a suspicious
appearance. Left my pottery with Don Antonio. He will send it
to San Juan by José Olivas.[399] Left at 8:45 A.M., Mr. Springer
accompanying me to the brow of the hill. I then crossed, following the trail, at the foot of the "Cerro Colorado," and between
it and the lower height. All these heights are of the same rock as
at Ojo Caliente. I thus saw the "Cerro Colorado" from three
sides, and everywhere, it presented the same appearance, and
there is not the slightest trace of lava, scoria, basalt, or pumice
stone. It grew very hot and sultry.

I descended, through many windings, into the sandy cañada.
Beyond it, abrupt heights of sand, with sabinos and cedros, disin-
tegrated rock into sand and detritus. Crossed that ridge and
struck the road, about six miles from the Ojo Caliente. Thunderclouds rising northwest. The weather exceedingly oppressive
and hot. Clouding. Landscape the same character; hills and
ridges of sand with sabinos and cedros.

At 11 A.M., after having had occasional glimpses at the "Cerro
del Pedernal"[400] (20 miles west-northwest of Abiquiu), the plain
of the "Rito Colorado" burst out into full view. It is perfectly
level, eight miles long, and from two to three-and-a-half miles
wide. Unfortunately, the little "Rito" runs along its eastern edge,
leaving the whole expanse without water towards the west, so
that only the smallest portion of the level, grassy, and treeless

plain is watered. Above the course of the western shore of the river (now partly dry) the heights descend abruptly, and in jagged gullies; in the west, the plain rises almost imperceptibly to the long line of a very low and perfectly flat-topped mesa, whose slopes and summit are densely studded with coniferae of the lower kind, junipers and cedars. In the southwest, the mountains of Abiquiu appear near, with frowning mesas beneath. The heights opposite San Juan and above Chamita are plainly visible, in the south, where the valley narrows. The chain beyond Santa Fe can be discerned and thence on the whole chain occupies the horizon until the east-northeast, unfolding the relative positions of the three groups most splendidly. The Santa Fe group, or the Sierra de Nambé, with "Baldy," is the most southerly; the "Truchas" occupy the center and are the highest; the "Jicarrita" flank it to the north. It is the best and most instructive view I have had of this chain and of its summits. I crossed the Rito at the lowest plaza.[401] It began to thunder northwest and north; the sky was all overcast and rain approaching. The plain is extremely fertile. Its houses are all strung along the rivulet. The church is two miles higher up, and I got there just when a slight shower was falling, the rain all pouring down in the mountains north and northeast —also south over Abiquiu. About a mile north of the upper place (where the church stands) the plain ceases, and the rivulet comes out of a gorge. It takes its source about 20 miles north-northwest of here, and 12 miles below, it empties into the Rio Chama. The latter takes its head nearly 100 miles to the northwest. The country west and northwest clear up to the Rio San Juan, is all mesa with interminable cañadas, several journeys long. It is well-watered. "Tierra Amarilla" is very cold.

Here [El Rito][402] I met, to my great delight, Father Grom. Kindest possible reception. The settlement is recent, and there are three plazitas, this one, the one at the crossing, and one between. From here to the ruins, six miles south; to Tierra Amarilla, 45 miles; to Abiquiu, 18 miles; to Ojo Caliente, ten miles straight, but about 12 miles the way I went. The church and presbytery are modern, the first Curacy established in 1852 and church commenced, the settlement in 1869, but there is an anterior "Merced" [earlier grant], now lost. Father Courbon is an old "settler." He knows the country exceedingly thoroughly and well.

As far as I could ascertain, there are no other ruins in the vicinity. The winters are not very cold, still snow remains eight days sometimes! What the people complain of, is lack of water. There is a little store here kept by a Jew.[403] The country is rich in game, deer, but no antelopes; bear ("negro" and "platiado" [black and grizzly]), no elk, and turkeys. I saw colossable beets and cabbage, also cauliflower, grown in Father Courbon's garden. The latter is quite extensive. It rained several times in the afternoon, and a very strong shower took place before sunset. We had just called on Pedro Jaramillo.[404] He stated that the first inhabitants came here in 1806 about, that is, between 1806 and 1816. Of other ruins, but the one south of here, he knows not. Climate not very cold in winter. After the storm it grew very cool. Night fine, almost chilly, wind northwest.

AUGUST 29: I left on foot for the ruins at 8:30 A.M. They are four miles south of the church, on the west bank of the Rito, about 500 feet distant from it, and in all 90 feet above the bed. [There] are gardenbeds and "banquitos" on the little expanse north of the ruins.* There is a rancho near by (north of it) where lives Lorenzo Martinez, who treated me very kindly. He speaks of another ruin, about seven to eight miles southwest on the Abiquiu road, and of an old acequia near by. Between this ranch and the ruins, and separated from the latter by a little ravine, are the gardenbeds on the other side. They are mostly level, although also on the brink of the slope.*

A border of heavy gravel marks the outline, principally where it is on the edge of the slope, the partitions are of smaller pieces. The soil is exceedingly light and very fertile. Today they raise beans and corn right in the midst of the ruins and also around them. The soil is largely gravelly nevertheless, and so are the hills mostly of gravel. The east side is very broken and rugged, columnar erosions appear, and the ridges from the west shut in gradually, having only a few cultivable basins along the Rito, on the whole not over a half-mile wide, and frequently intercepted by projections of the gravelly hills. Beautiful erosion formations on the east side, jutting out from beneath high crags. It seems to be reddish sandstone. To the northeast and north and north-northwest spreads the level plain of the valley of the Rito Colorado, only cut by the low ridge west of the ruins, which extends to the west about one-and-a-half miles.*

The ruins have an old appearance. Either they are much washed, or else very old. So is pottery. Similar to that of Ojo Caliente. Obsidian, basalt, and flint flakes. Metates, everything as usual. Many cedar posts protruding vertically from the ground. They are in rows, principally along the eastern border, at regular intervals of six to ten feet. Their diameter is seven to eight inches. At 2 P.M., Father Courbon came with his buggy and we left, descending the Rito for about three miles. Ranches on both sides of the stream, many abandoned, the people having gone north on account of lack of water for irrigation. Thus at the "Casita," they moved up near Tierra Amarilla. Distance to Abiquiu, 18 miles; San Juan, 27. The mesas below the Abiquiu Peak loomed up grandly, and in front of them high ridges of sand, hills 7 to 800 feet high, blown together by winds.

We soon turned to the southwest and saw the Chama River. It was muddy and red, a sign that it rained at the "Coyote" [present-day Coyote]. The Chama has three sources: the "Coyote" west; the "Gallina" north of west; and the "Nutrias" in Tierra Amarilla, north. The waters from the Coyote are red; those of the Gallina white, and the water from Tierra Amarilla is clear and limpid. Reached Abiquiu at 5 P.M.

Don Juan García and Frank Becker[405] are here. It is a very picturesque place. The Sierra de Picuries and the peaks of Taos are in full view. Evening clear and beautiful. The rocks are eaten and shaped by erosion.* A grand cañón opens to the west and northwest, and right behind the village the Peak of Abiquiu is visible. The valley is fertile, but subject to overflows of the Chama. High mesas border it on the right (south), whereas the other side is level, sandy, and gradually rising to turreted rocks and peaks of moderate height. In front of the village stands a long ridge of red rock curiously wrought, and behind white erosion formation, very remarkable. The village is on the south bank and steep hill.* [There are an] abandoned rancho and probably a tank, eight feet deep. The mounds are low and flat [and there is one], over whose entire length the road passes. The four other estufas are an average 30 to 40 feet in diameter, but one is like the big tank at the Ojo Caliente, vertical walls of stone. The pueblo was of adobe, and the walls about nine to twelve inches thick. It seldom exceeded two stories, if ever. Where there are three sets of rooms, the section is as follows:* the middle row being highest of all.

AUGUST 30: On the whole, Abiquiu is quite a romantic spot. It lies high above the river, in a nook, on a plateau which descends from the mountains behind by degrees. The Peak of Abiquiu closes the distance. Its slopes are grassy, but with few trees.* The soil is as usual, reddish and fertile, light, and very sandy in the valley. The heights are covered with dwarfish coniferae; in the bottom there are álamos, and along the river is underbrush of willows. The sight is handsome, with the view to the east, where the northern end of the Sierra Picuries and the two high peaks of Taos protrude.

As a general thing, at the Rito Colorado, at Taos, and in those latitudes, the crops are two weeks later than at San Juan, and at the Tierra Amarilla the wheat is cut in September. It snows there (at the "Cangelón")[406] in June, in the heights. That country is beautifully watered. The farther south, the scarcer the water supply becomes. Here at Abiquiu, the western range of the Cordillera skirting the Rio Grande terminates, and beyond it, are extensive mesas only, clear into Colorado, with deep and interminable cañones through which run considerable streams of permanent water. On these mesas there are a great number of pueblos. Eight miles higher up, towards the west-northwest, lies the ruins of a pueblo built of pumice-stone, like that of the "Potrero Viejo" and others, north of Cochiti.

Don Pedro Jaramillo told me that the bell at the Rito, the bell at the "Casita," were cast there, the former by one Luján from the Embudo. The former patron saint of Abiquiu was Saint Thomas Aquino [Aquinas]; near it is Santa Rosa.[407] Day cloudy in the morning, but soon cleared. Went up to the ruins. They are about 100 yards south of the stone, above the place on a slope. They are much ruined and reduced to mounds, but considerable excavations have been made in them.*

The walls of the pueblo have the usual thickness, about a foot; they are of adobe on rubble foundations. Pottery in every respect similar to that at Ojo Caliente and at the Rito. There is some obsidian, basalt, and lava. The old Pueblo of "Genízaros"[408] stood where the store and church are now, but the old church of Santa

Rosa de Abiquiu is still two miles farther down, or east, of here. At the Puente, there has been also a migration to the Tierra Amarilla, on account of lack of water and of inundations.* It is the Feast of Santa Rosa today and a great many people are up here from the Rio Grande selling fruit and visiting in general. It promises to become lively. Tomás Trujillo is here, and also some Indians of San Juan. Went to mass, but everything was crowded with people so that I had to stand outside.

[Here, Bandelier entered notes from Howard Stansbury's *Exploration and Survey of the Great Salt Lake of Utah*, etc. 1853 (p. 182). He also included detailed data from Captain J. S. Loud's *Table of Distances*, 1878.]

Went into the cañón above Abiquiu. Very handsome, fine mesas, abrupt, and a beautiful round place. On the other side, there are splendid erosion formations in white and yellow rock, and the crest northwest of Abiquiu narrows to a towering cliff of reddish brown rock. The plain is fertile, and there are some houses in it. Evening fine, quiet, but warm.

[Bandelier added notes here from *Report of the Commissioner of Agriculture*, 1881–1882 (p. 584); also 1884 (p. 490); 1883 (pp. 262–63, 274, 276.]

Father Courbon called on me this afternoon. I painted a splendid axe which Aaron [Adler] got from the upper ruins. His collection is valuable; there are especially stone axes, beads, and flint objects. He also has two fetishes, crude, but interesting. The festival passed off without much noise. Of course, the "Gallo" was tormented, and with it, the horses.[409] Night very quiet and calm.

AUGUST 31: There is a small round tower also on the steep ridge closing the mesita on the south side; hill very gravelly. Top soil very good; walls 10 to 12 inches, mostly adobe. Also rubble. Left early in the morning on horseback, with Becker and the mail.

We descended the valley for three miles to the "Puente," where we met a group of houses. Here lives Epimenio Quintana. About 75 feet steep gravelly declivity, above his house, and on his land, are the ruins.* Mounds are low and flat, but compartments plainly visible. Only one estufa, but a round tower of stone on the very edge of the slope, in an excellent position, so as to command the whole valley in every direction. The pottery is in every way identical with that of the other ruins, carved, plain, black-and-white, glossy, etc. Obsidian.

Quintana told me that bodies (skeletons and skulls) had been washed down a cut east of the ruins, as if the burials were outside the pueblo and to the east of it. He speaks of another ruin lower down the river, on the north bank, and of a few scattered small houses on the high hill tops. The bottom of Abiquiu River is fertile; álamos stand along the river bank, and for four miles down from Abiquiu there are a great number of abandoned Mexican ranchos, the people having moved north. The Navajos and Apaches have not, in the past 30 years, remained around here. The country farther down becomes more open, the mesas lower, but it is terribly sandy, so that the horse has trouble in moving. Thundershowers all around. At the crossing of the Chama, about a mile above Chamita, and before, I met many Indians from San Juan with loaded burros, armed, and on horseback. They go to the Rio de los Pinos to trade with the Utes! Reached San Juan at 3 P.M. Lost my watch on the road. J. C. Pearce is here. Letter from Joe. Evening clear and warm. Quiet. Dr. Ayres from Cincinnati is here. I forgot to mention that the Arroyo de Abiquiu is only four miles long, and the outcrop of a spring. It runs almost due south to north and has very clear, good water. The Chama is not considerable; it has much quick-sand.

SEPTEMBER

SEPTEMBER 1: Sultry and warm. Wrote to Professor Ratzel, to George [Hoffmann], and to E. W. Mudge. Then set to painting the plat of the "Tunque." Thunderstorm and hard rain about 4–5 P.M. Night quiet and clearing. Am very tired. Don Juan García gave me a remedy for my lip, which works splendidly.

SEPTEMBER 2: Beautiful morning, quiet and cool. Towards night-fall it clouded with a few thunderclaps from northwest and a sprinkle. Letter from Ratzel and Mr. Dronne. Lots of visitors. Don Dolores Romero[410] (Indian Agent), Mr. Smith, Simpson, Elkins,[411] and others. Painted all day. Lumbago coming again. My lip much better.

SEPTEMBER 3: Beautiful day again. Not as hot as formerly. Sunset magnificent. Wrote to Professor Ratzel; to the *N.Y. Staatszeitung;* to Father Navet, enclosing $20.—; to Eddy, enclosing $60.—. (Borrowed $80.— from Eldodt!); to Joe. Began, tonight, to teach writing to Juan José Chavez, son of old Francisco.

SEPTEMBER 4: Wrote to E. A. Allen. The pueblo at the Rito Colorado is called *"Se-pa-ue";* the other one to the right on a mesa is called *"Ponyim-pa-que."* Tehua names: . . . These names were given and others, as personal names, to Marshall when he took the census! Wrote to E. A. Allen, and to Professor S. F. Baird.[412] In the afternoon I went with the Chino to see his nasa [fish trap]. It closes one arm of the river, and is a fixed trap into which the strong current of the river drifts the fish and out of which they

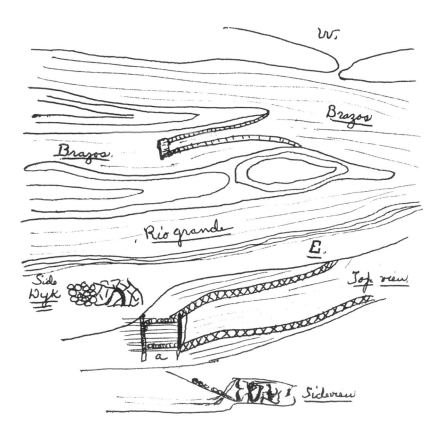

cannot escape any more. It is an ingenious thing, and when it closes a stream, not a fish can escape. It empties the whole breed at once. The side dams are a long cylindrical basket of branches filled with rocks. At the issue, a strong beam is placed across horizontally, and under the dykes. Over this beam the water falls through the sieve (a) and here the fish are caught and cannot get up the inclined plane. The former nets were made of yucca, selecting the interior leaves, which were toasted, then packed in little bundles, boiled, and finally chewed by little boys, to whom ears of corn were given in remuneration. Thus slimy and flexible, the net was tressed or braided out of them. Pueblo at the baths of Agua Caliente, *"Po-se-o-uinge."* A mile higher up on the east bank (the largest), *"Ho-ui-ri,"* opposite *"To-ma-yo"*; the small one at Abiquiu, *"Fe-jui."* Consulted Candelario; he gave me *osha*-root, to pulverize and apply, saying as much as "Similia, Similibus, curantur."

SEPTEMBER 5: I assorted, reassorted, and finally placed the rest of Eldodt's collection today. It took me until 3 P.M. Had a tremendous toothache all the while; my last upper molar, right-hand side, is decaying, and I suffer considerably from it. At night, had some little relief at last. It rained at night. Finished the text of "Fray Marcos." Night cool. It is dripping in my room like everything. (Melon is very bad for sores.)

SEPTEMBER 6: My toothache almost completely vanished over night, and I feel very much relieved. Wrote at the notes to "Fray Marcos." Swope and Colonel Wyncoop came at noon. It began to rain soon after noontime, and one thundershower chased the other with violent rain until after 3 P.M. when it ceased. Large quantities of water fell, and the thunder and lightning were very heavy. Little wind.

At 3 P.M., the herald of the *"Qö-sa-re"* went through the place with a cowbell, and cut his capers and pranks. We went out to see. About an hour afterwards, the whole group of *"Qö-sa-re"* came out; 11 men, and four women, all painted with white, and black circles around the eyes and mouths, singing, and in two rows. The men had old axes, painted sticks; they carried old leather "riatas" hung over their shoulders; three of them had shields on their backs; the women, a sunflower on each ear. The men wore foolscaps, white, striped black. They were dressed with more decency than those at Cochiti, but still the kilts and breechclouts were old. Their hair was loosed as usually worn, and not tied up in the topknot.

Candelario acted as drummer with the big drum. Thus they marched through both squares, singing improvisations, and cutting capers. It began to rain again. At sunset, the sky cleared in the west, and as the sun shone bright, it showed the "Truchas," the "Jicarrita," and the "Sierra de Nambé" all covered with snow. It was very cool. Don Dolores Romero came. He says that the people of Taos showed him a paper from 1613. (?) This is very doubtful. He also asserts that there are no ruins on the eastern slope of the mountains. This also is not correct. At night, fearful rain again, from the northwest with lightning and thunder. Had Juan José again for a lesson in reading and writing. The poor boy is painstaking. Finished the notes for "Fray Marcos." Sent the two tinajas to Dr. Eggert today by Mr. Swope.

SEPTEMBER 7: Beautiful day. Wrote to Mr. James Jackson, #184 Boulevard St. Germain, Paris, and sent MSS of "Fray Marcos"[413] to him. Eldodt left in the morning for Santa Fe. I began to paint at the "Qösare." In the afternoon, they marched out, 15 in all, Candelario drumming alongside of them. He wore behind each ear, feathers, of macaw, probably. There was a malinche along, but she wore only a long "plumet" of broom grass attached and sticking up from the back of her head, with two blue parrot feathers behind it. They danced and sang. Everybody almost was in good dress. After they reached the middle of the southern plaza, the governor and the other officers came each with a tray of fruit, melon, apples, squashes, corn, plums, etc. and emptied it on the ground. Nearly all the women and girls came and deposited the same kind of offerings around them. The dancers then trampled a part of it (the official part) to pieces, by dancing over it in a circle, all the while singing. The rest was carried to the other plaza, where the same performance was gone through also. On the whole, with the exception of this offering to the earth, it was much the same thing as the *"Qo-sha-re-pash-qa"* [Koshare Dance] at Cochiti. They wallowed in mud-puddles, entered the houses, played drunk, counterfeited [imitated] the priest, cut all sorts of silly and ugly capers.[414]

Dr. Ayres came this evening. He was very much pleased with the dance. Sunset beautiful. Cloudless and cool. Snow still on the mountains. "Quico" going away tomorrow.

SEPTEMBER 8: Dr. Ayres left this morning for the north. The dance of the *"Qö-sa-re"* is called also *"Ojua-jiare."* The head-dress is called *"Qosare-qa."* Both the *"Qosare"* and the *"Qui-ra-na"* are *"Pay-oj-que."* The *"Qui-ra-na"* are *to intercede for the crops when they have just sprouted;* the *"Qo-sa-re"* when *they are ripening.*[415] I read to Candelario the passage of Torquemada (Vol. I, p. 681).[416] He does not know of *"Cocapo," "Cacina"* in *"Ca-tzina,"* the *"Ojuas"* of the deer (game) which they paint as deer, and to which they apply for the chase. The same to the bear. This explains the word *"Cachina."* It is *"Catzina-Ojua."* He made the remark, "No mirastes que bonito se pusieron los Ojua ante ayer depuis del baile?"[417] This is very characteristic for their faith and creed. It appears that everything supernatural is *"Ojua"* and that *"Ojua"* is mostly personified by the clouds! At least this is the interpretation which I must give it.[418]

He does not recollect the name of *"Cocapo,"* but says that it may be a name used by those of Santa Clara, as they have other words and names in some cases, than those of San Juan. As to "Homace," there is a mesita beyond Chamita, which they call *"Oma-se."* It might be that the name may come from this hill, but Candelario is not positive about it. He says that the customs have greatly changed, but that their present customs are good. In the afternoon, Don Alejandro García came, and we walked across the river to Chamita. I skipped the Pueblo of *"Yuge-ouinge,"* or Yunque. This is evidently *the "Yuque-Yunque"* of Castañeda.[419] It was comparatively a small pueblo, having but one plaza, and it is much disturbed by the building of Mexican houses on or out of the ruins. Very large metates, pottery of all kinds, glossy, white-and-black, etc., obsidian, flint are scattered about. The metates are large, of lava, and without feet; [some] walls are excavated.* They show the usual thickness of a foot about, and appear to have been of adobe, but there is also stone work. I returned about 3 P.M. and painted again.

SEPTEMBER 9: Most beautiful day. Had a lot of young girls in my room this morning. They all wanted to see my painting of the

"Qo-sa-re." In the afternoon, Mr. Smith came. He is a very pleasant man, speaks Spanish, French, and English. Being born on the Islands of Canaria, his mother-tongue is Spanish.[420] He says that there are still descendants of the "Guanches," very tall men, broad-chested, dark complexion, and whole families of them with six fingers. (Two Thumbs) He says that they have a way of making soil there with vegetable mould produced by lava having overflowed timber. Beautiful night, cloudless, clear and cool. Very handsome. Painted most of the time.

SEPTEMBER 10: Last night I wrote to Mr. Balsiger, to Eddy, this morning early to Honorable A. Joseph, Ojo Caliente. Painted all day. At night I wrote to Don Joaquín García Ycazbalceta [Icazbalceta].[421] My attempts at figure painting are rather fortunate, and I hope to be able to make portraits after a short while.

SEPTEMBER 11: Mailed letter to Mexico. Painted all day. Letter from Joe. At night wrote to Joe, to Padre Navet, to Dr. Gerlich, to Pretorius, to Garrison at New York. Painted yet awhile at night.

SEPTEMBER 12: Wrote to Frost & Adams,[422] #33 & 35 Corn Hill, Boston, Mass. Very cool before sunrise. Clear. Painted at the headdress of the *"Saritye"* and with good result. Beautiful day. Eldodt returned tonight.

SEPTEMBER 13: Finished my painting. After dinner went to Santa Cruz with Becker and thence to Española. Santa Clara is only a mile-and-a-half south of it. Returned to Becker's for the night and spent a delightful time as there was pleasant Mexican society there. Dr. Romualdo Ortiz and others. Father Medina told me that he had once, during the time of the Navajo wars, witnessed the return of a war party at San Ildefonso. They brought back one scalp and three captive children. They halted a mile from the village a full day, where the people visited them in gala, with plentiful food, etc. The next day they entered in great state, while the people were executing a great "baile." The captives were beaten, cuffed; their hair was pulled, pinched, principally by the old women, who were the most cruel. He interfered.

SEPTEMBER 14: Returned leisurely on foot. Painted the mask of the "Chacuan." Wrote to Joe about coming here. Laguna, *"Tung-qua"*; Moqui, *"Joso-uinge."* There is also *"Zete-ojua,"* and *"Po-se-yemo."* *"T'han-se-ndo"* is our father, and *"Po-quio,"* our mother. The springs at Ojo Caliente are called *"Pose-ye Po-quinge."* Encarnación told me that he had slept there once and had, while awake, heard soft murmurs and melodious voices from beneath. There is also another laguna, "muy brava" [very rough], at the north, in the Sierra Blanca, whose waters smoothen themselves as soon as spoken to by Indians. Burial rites, etc., as at Acoma.

SEPTEMBER 15: Magnificent day. The dance of the basket ("Baile de la Jícara") is called *"Tung-Jiare,"* and is danced from February to April. The serrated instrument used by the Indians and called *"Ua'a"* is used for music at the Baile of the Jícara. The women carry it as a wand, and when the dance is over, then they set their baskets on the ground, inverted, place the *"Ua-a"* on it, and scrape the latter with the *"Ua-a-fe"* so as to produce a loud sound.[423] Painted all day at fans and masks. Good result. Night fine. Father Seux returned from Santa Fe with Mr. Brevourt[?].[424]

SEPTEMBER 16: Most splendid day. My paintings of masks are easily recognized as "Cachina" and as *"Ojua,"* and Candelario as well as old Chavez cautioned me against showing them to the Mexicans.[425] Letters from Joe and from Professor Norton[426] today. It is strange how superstitious these people are. They inhale the breath of my pictures of the Zuñi gods![427] The headdresses are all called *"Ojua,"* and the *"Ojua"* are the clouds. So are the *"Shi-uana."* The clouds represent to them the spiritual part of the bodies, whose qualities they worship. Thus *"Catzina Ojua,"* is the spirit of game, pictured by a deer, but the *"Ojua"* part of it is in the clouds. *"Tzete-Ojua"* is the round headdress made of eagle's feathers. *"Tze-fa"* is the headdress of the *"Sa-ritye."* Candelario at once recognized the *"Cha-cuani."* Wrote to Joe. They are rehearsing for the *"Te-inbe."*

SEPTEMBER 17: Wrote to Father Navet and to the *Staatszeitung* last night, and mailed all today. Beautiful day. The dance of next

Saturday is called *"Te-inbe Jiare."* The mask of the *"Shu-ma-kue"* is called here *"Zabio Pu-mo."* (Máscara de Abuelo [Grandfather mask]) The *"Cha-cuan"* is called *"Ke-ojua." "*Bear-*ojua," "Jang-ojua." "*Panther-*ojua"* is the yellow mask with brown snout. *"Po-vi-ye Ojua"* are the Mudheads. ("el que manda todas las flores de la Sierra" [who send all the mountain flowers]) In the afternoon I went to Candelario, and copied the altar *"Cen-te,"* also caught a glimpse of *"Que-mang,"* another god, kept in a leather case with bear claws around it. It is taken out in October. It is strange that the Tehuas begin at the north when they strew the sacred meal![428]

SEPTEMBER 18: Last night Father Courbon came. Painted the water god for Eldodt. Afterwards painted the female headdress, *"Ti-yu"* of the "Baile de la Jícara." In the evening, Stevenson and wife from Cincinnati, Ohio, Hughes and Brevourt [?] from Santa Fe came. Everybody here in expectation of the dance tomorrow.

SEPTEMBER 19: The stars rule the six regions. *"Agoio-zahue"* (blue star), the North. *"Agoio-zii"* (yellow star), the West. *"Agoio-pii"* (red star), the South. *"Agoio-zai"* (white star), the East. *"Agoio Nu-kung"* (black star), Above. *"Agoio Zang-gei"* (all colors), Below.[429] *Mai-tza-la-ima* is called here *"Tzi-o ue-no-ojua,"* and Ahuiuta, *"Tzi-zang Ojua."* The laguna whence they came, sallying from the bowels of the earth, is called *"Ojange Po-quinge"* and is in the Sierra Blanca, two days north of here. The noise of all kinds of animals is heard in the vicinity at night, and below is a beautiful pueblo whither all go after death, good and bad. Montezuma, *"Pose-ueve,"* and the whole story confirmed. Still, it appears to be much mixed with Spanish and Christian tales.[430] The dance was deferred today, and postponed until next Tuesday, owing to the death of a grandchild of the *"Pay-ojque."* (Four days of mourning.)

SEPTEMBER 20: Beautiful day. Painted all day after mass, painting a skull and crossbones for the church. Today the young men all went out on the rabbit hunt into the llanito east of here. The tale about the twin brothers of Zuñi is similar here; even identical.[431] *"Pose-ueve"* signifies, "he who goes, or comes, strewing along the morning-dew." Everything here seems to center in the *"Ojuas."*

Cechialatopa is called here *"Tze-ojua"* (Eagle *Ojua*). He clearly distinguishes between the white eagle and that god.

SEPTEMBER 21: Morning fine, but it soon grew very windy from the south, and the sky clouded. Painted in the afternoon. In the morning finished to arrange Eldodt's collection. It blew hard about 3 P.M. and when it cleared again, the Truchas were covered with snow. That snow vanished in a few hours afterwards. Sore eyes are going around in the pueblo. Tonight they are having their last rehearsal at the estufa. It is a beautiful night, cloudless, clear, and cool. Letter from Eddy. The poor boy is complaining bitterly.

SEPTEMBER 22: Splendid day. People are gathering for the dance of the *"Te-inbi,"* but as usual, they are delaying very much. January, *"Oyi-Po."* February—September, *"Ta-tza-Po,"* October, *"Poye-Po."* The dance began late in the afternoon. They marched out of the estufa in single file, the *"Qo-sa-re"* heading the line, then followed the *"Qui-ra-na,"* then the older men, Candelario, and the cacique. The *Ojique* was about in the middle of the line. Of the *"Quirana,"* there were only four. They wore a white bonnet with a single horn, instead of two as the *"Qosare."* Painted white and greyish brown. They had strings of apples around their bodies; so had many of the dancers. The officers were not painted. The cacique wore no other decoration than a crown of yellow flowers around the head. The *Ojique,* no flowers, but an eagle's feather behind the left ear, and a large collar with a magnificent iridescent shell dangling from it. Francisco wore a buckskin coat embroidered in front and behind with blue beads, a small greyish feather hanging in front, and a longer one behind, hanging. Candelario wore a bunch of yellow flowers over the claws. They marched, the women carrying baskets filled with fruit, the men, ears of corn, meat, etc. The baskets were carried on the heads. When they emerged into the plaza they began to circle around, and finally they formed a circle, the singers in the middle. Only one drum. The step was gentle and slow, and seldom there was any stamping. No headdress, only finery, and generally yellow flowers. When the circle had been formed, the *"Qo-sa-re"* formed a line across the middle. Then the circle divided into four groups, so that there [were] six in all. They began

to deposit their baskets and fruit, etc., and finally threw about fruit and corn, etc., all the while singing and dancing in the same slow, soft, and measured tone and rhythm. After the *"Qo-sare"* had blessed the fruits, lifting their hands, etc., they joined in the circle, and the *"Quirana"* entered the ring, and did the same. Then the four groups, one after another, followed. They strewed the food and fruit around plentifully. The *"Qosare"* cut their capers, as usual, but not as filthily, and they acted also as masters of ceremonies. Besides, there were other Indians as masters of ceremonies. They went through the same performance in front of the house of the Chino, and then they ate and distributed to the bystanders, melons, watermelons, apples, pears, etc. The dance ceased at sundown. Louis Baer came this afternoon.

SEPTEMBER 23: Candelario's office is called *"Tzi'ui,"* Francisco's *"Sa-mayo."* The *"Tzi-ojque"* is "el Tata de las Compañas" [the "parent" of the pueblo]; Miguel is the *"Qui-ra-na."* These four and the principal *"Qo-sare"* and the two caciques form the leading chiefs of superstition. The four [six, in all] groups of dancers of yesterday were: the *"Qosare,"* the *"Quirana,"* the

"Payojque," the *"Oyique,"* the *"Samayo,"* and the *"Tzi-ui."* He repeated that the *"Samayo"* had the beasts of the field under his control, deer, bear, buffalo, elk, etc.[432]

I then called upon him [Candelario Ortiz] for a collection of his medicines for Eldodt, and he gave me the following 13 charms, all in powders.

#1. *"Ojua-uo"* (flor de chalchihuite verde) [green turquoise powder] used for rain-making.

#2. *"Pung-ua-Fe Poe"* (flor de concha amarilla) [yellow shell powder] for making good weather.

#3. *"Qu-pi-Fe Poe"* (flor de coral) [coral powder] to further and propitiate the crops.

#4. *"Po-tzu-nu-Fe Poe"* (flor de chalchihuite blanco) [white turquoise powder] and *"Ju-danyi-Fe Poe"* (flor de concha morada) [violet shell powder]. Both powders mixed. Against eclipses of the sun. "Para que no se eclipse el sol." [So there will be no eclipse of the sun.]

#5. *"Po-tzang ge-uo"* (pulverized shells, shellbeads, turquoises and coral) To make all people rich and wealthy, and numerous.

#6. *"Agoyo-Fe Poe"* (flor de estrellas) [?]. To provide against bad weather following shooting-stars and meteors.

#7. *"Hi-ui-qui Poe"* ("flor del llano") [powdered soil?]. To maintain peace and good will among all men.

#8. *"Cempi Poe"* (Yerba del Manso). The great war-medicine, carried by the *"Tze-Ojque"* on the warpath.

#9. *"Tzi-Jyumo"* (possibly manganese ore, or hematite). To paint the faces of warriors, or men, when they enter the enemy's country.

#10. *"Ojua Ung-ue"* (either iron-glance [iron sulphide] or manganese ore). Paint used at the great celebration when the altar is used.

#11. *"Tzi-u-je-uano-Fe Poe"* (flor del rayo) [powdered lightning stones]. Against lightning strokes. This contains a flint in the shape of a crescent, artificially cut, but which he claims has been so shaped by lightning.

#12. *"Acome-Fe Poe"* (a yellow flower which grows abundantly in the eastern plains). Used by the *"Qo-sare"* to ripen the crops.

#13. *"Nan Sua"* (little stones from the seashore from Mexico). To prevent frost-bite, make thawing, keep the river from freezing, etc. A piece of it kept in the mouth protects against freezing, and powder of it thrown in the river, opens it or keeps the water running.

The vegetable powders, or those of dry *flowers,* ground, and pulverized. When used, the powder is mixed with cold water and spattered in the air with incantations and prayers suitable to the occasion. With #8, there is a beautiful limpid rock-crystal. There are certain years when he goes to gather the flowers. (*Flowers* for magic; *roots and herbs* for men's woes!!) He sells these charms or medicines sometimes very dear. Thus he gets sometimes 20 xícaras of pinole, and an extra-fine piece of buckskin. He claims that all the other big men of the tribe get their medicines from them [Candelario and Francisco?]. He told me that at the big celebration of the *Ojua,* they paint the "Pueblo de los Ojuas." He then showed me the "Madre." It is like a Zuñi medicine-wand of white plumes, bound around the quills with cord and twine, painted white, a very graceful and tasteful thing. A string of coral, turquoises, with iridescent shell pendants. It is placed before the altar, upright, with seventeen others, smaller ones. He also showed me a little wand, used for calling the *"Ojuas."* He told me that the mountain lion was "el compañero" of the *"Tanyi Ojua,"* and that the sacred meal was made of white and blue corn, but tinged yellow. Yellow corn is regarded as very bad.

Arranged to leave tomorrow P.M. with Francisco, Chino's youngest brother-in-law.

SEPTEMBER 24: Left at 2 P.M. on a little waggon, two horses, with Francisco Ortiz, brother of the wife of Chino. Got a letter from Captain Dougherty.[433] Leave-taking very affectionate. Reached San Ildefonso at night, and stopped with Alonzo Aguilar. Kind reception. He confirmed, and so did the boy Francisco, that the two small buffalo horns are used in the *"Qo-o Jyare"* when there is no entire buffalo head. Night beautiful. *"Tzi-re-ge"* is six miles from San Ildefonso. *"Sa-que-uy"* [Sankewi] is near by.

SEPTEMBER 25: Left at 4 A.M. Day fine and quiet. Grew hot, but remained almost cloudless, with very little wind. We followed the very sandy road along the eastern flank of the Mesa of *"Cyu-mo."* Cañada is *"Yu-ge."* It is all one long cañada, *"Tu-team-boyuge"* traversed by long arroyos and excessively sandy, until the top of the volcanic mesa on which stands the Tetilla. The road follows the mesa closely. There is water in a deep picturesque cleft called the Cañoncito, and farther on there is a little tinaja [water hole]. But the water dries occasionally in both places. There is considerable vegetation, mostly sabinos, which thins out to the top of the Mesa of the Tetilla, also good grass, chamizo and chapano. That mesa is level, barren and somewhat covered with lava. In general, lava caves, sandstone all through. Our waggon broke five times today. First, the rear-tongue [?], and had to unload. Then four times, the tires [rims] fell, twice on the descent from the mesa, which is an easy slope, but rocky. It was night when we reached the Arroyo of the Cieneguilla, and finally night, 10 P.M., when we got to the Ciénega, where we stopped at the house of Luis Vaca. Had been 18 hours without water.

SEPTEMBER 26: Left about 8 A.M. There are ruins at the Cieneguilla, and two miles from the Ciénega, in the cañón, where there is still a very fine stone church. This is probably *Cigu-ma* (*"Tzi-gu-ma"*).[434] The ruins are on the high mesas. The cañón is grand, growing more so towards the outlet. The Rio Santa Fé flows at the bottom like a small stream, and the road crosses it 19 times. It is only few [?]. Broke down twice and had to unload besides, at the house of Esquivel. Kind reception. Heavy and very cold shower, after which the sky cleared. The outlet is highly picturesque. Towering cliffs, closing in and out upon the very narrow bottom of the river. Reached Peña Blanca at sunset, safe, but very tired.

Found letters from Washington (Smithsonian Institution), E. W. Mudge, and from Pretorius. Reception very kind. My furniture is here; the bed is broken, but allright for the rest.

SEPTEMBER 27: Beautiful day. Not too warm. After mass, Don Nicolas [Lucero] remained with us awhile. Letter from the Bureau of Ethnology and bill from Frost & Adams. Wrote to Joe, to Eddy, to E. W. Mudge, to Dr. W. Eggert, and to Eldodt. Fixed the bedstead as best we could. Wrote to E. Pretorius.

SEPTEMBER 28: Bad night, but fine day, quiet and calm. Warmer than yesterday. Unpacked my boxes, allright so far. Father Navet went to the Bajada this afternoon. I wrote all afternoon at #3 of the article of the *Westliche Post,* and finished it. (10½ pages.)[435]

SEPTEMBER 29: Beautiful day again. They returned from the Bajada at noon. Wrote #4. The letters were mailed today by Cusick to Wallace. P. R. [Padre Ribera] had two children baptized here: one in 1882, Abel, and [the] other later, Dolores. The name is Vigil, and "padre no conocido." One he baptized himself under the heading "p.no conoc"!![436]

SEPTEMBER 30: Got letters today from Joe (2), Henry, Icazbalceta, Alphonse, Garrison (with enclosure from Dr. Moore), all friendly. Finished my article for the *Westliche Post.* It is cool, by the wind, but my eyes suffer. I see double again and cannot write.

OCTOBER

OCTOBER 1: Wrote until in the afternoon, and then walked across the vereda to Wallace. It is much nearer, only about four miles, and a pleasant walk across the gravelly lomas, where there is no sand. The border of the mesa is much cut up and leaves no room for sites of villages. Mailed my articles to Pretorius.[437] No letters. Returned late at night, content; still there is a worm inside from the constant worrying on account of that unhappy Bank. Shall I never have peace?

OCTOBER 2: I wrote all day at "Cibola." But always with that interior weight. It is very painfull; still, as there is no remedy, I must bear it and not murmur. God will help.

OCTOBER 3: Doña Soledad,[438] Teresa, and their little girl left with José for Santa Fe early. Juan Sanchez came. It slowly quieted down during the day, and grew pleasant and warm, but the haze continued. In the afternoon I went to Wallace with Sanchez, got a letter from Dr. Eggert, and walked back before sunset. Night beautiful and quiet.

OCTOBER 4: Walked over to the Pueblo [Cochiti]; the bridge is very good now, they have actually sunk "caissons" in the river. They are from eight to ten feet in diameter, and a basket of branches solidly interwoven, and filled with rocks. These pillars can, of course, not be touched by beavers, unless they eat the tree branches, and if the river rises, it can only float off the big hewn timbers which form the bridge as usual. It is far more solid than

the other bridge and more pleasant to walk. All the men of the Pueblo were out on the rabbit hunt, the cacique, Romero Chavez,[439] José Hilario [Montoya], etc. Kind reception. Juan José [Montoya] told me that the *"Tenbi-Jyare"* was called *"Shyey-yum"* here, and had not been danced for six or seven years past. It was danced for three days; the first, the *"Qo-sha-re"* and they threw about the fruit, of which the others ate freely, which none of them partook of it; the next day, the *"Qui-ra-na,"* when the *"Qo-sha-re"* could eat, and the last day, the whole tribe. Met Pacifico Vaca. At night wrote to Joe. Found out that José has stolen one of my shirts, the rascal.

OCTOBER 5: Finished the article on "Cibola" completely, [working] until tonight, and put a few lines to the editors along with it.[440] Had a call in the morning from both Juan José and José Hilario. They recognized at once the pictures. Juan José told me about the "Bajada de los Comanches." It took place last century, and the people of Cochiti carried from 2 to 300 scalps home with them. The place is at the entrance of the "Cañón del Qoye," and the Comanches, who had killed a man in the fields of Cochiti, were surprised on the top of the rock and when they attempted to descend, precipitated themselves headlong into the branches of a big "Pino réal" and were all killed. The "Cañón del Qoye" is thus called on account of a big tree, with notches cut into it, which protrudes from it.[441] At night Doña Soledad returned. A brisk wind began to blow from the south, and it blew chilly all night. I am through now with the *Staatszeitung* for a time and can write for other matters.

OCTOBER 6: Clear day, quiet, and fine. Wrote at my novel awhile, and then finished the portrait of Candelario Ortiz. Afterwards painted at the prayerplumes. Evening fine and clear. Arranged to go to Santo Domingo tomorrow.

OCTOBER 7: [For entries of October 7 and 8, Bandelier inadvertently wrote "April 7," "April 8," and "April 9." He corrected himself with the entry of October 9.] Beautiful morning, clear and pleasant. Father Navet very ill-humored, or rather, childish as usual. Left for Santo Domingo. Could not do anything except that *"Gui-puy"* is about a mile above Wallace, on the right bank of the river, [or] Arroyo de Galistéo. Got letter from Mr. Balsiger and from Eddy. Returned across the trail and found everything allright. The people of Santo Domingo are as obstinate, suspicious, and superstitious as usual, and the fact that I was introduced by the priest had certainly a very bad effect. The governor told me to leave the pueblo today, and to come back tomorrow, for the purpose of drawing, that today nothing could be done. So I left at once.[442]

The river is threatening the church badly, and, if not speedily stopped, its current will cause the bank (now about 30 feet high and vertical, and only 20 feet from the church) to fall, which will entail the fall of the edifice itself. The governor reiterated the story that the present old church was the first one built at Santo Domingo by the Spaniards. This is not true.[443]

OCTOBER 8: Finished the first chapter of my novel completely,[444] although I had a very friendly and highly interesting call by Juan José. I showed my drawing, and he talked freely and frankly. The fetishes he calls after the names of the animals. *"Moqatsh,"* *"Cohay-yo"* [mountain lion, bear], etc. The musical instrument he calls *"Uyano-uitz"* and they use it also in one of their dances. The masks are called *"Shi-ua-na,"* also *"Ku-pish-tai"* (spirits). The altar is called *"Ai-tshi,"* and, if used in the winter, it is named

"Tzi-pañy ai-tshi"; in summer, *"Qashpit Ai-tshi."* The yellow mask worn along with those of the Chacuana is called *"Capo-nay-ya-mish."* It is a *"Shiuana"* also.

Their tradition [at Cochiti] is that *"Sen-quit-ye"* (whom he identifies with *"Mai-tza-la-ima"* after having seen the latter pictures!) created the earth out of the four wombs ("de sus cuatro senos"), and that men first lived in the darkness. Afterwards the sun was created and shown. *"Sen-quit-ye"* then had a brother who was half good, half bad, and who therefore went south. In the remainder, he confirms the tradition of the Tehuas about *"Shi-pap,"* and the creation of the *"Qo-share"* and of the *"Quirana,"* that the first are summer people, and the latter winter people, that the former have to fast and pray for the ripening crops, and the latter, for the sprouting plants.

There are three chayanes at Cochiti, *"Hi-tshanyi Chayani,"* now the cacique by interim; *"Shquy Chayani"* (Romero Chavez); and the *"Shiqama Chayani,"* so that when the cacique and his two assistants are there, there are six, as at San Juan, besides the *"Qoshare naue"* and the *"Quirana naue."*[445] But there are now no caciques except at Jemez and at San Felipe; the others are all "ad interim" although they have their "novicios" which they educate as their successors, unless the Pueblo puts [in] a regular cacique again. The candidates for that office are, however, scarce, as it is a very heavy duty, the three having to fast alternately one week.[446] The *Chayani* now fast four days when the rains begin. The *Qoshare* and the *Quirana* form a brotherhood which runs through all the Pueblos, Zuñi included, and these have the right to dance in the dances, although the dress be different. They [Qoshare] belong to the lower; the *"Quirana,"* to the upper estufa.[447] There is to be a great hunt of hares and rabbits this week yet, preparatory to the harvest of corn, and the *Chayani* are therefore collecting herbs, etc. F. N. [Father Navet] returned tonight from the Placeres.

OCTOBER 9: The sandals of yucca are known here as shoes for the snow. The sea monsters from San Juan are called here, *"Tzitz Shruui"* [water snakes]. Wrote at my novel and painted.

OCTOBER 10: Father Navet went to the Bajada early. The name of the ruin at San Miguel is also *"Raty Cama-tzeshuma."*[448] The longer plumestick from San Juan is called *"Poshto-asht,"* that is, lightning. Juan José saw it used at Cia in the estufa; the ribbon of yucca extends and carries the feather far beyond the stick. (Most of their ceremonies are mere juggleries it seems.) In the afternoon I went to Cochiti, but there was nobody at home, all the men being out on a hunt, or, perhaps, on a secret dance in the woods! Had a little scare tonight, somebody rapping at the kitchen window for José.

OCTOBER 11: Joe's birthday. God be with her and consent to a speedy reunion. Finished the plumesticks at last, but could not go to mass, owing to a razor cut very near the jugular vein. Was afraid I had opened it. Wrote to Joe, and then went to Wallace at 11 A.M., about, on foot. Found letters: 2 from Joe, 1 from Mudge, 2 from W. C. Kueffner,[449] and 1 from Pilling.[450] The letters from Joe and from Mudge are good. I replied at once, from Wallace, to Mudge, Kueffner, and also to Pilling himself; staid until 4 P.M. and then returned home. Thus, dear Joe's birthday has brought news which sounds at least somewhat favorably. It is not, however, absolutely certain as yet. I shall go to Santa Fe next Saturday, and await there the result at Edwardsville and Joe's coming. Hope to God that I will not have any more trouble, and the letters seem to indicate it.

OCTOBER 12: Went to Cochiti early in the morning and returned at noon. Nothing new there. Luis Lucero told me that the round building at the Rito [de los Frijoles] was a tank, indeed, but made by the Indians. Wrote to Joe and to Eddy.

OCTOBER 13: Father Navet went to Zile while I worked at my novel, until late at night. Sent off my letters to Santa Fe.

OCTOBER 14: Wrote to Eldodt. Father Navet went to Cochiti. In the afternoon, [I] went to Wallace and got card from Mr. Dronne. Wrote to him and to Dr. Moore, from Wallace. There is trouble brewing between Santo Domingo and Cochiti on account of land.[451]

OCTOBER 15: Walked very little, wrote at the novel and painted some. On the whole I am fairly satisfied with the work; if only everything at home improves. I still say "Home" although it does not deserve it at all!

There is trouble brewing between Cochiti and Santo Domingo about a tract of land south of Zile which the former bought of Juana Baca. There is a "Petición" by Phelipe Tafoya [Here, Bandelier included extracts describing land boundaries in the disputed area.].

OCTOBER 16: I walked over to Wallace where I found a very good letter from Joe. Thank God! It is not absolutely certain yet, but still there appear grounds of hope, that I need not return [to Edwardsville]. I wish it were true. I then went with little Perry, son of Thos. McIlvain, to the ruins of *"Guipuy,"* or *"Guipua,"* the former Pueblo of Santo Domingo, which was washed away partly by the Arroyo of Galistéo. It is hardly discernible owing to the lowness of the mounds. There is an innumerable quantity of flint, broken stones, basalt, and pottery fragments about. The pottery is nearly all glossy. Many pieces appear new and bright; they are all broken into small bits and scattered very evenly on the whole area. Not a trace of estufas is visible or left. One building is partly washed away, and its western wall is very thick, about three feet, and seems to be of adobe, so that it looks as if it might have been the church![452] The ruins are much overgrown with chamiza and some *Opuntia.* They are a mile-and-a-half east of Wallace, and three-and-a-half miles from Santo Domingo, on the right bank of the arroyo, which has there washed out a vertical bank nearly 15 to 20 feet high in places. This bank is still crumbling. The situation [site] is rather low, and [has] a good outlook up and down the valley, which narrows only a mile beyond the 2nd bridge of the railroad.

OCTOBER 17: Cloudy like an early spring morning. Damp and quiet. Clouds breaking. Warm almost to sultriness. Went over to Wallace and got a few letters.[453] At night, José left us at last.

OCTOBER 18: Cold, blustering, and finally rain. Painted. Shall leave tomorrow for Santa Fe [with] José Pio García and a load of wheat to be ground there. At last the crisis comes.

OCTOBER 19: Splendid weather. Left at 8 A.M. The horses gave out soon, and in the bocas we had to unload. Killed a great spider, Mygale [bird spider, probably tarantula], on the road, at the entrance to the bocas. The church in the cañón is recent, and there is no pueblo there. But opposite the house of Germán Pino, on the banks of the Arroyo Hondo, are the great rubbish heaps of *"Tziguma."*[454] It is a mile from the "Golondrinas" and is called the "Alamo Solo." Not a tree. It is also a mile southwest of the Cieneguilla. A dismal looking place. Coyotes are abundant between Agua Fria and the Cieneguilla. They howled dismally at sunset. I left José Pio at sunset and walked ahead to Santa Fe, where I got at 7 P.M. Letter from Bradshaw. Must go.[455] Stopped at Koch's.

OCTOBER 20:[456] Beautiful day. Began calling around. Pearce, Gerdes, Governor Ritch, Indian Agency. Got letters sent to me from San Juan: 2 from Pearce, 1 from Henry, 1 from J. J. Tylor, New York. Wrote to Henry and Father Navet. Telegraphed to Mudge. Met Father Seux. At night, Dr. Eggert fell sick. Called on Dr. Longwill[457] and remained up till 5 A.M. when he got better.

OCTOBER 21: Day same. Unwell. Telegram. Must go. Called on Father Eguillon and Father Defouri. Wrote to Henry. Got letter from J. C. Pilling. Information wanted as usual. Met General Bradley[458] and the officers. Saw Preciliana Chavez. Santa Fe is beautiful. The weather splendid. And now I must leave. Well, I go, and get the best of it. I will find my own dear Joe.

OCTOBER 22: Left 9:30 A.M. Day splendid. Very unwell. Had good company; C. W. Whitney, Thos. Hill, Captain Heincke, Señor Vargas, etc. But that awful weight in my bosom! My God, what will become of poor Joe!

OCTOBER 23: Like pounding [?] Wired to Mudge from Lakin, Kansas. How flat and monotonous the country is. Clouded at last. Captain Heincke left us at Topeka at 3 A.M. next morning. Quieting down within.

OCTOBER 24: Boys and Vargas left me at Kansas City. Got to St. Louis at 7:30 P.M.; went directly to George [Hoffmann]. Kindest reception. Nothing new. Joe is well, and everything quiet so far.

OCTOBER 25: Fine, cool, but what a hazy atmosphere! Went to the depot at 7:30 A.M., but Athanas Hoffmann was there and told me not to go to Edwardsville, as Court had adjourned for a week. "It is likely that you will be indicted," he said; still it is not positive as yet. People have cooled down. Returned home [i. e., George Hoffmann's home, in St. Louis], slept in the afternoon, and at night went down with Hubert [Hoffmann][459] to meet Gustave [Bandelier]. Joe had not come, so I telegraphed to her, and then went home, where I met August Becker.[460] At night an explosion was heard, a [railroad] car having been blown up with dynamite.

OCTOBER 26: Cloudy. Wrote to J. D. [J. C.] Pilling, to E. W. Mudge, to J. J. Tylor (Albermarle House, New York). Joe came at 5 P.M. with Bertha [Huegy Lambelet]. Thank God, she is well and hearty, and we are together again. Great news; the people are quieter and ashamed. Spent the evening at home. Rain at night.

OCTOBER 27: Happy again. Joe is with me. Wrote card to T. W. McIlvain; letters to Henry, Father Navet, Koch, Eldodt, W. F. White,[461] and Captain Dougherty. Clouding more and more. At sunset, thunder and lightning. Slight rain. Grew cooler. How happy I am to have Joe again with me. It seems as if there had been no dark past at all.

OCTOBER 28: I got a note from Gustave calling me to town immediately. Went and met E. W. Mudge. He speaks hopefully, but I have to go to Edwardsville next Friday. The G. J. [Grand Jury] appears to be about decidedly in my favor, as far as the majority is concerned, Highland members alone excepted, who are of course influenced by fear, envy, or jealousy. As if that crew could ever hope to reach as far as I have attained. This is vanity which I trust God may yet forgive, but this thought is the only satisfaction, the only revenge, which I shall ever attempt to achieve, obtain or wreak upon the poor people that have persecuted me so obstinately. No more explosions heard.

OCTOBER 29: Wrote for the *"Westliche Post."* Got a letter from E. W. Mudge again, telling me not to come tomorrow. I replied to him at once, in conformity with his directions.

OCTOBER 30: There is no sky here, and no atmosphere. Went down town in the afternoon and called on Charles Boeschenstein. Returning, at 7 P.M. got a dispatch calling me to Edwardsville, also a letter from Henry. Must go, although my throat is very sore and bad, and the weather is inclement.

OCTOBER 31: Dark, cloudy, and lowering. Had a very bad night on account of my throat, which hurts very much. Left for Edwardsville at 7:50 A.M. Kindly received. Attorneys hopeful; so is Krome[462] of the assignees. Called on Sister Severa,[463] and met Mrs. Kyburtz. Good, faithful souls. It rained hard. Made an arrangement with Bradshaw and Krome to transfer the coal mine[464] to the assignees and the house to Mr. Bradshaw. Mudge assents to it. I remained till 6:30 P.M. and then left. It rained and turned cool. At St. Louis, the rain had ceased. My throat was very sore and painful, had a very bad night; no sleep and much pain.

NOVEMBER

NOVEMBER 1: Sick and sore. Went to Pauline and Annie at noon, with Hubert. Staid until 9 P.M. Gustave came. Ida Streiff[465] has a little baby, a daughter. Allright. Returned late. Throat very sore. Very bad night.

NOVEMBER 2: Very weak and suffering, although my throat is better. Taking quinine. Went to J. P. [Justice of the Peace] E. Cronin[466] to have my two Deeds acknowledged, but have to bring witnesses. Got a beautiful letter from Mr. Balsiger. Went down town in the afternoon and saw Mr. Collett [Collet], Pretorius, and G. J. Engelmann.[467] Met F. C. Ryhiner [Jr.][468] on the road.

NOVEMBER 3: Went to J. P. Cronin, but he refused to acknowledge and is right. Wrote to Mudge, to Father Navet, to Eldodt, Koch, and to Mr. Balsiger, also to Henry. Received, at last, the registered letter from Chamita; it was from J. Hermann, and enclosed an acknowledgment of service in the foreclosure of the Grimen-Weder Mortgage. I signed and mailed it to Highland at once. Wrote card to R. Streiff. Spent the evening at G. J. Engelmann's.

NOVEMBER 4: Wrote the whole day at my article for the *Westliche Post.* No news. It is exceedingly gloomy. Warm. Night quiet, dull. Streets awfully muddy. G. W. Cone called at Blanke & Bro.[469] for me, but George did not send him out.

NOVEMBER 5: Exceedingly disagreeable, hard to breathe. Joe and Celia [Hoffmann] went to town, while I staid, finishing #2 for the *Westliche Post.* They returned at noon and told me that they had met F. C. R. on the street. Mailed my second article to Pretorius. Very sultry, foggy, & disagreeable. Damp. Called with George at Dr. Alleyne's.[470]

NOVEMBER 6: Damp, windy, ugly, muddy, sultry, mean, cloudy, and detestable weather. Left for Edwardsville with Joe at 7:43 A.M. Met there Jac. Kleiner; nothing decided as yet. F. C. R. indeed wanted to turn State's evidence against me, but was not accepted. The poor, foolish boy. Was startled by being addressed by Gruaz[471] with many assurances of friendship. Left Joe at Sister Severa's. In the afternoon went with her to Ad. Suppiger,[472] and finally took supper at Robert Hagnauer's. Returned late.

NOVEMBER 7: Joe and Celia went to town early. [Bandelier made extracts, at length, from:] *"Reports upon Zoological Collections obtained from Portions of Nevada, Utah, California, Colorado, New Mexico, and Arizona"* in Vol. V of Surveys of G. M. Wheeler's West of the 100th Meridian, 1875.

[Bandelier also made extensive notes on:] *Relation du Voyage entrepris par feu M. Robert Cavelier, Sieur de la Salle, pour découvrir dans le golfe du Mexique l'embouchure du Flueve de Missisipy," "par son frere M. Cavelier, pretre de St. Sulpice, l'un des compagnons de ce voyage"* (J. M. Shea, 1858, N. York.) [He also worked with:] *"Relation ou Journal du Voyage du R. P. Jacques Gravier de la compagnée de Jesus en l'an 1700 depuis le pays des Illinois jusqu'à l'embouchure du Mississipy"* (p. 29).

Got a letter from Mr. Markham[473] and a telegram from the [assignors?] of F. R. & Co.; replied to the latter that I could not come on Monday. Wrote to Bradshaw. At Dr. Taussig's,[474] was very well received; he promised passes and half-fare for Hubert. Had to go back to the *Westliche Post* for another letter.

NOVEMBER 8: Fine day, according to notions of this country—cool and quiet. George's 46th birthday. Rud Streiff, August Becker and Emily, Henry Hoffmann and wife, spent the afternoon and evening. Very pleasant. Dr. Alleyne called also for a moment. Joe unwell, but improved.

NOVEMBER 9: Cloudless, but foggy. Got a letter from Eldodt this morning. [Work on] *Jesuit Relations* continued.

Met Gruaz and had a long talk with him. . . . I then went to Pretorius and got him to give me another letter which I mailed at once. Returned at home.

NOVEMBER 10: Very handsome day. Went to Edwardsville. At Edwardsville called first on Lizzie Hagnauer.[475] Not at home. Met Mrs. E. W. Mudge on the street. Then called on E. W. Mudge, who told me that Papa, F. C. R., and I were all three indicted in the same Bill. I concluded to give Bond, after taking advice. Bradshaw was against it at first but came to the conclusion finally that it was best to defer the trial. Saw Lorenz Winter,[476] Jno Bardill,[477] etc. Called on Sister Severa, on Adolph Suppiger and his wife. Had to testify in Court in the case of Ad. Ruegger against the assignees. (Attachment.) After I had been released by Court, the s-- o- b---- brought in a new indictment, so that I was brought to law quickly and quietly at once. It is an outrage and is looked upon as such at Edwardsville.[478] Saw General [W. C.] Kueffner; he warned me about G. W. Cone. Upon my return I found a letter from Cone. Very friendly, but I have to be on my guard in order to avoid an admission. It is very warm and damp; the air is heavy. I trust to God that this infamous persecution will cease at last and give me time to make an honest though modest living. It is all I care for, all I wish and pray for in this world. God will, at last, relieve me and help me to quietness and rest.

NOVEMBER 11: [Bandelier here made extensive notes on:] *"Ensayo Cronológico para la Historia general de la Florida desde el ano de 1512, que descubrió La Florida, Juan Ponce de Léon, hasta el de 1722, escrito por Don Gabriel de Cardenas y Cano"* (Andrés Gonzalez Barcia) *Madrid 1723* (Dec. IIIa) Año MDXL. [He also made notes on:] *"Journal historique de l'établissement des Francais à la Louisiane."* [Notations were also made on:] *"The Wor-*

thye & famous History of the Travailes, Discouvery, & Conquest, of that great Continent of Terra florida, being lively Paraleld, with that of our now Inhabited Virginia, etc." London 1611 (*Reprint of the Hackluyt Society, Vol. 8, 1851 "Gentleman of Elvas"*).

These copies I made at the Mercantile Library.[479] Went to see Dr. Taussig, and got his passes to El Paso. Called at the *Globe-Democrat* and made arrangements for correspondence. Received letter of Henry. Wrote to Mudge, cards to Father Navet and to Dr. Kinner.[480] On the street met Henry Hesse.[481] Spent the evening at Beckers very pleasantly. Joe went to Hospes, and was very kindly treated.

NOVEMBER 12: No news yet. Wrote to Mr. Balsiger. In the afternoon, went to Dr. Kinner's. Pleasant.

NOVEMBER 13: Cold, clear. Went down town in the afternoon. Got tickets and berths. Called on Dr. Engelmann. No news yet. Ready to leave tomorrow, although there might occur trouble. I have done my duty to the bondsman, as well as to the assignees.

NOVEMBER 14: Cold and clear. White frost. Got letters, from Gruaz, and one from Kueffner with papers to sign. Rosalie and Lizzie came in too. Left at 9:10 A.M. Traversed Missouri, passing Iron Mountain and Pilot Knob. Mountainous, although low. Pine trees covering the ridges. Entered Arkansas, low and marshy, all wooded. Warmer.

NOVEMBER 15: Clear, fine, and warmer. Awoke at Texarkana, on the boundaries of Texas, Louisiana, and Arkansas. Flat and timbered. Thence travelled south 73 miles along the Louisiana line in Texas, always in the timber belt, interspersed with cotton fields. Many negroes live here. The country is absolutely low and rolling. Yellow pine is the prevailing timber. We then turned west, through the timber belt, which gradually thinned out into oak, rather well cultivated prairie, rolling, with little towns. Reached Fort Worth at 8 P.M. Absolutely flat. Night beautiful.

NOVEMBER 16: Awoke in the desert. A long range of mesas, black, and several hundred feet high, cut across the level and barren landscape from southeast to northwest in the southwest. They can, by an unexperienced eye, easily be taken for a mountain chain. It appears that, in central Texas, there are similar and even higher ranges, from time to time, so that Cabeza de Vaca[482] could well speak of "sierras" in Texas. Vegetation stinted; yucca appears. At noon, the rocky soil increased. At Big Springs, we crossed the Colorado. Here there are rocky hills. Met Will Doud. Farther on, the Staked Plains came in sight. Grassy, with tree-like yucca, *Opuntia arborescens,* . . . cactuses and flat *Opuntiae.* Towards Douro, white sand appeared, forming low ranges of white hills.

Beyond Quito, the mountains at last appeared in the southwest, a long range. They are the Sierra San Martín, Pah-cut, and the Apache Mountains, all belonging to the Guadalupe Range. In the south, about 120 miles off, an isolated mountain loomed up, perhaps the Bonita. Crossed the Pecos at sunset. There is no valley, only a perfectly level plain, stretching out beyond it to the west, to the foot of the mountain ranges. Saw several herds of antelopes, and considerable cattle. We soon began to rise, and it became cooler. The Pecos is not over 100 yards wide; it runs in a cut of soil with vertical banks about 10–15 feet deep, somewhat similar to the Rio Casas Grandes, less the rank vegetation. Its course is swift, the waters muddy.

NOVEMBER 17: Reached El Paso at 3:25 A.M. and went to bed at the Pierson House. Warm, and many musquitoes. Slept well. Most beautiful morning and day. Left El Paso 10:30 A.M. Sky cloudless, the mountains bright and handsome. Reached at 11 P.M. Albuquerque, and met Eddy. Went to bed at 1 A.M., tired.

NOVEMBER 18: At Santa Fe, Mr. Koch came to receive us. Most friendly reception everywhere. Found a letter from Paris, unsatisfactory. The rest are all old letters. Called on the Archbishop, Father Eguillon, and several others. Joe is comparatively well. Found a good room for Hubert and boarding with Mrs. Bush.[483]

NOVEMBER 19: John Pearce, the good boy, allows me to write at his office. He is an excellent friend. Wrote and mailed to Kueffner, Mudge, to George, to Henry, to Engelmann, and to Gruaz. Mr. Smith called. At night grande "soirée musicale" at

Koch's. Joe had such pains that she could not assist. A whole host of people. Smith and wife, Gerdes and wife, Staab and wife,[484] Grunsfeld,[485] Miss Staab, Eddie Franz,[486] Hubert, etc. It was exceedingly pleasant, although very heterogeneous. Poor Joe had to be in bed.[487]

NOVEMBER 20: Wrote this journal at John's office, made a short call at the Doctor's [probably, William Eggert] before dinner with my wife. Got a letter from George. Fresh persecutions seem to be brewing. Night at Smith's.

NOVEMBER 21: Wrote to Mr. Kueffner, to Ottendorfer, and to Bradshaw. In the afternoon, I walked out with Joe and Hubert. Called on Mrs. Reed. Wrote to the Illinois *Staatszeitung*[488] also. Evening at the Doctor's.

NOVEMBER 22: Was at Pearce's nearly all day. Talked about painting the blasons, his and Vanderveer's. Evening at the Doctor's till late.

NOVEMBER 23: Painted the blason of Vanderveer's. Evening musical soirée at Koch's again. Shall start tomorrow.

NOVEMBER 24 TO NOVEMBER 28: [Tuesday to Saturday] Left for Peña Blanca at 9 A.M. and walked on, reaching there at 3 P.M. Tuesday. Father Navet not at home; nothing ready in the rooms. Weather fine, except Thursday night when it rained. Am very much disappointed. Juan Sanchez has not done anything at all. And Peña Blanca is so terribly quiet, so still. I cannot get Joe to such a place under no circumstances whatever. Saw a few Indians, Juan José, Victoriano, etc. On Saturday night the priest returned, early in the evening. He had been to San Rafael, to the festival, and had met there Father [John B.] Brun,[489] and also Father Badilla of San Juan. Zuñi now belongs to the latter parish. He [Father Navet] is sorry for the delay, but I cannot possibly wait any longer. I must go back to Santa Fe and see that we get settled. Wrote a correspondence of 25½ pp. for the *New York World,* and only 9 pp. to the *Westliche Post,*[490] and commenced a correspondence of *The Nation* on Land Grants. It is a beginning only, and God grant that it may prove successful. But another delay is inevitable, for I must move to Santa Fe at once. Peña Blanca is no place for us.

NOVEMBER 29: Beautiful day. Left for Wallace early, on foot. Got a letter from Mudge, rather favorable. Also one from Mr. Balsiger. Good so far. But nothing from Germany! It is so annoying. Am decided to leave. Returned in the afternoon. Father Navet went to the festival of the Cañada [de Cochiti]. It is the festival of Nuestra Señora de Guadalupe, but owing to the inclemency of the winter there, it is celebrated on the 30th of November, in place of the 12th of December.[491]

NOVEMBER 30: Beautiful day. I left Peña Blanca on foot for Wallace and mailed my letters and MSS. Then started on foot across the mesa, to the Bajada. It was very tiresome walking across the uneven and slightly soft ground. At the Bajada, I met a waggon, and took it to Agua Fria. Reached Santa Fe at nightfall. It was very soon arranged to take Mr. Schumann's house,[492] that is, the three rooms vacant in it, furnished, at $15.—per month. All we need to buy is a cooking-stove.

DECEMBER

DECEMBER 1: Beautiful springlike. Warm. Wrote at the Landgrant article at Pearce's office. Saw Dr. Meany. He is very well satisfied with my article.

DECEMBER 2: Like yesterday. Warm and beautiful. Wrote and worked, but made very little headway. Everything getting ready, our friends helping admirably. Landgrant article going very slow, but it is interesting and important work.

DECEMBER 3: Similar, clear. Worked, but did not make much headway. It is very difficult work, or at least such as needs exceedingly careful watching. There are points of law which I am unable to decide for myself. Evening at Koch's, after working with Pearce for awhile. Met Mr. Franz, Mr. Schieff, etc.

DECEMBER 4: Clouding, chilly. Worked at the same. At night, George Pradt[493] and Provencher[494] came and called. Pradt says that the Indians of Laguna have their stone idols, which they place under a painting of the bear, mountain lion, and snakes. At Acoma, they have three caciques now. Spent evening at the Doctor's [Eggert].

DECEMBER 5: Bitterly cold, and brisk wind from north. Left for Peña Blanca with José de la Cruz Quintana, and two waggons. Reached the Curacy at 1 P.M., packed up and sent them back at 3 P.M. Father Navet absent at Wallace and Santo Domingo. [He] returned at sunset, well pleased with the school arrangements at the latter pueblo. Sold my furniture to him at once.

DECEMBER 6: Beautiful day. After mass I walked over to Wallace, got a letter and returned to Cochiti, to witness the close of the dance of the *Quirana*. They only wear a little plume of the eagle's (rather down) on one side, and a down of "Cernícalo" [sparrow hawk] on the other side of the head, above each ear, fastened to the hair, paint: red. Good blankets, etc., but no other costumes.

Remained overnight with Juan José, who confirmed what he had told about baptism on the fourth day. He says that when one falls sick, the chayani, three of them, and an old woman, sit up with the patient, four days and four nights, praying and watching, fasting rigidly. They are not allowed to eat anything except some cornmeal in water, once every twenty-four hours, and there is a guard placed on the house, to prevent every Mexican, every female or male relative, to enter the building, or even to approach it. About 2 A.M. of the fifth day, they go to the river to wash and bathe themselves. Then food is brought to them from the house of the patient. The medicine is mostly herbs, incantations, and prayers to their idols. The *Qoshare* sing, pray, and dance only the first day, the other three days they simply fast and remain quiet in their estufa [Turquoise]. He is full of witchcraft-lore. He still recollects a man who once attempted to prevent the setting in of rain. He had a *"Yaya"* [literally, "mother," but here idol, or fetish] made of owls-feathers; cactus leaves, woodpeckers feathers, turkey-buzzards plumes were used by him, also; in June, ears of green corn, with very few grains, and he was trying to prevent the corn of the others to have grains at all! He was condemned to death, but not executed, though badly treated and finally disappeared in the Jornada del Muerto.[495] He himself [i.e., Juan José] was bewitched by a woman, who afterwards pursued him twice in the shape of a coyote. The second time he shot the coyote, wounding him in the skull. The woman died soon afterwards, and it was found that the top of her skull was fractured.

Nearly every knoll, prominent rock, peak, etc., contains an enchanted spirit, which they call up by throwing grains of corn at the place, and shouting to him to come forth and give them what they want of him. Thus one of these ghosts was invoked by a few young people at *"Ca-ca-ua,"* on the other side of the river beyond the milpas. He is said to reside at a gravel heap, and they threw grains of corn at the heap and called him to come out and fetch them a deer. He at once answered, and they fled; he pursued them across the river. The same season all died.

In the Cañada de la Peralta a similar occurrence took place, but they did not run, so the deer was brought to them invisibly, to the fireplace, where they transfixed him with arrows, invisibly to them also. They only saw him after he was dead. At the Cerro Poñil also.

But the queerest occurrence took place at Cia. There is a vein of chalchihuite blanco, which the people of Cia and Jemez wanted to reserve for themselves, and deprive the other Pueblos of its use. So the *Chayani* gathered all the people of the Pueblo one night, and they performed the rites for calling the ghost. He came to the door with a great noise like thunder, and asked what they wanted. He then scolded them, and said that the vein was free to all, and imposed upon them a penance of four days fasting and vomiting. They do not use poison for killing, only bows and arrows, and clubs. It is the capitan de la guerra who does it.[496]

The laguna on the Sierra de Santa Fe is called *"I-yanyi Qawash."* It is regarded as belonging to all the Pueblos together. The *"Shi-pap-u"* is above Conejos, and is the same as the "Laguna brava" of the Tehuas.

DECEMBER 7: Clouding. Cooling rapidly. Started with Adelaido [Montoya][497] on horseback for the Cieneguilla. Blowing hard on the mesa. At the brink of the mesa, I sent him back and walked home, the wind pushing me. Got to Santa Fe at 5 P.M.

DECEMBER 8: Feast of the Immaculate Conception. Went to mass at the Cathedral. Bitterly cold. Visiting, running back and forth. Mudge sent 65.—dollars from Bradshaw.

DECEMBER 9: Heavy snow overnight. Very wet and chilly. Wind northeast shifting to north. Grew very cold at night. Began to move in, put up stove, etc.

DECEMBER 10: Clearing. Cold morning. Mr. Koch came, with J. Lucero, to put up the bookstand. Continued to unpack and to put things in place. Very chilly.

DECEMBER 11: Got letter from George. Finished unpacking. Juan José came. Told me a story of a puma ripping up a bear at the Cañón del Pino. Witness: old Lauciano [Luciano] Lucero,[498] of the Cañada [de Cochiti]. Afterwards, they returned with Pedro, and brought me a coyote which Juan José had killed on the mesa this morning.
    Wrote to George a long letter.

DECEMBER 12: Beautiful sunrise. Cold. Feast of Nuestra Señora de Guadalupe today. A few cannon shots early in the morning, and brilliant fires last night all around.[499] Finished my article on Landgrants.

DECEMBER 13: Mr. Koch called in the morning. Wrote to Mr. Balsiger enclosing letter from T. Gruaz. In the afternoon, went down town with Joe. Called on Mrs. Bush, on the Archbishop, and Mr. Meany. Anastasio Martinez told me that the ruins southwest of Agua Fria are not those of a pueblo, but those of a rancho, formerly belonging to one of his ancestors. Began to write for the *Globe-Democrat.*

DECEMBER 14: Wrote further. Got a letter from Mr. Ottendorfer with $22.50. Evening at Mr. Meany's; the Dr. [Eggert], Vanderveer, and Max Frost[500] present. Satisfactory. Came home at midnight, and found the gate locked.

DECEMBER 15: Finished the first article for the *Globe-Democrat* and mailed it, as well as the Landgrant [article] for *The Nation.*[501] Began at the second letter to the *Globe-Democrat.* Pearce here again.

DECEMBER 16: Splendid day. Got a host of letters. From Alphonse, Mr. Balsiger, Dr. G. H. Moore. Wrote at a second article for *The Nation,* on Pueblo Landgrants. In the afternoon went down town for nothing at all. An utterly useless walk.

DECEMBER 17: Invited by Gerdes, but refused. In the afternoon went with Hinojos to call on Don Antonio Ortiz y Salazar.[502] He showed me fragments of the journal of Diego de Vargas,[503] that had been sold at public auction by Governor Pyle.[504] At nightfall, Joe came home and told me the Dr. was very sick. So I went down. Pearce was there already (he is an excellent nurse), and we remained up all night until 7 A.M. He [Eggert] isn't sick at all, only a cold.

DECEMBER 18: Finished my second paper for *The Nation.* In the afternoon called on Mrs. Staab, on the Doctor, and the Archbishop. There I met Father Antonio Jouvenceau.[505] He tells me there has been great drouth in Arizona; no rain at all last summer. Springs and ponds are drying up, and many people leaving Tucson. Same in Sonora. Dr. is playing sick man.

DECEMBER 19: Wrote to Henry and mailed the letter. Got my pamphlets from New York. Wrote to Dr. G. H. Moore, to Mr. Balsiger, and to Alphonse. Mailed 16 pamphlets. Rainy and wet all day.[506] Dr. Eggert better; thank the stars for it. Wrote to Mr. Ottendorfer.

DECEMBER 20: Went to mass, Father Antonio preached. Then to the Dr. He has got pneumonia, but just a very slight attack only.[507] Wrote to Mudge. Got letter from Mr. Balsiger about the house again. In the afternoon, Mr. Schumann, and Mr. Schafer called. Wrote to Gruaz and to Pretorius. Evening at Koch's; the moonlight most splendid, the snow on the peak of Abiquiu glistening like silver. I tried to paint today, but it became impossible owing to visitors. Wrote a few pages for the *Globe-Democrat.*

DECEMBER 21: Sunrise beautiful, but it soon clouded from the northwest. Sam Eldodt in town. He has many nice acquisitions, among them the stone idol *"Tzi-o-ueno Ojua."* Adelaido from Cochiti called very early and ate breakfast with us. He brought a letter from Juan José telling me that they were to dance Matachines on Friday, and Adelaido told me that there was to be a "Baile de la Cabellera" on Saturday; six "matalotes" and six "malinches" from each estufa. I went to Fornance and told him about going. He may go along. Wrote at #2 for the *Globe-Democrat.*

DECEMBER 22: Got books from Mr. Balsiger. Finished article for the *Globe-Democrat.* In the afternoon, spent a few hours in town with the Dr., Koch, Pearce, Fornance, and the Archbishop. Fornance told me that a medicine man of the Navajos had been shot once near Fort Wingate. Clothed in a wolfskin, he was trying to get certain parts of a human corpse for medicinal purposes. If he succeeds, it is allright, but the relations of the deceased have the faculty of killing him in case he is detected.

Father Antonio told me that, after the Arivaypa Massacre,[508] the Papagos who participated in it went into the brush for a whole month (he says 30 days) to fast and purify themselves. Their women brought them the food and invariably broke the vessels in which it was carried. After the fast was over, a big dance was on, every "jacal" had an eagle plume on top of it. The chief performers were two old women, their faces painted blue and holding the ends of a slat to which two Apache children (captives) were tied. These had to dance along with the rest. All faces painted.[509]

At night wrote to George, sending him my article for the *Globe-Democrat.*[510]

DECEMBER 23: No letters. Wrote for the *Westliche Post.* Called at the Dr.'s several times, on Pearce and at Koch's. In the afternoon, Father Antonio called. At night we got a Christmas gift from Eddy. Made a short call at Koch's. Wrote to Eddy.

DECEMBER 24: Got a letter from Gatschet.[511] He can wait until I write to him. It is really abusive, to beg such information from me without previously replying to my letters to the Ethnological Bureau [Bureau of Ethnology, Washington, D.C.]. In the afternoon, I finished the article for the *Westliche Post;* Mr. Frye and Fornance called. Went down to town, called on Dr., saw Pearce, and then staid at home! First Christmas with Joe for four years. Very quiet, but still alone with *her,* and that is a blessing.[512] It is a pleasant Christmas, all in poverty but still quiet. Night beautiful, balmy and quiet.

DECEMBER 25: Very quiet today. Went to Mass, and afterwards wrote at my novel. Joe has a very severe headache. At night, spent a few hours very pleasantly with Kochs. Joe slightly better. No letters.

DECEMBER 26: Left at 6 A.M. on horseback with Lt. Fornance. It was not cold at all. After sunrise, the clouds began to lift from the west in arched bands. Reached Peña Blanca at noon. Took a hasty dinner and then went on to Cochiti. They were dancing the *"Ah-ta-Tanyi."* It is not the scalp dance proper, but an imitation of it. The "Matadores" (or Matalotes) or *"Umpa"* [Ompi, or Warriors] are painted black; the front hair, combed down on the forehead, is painted with almagre; there is a crown of white down over the head and down the side-locks, and a feather of the painted eagle hanging down from the topknot. They are dressed in buckskin and white shirt, the buckskin dangling down to the ankles almost. Bead strings around the neck and an iridescent shell [probably abalone] suspended to them. In the left hand, a bow painted red, with eagles feathers at each end, some red-painted arrows. In the right hand, a wooden or iron-hatchet, also red. The estufas alternated: *"Tanyi"* and *"Shyuamo"* [Pumpkin and Turquoise], and each had its Malinche, or *"Tzima-ta-tanyi"* or *"Cu-cu."* One had two *"umpa";* the other, three. They came in, the *"Tanyi"* with the cacique, who was not painted, but wore three little plumes, white, one on each side-lock and one behind, and carried a black folded cape with red trimmings or embroidery without sleeves. It is strapped round the waist, and the arms are bare from above the elbows. Some of the men are painted yellow, mostly red. The *Qoshare* are dressed; they wear twigs of the "Pino réal" [spruce] on the head, and wreaths of the same around the body and neck. Cheeks painted bluish-white in a streak across the cheek-bones. The Malinche dressed like always, with the exception of a tuft of parrots plumes instead of the "O-ta-tinsht." To the right wrist a coyote skin was hanging. The song was the same as always.

They danced first in a cluster, then in four rows, the Malinche between them. Finally they knelt down in two rows, only the cacique and the umpa standing. Then the Malinche, with arms gracefully uplifted, and an arrow in the right hand, hopped from one end of the line to the other, between, thus blessing alternately each row. The cacique was directing the motions of her arms and hands, by indicating the motions with his arms. She acted very gracefully. Then another woman joined her, and another, so that three of them performed the blessing inside of the rows together. The Malinche was a woman, the two others were "widows." This blessing was the last performance, and during it, muskets and pistols were fired off from behind the lines by men standing. Previous to the blessing, however, those of one estufa (the one who had previously danced), sent a delegation of men with fruits, corn, onions, chile, etc. which they threw to the dancers. Those caught them, and then women came in from the houses, and threw also, very much like the "Tunles-Jian," and the dancers threw them to the children and people on the house tops.[513] I never saw so many Mexicans at a dance, and a great number of Navajos, men and women. They were selling blankets, and the Pueblos were making them drunk!!

At the last dance but one, a little boy came, dressed as Matalote, and then there was another dance by the "Tanyi" whereat the Malinche was a young girl. Otherwise, the Malinches are young married women. At the real scalp dance, the Matalotes are naked, painted black with "marmaja," and bands of white down around the knees, white feathers on the head, the leatherstraps around neck and shoulder. Four days total abstinence except once every 24 hours, also the Malinches. The "Umpa," in this case, are only men who have killed beasts of prey—eagles, bears, mountain lions, wolves, and *those animals who are nearest to man!*

A real scalp dance can only be celebrated when a fresh scalp is taken, in which case all those who have taken scalps previously celebrate the new one and "wash it in blood." Along with the "Shyuamo," there was an old man with two eagles plumes on the head. The dance stopped at sundown;[514] some of the Navajos were pretty drunk and the people certainly got cheap tilmas.

We returned to Peña Blanca. Father Navet is always the same; he is queer, stingy and liberal at the same time. His school at Santo Domingo is doing very well; there are 52 children now, and the old men are taking interest in it. They are learning the letters and singing well.

DECEMBER 27: Left Peña Blanca at 10 A.M. and went by the "Bocas." Joe is better. Nothing new. Letter from Captain Dougherty. Quiet. Hubert staid downtown for supper.

DECEMBER 28: Letter from Bradshaw. Went downtown and called on the Doctor, on Pearce, and on the Archbishop. Father Navet came, like a fool [it was a stormy day, with hail and snow], but then, he doesn't mind his horses! Wrote at Chapter III of my novel. It is progressing fairly. Koch called at night.

DECEMBER 29: Letter from Henry. My first article appeared in the *Globe-Democrat* of the 26th, with very full headings.[515] It [the weather] is very sloppy. Called at the Archbishop's but Navet and Ambrosio Ortiz were there, so I could not speak to him. Wrote at #3 for the *Globe-Democrat.* Meany called.

DECEMBER 30: Clear, very sloppy. Went to the Archbishop's and talked about the Apaches and the Navajos. In the afternoon, wrote for the *Globe-Democrat.* At night, first Spanish lesson at Meany's. He, Fornance, and Dr. Strong[516] present. Only introductory.[517] Afterwards at Koch's; pleasant.

DECEMBER 31: Chilly, thawing, and very sloppy. Warmer. Wrote. In the morning called downtown, and in the P.M., had to go downtown again for the Dr.'s sake. There was no eastern mail yesterday; today a mail came from the East. Evening at Koch's. Exceedingly pleasant. Goodby 1885. God grant that '86 be different.

1886

JANUARY 1: Got back at 2 A.M. [from party at the Koch's], very much pleased. May it be a happy prediction. It soon began to snow and the day was very ugly, chilly and wet. Called on Gerdes first; then with him drove around to Koch, Symington, Fischer,[518] Staab, W. Spiegelberg,[519] Griffin,[520] Prince, Creamer,[521] afterwards to the Archbishop [Salpointe] and to the Padre Vicar [Eguillon]. It began to snow fiercely at nightfall.

JANUARY 2: No letters. Nothing at all. It is very discouraging. Still, why should I complain? It snowed all day. Joe is very unwell, and I had to consult the Dr. [Eggert]. Finished #3 for the *Globe-Democrat* and sent it to G. Hoffmann. Complained about the *Westliche Post.* Wrote to Mr. Balsiger. Gave my Spanish lesson; only Meany and Fornance there.

JANUARY 3: Wrote to Dr. Hamy,[522] enclosing map, to Professor Ratzel and to Dr. W. Reiss, Berlin. Complaining everywhere and scolding. Wrote to Icazbalceta.[523] Joe is better, but still we preferred to stay at home on her account. It was stormy, and so I finished Chap. III of the Novel. What for?

JANUARY 4: Began to write No. 2 for the [*New York*] *World.* Then came a letter from George [Hoffmann], stating that the *Globe-Democrat* only paid $5 per column. It is miserable. But then, what else can I expect but misery! Joe is well, thank God! Mr. Schumann came. Evening quiet and pleasant.

JANUARY 5: Wrote #2 for the *World.* It is at least an occupation and a faint hope. Letter from E. A. Allen. Mrs. Koch came up and spent the afternoon. It is our Silver Wedding.[524] What may yet be in store for us we don't know, but at all events Joe is better. We got some very kind presents, but this does not compensate for the bitterness of the day. God is very cruel.

JANUARY 6: Wrote all day, finished, nearly, the #2 [article] for the *World!* Joe went out in the afternoon. What a diary! Nothing but deception and deception—after all the great afflictions of the past. And it is no use trying. Every endeavor is lost; nothing works! At night I had my lesson at Meany's. Only two! He returned my correspondence to the *World,* saying it was too long! So this is also for nothing. Everything is useless. We are absolutely doomed, and with all this, Highland, that nest of infidelity, treachery, and coarseness, prospers! God is very unjust or at least partial. He flatters those who despise him and tramps down those who bend their knees. So even that work is gone. I shall try again, but with what result? Hope, there, is none whatever.

JANUARY 7: Clouding, and so at home, too. Joe is sick, high fever, headache and pain in the spine. So even the worst comes! Let it come, and if God wants me to perish, let him have that satisfaction. No relief, no returns for work, nothing. A sick wife and no means to support her. Work, earnest work and not a cent! It is distressing. I am unwell myself, and very unwell too, at that. Unfit to write. Bitterly cold. Wrote to E. A. Allen, sending him the two papers written for the *World;* also to Bradshaw and to Pretorius.

JANUARY 8: Clear, beautiful, bitterly cold. Bad night for both of us. Joe is slightly improving, but I am ill. Unable to do anything the whole day. Cooked myself. Day quiet. Joe up at nightfall. Gradually improving.

JANUARY 9: Similar day. Quiet. All well again. Wrote at the Nambé affair for some German paper, I don't know which yet. In the afternoon, Fornance and wife called. At night, Spanish class.

JANUARY 10: Fine and cold. No mail from the East for two days. Always northerly wind. Remained quietly at home. Wrote at the Nambé tragedy. In the afternoon, had calls from Mr. and Mrs. Gerdes and from Mr. Schumann. Joe is better.

JANUARY 11: Less severely cold. Went down town, hunted in vain for the papers concerning the sorcery case of Nambé.

JANUARY 12: No eastern mail yet. Went down town. Funeral of Mrs. Fitzmorris. Went everywhere to find documents relative to Nambé. The occurrence took place in 1853, while Mr. Tompkins[525] was Circuit Clerk. Could not find anything at all, and the papers were probably burnt in 1859 when the old, former capitol was destroyed by fire (incendiarism).[526] But there was a trial at Santa Fe about it, as Mr. Ellison, Tompkins, and Epifanio Vigil[527] distinctly recalled. Finished my article for the *New York Bell. [etristische] Zeitung* on the Brujos of Nambé[528] and mailed it to Udo Brachvogel.[529] Night painted and wrote at the novel.

JANUARY 13: Very chilly, but fine. Began an article on our tour to Virginia in 1856.[530] Lesson at Meany's in the meantime. That's all.

JANUARY 14: Wrote in the morning. Went to Mrs. Catron[531] in the afternoon, and then to Dr. Strong, and finally to the Doctor.[532] News that the mail would come in at last.

JANUARY 15: Similar, very cold. Mail came in at last. Letters from Garrison and Parkman. Two letters from Mr. Balsiger. Wrote for *The Nation* another article, prefacing the two on land grants. Wrote to Garrison also and to Mr. Parkman.

JANUARY 16: Got from Pearce a document, Mss., formerly stolen from the Historical Society and returned to him as curator, recently. It is a so-called campaign document, concocted at Mexico when the invasion of New Mexico by Americans was imminent. Evidently, its object was to attract the Pueblos to the Mexican side.—*Copy:* [The next eight pages of the journals were devoted to a verbatim copy, in Spanish, of this document of 1846.]

[After the lengthy recording of the 1846 document in the entry of January 16, Bandelier made no further entries until January 28.]

JANUARY 28: Wrote at my novel, until today. No mail for a long time. The river rising gradually. First mail came yesterday. It brought me letters from Allen with $10., from the *Globe-Democrat.* No lesson; Mrs. Catron sick. Today, letter from Garrison. Wrote to Allen and to George [Hoffmann] last night. Finished copying the Montezuma Legend at last and returned it to Pearce. Had my usual lesson at Mrs. Catron in the afternoon, and Mrs. Preston[533] was there also. In the evening, lesson at Meany's,

Fornance alone there. Then went to Doctor's, Joe being at Mrs. Bush.

JANUARY 29: Wrote most of the time. Card to Pretorius. No letters today. Am working at Chapter VIII of the novel. It becomes very interesting to me to do this work.[534]

JANUARY 30: Letters from Mr. Parkman, from George, and from Henry. Finished Chapter VIII completely and wrote a card to Mr. Parkman. Lesson at Mr. Meany's tonight; afterwards at Lt. Fornance's. He told me of great ruins in the Navajo country.

JANUARY 31: Instead of going to church as I intended, I went to the Doctor's. Letters from Father Bourdier[535] and H. C. Lodge. In the afternoon to Fischers with the Dr., Koch, Mrs. Hartmann,[536] Schumann. Pleasant time. Wrote card to Garrison and to Captain Dougherty. Began Chapter IX of novel, and letter for the *Advertiser* at Boston.

FEBRUARY

FEBRUARY 1: Letter from W. C. Kueffner which I replied to by sending two cuts of appearance, signed. Wrote eight pages and sent them to the *Boston Advertiser,* J. C. Chamberlain,[537] Editor.

FEBRUARY 2: Went down town. No letters again. It [a heavy snowfall] looks much like a blockade. Still it clears, but the mud will be awful. Unwell again. Stomach out of order. Everybody complains of the weather as far as wet and snow are concerned, and José Olivas says he never found a winter yet with as much and persistent snow. Mr. Franz left for St. Louis today. I hope he will get there without trouble.

FEBRUARY 3: Got $7. from *The Nation.* Finished Chapter IX tonight. Mrs. Catron not disposed for a lesson today, but she will have to pay anyhow. At night, lesson to three only.

FEBRUARY 4: Wrote card to Garrison. Snowbound again. Wrote today on Chapter X. Dr. Calvert came to bother me. Wrote all night.

FEBRUARY 5: An abominable slop, for it is thawing very rapidly. Letter from Alphonse [Bandelier]. Charming, but sad. Hebler has forsaken him. All right. Let them go to h---. Finished Chapter X. Evening at Doctor's.

FEBRUARY 6: Went to town early, to copy Chapter IX of novel. Got a plaintive letter from Eddy [Edward B. Huegy]. Poor boy. We are ourselves as poor as Job and should help him! It is impossible—as much as we would like to do it. Afternoon, lesson at Mrs. Catron's. Evening lesson at Meany's and afterwards at Koch's.

FEBRUARY 7: Went to Mass; Father Eguillon preached—against free-schools. Got a letter from Don Joaquín [García Icazbalceta],[538] and one from Adolphe Vautier, very friendly. Hubert [Hoffmann][539] went hunting this A.M. That's all the boy is good for, and all he thinks of. Spent the afternoon pleasantly at Gerdes'. Finished plate of Rito Colorado ruins.[540] Hubert returned without game.

FEBRUARY 8: Signs of bad weather. Could hardly write, so drowsy and sleepy was I. Got two blocks of paper from George. Our river is rather high and turbulent. Water muddy, showing that snow begins to melt.

FEBRUARY 9: Got a letter from Mr. Parkman with $100.—. Thank God! Paid rent to Mr. Schumann up to date, and $18.— to Gerdes; left with Koch $65.—. Got a letter from Mr. [W. W.] Williams,[541] Editor of *Magazine of Western History*, at Cleveland, Ohio. It seems as if we were new-born. Bought a hat from Gerdes, on credit again ($2.50). Fixed the cooking stove with Eduard. Wrote to Mr. Parkman,[542] to Don Joaquín,[543] and to Eddy also. Bought a table.

FEBRUARY 10: No letters. Wrote but little. At night concert. Joe went. I gave my lesson, and then we met at the Doctor's. Concert indifferent.

FEBRUARY 11: Joe sick with headache and vomitings of bile. In bed all day. Consequently, I gave no lesson to Mrs. Catron. It is dreary, notwithstanding the fine weather. Wrote at my Report, advancing slowly. It is hard work.

FEBRUARY 12: Joe better. Card from George. Replied to it by card. Had a call from old Mr. Fischer;[544] [also] from the Kochs. Night at home, quietly.

FEBRUARY 13: Got a letter from E. A. Allen. Wrote to him and to Mr. Parkman. Gave lesson at Mrs. Catron's. Mr. Meany sick. Fornances got a baby yesterday. Spent evening at the Doctor's.

FEBRUARY 14: Wind very chilly from the north-northwest, so that Joe and I could not take a walk longer than about half an hour; it was too sharp and piercing. First night reading of the novel: Dr., Schumann, Mrs. Koch, Mrs. Hartmann, and Minnie. Till midnight.

FEBRUARY 15: Got a letter from Garrison, and the Apache book of Major Bourke.[545] It looks a mighty poor affair. Wrote at my Report. Evening at home with Joe.

FEBRUARY 16: Got $24.— from the *Staatszeitung*.[546] Went down town and made several calls and purchases. Paid my hat. Afternoon wrote. Mrs. Gold came. Night, reading.

FEBRUARY 17: No letters. Wrote all morning on Report. In the afternoon went down town. No lessons today. Spent a pleasant hour at Mrs. Catron's. Wrote to W. W. Williams, Cleveland, Ohio, and to Eddy. Saw some (two) old vessels from Mora County. They are glossy and well preserved. There are ruins in Mora County, mostly on elevations.

FEBRUARY 18: Left for the Arroyo Hondo at 9 A.M. It was cold and soon a very strong and cutting wind arose, from the northwest. We stumbled down south to the Arroyo Hondo, which is very deep and running with water now until close to Constantin's Ranch, above the railroad. There we crossed to the south side, the arroyo being at least 100 feet deep and rather abrupt banks. Snow still on the north slopes. (Sketch and description thereof as follows:) *A*: is a new house of stone, not quite finished and as yet

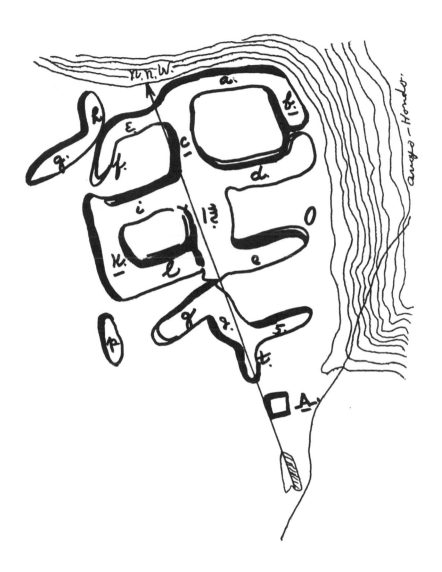

unoccupied. There are also some strips of pretty broken ground west, adjacent to the ruins.[547] The ruins lie on the very brink of the arroyo where the latter issues from the cañón, making a bend. There is a spring there, which is, of course, permanent. The depth is considerable and so steep that it appears next to vertical, although it can be climbed. There is scarcely any rock protruding. The height I estimate at 150 feet, about.

The ruin is old; the mounds, very densely packed and much abraded, are about six feet higher than the plazas; four estufas are faintly visible. It has been much excavated, and there is considerable broken pottery about, painted, black-and-white, red-and-black, black, red-and-white, orange. There is also corrugated and indented [pottery]. There are manos of metates, obsidian, flint, bones, and some charred corn. The general appearance of the ruin reminds of the great pueblos of the Ojo Caliente and the Rito Colorado.

In the immediate neighborhood the ground is level, and there is little brush, indicating thus that there has been former cultivation, but to the east of it rise heights, wooded and somewhat rocky through which breaks the arroyo. The view is open to the north, west, and south; to the northwest, west and southwest, the ground slopes, and the whole country until the Tetilla chain and the Cerrillos is open and distinct. It was therefore a good Indian position.* The distance of the ruin from the railroad is about one-and-a-quarter miles to the east. From Santa Fe, it [the ruin] is five-and-a-quarter miles in a direct line. We returned home about 3 P.M., Hubert killing a large rabbit on the way. In the meantime, Joe had had callers, Mrs. Haren,[548] Mrs. [Louis] Vollinger [Foellinger],[549] and Mrs. Hartmann. Evening, we read as usual.

FEBRUARY 19: Wrote card to W. P. Garrison. Wrote review of Bourke's book. Wrote at Report. Calls, Mrs. Staab and Anita.[550] At night, Dr. [Eggert] and Mrs. Bush.[551]

FEBRUARY 20: Birds singing, springlike. Wrote card to *New York-[er] Staatszeitung.* G. H. Jones, Waggon Mound [Wagon Mound], N. M., called on me this A.M. He told me that ruins were extant on Ocate Creek, west of Waggon Mound, and also on Canadian River, 25 miles east of Waggon Mound also. This is important, since it establishes a line of ruins north, and in the meridian of Pecos River. Mrs. Catron called in the afternoon. Evening at the Doctor's, and at G. Koch's. Pleasant. Got idol to paint [from Judge Prince].

FEBRUARY 21: Painted all day, at the idol. It is a very interesting piece. At night, reading; Eddy Franz came also. Pleasant evening.

FEBRUARY 22: Returned the idol to Judge and Mrs. Prince.[552] Afterwards, I went to Mrs. Catron's. Pleasant. Then to Koch's and finally home. Night quietly at home, writing at the novel.

FEBRUARY 23: Wrote all day at the novel. It snowed lightly at times. Reading at night.

FEBRUARY 24: Finished Chapter XI of the novel. Sent my review[553] of Bourke's book to *The Nation* today. Lesson at Mrs. Preston's and at Meany's. Returned early and wrote at Chapter XII.

FEBRUARY 25: Got a nice letter from Professor Ratzel today. It seems that one of his letters is lost, containing a portrait of Prince Louis of Bavaria. At night, had a pleasant call from Mr. Fischer and Miss Louisa.

FEBRUARY 26: Got letters today from Mr. Balsiger, Father Meckel, and from Hartmann. Wrote at the novel, and to Hartmann at night.

FEBRUARY 27: Gave my usual lessons. Wrote to Henry Kaune. Borrowed idol No. 2 from Judge Prince. Night at Mrs. Bush's with Joe. The Dr. at Staab's.

FEBRUARY 28: Painted; afterwards, wrote to Alphonse. Met S. Eldodt on the street down town. Reading at night. All present.

MARCH

MARCH 1: Letter from W. W. Williams. Father Grom called on us a moment. Joe went down town.

MARCH 2: Adelaido [Montoya] came from Cochiti. I showed him the pictures of the idols. He knew the first one, but says the other "es su companero [is its companion]." The first one (of lava) is called: Tjiare-qo; they are both medicine gods which they use in case of sickness. The cacique keeps them. Wrote at novel.

MARCH 3: Calmed towards morning. Quiet. Clouds breaking slowly.

Did not write any diary until the 21st of March. Sent, in the meantime, six chapters (of novel) to Professor Ratzel; wrote to him; to Bertha [Lambelet]; to Parkman; to Frank P. Smith;[554] to Bradshaw; etc. Got $13.— from *The Nation*.— Letters from Mr. Parkman, Frank P. Smith, Henry [Kaune]. Hubert went to Albuquerque and returned on the 20th, sound and safe. Weather variable; several sandstorms, each succeeded by snow and cold. Juan José [Montoya] sick; Pedro went after him on 20th at noon.

MARCH 21: Resumed my Journal again. Finished two more idols of Judge Prince. Wrote to Mr. Balsiger, to Bertha, and to W. W. Williams, Cleveland, Ohio. Mr. Schafer and Mr. Schumann called. Reading at night. (Pedro told me yesterday that: Scalp is "Ah-tze-ta." He also recognized the idols and calls them, like Adelaido, "U-ash-tesh-goro-o." Confirms besides what Adelaido said about them.)

MARCH 22: No letters. Today, I had visitors upon visitors. First, Lt. Fornance and Dr. Strong; afterwards, Mr. Meany and Van der Veer. The latter came to speak about French [?] lessons. At night, Schumann and old Mrs. Fischer.[555] Wrote at my novel.

MARCH 23: Beautiful, warm. Bees and other insects out. Luis Lucero and Luis Montoya came, about the Rito [de los Frijoles]. Went down to Pearce with them. Afterwards to Mrs. Edsdell and arranged for lessons. Got letter from the *Staats-Zeitung* with $26.25. Today, Priciliana got married to Juan de Jesús Martinez. He seems to be a right, good old man. In the afternoon, had a short call from Lt. Mumford,[556] about Mrs. Preston—fixing another time for the lessons. Joe spent the evening at Fischer's. Went after her at 11 P.M.

MARCH 24: In consequence of a call from Colonel Ed. Haren[557] yesterday, I went to see him at the Palace Hotel, and then with him, to Hartmann. Then to the photographer. In the afternoon, I gave a long lesson to Mrs. Preston and then called on Mr. Boyle.[558] Wrote at my novel. Lesson to Meany and Fornance at night.

MARCH 25: Old Mr. Fischer[559] called on me this afternoon to bid farewell. I wrote all day.

MARCH 26: Did go down town in the forenoon but still wrote most of the time. Received a letter from Mr. Parkman. Very kind. Hubert came back with four ducks. The hunt was not very satisfactory. Finished Chapter XVII.

MARCH 27: Gave my lesson to Mrs. Preston. In the afternoon, Joe had her "coffee": Kochs (3); Fischers (2); and Mrs. Foulinger [Foellinger]. I finished my correction and got three idols from Mrs. Prince. At night I wrote to Henry, to E. A. Allen, and to Udo Brachvogel.

MARCH 28: I painted all day, very assiduously, at the idols and succeeded in finishing all of them; also, the Dancer of the Scalp Dance from Cochiti. Night readings.

MARCH 29: Went down town to Archbishop Salpointe and to Father Eguillon, but the latter was not at home so I could not go to confession.

MARCH 30: Letter from Emma;[560] a disgusting trash of Highland gossip. I then went down town; to confession first, afterwards, to the Archbishop. Then to Mrs. Prince, who has bought an interesting lot of idols again—from Laguna. Then to Hayward[561] and to the Doctor. Wrote all afternoon. Joe went to Koch's. I remained at home. After supper, ran down to Koch's for a short moment and back again to write.

MARCH 31: Went to Communion early, Father Acorsini[562] administering it to me. Gave my lesson. Wrote all afternoon. News came of the surrender and subsequent (arrest) of Geronimo.[563] Lesson at night, as usual.

APRIL

APRIL 1: Letters from Henry and from H. Liebler. Eddy [Huegy, probably] came, quite a surprise. Spent the day with Eddy, showing him the town, etc. Evening at the Doctor's. Got a letter from Mr. J. G. Shea,[564] sent to Father Seux, who referred it to me.

APRIL 2: Letter from W. C. Kueffner with Deed to sign. Went down town, but could not find anybody. For the afternoon, drove to Fort Marcy,[565] Joe, Eddy, and Mrs. Bush. Dr. [Eggert, probably] and I walked out to Fischer's.[566] Quite a brisk blow of sand, very cool and strong, with some few drops of rain, but it quieted soon. Eddy left at night.

APRIL 3: Went down town and got $10 from Preston.[567] Gave my lesson. Finished my correction of the chapter. Old Dr. came and remained with us a short while. Very pleasant. Joe has headache, but I hope she will get over it. Eddy left last night at 11 P.M. He was very well pleased. The Dr. is dissatisfied about Mrs. Bush and yesterday. He is right. Otherwise, all right.

APRIL 4: Got letters from Frank P. Smith with $40.— in it; from Rochester friends. Mrs. Prince called, and we had a very pleasant time. Painted at the ground-plan of Batonapa![568] Reading at night.

APRIL 5: Letter from Eddy; wrote to Bertha [Lambelet]. Went downtown, paid $15.— to Gerdes. Paid the Brothers. In the afternoon, wrote at Chapter XIX. Joe went to Mrs. Gerdes. Took a little stroll at night. Also went to the Doctor.

APRIL 6: Louis Foellinger[569] suddenly left Mr. Schumann this morning. Hubert took his place temporarily. Call from the Doctor at noon. Wrote. Joe went out this afternoon to Mrs. Preston. She had a headache, but it improved toward nightfall. Went down town afterwards.

APRIL 7: The reason why Foellinger was discharged was—theft. It is too bad. The day clouded. No letters. Gave my lesson to Mrs. Preston. Met Marcus Eldodt.[570] Joe has severe headache. Coming home, I found a card from Purdy. He is sick in bed and lives very near to us. Called on him. About 3 P.M., it grew darker and darker and about 5 P.M. a furious sandstorm arose from the southwest, such as I have never witnessed before at Santa Fe! It was just fearful and lasted about one hour, when it subsided. Night quiet, cloudy, dull, and threatening. Lesson at Meany's.

APRIL 8: I finished Chapter XIX. Got letters from Udo Brachvogel and from *The Christian World.* Wrote to Brachvogel and sent him the portraits of the Qosare, of Candelario [Ortiz], and of Old Francisco [Chavez]. Wrote to Frank [P.] Smith, sent him three views of Popocatepetl; to J. G. Shea, to Padre Seux; to Adolphe Vautier.

APRIL 9: Wrote to George Hoffmann; to Father Louis Bourdier, Altar, Sonora; to Bertha and to Mr. Balsiger. Mrs. Staab, Anita, and Paul called. Went down town and sent two packages to Bertha. Mrs. Hartmann's birthday. At night, party at Koch's until midnight. Of course, "Smith" was there and played; Marcus Eldodt and wife, Gerdes and wife, etc. Mostly Jews. Pleasant.

APRIL 10: Wrote to Udo Brachvogel again about copyright. Gave my lesson to Mrs. Preston. Letter from Don Joaquín[571] with copy of the "Relación postrera de Sivola."[572] Called on the Archbishop with Joe, and afterwards at Dr. Strong's. Joe is feeling remarkably well. Lesson at Meany's. When I came home, Joe had suddenly an attack of ear-ringing, turning into headache overnight. There is no earthly apparent cause for this sudden illness.

APRIL 11: Joe has terrible headache; had to lay in bed all day, and I cooked as well as I knew. Dr. came up, also Schumann. José Hilario [Montoya] came with his family. Painted at the ground-plan of "Batonapa" but couldn't finish it on account of visitors. Joe better at night.

APRIL 12: The day abominable. One flurry of hail succeeded the other, very violent gusts of wind in the afternoon. Kochs could not leave. No berths. Mr. Koch called. Wrote at the article for the *Cosmopolitan.*

APRIL 13: I wrote at the article for the *Cosmopolitan.* Kochs left last night. Reading at night.

APRIL 14: Lesson at Mrs. Preston. Feliciano Depral [Prado] came to see about whitewashing the kitchen. Got "Yeso" [gypsum, whitewash], etc. Finished article for Rochester. Victoriano [Cordero] came from Cochiti and stayed a short while. The poor fellow was very hungry. Gave my lesson at Meany's. Then went to the Doctor's and read my article to all there. They made some useful corrections.

APRIL 15: Whitewashing the kitchen. Feliciano Prado. Sent off my article to Smith. At night the Doctor came and staid with us.

APRIL 16: Letter from Mr. Balsiger. Governor Ritch spent the evening and took supper with us. Delightful night. Indians have persecuted me all day. They are begging for Easter.

APRIL 17: No letters. It grows monotonous. Gave my lesson at noon. In the afternoon, Joe went to Fischer's, and I staid at home, finishing the copy of Chapter VII and writing to Ratzel also. Gave my lesson and then to the Dr.

APRIL 18: Went to Mass. Finished the groundplan of Batonapa. In the afternoon, Koch called; then the Doctor, and Mr. Schumann. At nightfall a very severe sandstorm broke out from the East, increasing in violence. The Dr. and Mrs. Bush called.

APRIL 19: Cloudy and covered and chilly; had whitewashing nonetheless. It is a horrible day and a worse night.

APRIL 20: River very high; bridge swept away, also one of the lower bridges. The railing of the bridge at San Miguel [Mission][573] has been blown down also.

APRIL 21: Koch and Dr. called in the afternoon. No lesson at Mrs. Preston's, but lesson at night at Meany's. Beautiful night, but Joe has headache again. Mail stopped by washouts.

APRIL 22: Joe has terrible headache again and is in bed. River is very high yet, but falling. Joe was very sick all day. It is almost distressing to see her thus suffering. Could not go to church. No mail.

APRIL 23: Mrs. Hartmann called and Minnie. A very dark and gloomy Good Friday. No mail. Washouts at Mora, Trinidad, south of Socorro, and on the Atlantic and Pacific Railroad.

APRIL 24: In the afternoon we had a short, but drenching snowfall with hail. Night quiet, cloudy, cool. The Misses Fischer[574] called. Finished my article on Cabeza de Vaca, with the annotations.[575] No lesson today. No mail.

APRIL 25: Easter Sunday. Both of us went to church. Each to his own. Beautiful day. Dined at the Doctor's. Gerdes called in the afternoon. No mail yet. Evening at the Doctor's with Koch. Water stopped since Tuesday.

APRIL 26: Wrote all day on Chapter XX. Joe went out calling. In the meantime, Koch called, and Miss Burden, with eggs. Water came again in the pipes today. No mail yet so far. Joe came back, quite satisfied with her visits. Wrote all evening.

APRIL 27: Similar [day], rather handsome. Mail at last. Letter from Henry. My right hand is almost useless. Cramp! Still, I finished Chapter XX. No money and nothing coming.

APRIL 28: Alike. Gave all my lessons. Quiet. In the afternoon, J. C. Pearce and Sam Eldodt called. Evening at Doctor's and at Koch's.

APRIL 29: Warm and pleasant. Painted. In the afternoon, Mr. Parsons and Dr. Strong came. Joe went out calling. Last night I wrote to Henry. Tonight wrote a few pages to Mrs. Parsons on Navajos. Joe has headache again.

APRIL 30: No letters! Joe felt unwell again, but soon improved. I finished Chapter XX of novel. Hand bothers me very much.

MAY

MAY 1: No letters. Spent all day in town for the Archbishop. In the afternoon out to Fischer's, where I saw Priciliana again. Evening lessons.

MAY 2: Dined at Doctor's. Call from John Pearce and the two Misses Manderfield.[576] Mr. Schumann took supper with us. Reading of Chapter XX [to] Dr. Eggert, Mr. Schumann, and Charles Hoffmann. No letters!

MAY 3: No letters. Wrote and mailed letters to Dr. Frenzel, Dr. Reiss, Berlin; to Mrs. Koch and to Udo Brachvogel; and card to F. P. Smith, Rochester, New York. My hand bothers me again. Wrote to Don Joaquín[577] and began to write to Mr. Balsiger. Evening at Fischer's. Very nice. Beautiful night, clear and quiet. Warm. Frogs crying.

MAY 4: Finished letter to Mr. Balsiger. No letters. Wrote to Father Meckel. Wrote also an article of six pages for *The Nation*, on the supposed Navajo troubles; letter to Garrison. Mrs. Meany called to invite us to supper. Hubert called at night. He's well and seems happy.

MAY 5: Letter from Ratzel and from F. P. Smith. No lesson at Mrs. Preston's. Dr. dined with us. Wrote to Ratzel and to Garrison again, about land grants. Evening at Meany's. Quiet and nice.

MAY 6: Finished and mailed the article on Santa Fe[578] for the *New York[er] Staatszeitung*. No letters.

MAY 7: Went down town and gave to Hartmann pp. 41–101, inclusive, of my Journal of 1880—for his Map of the Western Rio Grande Shores, north of Cochiti.[579] No letters for me. Finished copy of Chapter VIII; in the afternoon, had callers: Mr. and Mrs. Hartmann, Marcus Eldodt and wife. Pleasant afternoon.

MAY 8: Gave a lesson to Mrs. Preston and received $5.— from her husband. Louise Fischer came. No lesson at Meany's. Night beautiful. No letter.

MAY 9: Letter from F. P. Smith. Joe went to church. Koch called. In the afternoon, Governor Ritch, Schumann, Mrs. Hartmann and Minnie came. Evening at the Doctor's.

MAY 10: Wrote at Chapter XXI. No letters. Joe went down town and called on Mrs. Prince and on Mrs. Catron. Evening at Koch's with Marcus Eldodt and wife and Mr. Pessels.

MAY 11: Joe had to stay in bed until 3 P.M., when she improved and got up again. I finished Chapter XXI. Got a letter from W. W. Williams.

MAY 12: No letters. Gave lesson to Mrs. Preston; called on Mrs. Catron and on Fornance. Gave no lesson. Afterwards, went to the Doctor's where Fornance read us a paper on two dances of the Sioux. Very interesting. One is a dance recalling the Q'oshare; the other is the Sun Dance. Today at 7 P.M., I finished my novel! Thank God! I began it in 1883 and until the 28th of December, 1885, had only written two chapters, of 56 pages, about. The other 20 chapters of 420 pages, I consequently wrote in four months and fifteen days. If only the result justifies the work and time spent on it! That God alone can determine.[580]

MAY 13: [This entry and those for the 14th and 15th, Bandelier, for some unknown reason, recorded as December, rather than May.] Corrected the last two chapters. Wrote to Ratzel and sent Chapter VIII. No letters again. Mailed my letter. It is very disagreeable out, stormy, chilly, but no rain. Wrote at "Peru" for Rochester. Dr. Eggert and Mrs. Bush called.

MAY 14: No letters at all. It is almost desponding. We remained at home until the afternoon, when Joe went out calling. I finished the article on Peru and sent it to F. P. Smith tonight. Began to copy Chapter IX. Koch called this morning. He is brimfull of mother-in-law.

MAY 15: Lesson to Mrs. Preston. No lesson at Meany's. Spent the afternoon at Louise Fischer's. Very pleasant. Returned early and also retired very early. No letters today, yet.

MAY 16: Letters at last:—from Garrison, J. G. Shea, and Mrs. Prince. Could not go to church; too late. Wrote to J. G. Shea, #138, Catherine Street, Elizabeth, New Jersey, and mailed letter. Dined at the Doctor's with Fornance and his two ladies, Mr. and Mrs. Meany, and Mr. Dunlop,[581] the Episcopal Bishop. Pleasant. In the evening, concluded reading the novel, Dr. Eggert, Schumann, Koch, Mrs. Hartmann, and Marcus Eldodt being present.

MAY 17: Mailed "Kin and Clan"[582] to Buffalo and [wrote] to J. G. Shea. Got letter from Mr. Balsiger. I copied at Chapter IX all day and evening. Our money giving out already.

MAY 18: Got $15.— from *The Nation*. The first money for six weeks! Thank God! Wrote at Chapter IX, finishing the copy at night.

MAY 19: Mailed Chapter IX to Ratzel and pamphlets to Clotilde,[583] to Buffalo Historical Society, to George, Pretorius, and to Eddy. No lesson at Mrs. Preston's, but one at Meany's. I wrote, copying on Chapter X and beginning on "Iztac—Cihuatl [Ixtaccihuatl Mountain, southeast of Mexico City]." Joe got headache again.

MAY 20: Joe is free from headache. Went down town. Got a very friendly letter from Gruaz. Joe went down town; I wrote to Mr. Garrison and to Mr. Balsiger. To the former, about the "Belletristisches Journal," enclosing letter of U. Brachvogel. Met Don Andrés Tápia. Dr. Eggert has toothache and behaves like a baby. Met Koch, Meany, and others. Wrote but little today. Am not well disposed.

MAY 21: Mailed two pamphlets, one to Rattermann and one to Ottendorfer. Went to town early. Am tired of writing. My head is weak. So I went to painting groundplans. In the afternoon, Mrs. Hartmann, Minnie, and Annie Staab called. Before sunset we went to Fischer's. I went to singing at Alfredo Hinojos.[584]

MAY 22: Joe in bed all day with severe headache. Better at night. No lessons.

MAY 23: Staid at home until night. Got a letter from Papa![585] He is safe and well, thank God a thousand times for it. [Compare these comments with those in the entry of May 4, 1885.] Replied at once and communicated the news to Bertha, Clotilde, and to Mr. Balsiger. We are all so happy over it. He is alive and not in need at all. Louise Fischer was here all afternoon, and at night, Mr. Schumann. Our friends here are most happy at the news about Papa; they are as glad as we are, almost. It is a glorious day. And last year?

MAY 24: José Hilario [Montoya] called with two girls from Cochiti. Since four days, the Rio Grande rises very swiftly. It again threatens Santo Domingo. Got letter from Marcus Benjamin, New York, and Henry—with $10.—. Sang at Alfredo's. Mr. Gaertner[586] came with me.

MAY 25: Painted all day. Received letter from Padre Bourdier, Altar, Sonora.

MAY 26: No letter. Hartmann came in the afternoon. Evening at the Doctor's. He read us his lecture on Phrenology.

MAY 27: Letter from Consul H. Martens, St. Louis, informing us that my plates were at St. Louis—at last.[587] Replied at once. Evening at Hartmann's.

MAY 28: No letters. Morris' death's [first] anniversary, very sad day. Dispirited and disheartened. Almost despairing. The usual dull cloudiness in the afternoon. No resources, no money from nowhere. Everything looks gloomy and dreary.

MAY 29: Am better. Still coughing. Began to write to Gruaz. Letter from nobody. Gave lesson to Mrs. Preston, to Fornance, and to Meany. The Archbishop called me down. Father Stephan[588] was there. He looked at the drawings very closely and promises to do what he can for their publication.

MAY 30: Wrote to Papa, Gruaz, Garrison, and Brachvogel. Letter from Garrison. Afternoon at Gerdes'; night at Marcus Eldodt's. Pleasant. Still unwell.

MAY 31: Poem from Gruaz. Replied. Wrote to Henry. Joe went down town in the afternoon to see the procession of Decoration Day. Had a very bad night; therefore, indisposed to write at all.

JUNE

JUNE 1: Finished my paper on *Iztac-Cihuatl*.[589] No letters again.

JUNE 2: Gave my lessons everywhere. Got $6.75 today from Preston and from Fornance. Wrote on a paper for the *Missouri Republican* and finished it too. Evening at the Doctor's. He lectured on "the learned professions." Very interesting and well written.

JUNE 3: Mailed my article to Gruaz. Wrote to W. Williams. Wrote a paper for the *Boston Advertiser.* No mail. Called on Anita Staab, on the Doctor, and on Bishop Salpointe.

JUNE 4: Mailed paper to Boston. Letter from Mr. Balsiger and— my drawings from St. Louis. At last! Wrote at an article for Father Stephan. Wrote to Mr. Balsiger.

JUNE 5: Wrote to Dr. C. Walliser, Corner 11th and Mission Streets, San Francisco, California. Gave my lesson at Mrs. Preston's. Got my land grant manuscript at General Atkinson's[590] and sent it to Reverend J. A. Stephan, care of Muhlbauer and Behrle, #41 Lasalle St., Chicago, Illinois. Had a lesson at Fornance's and one at Meany's.

JUNE 6: Letter from Clotilde. I painted for the sake of diversion and rest. Mr. Schiff and Paul Staab came. Went down to the Plaza with Joe and then to Koch's.

JUNE 7: In despair, I went down to Archbishop Salpointe, who at once advanced me $100.—. Paid Mr. Schumann $30.—. Thank God! Mr. Koch had also given $10.— to Joe. She went down town in the afternoon. I wrote at "The Pueblo Indians and the Catholic Church." Evening at home, finished my article. Letter from George, very friendly.

JUNE 8: Wrote a short article for the *Westliche Post.* No letters. Joe at Fischer's in the afternoon. Read my article to the Archbishop. Mailed both papers with accompanying letters. Began to write for the *New York[er] Staatszeitung.*

JUNE 9: Got one load of wood from Juan José Romero ($1.50, paid for it). No lesson at Mrs. Preston's, Fornance also absent. Day as usual, Joe at home. Mr. Hartmann, wife, and niece called. Wrote at the article on the Mockingbird for the *Staatszeitung.* Night at Meany's, lesson; then at the Doctor's. No letters.

JUNE 10: No letters. Mailed "Spottvogel" [Mockingbird][591] to New York (for *Staatszeitung*); and to *The Nation,* five pages on pine timber of the Southwest.[592] Wrote to George Hoffmann. Fornance called with pottery from the Cebolla. He describes the ruin as fully circular and as situated in the valley. Mrs. Jacob Gold[593] called also, on Joe. There is another ruin near Cebolla, on the bluff. Pottery corrugated, black-and-white, red-and-black, brown-with-white, and white.

JUNE 11: General Bradley and wife called. Was lazy all day. Painted at the manta of the Malinche.[594] Letter from Gruaz, from Henry, and proof sheets from Cleveland. Corrected and mailed them back again.

JUNE 12: Was down town all morning, running about for Navajo interpreters, unsuccessfully; called on the Archbishop about the Pimas. No lesson at Mrs. Preston's nor at Meany's. Fornance, however, came. The day was the first handsome day since the 15th of May. Not a cloud. Night equally splendid. Mr. Meany read us a highly interesting paper on the origin of the House of Anjou. Came home about midnight. No letters at all for me.

JUNE 13: Mr. Schumann came and spent a few hours with us. Got letter from Gruaz and F. P. Smith. Received $25.— from the latter. Gave the check to Mr. Schumann, reserving $10.— for me on it. Wrote to Henry; to George; to Gruaz; and to F. P. Smith about Peru. He returned the article to me and will have to rewrite it. I get $1.70 per page, manuscript, for it.

The renter of Eddy told me that the old Pueblo of Nambé was four-and-a-half miles north of the Rio Tezuque, and that the old Pueblo of Tezuque was on the river itself, at Noodle's [Noetel's] Ranch.[595] In the afternoon we went to Manderfield's[596] with Pearce and spent the evening at Jacob Gold's very pleasantly.

JUNE 14: Letter for Joe from Mali; none for me. Called around in the morning everywhere; met Mr. Meyer, who lives at the Chaca near the ruins.[597] He invited me to go out with him once. Wrote on Peru.

JUNE 15: Wrote to Mali. Got letter from W. W. Williams, and one from the *Westliche Post* with $10.—. Wrote on "Peru." Spent the evening at Fischer's, very pleasantly.

JUNE 16: [Entries for this and the two subsequent days were begun with "May," rather than June.] Hubert has got chills and is in bed. [I] went down town. Am unwell myself, headache since last night. Father Defouri, Father Antonio [Jouvenceau], and Father Marilley [Mariller][598] called in the morning. Archbishop Salpointe left tonight. Lesson to Fornance and to Meany. Evening at the Doctor's. Gave a lecture on Indian pottery. Wrote a little, but very little on Peru. *Table of Distances and Elevation, Denver and Rio Grande Railway Co.* [Here, Bandelier devoted a half page to copying data obtained from Colonel Trevin.]

No letters. Today Joe Stinson shot a man, and Cross and a party named Hill had a fight on the street.[599] Evening, Louise Fischer came. Afterwards, her brother.

JUNE 18: Hubert has fever again. No letters. Went to guardmount with Father Antonio. Afterwards to Headquarters. In the afternoon, Joe went down [town] and, at night, to Koch's. Finished and mailed "Ancient Peruvians."[600] It was a disagreeable job.

JUNE 19: Hubert up again, which was some relief to Joe; still the boy is very weak. He is a helpless baby, has no energy, nothing, yields to the first blast. Lesson to Fornance, but none at Meany's. Wrote and mailed article #1, on the useful plants of the Southwest,[601] to Pretorius. Koch invited us to Fischer's, but we refused. Spent the evening at home, quietly. I wrote most of the time.

JUNE 20: Juan José came, then Victoriano and another Indian. Hubert also came; he is better but still weak. Brought one card from Garrison. Finished and mailed #2 for the *Westliche Post*. Had a long and intimate talk with Juan José. He recognized the idols as *"T'yiare Qo"* or idols used and held by the cacique, for medicine purposes. [Presumably, Bandelier showed Juan José the pictures he had made of the specimens borrowed from Judge and Mrs. Prince.] The same cacique used them for curing and is manufacturing them at Cochiti for sale![602] Some time ago, when the Pueblos were threatened by a bill passed against them by the territorial legislature, they secretly united with the Navajos, Utes, and even the Apaches, against Americans, in [case of] need.

Juan José is *chayan* and also *Shya-yaqqa* [medicine man and hunter]. He holds the fetishes of the Hunt, the panther, bear, etc., and they were transmitted to him through the last *Shya-yaqqa* who was his maternal grandfather. The *Shyayaqqa* command the animal dances, but the one who appears in the dances does it by command, without knowing the signification of what he does. The cacique, at the same time, is *Hishtanyi-Chayan* [Flint medicine man], *Shui-chayan* [Snake medicine man], *Mach-tohi Chayan* [?], *Potsho-Asht Chayan* [not translatable], *Hakanyi-Chayan* [Fire medicine man], and *Capina-Chayan* [? medicine man].[603] He is also the medicine man of war, and in the night before a campaign, blesses and paints the weapons. He goes along, or sends along, some of his household (*Qoye*) to represent him. His death in battle is always considered as a very great misfortune, a sign of utter defeat! He [Juan José] told me of an incident in the campaign against the Yutes,—when the *Hish-tanyi-chayan* was felled to the ground by a shot which merely perforated his shield, and his people were terribly frightened, thinking all was lost. But he recovered, and they finally whipped the Utes. This is interesting as in regard to the battle of Otum-pan,[604] and the real office held by the chieftain whose death decided the fate of that engagement.

Masewa and *Oyoyawa* are brothers—twins, but *Cenquitye* made everything. He also made two twin sisters, *Nau-tzi-te* and *Osh-tzi-te*. These quarrelled at the Casa Blanca near the Huajatoyas (Spanish Peaks) in Colorado and fought. The oldest one, Nautzite, gained the fight, and took the middle line (down the Rio Grande)—these now the Pueblo [Indians]; the other took the western line, and she was mother to the Navajos! *Oesh-tzi-te* left a peculiar medicine and a song in the Navajo language, and while the other Pueblos have the medicine and song of *Nautzite* alone, those of *Cochiti* and of *Jemez* possess also the former. Therefore, the people of Cochiti have a song in the Navajo language, and when the cacique there dies without a successor having been designated, and there is none able to step in his shoes, then they go to *Jemez* for a new cacique and also those of Jemez come to Cochiti for a cacique in similar instances. There is consequently a connection between these two Pueblos and the Navajos, which the latter acknowledge and they fear them in war since they have the same medicine. That medicine is called by him also *"comer lumbre"* (fire eating); therefore, the cacique is called *"Hakanyi Chayan."* The stick called *"Potsho-asht"* (lightning) is used by him in the estufa, and it is a part of that medicine too. When the Pueblos meet at Jemez (those of Zia, Santa Ana, etc.) to go to war against the Navajos, the warriors of Cochiti secretly meet those of Jemez in the estufa and have their weapons blessed by the cacique of Jemez also.[605]

Long before the coming of the Spaniards, when the Pueblo of Cochiti dwelt at *Cuapa,* there were two pueblos at Jemez, one below and another above. In the village above dwelt a man who had the medicine of *Oshtzite,* and he used to go down and cure the people of the lower village with it. To this, his folks objected and finally resolved to kill him. His *Yaya* [fetish, or "mother"] told him then that he would die on a certain day and so he called his grandson and told him about it, instructing him to gather his idols (the *Tyiare-qo*), his *Yaya,* and other traps and carry them to the cacique at *Cuapa* and stay with him until those of Jemez would call for him. That although the people acted very badly, he should not refuse to go and to become their cacique afterwards. Thus, it happened; the old man was killed by an arrowshot and the people burnt his effects. They also threw into the fire the *Yaya* but it refused to burn and flew upwards to heaven, saying to the people that, "in consequence of their action, maize would grow successively smaller for four years, and in the fifth year it would refuse to sprout and then great calamities would befall the people." With these words, she disappeared in the sky. The boy gathered the sacred things which his grandfather had concealed under a yucca plant and fled to *Cuapa,* where the cacique received him as his child and educated him to become a *chayan.* After the fifth year, his people came back to beg him to return, and he yielded to their entreaties and became cacique of Jemez. Therefore, the connection between the caciques of Jemez and Cochiti.

Witches are called *Qannat-Yaya;* brujos [warlocks], *Qutzema.* To become a *chayan,* one must be four years without touching a woman, without engaging in any altercation or strife and speaking ill of anybody. Afterwards, he should be trained to the office of medicine by the cacique and the other *chayani.* There are yet seven *Shya-yaqqa* [Hunters, i.e., members of the Hunt Society] at Cochiti.

JUNE 21: Juan José took breakfast with us. He told me also that the fact of killing for witchcraft was certain, but that it was done secretly and communicated secretly to all the other tribes. That only five or six years ago, two persons had been killed at Cia in a quiet way. They do not use poison but club them to death.

I wrote at Fray Marcos de Niza, finishing the text, thirteen pages.

JUNE 22: Finished notes to Fray Marcos and letter to it. Joe went out to Louise Fischer's. No letters again.

JUNE 23: Lesson to Fornance. In the morning, I called on Fiske;[606] he wanted, of course, information about historical points. Yesterday, I mailed my article on Fray Marcos[607] to W. W. Williams, Cleveland, Ohio. No letters.

JUNE 24: Yesterday, I wrote to Garrison again about Brachvogel. Joe went to the pic-nic with Hartmanns. I called on Mrs. Preston, Fiske, Doctor, Kochs, etc. Got letter from Dr. Walliser at last. Also called on Mrs. Henry Huning;[608] left card, as she was not at home. Called on Marcus Eldodt. Got *New York[er] Staatszeitung* with my article on Santa Fe in it. Wrote No. 3 for the *Westliche Post*. Mailed it. Joe came back, very well and elated at the pic-nic. Saw the Doctor and spent all evening with him.

JUNE 25: Finished No. IV for the *Westliche Post* and mailed it. Letters to Joe came, from Bertha and from old Widmer. Also a box with cactuses and "Waldmeister." Had some correspondence with Fiske about grants. In the evening we went to town. Hubert had again the chills. We saw Mrs. Henry Huning on the Plaza. Evening at Kochs'. Pleasant.

JUNE 26: Lesson to Fornance. No letters. Mrs. Koch returned this morning. She looks very well. There is something going on with the military, and I may yet be called upon to go to Arizona to enlist the Papagos or Pimas. In the evening went down to Kochs', both of us, but returned early.

JUNE 27: Hubert came, only to lie down with the fever all day. That boy is a bother and a load to us. He is good, but has no will, no energy; he is half-idiotic. I painted at the groundplan of Casas Grandes. In the afternoon, Mr. Schumann called. He took supper, and then we went to the Plaza, where I met General [Eugene Asa?] Carr[609] from St. Louis. Saw the Doctor. He had arranged with Mr. Fiske for me to study Law. So I am going to try and become a Lawyer! God grant it to amount to something at last. Went out to Fischer's afterwards, Schumann, the Doctor, and I. No letters.

JUNE 28: No letters again. Called on Fiske and on Mrs. Prince. Got my books from the binder and paid for them—$1.75. In the afternoon, slept long and afterwards wrote at the first part of "Geronimo" for the *New York[er] Staatszeitung*. Joe called on Staabs and afterwards went to Marcus Eldodt's. I went down there too at 9 P.M.

JUNE 29: No letters again. Called at General Carr's, on Doña Gregoria, and saw Father Rolly. Got book at Fiske's. It is Father Eguillon's Saint's Day, and I brought him a bouquet, which pleased him.[610] Wrote and mailed No. 1 of "Geronimo"[611] for the

New York[er] Staatszeitung. Joe went to Fischer's, and I followed; we took supper there.

JUNE 30: Got letter from Berlin. So so! Mailed No. 2 of "Geronimo." Went at the following book, loaned to me by Mr. Fiske for study: *"Institutes of American Law,"* by John Bouvier, edited by Daniel A. Gleason, 1872. (2 volumes). [Here, Bandelier devoted several pages of his journal to notes on his readings.]
Gave lesson to Fornance. He paid me $3.50.
Night beautiful. Letter from Dr. Frenzel, Berlin.

JULY

JULY 1: [Copying from Bouvier continued.]
Got letter from Smith with $25.—, and also letter from the Buffalo Historical Society. Mailed No. 5 to Pretorius.

JULY 2: Wrote to F. P. Smith, Rochester, N. Y. Letters from George and from W. W. Williams. Bad news from Celia. Cramp in my right hand, so much so that I can hardly write at all. Still, No. 6 for the *Westliche Post* was finished and mailed. Also wrote to George. Read Bouvier as usual. Went down town. Louise Fischer came to supper. Afterwards went to the music and then accompanied Louise home.

[Bandelier skipped entries from July 3 through July 6.]

JULY 7: Got $10.— from *The Nation.* Made everything ready for departure. Called around.

JULY 8: Left at 7 A.M.—Dr. Eggert, Fornance, Barnard, Judge Cross, Joe and the drivers, Needle and Kirk.[612] Drive most beautiful. Warm but not unpleasant. Kindest possible reception. [Probably at Eldodt's at San Juan Pueblo.] Unwell at night.

JULY 9: Beautiful. Left for the Cañón at 8 A.M. Drove to Santa Clara and then turned into the gorge. The water of the arroyo sinks a little above the pueblo, or about a mile from the river bank; all the rest of the way up, it is a clear, gushing, beautiful mountain stream, cool and full of mountain trout, black-speckled, the largest being about 12 inches long.[613] We drove up to a mile above the sawmill, or 13 miles. The first 11 miles are sandy and gravelly, bare, junipers and cedars being scattered about and considerable chaparro. It looks bare; the sides are steep, but only a few ledges are vertical. Rock friable, light gray, and in strata. Height of sides, two to three hundred feet; width of the valley about a quarter to a half of a mile. About one mile east of the old sawmill, tall pine timber begins, and the valley narrows and grows picturesque. There are open patches between trees. Oaks, cottonwood, and willows appear.

We camped about 2 P.M. Then the Doctor and I walked up about two miles. The cañón narrows; the sides grow higher and beautiful, truncated erosions appear on the slopes. These slopes are 4 to 600 feet high, very steep. It is beautiful, romantic. At a distance of about 14 miles, the cañón begins to turn to the west-southwest and southwest. It is very narrow and picturesque, and tree vegetation is not only abundant, it is also very varied and fine. The water is fine. Distance to the Valles [Valle Grande] 14 miles up the cañón. Whole length of the cañón, about 25 miles.

The Arroyo, or Rio, de Santa Clara springs from several springs on the east flank, about 13 miles southwest of the sawmill. The cañón has no ruins at all. It was always uninhabited, but now the Indians of Santa Clara inhabit the lower part in two places. We met some few cattle. Night most beautiful, cool and cloudless. A woman told me that the cañón was called *"O-ju-u."* Beetles not very frequent, still there are some. Not a crow, no other large animal either. Otters, but did not see any. Woodpeckers and turkeys in the woods.

JULY 10: Similar, and feeling much better. Went on top of the mesa. Ascent quite steep. On the brink, timber thinned and an open grassy plain began with a wide view to the east and northeast. Even the range of Taos and the Costilla visible. Very hot and the air very thin.

I proceeded due south along the base of the Pelado, about three miles. Promontories of white, friable, volcanic tufa jut out from beneath to the east. Their south side is invariably denuded and sometimes vertical, and there are very old caves in them. No water at all. Remains of tie-camps in the groves of pine timber and several trails, some of which are old. The western limit of the caves is therefore about 12–13 miles from the Rio Grande, and their eastern about six miles. They extend from the Cueva Pintada to *Shun-fin-ne*, [Shu-finné][614] or about 35 miles from south to north.

Due east, I saw *Pu-y-ie* [Puyé][615] as a hump with a cliff on the south and southeast. About a-quarter-of-a-mile south of it, is a similar rock with a few caves, and four miles north of the cañón, the long isolated rock of Shun-fin-ne rises high above the northern plateau. Towards Puye, the plain slopes gradually. Ravines traverse it, running towards the cañón. They are all timbered; I reached the Puye about noon. The south and southeast of the rock are all perforated, and there is a talus leading up to them, about 60 to 150 feet high, formed of debris tumbled down and on which only a few trees grew. Between this rock and the other on the south runs a timbered depression with a dry arroyo. There is water farther east but not permanent on the surface; still, it may always be had through excavation. Returned 5 A.M. [P.M. ?]. Moved camp three miles higher up the cañón.

On the level and sometimes treeless mesa, south of the cañón, there are remnants of foundations scattered in few places. There is little pottery about them. In one or two of them, I noticed trees having grown up. They are doubtlessly evidences of former cultivation—real small gardenbeds and the square ones are probably watch houses for the fields. The plain has no water, but the fall of rain and snow is enough for corn, squash, etc. For a length of six to ten miles, these signs of cultivation are, not abundant, but still they appear, and larger mounds, showing the existence of pueblo houses and even in the midst of groves and of high timber.

On a length of five miles, there are at least ten such mounds, including the pueblo on Folio 27. [See entry of July 12.] The houses were of white stone, very friable.

JULY 11: Sunday. Hot day, quiet and fine. Remained in camp all day, hunting beetles with fair success. Dr. in bad humor. He is very disagreeable, coarse, vulgar, and egotistical. It is no pleasure at all to be with him in camp. Still, I have the caves now at last. Yesterday I made about 18 miles.

JULY 12: Returned to the Puye directly and returned [to camp] about 5 P.M. Took water along. Measured several [ruins] and gathered pottery, it is not very abundant. Flint and obsidian about. Also nodules of obsidian in the rock. On the whole, they [the ruins] are an exact repetition of the Rito, only their situation is different. They are plastered with yellow clay, and there is a smoke escape cut out above the doorways. Floors are everywhere black and about two inches thick. Many holes for beams. On an average, they are only one story, but I saw two and three stories also. There are also beam holes indicating porches in front of the rock. The caves are singularly distributed, and they are high, over all timber and plainly visible at a great distance. It is a good position for defense and watch.

Before reaching the Puy-ie, I met ruins in the open air, on the plain about three miles north of it. It was quite a pueblo, and there are yet remains of walls of pumice stone, one foot thick.* The plain is fertile. But it has not a drop of permanent water. Still, as the edge of the cañón is very near, they may have got their drinking water there, although they had to go a mile, at least, down. The pottery is painted: black-upon-white, plain whitish, black, and corrugated. At the caves, I found some pottery and, besides, some glossy pieces (glazed ornamentation)[616] blackish and greenish upon red and upon brown.

There is another ruin, with much stone, north of the Puye. That house was probably two stories high.* All the other ruins are reduced to mere mounds of fine earth, and rather shapeless. In one of the rooms, the place of the metate stand is still visible. No chimneys, but occasionally a round smoke escape.

About a half-mile east of the ruins, another grassy plain begins with traces of former cultivation, guard huts, etc. The timber diminishes rapidly afterwards, and junipers and cedars take the place of pines. It finally disappears completely about five miles east. The top of the rock of Puye is well timbered. It is a gradual slope from the west-northwest and along the north side, a narrow ledge of grayish rock spans one-half of the height. The face of the rock on the south is white with iron stains. Sometimes the walls are vertical for 20 to 50 feet at most.

On the whole the trip was profitable. [Here, Bandelier sketched details of caves mentioned in the July 10 entry.]

The situation of the Puye is as follows: The spring is east or east-northeast of the cliff, and the whole cliff, about a mile long. The face is first to the south and then again to the southeast, and

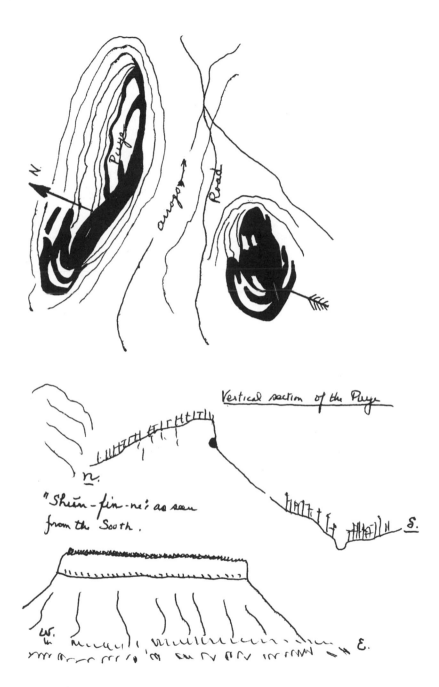

Puye

N

arroyo →

Road

Vertical section of the Puye

n.

"Shūn-fin-ni; as seen
from the South.

s.

W.

E.

the cliffhouses, or caves, are scattered along its face over the whole length.

There may have dwelt about 800 to 1000 souls in both cliffs. There is still a ruin on top of the Puye with walls 2 to 3 stories high and of stone.[617]

From here, *Shun-fin-ne* presents itself in the north. It is much higher than the Puye and also crowned with some little timber. It is a very bold object and rises high above the surrounding mesa and country. It is called "Cerro Blanco" owing to its color. Both rocks look much like enormous castles. *Shun-fin-ne* is also about a mile long.

JULY 13: Clear, but hot. Staid in and near to camp and gathered beetles. Kirk went to the Valle (14 miles). He found no ruins on the road, and in the Valle there is no tree and nothing. Only a creek like this one and much trout and grass. It's getting tiresome, on account of the Doctor and of the two others.

JULY 14: Beautiful. Very hot. Left 8 A.M. Went to Santa Clara, delivered my letter to the governor and had a long and pleasant talk. They have books from all the Pueblos of New Mexico, old ones, but do not know the dates.[618] They will look at them and read the dates and write to the Archbishop about them. They say that the Pueblo [Santa Clara], when the Spaniards first came, stood a little higher up on the arroyo and the church, where now is the old ruined convent. Now it has completely disappeared. San Ildefonso also stood on the opposite [i.e., from its present location] (west side) of the Rio Grande, where the meadow called "O-tzi-ma-e" is. The pueblo at "Pu-i-ye," was the old one of Santa Clara, and they also inhabited the caves. Drouth and war compelled them to abandon both. *Tzi-re-ge* was probably inhabited when the Spaniards came; still, this is not certain yet.[619]

Returned to San Juan on foot at 5 P.M., tired and glad to see Joe again. She is well and quiet.

JULY 15: Fine morning. Hot. Finished my diary and made some calls too. Saw Padre Seux, also old Francisco. Lola is sick, but the Chata is always the same good old girl. I began to paint at the picture of *Tzigo-umo Ojua.* It appears that while I was in the sierra, a number of men from San Juan went there also to perform certain rites. What it was, I could not fully ascertain. Sam [Eldodt], himself, did not know it, but Don Juan García, of course, suspected mischief. Joe has no headache at all. She feels light and well. The quietness has done her a great deal of good. Everybody is most kind and friendly.

JULY 16: Painted all day. In the afternoon, Rómulo Martinez came, going back to Santa Fe. Copied the *"Agoyo-Ojua,"* or Star-fetish. Saw old Francisco.

JULY 17: Painted the bear fetishes, *Ke-Ojua,* and began at the *Tze-Ojua* (eagle fetish) and the *Chang-Ojua* (panther fetish).

JULY 18: Thermometer rose to 101° again. In the afternoon, violent blow from the north-northeast but no rain. It is terribly dry. The pueblo is almost empty; the people are in the fields. This morning, early, a double homicide near La Joya.[620] An American stole a horse, and two Mexicans followed him at once. Result, the American and one Mexican killed. Pity for the Mexican!

Painted the *Ping-qu-cuan* (Toad fetish), used for throwing into the acequias when rain is needed very badly. Afternoon tremendously hot. Called on the Padre with Joe. Pleasant and quiet.

JULY 19: Quiet, hot morning. Went to see Candelario. He told me that the expedition to the sierra was to gather plants for to throw into the rivers and acequias in order to propitiate the coming of rain. There is "Pino real" [*Pinus clussiana*], "Alamito chico" [*Populus* sp.?], and others. The twin idols, *"To-a"* (the equivalents of *Maseua* and *Oyo-ya-ua,* and of the Zuñi twins)[621] are set up in a flat basket with yellow corn. They are of stone, faces painted black, with a brown frock, hood bordered white, and a crosslike ornament on the top. Stars are carved on the frock or gown. It looks much like coarse pictures of Franciscan monks, and it is very suggestive of Catholic origin![622] The yellow stone used for curing is called *"Jay-ye-uocane."* The black one is used for calling for rain and is termed *"Cua-cu."* Rain: *"Cua."* Thunder: *"Cua-ta."* Lightning: *"Tzigo-ue-no."* When the whites first came, says Candelario, *Tzirege* was occupied; so was *"Yuge-ouinge."*[623] The caves are the work of the Tehuas, who afterwards abandoned them owing to drouth and to hostilities of the Navajos.

The northern villages, however, those of Ojo Caliente, [El] Rito, and of Abiquiu, were in ruins at the time of Oñate. The pueblo at the Embudo is called: *"Tee-yi P-ho ouinge."*

Every meeting is begun with a prayer, short or long, according to the importance of the business. The journey to the sierra was undertaken at the instance of the cacique. The caciques and other medicine men cannot carry arms in war, only the *tze-ojke*, or medicine man of war, does carry weapons and may fight, the others not, and under no circumstances. The eagle, bear, and panther fetishes are used for curing, the former also for rain.

In the afternoon a very heavy thunderstorm from the west, raining hard in the Valles and in Abiquiu. Here, blast and a few drops. At night, windy and at last a slight shower. Harry S. Budd,[624] of Taos, came. He is a linguist (?) or rather a collector of words and sentences, and has already about 1000 words in the Taos language. Has evidently great aptitude, but is yet a great novice and has much to learn. Persevering, he is to intrusiveness and boldness and on the whole a bore. Complains about Washington too. Father Seux went to the Embudo today. At night, Archbishop Lamy came. Joe is tired from heat. There is no possibility to go out, for in the forenoon it is very hot, and in the afternoon commonly too windy and too dusty until night.

JULY 20: Drove Joe to the station[625] opposite Española and went back, stopping at Frank Becker's at Santa Cruz. Whole afternoon sultry, quiet. Budd left again for Taos. He is a big bore. Archbishop Lamy dined with us this noon. Budd is becoming quite a bore. He is sticky, forward, and indiscreet [*sic*]. Crocker is here from the Chama, and going there again.

JULY 21: Left on foot for Santa Fe at 9:30 A.M. Soon grew very hot. Called on Father Manuel Ribera[626] of Santa Cruz. After I left Pojuaque, a violent thunderstorm came up and drenched me completely till I reached Cuyamungue.[627] There I was stopped by the arroyo. It kept on drizzling and raining until I got to Tezuque. Reached Jud's rancho late and stopped there for the night. Hubert well; people most kind.

JULY 22: Have backache. Jud drove me to town with his shying horse. Joe well. Saw everybody. Letters from F. P. Smith, W. P. Garrison, and from A. G. Henry.[628] Slow, quiet rain in the afternoon. I slept. Went to bed early and am very tired.

JULY 23: Wrote to W. P. Garrison, to A. G. Henry, F. P. Smith, *Boston Advertiser,* W. W. Williams, *New Yorker Staatszeitung,* to Mr. Balsiger, to Dr. C. Walliser, No. 632 Hayes Street, San Francisco, California, to Alphonse, to C. H. Seybt, and mailed all ten letters together today. Lumbago, otherwise well. It is very pleasant here, so quiet, cool, and peaceable. Joe is perfectly well. The trip has done her good and me too. We are both fresh.

JULY 24: The rains have so far been very beneficial, but they have also stopped trains day before yesterday through washouts. I finished the "Nahr- und Nutz-pflanzen," VII and VIII, and mailed the first. Dr. Eggert called in the forenoon; Mrs. Catron and Louise Fischer in the afternoon, while Joe was not at home. General Palacio [Palacios][629] in town.

JULY 25: Were alone all day. I fixed my beetles and painted groundplans. It is wet yet on the ground.

JULY 26: No eastern mail has come in now since the 20th. Wrote at Letter #1, for the *Münchener Allgemeine Zeitung,* and mailed it to Professor Ratzel with a short letter. Have not been to town since the 23rd and have no desire to go, it is so beautiful out here.

JULY 27: Hubert came. He looks very well, and has gained 9 lbs. in two weeks. Mail at last. Letters from *New York[er] Staatszeitung* with $34.50, and from Cleveland with $14.25. Also card from George. Celia is better. Thank God for it. Went to town and got the money. G.A.R. [Grand Army of the Republic] here in masses. Wrote letter #2 for Munich.

JULY 28: Wrote #3 for Munich and mailed both, 2 and 3. Quiet day. Koch and Fornance called. The ground is getting dry again and needs water. Collection of beetles slowly increasing. Meeting at the Doctor's tonight, interesting. Mr. Wolff[630] present. But the old man is disagreeably peevish.

JULY 29: Hardly any beetles, except *Necrophoridae.* Wrote four pages for *The Nation* and mailed them.[631] Also mailed six bl'ks. to Honorable A. G. Henry, Greenville, Illinois. Called on several, among others, on Archbishop Salpointe. Went down town a second time, looking for V. but without result.

JULY 30: Went down town to the Archbishop's. Don Dolores Romero removed [?].[632] In the afternoon, Mr. Meany made us a friendly call.

JULY 31: Mailed letter and package to Mali for her birthday, and $1.— in cash too. Wrote at the article on caves for Rochester. Afternoon, went down town, to the Archbishop, to Doctor, etc. Wrote to F. P. Smith, Rochester, and to Sam Eldodt, sending G. Recipts [?] for Uncle Andrew. Louise called a moment. Met General Atkinson and General Bradley. Thus the month of July is over, and no news from Papa and from Ratzel.

AUGUST

AUGUST 1: Hard rain at last from noon to nearly 3 P.M. The river rose suddenly, but did not overflow. Was called to the Archbishop at 2 P.M. about Dolores Romero. Painted; Mr. Schumann came.

AUGUST 2: Eddy [Franz] brought us two letters, one from Pretorius and one from Papa! Good, thank God! Went down town in the forenoon and told about the letter. Wrote but little. Mr. Hartmann called. A slight sprinkle or shower, but the main storms passed south and east of us. Went down town in the afternoon, too; called on the Bishop. Agency matters look better. Papa's career has been a wonderful one indeed. Not one of his detractors at Highland would be capable of performing what he [did].

AUGUST 3: Papers and card from *New York[er] Staatszeitung;* also missing number from *Westliche Post.* Finished paper on cliff houses today. Mrs. Staab and Bertha called. Afterwards, we went to Fischer's. A severe thunderstorm came. The rain very heavy. So Joe remained at Fischer's overnight, and I went home.

AUGUST 4: Unwell, of course, from yesterday. Still, wrote at the letter to Father J. A. Stephan. In the afternoon, Mr. Schiff and Paul Staab came. Hubert was here all day. He looks well and feels good. Went to town early. Great scandal about the Presbyterian "Reverend" Jones[633] and the meeting of the Indian School.[634] Read at the Doctor's.

AUGUST 5: Mali's birthday. Poor child, it may be a very, very modest birthday for her. Those poor, good, innocent folks are even worse off than we are now. We have nothing to complain of. Wrote at the Massacre of Cholula for the *Staatszeitung.*

AUGUST 6: Wrote, but felt unwell. My birthday. Letter from Bertha, the children, and Rosalie. In the afternoon, Sam and Marcus Eldodt and the old Doctor called. Louise and her brother called and stayed until 10 P.M.

AUGUST 7: Another washout, no mail. Wrote to Henry and mailed also six photographs to Rochester, N.Y. Wrote to Papa, to Williams, to the *Staatszeitung* and to Lucien Carr.[635] Lesson to Fornance in the afternoon.

AUGUST 8: Began to translate Chapter I into English.[636] Hot. Letter from Henry. Louise Fischer called.

AUGUST 9: Night cool. Went out to Fischer's till 10 P.M. Pleasant.

AUGUST 10: Hot. Koch came. Afternoon cloudy, thundering. Finished translation of Chapter I and handed it to Meany. Evening at Koch's, very pleasant.

AUGUST 11: Letter from Papa. Went down town, saw the Bishop and others. Sent off first part of letters to Father Stephan. Afternoon at Meany's. No lesson at Fornance. Night reading at the Doctor's, but without him. He had had two teeth pulled and is now making a fool of himself again. Dr. Roehrich was present. I read Chapter I, and all were highly pleased.

AUGUST 12: As usual. Thence on, I interrupted my Journal [until August 22]. Got another letter from Papa. On Friday, I was surprised by Mahler's[637] visit. He was very friendly. But I mistrusted. The lecture on Friday night (13th of August) at the Post Hall,[638] was in sofar a success, as it pleased the people. But I spoke only 40 minutes. It was very hot. Ladd[639] was there too. There was not light enough for the drawings.

AUGUST 22: Sunday. On Sunday afternoon, we had plenty of visitors. First the three Staab girls. Afterwards, came the two Grunsfelds and Dr. Eggert. Then Mahler and Tamony.[640] At 8 P.M., Mr. Franz and Eddy.[641]

Translated Chapter II and read it on Tuesday, 17 August. On Wednesday, 18 August, left on foot for Peña Blanca. It rained till the Cieneguilla. Then sprinkled till the Bajada. Afterwards cleared and grew hot. Thursday, 19th, was the Mass for poor Juan José [Montoya] at Cochiti.[642] Poorly attended, but a modest, yet impressive ceremony. Ill. Very hot.

On Friday, 20th, left for Santa Fe, unwell, and reached there at 9 P.M. completely worn out. Already at Peña Blanca, I had heard that a pueblo existed there, west of the house of Juan Antonio Durán, where there are now fields, and the ruins are still to be seen. Metates and pottery, also walls, were seen. This was confirmed at the Bajada by Doña Quirina Vaca de Gallegos, who also stated that a number of idols of stone, painted red, were found and exhumed there. Her father gave them to the Cochiti Indians.

Peña Blanca is called *Qu Shiu-qo*. On Saturday, I was very much exhausted. Called on the Archbishop. Wrote to Cleveland, to Garrison, to Mr. Balsiger, to Pretorius. On Sunday, I got my article on the Mockingbird back again from New York and mailed it at once to Pretorius. Joe was unwell, and I am not feeling very strong either.

The whole day cloudy and cool, also rainy. I wrote at translations of Chapter III. Wrote to J. D. Warner and to Harry S. Budd. Mr. Hartmann called and took supper with us. Eddy went out to Tezuque. Flies very bad.

AUGUST 23: Letter from Papa. I finished my article on the Cholula Massacre and mailed it.[643] Fixed matters for the Archbishop. Monsignore Straniero[644] here, and I spent part of the evening with him about the drawings.

AUGUST 24: Went down town early and saw the Archbishop. He takes hold of the sale of the drawings for the purpose of presenting them to Pope Leo XIII.[645] Wrote again, and mailed, Article VI to Pretorius. Evening at Fischer's. Very fine. Got a letter from F. P. Smith, catalogue of Vick's, and *The Nation*. Mail late.

AUGUST 25: I translated on Chapter III. Night very dark and rainy. Quiet.

AUGUST 26: I finished Chapter III. Got a letter from J. D. Warner and replied to it at once. Began to write at the first chapter of the big book suggested by Archbishop Salpointe. In French.[646]

AUGUST 27: No letters for me. Wrote Article IV for the *Münchener Allgemeine,* and mailed to Ratzel with letter. Article VI to Pretorius. Archbishop home again. Evening at Meany's. The destruction of Santo Domingo took place on the 3rd of June and lasted one night and one day.[647]

AUGUST 28: Read at Meany's. Wrote out synopsis of work for the Pope in French. Got $25.00 from the *Westliche Post.* Fornance came.

AUGUST 29: Finished English translation of synopsis. Wrote to F. Coste.[648] Painted in Minnie's album. Louise came, also Mr. Schumann. Took supper with us. Wrote to F. P. Smith, Rochester, with order to Vick's, bulbs for S. Eldodt, $11.47.

AUGUST 30: Wrote and mailed article to Garrison on "Removal of the Apaches from Arizona."[649] Went out to Fischer's. Began to translate Chapter IV. Also to write to Papa. Got letter from Dr. Walliser. Poor fellow.

AUGUST 31: I worked at the translation of Chapter IV. It goes very slow. Wrote to Papa. Joe went down town this afternoon with Louise, and they were caught in the fearful rain. I gave

Chapter III to Mr. Varden[650] this morning to read. In German. Wrote to Alphonse.

SEPTEMBER

SEPTEMBER 1: Am ill disposed. No letters. Am losing faith in the success of—[sentence incomplete]. I went down town in the forenoon, also immediately after dinner. Saw Meany; the Doctor is on the rampage. Joe went to Fischer's. Translated at Chapter IV. They seem to take a lively interest in the matter. At night, reading at the Doctor's. It was tolerably pleasant.

SEPTEMBER 2: Fine morning, quiet and cool. Few clouds. Am not well, last night's beer spoiled my stomach completely. Went down town and then to Louisa Fischer, about beans for tomorrow. In the afternoon wrote, but with difficulty. It grew very beautiful, hazy perfect Indian summer.

SEPTEMBER 3: Walked out to Tezuque and spent a delightfully quiet and peaceable time with Hubert and Mrs. Jud. We went to Christian Noetel and found on his ranch, to the right of the road, in the cornfields, the ancient pueblo. It is partly washed away by the arroyo. The Rio Tezuque formed his wide bed in one night in 1855. Up to that time, the river had been narrow and lined by a thicket of cottonwoods, willows, etc. All these were washed away at once and since that time the water has been encroaching constantly, and is changing its course from one side to the other. Besides, the water from several springs comes in from southeast of Noetel's, and between his ranch and the chapel.

The pottery is mostly black-and-white. Metates, axes, arrowheads, etc. were formerly found here. I was told there were two more pueblos on the opposite (southwest) bank, on the high lomas. Edward Miller[651] told me that the Nambé affair really occurred in 1853, one year before his coming, which was in 1854. Noetel, although his memory is not as good, says the same.

At night, lecture by Judge Prince, on the Pueblo of the Potrero de las Vacas, which he calls "Pueblo Quemado" and *"Yapashi,"*[652] of course, because a number of stone idols were found there. The "Pinini story"[653] is there also. On the whole, the lecture was a very shallow thing, superficial and buncombe. Delightful night, but I had drunk too much coffee and remained sleepless.

SEPTEMBER 4: Letters from Garrison and Frank H. Cushing. Finished Chapter IV. Wrote to Cushing and mailed the letter. Fornance came. It rained until 4 P.M., slow, but steadily. Read Chapter IV, at Meany's, Fornance and Varden present.

SEPTEMBER 5: Letters from Papa and Pretorius. Good, old Papa! He sends us a present. His hard earned money! Joe went to church. [I] wrote to Papa, to Mr. Balsiger, to Henry, to Pretorius, to Dr. Walliser. In the afternoon, Joe went with Kochs to the Brewery while I staid at home and wrote the paper for Atkinson, 6 pages. At 6 P.M., Gerdes and wife called. Went down to Koch's at 8 P.M. and spent evening very pleasantly. General Bartlett[654] and wife were there, also Miss Webb.

SEPTEMBER 6: Went down town. Got letters from Mr. Balsiger, and F. P. Smith. The latter returned the manuscript of "Cliff Houses." Am not surprised. Vanderveer is going East tomorrow; he returned me the manuscript of Chapter II, English translation. Wrote to F. P. Smith and sent manuscript of Pearce's. Hubert came; I copied Chapter I for the *"Westliche Post,"* that is copied on Chapter I! Had callers, Don Dolores Romero and Florence, finally Hayoua[655] and Gervasio[656] from Cochiti. Could not keep the former, so I told him to come back tomorrow.

SEPTEMBER 7: Hayoua came: I see: *"sio qatshanyi qo"*; thou seest: *"sho qatshanyi qo"*; he sees: *"qo qastshanyi qo"*; we see: *"sio qatshanyi qo a"*; you [see]: *"shro qatshanyi qu a"*; they [see]: *"qo qatshanyi qu a."* I saw: *"sio qatsh"*; thou sawest: *"shro qatsh"*; he saw: *"qo qatsh"*; we saw: *"sio qatsh anyi"*; [you saw]: *"shro qatshanyi"*; [they saw]: *"qo qatshanyi."* I will see: *"nyo qatsh se"*; [thou willst see]: *"nyo qatsh sho"*; [he will see]: *"nyo qatsh qo"*; we will see: *"nyo qatshanyi ossu [?]"*; you will see: *"nyo qatsh sho"*; they will see: *"nyo qatshanyi qu so."* I shall see: *"sha e nyo qatsh se"*; thou shalt see: *"sha en yo qatsh sho"*; he shall [see]: *"shaenyoqatsh qo"*; we shall see: *"sha e nyo qatshsho"*; they shall see: *"sha enyo qatsh qo sa."* Where do you go to: *"Hai que tzoña sho?"* Animal fetishes, small, *"Uashtesh"*; human figures, small: *"Pa-at-yama."* Uncles: *"Sa-naua"*; Aunt: *"Sa nya nya."*

This has been the wettest day I ever saw in the Southwest. It is but a series of thunderstorms, all from the south and southeast. A very violent one, with very heavy wind and hail occurred about 4 P.M. Another began about 6 P.M., and it continued raining heavily.

Hayoua says that the *Shikama-Chayan* is one of the *Shyayak,* and that whenever they went to a great hunt (buffalo, etc.), he had to fit them out. The *Hishtanyi Chayan,* is the war medicine man; he may delegate one of the others, but only by his consent can they officiate, receive the warriors, paint them, etc., otherwise they are punished for it. The *Qoshare* have fasted, last week; so has the *Hishtanyi Chayan;* now the *Shkui Chayan* is fasting.[657]

Our river is on the rampage; it has torn away Boyle's bridge, flooded the bottom. No carriage, nor waggon, etc. can cross it. Our plank is going. Part of the railing of San Miguel bridge gone also. Down town a good deal of hail fell. The blow about 4 P.M. was very severe, still not a tree, not even a branch broke or tore. It may be said that there was one continuous thunderstorm all day, last night, and part of this night.

SEPTEMBER 8: Cloudy and dull all day. At sunset, a slight thunderstorm from the southwest. Night clearing, quiet and cool. River very high and roaring. Our plank gone. Finished copying Chapter I and sent it to Pretorius, with a letter. Began to translate II, but Mr. Meany is going to Pueblo, Colorado, so that there is no use in hurrying about it at all. I then went at copying Chapter II. No letters.

SEPTEMBER 9: Copied at Chapter II. Of course, it rained again in the afternoon, a very brisk thunderstorm from the west with rain and hail. This rain is sickening.

SEPTEMBER 10: Gloomy day, but no rain until late in the afternoon, when it came slowly from the east. Very chilly. I finished copying Chapter II and mailed it to Pretorius. Joe went to see Louise Fischer, it being her birthday. River still high. Got Boyeson's translation of Goethe's *Faust,* and found the following passages for Chapter V of the Romance: "Part of the Power which still produceth good, while ever scheming ill."[658] Also: "But small concern I feel for yonder world."[659]

SEPTEMBER 11: No letters. Copied at Chapter III. Louise came in the afternoon. My eyes hurt and am weak. It is always so dark that I see but little and must strain my eyesight beyond measure.

SEPTEMBER 12: Finished copying Chapter III. It began to rain hard about 9 A.M., and rained and rained unceasingly, with an occasional thunderclap at long intervals. Almost impossible to write, so dark it is. It rained all day almost uninterruptedly till dark. Wrote at Chapter IV and a letter to George Hoffmann. Mr. Schumann came and took supper with us.

SEPTEMBER 13: Very cool, clear. Yesterday, our little river was very high; today, it is falling. Letter from Ratzel, nothing positive in it. It is sickening. Wait, wait, and wait! Went down town. The Archbishop is home. His talk is good, the thing will probably go, but I must still—wait![660] First snow on Baldy this morning! Spent evening at Fischer's.

SEPTEMBER 14: Letter from *The Nation,* with $15.—. Thank God! Went down town, twice. Professor O. C. Marsh[661] is here from New Haven. Felt unwell, still copied on Chapter IV. The Jicarilla Apache call the Rio Grande: *"Cutz-oy,"* and Taos: *"Jua-ute."* Met a Tezuque Indian who told me that the pueblo on Noetel's ranch is called: *"Po-jyu uingge"*[662] and that the old Pueblo of Tezuque was not there. At night, Koch and Marcus Eldodt called.

SEPTEMBER 15: Finished Chapter IV, and mailed it. Nothing in the *Westliche Post,* as yet. Began at translation of Chapter V. Lesson to Fornance. Called at General Bradley's at night.

SEPTEMBER 16: Letter from Papa! All right so far. Nothing new. Wrote at Chapter V translation, finished it, and then began at German copy.

SEPTEMBER 17: Finished copying Chapter V. Louise came. Also Mrs. Gilman and Miss Dewey. Letter from Professor Hewett[663] of Ithaca. Mr. Meany returned. I finished copy of Chapter V. It is wonderful weather since Monday, and the river is falling daily.

SEPTEMBER 18: Still beautiful. Letter from Pretorius, negative; also from good Cushing with $100. Thank God! Then I ran down town, cashed it, and went on paying. Bought a dress for Joe. In the afternoon, Joe went to Mrs. Catron and to Hartmann's. Wrote to Cushing. Took supper at Hartmann's and then went over Chapter V with Mrs. Meany. Sent off the German of Chapter V.

SEPTEMBER 19: Painted the whole day at home, did not go to town at all. Joe went to Mrs. Gerdes with Louise.

SEPTEMBER 20: Wrote at—nothing. Painted, although I am not at all disposed to do anything of that sort. Evening at Meany's, reading of Chapter V. It strikes me as if they would not sufficiently appreciate the literary part and exigencies of the work. Must consult Dr. Strong also.

SEPTEMBER 21: Painted, but with little spirit. In the afternoon, we went to Fischer's where I met Dr. Strong and spoke to him. We spent the evening at the brewery and returned late.

SEPTEMBER 22: Koch came, and we went to town together. In the afternoon, Joe went to Manderfield's, and I painted. At the Doctor's, Mr. Meany read a paper about "Development in Christianity," in which paper he assailed Infallibility and the Immaculate Conception. There was little delicacy on his part in doing so, and I suspect the Doctor to be at the bottom of it with his foolish ideas of changing my religious opinion. He is a hypocrite.

SEPTEMBER 23: Translated at Chapter VI. Had little pleasure. No letters. Evening at home, quiet. Letter from Henry yesterday. Hubert also came; Father Mailluchet and Madlle Rousse.[664] One fifth of the arable lands in the Pecos Valley is swept away, and 6/7 of all crops are destroyed. 600 fanegas of wheat.[665] Grasshoppers are very bad; they have eaten up all the vegetables.

SEPTEMBER 24: Worked at Chapter VI and called on Dr. Strong. More and more, Meany's conduct looks suspicious to me. In the afternoon, Louise came, and her brother got her at 5 P.M.

SEPTEMBER 25: Wrote to Pretorius and to the *Staatszeitung*. Finished Chapter VI. Lesson to Fornance. Dr. Strong spent the evening with us. I read Chapter VI to him. Strong is well satisfied. No letters.

SEPTEMBER 26: No letters again. It is not surprising, for I have hardly written any myself. Joe has headache, and I put her to bed until 2 P.M. when she rose and felt well. I closed every shutter towards the porch and went to painting in the kitchen. Calls in the afternoon: Koch, Schumann, Chas. Hoffmann; Hartmann, Mr. Dittrich [E. W. Dietrich],[666] Mrs. H. Hartmann, Louise, and Miss Neber [Amalia Nehber].[667] Plenty, but not too many. The high mountains are turning yellow from sunflowers and it looks most beautiful. Joe is well again; the attack is not severe.

SEPTEMBER 27: Quiet, barely a breeze from the southeast. Flies are still very bad. Last night, the nasty dog, "Prinz," tore off our mosquito-net in the kitchen window and damaged two flower-plants. Letter from George, long, painful, yet he hopes. Poor Celia. Also letter from *Staatszeitung* with $18.—.[668] Thanks! Went down town. Wrote to the *New York[er] Staatszeitung* about Brachvogel, to George, and to Henry. Wonderful day. Joe is preparing to leave for Albuquerque. I called on Mrs. L. P. Shelden [Mrs. Lionel A. Sheldon, wife of former Governor of New Mexico, 1881–85][669] this P.M. at the Palace Hotel. He is in town also. Sunset and evening magnificent. Joe left for Albuquerque at 11:20 P.M. with Kochs. He himself was drunk, lost his hat, fell into the river, etc. Finally, they got off, and I went to see L., and then home.

SEPTEMBER 28: Day perfectly splendid. Breakfasted and dined at Mrs. Hartmann's. Called on Mrs. Hartmann, Sr., and Mrs. Fornance. Brought my blankets to washing. Painted at pottery and blankets.

SEPTEMBER 29: Heavy frost. Ice in the fields. Slept well. Breakfasted at Mother Helbig's. It is lonesome without Joe. Dined at Mrs. Hartmann's. In the afternoon, Fornance came. Went to Fischer's for supper, then spent the evening with Camillo Padilla,[670] partly at home, partly in his room, and also walking. Wrote to Joe, sending letter from Bertha.

SEPTEMBER 30: Letter from Joe. Day splendid, beyond all description, night cloudless. Painted. Wrote to Joe. Went to Dr. Strong. Found in his copy of Longfellow's translation of Dante the full—old English—text of the Legend of St. Brandan.[671] Also examined Canto XXVI. No letters.

OCTOBER

OCTOBER 1: Painted. The Archbishop is at home, and he directed me to begin at once.[672] Thank God. Called on Mr. Meany and on the Doctor. Evening with Camilo.

OCTOBER 2: Warm. Painted some. In the afternoon, painted for Jac. Gold. Called on Anita Staab and then on Louise. Took supper with the Archbishop.

OCTOBER 3: Joe returned at 8 A.M. Well and tired. Painted. Governor Ritch, Koch, Louise, and Mr. Schumann called. Letter from Pretorius. Governor Ritch told me that there are traces of an old pueblo on the west of the Sierra de San Andres, between Engle and his ranch, on the side of the road. Pottery and stone objects.

OCTOBER 4: Began on my work for Pope Leo XIII! May God help me.
Joe went to town in the afternoon. The band played again for the first time. Suffer from rheumatism in my back. Can hardly sit up.

OCTOBER 5: Remittance of *Magazine of Western History,* $16.50. Letter from Rosalie. Poor Celia. Wrote all day. In the afternoon, the Staab girls called; also Miss Schutz of El Paso. At night, began to write to Papa.

OCTOBER 6: Quiet. Wrote all day. Got book from Don Joaquín. Dr. Eggert called. Wrote all day at Chapter I of the new book and mailed letter to Papa. Am very well disposed.

OCTOBER 7: Letters from Henry, Don Joaquín, and Cushing. The latter is more than good. I am even in a quandary what to do, the work is almost too much for me at once.[673] Still, Joe says I shall take it.

It thundered in the afternoon, and the mountains are covering up again. Finished Chapter I. In the afternoon, Father Deraches[674] called, and I read my manuscript to him. He took it along for correction. Went down town with Joe. Night turned very beautiful, quiet and cool. Wrote to Don Joaquín[675] and to Mr. Pretorius. It is almost too good to be true. Thank God a thousand times for the good news from Cushing.

OCTOBER 8: Weather beautiful. Replied to Cushing. Worked at the notes for Chapter I. They give a good deal of trouble. Father Stephan arrived.

OCTOBER 9 TO 14: Today, I finished Chapter II, notes and all. I was almost worked to death. Had several interviews with Father Stephan and with the Archbishop. The whole thing seems to be arranged. On the 11th, was Joe's birthday, and could make her some presents, small but practical. It was the first of her birthdays since 1883 that we could celebrate together. 12th and 13 were most beautiful days, so is 14th. Cloudless and cold. Ice 1/4 of an inch thick. Arranged with Father Deraches to copy my manuscript for the Pope. It needs revision of its French at all events. I have considerable difficulty to write French anyhow. Letter from *Staatszeitung*, etc. Sunday—otherwise nothing. I intended to go to Santa Clara, but cannot do it this week. Must work. Bought the manuscript of Louis Felsenthal.[676] It is surely 1643 and covers a period in New Mexican history which is almost entirely unknown yet. Am glad I got it.

OCTOBER 15: Warming. It is a perfect delight, this weather. Letter from E. Pretorius. I fixed the wood this morning and then began work on Chapter III. Have a bad cold and could not write much. In the afternoon, Mrs. Fornance and the Lieutenant called, while Joe was down town.

OCTOBER 16: Passed a sleepless night on account of my cold. Ill. Letter from Garrison and the book of McLennan for review.[677] Went down town. Wrote on Chapter III. Wrote to E. Pretorius. Went to bed early. Quite unwell.

OCTOBER 17: Had a good sleep and feel much better. Yesterday, the Archbishop told me about the new plans. Mr. Dow[678] is going to establish a large wool factory here soon. Letter from F. Coste with $15.— from *Westliche Post.* Thanks! In the afternoon, we went to Fischer's and then, with Louise, walked out to the new Indian School.[679] The site is beautiful. At night, at the Archbishop's, reading. Koch, Schumann, and the three ladies called at night.

OCTOBER 18: A letter from Dr. Walliser. Bad cold. Finished Chapter III. Joe went down town and to Louise. I went to the Archbishop at night and read to him Chapter II. He is well pleased.

OCTOBER 19: No letters, perhaps even no mail. Mr. Meany left for Chicago last night, and now they are begging money to defray expenses of his trip. Later, letter from Don Joaquín. Wrote at Chapter IV. Cashed a check for $25.—, which Clotilde sent us for Papa. We must wait until we hear from him again. Went down town twice, paid my overcoat at Gerdes'.

OCTOBER 20: Finished Chapter IV this evening. Mrs. Hartmann called in the morning, and Louise came and spent the afternoon with Joe. Went to the concert tonight upon invitation of Mr. Schumann. Called on the Archbishop and on Father Stephan. Got $50 from the Archbishop. He leaves tonight for Baltimore.[680] Concert good, but audience small.

OCTOBER 21: Went to town in the forenoon and bought me a watch for $10.—. How things have greatly changed! But no pride, no buoyancy, lest the good prospects might vanish again like a dream. It feels like a dream anyhow.

Wrote at Chapter V. In the afternoon, Mrs. Jac. Gold came.

OCTOBER 22: I wrote on Chapter V. In the afternoon, Louise Fischer called. Night cold and clear.

OCTOBER 23: Letter from Cushing. Replied.[681] Finished Chapter V. Visit from Mrs. Koch about Eddy [Huegy, in Albuquerque]. He is always the same fool and presumptuous fellow.[682] I hope he will not come here.

OCTOBER 24: No letters. A most admirable day, perfectly cloudless, quiet and cool. Father Deraches wrote me a foolish letter, declining to copy. It is only laziness on his part. Went out to Fischer's. Louise and Gaertner had an accident today with the buggy. We walked over Fort Marcy. It was simply splendid. Staid at Fischers till 9 P.M. and got home safe. Am worried about my French work.

OCTOBER 25: Beautiful day, but Joe in bed. She had no headache, but is dizzy and cannot be up. Letter from Gruaz. I am free![683] Thank God, a million times! At last, at last! But Joe is very unwell. Finished the article for Frank Cushing. Went to town. I am in ugly mood, for Joe is sick. Towards night, she felt improved. Saw Koch about Eddy.

OCTOBER 26: Wrote review for Garrison and letter to him. Letters to: Mr. Balsiger, to Gruaz, and to Henry. Louise called, also Fornance. I was busy all day writing. Joe is well and hearty again.

OCTOBER 27: Letter from F. P. Smith, returning the manuscript on Peru. Singular. Circus today, and the whole town full of people. Hubert came. Commenced on Chapter VI but couldn't do much as I had to be down town nearly all day. Father Antonio took supper with us tonight. He goes to Acoma for children. Father Seux in town also.

OCTOBER 28: Letter from G. H. Jones, Naranjos, Mora County, with a fossil tooth. It was found 35 feet below the surface, and charcoal and human shinbones at 20 feet depth.

Hayoua and Serafín's son called, in uniform, from Cochiti. They are in quest of work. I recommended them to Father Stephan. Wrote at Chapter VI. Joe went to the great reception at [General] Bartlett's.

OCTOBER 29: I wrote at Chapter VI and finished it too. Joe went down town in the afternoon. Wrote to Frank P. Smith and to G. H. Jones. Also to George. Night most magnificent. It appears the old Doctor is after Miss Neber at Catron's. He has also spoiled it with Mrs. Catron.

OCTOBER 30: Pedro from Cochiti took breakfast with us and then went off again. Housecleaning, so I went down town in the morning to Pearce. Hubert came in again. Saw Felipe Ortiz, Jorge Ortiz, and José B. Ortiz about manuscripts from the seventeenth century. There may be some yet, but very few. Then went out to Lt. [Fornance] and to the brewery. Joe had her "Bohnenverein" [?] this afternoon, and I could not stay at home, nor work any, the whole day. Was rather "on a bum" for my part.

OCTOBER 31: No letters. Worked at Chapter VII. In the afternoon, we went out to the brewery and walked out with Louise on the road to Aztec Springs, about two miles. It was beautiful. The view is very handsome to the south and west. Quite lively wind from the south–southeast. Cool.

NOVEMBER

NOVEMBER 1: I wrote the whole day at Chapter VII and finished it too. Night very beautiful, cloudless and quiet. Great election excitement in town.

NOVEMBER 3: Two beautiful days [no entry for November 2]. Worked at Chapter VIII. Today, we had visitors: Mr. Dittrich and Reverend Mr. Winters, the Misses Manderfield, Dr. Strong with whole family; Mrs. Hartmann and Mrs. Meany. At night, Mr. Hartmann, Ad. Fischer,[684] Mr. Schumann came and spent the evening. Louise was here already. Between times, Adelaido [Montoya] from Cochiti. It was a perfect chase, fifteen calls today. One after another.

NOVEMBER 4: Letters: Papa (2), Gruaz, Mr. Balsiger, Padre Navet, and W. C. Kueffner. Mailed to him Acknowledgement. G. W. Garrels. Good news from Papa and Gruaz. Finished Chapter VIII. Joe went out calling.

NOVEMBER 5: Joe went to Louise. It clouded more and more. Night quiet and cool. Fine halo around the moon. Wrote at Chapter IX.

NOVEMBER 6: I finished Chapter IX. Letters from Seybt, from James Jackson, and Garrison. Joe went out calling in the afternoon to Mrs. Boyle and Mrs. Meany. At night went down town and found, quite unexpectedly, the Archbishop at home. Everything seems to be all right.

NOVEMBER 7: I wrote at Chapter X, but only two pages. It cleared in the afternoon. Mr. Schumann came, and we went out walking with him and Louise. In the evening, Koch called, and I had to go down to the Archbishop for him.

NOVEMBER 8: Letter from Cushing with $116. I went down and paid Mr. Schumann's bill and account. Left $30.— with Koch and gave $20.— to Hubert. Letter from Henry and one from Pauline. She is now at Albuquerque. I wrote to Cushing, to Gruaz, and to Mr. Balsiger. Hubert came to town. Went to the Archbishop's and read to him Chapter III and IV. Father Antonio was present also.

NOVEMBER 9: Wrote at Chapter X. I am getting a little tired. In the afternoon, Joe at home. We called on General Bradley at night, to excuse us for not coming to the reception on Thursday night. Then to Fornance's. Not at home. Finally, we dropped into Mrs. Jacob Gold's.

NOVEMBER 10: Finished Chapter X today. Fornance and wife came in the afternoon, also Louise.

NOVEMBER 11: Went down town in the morning and saw a number of people. Copied the manuscript of Don José B. Ortiz. It is from 1695–98, and 1755.[685] At night at the Archbishop's. Dow[686] from Tajique came. He says that there are no ruins east of the Salinas and west of the Rio Pecos. Joe was at Koch's in the afternoon. Trouble down there. Mother-in-law at the bottom.

NOVEMBER 12: Letter from Henry, announcing his baby.[687] Wrote at Chapter I for Cushing, but did not advance much today. Joe went to Louise in the afternoon.

NOVEMBER 13: Wrote at Chapter I the whole day, except in the morning, when I went down town. Cold and rather blustering. Grand Ball at night for General Miles.[688]

NOVEMBER 14: Letter from Papa. Finished my work for Cushing and mailed it.[689] In the afternoon, took a walk with Louise into the Santa Fe Cañón.

NOVEMBER 15: Wrote at Chapter I, Part I, for the Archbishop. It is very difficult. Joe went out to call.

NOVEMBER 16: Wrote all day at Chapter I. It is a very difficult job; especially the geological part. Went down town at 4 P.M. and met Lt. Gatewood.[690] Looks like more snow. We are very quiet and happy in our modest home. Thank God for it. Last night there was a big ball in honor of General Bradley, etc. Began to write to Papa.

NOVEMBER 17: Hubert came, and Louise, in the afternoon. I made a call at General Bradley. Met Captain Chance.[691] Wrote at Chapter I, Part I, for the Archbishop's book. It goes very slow and is difficult. Tedious work. Wrote to Papa.

NOVEMBER 18: I wrote all day. At night, got letters from Gruaz, Mr. Balsiger. Good, but F. C. R. [F. C. Ryhiner, Jr.] is at his old mean tricks again. I wish that fellow would let me alone once! I do not hurt him, why should he persecute me? General Bradley left tonight.

NOVEMBER 19: My typewriter came yesterday,[692] and Pearce helped me to arrange it. Now it works well, and I am writing with it quite easily. Last night I wrote to Cushing, to Mr. Balsiger, and to Henry. S. and M. Eldodt called.

NOVEMBER 20: Letters from F. P. Smith. Finished Chapter 1, Part I. Joe went to town and to Louise in the afternoon.

NOVEMBER 21: Wrote at Chapter II, Part I. In the afternoon, Louise came. Mr. Schumann came afterwards. I went down and called on Mr. Franz and on the Archbishop. Mr. Schumann brought us two tickets to the concert for tomorrow.

NOVEMBER 22: Was down town all day. First at the Archbishop's, where I drew $90.—. Paid Seligmans $20.—, Staab's $16.50; gave Koch $20.—. In the afternoon, helped Koch to fix the Post Hall for the concert. At night went to the concert with Cyrilla Manderfield. Woodside[693] and Eugenia Manderfield came along too. Concert very well attended. About 72 people. Gross result, $134.50.

NOVEMBER 23: Joe in bed with headache. Dreary, still what an improvement since last year! No water and bad wood, but I don't mind it much. Wrote at Chapter II. Father Antonio came; in the afternoon, Koch's. At night went to the Archbishop. Read Chapter I, Part I, to him and to Father Antonio. They are satisfied.

NOVEMBER 24: Joe better. Wrote and finished Chapter II, Part I. Mailed letter to Papa. Dr. and Meyer, from Cleveland, called. Began at Chapter III.

NOVEMBER 25: Thursday. Thanksgiving Day. We have every reason to be thankful to God for it. What a change since last year! God has been very, very good towards us, and we owe Him infinite thanks.

Day clear and not as cold as might be expected. Joe well again. We went down town about noon and took dinner at Koch's, a good, sensible, homelike dinner, turkey, of course. In the afternoon, Koch and I went out to the Indian School and then to the brewery. It was a magnificent afternoon, cold, but not a cloud, and the view superb. Spent the evening at Koch's also. The Panizzas came. Poor people, we can appreciate their feelings. A year ago today, we were in the same position, or very nearly so. God has been very, very good to us, and we owe Him thanks this day and always. May He help those poor people also as he has helped us. And may He keep us from pride, vanity, and sin.

NOVEMBER 26: Joe went to Louise in the afternoon. I was called up there also. Letter from Pauline. I wrote at Chapter III.

NOVEMBER 27: No letters. Finished the text of Chapter III. Hubert came in the afternoon. I went up to Louise and got the cauliflower.

NOVEMBER 28: Pearce came to dinner. He felt unwell. Schiff and Paul, also Koch came. Letter from Henry. After dinner, Pearce and I went out. Called on Father Defouri. Visited the Indian School. Picuries is called in the idiom of its people: *"Ping-gul-tça,"* so a Picuri boy told me. Took supper at Father Defouri's and then went home.

NOVEMBER 29: Telegram from George, calling Hubert home. Went down town and replied, also wired to Pauline. Koch came, and I rode out to Tezuque and got Hubert in with his trunk. Telegraphed to Pauline again. Hubert left at night for St. Louis.

NOVEMBER 30: No letters. It is getting very disagreeable. Wrote at Chapter IV. Nothing at all new about town. Joe went out in the afternoon and at night. I wrote till 9 P.M. and then went to Koch's also.

DECEMBER

DECEMBER 1: Letters from Cushing at last, and from C. W. Butterfield. Cushing is coming. So the trip to Mexico will probably take place. In the forenoon, Joe went to call on Mrs. Fornance. I went down town in the afternoon. Wrote at Chapter IV. Louise came.

DECEMBER 2: Went down town to make necessary calls. Saw Fornance. He told me about Cushing and the Zuñi Reservation, requesting him to speak to the Indians. Shall not forget it. In the afternoon, called on Governor Ritch and on Fornance. Wrote at Chapter IV.

DECEMBER 3: Wrote at Chapter IV. Fornance left at 10:20 P.M. I went to the depot to see them off. Joe is well. Nothing new at all. No letters. Finished Chapter IV.

DECEMBER 4: Finished the text of Chapter V. Went down town twice. In the evening at home and at work. Joe well.

DECEMBER 5: Wrote at notes and corrections in the morning. Koch called. In the afternoon, we went out to Louise and took a walk with her and Miss Neber. Fine, but chilly. Evening and night at home. It was a very pleasant day, on the whole.

DECEMBER 6: Finished Chapters IV and V. In the afternoon, Louise came, and at night Gaertner and Fischer. All three took supper with us. Very pleasant.

DECEMBER 7: Letter from Sylvester Baxter,[694] with $116.— (Thank God for it), and one from Father Navet. I went down town at once and paid my debts, then finished my Scrapbook.[695] In the afternoon, Mrs. Hartmann came, and, to my greatest surprise and joy, Otto Meysenburg![696] We spent the evening at Koch's.

DECEMBER 8: I wrote today to C. W. Butterfield, Madison, Wisconsin, to Sylvester Baxter, to Henry, and to Hubert, and mailed the letters also. In the forenoon, drove about with Meysenburg. Afternoon called on the Archbishop; Meysenburg left at night. I give him the full text of my novel along, to read, and do something for it, if he can.

DECEMBER 9: I wrote letters: to Garrison, Mr. Balsiger, James Jackson, Gruaz, and Dr. Walliser. In the afternoon, I was surprised by a very pleasant visit of Barthelmess![697] He has enlisted again, and is going to Fort Lewis, Colorado. He told me that there is more water in the mountains of northeastern Chihuahua than commonly believed. Ruins of large adobe, like those of Janos and Casas Grandes, begin in the Puertecito between the Sierra de la

Hacha and the Hachita, 15 miles west of the Espía, on the frontier line, but still within the United States territory. There are ruins on the Ojo del Perro, and three large ones near Fort Bayard.[698] Called on him at night. He is very well informed.

DECEMBER 10: Today is the anniversary of our moving in here. How different everything looks now! God has been very, very kind to us. Thousand thanks to Him and may we never become proud and forget ourselves towards Him! Wrote to Seybt, to Papa, and to Frank P. Smith. Not cold at all. Went to [Will] Tipton.[699] Father Navet called and spent the evening with us. Met Henry Holton[700] today. No trace of Cushing.

DECEMBER 11: Letters from Hubert, Henry, and W. C. Kueffner. Sent to the latter, 13 Certificates of Appearances. Went down town, gave Father Navet my manuscript, and the paper.[701] Saw the Archbishop and Father Garnier.[702] Wrote to Hubert. Began to write at Chapter I of Antiquities. It is an easy one.

DECEMBER 12: Sunday. (Nuestra Señora de Guadalupe Day.) Wrote at Chapter I (Antiquities). No letters, because mail came late. The train brought from 6 to 800 excursionists. They infest every part of the town. Eddy went hunting this A.M. with Caselo. Major Pessels came and took supper with us. Afterwards we went with him to Staab's. Rather pleasant. Gerdes and wife there.

DECEMBER 13: I went down town in the morning. No letters at all, and no Cushing either. It is very annoying. Finished Chapter I of Antiquities tonight.

DECEMBER 14: Began to write at Chapter II of Antiquities. Got $5.— from *The Nation*. Also a catalogue of the Boban Collections.[703] Wrote at once to Garrison for three or four books. Went down town, mailed the letter, bought a pair of pants, and saw Epifanio Vigil. He has a fragment of a book of the past century, containing royal instructions about the Presidio.[704] Afternoon quietly at home. Joe went down town. After supper, I went to Staab's and took leave, Mrs. Staab, Anita and Adde are going to

California tonight. Spent two hours at the Archbishop's, reading Chapter I of Antiquities.

DECEMBER 15: Wrote all day and night at Chapter II, Antiquities. It requires a good deal of work. No letters. In the afternoon Joe went out to Louise.

DECEMBER 16: Letter from Hubert: Celia died on the 12th.[705] Poor, good soul. I wrote to George at once. Also, telegram from Cushing. Have to meet him on the train tonight. Went down town. Stopped writing at Chapter II. Left for Albuquerque at 10:20 P.M. and met Father Antonio. Met Cushing at Lamy, in company with his two ladies,[706] Mr. Hodge,[707] and three Zuñis: Pala-ua-tiua and two young men.[708] Very, very pleasant on all sides. Frank looks rather as usual.

DECEMBER 17: Reached Albuquerque at 3 A.M., about. Found, at last, rooms at the Girard House.[709] Called at Altheimer's,[710] Huning's,[711] Candelaria's,[712] Father Gentile's,[713] and Father Durante's.[714] All very kind. Cushing says that the Indians of "Marata"[715] spoke another language than those of Zuñi. There are still some of them remaining alive at Zuñi. Financially, everything seems all right. Cushing telegraphed for $450.— to Boston. Saw Louis Baer and Professor N. A. Bibikov.[716] Spent the night with Cushing.

DECEMBER 18: Left Albuquerque at night, 5 A.M. at last. Got to Santa Fe at 9 A.M. Found Joe in bed at Koch's with severe headache. Extremely sleepy and tired. Letters from Mr. Balsiger. Slept nearly all day. Joe up at night, she feels well again. Good care, etc.

DECEMBER 19: Moved home again. Letters from Garrison and Butterfield. Replied to both. Very cold day, quiet and beautiful. Stayed at home. Nobody came.

DECEMBER 20: Wrote to Cushing about the Rio Gila. Louise came in the afternoon. In the morning, I went to Koch's to disarrange about Christmas. We can't be there always. They are good, kind people, but clumsy. Night cold and quiet. Bought a Christmas present for Joe. It seemed to please her much.

DECEMBER 21: Pleasant and warm. I went twice to Louise, carrying up the cacti. Copied the document about Albuquerque at the Surveyor General's Office.[717]

DECEMBER 22: Copied, for the Archbishop, the skeleton of my work in Spanish and in English. Joe went down town in the afternoon. Mr. Meany, D. D. Barrett from Washington, D.C., and Mr. Howard, called in the afternoon. At night, Mr. Meany called again.

DECEMBER 23: Letter from Baxter with $450. Stormed over town. Called on Mrs. Catron in the afternoon. Left money at the Bank.

DECEMBER 26: [No entries for December 24 and 25.] Spent a very pleasant Christmas. Eve at Louise's; Christmas night at Koch's. Got a nice Christmas card from Dr. C. Walliser yesterday and a letter from Fornance today. Yesterday, I wrote to Sam Eldodt, to Baxter, to Father Gentile, Father Navet, Mr. Huning, and to Don Joaquín.[718] Lots of kind presents last night. It was very pleasant. Marcus Eldodt, Mr. Franz and Eddy, and Miss Amalia Nehber were there also. Today it is cold but clear. We dined with Mr. Pessels at the Palace Hotel. Gerdes and wife and Mr. Wedeles[719] were there. Afterwards we called on Prestons, then walked out to the new Capitol[720] with Pearce, Louise, and Miss Nehber. Evening at Jac. Gold's.

DECEMBER 27: Packing. Running about, taking leave; took out Insurance Policy for two months. $5000. Left at 10:20 P.M. Pleasant and kind good-bye. Hope to return with good work done and material for more.[721] God bless Santa Fe and all the good people there.

DECEMBER 31: [No entries for December 28 through 30.] We reached Mexico at 8 A.M. today.

28th. 4:30 P.M. to El Paso. Trunk not there. Left check and key at the Wells & Fargo & Co., El Paso del Norte, and proceeded to Chihuahua.

29th. Sun rose at Chihuahua. A naked valley, mezquite, bare and abrupt mountains. Cerro de Tavalopa. At Chihuahua, the Rio[s] Sacramento and Chubisca meet. Tributaries of the Concho, also the Rio San Pablo. Hot Springs[722] in Chihuahua. Santa Rosalia, El Javali, Jalimes, San Diego del Monte, at 25–30 leguas southwest of the city, near Cusihuiriachi. The Tarahumares still wear sandals of yucca sometimes.[723] They dance the "Baile de los Tobosos." A horrible country. The road runs through a big flat, denuded, arid [country], only yucca and mezquite, tasajo, uña de gato, etc. It is much worse than Jornada. Absolutely treeless mountains on both sides. The [Rio] Concho mostly dry. Dusty and warm. Joe has severe headache.

30th. At Zacatecas. High plains, mountains almost out of sight. Desolate. Much *Yucca brevifolia.* Enormous trees. Farming on a large scale. Soon grew warmer as we descended to Aguas Calientes. Vegetation grew different. Opuntia enormous. Wild mountains. Much mining around Zacatecas. Also small lakes. Lagos at 3 P.M. Very fine vegetation. Night (supper) at Silao.[724] Weather fine.

31st. Beautiful volcanoes in sight. Joe well and full of joy and astonishment. Stopped at Hotel del Bazar.[725] Called on Don Joaquín. Exceedingly friendly. Everything ready for me. What a change in a year! God is favoring us, but let Him also preserve us from falling into excesses, temptation, and sin! He is good, very good, even when he strikes. God bless Papa, all our good friends, and all mankind. Letter from Seybt.

Happy New Year!

1887

JANUARY 1: Happy New Year! Took a walk with Joe to the Sócalo [Zócalo].[726] Such flowers, bouquets, roses, violets, bouvardias, magnolias, and many plants unknown. In the afternoon, called on Don Joaquín. He gave me the catalogue of his books, and Duro's[727] work on Peñalosa. It contains many interesting and valuable documents. In the evening, had a call from a young man who thought I was a miner and who therefore wanted to offer me a situation as director of a new mine. I, of course, declined but mentioned Bibikov; it may be something for him. Wrote to Koch.

JANUARY 2: Walked out to the Paseo[728] in the morning and moved to the Hotel Central. In the afternoon, went to the San Lázaro Station[729] to give Joe a glimpse of the volcanoes. Wrote to Papa, to Seybt, to Ad. Seligman, to the Archbishop, and to John Pearce. Formed the acquaintance of Mr. and Mrs. Crotti at the Café del Bazar where we take our meals. Beautiful music at the Sócalo at night and an immense throng of people. It was a true sight.

JANUARY 3: Went with Joe to the Museo Nacional.[730] There have been several additions, and the whole is in process of good arrangement. The so-called calendar stone[731] is there now, and there are a number of large pieces which were not in 1881. The garden is lovely. Trunk came all right, but it costs $16.35.[732] Nothing lost nor damaged. Wrote to George. Began copying tonight.

JANUARY 8: [No entries since that of January 3.] Always splendid weather. Still, since Tuesday, the plants in the Sócalo have suffered from light frost. Finished copying from Duro's work. Important documents. Got today letters from Papa. He is well. I saw Chavero[733] and Vigil.[734] Am crowded with gifts of books. Got Volume XV of the *Documentos inéditos*[735] for copying and returned Duro to Don Joaquín. Called on him twice. He presented me with Ribadeneiro.[736] Also Vasco de Puga.[737] Bought

Alegre[738] for $6. There is an immense amount of documents here. I am everywhere received in the kindest possible manner. The new library[739] is a magnificent building. Also at Abadiano.

JANUARY 9: Last night I wrote to Seybt and to Frank Cushing. Went out to Chapultepec [740] with Joe. It was splendid. The trees have suffered somewhat from caterpillars, and from drouth, and frost, but there are new ones planted, and other improvements. The view is simply grand. We greatly enjoyed it. Returned to the city, tired and hot. Evening at the Sócalo. Music and terrible throng of people, all happy and, of course, innocently noisy. Wrote to Mr. Schumann, to Sylvester Baxter, and to Mr. Balsiger.

JANUARY 10: Went to the Biblioteca Nacional[741] and saw Vigil. Then back to the hotel where I wrote at Chapter XII of Part II for the Archbishop. Then to Don Joaquín who presented me with Puga's "Cedulario." Then to the Biblioteca and with Vigil to the Palace[742] to call on Señor Mariscal, Minister of Foreign Affairs. Pleasant interview and permission to obtain everything at the Archives.[743] Then had a long talk with Vigil, while walking around on the Sócalo. It was splendid moonlight and the Sócalo magnificent. Joe had headache today, but it passed off well. Card from Mary S. [Suppiger?].[744]

JANUARY 11: Joe well again. Went to the Biblioteca, saw Vigil and glanced at Fray Zárate Salmerón's "Relaciones," etc. I see now that they are only abstracts. Then, I gave my Petition to the Secretary's doorkeeper and went to the Archives, where Señor Rubio[745] received me most cordially. But, what a mass of indispensable material!

The collection of Revillagigedo[746] has 4,000 pages to copy! I cannot possibly do justice to it alone. It is too much. So, after taking notes of what there is, I went home, wrote at Chapter XII, and then out to Don Joaquín, who leaves tomorrow for his hacienda. He approves of my plans fully. To copy as far as possible while here and for the rest, to have copied at 25 to 35 cents, the sheet. Music at the Sócalo. We strolled around a little, and then went home, where I wrote to the Archbishop, to Frank Cushing, and to Sylvester Baxter.

JANUARY 12: Went to the Archives and copied. Letter from Pearce. Bought the "Life of Father Antonio Margil de Jesús."[747] It is very difficult to buy books here. Abadiano has an enormous amount of books, but in the first place they are very dear. In the second, they don't know themselves what they have. Consequently, they don't sell. Copied on Fray Gerónimo de Zárate, Volume 2, "Historia":[748] [The next several journal pages were devoted to notes on this item and also to material from Gaspar de Villagrá's *Historia de la Nueva México, 1610.*][749]

These [above] copies were taken on the 13th. On the 12th, I copied at Father Gerónimo de Zárate. Felt rather unwell. We took a very long walk. Passed a miserable night. Joe has headache, and I could not sleep at all. Headache, nausea, catarrh, etc.

JANUARY 13: Felt very miserable. Sick and weak. Headache almost gone; nevertheless, I cannot eat and feel drowsy and dizzy. Went to the Archives and copied the above; then to the Biblioteca where I took Villagrá and the Laws. Met Señor Duarte and Señor Agreda.[750] Found out many things.

Until the 27th, I had many deceptions too. Wrote three chapters, got a few letters. Was snubbed at the Archbishop's and stopped at the Archives. Catarrh, headache, and everything else. The ways of work are always hard.

JANUARY 27: Wrote to Henry. Sent to Archbishop Salpointe Chapter XIV of Part II by mail with a few lines.[751] Copied. [These notations consisted of extracts from, rather than a complete copy of, Gaspar de Villagrá's "Historia de la Nueva México, 1610."]

Today, I got letter from Alphonse, at last. Thank God! He is well and kind, as always, anxiously inquiring for Papa. At the Archives, I stopped copying because of the order of the Minister, which claims: "Testimonio autorizado," that is: a $10. stamp to begin with, and $1. stamp for each sheet, in addition [Notes on Villagrá followed].

JANUARY 28: The whole of the Canto I and II (of Villagrá) is a discussion of the origin of the New Mexicans—of the Mexicans in New Mexico. Canto III, fol. 15, Fray Marcos de Nizza. [More notes from Villagrá followed.]

Wrote to Koch. Got letter from Mr. Balsiger. Went to the "Puente del Zacate" for book, but found nothing. Bought Volumes 3 and 4 of *Documentos inéditos del Archivo de Indias*. Went to the library with Joe. At night, we called on Señor Mariscal for the second time. Was very well received, and he promised to do what he could. Wrote to Eddy S. [?].

JANUARY 29: Letter from Mr. Schumann. Wrote to Gerdes and mailed the letter at 3 P.M. Wrote at the library until 1 P.M. Called on Don Antonio de Miera,[752] Calle San Agustín No. 1. Went to the Licenciado Duarte, but he was not at home. Went out to Don Joaquín and returned Villagrá. Got Ribas[753] in exchange. Called on the Licenciado Sepúlveda, but he was not at home. Padre Francisco de Florencia:[754] "Historia de la Provincia de la Compañia de Jesús de Nueva España," 1694. [Notations on this item followed; regarding Lib. I. Cap. II to XII, inclusive, Bandelier noted a few major points of interest.]

The first missions in Florida. The first coming of the Jesuits, agreeing with Alegre . . .

Lib. IV. Cap. I. (p. 202) The Bishop of Guadalajara, Don Francisco de Mendiola, asked for Jesuits. They sent him Padre Herman Suarez and Padre Juan Sanchez. The latter was a young priest yet, recently arrived. . . . The two priests went to Zacatecas.

(In general, Florencia occupies himself mostly with the first coming of the fathers to Mexico, and has nothing on Indian missions almost. He is, as usual, diffused, and only detailed on spiritual matters.)

Fray José de Arlegui. *Crónica de la santa Provincia de San Francisco de Zacatecas*, 1736[755] [Wagner (1937: II, 365–67) gave 1737]. [Bandelier then added almost a full journal page of notations on this source.]

It is an important work, but I was unable to find any reference to what tribe of Indians inhabited the Valley of Casas Grandes. Still, it appears that the buildings were in ruins and abandoned at that time [1640], and no traditions in regard to their origin.

JANUARY 30: Staid at home. Wrote at Chapter XI of 2nd Part. In the afternoon and after dinner, we went out to the Paséo Nuevo[756] and saw the [drives?]. Wrote to Ad. Fischer.

JANUARY 31: Got a lot of papers and letter from Clotilde at the Post Office. Went to the Archives. No reply yet from the Minister. Cannot do anything there. Bought Prieto's work on Tamaulipas.[757]

At the Archives, Señor Rubio told me that Conchos and Atotonilco are both in Chihuahua, but at some distance from each other. There is a mass of meteoric iron at the hacienda of San Gregorio, five leguas from Parral, and one at the hacienda of Concepción, one legua south of San Bartolomé (Allende) on the old road to the north! Of the former, there is a recollection of when it fell; of the latter, not. I finished Chapter XI, the text, tonight.

FEBRUARY

FEBRUARY 1: Wrote at the notes. Don Joaquín Sepúlveda called in the morning. Letter from Henry. He has trouble with Mali about her money. Bought the *Recopilación de Leyes de Indias*[758] for $10. Began the notes on Chapter XI. With the help I have now, I can do something. But the work is hard and difficult, and there is much research needed. God grant that it end well.

FEBRUARY 2: Everything is gala! The stores closed and everybody out. Finished Chapter XI and mailed it. Went to the library where I got permission to write my work there, and with my pen and ink. When I came home, I found letters. One from the Archbishop [Salpointe], very friendly, with $75. and one from Dr. Brühl.[759] The latter is a wonder and a surprise to me. Still it is very friendly. After 5 P.M., we went to Chapultepec. It was simply wonderfully beautiful. The draft of $75. I gave to Crotti. Wrote to Cushing and to the Archbishop.

FEBRUARY 3: Mailed my two letters. Then went to the library. I worked there until 3 P.M., making rapid advances. Then I stopped, and we went to dinner. Afterwards, at home, I continued writing. At night I got a letter from Baxter. Not satisfactory, but only owing to the fact that I did not state my plans. I did a good deal of work at Chapter I of the Third Part.

FEBRUARY 4: At the library, finished the text of the chapter and began on the notes. Crotti told me he had the books, at least several of them. In the afternoon it rained a little, a sprinkle only, but enough to borrow an umbrella from Crotti. Bought photographs. Tomorrow, there is national festival, and I cannot work until Monday.

FEBRUARY 5: Constitution Day.[760] Letter from Hubert. Wrote to Dr. Brühl. Great, gala day. At 6 A.M., 21 guns opened it. Then came a host of processions. Military; cavalry and infantry. Schools, working men, etc. with innumerable flags. It lasted until after 11 A.M. Porfirio Diaz[761] stood on the balcony, saluting the flags, etc., as they passed. He is a tall, handsome man. The Sócalo is all decorated with colored Chinese lanterns. We went around and looked at everything, including the flags of the consulates. Saw Germany, Spain, Portugal, Sweden and Norway, Peru, Chile, Honduras, the Dominican Republic, Belgium, the Swiss rag, and, of course, our own gridiron. The Mexican flag abounds. At night, the Palace, the Sócalo, and several rows of buildings were beautifully illuminated, but it soon began to rain from the east, with lightning from northeast and west, and we ran home. Wrote to F. Huning and began to write to Baxter also.

FEBRUARY 6: Finished and mailed letter to Baxter. It has twelve pages. Wrote to Papa, to Gruaz, and to John Pearce. Worked also at the notes. It was a very noisy Sunday. No letters.

FEBRUARY 7: Mailed my two letters. Dr. José Rubio, I met him on the street, and he told me that it was all right at the Archives. But I shall begin only tomorrow. Letter from Eddy [probably Huegy]. Finished Chapter I of Part III today and sent it to the Archbishop. Don Antonio Gutierrez[762] made us a very friendly call this morning. He is exceedingly kind. Father Augustin Fischer[763] expects me. Tonight, my boy told me [he] had the "Documentos" for me. I hope it is so, but doubt it yet. Wrote to Mr. Meany.

FEBRUARY 8: Went to the Archives and took a list of the documents in relation to New Mexico. They make about 1200 pages. Then I went to Guernsey. He was charming. A comical thing came out. The old gentleman who came with us from El Paso del

Norte is Señor Zazarmendi [Zarzamendi?], a friend of Baxter's, and to whom I am recommended. It is more than comical; it is almost ridiculous. In the afternoon, I began to write to Fornance. We staid at home, and I did not at all feel like working. I am actually apathic, slow, and lazy, unfit for work. Then the uncertainty about getting the books. Crotti has nothing yet.

FEBRUARY 9: Called on Don Antonio Gutierrez with my wife. Cantoral sick also. The boys had too much Sarah Bernhardt on the brain, I presume. In the afternoon, I called on Father Fischer with Don Antonio Gutierrez. It looks now as if I was going to get the books. Met Don Nicolás León of Morelia. At night, wrote to Mr. Schumann.

FEBRUARY 10: Went to the Archives and copied the Report of Archbishop Palafox y Mendoza (1642)[764] and began at that of Bonilla in New Mexico (1774).[765] Letter from Alphonse, with one of Ratzel enclosed. The Novel is not lost. Went after the books again, but—Quien sabe? It is terribly slow. At last, I obtained the fourth series, incomplete, but still the main things are there. Began to write to Alphonse.

FEBRUARY 11: Went to the Archives and copied. Found original documents from 1626 to 1639 in relation to New Mexico. These must be copied, but how? There is more and more work. We went to dinner. Then to Mrs. Crotti, and I left Joe there while I went to Don Antonio Gutierrez. At night, wrote to Alphonse. Wrote to Professor Ratzel also.

FEBRUARY 12: Beautiful day, but I could do nothing. There was no time left, as I was invited at Padre Fischer's. So Don Antonio and I went out there. Splendid dinner, wine excellent. Padre Muñez-Cano came, and we talked and talked about Cholula. Padre Campos[766] is still alive; Conchita died of consumption. Poor girl. Monica and Lupe are still at Puebla with their father and the Señor Cura. Otherwise, the people of Cholula are always the same. Wrote to Dr. Strong. No letters from nowhere. It is annoying, but I guess I will have to take it as it comes. The Padre promises to help me as much as he can, but it will take time. If only Baxter and Cushing sustain me, then I will get through all right, but time it takes at all events. And a good deal of it.

FEBRUARY 13: Met Mr. Bobo[767] on the Plaza. Bivins has swindled him to the tune of $5 to $7000. Met Agreda, Señor Gutierrez, Casilda, and Luisa called. Wrote to Father Navet. Got letter from the Archbishop and a card from Señor Zarzamendi. He cannot come this afternoon. Mailed photographs to Celia [?][768] Wrote to Mr. Balsiger. Joe and I called on Mrs. Crotti. The calls announced, [but she?] did not come. If they don't like it, they can lump it! About 8 P.M., we took a walk to the Sócalo; it was beautiful, but that terrible noise!

FEBRUARY 14: Letter from Henry. Went to the Archives and finished copying two documents. Then to the hotel and to dinner.

After this, owing to the condition of my right arm, I broke off this journal. I began again on Sunday, the 3rd of April, although with great difficulty. It is the contraction of muscles, and not the writer's cramp, that makes it so very difficult to use.[769]

In the interval, wrote at the Archives and at the hotel, and gathered much more than I, in fact, [expected]. Eusebio is helping me a good deal. Have now two copyists engaged, one at the library on Villa-Señor,[770] Volume II, and one here on the Rudo Ensayo;[771] besides, Antonio Gutierrez. The latter is slow "y muy borracho" [and very drunk]. During the 45 days of interruption of this journal, the following were the important days and occurrences.

FEBRUARY 24: Louis Huning and wife[772] surprised us suddenly. They staid until the following week and then went to the coast.

MARCH

MARCH 7: Joe and I went to Amecameca.[773] Beautiful and clear. The volcanoes splendidly near.

MARCH 10: Hunings returned from the coast.

MARCH 12: Professor Henry A. Ward[774] came. Spent the evening with us.

MARCH 14: Joe left for home with Hunings,[775] and I remained alone at the Hotel Central, until the 2nd of April, when I moved out to Padre Augustin Fischer's at San Cosme, where I now take up this journal again and hope to be able to continue it.

APRIL

APRIL 3: At the Parroquia of San Cosme and quiet for the first time in Mexico! Beautiful day. Good room. Fine view and,—*no noise.* The latter is the main thing. Yesterday, I mailed letters to Joe at Albuquerque, to F. Huning, to Gruaz, and to Henry. Today, I wrote to Alphonse and to George Hoffmann. Forgot to state that yesterday I also mailed letter to Mr. Schumann. It is wonderfully quiet here!

Antonio de León y Pinelo: *Tratado de Confirmaciones Reales,* 1628, Parte Ia, Cap. VII. f. 41. V.[776]

[Bandelier then made several pages of notes.]

(Here I stopped copying as Padre Fischer told me he had a duplicate copy of León y Pinelo, which I could get.)

Montemayor: "Sumarios."[777]

APRIL 4: Worked at the Archives until 2 P.M., making considerable advances. Had an interesting talk with Padre Fischer this evening, until Monsignor Gillod came at 9 P.M. when I retired. Copied six sheets today.

APRIL 5: Copied at the Archives. Met Treviño. Night before last, Padre Fischer told me that he had seen the Tonkaways, in Texas, eat human flesh![778] [More notations on Montemayor followed.]

APRIL 6: Today is a day of Joy! Letter from Papa, and a very nice one from dear Joe. She is getting "way up in the world," moving about on visiting tours, going into wine cellars, etc. Also got letter from Will Barnes.[779] Finished at last the copy of the documents on Otermín's retreat to El Paso.[780] Evening with the Padre.

APRIL 7: Went to Mass, which lasted over two hours. Padre Plancarte preached and Monsignor Guillo said Mass. Monsignor Gillod and Señor Menacho took dinner with us. I copied and slept. Monsignor Davis called in the afternoon. Padre Fischer suffering. Began to write to Joe tonight.

APRIL 8: Good Friday. Slept wonderfully, for the first time. Day rather like yesterday. Ceremonies began at 9 A.M. I went to the choir with Don Joaquín and Juan Martinez del Cerro;[781] lasted until 11 A.M. Finished letter to Joe.

[Notations on Montemayor's "Sumarios" followed.]

APRIL 9: Went to church at night with Luis García.[782] Padre Morales preached, but I could not understand a word, owing to bad acoustics. Went to town. Called on Don Antonio Gutierrez and sent bouquet to Doña Casilda. Got letters: from Papa, from Fornance, from Baxter (very unsatisfactory), from Bertha for Joe. Saw Eusebio, Crotti, Suger, etc. It is very unsatisfactory to keep on working and working without any result. And without any support. Wrote to Joe. Immense crowds.

APRIL 10: Painted. Don Antonio came and took dinner with us; also Monsignor Gillod.

[More notes on Montemayor's "Sumarios" followed.]

APRIL 11: Found at the hotel letters from Joe and from Mr. Balsiger. Wrote to Joe as soon as I came home. I copied the whole of Ayeta's letter of 1676 with documents annexed.[783] Made another application to Mariscal, this time for the *Ramo de Tierras*.[784]

APRIL 12: I had a very good sleep, and therefore rose early. Went to town and copied at the Declaraciones. Day as usual. Got a letter from Francis [Franz?] Huning. The Padre may go to Morelia for a few days.

APRIL 13: Got letter from Baxter and from Alphonse. Copied at the Archives; went home early and copied at Pedro de Rivera.[785] Padre Fischer gave me Beristain.[786] It is a perfect streak of luck that I have in contact with him.

APRIL 14: Went to town after writing a letter to Baxter, then to Guernsey and telegraphed to him [Baxter]. Did not work today, as I am too mad and waiting for reply besides. It is a miserable, mean situation; if Baxter's reply is not exactly favorable, I shall at once resign. I cannot stand this treatment any longer. Spent a rather poor evening and went to bed early.

APRIL 15: Got telegram from Mr. Baxter, very favorable. I at once mailed the letter to him and wrote another one to dear Joe. I got my books and am happy for the time being. Also got the copy of "Documentos," which Antonio has been doing. The boy is simply "borracho," and I will not give him any more work.

APRIL 16: Went to town. The permission to consult the Archives to their full extent is here. Thank God. Got the money at last, after much trouble. That British pup, Waters, would not accept the draft on the strength of the telegram, and Suger got mad and took and paid the draft himself. I at once bought Albarez–Abreu: "Victima Real Legal."[787] Got letter from Joe and replied to it at once. My chin is sore again. It is a very bad thing.

APRIL 17: The Cura presented me with Valarde's: *Retorica Christiana.*[788] Wrote to the Archbishop and to Papa. Justino Rubio dined with us.

APRIL 18: My chin being very sore, I consulted Dr. Flores, who gave me white precipitate diluted in cod liver oil, to anoint with, and brom-hydrate of quinine to take. Padre Fischer and Dr. Kaska left this morning very early for Morelia. Went to town only for a short time. No letters. Copied at the report of Rivera. Wrote to Dr. Walliser.

APRIL 19: Indoors all day. Chin improving. Finished to copy Rivera. I am decidedly improving, but will stay indoors until completely healed.

APRIL 20: Feel better. Went to the Archives and there found a series of very important documents, from 1604 on. They are the beginning of the complaints against the Franciscans in New Mexico and extend to 1639.[789] I copied, paleographing.

APRIL 21: Got letter from Joe with one from Alphonse. Copied at the Archives. At the hotel, Ribera is very sick.

APRIL 22: Copied at the Archives. Saw Crotti's, Aberto, etc. Took a big cold.

APRIL 23: Big Catarrh again. I am tumbling from Charybdis into Scylla. Bad chin, bad cold, etc. Copied. Bought *Villadiego*[790] for ten reales! Copied at the Archives. Padre Fischer came home at 7 P.M. He is very well pleased with his trip and has, among others, found another book from the 16th century, heretofore completely unknown. It is written in the Tarasca-idiom of Michoacan. Wrote to Joe.

APRIL 24: Suger told me that the $75.- draft had been protested. Was in very bad humor in consequence of it.

APRIL 27: [No entries for April 25 and 26.] Three dreary days spent in copying at the Archives. Wrote to the Archbishop on the 26th and mailed it today. Finished copying the documents of 1617.[791] They are very important. Letter from Joe at last. Returned Rivera to Don Joaquín on Sunday. Am going to make a catalogue of Father Fischer's library day after tomorrow.[792] Began copying again at Montemayor's—on Indians.

APRIL 28: Was about 24 hours without food—again. At last, I could not stand it any longer and talked to the Padre. I must have a regular breakfast. Then I can stand it. Wrote eight pages today, copying a whole document in series of documents of 1636.[793] They are exceedingly valuable. No letters. Wrote a short one to Joe.

APRIL 29: Met Zarzamendi. Copied another document from 1636. It is a series of acts and official papers about excommunication by the Franciscans in New Mexico and in 1636.[794] No letters. It is getting very lonesome. No letters, no money, only trouble and work. If I only could go home. Don Justino Rubio called on the Padre and took supper with us. It was a very interesting evening, full of new facts, but—what does it amount to?

APRIL 30: Went to the Archives and finished copying two documents. No letters. Nothing. No funds. Went home and began the catalogue of Father Fischer's pamphlets, etc. Volume I, alone, contains 167 documents.

MAY

MAY 1: Finished the volume of documents. Letter from the Archbishop and Father Gentile. Wrote to the Archbishop at once. It is almost distressing. If I only can get home! Soon, soon! As soon as possible! I am so terribly homesick. Cannot do anything for the Father now, for I must work head over heels at the Archives.

MAY 2: Went to the Archives and found the *Reales Cedulas* of 1631 and 1636.[795] Copied at the "Carta" of the Cabildo of Santa Fé, 1639.[796] It is terrible against the Franciscan missionaries. Father Fischer went out today. No letters.

MAY 3: Spent the day at the Archives.

MAY 4: Today I found, at last, the "Real Cedula" of 1643, about the assassination of Governor Don Luis N. Roxas [Rosas].[797] Besides, there is a whole lot of other cedulas of importance there, on New Mexico also.[798] There is a great step taken now towards completion of the work here, and I may calmly look forward to the arrival of funds, then pack up and go home.[799] Saw Don Joaquín and Vigil. There is a very bracing and lively atmosphere, cool and fine. I seem to live again. But no letters at all.

MAY 5: Great National Holiday.[800] I assisted José María Gutierrez and started him in making the catalogue of the Father's books. Went to town afterwards. Letter from Henry and a paper from Gruaz. Afterwards, the Father and I met, as arranged, at Don Joaquín's. Saw nothing of the whole festival. My foot very sore.

MAY 6: I went to the Archives. Finished copying there. Got two letters, one from Joe and one from Baxter. The latter is satisfactory so far, but the former made me very mad. Joe had not yet called on the Archbishop! It is utterly inconceivable.[801] Then there was also a painful letter from Papa. He is unwell, still, the hand is firm. I went to Guernsey, and they telegraph to Boston to see whether I can leave soon. It looks at least as if I was going to be relieved and could go home—at last! It is high time.

MAY 7: Went to the Archives and copied. Then drew $200. Handed the check (250.49) to Crotti and got $105 of him, [of] which I gave $80 to Father Fischer.

MAY 8: Splendid day. [Notes on Montemayor's "Sumarios" followed.] Went to town. No letters. Called at Don Antonio's, at Altamirano's (nobody at home), and, finally, at the German ministers!
[No entries from May 9 through May 23.][802]

MAY 24: I arrived at Santa Fe yesterday at 5:15 A.M. Found everything and everybody all right. At Los Lunas, where I spent the 22nd inst. with Hunings, I found out that there is a pueblo near Los Lunas, called San Clemente, and whose Tigua name is *Be-Juy-Tu-y,* or Pueblo del Arco Iris [Pueblo of the Rainbow].[803] It was a village of the Piros, and its ruins are almost one-half mile northeast of Los Lunas. Mr. Huning told me it was the Manzanares Grant. Today, I called around everywhere, and in the afternoon we went to Louise.

MAY 25: Went down town. Saw Hartmann and Meany. Letter from Mr. Balsiger. At noon, Dr. Strong called, soon after Dr. W. Eggert, and finally the Archbishop. The latter is very well pleased with my work so far. Wrote and mailed letters for Father Fischer, to Crotti, and to Don Joaquín.[804] Got letter from Mr. Balsiger. Fixed the flowers.

MAY 26: Wrote to Don Antonio Gutierrez and to Don Justino Rubio. Letter from F. Huning. Fixed our cactuses and the other plants. The porch, as now decorated with plants, looks exceedingly nice and well. Hartmann spent the evening with us and took supper. Eddy is sick.

MAY 27: Wrote to F. Huning, returning the letter of Schuster[805] to him. To Louis Huning, enclosing in the letter a ten dollar bill for the ten dollars Mrs. Huning lent me last Sunday. Also wrote to Don J. M. Vigil and to Guernsey, and mailed the German Vortrag [lecture] to the German minister at Mexico, one copy to Dr. F. Kaska, and to Altamirano; to Guernsey and to Janvier,[806] each, one copy of the *Romantic School.*[807] Letter from Henry. Wrote to Professor Norton and to S. Baxter. Louise came.

MAY 28: Wrote to Alphonse and went down town. No letters. I went out to the brewery and spent two hours with Dr. Strong very pleasantly and quietly, while Joe had her friends at home. Today, 3 to 400 Jicarrilla [*sic*] Apaches passed through Santa Fe;[808] I began on Chapter II of Part 3 and wrote eight pages.

MAY 29: I finished the text of my chapter. Kochs, Schumann, and Hubert took supper with us. Marcus Eldodt also called.

MAY 30: I worked the whole day at my chapter and only went down town for a few minutes at about 5 P.M. Could not finish the chapter fully, owing to my eyes.

MAY 31: Finished the chapter and began on #3. Went down town, bought four fuchsias for Joe, received at the Post Office papers from Papa—his articles on Venezuela in the *New Yorker Staatzeitung.*[809] At home, I began on #3. It is slow work, for the material is so large, and field new to me, almost. We went out to Fischer's at 5 P.M. and spent the evening very pleasantly.

JUNE

JUNE 1: Wrote on Chapter III all day, except when I went down to see Dr. Eggert and Father Deraches. Pessels took supper and spent the evening with us, and Hubert also came.

JUNE 2: Wrote on the third chapter all day and very nearly finished it. Joe went down town in the afternoon.

JUNE 3: Finished my chapter and took it down to the Archbishop's, where I met Father Seux. Letter from Henry. Louise Fischer and her niece called, and Joe went with them to Gerdes, but soon returned, and Louise staid with us. Father Mailluchet and his brother called. Grasshoppers are destroying the Pecos Valley completely.

JUNE 4: I began at the second chapter of the last part ... and finished it on Tuesday, the 14th. It has 46 pages, text, and eight pages, notes. Along with it go 256 groundplans and 16 photographs. The plans and photographs I deposited with Hartmann and the chapter, I gave the Archbishop. On the 8th of June, I got a friendly letter from Baxter, on the 11th, a ribbon for my typewriter. On the 13th, letters from Professor Norton, from Justino Rubio, and Henry. The latter is incomprehensible. On Sunday I was ill.

JUNE 14: I began at Chapter III of the seventh part. In the afternoon, Louise, Miss Gold, and Mrs. Staab called.

JUNE 15: I got my other typewriter ribbon this morning. Finished the chapter this night. It has 11 plans and two plates.

JUNE 16: Last night was the concert for the hospital, and Joe went with Hubert. I went down town. Got letter from Baxter with check for $50. Saw Sam Eldodt. Sent the $50. check (fifty dollars) to George Hoffmann at once. Set up my typewriter again and began on Chapter IV of Part VII. Chapter III and the 13 plates, I left with the Archbishop. Sam Eldodt spent the evening with us, taking supper. Also Marcus came, but only for a moment. It was really nice and agreeable.

JUNE 17: Began to assort the plates for Chapter IV and wrote at the Chapter. Spent the evening at Fischer's.

JUNE 18: Assorted the plates. Made arrangements for the binding, to be done here. In the afternoon, Joe had her usual coffee party. To my great surprise, J. C. Pilling from Washington called in company with Professor Thomson. It was very pleasant. I spent the evening with them at the Palace.

JUNE 19: Finished the plates to Chapter IV as far as scratching and titles are concerned.[810] Spent the evening at Koch's. Letter from Dr. Walliser.

JUNE 20: Painted all day. Evening tolerably fair.

JUNE 25: [No entries for period of June 21 through June 24.] The week passed off as usual. I finished two chapters and turned them over to the Archbishop, making seven in all, up to date, and in one month. Also arranged them for binding and arranged with the binder. Today wrote to Baxter, to Father Fischer, and to J. C. Pilling. Went to the brewery with Koch.

JUNE 26: Painted at the manta of the Malinche. Mr. Schumann came. Evening at the brewery. Mr. Hochmuth of St. Louis was there.

JUNE 27: Went down town and turned 101 plates over to the binder. Met Longuemare[811] and had a long talk with him about the Quivira. He is becoming very reasonable now. Called on the Archbishop and got $30. from him. Letter from George. Replied at once. Hartmann spent the evening with us. Began at Chapter VI, Part VII.

JUNE 28: Wrote steadily. Louise came in the afternoon. Of course it clouded in the afternoon and blew from the southeast and east and thundered around us. Louise was here all afternoon.

JUNE 29: Got a letter from Baxter with $116.—for June. Paid rent to 9th of July and all my little debts in town, except Fischer. Then finished the text of Chapter VI and went at the notes.

JUNE 30: No mail until noon. Finished Chapter VI completely and commenced on No. VII. I was called down to the Doctor's by Meany's son to assist at a reading, but went to the Archbishop's instead. I cannot afford to be with society that has no other object but entertainment.

J U L Y

JULY 1: Began on Chapter VII. Letter from Vigil, from Professor Ward, from Alphonse, and a card from Henry. He is on the way. Went to Staab's and spent rather a lonesome hour there. Joe goes tomorrow whether Henry arrives or not. It makes no difference. He has fooled us for fifteen months, and I don't feel like being fooled again.

JULY 2: No work today. Joe left with Koch's early, and Henry came.[812] So I ran about with him all day. At night, Hubert came, and we spent a pleasant evening all together. Henry is not yet decided as to what he will do. The country does not suit him. He is green yet and looks at everything with eastern eyes and ideas.

JULY 3: Have a slight headache. Dr. Eggert came and kept us for three-and-one-half-hours. In the afternoon, I went to Dr. Strong's. Evening, we spent at the brewery.

JULY 4: Festivities all right, as long as you keep out of it. Still, I had to go to the races. Evening at home.

JULY 5: Letter from Pilling. Joe came home tonight, sound, safe, and contented. She had a pleasant time at San Juan. Today, I took a room at Padilla's for Henry, and he slept there for the first time.

JULY 6: Wrote to Don Justino Rubio, to Baxter, and to Papa. Worked with Hartmann till 9 P.M. at the map.[813] Wrote also at Chapter VII, Part VII, but only a few pages. Eddy is sick. Hartmann and Louisa took supper with us, and afterwards Joe went with her and Henry to the music and thence to the brewery, too. No letters. I did not go to town the whole day.

JULY 7: I discontinued my journal until the evening of the 19th of July, when I make the following notes. The rain began on the 13th of July; Sunday, the 17th, and Tuesday, the 19th, were beautifully clear and cool. The first rise of the river took place on Friday, the 15th, after a violent storm from the south. It rained heavily nearly all afternoon of the 18th, from the south also. I finished Chapter VII, Part VII, and commenced at Chapter VIII, but had to work at the plates, etc., so that I could not finish it. One volume of the plates is in the printer's hands to be bound and will be finished this week yet, and he has now 100 plates more to bind, besides the plans, etc.

On the 12th of July, I wrote to Professor Ward, to F. P. Smith, enclosing a check for $11, and to Garrison, enclosing a check for $6. On the 18th, I wrote to Mr. Balsiger, to Seybt, to Meysenburg, to Baxter, to Cushing, and to Dr. Walliser. Today, I wrote to Dr. Brühl, to Papa, to Vigil, to Altamirano, to Peñafiel,[814] to A. Ernst,[815] to James Jackson, to Dr. Frenzel, to the *Ausland,* and to Alphonse. Sixteen letters in two days. On the 16th, I got the four books from Washington; on the 17th, a letter from Baxter, on the 18th, Ribas, and a letter from Father Fischer at last. Am tired. Henry is improving. Louise was here today. Joe went with her to the Plaza and then up to the brewery.

JULY 20: I finished the text of the very last chapter of the book without the notes. Quite a surprise: S. G. [*sic*] Evans[816] called! Spent the afternoon with him at the brewery. It was very pleasant, and the air was delightful. Henry was with us. At night Hubert called, and we spent quite a pleasant evening.

JULY 21: Letter from Alphonse, sending me one of James Vautier[817] which says that Aunt Sauvant is in very critical condition. Finished Chapter VIII, Part VIII; brought [it] down to the Archbishop and then began at Chapter I, Part V. Hartmann got a big boy today. Joe went to town early. We took supper at Koch's. The binding is going along nicely and first volume nearly done.

JULY 22: Letter from Garrison with receipts. Joe went up to Louise's in the afternoon, and I wrote all day and evening. No letters.

JULY 23: Finished Chapter I, Part V, and brought it down to the Archbishop. No letters. Book at the printers ready. In the evening, went to the Archbishop and had a nice little talk with him. Louise came for a moment.

JULY 24: Koch came up at 6 A.M. to tell us that the house of Rafael Lopez[818] had burnt down completely, with store, goods and all. Nothing saved and not insured. Poor man.

Went to Mass as usual. Father Garnier preached, and Father Rolly sang Mass. No letters. We left on foot for the north, Henry and I, and walked about five miles, due north of the brewery. Delightful view of the cañón very handsome.

JULY 25: An uneasy night. A little before 2 A.M. (somewhere about 1:30 A.M.), I felt what I thought to be two very slight earthquake shocks. I put this down as a memorandum, as I [am] not sure of it at all. Mr. Schumann, who has been to Las Vegas yesterday, told me that a certain Dr. Nauer assured him that there are ruins, with much pottery, at Las Peñitas, in southeastern San Miguel County. Also that the Yerba del Pueblo,[819] mashed and with pulverized sugar, was an excellent remedy against ants. It kills them slowly, but surely. Met Professor Longuemare. He is full of Quivira as usual. Joe had company, so I bummed about town. Joe not very well.

JULY 26: Letter from F. P. Smith. (He is now at New York.) Wrote all day at Chapter II, Part V. Mr. Franz arrived.

JULY 27: Letter from Mr. Balsiger. Joe sick and in bed, but better at night. Wrote at my Chapter II, Part V, finishing the text. This afternoon, young Houck,[820] Creamer's partner, was killed by an explosion of the soda apparatus while charging it. Gloom all over town. No music in the plaza. Got [?] and paid it.

JULY 28: Joe well again. Finished my Chapter and returned it. Got my plans in order to mount them. Letter from Papa. He is willing to come! Also one from Meysenburg. Louise called.

JULY 29: Henry assisted me in fixing my plates and plans today, but we stopped by nightfall, owing to a confusion in numbering. Miss Nehber called. I went down town. Hubert spent the evening with us. No letters.

JULY 30: I worked at the plates with Henry until 3 P.M. and then went out to the brewery to meet Dr. Strong. Joe went down town too. Both of us had a few pleasant hours, each in his way. At the Archbishop's, I met my old friend, the Governor of San Ildefonso. He confirmed the fact about the caves of Puyé as having belonged to the people of Santa Clara, and said that San Ildefonso, when the Spaniards came, stood on the west bank of the river, where Peragé is, or near by. Got a letter from Rubio.

JULY 31: Went to church and then to the Archbishop's and to the priests. In the afternoon, I wrote to Father Fischer. Epifanio Vigil called, then Koch. Spent the evening at the brewery with Schumann, Pessels, Hubert, and the usual crowd. It was very lively and pleasant.

AUGUST

AUGUST 1: We have all more or less headache. Got a letter from Texas. Shall not reply to it; it looks like fraud. Got my books, etc., from Mexico, together with a charming letter from Peñafiel. Wrote to him, and to Frank Cushing. Brought the third volume down to the binders. Tonight, there is again trouble between the old hag and Eddy. He went down town and [_?_ _?_ _?_] and then got drunk. She is a witch!

AUGUST 2: Began to work on Chapter III, Part V, with the machine. The hand is almost inserviceable. I wrote this on Friday, the 5th, and cannot recollect what I did on Tuesday. We had fine weather though, of this I am positive.

AUGUST 3: Today, I got very welcome letters. One is from Baxter with $116. and the other is from Don Joaquín.[821] Both are good! I went to town and paid Mr. Schumann $35. and then home in very good spirits. God is very good to me; much more than I deserve it; because I am a very great offender as towards Him! Well, I presume he does it on account of Joe, and so I take it as a gift, or present.

AUGUST 4: Wrote nearly all day, except in the morning, when I went down town for awhile. In the afternoon, Hartmann brought me the maps. In the forenoon, early, Don Abelardo Román called. At night: Pessels—Tuo [Duo] fasciunt collegium. [We two make a school.]

AUGUST 5: Got news of St. Louis earthquake.[822] It is very hot and dry. All gardens and fields are suffering, and if it does not rain very soon [what will be left?]. Finished Chapter III, Part V, today and brought it down to the Archbishop, where I met Father Lestra[823] of Socorro.

AUGUST 6: My birthday, and a very, very pleasant one at that. Present upon present came in from the good, kind people, but the nicest is from Joe, a beautiful cup and saucer. Letter from Mali. Finished six maps for the Atlas today, and brought them to the binder at once. At night, we had a little gathering of a few friends. It was very pleasant.

AUGUST 7: Henry and I took a stroll in the afternoon, and we called on Father Defouri and finally also at Koch's. At night, Mr. Franz, his daughter, and Eddy called. Hubert took supper with us.

AUGUST 8: Got a letter from Dr. Walliser, and in the afternoon, letters of congratulation from Rosalie and her brat. We scratched and fixed up the plates for Volume IV, and I brought them down to the binder. Mrs. Clara Fergusson (Clara Huning),[824] Mrs. Koch, and Minnie spent the evening with Joe til 5 P.M. At night, both Louises called. I accompanied them back to the brewery.

AUGUST 9: Very friendly letter from Dr. Brühl. Eddy and Henry are going out to Tezuque. I worked the whole day, finishing at last the "Manta de la Malinche," of Cochiti. At night, Joe went down town, and Father Navet arrived suddenly.

AUGUST 10: Father Navet took dinner with us, and I spent the afternoon with him. We went to Father Defouri together. I did not work anything today. Letter from Papa. And still no rain. Everything is terribly dry and if it does not rain soon even the corn will be lost.

AUGUST 11: At noon a thunderstorm broke out, and a succession of clouds emptied themselves over us with quite copious rains. At last the spell is broken! I finished the maps, working all day. No letters for me today, but Joe got one from Lizzie. I am glad the maps are done; they gave me a good deal of work, but now it's over at last.

AUGUST 12: Very friendly letter from Seybt. Went down town to the Archbishop, etc. He lent me a fragment of Velasco. Wrote to

Papa and to Alphonse. Hubert came at night. Commenced at Chapter IV, Part V, this afternoon.

AUGUST 13: Found a small spider in the kitchen, of the "Indian terror" species! I finished the text of Chapter V at noon and then went to the brewery, where I met Dr. Strong; Symington also came. At night, we had a call from Koch. Letter from Hodge. Frank Cushing is sick!

AUGUST 14: Went to Mass. Wrote in the afternoon: to Seybt, to Dr. Brühl, and to Meysenburg. Mr. Schumann and Mr. Franz called in the afternoon. Spent the evening, after 8 P.M., at the brewery.

AUGUST 15: Finished Chapter IV, Part V; Joe went calling. At night Hubert came. No letters for me, but Joe got one from Bertha. All well. I wrote to Mr. Balsiger.

AUGUST 16: I wrote and finished Chapter V, Part V, today and brought it down. Met Padre Gentile from Albuquerque. Louise was up in the afternoon. It is her usual day. Am again sore in my left mouth-corner. Wrote to Alois Widmer[825] tonight.

AUGUST 17: I wrote the whole day at Chapter I, Part VI, finishing the text. At night a heavy blow from the southeast, but it soon quieted. Night very cool.

AUGUST 18: Papa's birthday! Let us hope that he will be able to celebrate the next one with us here. Ad. Fischer's birthday also. I did not do much. Went up to the brewery in the morning. In the evening, we ran up there also and spent the evening. It was very nice. No letters. Trains very irregular again. Henry worked at the roof of the portal, but had to interrupt at noon. The sun is too hot yet for him.

AUGUST 19: Henry worked at the roof again. If the strips were here, he would finish it tomorrow. No letters. I finished Chapter I, Part VI, today, completely. Mrs. Bartlett and Miss Webb called in the afternoon. Our old woman is sick again today. Mr. Meany and the Doctor fell out this morning.

AUGUST 20: Henry fixed the roof as far as he could, but the strips not having been sent, he cannot finish it. I wrote at Chapter II, Part VI. Card from Baxter. Cushing is very sick. Poor boy. Our water supply is extremely unsettled; once gushing, again it stops suddenly. I wrote to Frank Cushing and to Baxter.

AUGUST 21: Last night at 8:40 P.M., about, while I was sitting at the east window of the kitchen, there was an extremely brilliant flash of bluish, electric light. It lasted longer than lightning and was brighter. It illuminated the corral and everything with a fearfully intense glare and remained thus for about five or ten seconds. About five minutes afterwards, a very distant rumbling noise, like an explosion or camera shot, seemed to proceed from the west. Morning foggy, then cleared.

Henry also saw what he thought was lightning and heard the sound, which was followed by a long roar, like that of an earthquake passing off. The old woman also saw it and heard it. She says it was in the west.

Father Garnier and Hubert both saw the meteor last night. It was very large, nearly the size of the moon, and flashed across the sky from east to west. The flash was seen by many and the detonation distinctly heard.

Joe went to church with Louise. I went to Mass and afterwards wrote to Dr. Walliser. No letters for us.

W. Spiegelberg also saw the meteor. The illumination appeared like that of electric light, bluish. The body somewhat larger than one half of the full moon, and the train, fiery red in the center. From what Hubert tells, the meteor exploded nearly over San Ildefonso and did not reach the horizon. The detonation was heard two to three minutes after the explosion. I wrote concerning it, to Ed. Johnson, Española.

Mr. Schumann and Mr. Franz came up in the afternoon. Joe and Henry went to the music, and I wrote to Ratzel and to Professor Horsford.[826] Began article for Haren also.

AUGUST 22: Finished Chapter II, Part VI. No letters. Joe went down town to Miss Franz.[827] Henry worked at a dough-board and at my typewriter.

AUGUST 23: John Jonsen, Norwegian carpenter, came to me with a letter from Ed. Johnson at Española. He saw the meteor explode, between 8 and 9 P.M., as he was returning home to Española from the Polvadera, by the trail crossing the mesa. It was dark and rainy, and he lost his way in the timber. A sudden brilliant flash of dazzling bluish light illuminated the whole country. A round body, as large as the full moon, appeared in the zenith. It was of a bluish color and at once exploded with a terrific, hissing noise and a loud report, the loudest he ever heard. Sparks flew in every direction and then fell down, most of them falling perpendicular. From his impression, it exploded east of him about two miles, somewhere about the Vallecito, or about 40–45 miles west of Santa Fe, as he thinks it was due west of Española.[828]

Dr. Brühl's book[829] came this morning by express. It is beautifully bound and seems to be a fair work. This A.M., Eddy showed me his sweet corn. It is eaten up by brown *Cetonidae,* who creep into the ears by dozens at one ear. Letters: from James Jackson, Paris, and from the *Ausland.* The latter places at my disposal RM: 200.85. I at once went down town and drew a draft for that amount in favor of the First National Bank.

Louise spent the afternoon with us. Began at Chapter III, Part VI. Wrote to Dr. Karl Müller, Stuttgart, and to Dr. Brühl. Volume IV bound and delivered.

AUGUST 24: Letters from: Baron von Waecker, Gotter, Mexico, and from the *National Zeitung,* announcing the sending of $26.04 for my article on "Chalchiuapan."[830] At last! Joe and Henry went down town. Joe with Miss Franz to Mrs. Willie Spiegelberg's[831] and to Mrs. Staab. Wrote at Chapter III, Part VI. Went down town also. Wind easterly. The west clear. Weeded the front of house.

AUGUST 25: Joe has got a slight attack of headache. The strips came yesterday at last, and Henry can begin today finishing the roof. If only I can find a situation for the good, faithful boy. He is so kind, so faithful and true.

Two very excellent letters, one from old Widmer and one from Father Meckel. Both very kind. Wrote and finished *text* of Chapter III, Part VI. Henry put the strips on. Joe went down town with Louise. Wrote to the German Minister at Mexico and to Father Meckel. Went down to Koch's. He went to Glorieta.

AUGUST 26: Finished Chapter III, Part VI, and brought the Chapter down to the Archbishop. Sent Chapter III, Part III, to Father Navet; finished the article for Haren and mailed it to him at East Las Vegas. Joe went up to Louise's. Ed out to Tezuque. Wrote W. P. Garrison about Bourke's "Snake Dance" of the Moqui.[832] Went down town and was suddenly taken ill at Mr. Schumann's. Had to go to bed. Hubert was up here.

AUGUST 27: Feeling better. Wrote on Chapter IV, Part VI. It is a rather difficult job. Wrote to Charley Kaune and painted a kind of would-be comical paper. No letters today, and nothing new at all.

AUGUST 28: Lost my pocket book! Don't know where. Went to Mass. Got letters, from Baxter with $116.—check, and one from Dr. Brühl. The novel seems to loom up at last. Wrote at once to Pretorius to send his chapters to Dr. G. Brühl. Wrote to S. Baxter and to Dr. Brühl also. Went down to Bartsch's[833] with Henry and then home, where I wrote at the notes of my chapter. Went up to Fischers.

AUGUST 29: At home, there must have been tall fussing. Eddy got terribly drunk out at Tezuque, and he came home only about 8 P.M. This morning, he is meek and has swollen eyes. The whole day magnificent beyond description. It was so beautiful that I sent Joe out of the house. Worked on Chapter IV, Part VI. Padre André called to bid good bye. He is sorry to go and hates to leave. No letters.

AUGUST 30: No letters. I worked at Chapter IV all day. Father Antonio called. He proposes to me to go to the Cañón de Chaca with him next week. I am undecided yet as to whether to go or not. Will see. Henry had again a slight attack of fever. I wrote at the notes. Henry went up home with Louise and came back to bring us the *Westliche Post.*

AUGUST 31: Went down town early and got, at the Post Office, letter from Peñafiel and all the manuscripts from Father Fischer which I had ordered. I went also to Wedeles, but could do nothing at all, on account of Marcus Eldodt. Wrote at Chapter IV, Part VI. Finished text. I am in bad humor all day in consequence of Eldodt. Went down town with Henry at night and spent an hour at Billy's with Koch.

SEPTEMBER

SEPTEMBER 1: Got news of Aunt Sauvant's death today by letters from Alphonse and Adolphe Vautier.[834] She was 86 years and nearly six months old. Requiescat in pacem! I am losing all my feelings for people abroad and in Switzerland especially. Alphonse excepted.

Letter from Camilo Padilla also. He is a good boy. Finished Chapter IV, Part VI, and delivered it too. Paid my bill at the *New Mexican*[835] and also that of the Archbishop's, but he paid it, himself, back, $38. Wrote to Meysenburg and to Padre Fischer. Hubert and Miss Nehber and Major Pessels called. Pleasant.

SEPTEMBER 2: At the Agency of the Pueblo Indians: Total number of Indians of the Pueblos in New Mexico (Moquis excepted) is 8,337; 2,101 children between 5 and 16 years of age, 780 at school. 4,068 males; 4,269 females. 2,279 males above 18 years; females 2,347. Taos, 377; Picuries, 108; San Juan, 370; San Ildefonso, 139; Santa Clara, 189; Nambé, 76; Pojuaque, 16; Tezuque, 91; Cochiti, 302; Santo Domingo, 917; San Felipe, 483; Santa Ana, 222; Cia, 106; Jemez, 518; Sandia, 120; Isleta, 1,022; Laguna, 1,152; Acoma, 582; Zuñi, 1,547.

I was down town nearly all forenoon. Called on Gerdes, on Ed. Deutsche, on Father Defouri, on Hartmann, etc. Wrote at Chapter V, Part VI. Henry had an attack of fever, but it passed off. Wrote to Alphonse and to Vick's. There is an outlook for Henry at last! Hubert called at night.

SEPTEMBER 3: Letter from Papa at last. Worked at Chapter V, Part VI. Henry will probably get a situation at Wedeles and Eldodt. We made a short call at General Grierson[836] and at Koch's. Afterwards, I had to go down again, and fell in with Pessels.

SEPTEMBER 4: Got "Ye Replie" from Charley Kaune. It is not bad. Henry has a situation at Wedeles![837] Thank God for it. Corrected and wrote at the Notes[838] in the afternoon. Hubert took dinner with us. In the afternoon, Mr. Franz and his daughter and young Louise were with us. As I wrote at the Notes at night, the suspicion grew very strong that the Laguna Grant is a forgery. I may be utterly mistaken, but it looks very suspicious. Either the author of the "Relación anónima" is grossly mistaken, or else the Grant cannot be from 1689.[839]

SEPTEMBER 5: Today, Henry began at Wedeles, etc. Letter from Garrison. Wrote at Chapter V, Part VI. Got my Novel back from Meysenburg.

SEPTEMBER 6: No letters. Wrote. Went to town early. Finished Chapter V, Part VI, and brought it down. Wrote to Dr. Brühl, to Meysenburg, and to Garrison. Hartmann, Louise, Hubert, and Fischer spent the evening with us. Shaw also called to see about Henry.

SEPTEMBER 7: No letters yet. Went up to Fischer's early in the morning with a basket of chile verde. Did not work much, only two pages of Chapter VI, Part VI. Felt weak and weary in my head. Wrote to James Jackson at Paris and sent him two maps. Wrote to the *National Zeitung* at Berlin; I feel tired of working, and it is time to get through with the French work at last. But it feels as if the last fifteen Chapters were harder than the first forty! Overwork, and then the disagreeable weather has something to do with it. Today it was sultry. Wrote to S. Eldodt about our proposed visit next week.

SEPTEMBER 8: Letters, from Charley, from Alphonse (a very good, kind letter too), and from Ratzel. This last letter is from the 20th of June, and it took the road to Buenos Aires again! Wrote at Chapter VI, [Part] VI. At night, went down to the priests and found there a torn copy of the "Sermones [en] Mexicano," and of the "Catecismo en Mexicano," of Fray Juan de la Anunciación. It is badly damaged, the title pages of the "Sermones" are gone, but the date is 1575, that is: 1577. It comes from the [convent]

Library of Santo Domingo [Pueblo].[840] Wrote to Don Joaquín[841] at once.

SEPTEMBER 9: Koch came up rather early, his wife is sick, and he wants Joe to come down and see her. So she went down town, while I wrote at my chapter. Mrs. Koch is indeed ill, but not so exceedingly dangerous. The good people are easily frightened and quite helpless at that. This is the first heavy and long rain of the summer. It still helps the corn. I went down town when the rain was over and there saw Sam Eldodt. Arranged for next week; if weather permits. At night went to Mrs. Staab, and Joe, to Koch's. She is better but weak.

SEPTEMBER 10: Letter from Meysenburg. Fischer called. Train bound at Española,[842] washout between here and San Ildefonso. Wrote at Chapter VI, Part VI. Joe went up to Louise; it is her birthday. Wrote to Alphonse and to Professor Ratzel.

SEPTEMBER 11: Letter from Father Meckel, favorable. Went to Mass and then to the Archbishop. He is satisfied. There is great baseball excitement in town and great foolishness in consequence. The people seem crazy. It's a perfect shame.[843] About 1 P.M., while Henry and I were at Bartsch's, a fearful shower broke out. Hubert was up in the afternoon, and Joe went down town after supper. I corrected at my Chapter VI and wrote to Father Meckel.

SEPTEMBER 12: I wrote at Chapter VI. It was so chilly that we put in the fuchsias and some of the cacti at nightfall. No letters.

SEPTEMBER 13: Finished Chapter VI, Part VI, today; brought it down to the Archbishop. Did not work in the afternoon. Night at Fischer's and down town. Louise was up in the afternoon.

SEPTEMBER 14: Went down town and with the Doctor to the Archbishop's, preparing to go to San Juan tomorrow. Sent the balance [?] of the *Revista* to Father Fischer, to Don Joaquín, and to Dr. Brühl. Koch is making a fool of himself again. It is a pity for the man, he is fundamentally good but very presuming and "soberbio" [haughty]. As to his woman, she and Minnie are nothing else but blockheads. Haughty, ridiculously proud, and good for nothing as far as work is concerned. We are going anyhow— just to show that they may do as they please!

SEPTEMBER 15: Left for San Juan with Joe and Louise. The trip is very pleasant, even handsome. The road makes a multitude of curves until it reaches the Rio Grande.[844] It rises to certainly 8,000 feet, then enters the Cañada de los Alamos and reaches the river through the Cañada Ancha, crossing it at the outlet of the Cañón below San Ildefonso and at the foot of "Shyu-ma." Sam Eldodt received us most kindly, and we felt perfectly at home. The Archbishop came and Father Garnier. The usual cavalcade, with the Padre at its head, went out to receive them.[845]

SEPTEMBER 16: I painted the vase from Abiquiu.[846] It was very pleasant, but the Indians are all gone to the ranchos and the pueblo is empty. The Archbishop and the two Padres left for the Embudo. Sam's collection has increased but little.

SEPTEMBER 17: Returned to Santa Fe. Letters: from Janvier, Garrison, and Mr. Balsiger. So my Mexican monographs, etc., shall be reprinted![847] We are tired out.

SEPTEMBER 18: Koch and Friedmann called, and they kept me from going to Mass. I then went down town with Hubert. Henry was busy all day at old man Debus' store, with Mr. Schumann taking up inventory. I wrote to Mr. Balsiger, to W. P. Garrison, to Putnam,[848] to Professor Norton, and to Janvier.[849]

SEPTEMBER 19: Last night I wrote yet to old Widmer, dating it today. The letter for Widmer was mailed today. The others, yesterday. I went down town and took a draft on Alliance Bank, London, for £20. and sent it to Papa at once. Finished Chapter VII, Part VI, and brought it down to Father Antonio. Joe went down town in the afternoon. On the whole, the day is pleasant. I went down town also at nightfall. No letters.

SEPTEMBER 20: No letters. Louise was here. I began at Chapter I, Part IV. At night, went up with Louise to the brewery. Hubert and Henry called. Today, Joe and Louise went and bought some things out of old man Debus' store.

SEPTEMBER 21: Joe all day in bed with a fearful headache. It is one of those fearful attacks again, which almost deprives her of consciousness. But by 3 P.M., it was over. Mrs. Jud called; also Dr. Thomas.[850] I wrote at my Chapter I, Part IV.

SEPTEMBER 22: No letters in the morning early. Finished text of Chapter I, Part IV, and began to write at the Notes. At night, Koch called.

SEPTEMBER 23: Letters from Rattermann and Dr. Brühl. Very kind and friendly. Joe went down town early, to the dressmaker, and in the afternoon to Louise. I finished Chapter I, Part IV, and brought it down after nightfall. Little thunder, but very heavy, drenching rain. Our roof leaked in the southwest corner, so we had to get up and put bowls, etc., under to catch the water that came through the ceiling.

SEPTEMBER 24: Letter from Father Meckel. Went down town in the morning. Koch and Louise spent the afternoon with us. Wrote at Chapter II, Part IV. Letter from Don Joaquín.

SEPTEMBER 25: Went to Mass. In the afternoon, corrected and wrote the notes to the first six pages. Mr. Schumann came and took supper with us. At night Koch called. River high.

SEPTEMBER 26: Letter from Papa. Went down town where I met Haren. Finished Chapter II, Part IV, late at night. Letter from Mali. She has decided not to come, owing to bad times in the East. Poor Bertha! Eddy was out all day, drinking and playing down town.

SEPTEMBER 27: Samuel Eldodt called and spent the evening with us. Louise up in the day.

SEPTEMBER 28: Jewish day of fasting and prayer.[851] Henry at home. Letter from Baxter with $116. Thank God! Wrote at Chapter (notes). Joe drove up to Fischers with Sam.

SEPTEMBER 29: Finished Chapter III, Part IV, and began at Chapter IV. Did not work much. Wrote to Mali, enclosing draft for $18.75; to Baxter; to Father Meckel, and to Don Joaquín.[852] Joe went down town in the afternoon. Henry and Hubert called late at night. Card from Garrison.

SEPTEMBER 30: Finished Chapter IV, Part IV. Joe went up to Louise. She is better.

OCTOBER

OCTOBER 1: Wrote at Chapter V, Part IV, finishing text.

OCTOBER 2: Wrote at notes. Joe very unwell, headache. In the afternoon, went to see Mr. Catron,[853] and then Louise. Hubert took dinner with us.

OCTOBER 3: Finished both Chapters V and VI, Part IV. No letters.

OCTOBER 4: Finished Chapter VII, Part V[IV?]. Louise called, and we accompanied her home. Henry came late, yet. I began at Chapter VIII, Part IV.

OCTOBER 5: No letters as yet. It is getting monotonous. Wrote and finished Chapter VIII, Part IV, and began at Chapter IX. Spent the evening in town with Henry.

OCTOBER 6: No letters! Wrote and finished Chapter IX, Part IV. Mrs. Spitz[854] and her sister called on Joe.

OCTOBER 7: Mails late. Went down town. Letter from Father Meckel. In the afternoon, I went with Griffin up to the Archbishop and showed him the books and plates. Met, by a mere accident, General Carr,[855] of the 6th Cavalry. Wrote a little, though not much, at Chapter X, Part IV.

OCTOBER 8: Mails late. At last a catalogue from Quaritsch and a box of cactus from Mary Suppiger. Went down town and called on General Carr. On the way back, I was accosted by Professor de Ceulmen from Ghent, Belgium. He was directed to me by Mr. Collett. So I had to tramp with him the whole afternoon. Did not write anything today, except one-and-one-half pages. Professor de Ceulmen told me that Fray Pedro de Gante, or de Mura, was properly "Van der Mur," and that the family is still living at Ghent.

OCTOBER 9: Letter from Dr. Brühl. Wrote at the notes of Chapter X. In the afternoon, Koch called.

OCTOBER 10: No letters. Went down town in the morning and in the afternoon. Wrote at Chapter X, Part IV.

OCTOBER 11: No letters. Joe's birthday. Finished my Chapter. The two Louises, Koch's [family], and Koch came in the afternoon. At night, Hubert and Henry came. Letter from Professor Norton. Nothing from Papa. It is strange.

OCTOBER 12: Began at Chapter XI, Part IV. Bad news of Charley Kaune.

OCTOBER 13: Eddy Franz put up our base-burner today. It looks fine, and he fixed it very well. No news from Charley.

OCTOBER 14: Bad news from Charley Kaune. He is dying. Poor, good boy. Henry is very despondent. Pessels also. He was thrown from his horse this morning and is lying, still unconscious, at the hospital. His condition is almost desperate, concussion of the brain. Finished Chapter XI, Part IV. Only one more, thank God! This has been a very sad day on the whole.

OCTOBER 15: Pessels died at 5 A.M. today! We shall miss him a good deal; he was a good friend to us. Telegram came, announcing Charlie Kaune's death, yesterday afternoon.[856] Poor Henry is very much dejected. I was down town, morning and in the afternoon. Wrote to Mrs. Kaune and to Dr. Brühl. No letters. Wrote to Papa and prepared a letter to Vicks for bulbs.

OCTOBER 16: No letters at all. I wrote to Father Navet. Went to Mass. In the afternoon, we both attended poor Pessel's funeral.[857] It was quite a long procession. The military band played, and the

K. T. [Knights Templars?] marched ahead. Afterwards, we went to the brewery.

OCTOBER 17: Eastern train thirteen hours late; southern train eighteen hours late. Henry's furniture came. I wrote the introduction and the title page, and at the last chapter! Eddy was down town all day, and came home hopelessly—beastly drunk. The old bitch is furious. If they only would leave soon, for it gets very disagreeable. Joe went down town, to Manderfield's, this afternoon. Letter from Papa at last. He won't come till March! Letter from Mr. Balsiger also.

OCTOBER 18: Letter from Father Meckel. He wants the books sent to St. Louis. *Finished the work for the Pope today!* Thank God for it a thousand times! He is very good! I have now finished the manuscript in eight months at most. Henry moved into his new quarters tonight. Louise was here.

OCTOBER 19: Wrote to Papa and to Padre Fischer. Also review[858] of Brinton's book: *Nahuatl Songs,* and sent it to Garrison. Got $90. from the Archbishop and gave Henry $50. of it. Spent a good deal of time down town, at Hartmann's and Koch's.

OCTOBER 20: Did the work for Mrs. Catron and brought it down to her. The whole of the Hartmann family spent the evening with us.

OCTOBER 21: Decided upon going to Peña Blanca tomorrow. Wrote to Father Meckel. Henry is making a big fool of himself. Am therefore divided upon going tomorrow. Wrote at the Zuñi history, the first four pages. Hubert came in the afternoon. Henry is at last resolved to stay. He is a silly, babyish fool.

OCTOBER 22: Left at 9:30 A.M. for the country and reached Peña Blanca at 7 P.M. All right. Met [Father] Ribera[859] at the Bajada. He is well fixed. On the whole, it was a pleasant walk, although I got tired.

OCTOBER 23: Am very tired, and less so physically than mentally. Remained indoors nearly all day. Father Navet has done very well. His copy is handsome, and he has finished already sixteen chapters, and among them, the longest ones.

OCTOBER 24: Wrote to Joe. David Vaca[860] called. Copied the "Nota" Fray Juan Caballero[861] about the idolatries of Cochiti, 1819. Measure of Father Navet's room: 19 × 14 1/2 feet. Copied the lists of the Franciscans of Santo Domingo, Cochiti, and Santa Ana from 1770, about, to 1830.[862] Crossed over to Zile at nightfall with José Sena,[863] on horseback, and stopped at the house of Don Antonio Baca.[864]

OCTOBER 25: I started from Zile about 8:30 A.M. The road crosses first the loma, and then an immense view expands to the north, east, and south. All the mountain chains develop to their full extent, and this view remains more or less in sight until 1 P.M. The road is mostly very sandy and therefore very tiresome. Ascent to the lomas sandy. Then a cañada opens, trenching and opening to the southeast and closing against the north. Several of these cañadas, all wooded with sabinos and with utterly dry arroyos, very deeply sandy, running through them, had to be traversed until I reached the mesa about noon. There, the view expanded to the south; the Sierra de Sandía looks very formidable, and the Sierra del Manzano appears, as well as the Ladrones, very distinctly. Here the sabinos are few and small. I killed a rattlesnake on the road, and saw some quails. Here the soil is hard and red. Afterwards a wild and picturesque cañón, running almost directly westward. Steep slopes, a heavy, dry arroyo, very unpleasant and painful. Sabinos, tree-like. The bottom very narrow, narrowing towards the western opening. The road drags through the bed of the arroyo, and finally crosses over to the northern slope, along which it winds high up above the bed to the end of the cañón. There the view opens to the west, the valley of the Rio Jemez, wooded hills, the river itself is partly visible in the southwest. Northwest, the chain of Jemez appears with the Cabezon [Peak] behind it, and due west, the Sierra de San Mateo [Mount Taylor].[865] East and north of the issue of the cañón, tremendous mesas arise to towering heights. Their aspect is very imposing, and the whole view impressive. Then the ascent began. It is terribly sandy and heavy, slope after slope in deep sand.

I reached Jemez at 6 P.M. Distance from Zile, 29 miles.* Height 5,056 feet. It is nearly a mile from the river. On the whole stretch not a human soul and not a drop of water. All desert and arid, though vegetation everywhere, even in the deepest sand. Reception at Jemez, the kindest possible.[866] Father [J. B.] Mariller, very friendly. They still cultivate some cotton here, many grapes, and the Indians (519 in all) make fair red wine![867]

OCTOBER 26: Names of the Pueblos in the Jemez dialect:[868] *Ua-la-to-ua*, San Diego (the pueblo); *Guin-se-ua* and *Amoxiumqua*, these are on the mesa between the San Diego and Guadalupe Rivers; San José de los Jemez, *A-tia-la-cua,* or *Pato-qua.* Those of *Amoxiumqua* came from San José lake, 75 miles to the northwest, where formerly was their first village. The second village is *Anu-qui-ci-qui,* between Salado and Jemez. The lake where the dead dwell, *Ua-buna-tota,* four days to the north. It is where they left from, in the beginning. There is a pueblo there. Cacique of Summer: *Ua-buna-jui;* Cacique of Winter: *Tzunta-jui,* child of ice.

[The remainder of Bandelier's notes on Jemez clans, kivas, officers, and societies were badly confused. Some of these data may be obtained from his *Final Report.*]

Peslia-so-de (a famous man, hunter, who wore a hunting costume of *Ua-buna-tota*). There is something like a Montezuma story connected with this man. He made a child to the niece of a man, but it was discovered. The girl pretended to have become pregnant alone. The uncle laid in wait and saw the boy come down and meet her. He made no opposition to their marriage, and the boy became a famous hunter and had his medicine from the lagune.

They make very little pottery at Jemez, only black. Mostly, use Cia pottery. On one occasion, the *Tzunta-jui* was called upon to make snow in summer, and he made it, very high, so they burnt him and his two assistants alive for it. They have winter and summer people also.[869] The magpie is the most beneficial bird because it "speaks correctly!" It derives its power from *Ua-buna-tota.* They have many fetishes and place them secretly behind the altar of the church to have them blessed. Are not at all strict with Father Mariller. He can go anywhere. Two estufas only. Marital customs as of old. The girls are even tried before marriage, and the boys chose in preference one who has a child already if possible.

From Jemez to San Diego, there are 13 miles.* Mariano gave me the names of 17 pueblos around Jemez, the most of which were inhabited when the Spaniards first came. He says that when they first appeared, it was because a man from Jemez went down the river into the Rio Grande Valley, and there he met a Spaniard on horseback. The Indian had never seen horses before, and the Spaniards told him they would be there in August. On the first of August, they came, but the whole story is mixed with reminiscences of the assault on the Mesa San Diego, and, even, I suspect, of the Insurrection of 1680. He claimed positively that the Piros are a part of the Jemez.[870]

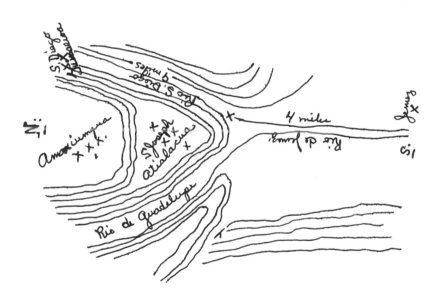

The situation of Jemez is quite striking. In front, are red mesas and [also] to the north, at the junction of the Guadalupe and San Diego streams. Very high and almost vertical. The climate is mild, but the soil is not good for wheat, whereas corn, grapes, etc., grow well. Grapes grow wild in the mountains. *Quila-jube* —Navajo. Queres—*Chachisca*.

OCTOBER 27: Father Mariller went to a wedding early this morning. Called around at Mariano's—Pecos: *P'-a-qui-lä*. North is yellow; west is green; east, white; south, red. Above, speckled; below, all colors![871] Wrote to Joe and sent the letter by a party going to Albuquerque.

First village north of Cia: *Qo-ha-sa-ya*. Opposite, on the other side: *Qa-qanatza-tia*, west of the river. War between the two because those of the latter stole the girls. Those of *Qa-qanatza-tia* went south to Mexico. The former went to Cia after having attempted to burn the other village with turpentine. The earliest village, also called *Tzia*, was opposite the present Jemez, on the other side of the river.[872] They were attacked by the Jemez, and the Taos and Pecos helped them. After four days fighting, the Jemez were defeated. Thereupon, the Jemez made an alliance with the Cochiti people, and these attacked old Cia, but were also repulsed after two days. Then the Cias attacked and fought the Cochiteños at the Potrero Viejo when these latter were living there and made peace. They still have communal crops. The crops are raised ostensibly for the cacique and accumulated at his house. There they are kept, and when there is any official work going on, the officers are fed from it. But in case of necessity, poor people receive their share from it also. Consequently they are in reality communal crops. The estufa is full of paintings, but it requires the permission of the *Ope-so-ma* to see it. With money, so the governor signified to me, everything can be obtained! This is significative.

About 4 P.M., Father Stephan, Father Parisis,[873] and Albert Benziger of Schwyz, son of Adelreich Benziger, came up from Bernalillo. We spent a pleasant evening, and I determined to go back with them. Since they came up to see me, it is but just that I should return with them.

OCTOBER 28: Started on horseback about 8 A.M. Father Mariller gave me a horse. The road follows the Rio de Jemez, crosses and recrosses it at San Isidro, and then goes down to Zia, where it crosses again to the west (or right) bank of the river. The river is not deep. Distance to Zia: 9 miles, thence about 15 to Bernalillo. Zia lies on a bluff, overhanging the river bank almost. The church appears large.[874] The heights on the banks decrease to the south. They become mere hills, studded with sabinos. The bottom is very sandy. Still, there is no comparison with the road from Peña Blanca, because it is level, and we have not to go down the slopes which, between the river and the towering mesas, are only accumulations of volcanic sand, deep and movable.

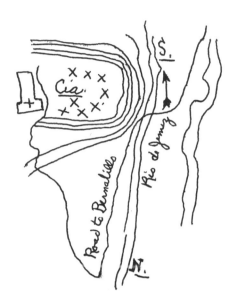

There are but very few ranchos in the river bottom, and San Isidro is a very small place only. Farther down, the road goes exclusively over the wooded lomas and not in the valley itself. The river becomes a little broader and is very muddy. Opposite Zia, the Rio Salado enters the Jemez and makes its waters alcaline. 8 or 9 miles below Zia, at the foot of the Mesa de Santa Ana, lies the Pueblo of Santa Ana, a little above the river bank. It looks well, with its large church and yellowish houses, two-stories high. The people have now their fields almost exclusively on the Rio Grande, 6 or 7 miles away.[875]

The road keeps exclusively on the other side of the river, so that I did not see the pueblo except from across. The river is wide, muddy, and the bank is high and cut-off sharp. Immense sand hills, bare and yellowish, cover the other (south or west)

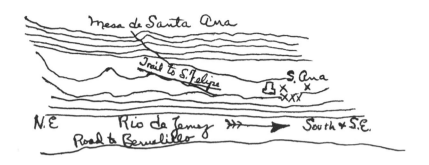

bank. The road winds and twists in and between them, very painful and slow motion.

After Santa Ana is out of sight, the crest of the mesa above the Rio Grande and Bernalillo appears, red, and dotted with sabinos. From that crest, an immense view spreads out. The Sierra de Sandía towers formidably. The Sierras de los Ladrones, de Socorro, of Magdalena, even, appear in the far south. All the mountains north and east appear, even the Truchas. The mesa is not level; it descends to the east rapidly. We reached Bernalillo about 5 P.M., my horse stumbling and being lame. Tired.

OCTOBER 29: Musquitos about, but not troublesome at all. They do not sting. Walked out to Sandia (four miles). Hot. I met Don José Gutierrez at Sandia, but could not do anything with the Indians. They are stubborn and told one lie after another. Thus, they said that *Puaray* (*Poa-ra-to*, or *Pura-ida*—worm people) was near the Alameda.[876] Of the Manzano, they refused to give the name but called it "Pueblo de la Campana." This is significative, also. Sandia[877] is a small Pueblo, but the houses appear clean inside. They are gathering the corn, and the crop is good. I returned to the parish about 3 P.M. and received a letter from Professor Seler.[878] Made provisional arrangements with Father Stephan for inspectorship of the Pueblos, at $25. per month, salary, and $150 for travelling expenses.[879] Wrote to Joe.

OCTOBER 30: Walked up from Bernalillo to Wallace in the afternoon and was very kindly treated by Mr. J. L. Morris.

OCTOBER 31: On foot to Peña Blanca, where I found, to my great displeasure, Dr. and Mrs. Seler. Still it went on passably and better than I expected. Walked on to the Bajada and stopped with Don José Rómulo Ribera.[880]

NOVEMBER

NOVEMBER 1: Went home by the way of the Cieneguilla. There are three pueblos there, at the Alamo-solo and at the Ciénega. The one at the Cieneguilla is called *"Tshiguma."*[881] Reached home at 4 P.M. Lizzie and her two children [Alice Amalia and Alfred William Kaune][882] were the first persons I saw. Found a mass of letters, but no money from Baxter. Joe well, thank God! Our people moving. Selers left tonight. Lizzie looks very poorly.

NOVEMBER 2: Got the copy of Benavides[883] at last. Bought part of the furniture of poor Pessels for $86. Mr. Schumann was up. He is very, very kind to us. Dear little Louise left this morning for Denver! We shall miss her very, very much. Henry is in better spirits. I wrote to Pretorius, to Baxter, to Don Joaquín,[884] and sent letters of recommendation [introduction] to Dr. Seler at Mexico, for Father Fischer, Chavero, Vigil, Peñafiel, and Altamirano.

NOVEMBER 3: No letters. Well, as God may please. Wrote at the history of Zuñi. Day quiet, except in the morning when the furniture came. Eddy moved the hogs today. But, what a slow, mean moving? Those people are the poorest wretches I have ever seen. Henry is acting very mean also. Poor Lizzie.

NOVEMBER 4: Beautiful, quiet, no letters. Work began in the corral today and also in the garden. I wrote as much for Baxter as I could, but was often disturbed. Moving began in earnest.

NOVEMBER 5: The old woman and the cows left! Planted tulips, Crown Imperials, hyacinths, and crocus. Sent the first four pages of the new chapter to Baxter. No letters. Henry and Lizzie moved in today. Glad they are gone. It is high time.

NOVEMBER 6: Went to Mass, and Joe, to church. Charley Hoffmann made a short call. In the afternoon, Koch and Mr. Schumann came, and we worked in the garden, all of us. Night cold, partly overcast. Wrote at the notes.

NOVEMBER 7: Beautiful weather. Wrote. No letters. From here on till Thursday evening [10th] almost always cloudless, but getting gradually cooler; especially the nights. On Tuesday, the 8th, I got letters from Baxter, with check for $116., from Captain Dougherty, from Father Meckel, and from Dr. Brühl. Thank God. I at once paid Wedeles $75. on account, to Mr. Schumann the rent until 9th inst. On Wednesday, the 9th, letter from the Museum at Leipzig. On Thursday, the 10th, I finished Part I, Chapter II, of the Documentary History of Zuñi[885] and sent it to Baxter. Gardening all the time. Henry acting a little less foolish. The garden looks beautiful now.

NOVEMBER 11: Broke one of the window panes this morning while splitting wood. Hubert came up and fixed it again. Wrote at Part II, Chapter II. Joe went up to Louise's. Wrote to Papa, to the Museum at Leipzig, and to Baxter. Also to J. Jackson, Paris.

NOVEMBER 12: Very early this morning, Pancratino Boll of Greenville (!!!) called. Quite a surprise. I then went down to see his wife and daughter. They were very friendly, but I don't care much about these kind of people anymore. Koch came back home with me. Mr. Schumann also came. Then—at last—Dr. Ten Kate[886] arrived. I spent the whole day and evening with him. We both like him.

NOVEMBER 13: Could not go to Mass, as I got up too late and on account of Ten Kate. Was with him all day. We went to the Archbishop and saw Father Antonio. In the afternoon, we drove out to Tezuque. Hubert came along. Letter from Baxter. We must make definite arrangements about future work. Evening at Koch's. Mr. Wedeles came also. Called at Archbishop Lamy also.

NOVEMBER 14: Archbishop Lamy told us yesterday that the first fruit trees which he imported across the plain cost him $10. to $15., each tree, by stage; he had to pay $10 per pound freight. Father Garnier and Alb. Benziger called early. Ten Kate and I walked out to Archbishop Lamy's. It was most beautiful and very pleasant. His ranchito is a lovely place.[887]

Father Stephan definitely agreed to employ me for one year at $25. per month, from the 1st of December next, and expenses for travelling.[888] I am very thankful for that to God and to my friends. Ten Kate and Benziger took supper with us. Both left tonight. My novel came back from Cincinnati.

NOVEMBER 15: Nothing new nor strange happened, except some little trouble about the water, so that Mr. Schumann had to come up and fix it. Atanasio was out the whole afternoon. He worked only in the morning. I went down town twice. Wrote at Part II, Chapter II, of Zuñi. Joe was at Lizzie's in the afternoon. Wrote to Baxter and to Frank Cushing.

NOVEMBER 16: Finished the text of Part II, Chapter II, this morning and corrected it in the afternoon. Atanasio did not come the whole day. Met Father Tanquerey of New York at the Archbishop's. He is an artist, there is no doubt. He repairs some of the old paintings. Gave me advice about the water colors.

NOVEMBER 17: Atanasio not here. Had to run around on account of it. At last he came, was sick, etc. I wrote on Part II, Chapter II. No letters.

NOVEMBER 18: Finished Part II, Chapter II, and mailed it. Joe went to Louise with Johanna Franz.[889] Had a long talk with the Archbishop. Koch is slowly, but surely ruining himself through pride and lazyness [sic]. It is a great pity, but it cannot be helped. He will not listen. Mr. Schumann came with Dobbins, the carpenter. Atanasio did not come. Letter from Garrison and from Louise Fischer.

NOVEMBER 19: Began at Chapter III, Part I. In the afternoon, Kochs were here. Went to get Atanasio to help me clean out the rooms, ready for the carpenter. Wrote to Baxter and to Captain Dougherty.

NOVEMBER 20: No letters. Both of us went to church. In the afternoon, we walked out to Fischer's with Lizzie, Henry, and the children. Evening at Henry's.

NOVEMBER 21: No letters yet. Wrote at Chapter III, Part I. Atanasio not here. In the afternoon, Joe in town.

NOVEMBER 22: Nobody at work. Finished text of Chapter III, Part I, and copied list of priests.[890] Fischer and Mr. Hartmann spent the afternoon with us. Am much afraid about work.

NOVEMBER 23: Atanasio and a carpenter at work—at last! Wrote some. Henry had a chill today. Copied data about San Felipe.[891]

NOVEMBER 24: Thanksgiving Day, but nobody pays any attention to it. All the stores are open! Wrote but little. Dougherty[892] worked all day with old man Jonsen. Atanasio worked all day too. Henry sick. We took dinner with them. Also supper. Joe is suffering very much from toothache; her right cheek swells. Had to make poultices until 10 P.M. Copied from the book of Santa Clara, wherein I found the handwriting of Fray Juan Minguez![893]

NOVEMBER 25: Atanasio and Dougherty both at work. Letter from C. Burton with blanks to sign. Joe better. Hard at work in the house. Wrote at Chapter III, Part I. Call from Dr. Strong and Mr. [Harry] Skinner. Wrote and sent off review of Brooks' book, *The Story of the American Indian*.[894] Joe well again.

NOVEMBER 26: No letters. Went down town. Putting up the ceilings. Wrote to Mr. Balsiger.

NOVEMBER 27: Letter from Ten Kate. Joe unwell. Still, she keeps up. Wrote to Ten Kate. Willie Spiegelberg and wife called. At night, I went to Dr. Strong's. When I returned, found Joe very ill. High fever, chills, but not much headache. This condition lasted all night. She got some relief after midnight, though.

NOVEMBER 28: Joe is better. Still, she must remain in bed. Eastern train fourteen hours late. Atanasio here. Finished Part I, Chapter III. Wrote to Dr. Brühl and to Baxter. Joe well again. Louisa and Julia Fischer called in the afternoon. Joe got up about 4 P.M.

NOVEMBER 29: Letter from Baxter at last. Satisfactory. Began to write for the Institute. Joe downtown in the afternoon. Mailed

Part I, Chapter III. Nobody but Atanasio at work. At night, wrote on "Irrigation" for *The Nation.* Quite unexpected and very pleasant call at night from Gerdes and wife.

NOVEMBER 30: Dittrich, Dougherty, and Atanasio here and at work—at last. Mailed article[895] to Garrison, and three acknowledgments of service: G. W. Garrels vs. S. B. Kelso; ditto vs. C. M. Casey; and ditto vs. Mary Logan—to C. W. Burton, Mount Vernon, Illinois. I moved my books tonight. They just fill the case.

DECEMBER

DECEMBER 1:[896] Letter from Baxter. Had an awful time with that ugly dog, Bismarck. Got him out at last. Mr. Dittrich and his boy, Atanasio, and Dougherty here. Paid Dougherty $6. for his work. Father Antonio took supper with us. Hubert came at night. Wrote to Baxter and mailed the letter. Joe went down town in the afternoon. Work is rapidly advancing here in the house.

DECEMBER 2: Atanasio went away, so that today does not count for Mr. Schumann. We moved the big cupboard today, from the hall to the kitchen. Could not write anything at all, except an index to a volume of manuscripts.[897] Wrote to Alphonse.

DECEMBER 3: Today, we moved into the kitchen! Two letters from Papa! Thank God! One from Father Navet. Atanasio worked for us, and I paid him $1.50 for it. Could not write at all today. Moving and trouble all around. But we feel happy because we are moving in.

DECEMBER 4: Letter from Dr. Seler—at last. Koch called. Pleasant. We are very happy in our newly fixed place. In the afternoon, Mr. Schumann and Mrs. Hartmann called. Spent the evening at Henry's. He is doing better, it seems.

DECEMBER 5: My room did not get quite ready yet. Paid Atanasio $1.25 for today. Hubert came. Wrote to Alphonse, to Papa, to Dr. Ernst, to Dr. Brühl, and to Father Navet. It is very annoying— that slowness of moving. Met H. [Brucke?] from St. Louis.

DECEMBER 6: Fixing going on as usual. It gets very annoying. Still, the work advances, but there is such slow progress. And no letters. My table is not done yet.

DECEMBER 7: No table. No letters. Very, very annoying. Dougherty is drunk.

DECEMBER 8: No table. No hands. No letter! It is sickening. Yesterday, we cleaned out the parlor and bedroom. Today, it is [the feast of] the Immaculate Conception, and neither Atanasio nor Manuelita are here, of course! Sent acknowledgment of service: Garrels vs. Rotramel, to C. W. Burton, Mount Vernon, Illinois. I could not do a thing again today. It being a holiday, nobody worked. Towards evening, the table came at last. Quiet and cold. I write this already on the new table. How nice the room is, how cosy [sic] and homelike! Wrote to Samuel Ward and Co., Boston, about writing paper.

DECEMBER 9: Letter from Ten Kate at last. Atanasio here, also Antonia Sena. Mr. Dittrich finishing. Wrote to Dr. Ten Kate and sent him two pamphlets. Today, at last, thank God, the whole house is finished and done, and we may consider ourselves as settled. If only Baxter would write! Began an article for the *New Yorker Staatszeitung* this evening.

DECEMBER 10: Wrote at report to the Institute in the morning. In the afternoon, Joe had her callers: Fischers, Kochs, and Johanna. I went down town, to the Archbishop and to Skinner. In the evening Henry, Lizzie, and Hubert came and spent the evening pleasantly with us.

DECEMBER 11: Joe in bed with headache. We staid up too late. Letter from Baxter with $116. check. Thank God for it. Replied to him at once. Took dinner at Lizzie's. In the afternoon, Mr. Schumann and Koch called. Schumann spent the whole evening with us. Very pleasant, as usual.

DECEMBER 12: Joe went to Fischers in the afternoon. I was rather dissolute today. Still, I wrote a little for the Institute. No letters. Wrote to Dr. Seler at Mexico, and to Louise Fischer.

DECEMBER 13: No letters. Henry babyish and contemptible again. I wrote little, for the Institute.

DECEMBER 16:[898] In the past two days, I finished the chapter for the Institute and sent it to Mr. Parkman,[899] and an article to the *New Yorker Staatszeitung*. Today, I copied at the Archives and took home a volume for copying.[900] Last night, my typewriter broke. Got letter from Paris and from Seybt, very friendly.

DECEMBER 17: Letter from Don Joaquín and card from *New York Herald*. I had considerable trouble with my typewriter and finally carried it down town again to Hudson for repairs. Wrote copies, in the afternoon and at night.

DECEMBER 18: Went to Mass. Harry Skinner came up with me. We dined at Lizzie's. In the afternoon, Preston and wife, [Mr.] Franz and Eddy called; also Hubert. Night starry and quiet. Were down at Lizzie's with Hubert.

DECEMBER 19: Letter from Garrison with $6.05. Balance due. Thank God! Eddy Franz left tonight. I copied at the Journal of Dominguez Mendoza.[901]

DECEMBER 20: Wrote and copied. Letter from Mr. Balsiger. I sent him $20. at once, per draft. Hubert called at night.

DECEMBER 21: Thermometer: –4° F. at 5 A.M. Water frozen in the conducts. Good-bye for the kitchen. Have to take it from the well now. Got my five pamphlets at last from Paris,[902] and a letter from Father Fischer by Rubio. The old man is very sick. While down town, I learned that my little and simple article on *Irrigation* is quite approved. In the afternoon, I copied. The girls called on Joe. Amado Chavez[903] called after supper. Today, I sent off three pamphlets on Fray Marcos: one to Rubio, one to Don Joaquín, and one to Father Fischer. Also a card to Seybt. During the whole day, thermometer at 10° F.

DECEMBER 22: Bitterly cold. Quiet. Was down town all day at the Surveyor General's Office, copying the Bernalillo Grant,[904] etc. Letters from Samuel Ward and Co., and from old man Widmer.

Wrote to Baxter about paper and copying. Joe retired early with headache. I copied yet.

DECEMBER 23: I write this on the 31st of December. I did not keep my diary, principally for the reason that my hand was almost out of use.[905] I received letters almost every day, and the news of the death of Father Fischer![906] Peace to his ashes! A very remarkable man gone. I wrote at once a number of letters: to Don Justino Rubio, to Peñafiel, to Don Joaquín,[907] and to Dr. Kaska. Weather cold. On the 30th, we had a heavy sandstorm, remarkable for the season, and snow afterwards. A light snow, but wet. Our Christmas celebration was plain, but still very pleasant. On the 25th, we were with Kochs. On the 27th, spent the evening with Franz's. Exceedingly pleasant. Today, 31st of December, it is clear and cold, but quiet. Fornance is here with wife and baby, also.

Last of the year 1887. Thank God for all he has given us! It was a prosperous year, blessed and happy! [This final paragraph was written by Bandelier in perpendicular lines across the rest of the entry of December 23.]

1888

JANUARY 1: Joe in bed with a strong bilious attack. I went to High Mass. It was beautiful. The Archbishop [J. B. Salpointe], himself, officiated, assisted by Father Mailluchet. Besides, Fathers Eguillon, Rolly, and Deraches were present. The Christian Brothers sang and played string music, and the San Francisco band[908] "blew" also. It nearly blew us away!

I took dinner at Lizzie's. In the afternoon, I stayed quietly at home, writing, until Sam and Marcos Eldodt called, and Joe got up also. In the evening, grand illumination, procession, etc. I went down to the Archbishop's and called on him and the Padre Vicario [Eguillon].

JANUARY 2: No letters. Spent the day visiting. Called mostly on people who did not receive officially. Kochs, of course, did.[909] Foolish and silly enough for that. Joe had only two callers, Dr. Eggert and Fornance.[910] At night we had a turkey. Schumann and [Mr.] Franz came and joined. It was just glorious.

JANUARY 3: No letters, but Emma Huegy had the cheek to send us a New Year's card. I went down town twice. Slept awhile. In the afternoon, Koch, Sam Eldodt, the three Koch ladies, and Goldsbury came up and staid until sunset. It was pleasant.

JANUARY 4: No letters. Henry made a fool of himself again. Went down town. I paid Koch and met Father Francolon. My hand troubles me so much that I can hardly write. Still I copied, for the holydays [sic] are over.

JANUARY 5: I wrote all day, though with great difficulty and pain. Joe went down town in the afternoon. Night calm, partly cloudy. Quietly at home, for it is our 27th anniversary of marriage.[911] How time flies! God is good to us; we are happier now than we ever were before. No letters today.

JANUARY 6: Letter from Dr. Walliser. I copied all day, though my hand is very painful.

JANUARY 7: Letter from Papa. I wrote the whole day and only went down town at night.

JANUARY 8: Baxter came! Spent day with us. We had an exceedingly pleasant time. He left at night.

JANUARY 9: Letters from Seler and Peñafiel. My old Indian came from San Ildefonso. He told me of their tradition on migration, saying: that all the tribes came from the north together, and that in the beginning they spoke but one language. But that on the way, and in Colorado, they quarrelled and finally dispersed, each band taking up its own idiom gradually. He asserts that the caves of the Pu-yé and Shu-finné were made and inhabited by the people of Santa Clara, San Juan, etc., that San Ildefonso first stood on the opposite bank of the Rio Grande, but that pressure from the Navajos, Yutes [Utes], etc. caused them to move across the river to a loma south of the present church. On the northern spur of that loma the first church was built. It was abandoned, as also the village, in consequence of the smallpox which had decimated the people.[912]

Joe went down town in the afternoon on account of Hubert [Hoffmann] being ill. Vanderver [Van der Veer] called. At night, letters from Norton and Parkman. I wrote to Seler and to Peñafiel.

JANUARY 10: Wrote at the second part of my report to the Institute [Archaeological Institute of America],[913] on the Indians of the Southwest in the 16th Century. Went down town in the afternoon. Archbishop Lamy very ill; his recovery is doubtful! Wrote to Dr. Walliser, to Seybt, and to Mr. Parkman.[914]

JANUARY 11: Wrote at Part II of report to the Institute. My hand very bad. Wrote to Professor Norton and to Dr. Brühl. John Pearce was up in the afternoon. Poor unhappy boy.

JANUARY 12: I attempted to write, but cannot. My right arm is useless. The typewriter, too, is out of order. Went up to Fischer's in the afternoon. Am quite discouraged. No letters, although both mails arrived. Archbishop Lamy is better today. Still, there is no reliance. Wrote to Mr. Balsiger.

JANUARY 13: I went down town and consulted Dr. [Norton B.] Strong.[915] He gives little hope. Still, relief appears possible. Saw Schumann and Willi Spiegelberg, also Pearce and Lt. Crittenden. No letters today. In the afternoon, Joe went down town. I painted, and then Dr. Strong came and spent the evening with us, a very pleasant, quiet evening. He has taken me under treatment now.

JANUARY 14: Painted, since I am prohibited from writing. Arm seems to be better. Went down town in the morning, to Koch's, etc. In the afternoon, to the brewery with Dr. Strong. Letter from Alphonse [Bandelier].

JANUARY 15: Remained indoors all day. Painted. No letters. Henry took the machine [typewriter] to repair it. In the afternoon Koch came, then Johanna Franz, finally Mr. Franz and Mr. Schumann. The latter three staid for supper. It was very pleasant. I have got Johanna's typewriter now and shall try to use it.

JANUARY 16: I wrote with Joh? Franz's typewriter, but had to go down town at night for information. Copied all day. Hand as usual. Joe went down town in the afternoon to call on Mrs. Catron with Johanna. Letter from Dr. Steinert, but I do not feel like replying to it. Am no longer a Swiss.

JANUARY 17: Mails all out of order. Went down town. Archbishop Lamy is fast declining. Called on Archbishop Salpointe, on Schumann, on Mrs. Strong. Letter from Peñafiel and book from Ten Kate. Finished the document of 1681. Went down town and called on Bishop Macheboeuf [Machebeuf].[916] At night, I wrote the report for him on the northern boundaries of Mexico and brought it down to him. Saw Meany also.

JANUARY 18: No letters. I wrote with the typewriter, copying at documents. Wrote all day; hand same, can hardly hold the pen. Louise and Julia [Fischer] called in the afternoon.

JANUARY 19: No mail so far. Copied with the machine. Letters from Papa and from Dr. Ernst. Spent the evening at Mr. Franz's very pleasantly.

JANUARY 20: Card from Father Meckel from Rome, dated January 1st. At noon, letter from Father Navet. In the afternoon, I wrote the Table of Contents for Parts IV and VII of the work for the Pope and then helped the Archbishop packing the Manuscript. It is complete now, and to leave for Rome by express. My hand is about the same. I copied some with the machine this forenoon.

JANUARY 21: Mails late. Letter from Baxter, at last. Copied. The document is becoming more and more interesting. In the afternoon, Joe went up to Fischer's, and I remained alone, copying all afternoon and evening. Wrote a few lines to Dr. Ernst, enclosing letter from Joe to Papa.

JANUARY 22: Copied. Letter from Dr. Brühl. Wrote to him and to Baxter. Took a short walk in the afternoon. It was rather cold. Mailed my three monographs to Peñafiel, also the "Romantic School." Koch came in the afternoon, and we went up to the brewery together. Went down to Henry's. Hubert was there also. He is now almost well.

JANUARY 23: Yesterday, Henry brought my typewriter again, and I'll see now how it works. I copied part of the time, but went to town several times. No letters. Got very mad today at our milkman; he is lying and careless. Will have to quit Piersoll on account of him.

JANUARY 24: Letters from Professor Norton, and Professor H. A. Ward. Sent off the manuscript to Rome by Express. Wrote to Father Meckel, enclosing the letter in one to Dr. O'Connell,[917] Rome. Took supper at Koch's. It was very pleasant.

JANUARY 25: Letter from Cushing at last. They expect me to leave after the 29th inst. as soon as practicable.[918] Also a letter from Eddy [Huegy]. Got a fine present of vegetables from Sam Eldodt. Copied. It is very hard work, as the document is in a horrible condition, decayed and mangled.

JANUARY 26: No letters. Joe in bed with headache. Joe in bed all day with a bilious attack. It was lonely and dreary. Copied, but had to go down town on account of Bishop Macheboeuf of Denver. At nightfall, went down town and returned a part of the manuscript to Sam Ellison.[919] Dr. Strong came up and spent the evening with us.

JANUARY 27: Friendly letter from Seybt. Dougherty at work today. In the afternoon, down town, at the Surveyor General's Office,[920] at work copying for Bishop Macheboeuf. Letter from Guernsey. Wrote to Jackson, Paris. Koch and Hubert called, and in the afternoon, Mrs. Hartmann, and Dr. Strong and his wife.

JANUARY 28: Letter from Mr. Balsiger. Dougherty is here. He finished the book case, and I paid A. Windsor $6.50 for it. Wrote to Seybt and to Colonel Haren. In the afternoon, Hartmanns called. They took supper with us. I finished copying at the Surveyor General's Office. It is an indifferent document on the whole.

JANUARY 29: Moved my books into the new case. In the afternoon, went up to the brewery with Henry, when the Doctor [Eggert], Schumann, Franz, and Dieckmann and Mrs. Dieckmann[921] called on Joe. The gentlemen then came up to the brewery, while Mrs. Dieckmann remained with Joe. We spent a pleasant hour together and returned home. At night, I wrote to Sam Eldodt, to Peñafiel, and to Guernsey. Joe went down to Lizzie's.

JANUARY 30: Lizzie unwell. Letter from Colonel Haren with Pass. Wrote to him, to Professor Ward, and received a telegram from Dr. Brühl. Meany spent the evening with us. Later, wrote to Father Parisis.

JANUARY 31: Letter from Bertha [Huegy Lambelet] with news of Uncle J. Weber's death. Wrote at once to Aunt Weber and to Professor Norton. In the afternoon, Dr. Eggert called; also Mrs. Koch and Minnie. Telegraphed to Cushing. I leave tonight; may God be with my dear little Joe meanwhile. Left at 10:20 P.M. Varden is on the same train.

FEBRUARY

FEBRUARY 1: Awoke at Socorro. Separated from Varden at Rincón. On the train at Deming, I met Mr. Reid, one of the owners of Carizalillo. He told me that since the earthquake of last May,[922] the volume of water at both of his springs is twice as large as before. He gave me a number of details about the Apache wars. At Deming, I met Mr. Conway.[923] On the road to Tucson, it rained and was very dark. I took no sleeper and had quite a pleasant time with Ignacio Garcia of Tucson. No sleep whatever.

FEBRUARY 2: No sleep at all. Got to Maricopa about 6 A.M. and to Tempe after 7 A.M. Everybody recognized me; everybody came to greet me. At 10 A.M. Garlick[924] came with the buckboard to drive me to the camp. There are two camps, both on the site of a ruined village.[925] Ten Katc, Baxter, Frank [Cushing], etc., are very kind.

The villages were large, and there is quite a number of them. That delta between the two rivers is very favorable for agriculture. No lack of water, as canals can be built across from the Salado to the Gila; and the soil is very good everywhere. It is a rich, reddish loam. It is warm and pleasant and everything is green. Small palm trees grow in the gardens. The population has much increased since 1883. Large canals are being constructed, and some are already done.

FEBRUARY 3: The finds of Cushing reveal nothing new at all, except one very interesting point, the manner in which these thick walls of clayey marl were constructed. They are not of adobe, or so-called "cajón," but simply "fascine" or rather "hurdles." In the main mound, which he calls the "citadel," the holes of the posts are still visible on both faces of the wall. They are about two-and-a-half to three-and-a-half feet apart, and the posts must have been three to four inches in diameter. From post to post, willow branches were woven, thus making a series of rectangular hurdles strongly connected and filled with earth. It is primitive "cajón work."

We had a long and satisfactory conference. The collections are large, but the pottery is only what I found at Show Low [present-day Showlow], Fort Apache, and on the upper Salado, etc. Corrugated pieces are rare.

FEBRUARY 4: Left Tempe for Phoenix after dinner with Garlick.

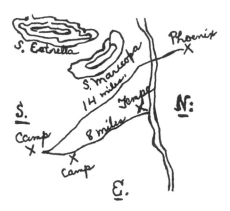

The road goes through the plain, winding around the base of the Sierra de Maricopa over to the Rio Salado. Distance from the camp to Phoenix fourteen miles; to Tempe six miles. Colossal cerci. Phoenix is on the level, about one-and-a-half miles north of the Salado. It has 4,000 inhabitants, and its aspect is very pleasing. It looks as if it was in a forest of álamos. Ditches (acequias) cut the country in every direction, and these are all lined with tall álamos. The town is well laid out, wide streets, and the houses mostly one story.

   Called on Father Jouvenceau.[926] He is well pleased with his situation. Left Phoenix by rail at 7 P.M., and it took us five hours to get to Maricopa, a distance of thirty-five miles.

FEBRUARY 5: Reached Tucson at 5 A.M. On the train, I met Mr. J. D. Walker[927] of Casa Grande. During the day, I saw Sander, Josefa Molina, Father Morin, Dr. Girard,[928] Father Gheldof, Sister Euphrasia, and Ignacio Garcia. Have had no sleep for several nights and still could go to bed at midnight only.

FEBRUARY 6: Walked out to Fort Lowell[929] early in the morning and spent the whole day and the night there, with Dr. Girard and his family. Exceedingly pleasant. At night, the Dr. gave a lecture on the dressing of wounds, hemorrhage especially.

FEBRUARY 7: Captain Mason[930] of the 4th [Cavalry] called. The Dr. drove me back to town, and we dined at Father Morin's. Left Tucson at 7 P.M., the train being late as usual. Saw Ignacio before I left.

FEBRUARY 8: Reached Deming at 11 A.M., having been delayed twelve-fourteen miles from the place by a wreck. At Deming, went to see Henry Holgate.[931] Chico[932] is in Sonora! At Babispe [Bavispe], eighty-three to eighty-four people were killed by the earthquake of last May. None of my special friends among them, however.[933] No casualties at Huachinera, Baserac, Granados, Nacori, Bacadehuachi, etc. But at Opoto, buildings were shattered, etc. North of Babispe, great rents and clefts formed, but as nobody lives there, there was no damage. At Tucson and Fort Lowell, walls cracked and the court house swayed visibly. Left Deming at 2 P.M. Met Reid again. Did not sleep.

FEBRUARY 9: Reached Santa Fe and home at 6 A.M., very tired. All well! Thank God! Went to sleep. While I slept, Dr. Brühl came. We went out in the afternoon together. The Dr. staid at the Palace Hotel. Found several letters.

FEBRUARY 10: We drove out to Tezuque [Tesuque]. At the pueblo, I was told that *Pose-yemo* was indeed a tradition of the northern Tehuas [Tewas]. We returned home pretty nigh frozen. The wind was very cutting. Night cold and clear. Mr. Dittrich [E. W. Dietrich][934] died.

FEBRUARY 11: Wrote to Cushing, to Sam Eldodt, to the [*New Yorker*] *Staatszeitung* and to Vick [mail order house], enclosing a check for $5.00. Made visits. Ready to leave Monday for Taos. Poor Hartmann, he came to ask for pall-bearer.

FEBRUARY 12: Went to Mass and in the afternoon to the funeral. Dr. Brühl moved to us in the morning. Wedeles called, and Mr. Schumann took supper with us. Spent the evening very pleasantly at Koch's. Marcus [Eldodt] was there also.

FEBRUARY 13: Left for San Juan. Arrived safely and spent the day most pleasantly. Nothing new up there, besides. Father Seux showed me books of the church from 1726.[935]

FEBRUARY 14: Left for Embudo at 10:42 A.M. The Truchas and the Jicarrita are heavily snowclad. Reached Embudo at noon and then took an open buckboard. Our driver was Macedonio Hidalgo.

The drive is beautiful. The Rio Grande flows through a deep cañón, very grand and romantic, past the Nasa, Rinconada, and Cieneguilla, to the Caja del Rio, where the rocks on the right hand side are gigantic. Then it turns off [to] the right at the Cieneguilla. Up a narrow, sandy valley, bordered on the right by the dark Sierra de Picuries [Picurís], pine-clad. It reaches, at last, the top of a ridge, seventeen miles from Embudo.

Thence, a magnificent view expands in all directions. The Sierra de Taos is very grand in the northeast, beyond the broad and level valley. In the north-northwest, the Sierra de San Antonio looms up, and in the southwest, the Sierra de Abiquiu with the Pedernal. The Rio Grande itself is invisible in the depth of a large, serpentine, and very deep cleft, a cañón with perpendicular walls, which cuts the plain like a Mexican deep barranca.

We reached the Ranchos de Taos at nightfall, and Fernandez de Taos at 7 P.M. Stopped at Dibble's.[936] I called at once on Father Valézy,[937] where I met Etienne Desgeorges. As I came, there also came a card from Father Eguillon stating that Archbishop Lamy had died yesterday, the 13th of February, at 8 A.M. Father Valézy therefore must leave tomorrow for Santa Fe, while we go to the pueblo.

The town is almost exclusively Mexican, and it contains about 2,000 inhabitants. The Rio de Taos, Rio de los Ranchos, etc. water the eastern half of the valley. Distance from Embudo: thirty-three miles and three miles to the pueblo. *Opuntia arborescens* abundant in the mountains.

FEBRUARY 15: Went to the pueblo, which really corresponds to the Braba of Castañeda.[938] The river runs between the two big houses. There are two foot-bridges across, both of heavy timbers. Seven estufas, all absolutely subterranean.

Each one of the two great buildings has its cacique, and they call him *Te-¢la-pa.* The old wall is still upright, in part. I could not, of course, do anything, as the good, old Doctor [Brühl] monopolized everything. Still it is a first reconnaissance only.

The school is going on well.[939] Indians friendly and rather communicative. They acknowledge that the old wall is very old; and even did not deny it when I suggested that it might have been built at the time of Popé and Chato.[940] In the afternoon, we called on Mr. Scheurig[941] and on Alex Gusdorf. On the whole, I am glad I came, for I can now go to Taos with knowledge of the country and people and stay longer and with greater profit.

FEBRUARY 16: The Pueblo of Taos lies at the outlet of a narrow valley coming in from the south-southeast at the base of the mountain. Through this valley, the Rio de Taos enters the plain. It is lined with beautiful álamos on both sides and as far down as the pueblo. The houses are five to seven stories high.[942]

I cannot help but admiring the fine description of Castañeda and of the "Relación del Suceso."[943] In conjunction with this, it struck me that the "Braba,"[944] or "Yuraba," might be "Uraua"! Upon my asking one of the people of Taos, he replied: "Eso es de los antiguos [That is of the ancients]" and smiled.

We left Taos at 7:30 A.M. with Desgeorges, passing by the rancho of Pedro Sanchez and by the little town of Cordoba.[945] Arrived at Embudo at 2 P.M. and at Santa Fe at 7 P.M. All well, thank God!

But a letter from Father Meckel is here, stating that my plates are probably lost![946] There is hope yet; the Italian vessel "Entella" has not landed, and it may come into port still. If lost, well, then it is lost, and that's all. We are able to live, and the plates were to me a source of much pleasure and knowledge. Nothing is safe in this world anyhow, and we must take things as they come.

During my absence, Joe has bought a sewing machine, and that is better than all the plates in the world. Funeral of Archbishop Lamy.

FEBRUARY 17: Joe had a severe spell of headache, but Dr. Brühl relieved her greatly. Letter from Ignacio Garcia. Wrote to Cushing. Made some calls. The Archbishop is rather depressed over the news from Rome [concerning the missing plates]. Sam Eldodt is here. Dr. Brühl left tonight for Tempe.

FEBRUARY 18: Yesterday we got water again in the kitchen, at an expense of $25. Wrote to Pitt and Scotts, 229 Broadway, New York; to Garrison, and to Monsignor O'Connell. No letters.

FEBRUARY 19: No trains from south or east, but the Denver train of last night brought a letter from the *Staatszeitung* with $10.50. Letter from John Pearce. Hubert came and staid all day. In the afternoon, Sam Eldodt came and took supper with us. Mr. Franz and Mr. Schumann also called. The former leaves for St. Louis tonight. I did some copying today. Wrote to John C. Pearce, 2340A Indiana Avenue, Chicago, Ill.

FEBRUARY 20: Letter from Dr. Girard. I copied somewhat, but had to go down town. I left $50. to my credit with Mr. Schumann; saw Hartmann, Samuel [Ellison, or Eldodt?] etc. In the afternoon, I was called down to the Archbishop's to look at some papers of Archbishop Lamy's. Wrote to Dr. Girard and to Ignacio Garcia. Louise and Julia up in the afternoon with Joe.

FEBRUARY 21: Last night, I still began to write to Mr. Balsiger. Whole day very ugly, blustering at intervals. Copied. Joe went to town in the afternoon. Telegram from Cushing. No mail. Finished and closed letter to Mr. Balsiger. Joe suddenly ill and had to go to bed, not headache, but dizzyness [*sic*] and nausea. Wrote to Cushing also. My hand is very bad.

FEBRUARY 22: Mail, but no letters. Finished copying the document of 1682. Went down town twice. Camilo [Padilla] came and spent evening with [us]. Joe better. She took a drive with Mrs. Staab.

FEBRUARY 23: No letters. Copied. Also wrote to L. Brown at Taos and to Cushing, by express; and sent him Squier's "Peru" and also Tschudi's "Peru."[947] At night, Camilo Padilla paid me visit, and tonight, Hubert called.

FEBRUARY 24: Copied. Father Antonio [Jouvenceau] called in the afternoon. No letters. Telegram from Pitt and Scott, New York.

Plates miscarried, but not yet lost, it seems. Wrote to Henry S. Budd. Also sent ribbon to Hammond Typewriter Company, 77 Nassau Street, New York, for re-inking, and wrote to them about it. Snow again. There seems to be no end to it this winter.

FEBRUARY 25: Wrote at Report for the Institute. Afternoon with Dr. Strong. Sent pamphlets to Cushing, to Clotilde, and to Gustav [Brühl]. No letters.

FEBRUARY 26: Went to Mass. It was Confirmation Day, and the cathedral, crowded. In the meantime, Koch had been at the house with Hubert. In the afternoon, Schumann came, and we all went out to the brewery. Very pleasant. No letters from no-where. After supper, we went to Henry's. Kaenter was there too, and Hubert.

FEBRUARY 27: No letters again. Atanasio at work for us. It is very, very strange that I get no letters at all. Copied. By express, there came a long letter from Cushing about the novel and the first five chapters of that novel also.[948]

I went down town, then copied again and also wrote at the Report to the Institute. Then Mr. Meany came, kindly volunteering to help me with the novel, which of course I accepted. In the evening, I began to write to Janvier[949] and to recopy and correct on the novel.

FEBRUARY 28: Letters from Garrison, Harry Budd, and a card from Dr. Brühl. Copied; then wrote for the Institute and finally at the novel. Wrote to Janvier, No. 20, 7th Avenue, New York, and mailed the letter. Joe went to Fischer's, and I accompanied her. In the evening, I went down to Mr. Meany's and he came up with me. The work I did at the novel is no good, and I destroyed the two pages. Got letters from James Jackson and Monsignor J. D. O'Connell. The outlook is better for the plates; the ship is not lost, but the plates are miscarried.

FEBRUARY 29: Card from Ten Kate. Mailed the first five chapters of the novel to Janvier, together with a few lines. Mrs. Hartmann made a short call. Copied and then wrote letters: to Cushing, Garrison, Dr. O'Connell, J. M. Vigil, James Jackson, at Paris, Dr. Walliser, Theodor Brühl.

MARCH

MARCH 1: Letter from Bertha [Lambelet]; Mali [Amalia Huegy] is coming only at the end of May. Copied, wrote for the Institute and translated at Chapter VII of the novel.

MARCH 2: I went down town and got, at the post office, a package of beautiful photographs sent by Mr. Jackson. In the afternoon, Louise and Julia came. Vicente and his associate put up the canvas in Papa's room. Copied, wrote, and translated. At night, Henry and Hubert came.

MARCH 3: Letter from John Pearce; he is better. I translated at the novel and wrote to Dr. Ten Kate. Mr. E. W. Meany spent the evening with us. We corrected the novel together.

MARCH 4: Went to Mass. Letter from Cushing. It is all right. In the afternoon, I went to see Father McCall at Father Defouri's and met Father Révion. Then with Koch to the brewery. Wrote to Harry Budd, and No. 6 to Cushing.

MARCH 5: Letter from R. A. Varden. Returned the documents to S. Ellison. Wrote at the Report for the Institute and translated some.

MARCH 6: Letters from the Hammond Typewriter Co. and from Professor Frothingham[950] of Baltimore. Wrote for the Institute and finished translation of Chapter VII of novel. Hubert called at night.

MARCH 7: Very unwell last night on account of too much beer. Feel bad today yet. This morning, we got two letters from Papa! Thank God! He is well and will sail from La Guayra [Venezuela], on the 9th inst. Also two letters from W. C. Kueffner. I returned acknowledgment at once. Went down town and then got a telegram from Pitt and Scott, New York. The plates are safe! Thank God also for it. Wrote for the Institute and translated a little too. Wrote to Varden, to Justino Rubio, and to Monsignor O'Connell. Joe down town in the afternoon.

MARCH 8: Letter from James Jackson. My monographs got to Paris all-right. Joe had another spell of headache, but the salve of Dr. Brühl took it away at once. Wrote for the Institute. Got two letters from F. Cushing, one with the check for $116. Left $100. with Mr. Schumann and sent a money order for $3.10 to the Hammond Typewriter Co. at New York. Crampton[951] came up here. Translated on Chapter VIII when John C. Pearce quite unexpectedly came. He had arrived this morning and is quite improved, but his left eye is half gone. His impressions of life in Chicago are not favorable; too much restlessness.

MARCH 9: Letters from Dr. Walliser and Harry Budd. I copied, translated and wrote. Went down town. Today, the news came of the death of the Emperor of Germany [Wilhelm I] at the age of 91.

MARCH 10: No letters. Wrote to Colonel Haren for a pass and to Frank Cushing, No. 7 [presumably, Chapter VII of the novel] by mail. Also to Father Navet. Went down town twice. In the afternoon, I met Mr. Boeninghoven[952] of the *Illinois Staatszeitung.* Night quiet, fine. Mr. Meany spent it here as usual. Today, I got from Ellison the sentence pronounced by Pedro Reneros de Posada[953] against the Indians captured by him at Santa Ana [Pueblo]. I copied it at once.

MARCH 11: Went to Mass, not very devoutly. The Archbishop leaves tonight for St. Louis. Letter from Peñafiel. [I] got a fierce "dolor de la rabadilla [backache]." Could hardly move. That comes from yesterday. Wrote to Dr. Walliser. Joe went to church also. In the afternoon, we went to the brewery, although Joe had a headache, and I, rheumatism of the worst kind. It was pleasant though; nevertheless, I suffered considerably. Boeninghoven, Schumann, Koch, Dr. Eggert were there. Also the agent of H. H. Bancroft.[954] Went to bed early, as the lumbago or rheumatism did not allow me to stay up.

MARCH 12: Lumbago rather worse although I put a strong sinapism on last night. Went down town early. Wrote two pages at my report. In the afternoon, Boeninghoven called, and I gave him seven letters for Mexico.

Got a letter from Janvier and a card from Mr. Balsiger, informing me of the death of Graffenried. Called on Felicitas Garcia[955] in the afternoon; she will give Joe some flowers. To Boeninghoven, I gave letters to Kaska and Guernsey and some cards. Wrote to Janvier.[956] At night Camilo came, also Koch and Hubert. Camilo is writing pretty well.

MARCH 13: Letter from Haren with Pass. Acknowledged reception. Card from Ten Kate. Our bulbs coming out nicely; we uncovered them today. I wrote and translated. John Pearce and Elbert called. Gave the latter orders to the aggregate amount of $14.60. "Daheim," $2; Macaulay, $7; Momensen [?], $5.60.

MARCH 14: Antonio Ortiz came in place of Atanasio, who is drunk since Sunday last. Wrote and translated. Sam Eldodt called, also Anita Staab and Felicitas Garcia; at night, Hubert. Card from James Jackson.

MARCH 15: Wrote six letters of introduction for Sam Eldodt.[957] Koch called; he wants to rent the outside orchard. Why, the Lord only knows! Did not strike a lick the whole day; I was lazy and good for nothing and shall confess it. Did not work; had no desires for anything, but bumming. In the afternoon, the girls came. I wrote to James Jackson.

MARCH 16: Letter from Vigil and from Mr. Balsiger. Wrote to Vigil and No. 8 to Cushing. Yesterday I paid to Antonio Ortiz $2.50 for two day's work. Could not do much as Brother Amian spent the afternoon with me. It was very pleasant. Wrote an article for *The Nation* and sent it off to Garrison. Worked but little.

MARCH 17: A very good letter from Franklin Beck. As Joe had her circle, I could not do anything and went out to the brewery, where I had a pleasant talk with Fischer and Gaertner. At night, Mr. Meany came and corrected the novel. Strike said to terminate tonight.

MARCH 18: A bad cold and lumbago worse again. Day may be fine yet, although it is cloudy at times and rather chilly. Did not go to church. Wrote letters: to Alphonse, Franklin Beck, Mr. Balsiger, and Dr. Brühl. In the afternoon, Gaertner called, then Hubert and Henry. Joe went down to Lizzie's. In the forenoon, Koch came and Spitz.[958] Wrote to Henry S. Budd. Conflicting rumors about the strike. The mail did not leave as no train went to Lamy.

MARCH 19: Letter from Rubio. Wrote to him and No. 9 to Cushing. Wrote for the Institute and also went down town. The mails are coming in now, slowly. It kept on snowing thick and fast, streets very muddy. I took quinine the whole day, and still have a very bad cold. Have nothing more to copy and yet do not feel like doing anything at the translation. My head is thick and heavy. I am unfit to work. I wrote to Professor Norton, Captain J. G. Bourke, and to Peñafiel.

MARCH 20: Letter from Baltimore. Went to the Brothers and got the copy of Sebastian de Herrera's testimony of 1681.[959] Copied it; also finished the Montezuma legend.[960] Joe spent the afternoon at Mrs. Catron's. Joe got a long letter from Eddy today. It is an entertaining document.

MARCH 21: Letter from Hammond T. W. Co. 1 Hectoliter = 2.-832 bushels. I went to see Antonio Ortiz y Salazar[961] and examined some of his old papers. Then to Uncle Sam Ellison,[962] where I got a whole lot of them. My cold is better.

MARCH 22: Henry made such a scene to Lizzie today, that we broke off all relations with him.[963] Copied. Hubert came at night. No letters.

MARCH 23: Returned to S. Ellison the document of 1713 and got one from 1681.[964] Was down town all morning settling up with the Archbishop and Koch's. Got a beautiful pipe from Jake's [Jake Gold's Curio Shop]. It is from Nambé. In the afternoon at home. My rheumatism is very bad. Copied. The girls came, and at night, Hubert.

MARCH 24: Letter from Sam Eldodt, and a telegram from Cushing. My rheumatism, very bad. Copied. Joe went to Fischers'

MARCH 25: Copied all day, as my rheumatism was too painful. Hubert came in the morning. No letters. My cold is nearly over, but the rheumatism is bad. Also the hand.

MARCH 26: Had a very bad night. Suffered a great deal, could not sleep. Walking and lying down equally painful. A sitting posture is the only one I can bear. The morning bright and clear, cool, quiet. Drove down and saw the Doctor. In the afternoon, I slept a little. The Dr. came, then Koch. Night cloudy. Much pain. I copied all afternoon, Uncle Ellison having lent me a new batch of documents.

MARCH 27: Horrible night. Pain excruciating. Very ill from pain. Letter from Cushing with check for $100. Much suffering all day. Copied. Dr. Strong came up in the afternoon. Pleasant. Also at night, and Hubert too.

MARCH 28: Pain still very strong. Copied. The Dr. came up in the morning. On the whole, the day was very painful. Wrote to Cushing and to Vigil.

MARCH 29: Splendid. Feel better. Went down town and enclosed a draft for $50. in a letter to Vigil and mailed it. Letters from Papa, Dr. Ernst, and Monsignor O'Connell. All right. Pain less violent. Day fine. I was down town nearly all day. Night fine. Wrote to Monsignor O'Connell.

MARCH 30: Went down town. Walking still painful. Wrote to Mali. Got books, etc. from Dr. Ernst. In the afternoon, Koch came. Also the girls. Ready to leave tonight for the Paso [El Paso], so I fixed up everything down town. At night, Hubert called.

MARCH 31: Left at 2:45 A.M. Trains on time. View beautiful in every direction. Reached El Paso at 6 P.M. and went to the Hotel Vendome. It is warm here, and pleasant, but still I feel that it will do me no good. W. H. Brown[965] died one-and-one-half years ago.

APRIL

APRIL 1: Found [Dr. ?] Hamy[966] and spent the morning with him. My sciatica is decidedly worse; I can barely walk ten steps. In the afternoon, went over to El Paso del Norte.[967] Everything is green there. The town considerably improved. Called on Emile Duchene and on Father Ortiz.[968] Both recognized me. Nicomedes [Lara or (y?) Leyva], the old scamp, had left over a year ago, taking the wife of old cacique, Manu Huero,[969] with him. It is a clear case of elopement. The couple is now at Las Cruces. This deranges my plans to some extent. Wrote to Joe and to Frank Cushing.

APRIL 2: Warm. Am a complete cripple again. Feverish at that. Was with Hamy most of the time and went to Paso del Norte with him. At night, severe cough began.

APRIL 3: Atrocious pain, much fever and catarrh. Still, I went over with Hamy and rented a room of Dr. Sebastian Vargas. The Padre showed me the "Primer Libro de Casamientos," begun in 1662 by Fray García de San Francisco. It contains the Act of Foundation (1659) and the blessing of the cornerstone (1662) of the present church. Shall copy them. Went to bed at 4 P.M. and had a violent chill. High fever all night. Very ill. While I was lying there, half dead from pain, chills, and heat, John F. Wielandy[970] surprised me with a very kind, friendly call. He is a Catholic now.

APRIL 4: Very weak. Still I moved across the river and copied.[971] Wrote to Joe also. Pain sometimes fearful. In the afternoon, we had an interview with Manu Huero at last. Hamy is now introduced to him. The old man was very glad to see me.

APRIL 5: A slight relief in pain. Finished copying and returned book to the Father.[972] Letter from Joe; nothing from Papa.

APRIL 6: Pain worse. Still, there seems to be some improvement. Took leave of everybody and got ten blanks from Peñafiel at the custom house. Then went back to El Paso, Texas, where at the Hotel, I found: Papa!! Thank God, after three long, sad years. The rest I need not write down. Felt well at once.

APRIL 7: Arrived home with Papa! How happy we are united again.[973] Joe is well. Papa slept well. Schumann, Koch, and Hubert called. Also Baby-Henry!![974] Hubert and Henry here in the evening. Gave $116. to Schumann.

APRIL 9: Quiet. Everything fine outside. Papa had a fine night and I also. Went down town. Everything seems so lovely again. Letters from Cushing and Wielandy. Papa is picking up gradually. Day remarkably fine. Sent book to Bourke and wrote to him, to Wielandy, to Mr. Balsiger, to Alphonse, Peñafiel, Cushing, and to Sam Eldodt. Wrote to Clotilde also. Papa and Joe went down to Baby-Henry.

APRIL 10: Went down town early. Letter. Vigil and W. Scott. Papa's trunks came. Archbishop at home. Saw Padre Coudert.[975] Wrote to W. Scott, to Bertha [Lambelet], Rosalie [Bandelier], Eddy [Huegy], and sent sample to J. M. Vigil. In the afternoon, Papa and Joe took their first stroll down town, while I copied at home. Papa's things came. He brought beautiful beetles, Orchideas, Fuchsias, and fine specimens of antiquities. Hubert came up tonight.

APRIL 11: Most beautiful. Papa is decidedly improving. Letter from E. Dufossé, Paris. In the afternoon, Dr. Strong called.

APRIL 12: Letters from Dr. Girard and Nacho [Ignacio] Garcia. Copied. Callers: Louise and Julia, and Hartmann and Hubert at night. Papa took a drive with Hartmann. Today, I irrigated the strawberries.

APRIL 13: No letters. Copied, irrigated, and worked. Had to go down town three times.

APRIL 14: No letters. Went and got a draft for francs, 75, and mailed it to E. Dufossé, Paris, for books. Wrote to Dr. Girard, and to E. Duchene, El Paso del Norte. In the afternoon, as Joe had her circle, Papa and I went to the brewery.

APRIL 15: Drove out to Tezuque; had a splendid drive. Went to the pueblo, [en route] stopped at Jud and the old woman. Papa seems very well pleased. Letter from Wielandy and from the *Evening Post.* Returned at 3 P.M. Lizzie is still unwell. Henry and Hubert came. Night quiet and fine. Koch came.

APRIL 16: Summer-like. Copied all day. In the afternoon, it thundered and so on. Tuesday. Hand became so bad, however, that

I could not write with it at all. On the 18th [Wednesday], Wielandy arrived. I copied with the machine. The weather cloudy, blustering on the 18th and 19th and constant threats of rain. Two slight sprinkles with thunder, one the 17th and one on the 19th. Papa very well and active. All the trees in bloom. On the 18th, two letters of Alphonse.

APRIL 20: Went down town with Papa. Letter from Walliser. Copied.

APRIL 21: In the afternoon, I copied the document of A.D. 1602 at the U.S. Surveyor General's Office.[976] Hubert came. No letters. Papa very well.

APRIL 22: Went up to the brewery, and then Mr. Schumann came home with me.

APRIL 23: I went down town and copied at the U.S. Surveyor General's Office. Letter from Mr. Balsiger.

APRIL 24: I copied at the U. S. Surveyor General's Office until 4 P.M. Letter from Captain Bourke.

APRIL 25: Letter from Harry S. Budd. Wrote to Cushing (No. 13), and report on work. Also to Vigil and to Captain Bourke. Hubert up.

APRIL 26: Towards evening, rain, turning into snow at nightfall! Poor blossoms! Letter from A. Nuñez Ortego. Wrote to him, to Padre Ortiz, and to Dr. Ernst.

APRIL 27: Letter from Professor Norton. Koch came in the afternoon.

APRIL 28: There is no damage as yet to fruit, at least in our garden. But the weather is abominable, though warmer than yesterday. Proof sheets came from Boston.

APRIL 29: Papa unwell. Letters from Seybt and Harry S. Budd. We walked up to the brewery and then, with the girls, up to the mesa. Coming home, Koch (of course) and Marcus Eldodt came. Wrote to Cushing (No. 14).

APRIL 30: Had a host of callers. The girls, Koch's women came in the afternoon. At night, Dr. Eggert; afterwards, Hubert and Miss Nehber. It was pleasant.

M A Y

MAY 1: No letters. At night, C. F. A. Fischer and the girls came. Also Hubert.

MAY 2: All these days I wrote at the Notes for the Institute, and Papa copied for me.[977] At night, Koch called.

MAY 3: Wrote, and Papa copied. Hubert up at night.

MAY 4: Letter from Professor Norton. I set to work at once at the Report which he asked.

MAY 5: I wrote to Professor Norton; sent him the Report he asked for, six pages text and sixteen pages Notes of Part I.[978] Went down town in the afternoon.

MAY 6: No letters. Wrote to Mr. Balsiger, to Hammond Typewriter Co., and to Cushing (No. 15); Koch was up here the whole afternoon. He is a veritable bore, bloated, pompous, and yet scheming. My machine broke, the main spring. Now I am in a nice fix again.

MAY 7: The mail has been very late, every day of the week, and today it came in at 9 A.M. Went to town with Papa. Letter from Hodge—Cushing, sick. Borrowed Francisco Delgado's[979] typewriter. In the afternoon, Koch was up again. Scene with Papa; he is always the same, and I got pretty angry when he wanted to leave us. This is played out for once; we will not stand it any longer.

MAY 8: All had a bad night, owing to Papa's conduct. Antonio at work today. Joe threatened with headache. No letters. Went to bed early.

MAY 9: Papa, a little less ugly, but Joe, in bed all day with very severe headache. Mrs. Hartmann came, and at night, Hubert. I copied and got some more documents. No letters again.

MAY 10: Day fine, but very busy. Baxter came. Out all day with him. Letter from Dr. Fritsch. Had a perfect stream of people here.

MAY 11: No letters. But at 3 P.M., a telegram from Eddy stating that Mali would be here tomorrow morning. Irrigated all afternoon and copied also. Hubert up here.

MAY 12: Mali arrived! No letters, but the books on Peru came back from Cushing.[980] It is getting monotonous. No money. So I went to the Archbishop and got $60, paid Winsor $5; to Spitz, $6.25; to Antonio, etc. In the afternoon, Joe had her circle, and so we went out, Papa on his side and I, on mine. At night, Koch and Hubert.

MAY 13: No letters from Cushing, but one from Dr. Brühl. Mexican Band (8th Cavalry) came. Hubert up, of course. In the afternoon, Papa and I went down to Koch's. He was alone and it was quite pleasant. Joe and Mali did not go to the concert. They went down to Lizzie's where we all took supper. I wrote a few lines to Bertha. Mr. Franz arrived this A.M. At night, a whole lot of visitors came: Franz, Schumann, Dr. Eggert, and Mr. K. . . . [Kaenter?].

MAY 14: Yesterday, I still wrote to Dr. W. A. Fritsch, at Evansville, Indiana. No letters! It is very disagreeable, indeed. Copied all day. Mrs. Gerdes[981] called today. Joe and Mali went down town in the morning.

MAY 15: This morning, Cushing's typewriter came, but in a terrible condition! Useless, completely useless! All broken! Wrote to Cushing. Returned typewriter to Francisco Delgado. It is exceedingly annoying. No letters. We made a call at Gerdes'. Very pleasant.

MAY 16: Letters from Ten Kate and from Hodge. Mailed Pima Vocabulary[982] to Peñafiel. Copied with the pen. Nine pages,

which is a good deal. Koch came up, of course; he has nothing else
to do! Hubert up, as usual.

MAY 17: Went down town early and staid all forenoon. No letters,
but the springs for my typewriter, from New York. Went up to
Fort Marcy with Mali. Ready to go.

MAY 18: I left Santa Fe on foot at 8:30 A.M. Stopped at Jud's for
half an hour. As I approached San Ildefonso, it sprinkled, thundered, and blew a short, cold blast. Reception at San Ildefonso
very friendly. First, had to attend to the business of a Jicarilla
Apache—Juan de Jesús, who is settled on the Rio del Oso and
cultivates land with his people.
    First, a preliminary junta [meeting], in which I explained my
ideas as well as I could; then a general meeting at night when all
the principals were there: the cacique (they have only one here),
Po-at-u-yo, the governor, etc. The meeting lasted till late and
terminated with a long prayer from the governor, but only after
the cacique and two more had left the junta.
    The people here deny knowing anything about the caves or
about the old pueblos opposite. In Apache, San Ildefonso is
called: *Qui-pli-plii*, and Santa Fe: *Jo-qŭ.*

MAY 19: Left San Ildefonso early and walked down to the railroad
bridge, three miles, and then along the railroad track, nine miles
to Española, where I met Alejandro [E. Campbell].[983] Wrote to
Joe and to Bartsch.[984] Am very tired and used up. Yesterday
twenty-four miles; today thirteen miles.
    Got to Santa Clara about 3 P.M. Kindest reception in the world
at Alejandro's. Doña Ramona unwell, but withal, I was received
with open arms. The situation at Santa Clara is critical, owing to
the division in the tribe. That division was explained to me fully
at night!
    There are two parties. One has been in power now for two
years, and the *Oyique*, the *Zihui*, the governor, and the *Quira-
na-Sendo*, belong to it. They are those who oppose Father Francolon. The other side has the *Payojque*, the *Tze-ojque* and the
Samayojque. The troubles come from the fact that the first party
recognizes, or claims the right to nominate, the governor,
whereas the other cluster claim it for the *Payojque* as *Po-a-tu-yo*,

or real cacique of the village.[985] The night was beautiful and cool, and we had a long talk outside. The people here claim positively that the caves of the Puyé, etc., and all the Pueblos around them, were inhabited by the Santa Claras. Those of San Ildefonso lived at *Tzirege, Perage,* [and] finally crossed the river to where they are now. *Kapo* was first about a half-mile west of the pueblo, near the outlet of the cañón.[986] The Laguna Peak: *Agatyona-Pii;* Sierra de las Truchas: *Qu-sa-pii;* and Baldy: *Poya-More-Pii.*

MAY 20: Beautiful day. The view from here is grand. The mountains in the east spread out to full length. Even the Jicarrita (in Tehua, *Jung-pii*) is visible. From opposite San Ildefonso, the Culebra and the Costilla are visible. Another name for the Rito de los Frijoles is *Tehua-tu.*[987] Got at the papers and copied one. Important. Took a room for a week.

MAY 21: The school here is in good order and progressing. Alejandro is well liked. He has now thirteen pupils.[988] The Pueblo is all at work on the acequia. Plenty of water in the arroyo and prospects of fine crops.

The oldest document I have seen here so far is from 1681, and the majority of the papers are "diligencias matrimoniales" and a number of church registers of every Pueblo, almost. They date as far back as 1694 in some instances. Among the "diligencias" are those of Pedro Ladron de Gubera[989] and others. I copied, then returned the copied documents to Felix Valverde [Velarde],[990] who is the keeper. Went to Española over noon. Got letter from Joe and my razor. Wrote to Joe. The night was delightfully clear, cool, and quiet. Copied until very nearly 11 P.M. Juan Diego Padilla told me today that the first chapel[991] stood on the bank of the arroyo, north of the pueblo, but I doubt it.

MAY 22: Copied. The village is almost empty of men, as they are all out on the acequia. I returned the copied originals and got new ones, still older. There is one from April and June 1680![992] Alejandro went to Española, so I wrote a few lines to Joe through him. Copied today eleven pages. All the documents are of the highest interest. Copied until after 10 P.M. Many Indians came visiting me.

MAY 23: Night good, but the Indians were rather stirring all the time. As often as I awoke, I heard them going about. Copied 10 pages. Went to Wallace[993] and got letter from Joe. Wrote to her, to Ten Kate, to Baxter, and to Dr. Brühl. Alejandro went to Española this evening with his guitar. There is a dance tonight, and he will play.

MAY 24: Bad night. Hardly any sleep at all. Copied. Night fine and cool. [Here, Bandelier recorded four lines, presumably of a song, and "Alejandro E. Campbell" was written alongside, in a hand other than Bandelier's. The lines are blurred and could not be meaningfully translated.]

Alejandro assured me that, when a child, he went with his family overland by way of the Manzano to Las Cruces and passed through the Quivira! Indians told him then that that was the Pueblo of Tabira! Alonzo Aguilar [of San Ildefonso] went with them as moso [servant] and he called the same pueblo: "La Gran Quivira."[994]

Staid up till 1 A.M. talking to the Indians. One of them told me that the present difficulty originated ten or eleven years ago, when they still cultivated land for the church. The cacique refused to allow his daughter to assist in getting the cornhusks for the church. He thereupon came to blows with the fiscal mayor, whom the governor had commanded to assist the cacique. A general row followed, and the division has been ever since. No remedy for it, unless the other Pueblos interfere. Outsiders cannot do anything.

MAY 25: Went to Española, wrote to Joe, and received a letter from her. Then, decided upon going to San Juan [Pueblo] for rest. Went there in a big blow of wind and dust.

MAY 26: Worked a little,[995] but on the whole felt lazy. Potatoes and chile slightly singed by the frost.

MAY 27: Copied a document belonging to Don Juan García.[996] Night less cold and rather clear. Nothing new here.

MAY 28: Wrote to Joe. Returned to Santa Clara. Letter from Joe.

MAY 29: Copied and finished documents about Fray Gerónimo de la Llana, 1759.[997] The altars of the church here bear date 1782 and were made by Fray Ramón Gonzalez.[998] The church is a big structure, very long and narrow. Nine-and-a-half pages [of documents] today. I have now, all told, seventy-two pages. Retired early, not having anything to copy.

MAY 30: Finished my copies, these last ones being the most valuable. About 2 P.M., Alejandro was suddenly arrested by Sheriff Louis Ortiz on a warrant from Mora County. I went bond on condition that somebody else would go in it too. Amount of bond, $200. Alejandro went to San Juan. He came back, released on his word.

I am through here now and return, so help God—with eighty-two pages of valuable documents.[999] Wrote to Mr. Parkman about l'Archévèque.[1000] José de Jesús Naranjo told me today that the old church of Santa Clara stood south of the present one.[1001] Am well satisfied so far.

MAY 31: Beautiful day. Cool. Ready to leave. Alejandro will copy for me the diligencias of Archévèque. Went over to Santa Cruz after writing to Joe from Española. Kindly received. Plenty of documents there also.

JUNE

JUNE 1: Wrote most of the day. The archives here are part of those from Santa Clara.[1002]

JUNE 2: Went over to Española and home by rail. At home, everything all right, thank God. Matters of salary explained, good letters, and all well. Koch and Hubert up, of course.

JUNE 3: Henry up. No letters. Arranged manuscripts. Wrote to Baxter, to Budd, and to Alejandro Campbell. In the afternoon, a host of callers. Still, we took a short walk yet.

JUNE 4: I was in town nearly all day. Got my pay from Father Stephan[1003] and left $200. with Mr. Schumann. Worked scarcely anything today.

JUNE 5: Copied. Letters from Cushing and Father Navet. The girls, Miss Nehber, Hubert, and [E. L.] Cole[1004] came after sunset.

JUNE 6: Today, Papa received the first letters from Venezuela. Copied.

JUNE 7: Letters from Alejandro and from Harry Budd. Wrote to F. H. Cushing, to Dr. Walliser, and to Captain Bourke. Before sunset, Wielandy came; afterwards, Koch. Father Francolon called.

JUNE 8: Letters from Dr. Brühl and Hodge. Had to go to the brewery. Archbishop lent me some documents. In the afternoon, Joe, Mali, and I took a drive to the heights of Tezuque and then to the Indian School. No picnic Sunday; Gaertner cannot go. Hubert came at nightfall.

JUNE 9: Letter from Baxter with check for April at last. Went down town in the forenoon, and left $60. with Schumann. In the afternoon, Joe had her circle, and I ran away to town. In the evening, Papa had a spell, but I stopped him pretty quick. Wrote to S. Baxter.

JUNE 10: Eastern mail came only at 5 P.M. Went to Mass. Went to the brewery with Henry and Hubert. Took a long walk, calling on the Manderfield girls. Letter from Alejandro.

JUNE 11: Antonio here. Wrote to Dr. Walliser and to Captain Bourke.

JUNE 16: I wrote to the Hammond Typewriter Co. and to Nuñez Ortego on the 14th, and to Mr. Parkman on the 15th.[1005] Dr. Strong spent the afternoon of the 14th [with us]. On the 15th, I began to copy at the U.S. Surveyor General's Office and copied the whole day and part of today, but it became so very hot up there, that I stopped and went to Dr. Strong's. All well, and Papa comparatively pleasant. Got letters from Mr. Parkman, from old Widmer, from Mrs. Parkman,[1006] and from Peñafiel. Very hot today. Koch left at night.

JUNE 17: Hot. Papa left on foot and alone for a long walk. He is determined to go. The old Doctor came, and I went up to the brewery with him. Papa came back about noon, tired. Hubert took dinner with us. In the afternoon, Tipton[1007] came. After supper, of course, Koch. He is a bore. No letters today.

JUNE 18: Went down town and copied at the U.S. Surveyor General's Office. Hartmann is better. Change in mails today.

JUNE 19: Was down town all day, copying. Finished the inventory of l'Archévèque. No letters again. At night, the Fischer girls, Miss Nehber, and Hubert called. Very pleasant evening.

JUNE 20: Copied all day at the Office. Letter from Dr. Obst, Leipzig. Yesterday, Papa commenced trimming vines, and today, the trees. This afternoon, the Staab girls called on Joe, and at night, Hubert for a moment. Miss Nehber leaves tonight for Europe.

JUNE 21: Began to write to Sam Eldodt last night; finished it today, also work at the Surveyor General's Office. Arranged with the Archbishop to go to the ranchito tomorrow with Papa. Papa cut the vines today. Mali sick all day. Joe went to the "guild" this afternoon.

JUNE 22: The Archbishop and Father Antonio drove us out to the ranchito, Papa and I, and we spent an exceedingly pleasant time. Returned home at 5 P.M. Mali is well again. No letters. Lizzie's birthday today.

JUNE 23: Papa irrigates well. Today, everything will be irrigated. I wrote at the Archbishop's, morning and afternoon. No letters. Evening most beautiful. Joe is in bed. It is less headache than nausea. Got well again at night.

JUNE 24: Henry began to pick cherries. Went to Mass. In the afternoon, Allard and Gonzalez came. Then I went to Dr. Eggert's and came home with Mr. Schumann, who took supper with us.

JUNE 25: Papa suffering from herniae. Had his truss fixed. Worked at the Archbishop's all day. Got nearly through. Father Mariller here. At night, beautiful illumination of the Brothers' College and fireworks. We went down to see it and quite unexpectedly met George Hoffmann and Emily Becker!! What a surprise! They had come by the Denver Road. Emily remained with us, while George staid at Koch's.

JUNE 26: In the morning, Koch came up with George and stayed till noon, all the while talking and managing the whole conversation. It was very disgusting! No letters. In the afternoon, Fathers Navet and Brun came. Solemn High Mass, nearly forty priests assisting. Evening at the brewery.

J U L Y

JULY 2:[1008] George and Emily left us last night, about 3 A.M., after spending not fully one week with us, and most pleasantly too. During all this week, I got but one letter—from Captain Bourke! It becomes very annoying.

Wrote to Hammond Typewriter Co. Also to Captain Bourke. No letters. In the afternoon, I went down town and saw Ed. Bartlett about the papers of David Miller.[1009] Got permission to copy them, but will not be able to see them before tomorrow morning. Papa acting mean again.

JULY 3: Antonio at work in the garden. Papa acting most foolishly. He is incorrigible. Got the repairs from Hammond T. W. Co., at last. Got after David Miller's papers. There is a lot of stuff, masonic, private, and incomplete recollections, notes about grants, in fact, all huddled together pellmell. It is difficult to get through. I avoided prying into anything and only selected those papers which, at first sight, were plainly old documents. These I took along, showed them to Captain Davis, offering to give him a receipt. He declined and referred me to Mr. Ed. L. Bartlett, who also refused to take any receipt. This was done in presence of Mr. Clancey [Frank W. Clancy],[1010] the partner of Catron! I copied one. Papa was very ugly all day. The girls called with gooseberries.

JULY 4: Card from Ten Kate and bill from the Hammond T. W. Co. Very cheap. Went down town. All full of people. Got some valuable documents from Sam Ellison. Last night, I got our ice-box.

The town is full of people, but we notice very little of the celebrations. Occasionally, we hear the music and the firecrackers. Papa as silly as ever! Tonight, our *Cereus grandiflora* blossomed. Boyle and wife, Felicitas, and Josefa came to see it.

JULY 5:[1011] Wrote to Cushing, to Ten Kate, to Dr. Brühl, and to Haren. Day similar. Papa ugly. No letters. The girls came in the afternoon. Returned the papers to Mr. Bartlett, except one, which Papa is copying.

JULY 6: No letters. *Lillium punctatum* opened today, beautifully. Boyle called to see it; also Felicitas. Copied.

JULY 7: No letters. Papa very silly and ugly. In the afternoon, we went up to the brewery with Dr. Strong. Dr. Eggert came up after 6 P.M., and we went down together. I took leave of Koch, Schumann, and Gerdes. Mrs. Hartmann and Hubert came up at night.

JULY 8: Papa in bed playing sick. Did not go to Mass. Letters from Harry Budd and E. L. Cole. The latter leaves Santa Fe, and it looks as if the so-called "University" was in a bad way.[1012] We spent the evening very pleasantly at the brewery. Henry, Lizzie, and the children came along.

JULY 9: Wrote to Louis Huning and to Garrison. Visit from Jesús Candelaria[1013] of Albuquerque.

JULY 10: No letters. It becomes disagreeable. I spent most of the day down town. Still copied some.

JULY 11: Left Santa Fe at 8 A.M. on foot. *T'-o-Bhi-pang-ge:* old Pueblo of Nambé, in the sierra, about eight miles northeast of Nambé. At the Chupadero: *Que-guayo. Agaaono:* in the Santo Helado. *Ka-a-iu,* also in the same direction.[1014]

I stopped at Jud's for about half an hour and then went on. A little beyond Muller's,[1015] I turned off to the left [?], but soon lost the trail and became entangled in a maze of arid "cuchillas" with steep slopes heading down into rents and washes. Wild but not picturesque. Trees are getting larger. With considerable exertion, always going to the northeast, I at last reached the ridge above the southern arm of the Rio de los Chupaderos and descended to the Chupaderos themselves, about five miles above Nambé, a fertile spot with some houses on it. It is encased by steep ledges, and there are many trees along the banks.

Descending the little stream, it soon ran out to a sandy and dry arroyo. At its junction with the western arm, the Rio de Nambé proper, the valley suddenly widens and becomes a level, well cultivated and about two miles broad from north to south. This is the valley of Nambé. It is very handsome and slopes gently to the west. The river hugs the southern loma. Many Mexican houses dot the valley, and the little Pueblo of Nambé with its tall church, stands in the midst of green fields. Many of the houses are empty and in ruins.[1016]

To my surprise, I met Desiderio from Tezuque there. Spent the afternoon with him and the governor pleasantly and then went down to the house of Juan Luján, about a mile farther west, where I was most kindly received and was told all about the brujos of 1855.[1017]

JULY 12: Reached Santa Cruz at noon, crossing by the trail to the Arroyo Seco, a desolate, arid, waterless stretch. It was very hot. Tired. Spent the afternoon and night at Santa Cruz very pleasantly at Father Francolon's. Clear, night quiet. They have had no rain for three months, but damaging hail four times. Everything looks dry and parched.

JULY 13: Father Francolon drove me over to Santa Clara. Letter from Joe, and wrote to her. At the Pueblo everything all right, except that Alejandro is not there. Got document to copy. Bourke here![1018]

JULY 14: About 2 P.M., a tremendous hail storm formed opposite San Ildefonso and moved northwards. West of us, the Rio de Santa Clara, which is dry, came suddenly high and roaring. They are working at the acequia now. Wheat is ripe for cutting at Nambé and here, and the people look forward to a fine crop. Tonight is cool; heretofor, the nights have been abominable. But the room is full of bedbugs and chicken-lice, and I have not slept any.

JULY 15: A few sprinkles. Gusts of wind from every quarter. Copied all day and night.

JULY 16: Went to Española and arranged with [Father L.] Rémuzon[1019] to go with him to the Valles [Valle Grande]. Letter from Joe and wrote to her. Finished copying late. Am through so far.

JULY 17: Tolerably clear in the morning and hot, very hot. Left for Española about 10 A.M. and got there, my shoes and the flask. Packed up the manuscripts and the mocassins [*sic*] and left them with Ed. Johnson. A little before noon we started—Father L. Rémuzon and I, he on horseback and with a loaded burro, I on foot.

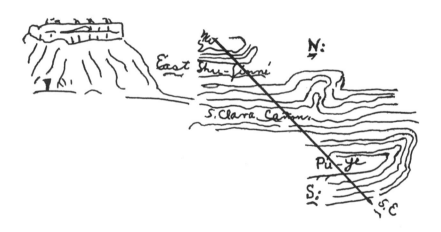

We crossed the mesa west of Española, rising to it by a long and steep "cuesta," then a barren plain, very good walking, to the low timber at the foot of the *Shu-fi-né* [Shu-finné]. This rock stands higher than the *Pu-yé,* [and it] is also higher from the base, steeper. The rocky crown, along which the caves are, is lower, and in extent it appears much smaller. Probably only one-third as many people lived in it. Otherwise, the conditions are similar. Timber around its base and no water nearer than the [Santa

Clara] Cañón, which is about a half-mile to the north of it.* There are two tiers of caves in places. On the road, we lost our burro, and while I remained in camp at the old saw mill, Rémuzon went after the animal and brought it in. Rémuzon shot a young skunk. He told me that he saw mountain sheep at the Jicarrita last week. Also traces of a small glacier. There is still much snow over there.

JULY 18: Our animals got away last night, and it took some time to find them. Left at 11 A.M. and ascended the Cañón. It is picturesque and grand. Towering wall and steep slopes. Dense forest of pine, álamos, pinyon [?], too, with the Rio de Santa Clara darting through it. Towards 4 P.M., it rained and grew very cold. As we approached the divide, beautiful grass and fine groves of álamos and pino real made their appearance. Raspberries and fine flowers. The divide is a dense forest of pino real and álamo. Stopped for the night at an empty log cabin, about two miles west of the "Bordo." Distance to the Bordo from Española: about 28 miles. Made 18 miles this afternoon. Sheepherders from Peña Blanca came to us. Saw grouse near the divide.

JULY 19: The descent from the divide is rapid. It follows a brook, is covered with tall grass, and beautiful groves of pino real and high straight álamos. Better than a description, a map will show.

From the divide to the source of the Rio de la Jara, three miles. Thence to the Valle Grande, or Valle de Toledo, two miles. Left this Valle south of us and traversed the Valle de Santa Rosa, three miles; then the Valle de San Antonio, four miles. Then into the Cañón de San Antonio to the Ojos, three miles. Total from Española: 43 miles. The divide must be about 10,000 feet; the Ojos de San Antonio, 8,500 feet.

The Valles are three beautiful, grassy basins, through which the Rio de San Antonio meanders. They are full of Atascaderos [bogs], and the stream is filled with trout. On the whole, it is the most beautiful country I have as yet seen in New Mexico. The Cañón de San Antonio is very narrow and picturesque. The rock seems to be volcanic. Vegetation grand. Got wet thoroughly, both by the rain and while fording the river. The hot springs (temp. about 110° F.) are at least 250 feet above the river and steep slope. The volume of water is considerable.

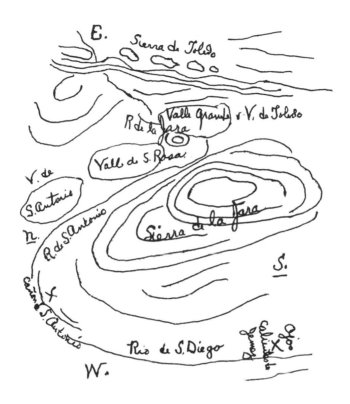

JULY 20: Spent the day at the Ojos. It was beautiful. I bathed twice. Many flowers. Lilies, iris, etc. Many beetles. In winter, it is very cold and frost still in May. Still they attempt to grow potatoes. The whole region is magnificent, and there is much game yet: principally bear and turkey. Some deer. Grouse is abundant. So is trout. Very heavy dews every night. The sheep herds are out of the Valles and grazing in the adjacent timbered slopes.[1020]

JULY 21: Left the Ojos about 10 A.M. and walked down to the Jemez Springs, distance 17 miles, with Mr. Judt. A beautiful trail, through thick woods, down the narrow and picturesque Cañón, through which the water rushes, clear and like a torrent. Five miles below San Antonio, at La Cueva, the Cañón de San Diego begins, wooded and very grand. Oak trees, quite tall, appear two miles beyond the Cueva. At La Cueva are the ranches of D'Arcy and Judt. Afterwards, it is uninhabited, but very beautiful for eight miles. The mountains gradually assume the mesa-formation, and they appear at least 700 feet, if not 1,000, above the gushing torrents of the river.

Very grand scenery, at "Seltzer Springs" by the road, four miles from the Jemez baths. Then the Cañón opens, and the road leaves the timber. Large deposits of native sulphur. At the saw-mill of Everhard, two miles farther on, the soda closes with a cataract of hot water [Soda Dam] and fine emerald green stalactites.[1021] The church of San Diego is a half-mile above the Ojos Calientes.

Six miles from San Antonio, southeast, are the sulphur springs with mud baths. They lie three miles from D'Arcy's to the left; going down, about the Seltzer Springs, we had quite a shower and got wet. It thundered all afternoon on all sides. Reached the Hot Springs about 3:30 P.M., where I met Koch, Schumann, Dr. Haroun,[1022] Gerdes, and Mr. L. Huning and family, all in good health and spirits; also Mariano Otero[1023] and family. Very pleasant and kind reception.

The baths lie in an open valley picturesquely framed by towering mesas. In the background, where the valley descends, the ruins of the church of San Diego[1024] are seen. The valley is oblong, about one-and-a-half to two miles long and a quarter-of-a-mile wide. To the right, or west, is the Potrero de los Garcias with three ruins on the top. To the left, the potreros bear also three ruins. Beyond the Rio de la Virgen, there is one ruin on the Potrero del Chisé and one on the Potrero de la Cebollita.[1025]

JULY 22: Walked up to San Diego with Schumann and Dr. Haroun. The church is of stone, and the walls are nearly eight feet thick. It is built against the slope and faces south. To the rear of the choir and half-way up the slope on the north is an octagonal watchtower which was entered from the church and has loopholes. It was two stories high. The convent is all gone, but the high wall remains in part. West of the church, on the slope towards the river, lies the ruin of the pueblo. The houses touch the western walls of the church. They were two stories high, walls of rough stones and of mud.* Two estufas are still visible. All over-

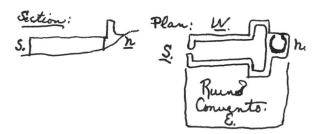

grown with very large *Opuntia* and some of them are the largest and tallest specimens I ever saw.

The pueblo was not large; it could accommodate about 500 people, and it does not extend to the water's edge. Pottery, obsidian, etc., as usual. Glossy specimens about. In the Valles and higher up the cañones, there are no traces of ruins.

About 4 P.M., the river suddenly rose and came very red—muddy. It rained heavily higher up. Mr. D'Arcy came. He tells me that on his place, he ploughed up pottery and that around there, on the second and third ledges above the bottoms of the cañones, also at the Cebolla, there are many ruins of detached houses. They were small and of stone. But no pueblos.

JULY 23: Rose at 4 A.M. and left at 5:30 with Koch and the others. Descended the cañón. It is beautiful. The river high and thick and red. The last mesa, the one forming the point, where the Rio de la Virgen joins the one of San Diego, and on top of which is San Joseph de los Jemez, is separated from the Mesa of Amoxiumqua by a depression. This is the section down to the junction of the two rivers:*

The valley is fertile, but still they have had but slight rains, although almost daily. At Jemez, found two letters, one from Joe and one from Haren. Remained with Father Mariller, while the others went on. Father Mariller told me about the two brujos of Cia [Zia], man and wife, killed in 1878. The man's name was Hilario, and he was shot and killed by one San Antonio. Afterwards, they killed his wife also, as she came and wanted to save her husband. But it is not certain that they were killed for the crime of sorcery. About that time, a young Mexican disappeared, and Hilario is said to have threatened to accuse the others of Cia to have murdered him. For this threat, he was killed. Padre [Manuel] Chavez[1026] was priest of Jemez at that time. The case is obscure and *not* clearly one of witchcraft. It may have been one of private revenge.[1027]

JULY 24: The Governor of the Pueblo, Agustín Cota, an Indian from Pecos, came. Will have another interview with him tonight. Miguel García of San Isidro told us about the Cia matter. When the Indian of Cia noticed that his life was threatened, he fled to Padre Manuel Chavez at Jemez, who sent him back to San Isidro with a letter for Don Miguel García, but he was not at home. So the Indian returned to Cia, late, hoping to reach his home unobserved, but they had spies out and as he came up the hill to the pueblo, he was shot and killed.

When Don Miguel went to Cia on the following day and asked of the Indians why they had done the deed, they simply replied: "Porque era muy Pícaro [Because he was very evil]." The Padre told me that last year an Indian of Jemez struck the cacique, who accused him before the governor. The latter condemned the Indian to be whipped, and to a fine of $50. The Indian was accordingly stripped, tied to a post in the plaza and received 25 lashes.

When the Indian of Jemez dies, guard is kept over his tomb for two days and two nights with firearms. I must correct about San Joseph de los Jemez![1028] It lies at the foot of the Mesa, not on the Mesa itself. See diagram:

Got a letter from Joe and wrote to her at once in reply. All well and happy, thank God! Father Mariller told me of a strange cachina [kachina] that he witnessed at Cia last spring. The Indians were in two files, the men on one side and the women on the other. Between was a little cart filled with cotton, looking much like a round cheese and a man shaking rattles. One man and one woman always came together, took hold of the idol and made some ceremonies with it.[1029]

JULY 25: Mass of Santiago. Afterwards, had a conference with the three Pecos Indians: Agustín Cota, José Miguel Vigil, and José Romero. The name of the Pueblo of Pecos is: *Tzi-quit-e;* of the tribe: *Pa-qui-ala.*

Names of the Pecos Indians, still alive:

José Miguel Vigil, married into Jemez.

Agustín Cota, married into Jemez.

José Romero, married into Jemez.

Lázaro Romero.

Juanita Vigil, 4 children.

Reyes Chama, [married to?] José Reyes Gallina, with children.

Rosita Romero, married to Armenta.

Francisco Romero.

Reyes Chama, married to José Antonio Vigil: seven children.

(21 in all)

El Pueblo de la Rueda: *Qu-uäng-ua-ba.*

Gusano Pueblo: *Se-yu-pai.*

San Antonio Pueblo: *Po-mo-jo-ua.*

Pajarito Pueblo: *Se-yu-pa-lo.*

When the Spaniards first came, the Pecos lived in one pueblo only, the one of *Tzi-quit-e* which is the great pueblo known today as old Pecos. This former village extended as far as Pajarito, and not beyond.

Those who came to Jemez in 1839–40 were six men and three women. The children all had died of mountain-fever.[1030]

About noon, Father Defouri arrived with his nephew Joseph and with a Frenchman from California, Mr. Vessé. We left in a buggy, Francisco Montoya Romero and I. Before reaching San Isidro, we caught a shower and a slight ducking. Reached Cia [Zia Pueblo].

The church is large, and the outer walls are asserted to be those of the church prior to 1680, the new walls being built inside of them. The appearance justifies the presumption of old age. The pueblo, it is said, was first east of its present situation.[1031] Even in the present day, the most of the houses (they are chiefly built of lava, small blocks in mud) are in ruins. We stopped at the house of the Sacristan, Juan de Dios, but only a moment.

Afterwards, we kept on the east side of the river, which is not as sandy as the other side, still sandy and heavy enough. We cut across a sandy and hilly promontory, on the south of which stands the Pueblo of Santa Ana,[1032] almost on the river bank and on a slope. It is larger in reality than it appears to be and, in fact, consists of three long streets. The houses are mostly with an upper story and resemble Acoma to some extent. The church is large and in tolerable repair. The altar painting is not very good, but there are two heads which, although badly disfigured by rain, etc. still appear fair. The governor told me that the first pueblo of Santa Ana was in the caja [box cañón], southeast of the present village. Thence they moved to the mesa and finally to where they are now.

Vespers,[1033] as Father Mariller came. While the ceremony was going on, they came on drum-beating and firing guns and as often as the words of "Gloria Patri" were pronounced, they rang the bells, beat the drum, and fired guns. Very few people attended Vespers.

JULY 26: As Mass was announced, they entered in a short procession. First, the fiscal, then two little horses on two legs, well made, and which a masked man followed, whipping them up. They are on two legs and played well by two men or grown boys, who are horse smiths at the same time. The little ponies are bridled and saddled and look well. Last night, it seems, they performed already some ceremonies with them, holding long talks to them in their idiom. Some Navajos here.

Last night, they held meetings in the estufas, blessing the caballitos [little horses]. Yesterday, they practiced [performed] the "gallo" at Jemez, Cia, and Santa Ana. During Mass, the same salutes were fired, and the drum beaten inside of the church at intervals. At the procession, the cross-bearer followed the drum-beater and the two little horses. The procession was followed by Indians on horseback. One of the little horsemen was an Indian, painted black, with bow and arrow; and other a Spaniard, with hat (old black common felt) and an old sword. In the second street, a bower, with fine tilmas, for the statues of the saints. The dance began at 1 P.M. First came the Qo-sha-re [Koshare] and danced in the churchyard; then followed the Qui-ra-na [Kwirena]. Afterwards, they went to the plaza.[1034]

I left soon, on foot, for Bernalillo, where I arrived at 4 P.M. Distance: nine miles, heavy sand, even on the mesa, very hot, but clear.

JULY 27: Spent the day at Bernalillo; visited Mariano Otero, Brother Gabriel, Schuster,[1035] Block,[1036] and José Gutierrez. Wrote a line to Joe.

In conversation, Father Parisis told me some facts about the big rattlesnakes, that convinced me of the existence, in caves, of huge reptiles of that species, which the Indians feed with rabbits and sacred meal. He cited the following instances:

1. While Father Fiallon [Joseph Fialon][1037] was at Bernalillo, the snake of the Indians of Sandia came down from the mountains to a grove near the pueblo. There it was discovered, and soon the people congregated. They made a great noise, caught rabbits, and fed the monster also with sacred meal and finally drove it back to its hole. The priest saw only the trail made by the snake, and it looked like the trace of a big timber.

2. While Father Parisis was at Isleta, and Indians confessed to him that they kept a large snake in a cavity of the Cerro del Ayro [?]. One man was specially charged with the duty of feeding it with rabbits and with meal. That keeper neglected his duty, and the snake came out and was discovered by some maidens. They gave the alarm, and the Indians at once ran out and managed to get the snake back to its hole. Later on, however, it escaped again; they followed the track as far as the Rio Puerco, where it vanished. Since then the people of Isleta gave up the custom.

3. Father Parisis visited San Diego de Jemez once with an Indian from Isleta. That Indian discovered in the rocks of the Mesa de los Garcias, a small opening closed by a plate of rock.

Removing the plate, he discovered an enormous snake coiled up inside of a cave. He ran back to inform the priest, who at once went to see. The snake was gone, but while it was not safe to venture inside, they still removed from near the entrance: tufts of rabbit hair and eagle's plumes, tied to little bunches!

In presence of these facts, I can hardly doubt the fact that big snakes are sometimes kept and treated as fetiches by the Pueblos.[1038]

JULY 28: Left Bernalillo on foot at 9 A.M. Reached Wallace at 4 P.M. and Peña Blanca at 6 P.M. Found Papa, hale and hearty, and a letter from Joe.

JULY 29: At Mass, Father Navet spoke well, and he related a case about witchcraft which I put down here. He was often begged by people to allow them to fill the sacred lamp with fresh oil *themselves.* Their object is, in so doing, to use the oil afterwards for killing the brujos. Doña Soledad also said that the custom of placing a broom across the doorway against witches is very common. They insert, in the eye of a needle, another needle crosswise, and this little cross of needles they fasten into one of the popotes [straws] of the broom.[1039]

I remained at Peña Blanca all day.

JULY 30: I left Peña Blanca at 5:30 A.M., stopped two hours at the Bajada,[1040] and reached home, tired and hot, at 6 P.M. Found everybody well. Thank God! Letters from Mrs. Cushing, Baxter, and the Hammond T. W. Co.

JULY 31: Went down town, and, in the afternoon, to Fischers. No letters.

AUGUST

AUGUST 1: Wrote to Baxter, Vigil, Pretorius, to Rémuzon, etc. Dr. Eggert came in the morning. Hartmann and wife took supper with us.

AUGUST 2: Father Ribera came. Letters from Dr. Ernst and others. Ready to start.

We started on the third and spent a pleasant time. Cannot hold the pen and therefore make it short.[1041] On the third went to Peña Blanca, where we met Father Antonio, who was very disagreeable. Next day to Santo Domingo (4th of August) where we saw a beautiful dance. *Ayash-tyu-cotz.* Next day to Cochiti about school.[1042] Father Fournier was there. He is priest of Hippone, in North Africa. Sunday, the 5th, was a beautiful, cloudless day, but very hot.

AUGUST 6: Reached Santa Fe at 11 A.M. Found letters from Baxter, with check; from Eldodt, Father Meckel. At night, the Fischer girls, Koch, Mrs. Hartmann, Henry, and Hubert came up. My hand is so bad I can hardly write.

AUGUST 7: No letters. Copied all day. After supper, Mr. Danckegny [Danckengny][1043] from Belen called. He is sick and at the hospital. Took cold at Jemez.

AUGUST 8: Antonio irrigating our garden. Letter from the Hammond Typewriter Co. Copied all day. At night, clear with brisk easterly breeze. Danckegny came, and we went together to the brewery. Afterwards, I called on the Doctor and at the Archbishop's. Hubert up at night. I wrote to Baxter and to Mr. Balsiger at night.

AUGUST 9: Copied. Letter from Seler. Wrote to Cushing and to the Hammond T. W. Co., mailing $1.07. Danckegny called.

AUGUST 10: It is terribly dry. Antonio finished irrigating today. It took 47 tanks and 62 extra buckets. I copied until 3:30 P.M. and then went to town. No letters. Hubert up at night. I wrote to Sam Eldodt. The drouth becomes alarming. We have enough water yet, but the Rio de Santa Fé is dry and the acequias feel it.

AUGUST 11: Letter from Padre Navet and Papa. Sent him, by express, . . . [?], two ounces rhubarb, and some papers. Obtained the three manuscripts from General Bartlett and gave him receipt for the same. Mahler in town. I copied a little. Wrote to Father Mariller and to Papa. Koch called.

AUGUST 12:[1044] Henry picking peaches. Letters from Hodge, Alphonse, and two checks from Cushing for Budd and a letter and draft for $25.— from Alphonse for Papa. Sent the checks to Budd, wrote to Cushing and to Papa also, enclosing letter and draft from Alphonse. Went to Mass. Very hot and dry. Saw Mr. Danckengny. In the afternoon it clouded more and more, it thundered and threatened rain. Still not a drop fell. I wrote to Father Meckel also. Spent the evening at the brewery with Henry. It was very pleasant.

AUGUST 13: I copied and, at night, wrote the two articles for *The Nation*[1045] and mailed them to Garrison. Circus in town. A horrible noise while the two musics were playing. I brought down to the binder the three manuscripts received from Bartlett.

AUGUST 14: I did not do anything today, beyond making the index for the volume of documents. Just when I was going down town with them, Mahler came. In the afternoon, I went down town, delivered the volume, and made several calls. Wielandy back; he is well satisfied with his trip. Met Danckengny. At night, Joe and Amalia went to the concert with Hubert.

AUGUST 15: Letters from Vigil, Hodge, Papa, and Camilo. Sent vouchers to Hodge.

I went down town, and in the evening we had Mahler, Wielandy for supper. Schumann and the Doctor came later. It was a delightful night and on the whole very pleasant. Marcos Eldodt's youngest child died today. Copied but very little today. The water is shut off and defense [it is forbidden] to irrigate, owing to limited supply in reservoirs. Signs of the times!

AUGUST 16: Letters from Budd and from Janvier. Funeral of Marcos' child this A.M. Poor little being, neglected by his mother.

In the afternoon I copied. At night, Henry and Hubert came.

AUGUST 17: At midnight a nice little shower. Morning dark clouds low over the mountains and showers, slow and gentle. There is no heavy rain as yet, but evidently it is coming. Thank God, for the water is giving out everywhere, even in the reservoir. The ground swallows every drop that falls.

I copied all day, in the forenoon at the novel, in the afternoon at my documents. In the evening, Mahler came to bid us good bye. Went to the Archbishop, but he had gone to Bernalillo.

I am now copying the novel according to Janvier's directions.[1046]

AUGUST 18: Letter from Papa. He is always the same grumbler, and never satisfied. Well, he must stand it, there is no way to get over it now.

I copied some at my novel and at 3 P.M., I went up to the brewery to meet Dr. Strong. Passed a few pleasant hours.

Evening beautiful. Hubert came up.

AUGUST 19: I copied at the novel. In the afternoon, Goebel[1047] and his wife called. Afterwards, Koch.

AUGUST 20: No letters either. Wrote to the Hammond T. W. Co.

The day remained hot, quiet and dry until 4 P.M. when suddenly a cloud opened directly above us, and it began to hail and afterwards to rain. This broke the ice. At sunset, another heavy shower from the northwest, and at 11 P.M. a third one. Everybody rejoices, for the rainy season appears to have begun at last. Air cool and quiet.

In the afternoon, Mr. Schumann called, and in the morning, Father Antonio. Just as the rain began, Ha-yo-ue arrived. He stays with us, in Papa's room. We talked nearly all night.

Ha-yo-ue told me that the *Cha-ya-ni* are invested by the capitán a guerra [war captain, or *masewa*] and by his lieutenant, the o-yo-ya-ua. The party who wishes to become *chayay* has to make the application himself directly. On the day set, the maseua and his brother, the oyoyaua, go to the place where the candidate is and sit on both sides of him, the maseua to the right and the oyoyaua to the left. Thereafter, the maseua and his brother are obliged to protect the *Chayani* all; they also have the duty to punish them, in case they do wrong. These two dignitaries, the maseua and the oyoyaua, are the representatives, upon earth, of the equivalents of the maseua *Q'o-Q'a-Tyumishe,* which in turn correspond to *Mai-Tza-La-Ima* and his brother *A-Hui-Uta* of Zuñi.

It is the rule, that the *Ho-Tsha-Nyi* [cacique] is always *Hish-Ta-Nyi Cha-Yan mayor* [Head Flint medicine man] (*Na-Ua* [chief]). He it is who holds in his power all the higher medicines. The *Shkuy-Chayan* [Giant Society head] and the *Shi-ka-ma Chayan* [Shikame Society head] are his assistants insofar that these three together are the *Yaya* ["mothers"], since they are those who intercede with the *Yaya-Tesh*, or higher good spirits, who fast and pray for the good of the tribe in general. But only the *Hotshanyi* has the medicines; the others have to go to him for whatever they need. The *Hish-tanyi Chayan* has also the great war-medicine, and he it is who prepares and fits out the warrior, previous to starting for a campaign. This, as for instance: the putting on of the war paint and anointing of the weapons with the sacred paints, etc. is done in the night before the departure. Only the *Hishtanyi Chayan,* or one of his assistants, has the right and power to do this. For it seems that the three great *chayani* are but the heads of so many departments, so to say: the *Hishtanyi* has under him a certain number of what might be called assistant *Hishtanyis;* the *Shkuy,* a certain number of assistant *Shkuys;* and the *Shikame,* also a band of *Shikame* assistants. Each can delegate his powers only to his particular assistants. All are medicine men, doctors, in addition to their higher arts and duties.

I gather that the *Uisht-Ya-Ka* is also the *Shkuy-Naua,* and the *Shay-Ka-Tze* is the *Shi-Ka-Ma-Na-Ua.* So there would be only three *yaya.* These are not permitted to listen to anything conducive to disorder or strife within the tribe. If in any meeting an angry discussion arises, or there are any signs of trouble, the *Yayas* must leave forthwith, and should they refuse, it is the duty of the maseua and of his brother, or lieutenant, to *compel* them to leave in case they do wish to stay.

When a war party returns with trophies, the *Hishtanyi* is the only one who dares go out to receive them, conduct them in triumph to the pueblo, and prepare them afterwards for the solemn dance with the scalps. Neither of the other two or any of their assistants can touch these matters. If they do it, they are exposed to grave punishment.[1048]

When anybody dies, they place in a corner of the room, or where he or she has expired, an ear of *blue corn* with barbs at the point, called *Ko-ton-a.*[1049] This ear represents the soul of the deceased, which still hovers about the place. Alongside of it, they put a small club. At the close of the fourth day, the three *chayanis* go there. One of them sings and prays, while another takes away the club and the ear of corn to some unknown place.

I forgot to state that when they first place the ear and the club, they surround these objects with a circle of crosses scratched in the floor. These crosses ... X X, are intended for the footprints of the bird called *Sha-shqa* or the paisano [roadrunner]. From the shape of such tracks, it is impossible to determine if the bird goes forward or backward. These tokens constitute a magic circle for the purpose of preventing evil spirits, or brujos, to find out where the soul of the deceased goes and thus protect that soul from their persecutions. When the ear and club are removed, while the singing and praying is going on, the last ceremony performed is the obliteration of the X-marks by one of the medicine men, and with the plume of an eagle. When the marks are all destroyed, the ceremony is over.

In regard to the origin of the Ko-sha-re and of the Cui-ra-na [Kwirena], the lore is about the same at Cochiti as it is at San Juan. There are some songs, still preserved, which say that the Koshare came down on the east side of the Rio Grande, while the Cuirana descended on the west, or mountainous side. But he says that all these tales are the subject of particular chants or songs, which are mostly known only to the initiated alone. Many of these songs are being lost through death of the old men.

About the Rito [de los Frijoles], he confirms the story, that the caves were originally inhabited by the Queres [Keres] and also made by them. He laughs at the name of *Yapashi,* given to the ruin on the Potrero de las Vacas.[1050]

In regard to the souls of good men, he asserts that they are going to "Our Mother." An ear of *blue* corn is the symbol of such a soul. They are *Ko-Pish-Tai,* also *Shiuana* [kachinas]. The Sun-father: *Se-Tshe-Ya-Nash-Tio,* is *Kopishtai* and *Shiuana* too; so is the Moon-mother: *Se-Tshe-A Naya.* The former resides also in the sun; the latter mostly in the moon, but not always.

Evil spirits are those of living men and those are the brujos: *Kan-At-Ya.* Demons properly, they have not in their aboriginal creed, for *Shu-at-yam* is, from what I can gather, but a Spanish Catholic idea and a corruption of the word and idea of "Satanas," "Satan," or "Sheitan [Shaitan, evil spirit]."

Consequently, there is in fact no evil principle [or principal?] in the higher, spiritual world. But the brujos have one superior, who is a living being and who is called *Kan-At-Ya Na-Ua*.[1051] They come together in caves or underground. After their death, they can do no more harm; therefore, it is a duty to kill them! But anyone who discovers a brujo must not disclose it. Otherwise, if he accuses him, he will die before that brujo. All he has to do is to kill him. In that case, the *Kanat-ya* will not die at once, but he will pine away for the lapse of several days and finally die, apparently of a natural death.

The symbol of the soul of a sorcerer is an ear of *violet* (not of yellow) corn. To this is attributed the gift of speech.[1052] In the absence of the witch, that corn will speak and say what the sorcerer or the witch would do meanwhile. Of a personal devil or demon, nothing is known, except through teachings of the Church. It seems that death is a final atonement for everything, and no punishment meted out whatever.[1053]

AUGUST 21: Concluded to ride to Peña Blanca with Hayoue tomorrow early. I take Koch's Navajo pony. The soil is already dried up fully and we can use much more rain yet.

At night, while it was raining hard, Hayoue related to us a great many things. There exist a kind of *Chayani* called: Fire Chayani, *Ha-ka-nyi* Chayani. They are a subdivision of the Hish-tanyi, and the Ho-tsha-nyi is now, at Cochiti, the only Fire Chayan existing still. Formerly, there used to be three or four of them. Hayoue recollects distinctly having seen, that they *ate fire!* This was done in a case of sickness and used as a cure. He describes the process as follows:

The Chayani met in the room of the sick individual. Each one held in hand a little broom-like tuft of grass (popote). They began to sing and, at a certain part of the song, the *Ha-ka-nyi Na-Ua*, who is the cacique always, bit off a part of the end of that broom which had previously been set on fire.

The broom was waved to the north, west, south, east, above, and below, in succession, and each time the chayani took a bite of the flaming grass and chewed it. After the Na-Ua had done this, the others performed the same operation in turn. Then the chewed ashes were spit into the face and on the body of the sick party, and he was thoroughly besmeared with them. This was the cure. He assures that the chayani did all this with perfect impunity, and he attributes it to the four or eight days rigorous and absolute fasting, which precedes such a ceremony *always*. If the fasting is done with perfect free will and carried out fully, then the chayani will eat the fire with total impunity; if not, they will suffer from it themselves. The same is the case with the *Fire Dance*. In it, the chayani, one after another, jump into a flaming pyre and dance in the very center of the flames. But should any of them fast irregularly, he will be scorched. If not, he can brave the fire.

He also mentioned, among others, one very remarkable trick, which *he himself* saw performed at his father's house. Some of the chayani placed a white screen in the background of a darkened room. Behind it and on the floor, they placed a round disk, painted yellow, representing the *sun*. Then they began to sing, and at the song the disk began to rise on the east corner of the disk [*sic;* screen], like the sun would in the heavens. When it reached the highest point of the curve (which corresponded with the middle of the screen), the song was interrupted, and the sun stopped also. When the singing began again, the sun resumed its motion, gradually declining toward the west until it touched the floor of that corner of the screen. He attributes this clever performance to the efficacy of the song exclusively.

Another very pretty trick is also done with an empty gourd, the top of which is perforated and has four eagle's plumes fastened to it. The bottom of that gourd is, of course, convex and cannot stand. Nevertheless, as soon as the song of the chayani begins, one of them gives it a very slight blow with the hand, and this causes it to stand up and to remain thus as long as the singing lasts, while the plumes quiver in a dancing motion.

Finally, he asserts that the growing and ripening of a maize plant in one day, between *sunrise* and *sunset* is performed by the *Navajos* today yet. The Pueblos did it also, but the *song that produced it is lost now!*

Everything is attributed by him to the magic powers of the *song* alone.[1054]

I wrote to Apolonio Vigil. We did not leave. At 6 o'clock, about, a very heavy thundershower broke out, and it rained copiously until 11 P.M. Very cool night, dark and windy.

AUGUST 22: Left at 7 A.M. on horseback with Hayoue. It appeared dark and raining at Santa Fe, but we had not rain at all until Peña Blanca where we reached at 2 P.M. Yesterday, the river came strong and very muddy, and the tops of the high sierra are covered with *snow*. Nearly three or four weeks earlier than last year. At Peña Blanca, everything all right. Papa happy; Fathers Navet, Antonio, Defouri, Fayet[1055] there. Antonio plays an ugly part. He is very much disliked by all. There was no Junta announced. I arranged with Florencia for Cochiti.

About 3 P.M., a tremendous thundershower broke out. It rained in torrents for nearly three hours, flooding everything. About Santo Domingo, hail destroyed the corn. After the rain, the Father Vicar General [Eguillon] and Father Deraches arrived in a buggy. They were not wet at all, since the shower did not extend farther east than the lomas nearest to Peña Blanca.

AUGUST 23: No rain today. Went over to Cochiti with Antonio. The river rose rapidly. We broke our waggon after crossing the first brazo. The Junta was quite a failure, still the matter of the Cochiti school is arranged so far. At Peña Blanca, Mass was said for the Father's mother. In the night, Fathers Parisis, Brun, and Ralliere[1056] had arrived. All left today. I remained alone, Papa having gone also with Fathers Defouri and Fayet. The night quite clear. At Santa Fe, rain all day.

AUGUST 24: Remained at Peña Blanca.

AUGUST 25: Fine day. Returned to Santa Fe. Found letters from Father Mariller, Dr. Brühl. All well at home. Papa is much better satisfied. Indeed, he feels well, now that the rainy season has set in. Everything looks fine.

AUGUST 26: Went to Jake Gold's and made the purchases for Dr. Brühl. Mr. Schumann came up in the forenoon. No letters, but the "Courrier des Estats Unis" came, which shows that *The Nation* has received my two contributions.

In the afternoon, Schumann and Koch came up. At 5:30 P.M., a heavy thunderstorm from the west. Snow on the sierra all gone now. Henry and Hubert hunted all day in the vicinity of Tezuque.

AUGUST 27: I copied somewhat at the novel, but had to go down town three times. At night, Hubert came up.

AUGUST 28: A host of letters from Frank Cushing, Baxter, Budd, the Hammond T. W. Co. I replied at once to Frank. I wrote the paper for Cushing.[1057] Ribera called and took supper with us.

AUGUST 29: Ribera came to breakfast. He wanted $25. Probably for losses in gambling! Today, we all went down town and had ourselves photographed. Turned out very well, it seems. A letter from Father Navet, and one from the Hammond Typewriter Co. In the afternoon, I went down town again. Joe went down town in the afternoon.

AUGUST 30: Letter from Seybt. Finished Chapter I of my novel. Cool and clear night, windy from the east. Callers: Dr. Eggert, Hartmann, and, at night, Gerdes and wife. Telegram from Professor Ward[1058] that he comes tomorrow. Everybody here remarkably well.

AUGUST 31: Professor Ward arrived this morning. Cloudless sky, quiet, beautiful morning. *No Rain!* It is getting very, very dry again.

I spent the day agreeably with Professor Ward. Wrote hurriedly to Father Navet and to R[Rob.]Clarke & Co., Cincinnati. No letters today. The night was clear and quiet for once. No signs of rain. Professor Ward leaves tonight again.

SEPTEMBER

SEPTEMBER 1: I wrote at the novel in the morning, and in the afternoon went up to the brewery to meet Dr. Strong. Papa came up also after us. No letters today. Joe had her "Kränzchen."

SEPTEMBER 2: It looks again like rain. ¿Quien sabe?
Wrote letters: to Dr. Brühl, to Cushing, to Janvier,[1059] Baxter, Father Mariller at Jemez, and to Garrison. Received $13.80 from *The Nation* today. Well paid for two hours work.

SEPTEMBER 3: Today, we had Antonio irrigating again! He used eighteen tanks. I wrote to the Hammond T. W. Co. enclosing $3.25 in a postal note and a Canadian dollar bill.

SEPTEMBER 4: Letters from Frothingham and Pretorius. Papa's articles rejected. Politics have the day. Replied to Frothingham. Called to Brother Amian. Wrote at the novel and copied also.

SEPTEMBER 5: Received the typewriter ribbons at last. The day was similar to the preceding one, dry, but calm. I wrote and copied all day. Mrs. Willie Spiegelberg called, but Joe had gone down town.

SEPTEMBER 6: Letter from Father Parisis. I copied nearly all day and wrote at the novel. Called on Father Defouri.

SEPTEMBER 7: Clear and very hot in the afternoon. Nothing. Letter from Mr. Balsiger and from Rob. Clarke & Co. I was down town three times today. Finished Chapter II of the novel in English. In the evening, Hubert came up. I wrote at Chapter III.

SEPTEMBER 8: Hot. No letters. I had to go down town early, which spoils the day for me as usual. Sent to Cushing the list of manuscripts copied and *bound.* Wrote to Father Parisis. Afternoon at the brewery with Dr. Strong.
   I am getting tired of those many conflicting corrections. In the end I shall go my own way, without consulting anybody at all.[1060]

SEPTEMBER 9: No letters. Went to Mass and then staid at home all day, writing and correcting type. Koch called in the afternoon; afterwards, Marcos Eldodt.

SEPTEMBER 10: No letters. For a few days, the flies are very troublesome again.
   In the afternoon, Louis Huning came; then a lot of people to gather peaches, whom I drove out, at once. They were not invited. Hubert up at night. Papa unwell from over haste and heat. I copied and wrote at the novel.

SEPTEMBER 11: No letters. Papa is better today. Finished copy of first part of the "Autos de Guerra" of 1696; returned it to Uncle Sam Ellison and got the second part to copy.[1061]

Father Navet and Doña Beatriz spent the afternoon with us.

SEPTEMBER 12: Finished Chapter IV of the novel today. Letter from Frank Cushing, with check. Met Father Seux, also Father Parisis.

SEPTEMBER 13: Day hot. Copied, and went to town. A grand excursion-party of Odd Fellows is in town, about 1800 people. Wrote to Haren for passes, and to Cushing. Miss Nehber is home again, hale and hearty. The Kochs were up this afternoon.

SEPTEMBER 14: No letters. Hot and dry. Drouth alarming.

SEPTEMBER 15: Clear day, hot and dry. At night strong wind again; from the east as usual. Went to the brewery with Dr. Strong in the afternoon. Copied every day. No letters again.

SEPTEMBER 16: I went to Mass as usual, while Hubert and Henry were up at the house. In the afternoon, wrote to Father Navet and copied. Very dry. We called on Miss Nehber, but she was not at home. In the afternoon, I made a short call at Father Defouri's. Letters from Mr. Balsiger and from Haren; the latter with the passes.

SEPTEMBER 17: I copied and wrote. Hot until 3 P.M. Hartmann called, also Julia, and at night, Hubert and Miss Nehber. Papa again very ugly at night, and correspondingly foolish.

SEPTEMBER 18: Last night, got a telegram from Cushing. I copied and finished the novel, Chapter IV. Hartmanns took supper with us. Mali in bed with headache. Papa is the cause of it. He is very ugly toward her.

SEPTEMBER 19: Harry Budd came. Spent the day with us. He brings word from Cushing to the effect that I may go along to

Taos with him. After much hesitation I concluded to go! At night, a fine, good shower at last. It lasted about two hours.

SEPTEMBER 20: We left Santa Fe at 9 A.M. The weather looked doubtful, but still it maintained itself during the day. At the Embudo,[1062] we had to take the conveyance of Albino Lopez. Reached Taos at 10 P.M. There had been a shower at Abiquiu[1063] in the afternoon. All the rivers are with water; still any man can ford them easily on foot.

SEPTEMBER 21: The mountains are glorious. Harry tells me that the Taos Indians are averse to have the sierra ascended by any-one except themselves. There is a small lake up there, where they perform secret ceremonies. Relighting of the sacred fire is done up there during the spring equinox. A tree is cut down with a stone axe, and the fire lighted with a fire drill. It is then carried to the pueblo by runners and distributed among the estufas and each quarter pertaining to each estufa.[1064]

In the afternoon, I went to Larkin Read,[1065] and I examined the paper of Don Santiago Valdés.[1066] Nothing! Neither is there anything, so far, at the court house. Spent the evening with Father Valézy. Harry went to the pueblo and spent the night there. The plain of Taos is the most fertile and best irri-gated of the Territory. Wrote to Joe. Wrote to Frank Cushing also.

SEPTEMBER 22: Harry staid at the pueblo last night. Beautiful morning. Harry came to get his traps. He is much elated over his prospects. Last night, Father Valézy told me the case of his being wounded. It occurred on the night of the 22nd to 23rd of Decem-ber 1865 at the hospital of Santa Fe and the [would-be] murderer was a crazy Mexican by the name of Teodosio.

I copied at the court house.[1067] My hand very, very bad. There are many Indians in town from the pueblo and also Jicarilla Apaches,[1068] males and females.

Father Valézy left this morning for Elizabethtown, or El Moreno.[1069] Distance: 36 miles. There are still descendants here, in the female line, of the Luceros de Godoy.[1070] They are the Martinez. I am also told that Don Nicolás Lucero of Peña Blanca is a descendant; probably. Here, I have seen almost everybody:

Scheurig, Gusdorf, Larkin Reed, [L.] Brown, Santaistévan, McClure,[1071] etc.

SEPTEMBER 23: Feel much better. Had callers. Xicarilla [Jicarilla] Apaches. They call Taos (the pueblo) "Imaki."–Picuries [Picurís]. Went out to the pueblo with [A.] Liebert and Scheurig. Harry, O.K.

SEPTEMBER 24:[1072] Yesterday, I noted that the Indians here were just thrashing their wheat. This shows that their harvest is just about over now and that they are consequently quite one month later than around Peña Blanca, San Juan, or Santa Clara, and San Ildefonso. The wild plums are ripe now, and people were out yesterday gathering them on the plain between the pueblo and Fernandez de Taos.

Harry wrote me a plaintive letter and I concluded, after consulting the physician (Dr. Kittridge [W. A. Kittrege])[1073] and Father Valézy, to send for the boy. An examination by the doctor proved, that there is only a little dysentery, so he should have left for the pueblo again. But the boy staid at Brown's for the night. Mariano Otero came, and a "grand Republican rally" was held at the court house. In the evening, I left with Gusdorf for the Ranchos [de Taos]. There, I met Husher and Bigelow[1074] going up to Taos. Staid overnight at the Ranchos, very well treated.

SEPTEMBER 25: Left the Ranchos de Taos at 8 A.M. Followed the beautiful little stream on an average to the southeast. A number of houses and fields line its course and about three miles from the Ranchos, it enters the cañón which at the beginning is rather narrow and encased by low wooded hills. The road is very good, and it keeps the left (east) side of the little river. The following is a sketch* of the whole road until Peñasco.

The distance, by the road, is 28 miles. I cut off about two miles by taking the trail to the right and going through high pine timber and leaving the cañón of the Rio de los Ranchos. I thus crossed an eastern spur of the Sierra de Picuries. The whole is well timbered with pino colorado, pinavete, and piñón. There are also some of the peculiar mountain álamos which line the valleys leading up to the Cumbre on the road to the Valles [Valle Grande]. Also oak which is turning yellow. This, together with the yellow blossoming artemisia, colors many of the higher slopes bright yellow at present.

In the woods, there are a great many magpies, fluttering about screaming and shouting to each other. Aside from these and some squirrels and handsome striped ground squirrels, the woods are deserted. Three successive, very long and steep ascents, which must be as high as 9,000, or nearly 9,500, feet, all densely timbered, lead at last to the crest, whence the Sierra Picuries appears to the right and close at hand, with its dark pine-clad humps and folds. The headwaters of the Rio del Pueblo are below like a narrow band of grass traversed by a dark ditch and encased by wooded slopes, whereas the mass of the Jicarrita, absolutely bare, rises in the southeast, and the Truchas also become visible.
. . .

It was quite cool on these heights and occasionally a glimpse was had of the Sierra de Taos. I descended into the vale of the Rio del Pueblo and followed its course downwards till about eight miles from the Peñasco, where I met the first houses. They are, in general, more carefully built than those on the Rio Abajo,[1075] more repaired, and there are many log houses daubed over with mud, which makes an excellent wall. After passing the settlement called Plaza del Rio del Pueblo, there was almost a constant string of ranchos. The right side of the slope was abrupt, the rock frequently protruding. The left side was more gentle in its slopes and more regularly wooded. There is splendid grass in these valleys are well as in the cañón. It is even thicker growing and stronger (though not as high) as the grass in the Valles. The cattle and horses are taller and of better build, also fatter, than anywhere in New Mexico, Taos, perhaps excepted. Crops all seemed excellent, with the exception of maize which has suffered from drouth, although it is far from being a complete failure. At the Vadito, I saw also a fair crop of peas. Thence, I crossed over to the south, into the valley of the Peñasco proper. That is a lovely, narrow vale, with a fine and limpid stream, rushing through it, and homes and ranchos scattered everywhere in nooks.

Therefore, the name of "Los Rincones" commonly given to the whole valley and its settlements. The church is small, but everything looks comparatively neat. Hearty reception by Father F. Guyot.[1076] He leads a very tranquil life, with small resources. In winter, it is very cold, and the winters are long and disagreeable.

But the summers are cool and quiet. They have had no rain scarcely this summer, still crops are good, for there is an abundance of water for irrigation. Father Guyot has a little garden with splendid cabbage and lettuce. The table is plain, but it is good.

SEPTEMBER 26: Fine day, but hot. Copied from the books of the church.[1077] Witchcraft is still in full blast here. So are the Penitentes.[1078] We drove over to Picuries in the afternoon. The pueblo lies at the foot of the slope of the sierra in a dark and sombre spot, on gray hillocks resembling rubbish piles which some of them manifestly are. There are about thirty families, half of which are Mexicans. The Indians, simple minded, very superstitious, but friendly. The old church has completely disappeared; it lay to the east of the present one, which is small, but clean. No dates. The old church was burnt by the Comanches, either late last century or in the first years of the present century.[1079]

SEPTEMBER 27: I left the Peñasco a little after 8 A.M. and wandered down the valley to the Junta de los Rios, where the valley terminates and the two rivers, of the Pueblo and of the Peñasco, join. Hereafter, it is called the Rio del Embudo. I ascended the mountains to the southwest. They form like a bridge between the Sierra de Picuries and the mountains around the gorge of the Embudo. They are pine-clad and entirely desert [ed?].

After climbing (on a good road) to the top of the ridge on the north of the river, I had to follow two cuchillas, long, broad, and with an almost perfectly level top, which is at least two to three miles long in each case. From the second one of these cuchillas, I saw the mountains of Abiquiu again and also, for a moment, the Cerro de San Antonio in the north. Then the descent began into the gorges surrounding the Embudo. A long and very steep descent it is, and I can hardly conceive how even empty wagons can ascend on this Cuesta de Picuries, so steep it appears. At the foot, a narrow arroyo leads through a rocky gateway of gneiss, and, following the arroyo, I descended into the bottom of the Embudo River.

The town of Embudo lies on its southern bank. It is small. Stopped at Pablo Sanchez' for an hour. No ruins about. Distance from Peñasco: 15 miles, at least. Distance from the railroad station: 5 miles. Here I determined upon going directly to San Juan. A good trail leads almost due south, up a sandy arroyo, encased by much worn and jagged rocks, nearly five miles to a cuesta, whence the upper valley of San Juan, from La Joya on to very nearly the Pueblo, spreads out below, very suddenly and strikingly.

In the distance, the top of the mesa of Shyumo (south of San Ildefonso) looms up and the Abiquiu Range is near and rather bold, though hazy today. The Jicarrita, as well as the Truchas, are almost due east. The plain is about three miles broad and level, also well cultivated. La Joya comes first, then El Bosque, Los Luceros, finally Plaza del Alcalde and San Juan. Reached that Pueblo at 8 P.M.; found Joe all right, with several letters. Husher here also. Thank God, everything is well, and I am, so far, again. Tired and weary. Must have walked about thirty-four miles today.

SEPTEMBER 28: Husher photographed Chamita. In the afternoon, we went over. The tradition of San Gabriel del Yunque is very distinct in the minds of the people. It must have stood west of the old pueblo of *Yuge-Uing-ge,* where there are cornfields now. But every trace of the remains has disappeared.[1080] Beautiful view of San Juan from the ridge above the river.

I begin to find out [about] Budd.

SEPTEMBER 29: We left San Juan in the afternoon with Husher, who remained at Española. Returned to Santa Fe, where it had just been raining very slightly. Quite a rain fell on the ridges north of the town. Everybody well.

SEPTEMBER 30: Bigelow here. In the afternoon, went out to the brewery with him, Henry, and Hubert. Night quiet and cool. It is now decided that I go to Zuñi on Tuesday night.

OCTOBER

OCTOBER 1: Not a letter. Returned the manuscript of the Franciscan letters to Don Diego de Vargas (1696)[1081] to Sam Ellison. Called on Bigelow and went down town in general.

Everything so far ready for tomorrow night. But I am tired of leaving, and if Papa only would be a little more pleasant, I would not have any thought of leaving. But he is always the same. His last years have not changed him in the least, he is always the same —wants to be "boss." We won't be bossed by him, *however,—so much is sure.*

I wrote a few hurried lines to Henry Holgate at Deming. Dr. N. Strong had the kindness to come up and spent the evening with me, correcting the fourth chapter of the novel. He returned late and it was pitch-dark.

OCTOBER 2: No letters for me. I prepared to go this evening to Zuñi and at once went down town. Husher had come; so he and Bigelow came up to dinner with us. Both appeared to be very nice people. Husher, of course, is young yet, very young; but Bigelow is a staid, quiet, sensible man of good education and much more knowledge than he claims to possess. After dinner we went with Joe to the different churches and chapels, also to the museum.[1082] Father Deraches was extremely kind and showed us the church ornaments. Some of them are really beautiful. Afterwards, we, as usual, wound up at the brewery. Papa continued foolishly ill-humored. It is a sad sight, to see the old man always grumbling and dissatisfied, whereas we do everything to make him comfortable. He ought to see it and to behave in consequence.

We left at 10:40 P.M.

OCTOBER 3: Reached Albuquerque at 3 A.M. and went to the San Felipe Hotel. Day warm. Saw many people and got a pass. Called on all the Hunings, on Louis & Franz. Met Willie Borchert.[1083] Professor Bibikov, etc. Called also on Father Durante.

OCTOBER 4: Left Albuquerque about 3 A.M. and reached Manuelito[1084] at 11 A.M. Left on foot with Husher, while Mr. Bigelow and Hubert staid at Manuelito. Road dry, but very sandy. About five miles to the south, we entered a beautiful cañón, very nearly five miles long and extremely picturesque. At the entrance are very well preserved ruins on the rocky cliffs. Walls one and part of two stories high, with loopholes. Also small caves with walled fronts. Groves of timber in the bottom and on the rocks.

A fine spring at the southern end, ten miles from Manuelito. Then a rolling, sandy, tableland seven miles to Daniel Dubois.[1085] Beautiful spring. Then again tableland, rolling, with timber in groves, but low. Saw the Sierra Blanca, the Escudilla, and finally the Sierra del Dátil. Reached Zuñi at 10 P.M.

OCTOBER 5: The kindest reception possible! William and George Pradt are here. Council in Mr. Graham's[1086] house about the schools. At night, a long and important "talk" with Na-yu-tshi and Pa-la-ua-ti-ua with Cushing.[1087]

The Zipias are the *Tzipia-Kué*, a tribe formerly related to the Zuñi, and west of them. The Cocoyes may be the *Coco-Kué*, a now extinct branch of the Zuñi, also west and south-southwest, and it is said they always used to dress in fine cotton robes. Tusayan is *Usaya-Kué*, or *Usayan* in the possessive, an ancient name for the largest Moqui [Hopi] Pueblo in former times. Topax is *Topax-Topan*, a name still used in the dances and coming from the southwest, from the vicinity of Round Valley.

Wrote to Joe.

OCTOBER 6: Heavy sandstorm in the afternoon. Nothing new. Listened to Cushing's fine paper for Berlin.[1088]

OCTOBER 7: Cushing, Husher, and Hubert went out to Hauicu [Hawikuh],[1089] and I took a drive with Mrs. Cushing as far as past Pinaua [Pinawa].[1090] At night a few showers. At last, for they have had but one rain all summer.

Copied and made abstracts from the church books.[1091] Called on Graham, who told me he had seen the Snake Dance at Moqui and confirms Bourke. He says among other things that the dancers, etc, are frequently bitten by the snakes, but pay no attention to it. After the dance is over, they all go and wash themselves with some greenish liquid held in store for the purpose and which may be some unknown antidote.[1092]

OCTOBER 8: Left for Hauicu at 8:30 A.M. with Mrs. Cushing in her buggy. She drove me about three miles and past A-Pinaua. Beautiful road to Hauicu. Caught up with Cushing, etc. beyond the little village at Ojo Caliente. Thence we went on the mesa where the ruins of Chyana-ué (Canabi!) stand. There is still a chapel there, showing that the pueblo was one of the seven and evidently a visita of Hauicu. The chapel is small and of stone. Its walls are about two feet thick and from seven to twelve feet high. It faces the east.* The front wall has disappeared. Length, about forty feet. No apparent trace of a convent. The pueblo was quite large. . . . In a straight line, it is about one-and-a-half miles east-southeast of Hauicu.[1093]

The sides of the mesa are steep, but the mesa extends on both sides of the pueblo, so that it cannot have been the Cibola of Coronado, whereas Hauicu answers the description perfectly.[1094] East of Chyanaué, about five miles, on a cuchilla, there are a series of caches with charred maize and several small houses. Broken pottery, metates, and hammers of stone, about. No graves found after short prospecting. Returned to Zuñi about 7 P.M. Saw a tarantula today.

OCTOBER 9:[1095] Bigelow left us this morning with Garlick. Am sorry to lose him. General and Mrs. Carr and Clark Carr here from [Fort] Wingate, but they soon left for their ranch. Wrote to Joe.

Moved into Husher's tent. There are over a hundred wagons owned by the Indians of Zuñi, and two of them think of buying buggies. Got money.

There is a very old and very regular trail leading directly from Hauicu through to Acoma and the Rio Grande, and from it another trail branches off to Cia. There are considerable ruins on this trail; it passes south of Toyoalana [Thunder Mountain] and is well known to the Indians.

In the afternoon, Hubert, Husher, and I went over to Pinaua. Everything is very badly ruined, and where the pueblo is (left side of the road), there is nothing but a series of rubbish heaps and thick ridges of rubbish left. The pueblo was a one-house structure and small. On the opposite (south) side of the road, there is a mound with a square watchtower on it, and this might possibly be the ruins of a chapel forty by fifteen feet. But there is no certainty to be acquired without excavations. Cushing showed us a bone (human) just excavated, the os coccix [sic], which has a white arrowhead imbedded in it. The bone was much corroded. There were three men buried together which all showed traces of a violent death. Slight earthquake shock at 10:20 P.M.

OCTOBER 10: Graham told me that killing of witches is going on lively. South of the ruins and outside of them, a perfect skeleton was discovered. It was a man, and he lies on his side, doubled up, without ornaments at all. It was evidently buried like a dog. Cushing says this is witchcraft burial. Might be the body of Fray Juan del Bal,[1096] killed here in 1680. (?) ¿Quien Sabe?

Three years ago, a man killed a woman here with an axe for witchcraft. He was acquitted by the Territorial Courts at Albuquerque. Spent an hour with the governor and at his house.

OCTOBER 11: There are reports, or rumors, of an old church on top of Inscription Rock. I doubt it very much, however. This morning, we found out that there was a church or chapel at *Ketship-a-uan,*[1097] a little this side of Chyanaué. It is still standing, and Cushing has seen it. It is one of the seven of Cibola, according to tradition. Hubert left for home this morning. Cushing and Husher went to some northern ruins, and I copied.[1098] Two letters from Joe came tonight, and Budd did not come in. The three skeletons found have been evidently scalped by Pueblo Indians (Moquis).[1099]

OCTOBER 12: Wrote to Joe, and a letter of recommendation to Garrison for Frank [Cushing]. The day remained beautiful, but warm. I got from Frank, $100., giving two vouchers (in duplicates), one for $62.35 and one for $37.65. Sent to Mr. Schumann, $70., and kept $30., in cash. Wrote to Dr. Moore, a letter of introduction for Cushing. Copied.

OCTOBER 13: As there were no signs of departure yet, I left on foot for the Pescado at noon, arriving there about 4:30 P.M. Distance: Twenty miles. The settlement of the Pescado consists of about four inhabited dwellings of adobes and stone. It stands on a hill whose crest is formed by an outcrop of black lava, whereas the rocks on the sides of the cañón are red. These sides are wooded, but the cañón itself is bare, grassy, and cultivated by irrigation from the very large and cool spring. The ruins of Heshota Tzina.[1100] The two pueblos were round, tolerably large, and almost contiguous. Little pottery about, also obsidian.

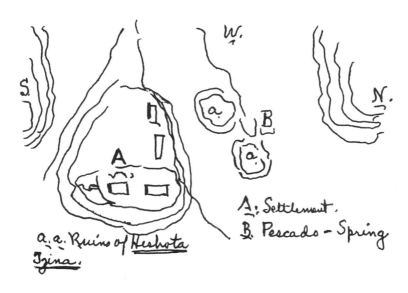

A.: Settlement.
B. Pescado - Spring

a. a. Ruins of Heshota Tzina.

Had a talk with Ramón Luna who lives here. He confirms about *Usaya-Kué* and *Tzipia-Kué.* Beautiful night, but no trace of Cushing.

OCTOBER 14: Beautiful day. Not a cloud. Set out at 7 A.M. and lost my way, reaching at last the Morro [El Morro][1101] a little after 3 P.M., tired, hungry and thirsty. Not a drop of water on the whole

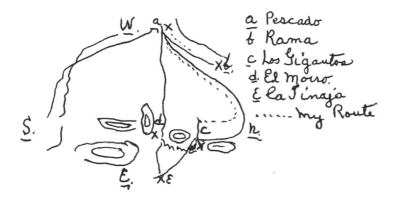

a Pescado
b Rama
c Los Gigantes
d. El morro.
E la Tinaja
.... my Route

route. Made at least twenty-five miles on foot and six, on horseback to the Tinaja.[1102] Found our men all at the Morro. There are two ruins on top of the [Inscription] Rock, but no church, and Ramón Castro says that as the houses were built on the rock, and there are several stairs still visible, it will be hard to find anything of value.[1103]

The country is barren. Groves of pine timber cover all the elevations and rocks, but the bottom and plains are bare, dry, and dreary. Between the Gigantes, and the Morro, and the Tinaja, the country is covered with low hills of lava and scoria, much worn, separated by hills of sand, on which isolated, tall pines grow. The mesas, on the contrary, are of white, red, and greyish stratified rock, and the sides, often picturesquely eroded. The Tinaja lies in a long valley, flanked on the east by a low, wooded border. By the road, it is seven miles east of the Morro. Spent the night there, at the house of Leopoldo Mazón. Kindly treated. There is no water at the Morro.

OCTOBER 15: There is a ruin right here, where the house of Epitacio Mazón stands. Another lies a mile southeast from here, and still another, four to five miles in the timber.

[On the next five pages, #47 front and back, #48 front and back, and #49 front, Bandelier copied various inscriptions. As evidenced by the reproductions in the present volume, he made dual entries of a number, the first being more of a "true copy," and the second, an attempt at editing the inscriptions. The present editors have combined the variations, with additional editing, into a single roster of thirty-six entries.]

No. 1. Aqui estobo el Genl D^n D^o/De varg^s q^n [quien] conquisto
       a nra. S.$^{[ta]}$ Fe, y a la R^l/Corona todo el Nuebo/ México
       a su costa/año de 1692.
No. 2. Lieut: McCook/1851.
No. 3. Este Paraje es de Albaro Garzia.
No. 4. Ju^a [Juan] Garsya 1636 (in a little cave).
No. 5. Pero Sanch[ez] . . .
No. 6. Maj. J. R. Hagner/1852 U.S.A.
No. 7. El Cap^n Juan de Uribarri.
No. 8. Por aqui paso Francisco Lopez a nueve de Julio.
No. 9. Casados 1727.

No. 10. Por aqui pazo el Alferez Real Joseph de Payba Basconzelos el año que trujo el Cauildo del Reyno a su costa a
18. de feb° de 1726 años.

No. 11. Pasamos por aqui el Sarjento mayor y el capitan Juª de
Archuleta y el aiudante diego Martin. . . . . . . 1636.

No. 12. Paso por aqui el adelantado don Juan de Oñate al descubrimiento de la mar del Sur a 16. de Abril 1604.[1104]

No. 13. Pedro Romero[1105] i 1580.

No. 14. Salʳ olguin [Holguin].

No. 15. Pase por aqui Francisco de A[naya] Alma[zan].

North Side

No. 16. Año de 1716 alos 26. de agosto paso por aqui Don feliz
Martinez Governᵒʳ y Capⁿ Genˡ de este Rⁿᵒ a la Reduc-
cion y Conqᵗᵃ de Moqui . . . Rᵈᵒ P. F. Antonio Camargo
Custodio y Juez eclesiastico.

No. 17. El dia 28. de Sept. de 1737 llego aqui el Bachiller Don
Ygnacio de Arrasain.

No. 18. Dia 28 de Sepᵉ de 1737 años llego aqui el Illᵐᵒ Sr. Dr.
Don Martín Elizaecoechea Obispo de Durango y el dia
29. paso a Zuñi.

No. 19. Aqui . . . . . . [Gober]nador Don Francisco Manuel de
Sylva Nieto. . . . que lo ynpucible tiene ya sujeto Su Brazo
yndubitable y su Balor con los carros del Rei nuestro
Señor Cosa Que solo el Puso en este efecto. . . . de Ab-
gosto y Seis cientas Beinte y Nuevo Quebo yba y a cuñi
Paso y la felleue.

No. 20. Juan Gonzalez 1629.

No. 21. Agustin de ynojos [Hinojos].

No. 22. El dia 14. de Julio de 1736. Paso por aqui el General Juan
Paez Hurtado, Visitador.

No. 23. El Capitan general de las provincias del Nueuo México
Por el Rey nuestro Señor Paso por aqui de vuelta de los
pueblos de Zuñi a los 29 de Julio del año de 1629. los puso
en pas a su pedimento y pidiendole su favor como Vasal-
los de su Magestad y de nuevo dieron la obediencia todo
lo que hizo con el agasaxe celo y prudencia como tan
christianisimo. . . . tam particular y gallardo Soldado de

inacabable y lo ad.memoria . . . . . . y en su Compania el Cabo Joseph Truxillo.

No. 24. Diego Luzero de Godoy.[1106]

No. 25. Lt. J. H. Simpson + R. H. Kern, artist visited and copied these inscriptions. September 17, 1849.

No. 26. Roque Gomes [Gomez].

No. 27. Luys [Luis] Pacheco.

No. 28. Antonio de Salas.

No. 29. Vicente Cisneros.

No. 30. Alonso Varela.

No. 31. Fran[co] Varela.

No. 32. Diego Belasques [Velasquez].

No. 33. Nicolas Luzero de Godoy.

No. 34. Cristobal Perez.

No. 35. L. [Lt.] Sitgreave U. S. A.—Aug. 30, 1851.

No. 36. R. H. Kern 1851.

Nos. 1 to 15 are on the south side of the projecting point. Nos. 16 to 34 are on the north side; Nos. 35 and 36, on the east front.

Left the Rock at 6 P.M., taking leave. Spent the night at the Tinaja. The ruin is not east, but north, of here, five miles, in the valley and at the entrance of a cañón.

OCTOBER 16: Copied the Inscriptions [into my journal]. Left the Tinaja at 11:30 A.M. Arrived at the house of Don José María Mares at the Gallinita at 4 P.M., but hardly walked more than three hours, crossing the crests of the Sierra de Zuñi. The whole road is through high and fine pine timber. Nowhere can any view be obtained at all.

Rising from the Tinaja, there is first a mile-and-a-half of deep, white sand, then red, sandy soil. All very heavy. Then firm ground, sometimes rocky. The ascent is fully eight miles long. The descent is rapid at first and finally very gradual to the Gallinas. As soon as the descent begins, the rocks and soil become deep red. It must be very fertile, but not a drop of permanent water! The Gallina, where lives Leandro Mares, is a fertile spot, and he raises excellent and beautiful potatoes. But the bottoms are very narrow and not of any length. The hills, covered with high timber, crowd in upon them from every side. The water is excellent, but it is all from wells. Nothing to irrigate with.

Bandelier as a young man, 1863

Burro Alley, Santa Fe

Palace Hotel, Santa Fe

Bandelier's journal entry for
October 15, 1888

15. of October a. v. 1888. Monday.]   N°. 47.

There is a Ruin right here, where the house of Epitacio
Matzon stands: another lies 1. mile S.E. from here, a
third another 4–5. miles, in the timber.

"Aqui estobo el Gen.¹ b⁴ D°. [De] Vargas 9ᵗᵉ Conquista
A rᵃ S, Fē, y a La R⁴.] Corona todo el nueb[o] mexico
a su costa] año de 1692.] A.P.L.

2ʸ Liut: M.ᶜ Cook,] 1851.]   Esto Paraje es de Albaro
4 Ju⁴ʸ Garsy A. 1636.   garzia. ' 3,

Pero Sanch.⁵...]   Maj. J. R. Hagner.
                    1822   U.S.a. 6.]

Eo[...]Romero[...]   ]

                                                        16.
año de 1716. alos 26. de ag⁺ paso por aqui D.ⁿ
feliz Martinez Gouron~ y Cap.ⁿ Gen.ᵗ de este R[eino]/
ala Reduxion y conq.ᵗᵒ el moqui...... P.O.R.ᵃ
R. P. Antonio Camargo Custodio y Juez eclesiast.

el dia 28. de Se.⁰ de 1737. llego aqui el B.ʳ D. Juan
Ygnacio Darrasain. 17.

15ᵗᵃ 28. de Sp⁴ de 1737. el llego aqui El. Ilᵐᵒ S. D.ⁿ
D.ⁿ Mᵐ D. Elizacoechea Obpᵒ D. Durango Y el dia
2 A. Paso a Zuni. 18.

No. 1. to 15, are on the South side of this projecting point. Nos. 16. to 34. on the north side. Nos. 35. & 36. on the East point.

W.

Morro.

No. 35. & 36.

No 1. –15.

No. 16. –34.

Road.

Lava and Sand.

N.

S.

mesa negra.

Lava.

Lava.

East.

No. 1.	aquí estubo el Genl. Dn. Dº. de Vargas quien conquistó a nra Sta Fe y a la Real Corona todo el Nuebo México a su costa año de 1692.
No. 3.	Este Paraje es de Albaro Garzia.
No. 4.	Juan Garsya. 1636. (in a little cave.)
no. 7	El capn. Juan de Uribarrí.
No. 8.	Por aquí paso Francisco Lopez a nueve de Julio.

No. 9. | Casados. 1727.

No. 10. | Por aqui pazo el Alferez Real Joseph
de Payba Basconzelos el año que trujo
el Cavildo del Reyno a su costa a 18. de Feb.º
de 1726. años.

No. 11. | Pasamos por aqui el Sarjento mayor
y el capitan Jen.ª de Archuleta Jel ayudente
diego Martin . . . . 1636.

No. 12. | Paso por aqui el adelantado don Juan
de Oriate al descubrimiento de la mar del
Sur A 16. d. Abril 1604.

No. 14. | Salvador Holguin.

No. 15. | Pase por aqui Francisco de Anaya
Almazan.

North Side.

No. 16. | Año d. 1716 alos 26. de agosto paso por
aqui Bon feliz Martinez Governº. y Capn Genbl
de este Rnº ala Reducion y Congª du Moqui . . .
. . . Rdo P. J. Antonio Camargo Custodio y Juez
eclesiastico.

No. 17. | El dia 28. de Septº. de 1737, llego aqui
el Bachillr Bon Ygnacio de Arrasain.

No. 18. | Dia 28. de Sep.º de 1737. años llegó aqui
el Illmo Sr D.º Bon martin Elizaecoechea Obispo
de Durango Jel dia 29. paso a Zuñi.

No. 19. | aqui . . . . . nador Bon Francisco Manuel
de Sylva Nieto . . . . Iun lo ynpucible tiene ya su =
= jeto Su Brazo yndubitable y su Balor con los
carros del Rei nuestro Señor Cosa Que solo el Puso
en este efecto . . . . De Abgosto y Suiscientos Beinte y
Nuebo Quebo yba y a cuñi Paso y la fellere.

agustyn de ynojos [1629?] [21,]   y en su Compañia el
Cabo Joseph Trugillo

El día 14 de Julio de 1736. Paso Por aqui el Gen.l
Jun Paez Hurtado Vaysitador. 22.

El cap.n gnl. de las pro.as del nuebo mex.o Passo el Rey
n.ro S.r Passo por aqui de buelta de los pueblos de
Zuñi a los 29. de Julio del año de 1629. los puso
en paz a su pedim.to y pidiendolo Su fabor como ba-
-sallos de su mag.d y de nuebo dieron la obidiencia
todo lo que hizo con el agassaxo selo y prudencia
como ta.n christiano ... tan particular y gallardo
soldado de ynacabable y lo edamemo. 23.

D.o Lugero de Godoy [24.]   Lt. J.H. Simpson & R. H. Kern
                          artist visited an copied this in-
scription Septembr 17, 18, 1849, 25.

Roque gomes [26.] — lugo pacheco [27.] Antonio de Zalas [28.]
Bysento Sagueros ê [29.]

Alonso Varela [30]; Fran.co Varela [31.]

Diego Belasquis [32.]   El cap.n de Uribarri 7.

Nico.as Lugero de Godoy [33.]   p aqui paso fran.co Lopes
                            el viente de Julio. 8.

xptobal Perus [34.]   Paso por aqui el soldado Jondodos

[illegible crossed-out line]
                                          Casado 1724 [2.]

Por aqui paso el Alfer.s R.l Joseph de
Jaybra Basconzelos el año q.e truxo el Caual.to
del Reyno a su costa a 18. de feb. de 1726.
años. 10.

15. of October a.w. 1888. monday.)   Nº 49.

Pasamos por aquí el Sargento mayor y el capi=
tan Juª de Archuleta y el ayudante diego
Martin...... 16 bb.   11.

L. Sitgreave. U.S.Aº. 35. — Aug. 30.1851. | R.H.Kern,
                                            | 1851. 3 b.

Passo por aquí el adelantado don Juº de Oñate
al descubrimiento de la mar del Sur a 16 de
Abril 1604. 12.

Pedro Romero i 1580. 13. | Salbº olguin 14.

Passo por aquí Franº de A....... Alma 15.

_____

Nº 20.	Juan Gonzalez. 1629.
Nº 21.	Agustín de Hinojos.
Nº 22.	El día 14. de Julio de 1736. Paso por aquí el General Juan Paez Hurtado Visitador. — y en su Compañía el Cabo Joseph Trucillo.
Nº 23.	El Capitan general de esas provincias del Nuevo mexico Por el Rey nuestro señor Paso por aquí de vuelta de los pueblos de Zuñi a los 29 de Julio del año de 1629. los puso en paz a su pedimento y pidiendole su favor como Vasallos de su magestad y de nuevo dieron la obediencia todo lo que hizo con el agasaco celo y prudencia como tan christianisimo..... tan particular y gallardo Soldado de ina=cabable y lo ad memoria.....

24.	diego Luzero de Godoy.	26.	Roque Gomez.
27.	Luis Pacheco	28.	Antonio de Salas.
29.	Vicente Cisneros.	32.	diego Velazquez.

Agua Fria is about two-and-a-half miles from here, nearly west. Night cool and quiet. Mein host is a cousin of Francisco Chavez, Sheriff.[1107]

OCTOBER 17: Slept fairly. Left on foot for San Rafael about 8 A.M., but was overtaken by a waggon, driven by Francisco Vargas of the Gallina. The country, to the entrance of the Cañón de Zuñi, is wooded and handsome, but desert[ed?]. At the entrance of the cañón, a huge lava flow appears, much corrugated and blown up. It is said to come from the north, but there are craters south of Agua Fria also. The cañón itself is very beautiful. Its rugged and rocky sides of grey, yellow, and reddish rocks rise in picturesque crags and clefts. In the bottom (which is quite narrow), the lava appears in spots, blown up, in corruscations [*sic*], dendritic almost; black, brown, and reddish. Few trees dot the narrow bottom, and not a drop of water. The cliffs vary in height from two to five hundred feet. The whole length of the cañón is eight miles, and it winds in and out like a serpent. All the while, the road inclines downwards. At the eastern outlet, the Sierra de San Mateo [Mount Taylor] bursts into view.

Reached San Rafael about 2 P.M. and found nobody at home. Went on to Grant [Grants][1108] and spent the night there with Emil Bibo.[1109] Letter from Joe.

Francisco Vega told me that the trail to Acoma passes by the old pueblos of the Cebolla and Cebollita and near the Cerro de la Cabra, where it is said there are some inscriptions.

OCTOBER 18: Very bad day. Violent blows, with sand and dust, from the southwest and some little rain. Remained at Grant's with C. F. Lummis.[1110] Wrote to Joe and received another letter from her, enclosing one from Don J. M. Vigil.

Lummis told me the Acoma tradition of the Mesa Encantada.[1111] The Acomas had their pueblo up there originally, and the ascent was by a piece of rock, detached, but still leaning up against the top. One day, while all but three women were down in the bottom in the fields, a cloudburst took place, and the rock fell, leaving the women up there to die of hunger. The tribe then moved to their present location.[1112]

OCTOBER 19: Spent the day[1113] at San Rafael with the Padre [John B. Brun]. Returned to Grants and met Roman Baca who, with Don José Sena, went to San Rafael. Junio Chavez also came. So concluded to stay at Grant's with Lochner.

OCTOBER 20: Very strong rain from the east all night, continuing in the morning. Chilly. No go today probably, as it looks bad. The ground here is red, and it gets very sticky through rain and heavy for foot travel. Wrote to José M. Vigil and to Joe. Still raining or rather drizzling. It stopped at last in the afternoon and appeared to clear up, so I started ahead on foot, leaving the railroad three miles from Grants and proceeding about two miles farther into the deserted plain.*

There I was overtaken by Junio Chavez and Eucario Garcia with horses, one of which I mounted. Soon a furious rainstorm, with small hail, thunder, and lightning, broke out, and the rain (very cold at that) kept on very heavily all night. We were made one mass of mud, and everything completely drenched. It was a fearful ride, through the dark night, the roads full of water and very slippery; the plain made one lake almost. My horse fell and rolled over, but, while I flew over his head, still I was not the least injured.

Reached San Mateo at 9:30 P.M. and were hospitably received and warmed up at the house of Don Casimiro Garcia, Eucario's father. My coat is in shreds; papers and everything are in a most lamentable condition, having ridden twenty miles in that fearful rain. Of the country, I saw nothing, beyond that the road is very level and the soil, dark red for about ten miles and excessively sticky. They have had no rain for about one year. The wheat is poor; corn, good!

OCTOBER 21: Went on to the house of Don Manuel Chavez[1114] in the rain and got wet again. Don Manuel is sick in bed; Amado [Chaves] has gone to Grant's to telegraph for a physician; the house, handsome and large, is flooded by rain through a leaking roof, and I am weary, unable to go out and without work. This part of the trip is a bad failure. I should have gone home, rather than try God in this attempt. He now interposes His will, and I will not strain anything.

San Mateo is a scattered place in a valley which is fertile, but without irrigation. All along the road, for 28 miles, are scattered the dangerous sumideros, or hidden springs, with nothing to indicate their presence on the surface. They are pits, constantly

filled with liquid mud beneath a thin upper crust. Anyone drop-
ping into them must perish unless help is on the spot.

Distance from here to: Rancho del Dado: 15 miles; Azabache:
30 miles; Cañón Juan Tafoya: 22 miles; Casa Salazar: 45 miles;
Cabezón: 45 miles; Grant's: 25 miles. Made a short call to Don
Manuel Chavez. He is very weak.

OCTOBER 22: There is some beautiful pottery in the house, coming from the ruins, corrugated and painted red. Also one piece
with the upper half painted red and black and the lower half
finely indented. Another bowl, painted and with designs as handsome as any of Casas Grandes. It snowed lightly all day, but in the
afternoon, the sun came out and before night the sky fully
cleared, displaying the sierra [Mount Taylor] covered with snow.
A very handsome sight. Amado returned from Grant's. Politics
and politics, nothing else than politics!

OCTOBER 23: Left with Trinio for Grants. The ground is too wet
and muddy to permit going to the Rio Puerco. At Grants I met
Dr. Marchand, also Father Durante. Resolved upon going home
at once. Lochner is here. All is politics, nothing but politics. It is
absolutely disgusting.

OCTOBER 27: I write this at home [with typewriter]. On the 24th,
I left for Albuquerque by freight, with Louis Baer.[1115] The day
was beautiful. At Laguna I met Pradt. At Albuquerque went to
Tammony and also took a room at Mrs. Woerner's at the Old
Town. Called on the Jesuits, where Fathers Gentile[1116] and Carlos Personné received me most charmingly and at once placed
the books at my disposal. Copied at night.[1117] Called on Rupe
[Ruppe].[1118] On the 25th, I finished copying and spent the evening at Hunings; left for Santa Fe at 11 P.M. On the 26th, I arrived
at 4 A.M. All well at home. Thank God!

Letters from several parties. Nothing very new at all. Today it
is very beautiful again, but chilly. Budd is here again. The boy
becomes a nightmare to me. I spoke to Schumann; he seems to
like the ideas which I told him. Verémos. [We will see.] Today,
I put my letters, etc., in order; sent the legal document to C. H.
Burton at Mount Vernon, Illinois; and went down town again in
the forenoon to call on the Fathers. The Archbishop is not here.

In the afternoon, I went to the brewery with Dr. Strong. At night, Hubert came up.

OCTOBER 28: Finished revising Papa's copy. Sent $7. to Louis Huning and $5. to Louis. Went to the brewery in the afternoon with Joe and Henry. Amalia drove to Tezuque with Hubert.

OCTOBER 29: Wrote letters: two to Hodge; to Father Guyot; to Father Mariller; and sent pamphlet to the former. Also wrote to Rubio at Mexico. I began my report to Cushing on the inscriptions. In town, everybody is crazy on elections; it is absolutely disgusting in every respect. The fellow Budd is here still.

OCTOBER 30: Finished my report on inscriptions.[1119] Thermometer at noon: 59° F. Called on the old Doctor [Eggert]. He is always the same. Franz arrived today. I copied documents and also forwarded pamphlets to Fathers Brun, Mariller, and Francolon. Dr. Strong, his wife, and Mrs. Harlow called in the afternoon; Hubert, at night.

OCTOBER 31: Wrote to Seybt, Bourke, and Cushing. Finished copying and got new material. Went down town and paid a visit to Brother Amian. Got photographs of our place. Met Fiske and Budd.

NOVEMBER

NOVEMBER 1: I copied all day. Went to town in the afternoon for half an hour only. No letters.

NOVEMBER 2: Magnificent morning. Not a cloud in the deep blue sky. Very little additional snow fell on the high sierras yesterday. But today, nature is indescribably beautiful. Wind north, cold, and invigorating in the extreme. It remained beautiful, cloudless, and cool all day along. I copied and Papa also. Joe and Julia went to Koch's in the afternoon. Night fine, calm, quiet. Hubert called. I copied all night.

NOVEMBER 3: I copied. Letter from Hodge; all well at Zuñi. Joe and Mali went down town, and I, to the brewery with the doctor as usual.

NOVEMBER 4: Letters from: Ten Kate; from Joe and Budd, both returned from Jemez; from C. H. Burton and Judge Hazeldine.[1120] I wrote to Ten Kate and sent to Burton the document he had remitted for signature. Joe in bed with headache all day, although the attack was not as persistent as formerly. In the afternoon, Louise and Julia came; at night, Miss Nehber and Hubert. In the afternoon, we went to the brewery: Schumann, Dr. Eggert, and I. It was not at all pleasant, however, on account of politics and drunkenness. I wish this election business was over. It is a perfect nuisance. Joe got well about 3 P.M., but she is very much weakened.

NOVEMBER 5: Letter from L. Huning. Budd came again, and, in order to get rid of him, I wrote again to Hodge for his baggage. Brought back some documents to Ellison and got some new ones. Town filled with election fools.

I went down town twice today. Every time the town looks worse owing to increasing throngs on the streets. Called on Brother Amian. Joe well.

NOVEMBER 6: Tuesday. Election Day! Carriages with "intelligent voters" are driving past here to the schoolhouse where are the polls. This system of popular suffrage is a mean farce.[1121]

I translated at chapter V of the novel. Letter from Liebert. Budd has borrowed $10. from him. The mean scrub! I shall try to do the best I can for the poor fellow, for he has been swindled evidently. In the afternoon, Koch came and was quite reasonable and modest. Joe went down town. At night, I went down town too, hoping to get to see some fun, but in vain. Nobody was on the street, and in order not to wait too long, I went home early.

NOVEMBER 7: Letter from Husher; he writes that he must go to Mexico. Sorry to lose him. Finished chapter V of the novel.

Wrote to Husher and went down town in the afternoon. It snowed all afternoon. Much excitement in town about elections.

NOVEMBER 8: Letter from Judge Hazeldine. Copied again. It will not do to work too eagerly at the novel; it tires my faculties too much. Went down town twice. Nothing new except politics. In the afternoon, Joe and Mali went to Lizzie. At night, I wrote to Liebert about Budd.

NOVEMBER 9: The letter which I wrote to Liebert last night I burnt. I copied. No letters. Nothing new at all. [Benjamin] Harrison is said to be elected. Tonight, I heard the news of the murder of poor Provencher.[1122] I copied all day except when I had to go to town. Joe and Mali went to town also. The political excitement seems almost over for the present. Papa also is becoming more reasonable. Hubert came tonight.

NOVEMBER 10: Letter from Rubio. Copied in the forenoon, and in the afternoon went to the brewery with Dr. Strong. It is our last visit there. He leaves next week. His post will be Fort Schuyler, New York. Met Theodore Fischer.[1123] The brewery will remain as it is. At noon, received a letter from Cushing with the monthly check. Very friendly.

NOVEMBER 11: Settled with Mali today. I remain owing to her, $100. Gave her a note for it today.

Yesterday, while at the brewery, they told me of the find of a skeleton while excavating a ditch for irrigating, or water storing purposes. The skull and many bones they preserved, and I told them to keep them for us. The skeleton was found at a depth of three feet below the surface, almost on the dividing line between the black loam and a yellowish, indurated clay. As regards the posture of the skeleton, I am unable to decide, but I requested Gaertner to leave the place undisturbed. In the afternoon, went to the brewery with Henry, and the evening we spent at Henry's. Pleasant.

NOVEMBER 12: No letter for me, but one from little Karl [Carl F. Huegy, probably][1124] with the announcement that the widow Brossard had married Henry Weinheimer. I wish them all kind of happiness and every possible bliss. Both he and she, have been meanly treated by the people of Highland.

I finished copying the Trial of Dirucaca[1125] today. It is highly important. No news for me. Antonio worked the whole day in the garden, and Papa cut the roses. Hubert and Henry were up at night. It was pleasant.

NOVEMBER 13: Antonio at work again. The boy is very good. He got through with his work at noon, as it is too cold for pruning and trimming trees. Papa, of course, cannot do it; he suffers from cold and from the altitude. I do not understand anything about it. Copied some in the afternoon. Mr. and Mrs. Hartmann spent the evening with us. It was very pleasant. He is always good and instructive company, and she is a very nice woman.

NOVEMBER 14: Letter from Hodge. Copied. At night, I had Carlos Scheurig. Hubert and Miss Nehber came up. Papa and Koch go to San Juan tomorrow.

NOVEMBER 15: Papa and Koch left for San Juan today. Cool. Copied. Dr. Strong left for New York with his family. Copied. No letters.

NOVEMBER 16: Quiet. Finished copies and returned the papers to Ellison. Got two books from Father Deraches and returned them also after copying lists of custodians, etc.[1126]

NOVEMBER 17: Letter from Mr. Balsiger. I wrote to him, to A. Liebert, Taos, to Dr. Walliser, and to Father Brun. In the afternoon, I went to town, while Joe had company, Fishers and Kochs. I called on Father Defouri. Papa came home from San Juan and very much dissatisfied and displeased. He is also chilled through and through, as might be expected by such weather and on such a trip! Still he might be a little more reasonable.

NOVEMBER 18: Letter from Father Guyot. Went to High Mass. Wrote a note to Father Guyot. In the afternoon, Koch, then Dr. Eggert, Franz, and Schumann came; then, Henry, Hubert, Kaenter, and Elbring. Papa is better today. He gets over his cold and is in better humor also. Wrote to the Hammond T. W. Co. At night, Theodore Fischer and Louise came. Pleasant evening.

NOVEMBER 19: No letters. Began to write at the report for the Institute. Joe and Mali went down town.

NOVEMBER 20: Copied. Letter from F. Cushing. Wrote at the report. Mrs. Fiske came, also Schumann. Letter from Cushing at night.

NOVEMBER 21: Wrote to Cushing. Copied and wrote. Nothing new. Letters from A. Liebert and from Husher. Wrote at my report. Papa very good.

NOVEMBER 22: Returned document to Ellison and got the vindication of Diego de Vargas from 1703.[1127] In the afternoon, Lummis came and to supper we had Father Mailluchet.

NOVEMBER 23: Could not do anything until 3 P.M, Lummis being here to dinner. Then copied. Minnie Hilgert left for St. Louis today, with Franz and Theodore Fischer. Copied.

NOVEMBER 24: Finished copying and returned [the document] to Ellison. In the afternoon, I went to Tipton and copied. There is still more at the Surveyor General's Office. At night, wrote to Dr. Brühl and to George Hoffmann.

NOVEMBER 25: Letter from Mr. Balsiger, with P.O. order for Mali. Replied to him at once. Wrote, and then went down town with Henry in the afternoon.

NOVEMBER 26: About eight inches of very heavy, wet snow. It took José Vigil and Marcelino nearly the whole day to clean the roofs and around the house. In the afternoon, Father Navet unexpectedly came with Teresa and Ophelia.[1128] Also a long and handsome letter from Cushing.

NOVEMBER 27: Letter from Father Brun. Card from Father Mailluchet. Went down town in the afternoon. At night, Bishop Matz[1129] of Denver having arrived, we went to call on him at the Archbishop's and afterwards called at Father Vicar's.

NOVEMBER 28: Letter from the Hammond Typewriter Co. Father Navet and the girls left this afternoon. Wrote.

NOVEMBER 29: Thanksgiving Day. Indeed, I have reasons to be deeply grateful sofar and always. Letter from Hodge. Wrote to Father Mailluchet. We spent the day at Fischers very pleasantly. Finished chapter VI of the novel in English.

NOVEMBER 30: No letters. Have a serious cold. Feel quite ill.

DECEMBER

DECEMBER 1: Joe is in bed all day with a very severe cold. I copied at the novel nevertheless. Letter from Captain Bourke. Went down town but once. I feel very bad about my head.

I write this on Tuesday [December 4]. Was in bed all day Sunday.

DECEMBER 4: Yesterday I had a good letter from Cushing. Wrote to him, to Husher, and to Hodge. Got letter from Father Navet.

Today, Koch came up in a flurry. He had got hold of the letter from George to Hubert. I pity the poor woman, but she is the cause of everything, and he is more to be pitied than anybody else.

I was down town nearly all day. Got letter from Cushing with check. Also letter from Father Francolon. Wrote to Cushing, to Alejandro Campbell, and to Father Navet. To the latter, I sent postal note order for $1.50. At night, Henry was up.

DECEMBER 5: Letters from Hayoue and from Dr. Walliser. I wrote at the report for the Institute, as I cannot get anything from the archives. In the afternoon, the Fischer girls came, and Louise announced us the news that Frank Hunter[1130] has arrived and that they are going to be *married tomorrow!!* This is quite unexpected. I wish them every happiness and bliss. Louise deserves it richly. At night Hubert called.

DECEMBER 6: Papa well again. Tomorrow, Louise Fischer will get married and leave. I copied the notes. At night, Tipton came up, and afterwards Louise, Julia, and Frank Hunter.

DECEMBER 7: [For the entries of the 7th, 8th, and 9th, Bandelier wrote November rather than December.] Burial of Manderfield.[1131]

Louise and Frank Hunter were married today by Mr. Meany, and they left at 2:30 P.M. God be with them! I wrote at the notes to my report. Henry came up; also, Hubert and Miss Nehber. Letters from Alejandro Campbell and Apolonio Vigil.

DECEMBER 8: Joe and Mali went down town in the afternoon. I wrote at my report, as I cannot have any papers out of the archives. Papa made a fool of himself again.

DECEMBER 9: No letters. Lizzie Kaune got a boy [Charles Harrison Kaune] this morning at 3 A.M. I went to the Church of Guadalupe, instead of the cathedral.[1132] They have fire at Guadalupe at least. Wrote to Hayouä at Albuquerque. Affirmatively, but for February only. In the afternoon, I went to the brewery with Schumann and Koch. Fine. Wrote to Louise Fischer.

DECEMBER 10: Went to the Surveyor General's Office and copied. Letter from Robert Lambhorn and telegram from Cushing. Nothing new besides. Machines make trouble again. They seem to be a failure after all.

DECEMBER 11: More cloudy. Quiet. Northerly breeze.

I kept no journal the whole week, owing to the fact that I worked at the Surveyor General's Office and at night at home on Part II of my Report to the Institute. The weather was cold all the time, and on the 13th it snowed and flurried all day. It was particularly cold on the 16th and 17th. Papa was very ugly all this time, so much so that we lose all sympathy for him. On the evening of the 17th, I finished my Part II of the Report and sent it to Professor Norton with a letter accompanying it.[1133]

Joe has acute rheumatism and went to bed early. I too suffer from backache. Beautiful moonlights.

DECEMBER 18: Wrote all day at the U. S. Surveyor General's Office. Dr. Zavala[1134] came up to the offices too. No letters, but the military and the band came today, 10th Infantry, from Fort Union.

DECEMBER 19: Copied at the Surveyor General's. There is a document there from 1788, according to which, at that date, the leagues assigned to Santa Clara had not been surveyed, and the lands of the Pueblo, on the east side [of the village] did not go across the Rio Grande, but lay all on the west side. No letters. I wrote at the novel at night.

DECEMBER 20: During the day, I worked at the Surveyor General's.

DECEMBER 21: Finished work at the U. S. Surveyor General's Office today. Copied at my novel at home in the evening. No letters.

DECEMBER 22: Joe had her circle, and so I had to go bumming in the afternoon. Got some documents from Ellison. Christmas card from Janvier.

DECEMBER 23: Went to Mass. Letter from Widmer. Chilly and the weather still unsettled. A heavy snow must have fallen in the mountains. In the afternoon, up to the brewery with Koch and with Dr. Zavala.

DECEMBER 24: Had to go down town frequently on account of Christmas. Nevertheless, copied some. Christmas Night. Cloudy and cold. Otherwise very pleasant. No letters for me.

DECEMBER 25: We had a nice Christmas dinner at Lizzie's. Papa, who until last night was acting very ugly, suddenly changed. I finished Chapter X of the novel and then went up to the brewery with the usual parties. No letters.

DECEMBER 26: I copied.[1135] No letters; it is rather annoying. Christmas presents still coming in.

DECEMBER 27: A few unimportant letters. I decided upon devoting the days till after New Year's to the novel. Papa is copying for me in the meantime, so that the work is going on anyhow. Joe and Mali are well, and Papa is very nice.

DECEMBER 28: Wrote and then went down town for a moment. In the afternoon, Zavala called.

DECEMBER 29: Copied. No letters. Nothing new besides.

DECEMBER 30: Letter from Ten Kate. Poor fellow. Finished Chapter XI and began No. XII. Went up to the brewery a short while.

DECEMBER 31: Cold and half cloudy. Busy all day. Writing and finally preparing for tomorrow. Thermometer, early in the morning, 12°. It cleared in the afternoon.

This is the last day of another so far fortunate year. We have succeeded in bringing Papa back, but with him we have secured a cloud in our otherwise happy sky. Well, God has so disposed, and we must take it as it comes. We staid up till 10 P.M. and then retired very quietly. God be thanked for all He has done for us this year also.

NOTES

PREFACE

1. Considerable correspondence by Dr. Edgar L. Hewett, Mrs. Fanny R. Bandelier, Mr. Paul A. F. Walter, and Dr. Leslie A. White, as well as Wilson-Erickson, Inc., regarding this typescript is in the Bandelier Collection, Museum of New Mexico files.

In October 1936, Mrs. Bandelier wrote Dr. Hewett saying that the book was supposed to have come out in 1935 and that she understood it "will be delayed until next year." In reply, Dr. Hewett suggested she send a typewritten copy to be considered for publication during the Centennial Year [1940], if she were not fully bound to the Press of the Pioneers. Nothing further came of this, as Mrs. Bandelier died later that same fall of 1936.

Because Dr. Leslie A. White was editing the Bandelier-Morgan letters, he was also interested in this manuscript. In a letter to Mr. Paul A. F. Walter, Santa Fe, on March 24, 1937, Dr. White wrote, "I have just had a note from Wilson-Erickson, Inc., 33 W. 42nd St. N.Y.C., in reply to an inquiry directed by me to the Press of the Pioneers, to the effect that the publication of the Bandelier Journals has been abandoned, due to the death of Mrs. Bandelier. I cannot understand this. I had understood that the Journals were actually in press. It will be a shame not to have them published. . . .

"I certainly hope that Dr. Hewett will succeed in getting some information concerning Mrs. Bandelier's effects. . . ."

On July 19, 1937, Dr. Hewett wrote Dr. White: "We have received from the New York people a complete copy of the journal manuscript which they had undertaken to publish. It does not, however, include the introduction of Mrs. Austin, or the illustrations referred to in their announcement of the publication in 1934."

2. An unsigned note, "Bandelier Material Enriches School Library," in *El Palacio* of August–September 1937 briefly announced the arrival of various items of Bandelieriana, according to the will of Fanny R. Bandelier, who had died November 10, 1936, in Nashville, Tennessee. The most significant part of the collection was the series of notebooks, extending from 1880 to 1907 and containing Bandelier's journal pages for those years (Anonymous 1937: 49–50).

3. These notations on the weather undoubtedly reflected an early interest of Bandelier. Goad (1938: 78) stated that "Bandelier showed his scientific bent by publishing in the [*Der Highland*] *Bote*, . . .a series of meteorological observations. The last of these articles was published in *Die Union* in January, 1869." The Smithsonian Institution (1874: 92) reported that A. F. Bandelier, Jr., made observations for Highland, Illinois, for the period 1860–64. An earlier report of the Smithsonian (1864: 65) had listed him as Adolphus F. Bandelier, Jr., making observations for Highland, Illinois, Madison County, 38' 45" North Latitude, 89' 46" West Longitude, using the barometer, thermometer, and psychrometer. It was noted that it was fairly common for scientists of that period to do this. Dr. George Engelmann (see n 467) reputedly kept meteorological records for forty-seven years, a longer period, it is believed, than that of any other man in America (National Academy of Science 1902: 9). Bandelier's interests in this regard were also reflected from time to time in the detail he sought and recorded for various informants' tribal cosmologies.

4. In the earlier volumes, there has been a comment at this point in the Preface regarding the omission of notations on Bandelier's photographic plates, since these had "never come to light" and retention of these notes appeared pointless. Subsequent research has indicated that many of these early plates were, in fact, destroyed.

However, in a letter from Bandelier to Francis Parkman (Bandelier-Parkman letters in the Massachusetts Historical Society) dated November 16, 1890, Bandelier wrote, "Last month I was also fortunate enough to secure again the photographic views of those Antiquities which are perhaps the most striking ones in the Southwest. [This was undoubtedly due to the efforts of Charles F. Lummis. In correspondence in the Bandelier Collection in the Museum of New Mexico Library from Goad to Hewett there is a letter reporting Goad's progress on his fieldwork and biography of Bandelier. He noted, "Of great interest will be several Lummis photographs of New Mexico Pueblos and ruins with Bandelier's notes written on the backs of the mountings."] The Negatives taken in 1880 had been destroyed by the Photographer before his death, which occurred at El Paso three years ago, as there was no sale for the views anymore."

In Ritch (1882: facing p. 43), W. Henry Brown, "Photographer—West Side of the Plaza, Up Stairs—Santa Fe, N.M." has a full page advertisement of "Eight different series as follows: l. Santa Fe, N.M. 2. The Indian Pueblo (Town) of Tesuque. 3. The Indian Pueblo of San Juan. 4. The Indian Pueblo of San Domingo. 5. The Ruins of Pecos Pueblo (Town). 6. The Cliff Dwellings of Cochiti and vicinity. 7. The Cerrillos Mines. 8. Trip from Trinidad, Col., to El Paso, Texas." Judging from the advertisement, both stereoscopic and 5" X 8" views were available in these series.

Bandelier had arrived in Santa Fe for his first fieldwork on August 23, 1880, and as the journal entry of August 25, 1880, indicated (Lange and Riley 1966: 72), he lost no time in seeking out professional photographers to assist him. "Bennett and Brown photo offer, 5 X 8 plates. Will do the work and give twelve prints from each plate, at cost, they keeping the plates." Presumably, at least some pictures that Bennett and Brown took for Bandelier were among those cited in the preceding paragraph.

Careful reading of the journals indicates that it was not until the fall of 1882 that Bandelier began to do his own photography, and that he had depended on Bennett and Brown in the meantime for his photography. Goad (1939: 71) noted that in the summer of 1880 while in the East making preparations for his fieldwork Bandelier "collected photographic supplies in New York" (see also Lange and Riley 1966: 24).

On July 30, 1882, Bandelier had written Parkman, "Finally I made a photographic tour to Cochiti again where I secured at last plates of the *dance*. But they are very imperfect, notwithstanding the great trouble we took. [Brown was with Bandelier at Cochiti to photograph the July 14 Corn Dance. See Lange and Riley 1966: 341.] The wet process is far too cumbersome, and too slow, and after the experience I have now had at Acoma and at Cochiti I shall not start again unless it be with a dryplate outfit. I have now learned enough to be able to take my own views and it would be impossible to take a photographer along hereafter. The Expenses for photographs have been enormous and they can all be avoided. Photography and excavation. I have both tried now and have become thoroughly disgusted with both of them."

However, by October 2, 1882, Bandelier had had a change of heart and wrote Parkman requesting among other items of equipment for the field, "One dry-plate photographic apparatus,—plates 5. X 8.—50 plates. But the whole should be as light as possible, so that it needs no packmule, but that I can carry it myself.—The Tripod of wire, and should you be unable to procure them I can have one made here." On November 20, 1882, he wrote to Parkman, "Shortly I shall send you drawings and photographs. The Machine and plates work splendidly." In another letter to Parkman on December 1, 1882, he wrote, "a draft for my photographic plates (6 doz.) which have at last come." In the entry of December 16, 1882, Bandelier wrote, " . . . and at 9 P.M. went with Bennett to the Gallery. He talked good sound photography to me for a long time. My plates have come and they are well paid for. [Worth the cost?] They are Cramer and Norton's, better packed than Eastman's and guaranteed to be more rapid." The entries from December 19 to December 31, 1882, all contained references to photographs Bandelier was making. In most instances he carefully noted the length of exposure (Lange and Riley 1966: 377–91). The reader shares Bandelier's frustration in the December 21, 1882, entry (p. 381), as he noted, "The ruin is largely overgrown with high *Opuntia*, and the work in deep snow is very difficult. Photographed, but Plate #7 would not go up, so I let down #8 and could not move either. Had to take them out, kicked over the instrument, split the wood, cursed amazingly, and finally took the view again, 11 seconds time. But am afraid my camera is spoilt." Apparently the camera was not ruined, as Bandelier continued taking photographs for the remainder of the month, and the editors have found no later entry which indicated the plates were spoiled. On December 29, 1882, he noted, "I fixed my camera with glue. ..." On January 21, 1883, Bandelier wrote, "shipped my photographs, box, etc. to Brown on the 20th. Am anxious to know how they turn out" (Lange and Riley 1970: 19). On January 25, he noted (p. 20), "Photographs from Brown," and on January 27 (p. 20), "Got letter from Brown. 18 [photographic] plates OK." After receiving the actual photographs, his entry said on January 28 (p. 20), "Got photographs; OK. . . . Wrote to Brown returning photographs, and sent photographs to Bernays, to Matthews, to Frank Smith, and Rev. Adams." Whether at this point Bandelier was giving Brown the original plate in lieu of paying him for developing the plates is not clear. It has not been possible for the editors to learn how many of Bandelier's original photographs are still in existence. With his initial arrangement with Bennett and Brown to receive twelve copies and from numerous letters like that just cited in which he noted sending photographs to various people, there is still a chance that at least some of these do exist.

Since reading the entries pertaining to the preparation of the *Histoire* and examining Father Burrus's Catalogue and studying slides of the illustrations, the editors believe that at least some of Bennett and Brown's pictures taken in the early 1880s and some that Bandelier himself took in late 1882 and early 1883 were incorporated in the *Histoire*. His drawing is discussed in greater detail in n 339. That Bandelier often painted or sketched rather than taking photographs is evident from the journals.

NOTES

1885

5. This was Alphonse Bandelier, a cousin of Adolph; over the years, there was a periodic exchange of correspondence between the two men. As shown in the journal entries of late 1884 and early 1885, the two were together a number of times during Adolph's visit to Switzerland regarding affairs of the F. Ryhiner & Co. bank and also various scholarly interests. Hobbs (1942a; 1942b: 118n25) was told by Elizabeth Bandelier Kaune that Alphonse lived in Bern, Switzerland, and had visited the family in Highland, Illinois, once when Elizabeth, or Lizzie, was a child.

6. Bandelier had visited Mr. Desgranges in Carouge, December 27, 1884, and had been shown "his manufacture of pottery . . ." (Lange and Riley 1970: 353).

7. Mr. Hebler remains without further identification. Bandelier's correspondence with him began at least as early as October 22, 1880. In addition to letters, Bandelier noted sending a map to Hebler from Peña Blanca, New Mexico, April 17, 1882, which suggests their relationship was in scholarly concerns as well as in business matters. From journal entries of late 1884 (Lange and Riley 1970: 350–51), it is clear that Bandelier had resorted to Mr. Hebler as a confidant regarding the deteriorating business situation in Highland.

In the list of European creditors of the F. Ryhiner & Co. bank published in the *Weekly Telephone* of May 6, 1885, Louis Hebler of Bern was given with an investment of 12,200 francs, while a Charles Hebler-Haller of Bern was listed with an investment of 50,000 francs.

8. Professor B. Studer, Ordinarius for Mineralogy and Geology at the University of Bern until 1870, had been visited by Bandelier at the Museum of Natural History in that city on November 27, 1884, soon after his arrival in Bern. Bandelier had also "spent a pleasant hour" on December 2 with Studer who had "received me most charmingly" (Lange and Riley 1970: 350–51). In a list of books in the Bandelier Collection, Museum of New Mexico Library, was the following item: "Studer, B.: *Lehrbuch der Physikalischen Geographie und Geologie*, Bern, 1844."

In the May 6, 1885, issue of the *Weekly Telephone*, a Bernhard Studer of Bern was listed with the amount of 5,000 francs among the European creditors of the F. Ryhiner & Co. bank. This may well have been Professor B. Studer.

In our first volume (Lange and Riley 1966: 9), we followed Hodge (1932: 353) in stating that Bandelier had studied under Professor Studer at Bern in 1857. However, this statement was corrected in our second volume (1970: 2); the editors agree with Charles Gallenkamp (personal communication) and with White (1940: I, 5n4), who have pointed out that, according to University of Bern records, the Bandelier who studied under Professor Studer in the period from 1858 to 1867 was Alph., not Adolph. This may well have been Bandelier's cousin, Alphonse (see n 5).

9. Bandelier had seen Mr. de Bùren of Bern, Switzerland, presumably on business matters, on December 6, 1884 (Lange and Riley 1970: 352).

10. Armand Guys, a Frenchman, of Boston, had been a fellow passenger on the S. S. *Lessing* when Bandelier went to Europe in late 1884 (see journal entry for November 13, 1884, in Lange and Riley 1970: 348).

11. In 1885, Bishop John Baptist Salpointe became the Archbishop of Santa Fe, having been coadjutor to Archbishop John B. Lamy for a brief period prior to this. Born in France in 1825, Salpointe attended the Clermont-Ferrand Seminary and, in 1851, was ordained a priest. He taught at this seminary from 1855 to 1859 and then came to the United States as a missionary in the Diocese of Santa Fe. He served as priest of the Mora parish, New Mexico, for six years and in 1866 he was appointed by Bishop Lamy to the new position of Vicar General for the Missions of Arizona. In 1868, he was appointed the first Bishop of Arizona. Bandelier had made his acquaintance in 1884 in Tucson (Lange and Riley 1970: 328).

As later journal entries of this volume show, the two men saw each other frequently; it was Salpointe who commissioned Bandelier to write the *Histoire* for the Pope's Jubilee. Following his retirement as Archbishop of Santa Fe in 1894, Salpointe devoted much time to research on church history in the Southwest, a subject on which his personal experiences well qualified him. His book, *Soldiers of the Cross,* was published in 1898; it was reprinted in 1967. Salpointe died in Tucson on July 15, 1898 (Lange and Riley 1970: 387n244; Salpointe 1898).

12. Dr. William Eggert, first homeopathic physician in New Mexico Territory, lived in Santa Fe during the 1880s and 1890s. Born in Germany, Eggert was educated in New York and went to Santa Fe after living in Indianapolis. He was active in territorial medical affairs and was a medical writer of national reputation. A friend and steady correspondent of Bandelier, Dr. Eggert also assisted Bandelier with his writing in German for publication (Lange and Riley 1970: 379n171).

13. Father Ignacio María Grom had been brought to New Mexico by Bishop Lamy; he served a parish at Belen and became acquainted with Bandelier there and elsewhere in the diocese (Chavez 1957: 259; Salpointe 1898: 282). Salpointe (1893: 9) listed Father María Ignatius Grom at St. Joseph's in Tierra Amarilla in 1888.

14. Father León Mailluchet, of Porrentruy, Franch-Compte, France, was a parish priest in the Pecos–Las Vegas area during the 1880s (Salpointe 1898: 273).

15. Lieutenant Charles Pinckney Elliott, a South Carolinian and West Point graduate, became a 2d lt. in the Thirteenth Infantry, June 13, 1882, later transferring to the Fourth Cavalry. In 1888, he became a 1st lt., and he retired in 1898 as captain (Heitman 1903: I, 401). Bandelier met him on the train on October 23, 1883, at which time Elliott was stationed at Fort Cummings (Lange and Riley 1970: 152).

16. This was Josephine Huegy Bandelier, the daughter of Moritz, or Maurice, Huegy and Josephine Suppiger Huegy; she was born October 11, 1836 (White 1940: I, 64). Joe and Adolph were married January 5, 1862, in Highland. There were no children from this marriage. Joe died December 11, 1892, in Lima, Peru.

Although Joe's name is mentioned frequently in the journals, it was only on rare occasions that Bandelier expressed his feelings for her. In the context of the bank's failure and the resulting suicide of Josephine's brother, Maurice, from correspondence which has survived (e.g., Bandelier's letters to Francis Parkman and to Joaquín García Icazbalceta), and from the journal entries of the years 1885 through 1888, the reader becomes more aware of Bandelier's devotion to Joe. Then, too, following the Bandeliers' move to Santa Fe in late 1885, the journals often recorded Joe's activities as well as those of Bandelier, thus giving the reader a better understanding of Joe as a person. In spite of its being an era when women took to their beds for the slightest illness, it does seem that Joe did in fact not enjoy good health. On occasion, she accompanied her husband on rather strenuous trips or went with him to Indian ceremonies and in this sense shared an interest in his work. The journals reveal that their home was always open to the men with whom Bandelier was working and also that Joe had made a life for herself in Santa Fe. The Bandeliers also had a number of mutual friends whom they saw frequently.

Various relatives both from her family and from Bandelier's lived with them from time to time, often for extended periods. Probably the most trying was Bandelier's father, Adolphe E., who, having deserted them at the time of the bank failure, later returned, as the journals of this volume relate, to make his home with Adolph and Joe in Santa Fe until they moved to Peru in 1892. Bandelier never indicated that Joe felt this was a hardship, but her frequent illnesses may very well have reflected life with this difficult personality.

17. On November 26, 1884, Bandelier had seen Mr. Aebi in Bern (Lange and Riley 1970: 350). The context of the present entry suggests that Bandelier was seeing Mr. Aebi on bank matters.

In the *Weekly Telephone* (Vol. III, No. 15, p.4) of June 2, 1885, a list of European creditors of the F. Ryhiner & Co. bank was printed. Among those listed was Rudolph Aebi of Berne, with a figure of 32,000 francs, the fifth most heavily involved of the 244 creditors, whose holdings ranged from 184,000 to 400 francs. It is probable that "Mr. Aebi" was the Rudolph Aebi of the news account. Also listed in the *Telephone* story were Mary Aebi-Ringier (22,000 frs.) and Marie Aebi Ringier (7,000 frs.).

18. Mr. J. U. Burckhardt was associated with Gruner-Haller and Company of Bern. He had participated in a conference in Bern held with Bandelier (Lange and Riley 1970: 351) and was very much involved in matters relating to the F. Ryhiner & Co. bank, as is evident from this journal entry. It is also evident here and in subsequent entries that Bandelier was favorably disposed toward Mr. Burckhardt.

The *Weekly Telephone,* May 6, 1885, reported, "The house (Gruner-Haller & Co., of Berne) representing the Swiss creditors, then sent by the latter's request one of its members, Mr. J. U. Burkhart [*sic*], to Highland who found everything as represented by F. Ryhiner & Co., whereupon the latter offered said creditors two propositions. The first was (based upon their statement) a reduction of all claims to 60 per cent, to be paid off in twelve years, with four per cent interest from Jan. lst 1886; the second was for 50 per cent, $130,000, to be paid in real estate (valued at $132,157.00 in their statement) transferred to said creditors, and $52,070.14 in cash to be paid off in six years. Mr. Burkart [*sic*] and his firm then recommend that the second proposition, as representing net about 30 per cent, be accepted, since the first proposition meant only a reduction of capital and interest without security for the new obligation."

19. Professor Adolf Bastian (1826–1905), German ethnologist, traveled widely, wrote extensively, and achieved prominence in developing museums and collections. (See Lowie [1937: 30–38] for a discussion of his importance.) Bandelier's entry of March 9, 1885, recorded his brief appraisal of Bastian.

20. The journal entry of December 8, 1884, noted that Bandelier had met Adolphe. Adolphe has been identified as "perhaps another, younger, cousin; possibly a brother or a son of Alphonse" (Lange and Riley 1970: 439n168). In the index (Lange and Riley 1970: 482), he is entered as "[Bandelier?], Adolphe (Bern, Switzerland)." The reader will note that in the January 12, 1885, entry Bandelier referred to him as "an excellent and feeling boy."

21. On December 26, 1884, Bandelier had attended a theater party. Among the names given, the editors were unsure of one, which they published as "Brun[?]" (Lange and Riley 1970: 352). This may well have been the same person.

22. This was Hippolyte Jean Gosse (1834–1901), a citizen of Geneva. Gosse was an expert on European prehistory and wrote extensively on aspects of the prehistory of central Europe (Library of Congress 1943a: 181).

23. On December 8, 1884, Bandelier noted Mr. Limer as one of the acquaintances he had made, seemingly at Geneva (Lange and Riley 1970: 352).

24. Dr. George H. Moore (1823–92), librarian, historian, bibliographer; he became Librarian of the Lenox Library, New York City, in 1879 (Jacobs 1960: I, 121). Bandelier's correspondence with him seems to have begun at least by that time (Lange and Riley 1970: 437n159). When in New York, Bandelier visited Dr. Moore and the Lenox Library. The Lenox Library today is part of the New York Public Library.

25. Rather extensive information was given about Francis Parkman in our earlier volume (Lange and Riley 1970: 366n72). As the indices of both Volumes I and II indicate, Bandelier carried on an extensive correspondence with Parkman. Through correspondence with Dr. Wilbur R. Jacobs, editor of two volumes of Parkman letters (1960), the editors learned that additional letters from Bandelier to Parkman were in the holdings of the Massachusetts Historical Society and subsequently obtained copies of all letters written during the period of our concern. These letters have been most helpful in that they frequently contained expansions of mere notes in the journal entries. They also reflected Bandelier's feelings about his work, often in greater detail than was expressed in the journals. At least portions of these letters will be of valuable aid to the editors as they make their appraisal of Bandelier's contributions to Southwestern studies as a part of the fourth and final volume.

26. This was Moisé Vautier (see entry of April 4, 1885). The Vautier family lived in Carouge, near Geneva, Switzerland; they appear to have been related to the Bandeliers. The precise relationship, however, remains obscure.

27. This was most probably the Swiss geologist, Karl (Carl) Christoph Vogt (1817–95), a colleague of Bernard Studer of Bern. Vogt was Professor of Natural History at Geneva (Library of Congress 1946: 100; British Museum 1964: 106–7).

28. As of the time of Bandelier's visit, Alsace was a part of Germany rather than France.

29. Members of the Bernays family living in Highland and also in St. Louis were friends of the Bandeliers. The precise relationship between these families and Helen Bernays has

not been established. The reader is referred to the biography of Augustus Charles Bernays by Thekla Bernays (1912). See Lange and Riley (1970) for information on several members of the Bernays family mentioned by Bandelier in his 1883–84 journals.

30. Mr. H. Mohr of Stuttgart was apparently the father of Dr. Hans Mohr, a physician and friend of the Bandelier family in Highland (see April 14, 1885, entry).

31. It was only natural for Bandelier to contact *Das Ausland* while in Stuttgart. As noted in Lange and Riley (1970: 365n61), *Das Ausland* was published in Stuttgart and München, Germany, between 1828 and 1894, volumes I through LXVII appearing in that interval (see Hodge 1907–10: II, 1180). Hobbs (1942b: 113n12) named Friedrich Ratzel, German geographer, anthropogeographer, and writer, as one of the editors of *Das Ausland,* in which many of Bandelier's works were published. Through the kindness of Dr. Christa Bausch, formerly of the Landesmuseum of Stuttgart, and a visitor on the Anthropology staff at Southern Illinois University, Carbondale, in 1967–68, the editors obtained Xerox copies of Bandelier's *Das Ausland* publications for the years of his Southwestern journals, 1880–92. Whenever possible, the editors have correlated the journal entries with the published *Ausland* articles. As the entry of February 5, 1885, indicated, Bandelier on several occasions met Professor Ratzel in Munich. As late as 1884, Professor Ratzel's name had appeared as editor on the masthead of *Das Ausland.* The editors have not been able to learn more of either Mr. Koch or Dr. Müller but presume they were editors of *Das Ausland.*

32. Whether "Dr." in this entry referred to Dr. Hans Mohr of Highland or to Dr. Hans Mohr of Brooklyn, New York, with whom Bandelier had spent an evening prior to sailing for Europe late in 1884 and whom he visited upon his return (see April 1, 1885, entry), is not clear. The relationship between the two Dr. H. Mohrs has not been established, and it is also possible that there was but one Dr. H. Mohr, a resident of Highland, who happened to be in the East both times Bandelier mentioned seeing "Dr. Mohr."

33. On this date, February 3, 1885, Bandelier's paper, "The Romantic School in American Archaeology," was read before a meeting of the New York Historical Society. It was printed in the *Papers of the New York Historical Society,* February 5, 1885. The fourteen-page article was reprinted in New York by Trow's Printing and Bookbinding Company, also in 1885 (Lange and Riley 1966: 43, 43n28). In Volume 2 of the *American Antiquarian,* there was a note that a copy of this paper was in the Ayer Collection [Newberry Library] and that the New York Public Library had the author's presentation copy.

34. The fact that Bandelier placed a question mark after the date 1526 is perhaps significant here. It is also interesting that he made no notes after observing that this was a written rather than a printed edition (see also n 39).

In a letter to Morgan dated November 24, 1876 (White 1940: II, 13), Bandelier had commented that he had ordered Oviedo's *Historia general de las Indias, &c.* and another book, costly but still cheap at the prices asked. "It may be possible that in Oviedo, who was a very good observer and a juris-consult too, by education at least, if not in practice, we find some indications of the gens. . . ." In a footnote on Oviedo's works, White added: "Gonzalo Fernando de Oviedo (1478–1557), Spanish historian. He was in Middle America in 1514; became official chronicler of the Indies; chief work: *Historia natural y general de las Indias,* in 50 books." White did not indicate where or when this work was published.

Waterman (1917: 251), discussing Bandelier's historical sources, gave a date of 1525 for Oviedo, at the same time noting that some dates given were conjectural. In his bibliography, he cited: "Oviedo y Valdés, Gonzalo Fernandez de, *Historia general y natural de las Indias.* (Composed 1525–1550.) Madrid, Real Academia de Historia (four folio volumes), 1851."

Wagner (1937), in his bibliography, gave "Fernández de Oviedo y Valdés, Gonzalo. *Historia general y natural de las Indias, islos y tierra-firme del Mar Oceano.* Madrid, 1851–55. 4 vols. A small part of this work had been previously printed in 1535 and 1557, and great difficulty was experienced in getting together the manuscript of the remainder. As it is, the work was not finished, there being a number of chapter headings inserted for chapters never filled out; and besides Oviedo promised another volume to bring up to 1550 the history of New Spain. His account of that country ends about 1540 or 1541. The book is an immense storehouse of facts recited without much order or plan. What is needed is an index, for unless one has read the entire work it is not possible to be certain that it does not contain an account of some particular occurrence."

Bandelier, in his *Report of an Archaeological Tour in Mexico in 1881* (1884: 5-6n3), cited yet another edition: Gonzálo Fernando de Oviedo y Valdes, *Historia natural y general de las Indias,* reprinted by the late Don José Amador de los Rios, in 1853.

35. The New or Neue Pinakothek in Munich was begun in 1846 but was not completed until 1853, after Ludwig I's abdication. It was built to house contemporary paintings in contrast to the Old or Alte Pinakothek (see n 43), which was a repository for old paintings (Wadleigh 1910: 162; Baedeker 1909: 242). Wadleigh wrote, "It is a lamentable failure as a work of architecture, the only complete and undeniable failure among Ludwig's twenty-five public monuments."

36. The editors feel that Bandelier was referring to the Royal Library, the Hof-und Staats-Bibliothek, in Munich when he wrote R. B. Library in this entry. In 1832, Ludwig I had entrusted Gärtner with the designs for this library. Its architecture was a combination of Florentine style with the early German round arch. The building was completed in 1843 (Wadleigh 1910: 165; Baedeker 1909: 222).

37. For a more detailed description of John de Laet's abstract, see Hodge, Hammond, and Rey (1945: 25–26). Though this book deals primarily with the Benavides Memorial of 1634, a manuscript found after Bandelier's death, it also includes data on the Benavides Memorial of 1630, to which Bandelier made reference in this entry. Mrs. Edward E. Ayer's translation of the 1630 Memorial was extensively annotated by Hodge and Lummis (Ayer 1916). Wagner (1937: I, 227–34) gave data not only on the various copies and editions of the 1630 Memorial but biographical material about Fray Alonso de Benavides as well.

38. Jean, or Joan, Blaeu (1596–1673) was a Dutch cartographer. Bandelier had cited Jean Blaeu, *Douzième livre de la Géographie Blaviane,* Amsterdam, 1667, in his Pecos report (1881b [1883 ed.]: 20n1). Hodge (1907–10: II, 1183) cited the same publication and added "[Quoted as Blaeu, Atlas, Vol. XII.]." This was the same volume to which Bandelier made reference in this entry.

In discussing the older cartography of New Mexico, Bandelier (1910a: 26) wrote, "It is through the work of Benavides that more correct ideas of New Mexican geography were gained and a somewhat more accurate and detailed nomenclature was introduced, since the *Géographie Blaviane* of 1667 by the Dutch cartographer contains a map of the region far superior to any hitherto published."

39. Undoubtedly, this edition of Oviedo that Bandelier examined in the Royal Archives in Munich was the partial publication by Oviedo referred to by Wagner in n 34 in the present volume. Bandelier must also have been aware that this edition of Oviedo's work was not complete and, accordingly, continued to search in the European archives and libraries for additional portions of Oviedo's work.

40. The sources in the Royal Archives examined by Bandelier were noted as follows: Padre Andrés Cavo, "Los tres Siglos en México durante el Gobierno Español," edited by

C. M. Bustamente, Mexico, 1836, Vol. II, Part IIª, Lib. VIII, and Francisco Pimentel, "Memoria sobre las las [?] Causas que han originado la situacion actual de la Raza indígena de México y Medios de Remediarla," Part I, 1864. (The first of these two items was cited by Espinosa [1942: 383] as "CAVO, ANDRÉS. *Los Tres Siglos de Méjico durante el Gobierno Español hasta la Entrada del Ejército Trigarante*. Publicada con Notas y Suplemento en 1836 por el Licenciado D. Carlos de Bustamente. Jalapa, 1870.")

41. Moritz Wagner (1813–87) was a German natural historian and evolutionist who traveled extensively in both North and South America between 1850 and 1860. Wagner was also professor at the Ludwig—Maximilians Universität in Munich (Library of Congress 1946: 459–60; British Museum 1964: 471).

42. Captain James Cook (1728–79) was a British explorer who made three extremely important voyages of discovery between 1768 and 1779. Son of an English day laborer, Cook was apprenticed to a ship owner at the age of 17. He eventually worked himself up to the command of a ship. In 1755, Cook volunteered for duty in the British navy and in 1757 was given a naval command. After the war with France, Cook's skill in mathematics and astronomy, as well as his maritime skills, led him to continue in British naval service on a series of scientific surveys.

In 1768, Cook was commissioned as lieutenant in charge of the vessel *Endeavour Bark*. His exploits included discovery of the Society Islands, the charting of much of New Zealand and the east cost of Australia, and considerable ethnological and botanical work on Tahiti. Returning in 1771, Cook was promoted to commander and in 1772 left England again with two ships, the *Resolution* and the *Adventure*. Exploring the Antarctic waters for three southern summers, 1772–73, 1773–74, and 1775, Cook laid the groundwork for an understanding of the geography of the extreme south; between these explorations, he also visited much of Polynesia. Returning to England in 1775, Cook was elected a Fellow of the Royal Society and was promoted to the rank of captain. He almost immediately volunteered to make still another voyage, again in the *Resolution,* with the *Discovery* as escort. On this third voyage, Cook discovered Hawaii, explored the Northwest Coast of North America, and, on returning to Hawaii, was killed in a minor skirmish with the Polynesian natives there.

Ethnographic collections by Cook from his various voyages have found their way into museums in a number of countries. His voyages make up some of the world's greatest sea adventures. For a discussion of Cook's life and voyages, see Beaglehole (1966: 229–315).

43. The Alte Pinakothek, built by Ludwig I of Bavaria and housing one of the famous European art collections, was completed in 1833. It marked the beginning of Munich as an art center. Bandelier, a man of culture, undoubtedly found genuine satisfaction in his visit to this art museum. Since Bandelier himself had begun painting (see n 339), the art works he found there had increased meaning to him and his comments in this entry showed his appreciation. Ludwig I had built the Alte Pinakothek to show the development of European art (Wadleigh 1910: 162, 255).

44. Of the painters named, the editors have singled out Zurbarán for special mention. Francisco de Zurbarán was born in Spain in 1598. Art historians vary in his death date, but the consensus seems to be that it took place between 1661 and 1664. He received his training in Seville. Before he had reached the age of thirty-five, he had been appointed painter to the king. In a list of the chief works of Zurbarán Stirling-Maxwell (1910: 294) noted a St. Francis of Assisi at the Pinakothek in Munich. Presumably, this was the painting Bandelier had reference to in this journal entry, as it was the only Zurbarán listed at the Alte Pinakothek (Baedeker 1909: 242). Of Zurbarán, Stirling-Maxwell (1910: 187) wrote, "He is the peculiar painter of monks, as Raphael is of Madonnas and Ribera of martyrdoms; he studied the Spanish friar, and painted him with as high a relish as Titian painted the Venetian noble and Vandyck the gentleman of England." He studied the

Carthusian monks in their native cloisters and painted for a number of the orders (pp. 182–83).

Bandelier's noting of the Zurbarán in Munich might have gone without comment by the editors if they had not found two letters in the Bandelier-Hewett correspondence of the Bandelier Collection at the Museum of New Mexico Library, written in 1910, from New York City, apparently in response to a query from Hewett concerning the Franciscan habit. These letters are reproduced below.

521 W. 158th St. June 29th. 1910.

My dear Hewett.

There are seven different Habits of the Franciscan Order. For your purpose you may adopt the original one worn by S. Francis of Assisi, Fray Marcos of Nizza and San Pedro of Alcántara. The color is a grayish brown or brownish gray (beast color). They wear the cowl and a short cape of the same color and material. The cord is white with a rosary to which pend seven decades. No shoes, only sandals, heads always bare with the great tonsure that leaves only about three-finger's breath [sic] of hair around the skull. The color of the cassock has gradually been changed into chestnut-brown for the regular Observants and Capuchins, but the Recollects (founded 1592) preserve the original habit of St. Francis as well as the Minorites. The blue Franciscans and those whose coat is purplish brown are exclusively Spanish and I doubt whether any of them came to New Mexico. The garment need not be painted very clean nor the cord snow-white! I do not know when the change to chestnut-brown became more general but know that at least one of the female ramifications of the Franciscans wore it in the middle of the sixteenth century.

Yours very truly.

Ad. F. Bandelier

521 W. 158th St. July 12th. 1910.

My dear Hewett.

When I wrote you I omitted mentioning that no Fransiscan of the regular Observants should be painted with a beard. It might not be amiss however to place, but in the background, a Capuchin in brown and with a beard, just for variety's sake. While it is not certain that Capuchins accompanied Vargas there is no great anachronism in putting one of them there as there were Capuchins in New Mexico in the second half of the seventeenth century. The great authority for the Franciscan habit of the Regular Order would be of course the paintings of Francisco Zurbaran (1598–1663). i [sic] have one original by him but will not let it go out of my hands.

Kindest regards from both of us,

Yours as usual:

Ad. F. Bandelier

P. S.: The Capuchin reform was instituted 1525. The frock is chestnut-brown with a white cord and they are the only Franciscans who can wear beards without special license.

The editors are unaware of information concerning Bandelier's acquisition of an original Zurbarán. The Encyclopaedia Britannica cited records of large numbers of Zurbarán's paintings destined for Peru in 1647. It is possible that Bandelier acquired one of these during his work in South America after leaving the Southwest in 1892.

We are interested, however, in light of Bandelier's comments about beards, to find that an original Zurbarán, entitled St. Francis, 1630–32, in the City Art Museum of St. Louis, has a beard, as does a print of the original of Saint Francis by Zurbarán in the Milwaukee Art Center Collection. In both of these examples, St. Francis is portrayed holding a human skull. The use of light and shadows immediately catches the viewer's eye. It is not surprising that Bandelier was interested in the Franciscan habit as of the time of the first Spaniards in the New World. As of 1910, he believed the artist who had depicted this habit most accurately was Francisco de Zurbarán.

45. The letter mentioned in this entry was definitely written by Padre Kino to Padre Zignis. However, the next few lines were quite illegible, partly in Latin, and, all in all, were virtually indecipherable. Whether these lines briefed the letter or were notations on other items examined by Bandelier remains uncertain (see ns 46 and 47).

46. This was the celebrated Jesuit missionary, Father Eusebio Francisco Kino (1645–1711), a Tyrolese Italian. As of Bandelier's time, he was thought to have been of German ancestry, hence the Father Kühne (or Kuehne) of Bandelier's writings. Bandelier commonly added "or Father Kino" to such designations. On occasion, as in this entry, he used only "Padre Kino."

An autobiography of Kino found by Bolton, after Bandelier's death, and published in 1919 (Bolton 1936: 29, 29n1, 30), established the missionary's ancestry as Italian and his name as Chino (or Chini) and not Kühn. In Spain and Spanish-America, the missionary generally wrote his name as Kino (p. 28). Bandelier made extensive use of Kino's writings, particularly in regard to Mexico and Arizona (see Lange and Riley 1966; 1970). However, in the comprehensive book on Kino by Bolton, cited above, it is singular that he made no reference to Bandelier, either in his text or in his bibliography.

Burrus (1969b: 54) indicated that Chapter IV of Part IV of the *Histoire* dealt with the Jesuit efforts in Sonora and Arizona, 1680–1700, mainly those of Fathers Kino and Salvatierra.

47. Padre Paulus Zignis has not been identified; in contrast to subsequent notations, possibly on the letter from Kino to Zignis (see n 45), the name Zignis was very clearly written in the original journals. Bolton (1936: 600) listed one and possibly two letters from Kino to Zingnis. These were original manuscripts, in Latin, in the Bayerische Hauptstaatsarchiv, München. Though Zingnis was listed in Bolton's index as Father Paul Zingnis and there were brief references in his text to the manuscripts cited, Father Zingnis was not further identified.

48. Bandelier's notes on this date were taken from a number of folios (No. 2, 6, 7, 9, 19, 22, 33, 40–41, 83, 87, and 543) of the following item: "Conquysta de Mexyco y otros Reynos y Provyncyas de la Nueva España que hyzo el Gran Capytan Fernan⁴⁰ Cortes. Su autor Don Domingo de San Anton Muñoz Quauhtleheranitizui. Se halla la copia original de esta Historia (que hasta ahora no se ha descubierto su autor ni dado á luz) en letra antigua en la Libreria del Colegio de San Pedro y San Pablo de la Cuidad de Mex⁵⁰ con la que se sacó esta copia para el Sr. Br. Don José Maria Espino, el ano de 1808." (Mark of J. M. Andrade.)

49. In the Bandelier Collection in the Museum of New Mexico is a letter of introduction in German for Samuel Eldodt (see n 77) from "Ad. F. Bandelier" to Dr. Simonsfeld, dated Santa Fe, New Mexico, March 15, 1888. The envelope was addressed to Dr. Julius Simonsfeld at Königl. Hülfs-bibliothek. München.

50. The "so-called novel" to which Bandelier referred in this entry was *Die Köshare* (see also n 73). He had started this novel on August 24, 1883 (Lange and Riley 1970: 146, 402n367); and, as the journal entries of this present volume show, he had completed only

two chapters by the end of 1885. He finished the novel, in German, on May 12, 1886, writing the last twenty chapters in four-and-one-half months, all by hand (see also n 580). In the files of the Bandelier Collection at the Museum of New Mexico Library is the following clipping on *Die Köshare* from *The Evening Post*, New York, Monday, March 17, 1890: "Mr. A. F. Bandelier has been publishing in the New York *Belletristisches Journal* since the new year a serial story, 'Die Kö-Sha-Re,' illustrative of the Pueblo Indians of New Mexico. The role of novelist is somewhat new for this scholar, but it cannot be said that he is going beyond his last. In fact, no one is so competent as he to attempt this portrayal. The *Journal* has just entered its thirty-ninth volume, under the editorship of Dr. Julius Goebel. Its range is wide, from politics to music, literature, and current events. The form of the paper is inconveniently large, judged by American standards, and in the finer type the Gothic letter becomes sufficiently trying." The editors in 1969 obtained Xerox copies of all installments of the novel in the *Belletristisches Journal* through the cooperation of the New York Public Library. From examination of these pages, it is clear that the German version was appreciably shorter than the ultimate English form, *The Delight Makers.*

By August 1886 (see entry of August 8), Bandelier had begun the translation of his novel into English and also its expansion and elaboration. The resulting novel, *The Delight Makers* (see n 636), has become a classic in American literature.

Normally, our editorial policy has been to reserve the note about a publication by Bandelier until it appeared in print. Although neither *Die Köshare* nor *The Delight Makers* was published until 1890, the reader needs to be aware that in this volume of the journals, Volume III, references are made both to the German novel and to the English version with Bandelier frequently failing to distinguish between the two.

In the journal entries of 1889 and 1890, Volume IV, the matter is further complicated. Bandelier, in April and again in September 1889, wrote the beginning chapters of a second novel, entitled "Fray Luis the Lay-Brother. A Reminiscence of Coronado's March." On March 15, 1890, he noted beginning rewriting "the German text of the novel." This may have referred to an expansion of *Die Köshare*, to a translation of the 1889 novel, or to an entirely different work. The editors have been unable to learn anything further.

51. Professor Michel, or Michael, Bernays was widely recognized for his significant work in clarifying the texts of Goethe, Schiller, Shakespeare, and others (Bernays 1912: 14). Elsewhere (p. 81), Professor Bernays was referred to as "the celebrated lecturer on the history of literature at Leipzig and Munich, far-famed also as a student of Goethe and Shakespeare."

52. C. H. Seybt had been a business partner of Bandelier in the Confidence Coal and Mining Co. (see n 97). Apparently Bandelier saw in Mr. and Mrs. Lane (see also February 20 entry) unpleasant traits that he had previously known in Seybt. At no other time had Bandelier expressed a dislike for Seybt, as far as the editors are aware. Biographical data were given in Lange and Riley (1970: 397n334). Gould (1885: 1060) listed Charles H. Seybt with a residence in Highland but in the flour business in St. Louis.

53. This was most probably Professor Rudolph Ludwig Karl Virchow (1821–1902), German scientist, teacher, and political leader. His most important contributions were in the study of diseases, although he wrote in archaeology and anthropology as well (see Penniman 1952: 109–11).

54. Bandelier met with Dr. W. Reiss on a number of occasions in Berlin. An entry while on shipboard, March 26, 1885, noted the finishing of "my letters in four envelopes, all directed to Dr. Reiss, 38 pages. Hope it will be accepted." The editors suggest this may have been a draft of "San Bernardino Chalchihuapan. Ein mexikanisches Abenteuer" (see ns 230, 287, and 830). On June 12, 1885, Bandelier noted receiving a letter from Miss

Anna Reiss (see n 210). As the cited notes indicate, Bandelier began writing for the *National Zeitung* on June 15. On June 27, he finished this manuscript and mailed it to Dr. Carl Frenzel. The entry of the following day noted that he wrote to both Dr. Reiss and Miss Reiss. Perhaps Dr. Reiss had been instrumental in the publication arrangements for the manuscript.

For the 7th Meeting of the Congrès International des Américanistes, held in Berlin, October 2–5, 1888, Dr. Reiss served as President of the Organization Committee. He was further identified as President of the Berlin Society for Anthropology, Ethnology, and Prehistory as well as the Acting President of the Society for Geography (Congrès International des Américanistes 1890: 1, 25).

55. Designations of the sources annotated by Bandelier were as follows:

Carlos de Siguenza y Gongora, "Mercurio volante con la noticia de la Recuperacion de la Provincias del Nuevo Mexico conseguida por D. Diego de Vargas, Zapata, y Ponze de Leon, Governador y Capitan General de aquel Reyno," Mexico, 1693. (Folios 2, 3, 4, 5, 14, 15, and 16.)

Fray Balthasar de Medina, "Chronica de la Santa Provincia de San Diego de Mexico, de Religiosos Descalços de N. S. P. S. Francisco en la Nueva Espana," Mexico, 1682. (Lib. IV, Cap. VII, fol. 160[?], 169; Lib. IV, Cap. XX, fol. 199.)

(The above at the Royal Library.)
(The following at the Library of the Geographical Society.)

Charles P. Stone, "Notes on the State of Sonora," Washington, 1861.

José Maria Perez Hernandez, "Compendio de la Geografía del Estado de Sonora," Mexico, 1872.

Eduardo Pierron, "Datos para la Geografía del Imperio Mexicano," Mexico, 1866.

Vivien de Saint Martin, "Rapport sur l'Etat actuel de la Geographie de Mexique," Paris, 1865.

56. The items selected for annotation by Bandelier were as follows:

Boletin de la Sociedad mexicana de Geografía y Estadistica, Vol. II, 1850, No. 13, "Noticias historicas," Ures, 8 de Marzo de 1850, J. Lucas Biso.

Boletin, Tomo III. "Inspeccion de las Colonias Militares de Chihuahua."

Boletin, Vol. V. Pedro García-Conde, "Ensayo Estadístico sobre el estado de Chihuahua."

Boletin, Vol. VIII. José Francisco Velasco, "Noticias estadísticas del Estado de Sonora."

"Rudo Ensayo, tentativa de una provencional Descripcion Geographica de la Provincia de Sonora, sus Terminos y confinantes," published by Buckingham Smith, author unknown but wrote about 1761–62.

57. This may have been the German botanist, Paul Friedrich August Ascherson (1834–1919) (Library of Congress 1942: 492).

58. The "Rudo Ensayo," on which Bandelier was commenting here, is the last item listed in n 56. At this point, Bandelier began recording lengthy notations, constituting the better part of twenty-one pages (pp. 11–20, fronts and backs; p. 21, front) and extending over his journals of February 27 and 28 and March 1.

Bandelier considered this document of sufficient importance that, in 1887, when he was in Mexico City, he employed a copyist to transcribe the entire document (see n 771).

Subsequently, Bandelier included additional comments in footnotes of his *Final Report* (1890–92: I, 77n1). "The *Rudo Ensayo,* published by Buckingham Smith in 1863, is the same as the *Descripcion Geográfica.*" On the same page (p. 77n3), he added, "The *Descripcion Geográfica,* or *Rudo Ensayo,* appears to be the source from which Alegre gained his information on the plants, etc. of Sonora. The work of Pfefferkorn, *Beschreibung der Landschaft Sonora,* also contains information, but it may have come from the same source, since the *Beschreibung* is posterior to the *Descripcion* by thirty years, and P. Pfefferkorn was in Sonora when the *Descripcion* was written. . . . As for the author of the *Descripcion*, I am convinced it was the Padre Nentwig, S. J., priest at Huassavas in eastern Sonora."

59. On this date, March 2, Bandelier recorded notes on Ignaz Pfefferkorn's "Beschreibung der Landschaft Sonora samt andern merkwürdigen Nachrichten von dem inneren Theilen Neu-Spanien," Cöln, 1794. His annotations covered most of seven pages (p. 20, back; pp. 21–23, fronts and backs).

Next, notes on Alegre's "Historia de la Compañia de Jesus en Nueva España," published by C. M. de Bustamente, Mexico, 1841, were made; the major portion of the notes were on Vol. I, with much briefer notes on Vols. II and III. (Bandelier's notes began in the March 2 entry, continued in that for March 4, and ended with the March 5 entry; in the journals, this appeared on the lower half of the back of p. 23 and continued, with some interruptions, through most of the back of p. 26.)

60. Dr. Hermann Gerlich was listed by Gould (1880: 400) as a consul at the German Consulate in St. Louis. Though Bandelier in this entry had called on him in Berlin, earlier journal entries indicated that at least some correspondence had taken place while Dr. Gerlich was still in St. Louis (Lange and Riley 1966; 1970).

On November 22, 1882, Bandelier's journal noted that he had purchased a collection for the Berlin Museum (Lange and Riley 1966: 360). On November 18 (p. 358) Bandelier had had a letter from the German Consulate and on November 23 (p. 362) Bandelier had written to Dr. Gerlich. Presumably this correspondence dealt with the purchase of the collection for the Berlin Museum. On November 23, Bandelier had also written Dr. George Engelmann; this letter has survived and is in the Engelmann Correspondence of the Missouri Botanical Garden (see n 467). In this letter Bandelier referred to Gerlich as the consul in St. Louis and described in detail his purchases for the Berlin Museum.

61. In addition to completing his notations on Alegre (which he had begun on March 2), Bandelier listed several other sources with hardly any additional comment on each.

P. Joseph Stöcklein, "Der neue Weltbott, etc."

Juan Domingo Arricivita, "Crónica seráfica y apostólica."

62. The editors have been puzzled by this entry in which Dr. Gerlich indicated he would attempt to sell Bandelier's drawings for him.

Careful reading of the journals from September 1884 to this entry of March 12, 1885, suggests that coupled with a desire to have his drawings reproduced for publication in the *Final Report* was the underlying thought in Bandelier's mind that the original drawings might have some monetary value. On September 12, 1884, he commented in his journal (Lange and Riley 1970: 345), "God grant that my drawings may 'draw'!" On September 14, just two days later, he noted in his journal, "Mr. Parkman admired my drawings very much. He is of opinion that they are very saleable." Actually, as early as November 20, 1882, Bandelier had written Parkman (Bandelier-Parkman letters: Mass. Hist. Society), "The drawings please send to my wife after Prof. Norton has seen them, —unless they can be sold."

In late 1884, Bandelier had left for Europe and the impression he had given was that he hoped to have his colored illustrations reproduced more cheaply and accurately there. On November 6, 1884, he had written Icazbalceta (Lange and Riley 1970: 438n163), "The time I lost in Boston is to blame for not having written before. I had to write up the last work [*Final Report*] that will come out on New Mexico, Arizona, Sonora, and Chihuahua. Because of its extraordinary length, its publication will necessarily be delayed. An atlas of 300 pages of illustrations will accompany the three volumes of text. The cost of reproduction in several colors is more than 25 thousand pesos and is one of the reasons that I go to Europe where this work is done better and more cheaply." On September 10, 1885, Bandelier mentioned the drawings again in a letter to Icazbalceta (see n 421), "At the same time I keep studying, increasing the collection of drawings and plans of the ruins. This collection, according to the most important artists of Germany will have a minimum value of 30,000 pesos. I am negotiating with the Prussian government to sell them the originals, but I doubt that we will arrive at any agreement."

On November 12, 1884 (see Lange and Riley 1970: 439n164), Bandelier's departure was noted in the *Weekly Telephone*. "After a short stay of only about one week Prof. Bandelier has again left us. . . . Since the illustrations for his grand work cannot be furnithed [furnished] as desired in this country, he now leaves for Europe to make arrangements there with the most prominent of artists, the text of his books, however, will be printed in America."

On April 5, 1885, upon his return from Europe, Bandelier had written Parkman (see n 73), "In regard to the publication of the main work, it is not possible to speak definitely yet, but neither is it at all improbable that it will be published in the German language, and under the auspices of the Prussian government." Whether by this time he had reconciled himself to the fact that his drawings and "main work" could not be published together because he had found no one to underwrite the expense is not clear. (Entries in our fourth and final volume cover final preparations and publishing of the *Final Report*.) Perhaps, his leaving the drawings with Dr. Gerlich was an admission of this fact. Bandelier obviously had a responsibility to the Archaeological Institute of America to publish on the fieldwork they had supported. Publication in German would have been essentially a translation of the work done for the Institute. To publish the same material in several languages was not an uncommon practice for Bandelier (or for others), as journal entries and the bibliography for this volume indicate.

That there was considerable confusion as to Bandelier's intentions even in his day was evidenced by this sentence in the *Santa Fe New Mexican Review* of June 6, 1885 (p. 4): "During his recent visit to Germany he [Prof. Bandelier] displayed some scientific writings and drawings concerning the southwest which were highly complimented by all the leading scientists of the empire, and the Imperial government has decided to publish them at a cost of $100,000."

An explanation for so many conflicting accounts was undoubtedly the fact that Bandelier's trip to Europe had had multiple purposes; one was related to his professional career, and another was to serve as agent for his father in negotiations with the Swiss creditors of the F. Ryhiner & Co. bank. No doubt it was to the bank's advantage that Bandelier had other obvious and legitimate business in Europe at that time.

Dr. Gerlich did not succeed in selling the drawings, as they were returned to the St. Louis consulate (see entry of May 27, 1886). Bandelier continued to sketch, draw, and paint for several years; together with a number of photographs (see n 4), many of his paintings were ultimately used in the *Histoire* presented to Pope Leo XIII, as later journal entries of this volume indicate.

Though the *Histoire* manuscript has only recently been found again (see Burrus 1969b: 13–14), the availability of the accompanying illustrations has been known at least since Bloom's research in the 1930s. Seemingly, very few scholars have made use of them, however. Kubler (1940) used many of the groundplans, as did Bandelier himself in the *Final Report* (1890–92). The editors visited the Vatican Film Library, St. Louis University, in March 1959 and examined the slides made of the *Histoire* illustrations; in the spring of 1970, through the cooperation of Father Ernest J. Burrus, S. J., Father Lowrie J. Daly, S. J., and the Office of Research and Projects, Graduate School, Southern Illinois University, we succeeded in acquiring a complete set of these slides. According to Burrus (1969b: 13), he had assisted in obtaining copies of these slides for the Bancroft Library at Berkeley; the Amerind Foundation at Dragoon, Arizona; and the University of Arizona, Tucson, as well as the set already mentioned at St. Louis University. His Catalogue (1969b) and the Supplement (1969c) will undoubtedly serve to increase the public awareness of them.

They deserve to be better known, as they are significant source materials for archaeologists, ethnologists, and historians as well as having considerable artistic value.

The editors would also like to mention that in the Bandelier Collection, Museum of New Mexico Library, there was a hardbound album with a number of unmounted, assorted watercolors, as well as lithographs from drawings by Bandelier. Primarily, these were of Mexico and South America, but we noted three watercolors important in the context of these Southwestern Journals: (1) Loom of Chavez at Cochiti, November 22, 1880; (2) Shield of Victoriano of Cochiti, November 21, 1881; and (3) Pot from Eldodt Collection, San Juan, undated.

63. This was Mrs. George Hoffmann of St. Louis, a cousin of Josephine Huegy Bandelier on her mother's side (Hobbs 1942a). It is curious, and seemingly an editorial error, that in Hobbs 1942b (p. 112n5) George Hoffmann was identified as the cousin of Joe rather than Mrs. Hoffmann. Hobbs's notes from the personal interview of June 10, 1942, with Mrs. Elizabeth Bandelier Kaune, cited as 1942a in the bibliography, stated, "Mrs. George Hoffmann and Mrs. August (Emily) Becker were cousins of Josephine Huegy Bandelier on her mother's side; Hubert was George's son, who came to Santa Fe for his health (after 1882) and died in Denver of tuberculosis. Cilla H. (Sept. 13, 1883), George's wife." In the journals, Bandelier referred to her either as Cilla or Celia.

The Edwardsville *Intelligencer* of May 12, 1886 (Vol. 24, Whole No. 1228, p. 8), noted "Mrs. Geo. Hoffmann and Mrs. Becker, of St. Louis, were guests of their cousin, Mrs. Mary Suppiger, several days last week. George Hoffmann came out Sunday to spend the day." Mrs. Mary Suppiger was the widow of Robert Suppiger, a maternal cousin of Josephine Huegy Bandelier (Lange and Riley 1970: 401n364).

64. Pauline's identity has still not been established. The name has no meaning to surviving relatives either on the Bandelier or Huegy sides of the family. Considerable effort has gone into trying to identify her, and the editors wish to express their appreciation to Mrs. Mary Blumenthal, Librarian of the Clinton P. Anderson Library, University of New Mexico, for suggesting we write Mrs. Spencer C. Browne, a daughter of H. B. and Clara Huning Fergusson, since Pauline's name appeared frequently in the journals in association with that of Clara Huning. Mrs. Browne has written several letters and suggested other Huning relatives to whom we have written. They, in turn, have also been most cooperative, but have been unable to help with the identification of Pauline.

The editors are grateful to Ernst H. Blumenthal, Jr., and his wife for their personal interest and their attempts to identify Pauline. The feeling persists that she was a close friend or even a relative of the Bandeliers. A second Bandelier Scrapbook was found during the summer of 1969 in the Bandelier Collection of the Museum of New Mexico. It was inscribed, "To Papa from Paulina." Pauline's name was found frequently in conjunction with that of Annie (Borchert; see n 65), as in this entry. Here they were in St. Louis, together, to welcome Bandelier home from Europe. In other instances, they were in Albuquerque. In 1882, Pauline had traveled from St. Louis on the train as far as Las Vegas, New Mexico, with the Bandeliers. At the time of Celia (Mrs. George) Hoffmann's final illness, when Hubert, the son, returned to St. Louis, Bandelier also wired Pauline. As far as the editors are aware, Hubert was the only child of the George Hoffmanns. In Volume II, the editors (1970: 332) wrote "Pauline [Borchert?]" in one entry, but they are less inclined at this time to designate even tentatively a surname for Pauline.

65. This was Annie Borchert, wife of William M. Though the Bandeliers were both in Albuquerque in June 1882 (Lange and Riley 1966: 310, 317, 325, 326), no mention was made of Annie. Willie was mentioned twice (pp. 309, 310), but at that time the editors were not sufficiently confident to identify him as William Borchert. In the February 1, 1883, entry (Lange and Riley 1970:23), Bandelier saw Willie in Albuquerque, noting that Annie was with Joe (presumably in Highland). Additional entries of Volume II indicate

that Bandelier saw both Annie and Will Borchert on several occasions in Albuquerque, and that Joe corresponded with Annie. On October 21, 1883, Bandelier (and Joe?), at the George Hoffmanns' in St. Louis, joined in a birthday toast to the absent Annie Borchert (p. 151).

At the time of the April 3, 1885, entry, Annie was in St. Louis to meet Bandelier on his return from Europe. The Borcherts then seemed to be living in St. Louis; Gould's directory (1885:135) listed William Borchert as a salesman for J. Weil & Bro. Similar listings were found for 1874 and 1875. He was again listed in 1886, but no Borchert was listed in 1887. However, in 1888, Gould (p. 182) listed Anna J. Borchert as "Wid. William." The editors are puzzled by this notation in light of data presented in n 1083, assuming that there were not two individuals with identical given names and surnames married to wives with identical given names.

66. This was Maurice Huegy (1840–85), brother of Joe, Bandelier's wife, and son of Moritz, one of the three original partners in the F. Ryhiner & Co. bank. Raised with Bandelier and tutored by the elder Bandelier, Maurice and F. C. Ryhiner, Jr., had long been accustomed to respect the elder Bandelier (Eggen 1933). Maurice's son, Carl, was an important informant for Goad at the time of Goad's research in Highland in the late 1930s (Goad 1939: 2). In turn, the present editors are indebted to Carl's son, Harvey Huegy.

67. E. A. Allen published *Prehistoric World: or, Vanquished Races,* Cincinnati, 1885. In summarizing his activities from October 16 to November 5, 1884, because he had been unable to keep his journal, Bandelier wrote, "I also corrected a manuscript for E. A. Allen of Cincinnati, Ohio, and sent it back to him on the 4th, A.M." (Lange and Riley 1970: 347).

68. While Bandelier also referred to Frederick B. Suppiger (n 168) as "Fritz," the editors believe that the "Fritz" referred to here was F. C. Ryhiner, Jr., the son of one of the three original partners in the F. C. Ryhiner & Co. bank of Highland, and at the time of this entry himself a partner, succeeding his father who had died in 1879. It would be expected that Bandelier would contact him promptly upon his return to discuss the condition of the bank. The preceding entry indicated that Papa (Adolphe E. Bandelier) and Morris (Huegy), the other partners, had met Bandelier at the Highland station, taking an early opportunity to gain information on Bandelier's trip to Switzerland and to provide him with news about the situation at the bank.

F. C. Ryhiner, Jr., was born in Highland in 1846. He died in the state of Washington in 1899. He was the son of Dr. Frederick C. and Josephine Suppiger Ryhiner. He had been Bandelier's close friend since boyhood and in the journal entries Bandelier often referred to him as "Fritz" (Lange and Riley 1970: 398n343). Spencer (1937: 192) noted that he was a bachelor and had few family ties to hold him in Highland. Data on his sister, Louisa, are given in n 122.

As the bank failure became imminent, the journal entries revealed Bandelier's frustrations at being the one on whom responsibility for a solution seemed to rest. Any former warmth for his friend disappeared, and "Fritz" was replaced by such designations as FCR, or the more formal F. C. Ryhiner (see n 468).

69. Lange and Riley (1970: 360–61n35) provided a brief discussion of various members of the Bernays family, of Highland and St. Louis; there were apparently members of the family still in Germany at the time of Bandelier's visit (Bernays 1912: 54–55; Eggen 1933: 36; Hyde 1896: 14; and Spencer 1937: 84, 154).

70. Adolph Müller [Mueller] was the first treasurer of Highland when it was changed from a village to a city form of government in 1884. He was also a charter member of the Knights of Honor Lodge in 1879 (Spencer 1937: 186, 229). The Biographical Publishing Co. (1894: 272–73) noted, among other data, that Mueller was born in Stargard, Prussia, on August 29, 1835, and came to this country in 1860. Following service in the

Union Army, Mueller returned to his drug business in St. Louis and in Trenton, Illinois, moving to Highland in 1869. He was active in civic affairs and a stockholder in various Highland business enterprises. Polk and Danser (1884b: 1003) listed him as a druggist. Eggen (1933: 88) gave him as a dealer in drugs, school books, and albums.

71. In the Highland column of the March 18, 1885, issue of the *Intelligencer* (#1166), Edwardsville, it was noted that "Dr. Schloetzer will occupy the building vacated by Mr. M. Stamm."

72. Bertha Huegy Lambelet, widow of Charles (deceased September 16, 1884), was a sister of Josephine Huegy Bandelier. There were three children, Fanny, Edmund, and Oscar. In later years, Bertha and another sister, Amalia, made their home with Oscar (a widower) in Marysville, Ohio (Harvey Huegy, personal communication, March 7, 1969).

73. This letter to Parkman was found in the files of the Massachusetts Historical Society:

Highland, Ill., 5. April 1885.

Dear Mr. Parkman!

Day before yesterday I at last arrived home, after a very successful tour in Europe; more particularly through Germany.—In a few days, I shall go to work on my Report, to which I intend to give all the desirable conciseness and brevity.—In regard to the publication of the main work, it is not possible to speak definitely yet, but neither is it at all improbable that it will be published in the German language, and under the auspices of the Prussian government. The receptions which I enjoyed both at Munich and at Berlin were of the most flattering kind, and have created relations which cannot fail to be very beneficial to me in the future.—Among others, the historical novel which I began to write, was received with decided approval and encouragement.—I shall therefore stay at home for the time being, and work up my materials in any shape and in anyone [*sic*] of the four idioms at my command,—as may appear desirable or advantageous in the future.—

I had begged Mr. Greenleaf to send a few copies of my book to some parties in Europe. It occurred to me afterwards that, in doing this, I had inconsiderately overstepped the limits. That book is too costly for this kind of distribution. — It is a book for *sale*, and I shall therefore buy what I need of it. —Saw Prof. Ware at N. York. He wants a Lecture, but I have to defer it until my return East.

With my best regards to Miss Parkman, I remain

Very respectfully,

Ad. F. Bandelier

74. Bandelier mentioned Graffenried several times in the journals, often together with Wachsmuth (n 114), in the course of visits made to the farm that Bandelier's father had a mile northeast of Highland. Hobbs (1942a) noted that Rudolph von Graffenried was apparently of some financial means and was said to have been of a titled Swiss family. On two occasions in 1884, Mr. Graffenried had given Bandelier financial aid (Lange and Riley 1970: 342, 347). Several Graffenrieds were on the list of European creditors published after the bank's failure. Bandelier expressed his gratitude for Mr. Graffenried's continued loyalty in the aftermath of the bank failure in his entry of May 20, 1885.

75. Father Joseph Meckel was the Catholic priest in Highland at this time. The Biographical Publishing Company (1894: 335–37) gave the following data. Reverend Clement Joseph Meckel, pastor of St. Paul's Catholic Church of Highland, was born in

Muenster, Westphalia, Germany, on November 10, 1843. In October of 1869, he came to the United States and was rector of a church at Olney, Illinois. Between this time and 1876, the year he went to Highland, he served in various parishes and capacities in conjunction with the church. In 1878 he built St. Joseph's Hospital at Highland. In 1888, in company with Father Cluse, priest of the diocese of Belleville, Father Meckel made an extensive tour of the Old World, traveling through Germany, Switzerland, France, Italy, Palestine, and Egypt (see entry of February 16, 1888). Eggen (1933: 44) added that after his successful pastorate in Highland, Father Meckel was sent to St. Mary's, Alton, Illinois, where he died in 1896.

76. Frank Hamilton Cushing (1857–1900) went with Major J. W. Powell's expedition to New Mexico in 1879; he lived at Zuñi Pueblo until the spring of 1884. Cushing wrote a number of major publications regarding various aspects of Zuñi culture. Bandelier had visited Cushing at Zuñi and had been greatly impressed by his rapport in the pueblo and his fieldwork (see Lange and Riley 1970). The two men, both pioneers in Southwestern anthropology, shared numerous professional interests and viewpoints. Hodge (1914: 353), a contemporary, in his obituary of Bandelier, specifically commented on the friendship between Cushing and Bandelier and Bandelier's genuine esteem for Cushing.

77. Samuel Eldodt, a native of Westphalia, Germany, came to the United States in 1868 after his brothers, Mark and Nathan, who had come in 1851; they were merchants. In the 1880s, Samuel had a store at San Juan Pueblo, with similar business interests elsewhere in the vicinity. He spoke several European languages, and he was knowledgeable in details of Indian life, all of which made him a valued acquaintance for Bandelier. Eldodt later became involved in politics in New Mexico (see also Lange and Riley 1966: 409–10; 1970: 410–11n446).

78. This was Wendell Phillips Garrison, literary editor of *The Nation*, 1865–1906 (Lange and Riley 1970: 436n150). Bandelier reviewed many books and wrote many articles for this magazine.

79. John Balsiger was an old friend of the Bandelier family; he had gone with Bandelier's father from Switzerland to Brazil, both eventually going to Highland. According to the *Weekly Telephone* of April 8, 1885, "John Balsiger has associated himself with Henry Riniker in the notarial business" (for further data, see Lange and Riley 1970: 399n347).

In the *Weekly Telephone* of September 2, 1885 (No. 28, p. 1), there was a brief note, "John Balsiger occupies the Bandelier residence since yesterday." Balsiger, together with John Blattner, had provided the security for the bond posted for Bandelier and Maurice Huegy following the closing of the F. Ryhiner & Co. bank (see entry of May 21, 1885, and n 155).

80. Mrs. Rentschler was presumably the wife of Reverend George Rentschler of the Christian Church of Highland, who was listed in Polk and Danser (1884b: 1003).

81. Louis E. Kinne was a cousin of Josephine Huegy Bandelier (Hobbs 1940a). His father was Charles Kinne, whom Bandelier referred to as "Uncle Kinne" in his journal entry, August 16, 1883 (Lange and Riley 1970: 145). Both father and son figured prominently in Highland history (see Spencer 1937; Lange and Riley 1970: 400n345).

82. See n 115.

83. John Wildi had a variety of business interests in Highland: the general merchandising firm of Ammann and Wildi; the Highland Embroidery Works in which he was a partner; and in 1885, the Helvetia Milk Company. In this enterprise, he was the youngest of the board of directors and served as secretary-treasurer for several years. Later he founded another milk company and built another plant in Ohio in 1907. Wildi died in Highland in 1910 (Spencer 1937: 55, 200, 201, 206, 207, 211, 218).

84. This letter, dated April 8, 1885, in Highland, was included among those published by White and Bernal (1960: 278–79); our translation follows:

Dear Friend

Happily I returned on the fourth of the current month and found my wife to be in good health but anxious to see me again after a separation of almost sixteen months [Here, White and Bernal suggested that Mrs. Bandelier was probably not in Highland in November 1884; otherwise the sixteen months of separation was obscure. Journal entries for 1883 and 1884 change the perspective on this point. Joe was in Highland during November 1884. Bandelier and Joe had been together in Highland, as of April 8, 1885, a total of about two weeks out of the preceding seven months; seven or eight weeks out of the past eighteen months; and before that, in 1883, had been together from July 13 to October 22.], a separation which was unavoidable, in the first place, for the very simple reason that I did not have the means for our support, and secondly, because I had to finish with the work already started and had to consolidate the results already acquired.

At the present moment I am facing a serious problem, and if I keep you informed, it is to give you the explanation I owe you and not with the intention to bother you. In the most courteous manner, I beg you to keep absolute secrecy, so it will not be divulged what, until today, has been a secret, and one which will not see light for some weeks. If I am not mistaken, I made known to you some time ago in your house on the shores of San Cosme, the distressing, if not terrible, life I had in my father's business, as much his fault as his partners. I left the business in 1880, because my life there was becoming impossible, and I had to leave the administration in the hands of others. Since then, I have had the sad satisfaction (if one can find satisfaction in it) of seeing how that business was declining; this has reached the point where they are now asking me to come back and, again, take over its control. The reputation of my father, and, of course, mine too, are involved in this affair. If I went back to Europe, it was with the intention to save the business and to try to find an answer for the situation (that coincided with my own affairs there). I think I have succeeded even though the last word has not been said. If the strong affection I profess for the well-being of the town in which I have resided for the last thirty-six years and the complete sacrifice of any personal feelings cannot bring a solution to this problem, then, my dear friend, I have no other alternative than to immigrate. I will go, naturally, to Mexico, seeking any kind of job no matter how modest and wherever it is. My wife, when arrangements are made, will accompany me. If this should happen, I implore you to advise me where I should go and to let me know if any possibility of finding a job exists.

All this I make known to you with the previous knowledge and consent of my wife, who has decided to follow me. The dislike which I have always had for this country and its people has finally become contagious and if they will not do right in that which begs for justice and follow their own self-interest, then how in the world can my wife and I expect to find an independent life? Needless to say, if we go to Mexico, it is to become Mexican; for that matter, we are not far from being [Mexicans].

Meanwhile, I will do whatever is possible to avoid the sad necessity of immigration. I hope that this will not be necessary, but in such case I want to be prepared and not to grope in the dark.

I would appreciate your answer as soon as possible; we will be eternally grateful for this demonstration of your friendship. I have nothing to tell you in the field of science. In about two weeks, I will be more informed and could write you with more calmness than I have at this moment.

Regards for all. Your grateful friend and servant.

Ad. F. Bandelier

I write faster than I should, but the time———!

Don Joaquín García Icazbalceta (1825–94) was an outstanding historian and writer who became, in the mid-nineteenth century, one of Mexico's leading authorities on history, linguistics, bibliography, and geography. One of his best known works was the *Colección de documentos para la historia de México.*

The correspondence between Don Joaquín and Bandelier began in 1875; the two men did not meet until March 1881. Aside from their shared scholarly interests, an additional bond between the two men came from the fact that Don Joaquín served as sponsor when Bandelier entered the Roman Catholic Church in Cholula, Puebla, July 31, 1881 (White and Bernal 1960: 248n1; see also Lange and Riley 1970: 4, 360n33).

85. In both Volume I and Volume II, references have been made by Bandelier in his journals to the "foundry" or to the Highland Mechanical Works. For background and history of the Highland Foundry, Highland Mechanical Works, and Bandelier's involvement, see Lange and Riley 1966: 18; 1970: 143–44, 397n334, 398n339, and 398n340.

The *Intelligencer* of April 15, 1885, #1170, noted that on Wednesday night, April 8, the Highland Mechanical Works were ablaze. Both the newspaper account and this entry indicated that it was a total loss; n 92 indicates otherwise. The newspaper also commented that there was no insurance and shared Bandelier's feeling that it was arson.

86. The confusion noted previously (Lange and Riley 1970: 398n341) concerning two John Blattners, both of whom were important in Highland history, persists. Bandelier either used Mr. Blattner or Blattner in his entries, and the *Weekly Telephone* of April 22, 1885 (No. 9, p. 1), used no identifying initial when it commented that John Blattner was a successful candidate for city attorney. Elsewhere on the same page of the *Telephone* were the following two items, some eight inches apart in the "Personal" column:

John Blattner has recovered from his recent illness.
J. R. Blattner, who has been suffering severely several weeks of rheumatism, was seen on the streets again.

Was this the same person or two individuals? To further complicate the matter, the *Telephone* of April 1, 1885 (No. 6), mentioned Joseph Blattner in connection with "a new feed trough."

The May 21, 1885, entry stated that following Bandelier's arrest, he was released on bond signed by Blattner and Mr. Balsiger.

87. This was Henry Weinheimer, who was a partner in a mercantile business in Highland in the 1850s. He had come to Highland in 1853 from St. Louis and in 1856 bought the Kempff Pharmacy Building, which John Boeschenstein had erected about eight years earlier. He became a prosperous merchant but still found time to serve on the first board of aldermen and to participate in formation of the village government. In 1867, Weinheimer served on a committee to raise money to bring a railroad to Highland. He built the Laura Everette home, a pretentious residence in those days. In 1872, Weinheimer was elected to the legislature, but served only one term. Whether he was a candidate for reelection in 1874, Spencer could not determine. He continued to reside in Highland for a number of years. The *Weekly Telephone* of April 22, 1885 (No. 9, p. 1), announced that Henry Weinheimer was selling property with a view to leaving Highland. Weinheimer died in St. Louis in 1891 and was buried in Highland (Spencer 1937: 54, 129–30, 142, 223).

88. Precise identification of "Aunt Sauvant" has not been possible. On September 1, 1887, Bandelier received from Europe letters from his cousin, Alphonse Bandelier, and also from Adolphe Vautier, which informed him of Aunt Sauvant's death. She was eighty-six years "and nearly six months" old. A Cecil Sauvant-Bandelier of Bern appeared in the list of European creditors published in Highland after the failure of the bank (*Weekly Telephone,* May 6, 1885).

89. Bandelier had called on Mr. O. Ottendorfer on September 1 and again on September 6 when he was in New York on a brief eastern trip prior to his trip to Europe later in the fall and winter of 1884–85 (Lange and Riley 1970: 343). Ottendorfer and Rittig (Bandelier's Rittich) were both with the *New Yorker Staatszeitung,* and Bandelier seemingly discussed with them his novel, *Die Köshare* (which ultimately became *The Delight Makers*), and other publications (see ns 115 and 440).

90. As noted in Lange and Riley (1970: 397n332), Andrew W. Metcalf was a partner in the legal firm of Metcalf and Bradshaw in Edwardsville, Illinois (see n 133 for details of this firm). Apparently, in this entry, Bandelier was seeking legal advice in regard to the losses from the recent foundry fire. The F. Ryhiner & Co. bank held title to the property. Other data on the foundry are given in Lange and Riley (1970: 397n334, 398n339, 398n340).

91. Polk and Danser (1884b: 869) listed Michael G. Dale as lawyer and county judge, Edwardsville.

92. An item in the *Intelligencer* (April 22, 1885, #1171) aided in this identification. It reported that William Ellison & Son of St. Louis had purchased light machinery (from the Highland Mechanical Works) and shipped it to their St. Louis foundry. Gould (1880: 332) listed "William Ellison, mach., 913 N. Main." Though the Highland Business Directory for 1883 (Eggen 1933: 87–88) had listed Ellison and Son Foundry and Mechanical Works, Polk and Danser's Directory (1884b) for the following year made no mention of it. Presumably, it had moved to St. Louis in the interim.

In the October 16 and October 17 entries of 1883, Ellison was not identified. With the above data and from the context, there can be no doubt that it was Ellison of the St. Louis Foundry.

This April 12 journal entry was apparently a preliminary to the purchase reported in the Edwardsville *Intelligencer* cited above. For related information, see n 85.

Bandelier's irritation at continued involvement with business matters, though no longer officially connected with the bank, which the editors have noted as a running undercurrent throughout the journals, was loudly voiced by Bandelier here.

93. This was Jacob Brunnschweiler of Highland. He was a partner in F. A. Gleyre and Co., which was founded in 1874 (Lange and Riley 1970: 398n340). Locally, this company was referred to as the Highland Mechanical Works, the Highland Foundry, or as in Bandelier's journals, simply "the foundry." At this time Brunnschweiler along with Ellison and his son (see n 92) and Morris Huegy were appraising the fire damage to the foundry. The entry is but one example of many of Bandelier's irritation at his continued involvement in business matters.

The *Weekly Telephone* of April 22, 1885 (No. 9, p. 1) stated that "Jacob Brunschweiler and wife will depart for Switzerland soon."

94. Hobbs (1940a) identified Mrs. Weber as an aunt of Josephine Huegy Bandelier. In December 1880, Bandelier had "spent an hour at Weber's" on the day before Christmas (Lange and Riley 1966: 235). She may have been the wife of Jacob Weber mentioned in Spencer (1937: 61, 95, 124).

95. Dr. John B. Knoebel practiced medicine in the Highland area for many years. According to Spencer (1937: 199), Dr. Knoebel was chosen as first president of the board

of trustees of the Helvetia Milk Condensing Co. in 1885, a position he resigned at the end of his first year.

96. Eggen (1933: 88) gave a Dr. A. Sacconi as a physician in Highland with office north of the Catholic church. In Polk and Danser (1884b: 1003), the name was erroneously listed as Saccom, A., physician in Highland.

97. E. C. Springer and W. F. Springer appeared as Attorneys-at-Law and Solicitors for Complaintant in the Edwardsville newspaper, the *Intelligencer,* of February 3, 1885 (Vol. 23, No. 1160). Journal entries of 1883–84 (Lange and Riley: 1970) show that Bandelier corresponded from time to time with E. C. Springer. When the nature of the correspondence was indicated in the entries, the letters and cards to Springer were consistently concerned with the coal mine. This coal mine had been a concern of Bandelier over an extended period of time (see n 464). In his journal entry of August 16, 1884 (p. 341), Bandelier had noted, "E. C. Springer came last night, and we had a long and serious talk. He left this morning." In the accompanying note (p. 434n136), the editors referred to the general awareness of the Bandelier family and others of the deteriorating condition of the F. Ryhiner & Co. bank. Two days later, Bandelier wrote in his journal (p. 341), "I went to the mine and found everything in very good condition. But it would be imprudent to sell land now. Reported to Seybt." Springer's name was not mentioned again in the journals. Other Edwardsville lawyers' names appeared, however, in conjunction with the closing of the bank and the final settlement.

98. This volume was John G. Bourke's *The Snake Dance of the Moquis of Arizona . . . with an account of the Tablet Dance of the Pueblo of Santo Domingo* (Charles Scribner's Sons, New York, 1884. 371 pp.).

Bandelier held Bourke and his writings in high regard although in a review of Bourke's *An Apache Campaign in the Sierra Madre* (1886), Bandelier was critical (see n 553). While various obituaries stated Bourke was born in 1843, Bloom (1933: 1n2) explained that 1846 was the correct date. Bourke died June 8, 1896, in Philadelphia, his birthplace. He graduated from West Point in 1869, having served in the Civil War prior to his appointment to the academy. His life span paralleled great changes in the West; this was especially true of the post–Civil War decades which he experienced on the Plains and in the Southwest. Bloom (pp. 1–15) provided a résumé of Bourke's life and also listed his bibliography, revealing a rather wide range of interests—ethnography of several tribes, military campaigns, and folklore. At the time of his death, Bourke held memberships in several scientific organizations and was serving as president of the American Folk-Lore Society. An obituary by F. W. Hodge appeared in the *American Anthropologist,* Vol. IX, o.s., 1896, pp. 245–48.

99. "Lame" Bernays referred to Bernard, one of four sons of Dr. George and Minna Döring Bernays. Earlier (Lange and Riley 1970: 338, 433n127), "Lame" was misread from Bandelier's handwriting as "Layne," with the consequent inability to identify this individual more precisely. In the first volume (1966: 132), Bandelier's handwriting was also misread, resulting in the name being rendered as "B. F. Bensays" rather than "B. F. Bernays."

Bernard F. Bernays came to Highland with relatives in 1854. He was a lover of art, and after fleeing Germany in 1848, had acquired several Flemish paintings "for a song" in Holland. His Highland home held numerous art works, and this collection was eventually given to Dr. Augustus Charles Bernays, an eminent St. Louis physician. When cleaned, the Flemish paintings were found to be of real value, and they were placed in the care of the St. Louis Museum of Fine Art (Bernays 1912: 54–55). Additional data on this family are briefed in Lange and Riley (1970: 360–61n35).

100. Hobbs (1940a) identified Widmer as the hired man, apparently on the farm of Adolphe E. Bandelier. Widmer's wife had died April 22, 1884 (*Weekly Telephone* 1884).

A native of Switzerland, Widmer later returned there and died. Bandelier's journal for New Year's Eve, 1880, recorded, "We spent the evening quietly at home, Widmer, Joe, Maly, and I, talking."

101. In the April 7 entry of this journal, Bandelier had promised the Turners (members of the Turnverein) that he would speak on the anniversary (and he erroneously wrote 25th instead of 20th) of Lincoln's death. The *Intelligencer* of April 22, 1885, #1171, briefly reported that addresses were given by Bandelier in German and Arthur Parkinson in English at the Turner Hall the previous Wednesday.

From time to time in the journals, Bandelier, though a U.S. citizen, expressed his dislike for the country and its people. Usually, as is the case here, he gave vent to these feelings when his own personal life was in crisis.

The *Weekly Telephone* reported the event in greater detail. The same issue (Volume III, No. 7, April 8, 1885) that announced Bandelier's return from Europe also stated, "A Lincoln Memorial Celebration will be held at Highland Turners Hall next Wednesday evening—free to all, of course. Our renowned fellow-citizen Ad. F. Bandelier will deliver the address." Following the event, the *Weekly Telephone* (Volume III, No. 9, April 22, 1885) commented, "The Lincoln Memorial Celebration at Turners' Hall last Wednesday was well attended. The stage was appropriately decorated and the ceremonies consisted in music furnished by Mr. Eichhorn and Mrs. W. J. Appel, and speaking in german [*sic*] by Prof. Ad. F. Bandelier in an extraordinary thoughtful and impressive manner, concluded by an able and well received short off hand address in english [*sic*] by Mr. Arthur Parkinson."

102. Although Bandelier made no journal mention of it, perhaps absorbed in a variety of local matters, the *Weekly Telephone* of April 15, 1885 (No. 8, p. 4), carried the following letter from Bandelier's brother-in-law, Edward B. Huegy.

FROM NEW MEXICO

Albuquerque, New Mexico.

March 22, 1885.

EDITOR OF TELEPHONE:

When I remember the cold northern blasts and snows that you people in Highland have been subject to this winter, and the mud and rains of your early spring, I cannot help pitying you, and at the same time wishing that all my friends could just enjoy one of those perfect days that we have here in New Mexico. Just think of it, but one fall of snow during the entire frosty winter, and that laid upon the ground just one day. While down here in the Rio Grande valley, at Albuquerque, we are revelling in sunshine and warmth, the tall peaks of the Sandia range of mountains, only fifteen miles away, are clothed in a raiment of pure white, lending a contrast to the beautiful landscape that I am sure all of you would be delighted to see.

The weather has been delightful during the past month, neither too warm nor too cold, but just perfect for out door exercise, such as riding, ball playing and walking.

Think of [New] Albuquerque not yet four years old, lit up at night with gas and electric lights. Of the latter there are now fifty in use, giving the city a most brilliant appearance in the evening. Why Highland is eight or nine times as old, and yet you have no such advantages. True, you have manufactories and dairies in abundance, but we have a broad river and the best farming land in the world, while the plains about us are dotted with thousands of head of sheep and cattle.

Albuquerque is a great wool centre, shipping from fifteen to twenty car loads a day during the busy season.

I met Mr. D. C. Jaccard, of St. Louis, well known in Highland, in this city yesterday, and he expressed himself as greatly pleased with our climate and town.

We have seven churches and a new brick hotel just completed. This latter building is the largest and finest in the southwest. More anon.

E. B. Huegy

103. This was Richard Hospes of St. Louis. Bandelier often wrote to him and consulted with him on business matters. Hospes was born at Augusta, Missouri, December 25, 1838, and in early life moved with his family to St. Louis. Well educated in the public schools, he began an apprenticeship in banking at the age of sixteen. He worked his way up in the German Savings Institution of St. Louis; as chief executive officer, he was instrumental in making the Institution one of the leading banking houses of St. Louis. He married Johanna Bentzen of Dubuque, Iowa, in 1862 (Kargau n.d.: 165; see also Gould's St. Louis Directories—1881: 549; 1885: 571; 1890: 637; Hyde and Conard 1899: II, 1050–51).

104. This "fatal Dispatch" was most probably a cable to Mr. Burckhardt from the Gruner-Haller and Company, Bern, announcing their decision not to support further the F. Ryhiner & Co. bank of Highland (see entry of January 6, 1885).

105. In an advertisement in a *Fest-Kalendar* (Helvetia Schützen-Gesellschaft 1883: 129), Dr. Hans Mohr was given as "Arzt, Mundarzt und Geburtshilfer (früher Assistenz-Artz an der Chirug. Klinik des Julius-Hospitals zu Würzburg, sowie der Entbindungs-Anstalt in Stuttgart.) Highland, Illinois. Consultationen in deutscher, englischer, und französischer Sprache." ["Physician, Dentist, Obstetrician (earlier, Assistant Physician at the Surgical Clinic of the Julius Hospital at Würzburg, likewise at the Maternity Hospital in Stuttgart.) Highland, Illinois. Consultations in the German, English, and French languages."] See also ns 30 and 32.

106. "Uncle Kinne," referred to here, was Charles Kinne (original form of the name was Kuenne) who was the father of Louis E. Kinne (see n 81), identified by Hobbs (1940a) as a cousin of Josephine Huegy Bandelier.

Charles Kinne first emigrated from Saxony, Germany, to Louisville, Kentucky. Because of his dislike for slavery, he moved in March 1840 to Highland. He was a saddler and harness maker and, like Bandelier's father, contributed much to the early growth of Highland. He was postmaster during the Civil War, having been commissioned by Lincoln in 1861. In 1869, he was elected president of the board of trustees of the village of Highland (Spencer 1937: 42, 158, 225, 232).

107. Edward B. Wickenhauser was born in Highland, September 27, 1848, and died in St. Louis on April 22, 1885. He learned the saddler profession in Highland, and afterwards worked for one year at the *Highland Bote* printing office. In 1868, he moved to St. Louis and entered the firm of H. T. Simon & Gregory, advancing to first bookkeeper (*Weekly Telephone,* Vol. III, No. 11, May 6, 1885, p. 1).

108. The *Weekly Telephone* of April 29, 1885 (Volume III, No. 10), reported the death of Mrs. Caroline Speckart nee Bellm, wife of Mr. Joseph Speckart.

109. This was probably Franklin Beck, a clerk in the bank. In Spencer's account of the bank failure, he wrote: "The men who were active in the bank at the time of the failure were the four named above [F. C. Ryhiner, Moritz Huegy, A. E. Bandelier, A. F. Bandelier] and Franklin Beck, then a very popular and well liked young man, who was employed as a clerk" (Spencer 1937: 191).

110. Henry S. Kaune of Breese, Illinois, had married Bandelier's cousin, Elizabeth (Lizzie) C. Bandelier, on September 13, 1883, in Highland (Lange and Riley 1970: 148).

Henry was one of three sons of Charles H. and Ernestine Weidner Kaune (see n 111). The sons were given the Eagle Star Flour Mill in Breese upon their father's retirement in 1876. As later journal entries reveal, Henry moved to Santa Fe in 1887, Lizzie and their two children following him a few months later. He and his descendants played prominent roles in the growth and development of Santa Fe.

During this period of financial crisis in Highland, Henry stood loyally by Bandelier, assisting him whenever possible. The May 12, 1885, entry noted that Bandelier had given power of attorney to Henry before leaving for Santa Fe.

Henry was born in Jamestown, Illinois, January 8, 1855 (Twitchell 1911–17: IV, 64–65). He died in Santa Fe on July 4, 1933, at the age of seventy-eight. It is interesting that family records shown the editors gave Henry's birth year as 1857, although they agreed on the death date and age. The discrepancy could not be explained and seemingly was a simple error in noting the birth year.

111. As noted in n 110, William G. Kaune, Henry Spencer Kaune, and Charles A. Kaune, the three sons of Charles H. Kaune, had been given the Eagle Star Flour Mill in 1876 upon their father's retirement. Charles A. Kaune died early in life, and Henry Spencer Kaune left the partnership in 1887 and moved to Santa Fe, New Mexico, leaving William G. Kaune the sole proprietor of the mill. In 1891, William retired from the mill, selling it to Koch Bros. In 1874, he had married Sarah A. Donne, a daughter of Robert and Gertrude Donne, pioneers of Breese.

After 1891, William G. Kaune was connected with the Kerens & Donnewald Coal Co. at Edwardsville. He died, after a short illness, on July 4, 1906. (Both the family Bible and the Breese Centennial Booklet say he died at the age of 52 though the family Bible clearly records his birth year as 1851.) During his lifetime, he held a number of responsible positions. He was president of the board of trustees of the Village of Breese; treasurer, clerk, and supervisor of the township; state treasurer of the Catholic Knights of Illinois; member of the Catholic Knights of America and the Merchants Exchange of St. Louis. In 1887, he was elected to the House of Representatives, 35th General Assembly at Springfield, Illinois. William G. Kaune attended McKendree College at Lebanon, Illinois, St. Joseph's at Teutopolis, and Christian Brothers College at St. Louis (Casey et al. 1956: 27–28).

In June 1969, the editors had the privilege of examining the family Bible of William G. Kaune and Sarah A. Donne Kaune in possession of Charles T. Casey, whose wife, (Mary) Olivia Kaune, was their fifth child. Mr. Casey, born August 15, 1878, was still living in the Kaune family home at North Third and Chestnut Streets in Breese, Illinois, with his son, Charles B. Casey. Mary Olivia Kaune Casey had died on June 20, 1968. The death of Benjamin Eugene Kaune, referred to in the journals, was entered in the Bible as of April 23, 1885. He had been born on April 12, 1884.

112. H. Hartmann had drawn a map of N.E. Sonora and N.W. Chihuahua based on Bandelier's journal data. Hartmann had completed this map in October 1884; it was published by the U.S. War Department (see Lange and Riley 1970: 333, 430–31n108). Bandelier later used this map in his *Final Report* (1890–92: I, end of volume). For a reproduction of this map, see Lange and Riley 1970: 474–75.

113. This comment may have referred to the quarrels between Britain and France over Egypt and the Sudan, or to the threat of war between Britain and Russia along the Afghan frontier, or to both situations (see *The Nation*, April 30, 1885: 351–55).

114. Bandelier's father had a large home on a forty-acre tract a mile northeast of Highland (Lange and Riley 1966: 7). As suggested in Lange and Riley (1970: 404n383) and borne out by this entry, the editors feel that Mr. Wachsmuth was a rural neighbor of the Bandeliers.

115. Bandelier's article "Cibola I" appeared in seven installments in the *New Yorker Staatszeitung,* Sonntagsblatt, May 24, 31; June 7, 14, 21, 28; and July 5, 1885. "Cibola II," a second series, appeared later that year in four units: October 25, November 1, 8, and 15 (see also n 89).

116. This identification of Dr. Hoffmann remains conjectural. It is possible that this was Wendelin Hoffmann, who was a German consul in St. Louis (Gould 1885: 558). Since Dr. [Hermann] Gerlich, whose name preceded Dr. Hoffmann's in this entry, had also been a German consul in St. Louis (see n 60) and since Bandelier was writing to them about "Papa" [Adolphe Eugene Bandelier], at a time when the senior Bandelier was contemplating leaving the country, it is perhaps not too much to assume that Wendelin Hoffmann was the Dr. Hoffmann of this entry.

The editors are aware of only two other references to a "Dr. Hoffmann" in the journals. On December 8, 1880 (Lange and Riley 1966: 229), Bandelier had received a letter from Dr. W. J. Hoffmann. The editors feel that this was the Dr. Hoffmann who was doing fieldwork for the Bureau of Ethnology, Washington. The second mention of a Dr. Hoffmann was in a January 22, 1892, entry when Bandelier was in New York City and was making arrangements with Dr. Goebel for a lecture at which time he had "met Dr. Hoffmann." In the *American Anthropologist* of January 1894, Dr. Hoffmann had a brief note published (p. 128) on "Beliefs Concerning Rattlesnake Bites." It was signed, "W. J. Hoffmann, M. D."

117. The "Personal" column of the *Weekly Telephone,* April 29, 1885, carried the following item: "Father Bandelier departed for the New Orleans Exposition Monday, and will probably go to Cuba from there."

Spencer (1937: 192), in writing on A. E. Bandelier and his role in the bank failure, commented, "So far as we could learn not much attempt was ever made to prosecute him. Perhaps it would have been could he have been found at the time, but he could not be located for a few years after that time. Several years later it was learned he was living with his son in Arizona [*sic*]. When very advanced in age he returned to his native Switzerland where he died in 1895 at the age of 85 years."

The editors do not know whether Adolphe E. Bandelier ever lived in Cuba. Research on subsequent journal entries reveals that he did live in Venezuela for a period prior to his return (see n 809) and that from that country he had earlier reestablished contact with his son (see n 585). He later lived with his son in Santa Fe, but not in Arizona as Spencer had indicated.

Circumstances surrounding A. E. Bandelier's return to Switzerland and the exact date of his death are not known to the editors. Some correspondence indicated that he stopped in St. Louis to see friends and relatives en route to Europe. There is one letter from A. E. Bandelier to Samuel Eldodt at San Juan, New Mexico, in the Bandelier Collection of the Museum of New Mexico; it has a Santa Fe postmark and bears the date, "Jul 16/96." This suggests that Spencer's date for A. E. Bandelier's death was incorrect.

This letter, and two earlier ones, all in German script from Adolphe E. Bandelier to Samuel Eldodt, Chamita, N.M., were transcribed and translated for the editors by Dr. Benjamin Jegers. The 1896 letter expressed gratitude to Mr. Eldodt and informed him that the senior Bandelier was leaving Santa Fe for Switzerland, never to return. The earlier letters told Eldodt of Adolph F. Bandelier's marriage to Miss Fanny Ritter and gave the Bandeliers' temporary address in Lima, Peru. These two letters, also written from Santa Fe, were dated December 17, 1893, and December 20, 1893, respectively.

118. This letter, now lost, was an answer to Bandelier's long letter of April 8. From Bandelier's subsequent letter of May 6, it would seem that García Icazbalceta had offered to help the Bandelier family resettle in Mexico.

119. Eggen (1933: 87) listed a Dr. P. F. Hellmuth, dentist, opposite from the Eagle Hotel; in Polk and Danser (1884b: 1004) a Phillip G. Hellmuth was listed as a Highland dentist. Spencer (1937: 191) credited Mrs. Helmuth [*sic*] as the bearer of the news of the impending financial disaster: "The first thing that started uneasiness in Highland about it was reports brought from Switzerland by Mrs. Helmuth, who had returned from a visit there. The deposits of Swiss people in the bank almost equalled those of the Highland people, and she brought word that they had banded together for the protection of their interests. That caused alarm here, withdrawals followed, and when the rumor was verified the failure followed."

120. This was Professor William R. Ware of New York and Boston. Professor Ware had called on Bandelier in New York in November 1884 on the day that Bandelier embarked for Europe. His assistance in teaching Bandelier to paint and draw is discussed in n 339 (consult Lange and Riley 1970: 418–19n4, 435n148 for further information).

121. George Roth had been in the hardware and implement business in Highland and later (1893) was the largest stockholder of the Helvetia Milk Condensing Co. of Highland (Lange and Riley 1970: 396–97n331).

122. The N. H. Thedinga of this entry was the husband of Louisa Thedinga, identified previously (Lange and Riley 1970: 398n343) as the daughter of Dr. Frederick C. and Josephine Suppiger Ryhiner of Highland, and the sister of Frederick C. Ryhiner, Jr. In the entry of May 4, 1885, Bandelier referred to him as Hermann Thedinga. The *Intelligencer Supplement* (Vol. 23, No. 1173) for May 6, 1885, noted that Mr. Herman Thedinga of Dubuque was visiting his brother-in-law, Fred C. Ryhiner.

123. There was a common feeling in the Highland area at the time of the bank failure that some of the bank's assets had been used to finance Bandelier's extensive travels and research and also the erroneous impression that Bandelier was a full partner in the bank, all of which helps to explain the rising feeling against him. The intensity of this resentment was reflected in the May 14, 1885, *St. Louis Globe Democrat* article quoted in n 148.

A month later, the June 16 issue of the *Weekly Telephone* carried this item:

Among the doubtful notes reported by the assignees of F. Ryhiner & Co. to the court we find the following given by the Bandelier family:

Feb. 18, '67, Ad. F. Bandelier, Josephine Bandelier, and Ad. Eugene Bandelier (interest paid up to 1st Jan. '77)	$4,000.00
Aug. 31, '78, the same	27,289.00
Jan. 2, '80, the same	18,316.06
Dec. 14, '80, Josephine and Ad. Eug. Bandelier $5,491.83, paid on this June 1st '81 $1,535.45, leaving a balance due of	3,956.38
Ledger balance due when bank closed	2,569.99
	$56,131.43

This is all they owe (without the interest thereon, which, if added, would make the sum considerably higher). In last week's *Union* one note of $1,000 and four of $500 each, by H. G. Bohn to Ad. F. Bandelier, Oct. 1st, 1878, were also added to the above account, making it higher by $3,000. This was an error. The notes were payable to Bandelier, who transferred them to the bank and received credit for the amount.

The accounts of Bandelier father and son were not kept separately, but combined. The large amounts for which they gave notes were not drawn at one time, but in small sums of less than one dollar up to several thousand dollars during the periods intervening between the different notes issued. To balance their accounts they gave the notes. A glance at the above list of notes shows that from Aug. '78 up to Dec. '80, in two years and four months, they overdrew their account by the unusually large sum of $23,807.89, while since then up to the collapse, in four years and four months, they remained in debt only $2,569.99. Until an explanation is given for the large amount received between '78 and '80, everyone may draw his own conclusions.

The other partners of the firm, Huegy and Ryhiner, did not draw more than they needed for their living and generally had a balance in their favor.

In some of our exchanges the asertion [sic] was made that Ad. F. Bandelier was not a partner in the bank. This is true as far as the law may teach [reach ?] him, but judging from the books he seems to have enjoyed the privileges of such nevertheless; and the fact that for years he acted for his father and was sent to Switzerland with the important mission to effect a settlement with the European creditors, is sufficient evidence that he was fully posted on the condition of the bank.

The notes mentioned above are classed among the doubtful accounts by the assignees, since the Bandelier property here will bring only a small percentage of the debt.

Goad (1939: 119) commented that even in 1937–38 he still found the name of Bandelier to be an "anathema" in Highland. The editors found some degree of credulity among the Bandelier-Huegy descendants for this feeling that Bandelier had made use of funds which were not rightfully his for purposes of research. The editors feel, however, that the publication of Bandelier's journals as of the period before and after the bank failure should serve to answer certain lingering doubts (see ns 134 and 158).

124. George Hoffmann's wife, Celia or Cilla, was a cousin of Josephine Huegy Bandelier (see n 63). As early as 1873, the name of George Hoffmann appeared as bookkeeper for Blanke & Bro. in St. Louis in Gould's directory (Gould 1873: 401). Blanke & Bro. was a candy company (see n 469). Hoffmann continued to be employed by this company, advancing to cashier and then secretary, the latter position being held as of the time of this entry (Gould 1881: 536; 1885: 557).

George Hoffmann was a year older than Bandelier, and the two were close friends. Besides maintaining frequent social exchanges, George and Celia Hoffmann frequently came to the aid of Adolph and Joe Bandelier in family and business matters, as the journal entries repeatedly indicate. Further indication of the esteem in which these families held each other is evidenced by the fact that the Hoffmann son, Hubert, was to accompany the Bandeliers to New Mexico in November 1885 because of poor health (see n 459).

125. This was Elizabeth Bandelier Kaune, Mrs. Henry S., the daughter of Rosalie Lipps and Emil Paul Bandelier. On occasion, she was also referred to as "Elise." She was born in Highland, Illinois, June 23, 1861 (see Lange and Riley 1970: 369–70n92), and her obituary appeared in the *Santa Fe New Mexican* of July 19, 1954. After her father's death in 1873, Elizabeth made her home with the Adolph F. Bandeliers, who had no children of their own.

In the literature, she has been frequently referred to as Adolph F. Bandelier's niece, and the editors were guilty of perpetuating this error in Volume I (Lange and Riley 1966: 18n9). The reader's attention is called to significant corrections in biographical data regarding the Emil Bandelier family in our second volume (1970: xiv and 358n24; see also n 127 of the present volume).

Actually, Lizzie was a cousin of Adolph F. Bandelier; the terms "uncle" and "niece" were used in the family but were not indicative of their true relationship. Of interest in this regard is a letter from Bandelier to Parkman, written April 9, 1883, from "San Juan, Apache County, Arizona": ". . . I have to ask one special permission. In the coming month of June our adopted daughter will be married. I would like very much to be permitted to dash home for one or two weeks at that time."

This was Lizzie's marriage to Henry S. Kaune, which, interestingly, did not take place until mid-September (1970: 148); with no further comment or word of explanation, Bandelier had continued his fieldwork, not returning to Highland until July 13. Except for the reference to Lizzie in the Parkman letter, the editors have no knowledge of Lizzie's having been legally adopted.

As entries from November 1, 1887, on reveal, the Kaunes moved to Santa Fe. Mrs. R. L. Ormsbee, youngest child of Elizabeth Bandelier and Henry S. Kaune, who now lives in the "Adolph Bandelier House" in Santa Fe (see n 492), has been most cordial in assisting the editors on several occasions. Notes on the interviews with Mrs. Kaune (Hobbs 1940a; 1942a), now in the Bandelier Collection of the Museum of New Mexico, have been invaluable.

126. The Edwardsville newspaper, the *Intelligencer* (Vol. 23, No. 1176), noted on May 27, 1885: "The arrest of Maurice Huegy and Ad. Bandelier, last Thursday evening, caused considerable excitement. An eager crowd gathered in front of Squire Riniker's office, expecting to see the parties under arrest sent to jail, but in this they were disappointed. Messrs. John Blattner and John Balsiger signed the prisoners' bond of $1,000 to appear before Squire Riniker on Thursday next. They were dismissed and accompanied home by Constable H. E. Todd and Marshall John Garbald." The *Weekly Telephone*, May 13, 1885, had announced that Mayor Suppiger had appointed John Garbald to be marshall. The issue of July 29, 1885, noted that "Marshall Garbald having resigned, the former Marshall, Chas. Britsch, was again appointed in his place."

127. In the 1880–82 journals (Lange and Riley 1966: 343), Rosalie was misidentified as Rosalie Bandelier, a sister of Adolphe E. Bandelier; this error was corrected in our second volume (1970: 358n24; see also 1970: xiv). Rosalie was the wife of Emil Paul Bandelier (born in Sornetan, Canton Bern, Switzerland, May 14, 1834, and died in Breese, Illinois, August 10, 1873); Rosalie B. Lipps was born in Switzerland in 1835, married in Sornetan March 17, 1858, came to America with her husband, and settled in Breese. She died in 1924 in Stillwater, Oklahoma.

As noted in our second volume, three children from this marriage grew to maturity, Elizabeth, Gustave, and Emma. Widowed in 1873, Rosalie assumed the care of the Adolphe E. Bandelier household after the death of the Swiss maid, Annali Näfiger, early in the 1880s (Hobbs 1940a). Records of St. John's Church, Breese, enable us now to add that there was a fourth child of Emil and Rosalie Bandelier; this was Paul Friederich, born May 5, 1862, and died August 22, 1863 (on the tombstone, this latter date reads "18 August 1863").

The basis for Bandelier's comment in this entry is not clear.

128. Henry Meyer was listed in Polk and Danser (1884b: 1003) as the owner of a Highland saloon. Eggen (1933: 88) gave him as a wholesale liquor dealer and manufacturer of cigars.

129. No positive identification of Mrs. Brossard has been possible. In 1867, a C. Brossard had subscribed funds to aid in bringing the railroad to Highland (Spencer 1937: 142).

130. Mali was Amalia Huegy, a sister of Josephine Huegy Bandelier. The story of her identification was told and acknowledged in Volume II (Lange and Riley 1970: 399n344).

She was born August 5, 1850, the daughter of Moritz and Josephine Suppiger Huegy. She never married and died October 10, 1910. She is pictured with Josephine and Adolph F. Bandelier and Adolphe E. Bandelier in Volume I (Lange and Riley 1966).

131. H. Todd and Co. is listed in Polk and Danser (1884b: 1004) as a livestock dealer in Highland. Spencer (1937: 228, 229) noted his membership in the Grand Master of Masons and the Knights of Honor. At this time, Todd was serving as constable (*Weekly Telephone*, June 2, 1885).

132. Spencer (1937: 186, 216) noted that Adolph Ruegger had been elected as county treasurer in 1877 and as an alderman in the first city election in Highland in May 1884.

He was born in Highland in 1850 of Swiss parents, George and Josephine Durer Ruegger. His father, an early sheriff of Madison County, died in 1869 and his mother later married Timothy Gruaz (see n 471).

Adolph Ruegger was educated in the Highland schools and attended St. Louis University. He was in the real estate business with his stepfather until his election as county treasurer, which position he held until 1882. After this he became secretary and treasurer of the Highland Milling Company. In 1878, he had married Louisa Wiggenhauser of New Orleans (Biographical Publishing Co. 1894: 177–78).

133. In addition to the biographical data on William P. Bradshaw given in Lange and Riley (1970: 396n330), the Biographical Publishing Co. (1894: 141–42) provided further information. Mr. Bradshaw was born in Fairfield, Illinois, on April 7, 1846, the son of Greenup and Mary (Boze) Bradshaw. He alternated work on the family farm with attendance at local schools. At the age of nineteen, he went to McKendree College, graduating in 1869. He went directly to Edwardsville and entered the law office of Dale & Burnett. After two years, he was admitted to the bar. In 1874, he formed a partnership with A. W. Metcalf, which in December 1889 was dissolved by mutual consent. He had married Sallie H. Harrison at Lexington, Missouri, in 1876.

134. Bandelier's failure to include himself with those whom Bradshaw exonerated strongly suggests that Bandelier was, indeed, free of blame—except in the minds of those who did not understand his true relationship to the F. Ryhiner & Co. bank or to those who involved him nevertheless in their frustration in failing to have the elder Bandelier apprehended. Bandelier's letter of April 8, to García Icazbalceta, stated that he had left the bank in 1880 (see n 84).

135. It is possible, if not probable, that the Vautiers were relatives of the Bandeliers. Recently, the editors became aware of a Swiss descendant of the Bandelier family and have been in correspondence with him. To date, however, we have no significant information from this source.

136. The following is a translation of the letter, dated May 6, 1885, from Bandelier to Don Joaquín García Icazbalceta (White and Bernal 1960: 280):

> Thanks, many thanks for your letter. The misfortune has now occurred; complete ruin has come. I have neither the time nor the spirit to give you details of the disaster. It suffices to know that after 25 years of having lived in a state of dependence on and slavery to my father he has fled to escape the outcry and to throw on my shoulders the responsibility of his acts. Ruined, without a cent, detained here for some days and without the possibility of earning a living, we exist thanks to a sister of my wife. I hope to obtain help to reach Santa Fe, New Mexico, where I shall try to obtain some employment. If I am not able to find anything, forced by necessity, I shall leave for Mexico.

My wife will remain for the time being with her sister [Bertha Lambelet]. I shall write you more from Santa Fe.

Yours gratefully but wretched

Ad. F. Bandelier

137. In this entry, Bandelier was referring to a Highland newspaper, the *Weekly Telephone*. The reader will find a detailed discussion of Highland newspapers in Lange and Riley 1970 (pp. 395–96n325). In that note (p. 396), the editors also commented that Goad (1939: 121) had cited the *Weekly Telephone*, Vol. III, No. 16, June 9, 1885, but that they had been able to find only one volume (II, Nos. 1–52, Feb. 26, 1884–Feb. 18, 1885) during their research at Highland.

In the summer of 1969, while working with the Bandelier Collection at the Library of the Museum of New Mexico, Santa Fe, the editors found a bound original copy of Vol. III of the *Telephone* and also correspondence which revealed that A. P. Spencer, editor of the *Highland News Leader*, successor to the *Weekly Telephone*, had presented this copy of Volume III to the Museum of New Mexico for the Bandelier materials then being gathered through the efforts of Edgar F. Goad and Edgar Lee Hewett in association with Goad's doctoral dissertation on Bandelier at the University of Southern California and also with the preparations for the Bandelier Centennial in Santa Fe in 1940.

138. The editors presume this was the wife of Mr. Kieburtz who was mentioned in the July 26 and 27, 1883, entry (Lange and Riley 1970: 143) as having been a witness with George Roth. It was on the basis of this entry that the spelling has been corrected in the 1885 entry.

139. This was Oscar Wilks A. Collet. Bandelier and Collet corresponded frequently. Born in Edwardsville, Illinois, August 4, 1821, Collet attended the Jesuit University in St. Louis. He and Bandelier shared many historic and scientific interests (see Burrus 1967; Lange and Riley 1970: 361n38, 370n98, 435n145).

140. The editors interpret this cryptic reference to Huaynopa being "on the train with Henry" as meaning that Henry [Kaune] had been entrusted with carrying the manuscript by this name, or, possibly, that the mail with this manuscript had come or gone at the same time Henry had. On March 15, 1890, Bandelier wrote, "Mailed remainder of Huaynopa to St. Louis." His March 13, 1890, entry noted that the article was for the *Westliche Post*. Bandelier had visited Huaynopa in Sonora in 1884 (Lange and Riley 1970: 225, 258, 259, 261, 289).

141. This was undoubtedly Mrs. Frank Hamilton Cushing. Bandelier had visited the Cushings at Zuñi Pueblo in 1883 (see Lange and Riley 1970: 45, 54, 69, 147, 375n136).

142. This was Gustave Bandelier, son of Emil and Rosalie Lipps Bandelier. The reader is referred to the Preface of Volume II (Lange and Riley 1970: xiv), where significant biographical corrections have been made concerning data presented in Volume I (1966) about Emil Bandelier and his children, Elizabeth, Gustave, and Emma. A detailed biographical sketch of Gustave Adolph Bandelier appeared in Volume II (1970: 403n374).

In Gould (1883: 110), Gustave A. Bandelier's name appeared as a clerk at Blanke & Bro. Candy Co. in St. Louis (see n 469). He continued to be employed there, at least sporadically, and he and his mother, Rosalie Lipps Bandelier, were listed with the same address, 4235 Evans Avenue, in the 1888 edition of Gould (p. 117). Gustave's son, George, of Stillwater, Oklahoma, was most helpful in clarifying family data during personal interviews in August 1969.

143. Emma Wilborn Huegy, wife of Maurice, or Morris, was born in 1855 and died in 1896 (see n 66).

144. Jacob Kleiner was listed by Spencer (1937: 196) as a committee member to solicit stock for the Helvetia Milk Condensing Co., Highland.

145. This was the second part of the first series of articles on Cibola which appeared in the *New Yorker Staatszeitung* in the late spring and early summer of 1885. It is noteworthy that these pages were written, or at least put into final form for publication, during the strenuous and upsetting events surrounding the final days of the F. Ryhiner & Co. bank (see also n 115).

146. Frederick C. Ryhiner, Jr., apparently went directly to Dubuque, Iowa, where his sister and brother-in-law lived. (See n 169, the content of which makes Bandelier's characterization of Ryhiner's departure "on the sly" a bit harsh.)

147. In the *Intelligencer* (Edwardsville) of May 13, 1885 (Vol. 23, Whole No. 1,174, p. 1), the following data appeared under the heading, "F. Ryhiner & Co.":

> . . .A number of garnishments were served on the German Savings Institute, St. Louis, by St. Louis and Quincy, creditors of the bank. The amount owing to these creditors is said not to be due yet. It is understood that a strong fight will be made to set aside these garnishments as also the attachments issued by courts in this county, and have all creditors share alike. From present appearances there will be considerable litigation in settling affairs, not least of which will be caused by defective titles to some of the lands in counties south and east of this. It is also stated that a large number of mortgages will have to be foreclosed and the lands sold by the master. In the shape in which the the matter now is it is not likely that most creditors will realize over fifteen or twenty per cent. A more accurate guess can be made after the assignees file their inventory.

148. This article appeared in the *St. Louis Globe Democrat* of Thursday morning, May 14, 1885 (p. 4, column 2) under the headings: The Highland Bank Failure; Another Partner Leaves the Scene of Trouble; The Assignees at Work; and Lowly Creditors. The "Special Dispatch to the Globe Democrat," dated May 13, from Highland read as follows:

> New developments still continue to present themselves in the Highland Bank failure. Before A. E. Bandalier [*sic*], the President of the bank, took his departure for Cuba (that is where he said he was going), he gave his son, Adolph Bandalier [*sic*], a power of attorney to handle all his business in the best possible way. Since the schedule of assets, made by the bank a few days ago, came out, it shows that his son is under obligations to the bank for $86,000, which he drew out at different times without giving any security. His personal effects are of no worth comparatively, and his notes, which he gave the bank, are worthless. The citizens are enraged over his action. Before the bank failed he was considered perfectly solid by all. Everyone respected and honored him, and the confidence shown in him was of the highest character. He is rather widely known as a historian, as he has been for several years working on a history of Mexico. Since the failure people have changed their warm feeling to that of hatred. Yesterday there were reports flying that some of the citizens had gone to Edwardsville and sworn out warrants for the arrest of Adolph Bandalier [*sic*], F. Ryhiner and M. Huegy, but they have proven untrue. Mr. Ryhiner has been almost crazed since the failure. Upon hearing the report that the partners were to be arrested he took flight. It is supposed he went to Lebanon, about seventeen miles distant, where he took the train for East St. Louis, thence to Dubuque, Io., where he has a sister living. One of the assignees was interviewed at once. The following questions were asked and answered: "Where is Mr. Ryhiner?" "As far as we know, he is in Dubuque, Io." "When did he go?" "Yesterday afternoon." "What was [*sic*] his general actions and condition of his mind before leaving?" "His

actions were like those of a man almost crazed. He walked the floor continually, and frequently talked of suicide if the trouble continued. He was exceedingly nervous, and every little noise seemed to frighten him. I think Mr. Ryhiner is clear of any fraudulent scheme and if he had only had the power to resist the propositions of Mr. A. E. Bandalier, he would have done so, but Bandalier had him under his influence." Generally among the people sympathy is expressed for Mr. Ryhiner and Mr. Huegy. The latter gentleman is a very quiet man and would not be suspected of being connected with any outrageous scheme, but it is thought that Mr. Bandalier had both the latter gentlemen under his control so that they would act as he directed. Nothing has been heard from Mr. Bandalier since the letter received from him dated New Orleans addressed to his son. His whereabouts is unknown to the public, but may be known by his relatives. The assignees are working diligently on the assets of the bank and endeavoring to obtain the real value of the lands, etc., belonging to the bank. They are getting along very nicely with their work, but say it will be some time before their statement will be submitted to the people.

This city has been overrun with a class of people who it was supposed had scarcely enough to keep soul and body together. Among those are found very heavy creditors of the bank. For example, an old washerwoman who has been washing for several years, and who was thought to be worth nothing, turns out to be a creditor of the bank to the amount of about $4,000. Many such instances as this have come to view.

149. John H. Hermann was listed by Polk and Danser (1884b: 1003) as a partner in the flour mill known as Henry Hermann & Co. Other partners were: Henry and Emil Hermann and Charles Seybe [Seybt]. Eggen (1933: 87) referred to this company as Hermann & Co., proprietors of Enterprise Flouring Mills. John Hermann was elected alderman in the first Highland election in May 1884 (Spencer 1937: 186).

In Brink's *History of Madison County, Illinois* (1882: 430), under a discussion of Highland City Mills, Henry Hermann, John Leder, and C. H. Seybt were the original partners; with a subsequent change, there were seven shares of capital stock. Henry Hermann and C. H. Seybt each owned two; John Hermann, Emil Hermann, and Mrs. Blakeman each had one share. The previous year's transactions amounted to over $300,000; the products were favorably known in both hemispheres, commanding "first prices."

150. Adolph F. Bandelier's mother was Marie Senn Bandelier. She died in Highland in 1855, when Bandelier was fifteen years old. The Swiss maid, Annali Näfiger, who had accompanied Mrs. Bandelier and Adolph to America from Switzerland when Bandelier's father sent for them, stayed on to care for them after Mrs. Bandelier's death.

151. On May 6, 1885, the *Weekly Telephone* (Vol. III, No. 11) had given front page coverage to the "Terrible Crash!" In this article was the following statement: "In our desire to get at facts, we tried to secure a copy of the much talked of circular, and succeeded after considerable exertion." The article then went on to condense the pertinent information about the liabilities and assets of the F. Ryhiner & Co. bank and to discuss causes and possible solutions. The article placed Adolph F. Bandelier in a bad light. Presumably, his May 7 entry, "The *Telephone* is heard," had reference to the issue. In that entry, however, Bandelier had made no comment on a circular.

Interestingly, in the Catron Collection in the Coronado Room, University of New Mexico Library, among various Bandelier papers, was an almost illegible four-page document in longhand, in German script, dated Bern, 10 April, 1885. With the help of the *Weekly Telephone* article, it has been possible to decipher some of the names, and the financial figures given as liabilities and assets in the *Weekly Telephone* parallel exactly the figures in the document, both presenting a financial statement for December 31, 1884.

354   BANDELIER'S SOUTHWESTERN JOURNALS

In the margins of two pages of the Bern document were written "Abbreviated from circular" and "Abreviated [*sic*] from Gruner-Haller circular." It is unclear how this document found its way into the Catron Collection.

152. As noted (n 95), Dr. Knoebel was president of the board of the Helvetia Milk Condensing Company at the time. Dr. Schmidt, initially a physician in Highland, became a chemist in the employ of Dr. Knoebel's company. Spencer (1937: 203–4) noted that, as of 1887, "... there was a practicing physician in Highland named Dr. Werner Schmidt. He had studied at the best universities in Germany and was highly schooled, being especially proficient in chemistry. He had been practicing medicine for a year or two in Highland but with no great degree of success. ... Since his medical practice did not bring him any big return, he readily agreed to give it up to enter the employ of the Milk Co. and assist in making the necessary experiments so that a system of sterilization of milk could be arrived at that would work at all times."

153. This challenge to a duel is particularly astonishing when viewed in terms of Illinois history. Dueling was outlawed as early as 1810, in territorial times (Carter 1950: 632), and only one subsequent duel (in 1819) was recorded. The victor, a William Bennett, was charged with murder and hanged. The circumstances of the duel were strange. It had been planned as a joke on Bennett, the seconds supposedly loading the guns with powder only. Bennett was charged with surreptitiously adding a bullet (Ford 1945: 54–55; see also Baldick 1965: 123–25). In view of the strong disapproval of dueling, it is hard to believe that Dr. Knoebel seriously intended to go through with the affair. If, indeed, he did intend to do so, it reveals dramatically the high state of tension in Highland at that time.

The following story, appearing in the *Weekly Telephone* of May 6, 1885, suggests a possible explanation for Dr. Knoebel's frustration and anger—even to the seemingly improbable point of issuing a challenge. As noted elsewhere, Knoebel was president of the board of the newly formed Milk Condensing Company.

> ... The treasurer of the Milk Condensing Company, Mr. Wildi, being anxious for the money of the new enterprise deposited there, without delay interviewed one of the firm and was informed that the circular in question need be no cause for alarm, since it concerned only their European business, which would not affect the American creditors, that they were able to meet all regular payments without embarrassment if only no sudden and unusual "run" on them occurred. This declaration and re-assurances made the following morning by Ad. F. Bandelier, the representative of his father A. E. Bandelier, senior of the firm, absent at New Orleans, were taken in good faith as satisfactory by the directors of the Milk Condensing Co. as well as by the business men with but a few exceptions, and all agreed not to draw their deposits in order to prevent the threatened rush. Public sentiment was then yet (again with exceptions) so strongly in favor of the bank that the detrimental report concerning it was emphatically considered a slander. But distrust, once let loose, spread, hastened by more or less plausible conjectures, and combinations based upon the absence of Bandelier Senior (the chief of the firm), an onslaught by others occured [*sic*] nevertheless, lasting throughout Wednesday and Thursday morning until ten o'clock, when they succumbed to the inevitable and closed their doors, thus after all making to a fact the sad event, which by the friends of the house was generally held and hoped impossible.

154. In Polk and Danser (1884b: 1003), Henry Riniker is listed as Justice of the Peace, Notary Public, Real Estate, Insurance, and Collection Agent. Spencer (1937: 192, 229) spelled the name "Rinaker." He was a member of the Highland Knights of Honor Lodge

and in his account of the bank failure, Spencer said that A. F. Bandelier was arraigned before Squire Rinaker and bound over to Circuit Court.

155. The correct spelling of this name seems to be "Unterrainer." Polk and Danser (1884b: 1004) listed John A. Unterrainer as a cutler in Highland.

The May 27, 1885, *Weekly Telephone* carried the following account of this warrant for arrest. "Upon complaint of J. A. Unterrainer a warrant for the arrest of F. C. Ryhiner, Ad. E. Bandelier, Maurice Huegy, and Ad. F. Bandelier was issued for taking money on deposit while the firm F. Ryhiner & Co. was insolvent. But since Ad. E. Bandelier and F. C. Ryhiner had departed from Highland only Mr. Huegy and Ad. F. Bandelier could be brought before Squire Riniker last Thursday evening, where they were jointly placed under $1,000 bond by states attorney McNulty for their appearance tomorrow, Thursday at 10 o'clock A.M. John Blattner and John Balsiger gave the security. The trial will no doubt be interesting."

156. Yager has not been identified. Hermann may well have been John H. Hermann, a bank assignee (Norton 1912: I, 534–35). Further information on John H. Hermann, and also on Henry and Emil Hermann, is given in n 149.

157. Xavier Suppiger was one of four trustees elected in the first village election of Highland in 1865 (Spencer 1937: 128). He was Josephine Huegy Bandelier's uncle on her mother's side (Hobbs 1940a).

158. Maurice had shot himself with a revolver; almost oblivious to the family tragedy, community leaders hardly paused, as the journal entries reveal, but pressed on with their actions against anyone they could, in other words, Bandelier alone.

Several weeks later, there was an editorial in the Edwardsville paper, the *Intelligencer*, June 3, 1885, which seriously scolded the residents of Highland for their unreasonable resort to mob action which threatened to violate due process in the days following the bank failure of May 5, several weeks earlier.

The *Intelligencer* openly deplored the attitudes which drove Maurice Huegy, a hitherto acknowledged community leader and highly respected individual, to suicide. Consequently, the editorial pointed out, aside from this unfortunate event, per se, the community of Highland had deprived itself of the capable services of the person best qualified to direct the liquidation of the bank's assets. Accordingly, all would suffer.

159. Goad (1939:119) reported that he found the name of Bandelier to have been an "anathema" in Highland. "Even today [1937–38] he is remembered, if at all, with bitterness, however proud the townspeople may have been of his achievements as a scholar. An excellent example can be found in the *Highland News Leader,* as of 1927: 42 years ago, Ryhiner and Co. bank at Highland failed for a large sum of money. Adolph F. Bandelier was cashier. At that date, the people here wanted to hang him. The President of the United States later named a large park in the West in his honor—'Bandelier Park.' Yes, times changed!" (clipping in the Library of the Museum of New Mexico).

The above quotation contains several misstatements: (1) Bandelier was not cashier; (2) the *Telephone* account of events of the time (June 2,1885) maintained the threat to hang Bandelier was not in earnest (rationalization in retrospect, perhaps?); and (3) President Wilson set aside a national monument and not a park in Bandelier's honor.

The seriousness of such misrepresentations may be seen in a news item in the *Highland News Leader,* July 7, 1937. Announcing Goad's presence in the community as a representative of the Museum of New Mexico in search of Bandelier data, the announcement continued: "None but our older people have any personal recollection of Mr. Bandelier, and theirs is not a very pleasant one. Prior and up to 1885 he was active in the management of the F. Ryhiner & Co. bank and after the failure of that institution he was held to the Madison County grand jury on the charge of having solicited deposits for the bank after he knew it was insolvent. No one in Highland would go his bail, and he spent one night in jail at Edwardsville [Goad maintained this was as a guest of the Sheriff, but Bandelier's account of the episode fails to support Goad on this]. The next day some Edwardsville people went his bail, and he left for New Mexico [actually on June 2, after a few days in St. Louis]. He was indicted by grand jury but never appeared for trial. Whether or not his bondsmen paid, we do not know. Probably not. [The journal entries of late October and November 1885 leave many of these details somewhat obscure.] At any rate he was never in Highland but once after that. About two years later he came here one evening, but left before daylight and only a few of his most intimate friends knew of his presence here. [Goad denied the accuracy of this episode.] Time has lessened the bitterness that existed then, and Highland people will likely give Mr. Goad every assistance in his investigations." (This clipping, with marginal notations, is included among the files relating to Goad's research in the Library of the Museum of New Mexico.)

160. Lange and Riley (1966: 47) quoted an article from the *Weekly Telephone* which used D. W. Mudge. Bandelier referred to him as Will Mudge and the Biographical Publishing Co. (1894: 156–57) as Elliott W. Mudge. As far as the editors can tell, these names all refer to the same person.

Elliott W. Mudge was born June 17, 1845, in Madison County, the son of Solomon H. and Susan Dodge Mudge. The Mudge family traced its ancestry back to New England and the Revolutionary War. Elliott W. Mudge received his education from private tutors and then attended Washington University in St. Louis and Flushing Institute of Long Island. He served in the Confederate Army and after the war moved to St. Louis, where he was a merchant for two years, then returned to the family homestead in Madison County. In 1868, in Collinsville, he married Fannie, daughter of John L. and Mary (Bradshaw) Clarke. In 1880, he moved to Edwardsville where he was a prominent figure in business and civic affairs.

161. Hugh E. Bayle of Edwardsville was listed as Madison County Clerk in Polk and Danser (1884b: 869).

162. In Polk and Danser (1884b: 870), Athanas Hoffmann was given as the proprietor of the Hoffmann House and Saloon in Edwardsville. Brink (1882: 555) added that he had been born in Baden, Germany, and had come to Madison County in 1868.

163. In the February 3, 1885, issue of the *Intelligencer,* Robert Hagnauer was mentioned as clerk of the circuit court of Edwardsville.

Spencer (1937: 216) wrote that Robert Hagnauer had been the only man from Highland to fill the office of circuit clerk. He was elected in 1880 on the Democratic ticket and served altogether for a period of twelve years. He was educated at Normal, Illinois, and clerked in a store at Sebastopol. Hagnauer was in the hardware business in Highland at the time of his election. After leaving office, he resided in towns in the western portion of Madison County until his death.

Providing additional data, the Biographical Publishing Co. (1894: 227–28) noted that Hagnauer was born February 11, 1848, near Highland, the son of William and Johanna (Suppiger) Hagnauer, a pioneer Swiss family. He married Elisa Felder in October 1872. This account gave 1884 as the date of his election as circuit clerk (p. 227).

164. In quoting the *Weekly Telephone* of June 2, 1885, in the Introduction to Volume I (Lange and Riley 1966: 47), which said "Bandelier was lodged in jail that night but the following morning Athanas Hoffman, D. W. [*sic*] Mudge, and Chas. Boeschenstein signed his bond, whereupon he was released to appear again when his trial comes up," the editors had inserted in brackets the following sentence: "Goad was told by Mr. Charles Boeschenstein, President of the Edwardsville National Bank, that Bandelier actually stayed in the sheriff's house as a guest." That Bandelier actually spent the night in jail as stated in the June 2, 1885, *Weekly Telephone* article is supported by this journal entry of Bandelier's and negates Goad's comment. It should be remembered that Goad's biogra-

phy and appraisal were submitted as a dissertation in 1939 and that his research in Edwardsville and Highland had taken place about fifty years after the bank failure. The Introduction to Volume II stated that Bandelier spent the night in jail (1970: 6), but the detailed correction of Volume I has been intentionally delayed until this entry in Volume III.

165. In 1883, Charles Boeschenstein, who had owned the *Highland Herald*, moved to Edwardsville, combining the *Herald* with the *Intelligencer*, which he had just purchased (Lange and Riley 1970: 396n325). An advertisement in Polk and Danser (1884b: 869) showed him as "Proprietor of the Edwardsville Intelligencer Printing House, (D.)," doing book and job printing. The *Intelligencer*, a weekly, was advertised as being the oldest Democratic paper in the county.

"Young Charley Boeschenstein" was the son of Charles Boeschenstein who was a nephew of John Boeschenstein; both of the latter were Swiss immigrants and prominent early Highland citizens (Spencer 1937: 54).

In the journal entry of March 1, 1882, Bandelier mentioned his making a new Will—presumably as he was preparing to return to the Southwest and further fieldwork. "Witnesses: Cha's Boeschenstein S'r and jr, ..." For comparison, see ns 158 and 164.

166. Bandelier's contrasting of Edwardsville and Highland in terms of people's attitudes toward him warrants elaboration. Goad (1939: 118) cited Carl Huegy in stating, "Black powder bombs had been exploded on Maurice Huegy's lawn. The town was in an ugly mood." In the *Weekly Telephone* of June 2, 1885, an account of events included the following: "The prisoner [Bandelier] was taken to the depot at 3:00 o'clock to be brought by train to Edwardsville, where he was to be placed in jail; but as the train was delayed several hours by washouts, a carriage was procured, in which the prisoner, constable Todd and W. P. Bradshaw drove off. The crowd which had gathered at Riniker's [The Justice's] office and at the depot, was of course more or less excited, but the threats of 'hang him,' etc., were not made in earnest, but intended only to scare. The man displaying the rope said he expected a bull calf to arrive with the train, and the fact is that he did receive the animal the next day...."

For comparison, see ns 158, 164, and 165.

167. Dr. Emil Preetorius of St. Louis was president of the *Westliche Post* Association (Gould 1886: 943). The *Westliche Post* was a German-language newspaper and from time to time, as journal entries indicate, Bandelier sold articles to it. Bandelier consistently spelled the name Pretorius. Dr. Preetorius had been Chief Editor since 1864 (see Lange and Riley 1970: 386–87n242 for added data on both Preetorius and the *Westliche Post*).

168. Frederick B. Suppiger was born in Highland, July 21, 1852, the son of Godfrey M. and Caroline Pagan Suppiger, both Swiss emigrants. He was educated in the local schools and at Charleston, Illinois, and later studied at Lausanne and Zurich in Switzerland. He married Paulina Felder, daughter of the late Dr. Felder, in 1876. In 1880, he entered the lumber business as a member of the Thorp, Kinne & Suppiger firm. In 1888, he disposed of this interest and established his present business, also in lumber (Biographical Publishing Co. 1894: 203–4). Suppiger was the last mayor of Highland, as a village, 1880–84, and also the first mayor, "under City Organization," 1884–89 (Spencer 1937: 273).

169. After Bandelier's departure from Highland, several items, reported in the *Weekly Telephone* during the following weeks, are noteworthy here.

In the June 2 issue, it was reported that there had been a letter from F. Ryhiner in Dubuque to J. C. Ammann (one of the bank assignees) saying that he "would come when needed" and that he would prefer to come voluntarily rather than to have someone sent to bring him.

The July 29 issue reported that "Last Wednesday [July 22] F. C. Ryhiner, member of the late bank firm and his brother-in-law, H. Thedinga of Dubuque, Iowa, accompanied by Attorney Chas. Wise of Alton, arrived here to give bond for his wife [Louisa Ryhiner Thedinga] as part of the Ryhiner personal property and real estate, and the court has accordingly appointed appraisers for the purpose. No claim was made, however, on the amount due the late Mrs. Ryhiner. [sic] by the bank" (see also n 68).

In the September 2 issue, it was noted that "J. H. Hermann, one of the bank assignees, inspected a large tract of land, which is to be sold at public sale, near Caseyville on Monday. It embraces about five hundred acres, partly good and partly swampy, and was taken by the bank as payment for a debt of $16,000. It is supposed that from $10 to $15 per acre will only be realized now."

A comment in the September 23 issue was a bit more optimistic. "The bottom lands of our defunct bank will be sold at Belleville Oct. 10th. A large portion ought to bring good prices, since it is located near Caseyville and generally yealds [sic] good crops."

Further data on the period following the bank's failure must be sought in sources other than the Highland *Weekly Telephone*, which ceased publication after the printing of October 7, 1885, Volume III, No. 33, its "Final issue" (see n 137).

170. The Tarahumares (or Tarahumara, or Tarahumar) Indians constitute one of the larger groups in northern Mexico. They live in the mountainous country of Chihuahua, and some families do, indeed, inhabit caves (see Pennington 1963 for a recent study of this tribe).

171. Bandelier had made the acquaintance of Father Salvador Personnet on his earlier trips to New Mexico. Father Personnet had served in both Albuquerque and Las Vegas. He was president of the Jesuit Academy at Las Vegas, 1878–82, and then succeeded Father Gasparri as parish priest of Old Town in Albuquerque (Lange and Riley 1966; 1970).

172. The name Lamy, honoring Archbishop John B. Lamy, was given to the junction of the AT&SFRR main line and the spur which was extended into Santa Fe in 1880. On September 29, 1857, Bishop Lamy had taken the area referred to as the Lamy Grant, a tract of irregular shape, in trust for the Catholic Church (Pearce 1965: 84).

173. While it is difficult to determine Reed's identity with any degree of certainty, it may well have been Samuel T. Reed with whom Bandelier had had supper in Santa Fe in October 1883 (Lange and Riley 1970: 153, 405n397). Reed was listed in Polk and Danser (1884a: 353) as in the real estate and mining business, with an office over the First National Bank of Santa Fe.

174. Since Bandelier was so unspecific, it is most probable that this was David J. Miller, Chief Clerk, Surveyor General's Office, Santa Fé. Bandelier had made his acquaintance when he first arrived in Santa Fe in the late summer of 1880, and with numerous common interests they remained friends over the years (see Lange and Riley 1966: 413–14; 1970: 368n84). Miller, a native of Alabama, was fifty-seven years old when he died in St. Louis on December 22, 1887 (*Santa Fe Daily New Mexican*, December 28, 1887, No. 263, p.4).

175. Herlow's Hotel was operated by Paul F. Herlow. It was located on San Francisco Street; a livery stable was in conjunction with it (McKenney 1882–83: 340; Polk and Danser 1884a: 352; *Santa Fé New Mexican Review*, 1884).

Herlow was a pioneer settler in the Southwest, living some twenty years in Santa Fe. He served with the 2d California Infantry and the 2d California Cavalry during the Civil War; he enlisted September 2, 1861, reenlisted October 18, 1864, and was mustered out May 13, 1866. He was married and had three children. His death "last night" was carried in the *Weekly New Mexican Review* of September 20, 1888 (p.3); he was about fifty-eight.

176. Apparently, the warm welcome given Bandelier in Santa Fe influenced him to

remain in New Mexico rather than going on to Mexico, as he had suggested he might do in his April 8 letter to García Icazbalceta (n 84). (In this regard, see also his letter of September 10, 1885 [n 421], again to García Icazbalceta.)

The *Santa Fe New Mexican Review* of June 2, 1885, noted his return with the following words: "Prof. A. F. Bandelier's legion of friends throughout the southwest will be pleased to learn that he has returned to Santa Fe after an extended sojourn in Europe."

The *Weekly Telephone* of June 16, 1885, picked up this item, repeating it more or less and adding further, bitter comment. "The Santa Fe, N. M., *Review* says: 'Prof. Bandelier's legion of friends throughout the entire South-West will be glad to hear of his return to Santa Fe after an extended trip to Europe.' To this the *Union* of here remarks: 'We can assure that paper that he left behind him here a legion of friends who are very sorry that he has become *so dear* to them.' "

177. Jean Baptiste Lamy was born in Lempdes, France, October 11, 1814. He attended the Seminary of Montferrand, France, and was ordained a priest in the Roman Catholic Church in 1838. Lamy came to America in 1839 as a missionary, serving first in Ohio and later in Kentucky. He was named Vicar Apostolic of New Mexico, and Bishop of Agathon in 1850, becoming Bishop of Santa Fe in 1853 and Archbishop in 1875. He resigned as Archbishop in 1885. The Santa Fe Diocese included New Mexico, Arizona, and parts of Colorado, Utah, and Nevada, and was expanded to take in the whole of Colorado in 1860. An untiring worker, Lamy induced the Sisters of Loretto to found a settlement in Santa Fe in 1852, and the Christian Brothers in 1867. With their help, he actively promoted the building of schools and churches. He died on February 13, 1888. The famous novel by Willa Cather, *Death Comes for the Archbishop* (1927), was based on Lamy's life (*Who Was Who* 1963: 301).

By recruiting priests from France, for the most part, Lamy added the considerable influence of another culture, the French, to the existing Indian and Spanish cultures. This also had an appreciable impact on the Catholic Church in the Southwest, which, prior to Lamy being named bishop, had received instructions for nearly three centuries from Mexico, and earlier from Spain. The extent of the French influence has generally been overlooked. For other data on Archbishop Lamy and Bandelier's associations with him, see Lange and Riley 1966; 1970.

178. Polk and Danser (1884a: 352) listed Gerard D. Koch as a dealer in lumber, hardware, and builder's materials on Lower San Francisco in Santa Fe. Mrs. G. D. Koch was listed as a music teacher. Earlier, Koch was a partner in "Eldodt & Koch, Dealers in all kinds of Merchandise, Dry Goods, Groceries &c., San Juan, New Mexico, and Abiquiu, New Mexico" (Huggins 1876).

179. This was John C. Pearce, listed by McKenney (1882–83: 340) as a metallurgist and assayer in Santa Fe.

180. No such catalogue has survived; seemingly, Bandelier had catalogued the collection in the archaeological museum of the new cathedral, referred to in n 195.

181. Father Michael Rolly [Rolli], assistant priest of the Cathedral of Santa Fe in the 1880s (Salpointe 1898: 273). Father Rolly had served as priest at Jemez, San Diego Parish, 1872–76 (Lamy Memorial 1950: 63).

182. This was Reverend Francis Gatignol, listed in the Lamy Memorial (1950: 53–54) as priest of Belen from 1885 to 1901. In this entry, Bandelier misspelled the name, Gatignalles, but in a paper in the Catron Collection which made reference to the discovery of these epitaphs, Bandelier referred to him as Father Gatignol. He was among the priests brought to New Mexico by Bishop Lamy (Salpointe 1898: 282).

183. In the building of the present-day Santa Fe Cathedral of St. Francis, begun in 1869, Bishop Lamy planned the construction so that church services would not be inter-

rupted. The old adobe Parroquia was to be enclosed by the new Romanesque stone cathedral. (See n 1132 and Anonymous 1972: 58–59 for additional data on the construction and history of the cathedral.)

At the time of discovery of the two priests' cyst, the interior of the new cathedral was nearing completion. Because of the method of construction, it was at that time necessary to remove much of the adobe of the old Parroquia from within the completed exterior shell of the new cathedral. The rear portion of the old Parroquia was to be closed off and a new altar erected in front of the partition. Von Wuthenau (1935: 194) described this partition as initially of canvas and later, probably in 1894, a permanent wall. The old stone *reredos* was to remain in the room behind the new altar, and this room was to become a museum (see Salpointe 1898: 205 and ns 180, 195, and 1082).

For the history and descriptions of the stone *reredos*, see Von Wuthenau (1935: 175–94), Adams (1947: 327–41), Adams and Chavez (1956: 32–57), Galvin (1966: 41), and Anonymous (1972: 48–49). Now a focal point of the Church of Cristo Rey in Santa Fe, the *reredos* as it currently appears is shown in color as the frontispiece of Adams and Chavez (1956).

It was at this stage in the cathedral construction that Fathers Rolly and Gatignol summoned Bandelier to the church to see the "side of a cyst" they had found while opening the north wall of the choir. Bandelier described it as "of brick and coated with a thin film of cement." An undated photograph by C. F. Lummis showed the *reredos* and the side of the cyst on the north wall. This photograph was reproduced by Von Wuthenau (1935: facing 190) and by Hodge, Hammond, and Rey (1945: Pl.IX, facing 92). Although presumably made later than 1885, it is the only photograph known to the editors showing this feature.

It is important to note here that although Governor Marín del Valle was responsible for bringing the friars' remains to the Parroquia in Santa Fe in 1759 (see n 184) and for commissioning the *reredos* in 1760, the remains and the *reredos* had not always been in the same church. The *reredos* was originally commissioned for the Chapel of Our Lady of Light, later known as La Castrense, where it was used until 1859, when the land on which that chapel stood was sold. Bishop Lamy then brought the *reredos* to the Parroquia. Von Wuthenau (1935: 194) noted that it was placed at the back wall of the apse behind the main altar and used continuously "for over twenty years in the principal church of the city."

As far as the editors are aware, the priests' remains were, in 1885, in the original location in which Governor Marín del Valle had placed them. But as this entry and the quotation from Defouri suggest, some alteration of the wall must have occurred. Bandelier noted "opening the north wall of the choir"; Defouri wrote of "behind the wainscoting" and then noted Bishop Zubiría's having the sepulchre opened to venerate the remains, which would imply that they had earlier been more accessible than in Bandelier's time.

It is pertinent to this discussion that in an unpublished manuscript of "Inscriptions" (Catron Collection PC 29 807), Bandelier quoted the inscriptions given in this journal entry and noted, "The above two inscriptions were discovered on the 3d of June, 1885, by Reverend Father Rolly, Father Gatignol, and me, at the time when the old Altar of the cathedral was being removed to its present place." This suggests that when the *reredos* was placed in the Parroquia in 1859, it was placed in such a position as to conceal the inscriptions. Bandelier located them as appearing "on the north side of the old choir."

It is important to emphasize again the June 3, 1885, entry date, as it has been erroneously cited in the literature as June 2, 1880, even by Bandelier himself (see n 184). As noted in this journal entry, Bandelier called on Defouri that same night.

These remains were later described by Father Defouri (1887: 146):

Behind the altar of the old cathedral are two treasures that ought to be recorded here, and will be kept most sacredly in the new. Behind the wainscoting on the north side, is a double headstone covering a sepulchre in which are contained the bones of the body of the Venerable Geronimo de la Llana—an apostolic man of the Order of St. Francis—which were brought from Guarac [Cuarac, Quarai] de las Salinas on the 1st of April, 1759, at the cost of the Governor Francis Antonio Marin del Valle, and placed there. Also, the bones of the body of the Venerable Asencio Zarate, of the Order of St. Francis, brought from the ruins of the old church of St. Lawrence of Picuries, on the 8th of April, 1759, and located in the parish of the city of Santa Fe on the 31st of August of the same year. [According to Bandelier, however, Zárate's remains were brought to Santa Fe May 8, 1759, and both priests' remains were reburied in the Parroquia on August 11, 1759. See journal entry of June 3, 1885, and also ns 184 and 185.] It is known that whenever the saintly Zubiría, Bishop of Durango, came to Santa Fe, he ordered the opening of the sepulchres to venerate the relics brought there from afar.

The whole of the wall of the old sanctuary is a stone monument of this same Governor del Valle and his spouse. It is a rare monument and worthy of the utmost care.

Defouri (1893: 70–73) later repeated various details, still somewhat divergent from those of Bandelier. Chavez (1957: 37) listed an item, dated 1758, regarding the purchase of a house and lot by Governor Marín del Valle and his wife for the erection of the Chapel of Our Lady of Light. The stone altar piece was originally there; later, it was moved to the Parroquia.

In his *Final Report*, Bandelier commented only very briefly on the burial of Fray Gerónimo de la Llana (1890–92: II, 261, 261n3). Bandelier made no mention of Fray Asencio de Zárate in his *Final Report*. His most complete account of the priests' remains appeared in 1890 in a Santa Fe newspaper article (see n 184).

Reference has been made earlier to an unpublished manuscript by Bandelier on "Inscriptions." Of interest here, but not noted in the journals, were those labeled, "Inscriptions at the base of the old Chancel of the Cathedral in the town of Santa Fe." The identical inscriptions appeared in Salpointe (1898: 205). Abert in 1846 had also noted them and copied and translated them when this piece of stonework, the *reredos*, was in La Castrense (Galvin 1966: 41). Although Abert thought this was a tombstone of Governor Marín del Valle, his account is of interest in that he described the *reredos* while it was still in the chapel for which it was commissioned. Abert noted the inscriptions on the *reredos*, but he made no mention of the wall inscriptions nor of the priests' remains when he described the interior of the Parroquia in October 1846 (p. 40).

As the June 5, 1885, entry indicated, Bandelier gave copies of the epitaphs from the wall of the Parroquia to Salpointe. Salpointe subsequently gave his account and translation, referring to the document which was in the archives of the cathedral (Salpointe 1898: 99, 100, 287). Although de la Llana's death date (1659) was correctly cited on p. 100, it was incorrectly given as 1569 on p. 287 in Salpointe's account.

Also, Salpointe (1898: 99–100), like Defouri and Chavez, gave the burial dates in the Parroquia for the two friars as August 31, 1759, rather than the August 11 date of Bandelier's June 3, 1885, journal entry and Bandelier's newspaper article (n 184).

Twitchell (1923: 38n2) stated, "Under the high altar in the old Parroquia rest the remains of the Re-conquistador General de Vargas, and also those of the Fray Geronimo de la Llana (who established the mission of Quarai in 1642, died in Tajique July 19, 1659) and Fray Asencio Zarate (who served at Picuris, dying there in 1632)." [Twitchell's details should be carefully compared with data elsewhere in this note and also in n 184 for discrepancies regarding Fray Gerónimo. Also, Twitchell's "under the high altar" does not seem accurate as the burial place of the two friars.]

The American Guide Series volume on New Mexico (1940: 202) is at variance about De Vargas as well. "Tradition has long placed the remains of the great re-conqueror, De Vargas, under the cathedral altar, but late researches indicate he is elsewhere." Of the burials, it says, "Two friars who came to New Mexico more than three hundred years ago lie buried beneath the board markers set into the east [sic] wall of this room. These are the only known graves of the fifty-three Franciscans who came with the Conquistadores" (p. 202).

In 1965, Fray Angelico Chavez (1965: 101–15) published "The Unique Tomb of Fathers Zarate and de la Llana in Santa Fe." The reader is referred to this article for many additional details. Not noted by Bandelier was a Franciscan knotted cord carved into the slab in the shape of a reclining figure eight with each of the ovals of the figure eight having one of the inscriptions (p. 102). Chavez cited the June 2, 1880, date for Bandelier but did not give his source for this date. Chavez also noted (p. 104) four short pieces of square beam which were around the front of the casket, details which Bandelier did not record. These beams showed clearly in the Lummis photograph to which Chavez also referred. Chavez also commented on the discrepancies between the easily viewed casket at the time of Bishop Zubiría's visits, in 1833, 1845, and 1850, and the subsequently enclosed tomb with the slab and beams of the Lummis photograph (p. 104).

Chavez (1965: 114n10) questioned further how or why Fray Francisco Atanasio Domínguez missed mentioning the casket in 1776. "Was it perhaps out of sight under the altar table? Or it may never have been in a wall niche until placed there *with the beams* in the nineteenth century." The editors tend to agree with Father Chavez that some of these questions may never be resolved.

Whether the beams might have yielded borings for possible tree ring datings, as occurred in the choir loft at the Nuestra Señora de Guadalupe Chapel, in which beams from La Castrense were thought to have been reused (Anonymous 1972: 20–21), has, to the editors' knowledge, never been tested. However, these questions are perhaps minor considerations in comparison to Father Chavez's major discovery regarding the tomb.

Father Chavez was asked to direct the restoration of La Conquistadora Chapel, which like the old sanctuary behind the altar in the new cathedral, with its tomb and *reredos,* was the only remaining part of the 1714–17 church, or Parroquia. After the *reredos* was moved to Cristo Rey Church in 1940, the museum specimens were removed and only the tomb remained in the wall of what had become a deserted storeroom. Both curious and solicitous about the early priests of his order, Father Chavez chipped away at the upper beam and discovered a "well-proportioned stone casket and, under its two removable lids, further inked inscriptions which no light had faded" (p. 104). Photographs of the opened stone casket and the two inked inscriptions were included opposite pp. 104–5. Father Chavez then had a contractor open a "niche in the left-hand side wall of the Conquistadora Chapel, and thither we reverently carried this 'treasure' on March 15, 1957, as I recorded in my notes along with measurements of the reliquary" (p. 104). . . . "The casket is a block of white chalky stone, 41 inches long, 21 inches wide, and 12 ½ inches high. [Chavez was of the opinion that this was the same stone used for the *reredos* (pp. 107–8).] Two compartments were neatly carved inside, leaving an outer wall 2 ¼ inches thick and a center partition 2 inches thick. Two identical covers had been cut from the same kind of stone to fit loosely over the twin compartments, each lid about 2 inches thick, beveled down to an inch around the outer edges. On the center of each lid a solid copper hasp was attached by means of two copper bolts driven through the stone and riveted on the underside. In each compartment a few bones showed among the moldy folds of eighteenth-century blue Franciscan habits, in which they had been wrapped and then stuffed into each section. I did not extract the bundles to see if any skulls or crania were inside. The habit around Father Zárate's remains was of a rough woolen weave, while Father de la Llana's was of a finer serge, the color of both fabrics unfaded, similar in appearance to the denim used for western 'Levi's,' though much softer. I snipped off a piece of each habit, and of a knotted cord, to preserve as the only known samples of the blue habit worn by the old Franciscans of New Mexico." [The reader with a special interest in the Franciscan habit will want to consult Chavez's note (p. 113n6).] Chavez's statement would indicate that at the time of reburial by del Valle the remains had been rewrapped, as their original interment habits would have been seventeenth century. See also n 44 on the Franciscan habit and Galvin (1966: 40) for Abert's comments on two wax, life-size, figures of priests in the Parroquia in 1846, one in white, and the other in blue.

Chavez continued, "Just as big a surprise were the inscriptions, inked in lower case letters, beneath the lid. . . . " The reader is referred to pp. 105–6 of Chavez for his recording of the Spanish inscriptions. His translations (p. 106), however, are quoted here completely:

> This Venerable Father Friar Asencio Zárate lay buried inside the ancient Church of St. Lawrence of Picuris a hundred and twenty-seven years until he was removed by the Lord Governor Marín. He was a man admirable in penance and prayer through whom God worked some wonders. He passed on to the Lord full of merits and with the fame of sanctity in 1632. These two venerable Fathers were finally buried here by the (Very Reverend) Jubileed Friar Jacobo de Castro, ex-Custos of Tampico and present re-elected Custos of this Holy Custody in his 7th year [in office A.C.]. These venerable bones went forth from the Royal Palace, where they were kept, the troop of the Royal Garrison and Militia marching with all pomp, with much rejoicing and the solace of all the inhabitants of this Kingdom. The Reverend Father Friar Tomás Murciano de la Cruz, ex-Custos of said Custody, preached the eulogy.
>
> This Venerable Father Friar Gerónimo de la Llana was a native of Mexico City where he made his profession. He passed over to this Custody of New Mexico to brighten these Regions with his exemplary teaching and virtue. He was the oracle of this Custody. Full of merits he went to enjoy the fruit of his labors at the afore-mentioned Pueblo of Quarac, where he lay buried for a hundred years.

Chavez was in error in citing 1699 as the date on which Father Freytas had disinterred Father de la Llana's remains (p.106). The correct date was 1669.

Chavez (p.106) made this additional comment: "It is interesting to note how phrases from Vetancurt's *Menologio* are incorporated into these inscriptions." From examination of the documents relating to Father Gerónimo de la Llana copied by Bandelier at Santa Clara Pueblo in May 1888 (see n 997), it appears that the governor, on the basis of the 1706 Fleytas letter which he copied September 10, 1758, decided to search for the remains of both de la Llana at Quarai and Zárate at Picuris and bring them back to Santa Fe for permanent burial.

One document copied by Bandelier stated clearly that on April 7, 1759, Governor Marín del Valle solicited the *Teatro Mexicano* by Vetancurt; both the *Crónica* and *Menologio* of the *Teatro Mexicano* pertained to New Mexico. It is not unreasonable to assume that Governor del Valle, with a copy of Vetancurt in his possession, might well have consulted it for the inscriptions that were to be placed on the interiors of the sepulchre lids.

The histories of these two Franciscan priests and Bandelier's "free" translations of the wall inscriptions, as well as the early documents he found regarding these priests, are discussed in ns 184 and 185.

184. This inscription concerning Fray Gerónimo de la Llana and "freely translated" was given, together with the Father Asencio de Zárate inscription (n 185), in reverse order, in an unsigned article in the *Santa Fe Daily New Mexican,* May 10, 1890.

The editors first became aware of this article in July 1969, when going through the Bandelier Collection in the Library of the Museum of New Mexico. It was pasted in a scrapbook referred to as the New Mexico Bandelier Scrapbook, to distinguish it from the Bandelier Scrapbook sent to the editors by Professor Fred Eggan (see n 695 for data on these scrapbooks). Both scrapbooks were heterogeneous collections of newspaper and magazine clippings, primarily but not exclusively of articles written by Bandelier. At the time, the editors photocopied a portion of this article, not knowing positively that Bandelier had written it, although next to it in the scrapbook was a signed article by "Ad. F. Bandelier." The fact that the 1880 date in the article did not correspond to the date of the journal entry for these two inscriptions immediately caught our attention, and it was filed as additional background data for this note.

In April 1970, in response to queries from Dr. John P. Wilson, Curator of Historical Archaeology, Museum of New Mexico, about data we might have on Father Gerónimo de la Llana to supplement those available in the *Final Report,* the editors referred him to this scrapbook newspaper article, as well as sending him a Xerox copy of the 1759 Santa Clara manuscript found and copied by Bandelier in May 1888, which pertained to Father de la Llana (n 997). The editors also sent Wilson the associated journal entries, as well as a Xerox copy of a 1636 letter from Fray de la Llana (n 794). Wilson then copied the entire newspaper article, sending us a copy, which is reproduced in this note. Wilson spoke of this as a "much fuller account than he [Bandelier] included in his *Final Report.* It must have been Bandelier himself that wrote the article; I don't see how anyone else could have maintained the accuracy. The article is an adequate summary of the 1759 original . . . although many details are omitted."

Through additional evidence since this exchange of correspondence, Bandelier's authorship of the article has been established. In editing the fourth and final volume of the journals, the editors found that in Bandelier's April 29, 1890, entry, he noted that he was to furnish monthly eight columns to the *New Mexican,* "of a generally interesting reading matter with special attention to New Mexico." This, presumably, was one of the early articles furnished by Bandelier. Chavez (1965: 103) quoted from this or an identically worded article, attributing it to Bandelier. Chavez also used the 1880 date (see n 183), but as this journal entry clearly established, the correct date was June 3, 1885.

To the editors' knowledge, Bandelier did not publish these data elsewhere, so the article has been quoted in its entirety here. Twitchell (1911–17: IV, 491–94) included the same account, with only minor variations. Twitchell gave no source for his data, other than crediting the account to Bandelier (p. 491). Subsequently, Walter (1931: 11–15) used the data presented by Twitchell. Since discrepancies are apparent in this newspaper article and the interpretations of it, it has been reproduced in its entirety with the present editors inserting additional commentaries [*1, *2, etc.].

Santa Fe Daily New Mexican, Saturday, May 10, 1890, Vol. 27, No. 68.

The Franciscan Sepulchres in The Cathedral at Santa Fe

On the 2d of June 1880 [*1], while preparing to remove the altar of the old cathedral of Santa Fe, preliminary to closing the rear portion of the present edifice, Father Rolly (lately deceased) and Father Gatignol (now curate at Belen) noticed, in the wall of the old structure, two ancient inscriptions. Upon deciphering them they proved to indicate the place where two cysts had been immured, each of which inclosed the remains of a Franciscan monk from the

17th century. The inscriptions were carefully cleaned from the adobe which had accumulated over them, and to-day they can be seen, together with the chancel [*2] dedicated to the parish church of Santa Fe by the governor, Don Francisco Marin del Valle, in 1761, in the vacant room behind the main altar. [*3]

A free translation of the two inscriptions conveys the following information:

No. 1. Here lie the remains of the Venerable Father Asencio de Zarate, of the order of Saint Francis, etc., which were taken out of the ruins of the ancient church of San Lorenzo of Picuris, on the 8th day of May, 1759, and were transferred to this parish church of the town of Santa Fe, 11th of August of the said year. [*4] (The inscription further states that the transfer of the remains of the monk referred to below took place on the same day.)

No. 2. Here rest the remains of the Ven. Father Geronimo de la Llana, etc., of the order of Saint Francis, which were taken from the ruined mission of Quarac at the Salines, on the 1st day of April, 1759, by the governor, Don Francisco Antonio Marin del Valle, governor and captain general of the kingdom, at the expense of whom this sepulchre was constructed.

We repeat that the above are not strictly translations of the inscriptions, but merely convey the substance of their texts.

So far these two tombs have been the only ones from the 17th century identified in New Mexico. The sepulchre of Fray Juan de Jesus, the priest whom the Indians of Jemez murdered on the 10th of August, 1680, may yet be discovered, but so far it has not been attempted. [*5]

Concerning the first one of the two Franciscans whose remains are at the cathedral, documentary information is slight. The date and place of his birth are not given in the authors who treat of the ancient New Mexican missions, but it is known he stood in high repute for his virtues and as an educator of the Indians. He was sent to the mission of Picuries, and died there on the 13th of December, 1632. That his body had been interred in the church of that pueblo was a well known fact in the 17th century. [*6]

Much more definite data exist in regard to Fray Geronimo de la Llana. He was a native of the City of Mexico, the son of Juan de la Llana and Dona Isabel de la Raya. His father was a Spaniard, his mother a Creole lady from Mexico. He entered the Franciscan order on the 21st of November, 1629, and soon distinguished himself by his learning. When he came to New Mexico is not known, but it must have been previous to 1636, since we are in possession of a note written by him at Santa Fe in that year. [*7] Vetancurt says of him: "He became the oracle of that custody, and a model for the people." The last years of his life were spent at the pueblo and mission of Cuaray or Cuarac, five miles southeast [sic] of the present town of Manzano, where he died (among the Tigua Indians) on the 19th of July, 1659. His body was interred in the church of Cuaray, the ruins of which to-day constitute one of the most picturesque objects among New Mexican antiquities. [*8]

As late as 1706 there still lived Indians who remembered Fray Geronimo de la Llana well, and spoke in glowing words of his virtues; nay of miracles which he should have performed. Among the Spanish population his name was but faintly remembered. In that same year, however, a letter was written to New Mexico by a monk who has lately acquired some celebrity (in connection with the notorious governor of New Mexico, Don Diego Dionisio de Peñalosa, the latter having attributed to that monk a report on a supposed expedition of his to the northeast. It is abundantly proven that the report in question was written by Peñalosa himself and that the friar had nothing to do with the document or with the purported expedition). [*9] That friar was Fray Nicolas de Freytas (a Portuguese) [*10] and he certified to the fact that in 1669 he disinterred the body of Fray Geronimo de la Llana inside the church of Cuarac or Cuaray and removed it to another place in the same edifice near the altar, and where it was less exposed to humidity.

The pueblos around the salt basin of the Manzano were in the 17th century at least six, perhaps seven in number. It is not certain yet whether there was an Indian village at the Manzano after the occupation of New Mexico by the Spaniards, although the presumption is in favor of it. The six pueblos, about the existence of which there can be no doubt, are, from north to south: Chilili, Tajique and Cuaray, all inhabited by Tiguas; Abo, Tenabo and Tabira, inhabited by Piros. [*11] The latter is the place now falsely called "Gran Quivira." [*12] There was also a village of Jumanos in that vicinity, but its location is not yet difinitely [sic] ascertained. [*13]

The abandonment and ruin of these villages, all of which were the seat of missions and therefore provided with churches, from documents in our possession, have taken place between the years 1669 and 1675. The villages were abandoned successively, Tabira (Quivira) [*14] being in all probability the first. Of the three Tigua pueblos, Cuaray was the earliest one forsaken. The people took along with them the body of Fray Geronimo de la Llana, placing it, in its rude wooden coffin, to the right side of the altar of the church of Tajique. [*15] When the latter village and that of Chilili had to be abandoned, and their Indians fled to Isleta, the distance did not allow them to carry along the remains of their beloved priest. So the body of Fray Gernimo [sic] de la Llana, after having been twice displaced by pious hands within fifteen years after his decease, remained for eighty-five years in the decaying temple of Tajique, at the mercy of the Apaches, then sole masters of all the region south and southeast of Galisteo. Still the savages did not disturb [sic] the body, either because they never noticed it, or owing to superstitious dread.

It is not devoid of interest to notice here how soon after the abandonment of what were then called the "Missions of the Salines" distinct recollections concerning their fate and even their location became confused. It may be said that twenty years after their depopulation they had faded out of sight. [*16] Still, in documents from the years 1683 and '84, Indians from Tabira, Abo and Cuaray appear as testifying witnesses. But they all dwelt at El Paso del Norte, where their ultimate descendants to-day occupy the villages of Senecu and Isleta del Sur. But after the terrible blow which the insurrection of 1680 inflicted upon Spanish power and prospects, and in the desperate efforts made for reconquest afterward and the excitement attending them the Manzano region was completely given up. The Apaches swayed over the whole of southeastern New Mexico, any attempt at colonization was out of the question with the feeble means of which the Spanish authorities could dispose; in fact they had more than enough to do to hold their own in the Rio Grande valley and its adjacent sections, without thinking of districts outlying upon the great plains.

This complete neglect of the ancient missions around the salt lagunes [sic] is curiously exemplified in the proceedings of recovery of the body of Fray Geronimo de la Llana in 1759. Gov. Marin del Valle had taken cognizance of the letter written by Father Freytas in 1706, and he determined upon making search for the relic. [*17] He therefore caused the work of Fray Augustin de

Vetancurt, entitled "Teatro Mexicano" (1698), to be sent him from Mexico [*18], and in it found a description of the old missions, which, however, contains some geographical errors [*19]. On March 30 the party, consisting of the governor, several officers, a notary and three priests, escorted by two squads of soldiers and thirty-five Indians, reached the ruins of Cuaray. The most diligent search revealed no trace of the body. Thereupon one of the Indians informed the governor of a tradition to the effect that the corpse had been removed to Tajique, and the curious discussion arose, whether Cuaray was Tajique or Tajique Cuaray. None of those present could solve the riddle, although it was manifest that the party was actually on the site of Cuaray, about twenty miles southeast of Tajique. Orders were given to return to the latter place, where the ruins of the church and pueblo were still (and are to-day) plainly visible, and very soon the precious relic was found. Enough remained of the vestments to show that it was the body of a Franciscan monk, pieces of cloth and the rosary being still intact. But of the parchment which, according to the certificate of Father Freytas, the latter had placed in the folded hands of the dead, no trace was left. The remains were carefully exhumed, placed in a casket especially brought along for the purpose and carried to Santa Fe, where they were placed in the cyst rediscovered five years ago. [*20] The inscription, however, which locates the find at Cuaray is erroneous. The village where the remains of Fray Geronimo de la Llana were exhumed for the last time was Tajique, whither the pious love of his parishioners had removed his body. [*21]

Three times in 100 years was the resting place of that venerable monk disturbed, and always in the best and most pious intentions of saving it from eventual desecration. Exactly 100 years after his death, they suffered their last transfer, and to a place where, it may be confidently expected, they will forever remain. [*22] Of the manner in which the remains of Fray Asencio de Zarate were secured, we have as yet no positive information. [*23] In that case, as well as in the instance of Father de la Llana, a full "proces verbal" was certainly executed. But the papers have disappeared or are perhaps lost, a fate only too common with historical documents in New Mexico, and one to which a great many other manuscripts here may still be exposed, unless steps are taken toward their publication. [*24]

[*1] The date of June 2, 1880, was obviously erroneous, as clearly shown by Bandelier's entry of June 3, 1885. This latter date was further substantiated by the phrase toward the end of this article, written in 1890, where Bandelier wrote, " . . . rediscovered five years ago."

[*2] Bandelier was apparently not aware that the chancel, the *reredos*, had originally been at La Castrense, the military chapel on the Santa Fe plaza.

[*3] The *reredos* was moved to the Cristo Rey Church, Santa Fe, in 1940 at the time this church was built. Chavez moved the friars' remains and the accompanying inscriptions to La Conquistadora Chapel of the Santa Fe Cathedral in 1957.

[*4] Bandelier consistently used August 11, 1759, as the date for the reinterment of the remains of both Father Zárate and Father de la Llana by Governor Marín del Valle in the Parroquia. August 31 was the date given by Defouri (1887; 1893), Salpointe (1898), and Chavez (1965).

[*5] It is interesting to note that Bandelier subsequently in his *Final Report* (1890–92: II, 210n3) stated that "The remains of Fray Juan de Jesús were exhumed by Diego de Vargas on the 8th of August, 1694. They were found in the first square of the pueblo close to an estufa, and showed that the body had been pierced by an arrow. The shaft of the arrow was found with the skeleton."

[*6] It is curious that Bandelier in this article did not cite the paragraph from Father Nicolás de Fleytas's letter (White and Bernal 1960: 318) which revealed that Father Fleytas, in addition to reinterring Fray Gerónimo de la Llana's remains at Quarai in 1669, had also reburied the remains of Fray Asencio de Zárate at Picuris that same year (see translation of the Fleytas letter in n 997). Bandelier's inclusion of this document in his letter to Icazbalceta was the only reference that Bandelier made to Father Zárate's reburial by Father Fleytas, as far as the editors are aware (see n 185).

[*7] See n 794.

[*8] According to the contents of Bandelier's letter to García Icazbalceta, dated June 20, 1891, Father Fleytas had originally buried Father de la Llana at Quarai, or Quarac (see n 997).

[*9] Peñalosa's use of Father Freytas's name will be further discussed in Volume IV (see also ns 564 and 727). Bandelier (1890–92: I, 173n2) commented upon "the pretended reports of Diego de Peñalosa" and added related comments, including a correction of Freytas to Fleytas.

[*10] The editors seriously question the basis on which Bandelier established Freytas's nationality as Portuguese (White and Bernal 1960: 312). This letter to Icazbalceta with our English translation will appear at its appropriate journal entry date in Volume IV (see also n 997).

[*11] Wilson (1973: 15) chose to designate the people of these last three pueblos as Tompiros rather than Piros. Together with the three Tiwa, or Tigua, pueblos, they constituted the Province of Las Salinas, in reference to the salt lakes in the vicinity.

[*12] Bandelier (1890–92: I, 131) made a comparable statement in his *Final Report:* ". . . there was Ta-bir-a, now famous under the misleading surname of 'La Gran Quivira.' " See n 811 for a discussion of the confusion surrounding these and other ruin names in the Salinas area (see also the journal entry of May 24, 1888).

[*13] See Hayes (1968) for identification of Pueblo de las Humanas.

[*14] Bandelier often equated Tabira with Quivira; on occasion, he also used Quivira to refer both to the Great Plains and to the ruin at Gran Quivira. See Burrus (1967) and note *12, above.

[*15] The editors recognize conflicting accounts regarding Bandelier's statement and statements by others (Kubler and Chavez) on the removal of de la Llana's remains from Quarai and reburial at Tajique (Bandelier 1890–92: II, 258, 258n1, 261–62, 261–62n3). However, Twitchell (1911–17: IV) and Walter (1931: 15) did not take issue on this point with Bandelier, nor did Wilson (1973) in his recent paper.

[*16] See Twitchell (1911–17: IV, 500–1); Hayes (1968: 36); Bandelier (1890–92: I, 131n2; II, 257n1, 258, 261, 262, 264).

[*17] Bandelier had found these documents in 1888 at Santa Clara Pueblo, including the copy of the Freytas letter of 1706 (see n 997). Nowhere did Bandelier indicate that Governor Marín del Valle's confirmation of the 1706 Freytas letter occurred on September 10, 1758 (White and Bernal 1960: 318–19). The actual trip to bring de la Llana's remains to Santa Fe did not take place until late March of 1759. Bandelier did not incorporate Roybal's feeling that others had searched for these remains.

[*18] Bandelier's sequence here was misleading; while searching for the remains, Marín del Valle recalled Vetancurt's account and consulted the *Teatro Mexicano* after his return. Bandelier and Scholes both cited an edition of 1870–71; the editors had access to a 1961 edition, including both the *Crónica* and the *Menologio*. Bandelier used Vetancurt extensively for data on Father de la Llana, but failed to cite Vetancurt on Zárate (Vetancurt 1961: IV, 327–28).

[*19] Bandelier (1890–92: II, 261n3) elaborated on these errors in Vetancurt and made accompanying remarks as follows: " . . . There is hardly any doubt that the body, when exhumed one hundred years after his death, was found at Tajique, and not at Cuaray,

according to the testimony of the Indian Ché, contained in the same documents. Vetan-curt, however, inverts the order of the pueblos, by placing Cuaray three leagues (nine miles) south of Chilili, and Tajique six miles farther south. The distances are of course incorrect, and the order in which the pueblos are enumerated still more so. From Chilili to Tajique is at least twelve miles, and thence to Cuaray or Punta de Agua the same (military measure 11.51 miles). Furthermore, it is well established that the pueblos were then where they are now. Such inaccuracies are numerous in Vetancurt's otherwise valuable book. He errs in geographical statements, and sometimes in dates. This is not to be wondered at, since he himself was never in New Mexico, and wrote at a time when that province was still inaccessible to Spaniards and priests. But it is well to call attention to such mistakes, as they might mislead students who are not well acquainted with the localities."

[*20] Bandelier was not aware that the remains of both friars had been kept for a time at the Palace of the Governors (Chavez 1965: 106, 107).

[*21] See note *15.

[*22] Chavez, in 1957, moved the remains of both friars to La Conquistadora Chapel in the Santa Fe Cathedral (Chavez 1965: 104–5).

[*23] Chavez (1965: 107) questioned how the identification of Zárate's remains had occurred. From the 1706 Fleytas letter, Governor Marín del Valle was aware that Father Zárate had been buried at Picuris (see note *6).

[*24] Ironically, even the documents on which Bandelier based this account have apparently disappeared since that time, and Bandelier's copies, in the Catron Collection (PC 29 807) at the University of New Mexico and in the Hemenway Expedition papers at Peabody Museum Library, Harvard University, are the only ones that have survived to the present time (see n 997). Bandelier was one of the few to express publicly his concern over the historical documents of New Mexico.

Defouri (1887: 146; 1893: 70–73) also gave accounts of these inscriptions and their histories. Discrepancies with Bandelier's data about Fray Gerónimo de la Llana have already been noted in n 183.

Much of Bandelier's account was based on documents found by Bandelier at Santa Clara Pueblo (see entry of May 29, 1888, and n 997 where a complete translation has been included). Since Bandelier's time, the originals have apparently been lost (Salpointe 1898: 99–100; Chavez 1965: 114n7; n 618) making Bandelier's copies the more valuable. In Bandelier's letter of June 20, 1891, to Icazbalceta (White and Bernal 1960: 318), Bandelier noted that "The Original [Diligencias Practicadas sobre la solicitud del Cuerpo del Vener-able Padre Fray Gerónimo de la Llana] can be found in the ecclesiastical archive which up to a year ago, was in the hands of the Indians of KA-PO or Santa Clara." [Translation ours.]

While in Mexico in 1887, Bandelier had also copied a letter from Father Jerónimo de la Llana (see entry of April 27, 1887, and n 794).

Bandelier's copies of these documents cited here are in the Hemenway Collection in the Peabody Museum of Harvard University and copies of at least some of them are in the Catron Collection (PC 29 807), University of New Mexico Special Collections, University of New Mexico Library (see n 618).

Chavez's discovery of additional inscriptions on the interior of the tomb lids (Chavez 1965: 104–6) has already been noted in n 183 and their translations quoted. Chavez also recorded and translated the inscription of Fray Gerónimo de la Llana from the cathedral wall; Bandelier, in the journal entry of June 3, 1885, however, gave the date as August 11 rather than the August 31 date of Chavez. August 11 also was the date appearing in a manuscript on inscriptions compiled by Bandelier and ultimately included in the Ca-tron Collections (PC 29 807) (see n 183).

In addition, Chavez incorporated Vetancurt's account (pp. 111–12). The reader is referred to the entire article by Father Chavez including the extensive footnotes (pp. 101–15) for additional data on Father Gerónimo de la Llana and for the discussion by Chavez of many details that appeared in the newspaper article.

Perhaps there will be additional, or new, data on Father de la Llana when Burrus completes his translation of Bandelier's *Histoire*, as de la Llana's name appeared in Bandelier's table of contents as translated by Burrus (1969b).

Hodge, Hammond, and Rey (1945) noted Father Jerónimo de la Llana at Isleta in 1634 (p. 256) and at Tajique in 1636 (p. 257). In an editorial note (p. 257n75), Hodge, Hammond, and Rey commented, "Date of the founding of the convent at Tajique is not known exactly. . . . Fray Jerónimo de la Llana was [guardian] in 1636." Though Hodge, Hammond, and Rey made no mention of Father de la Llana at Quarai, their comments on Quarai are pertinent to this discussion. *"Quarái,* spelled Cuarac in the 17th century documents, may have had a convent as early as 1628. At least, there is reference to Fray Juan Gutiérrez de la Chica as guardian of Nuestra Señora de le Concepción de Querac in that year; it would hardly seem that this could have been anything but Cuarac. Perea served there in the 1630's, Cuarac becoming the official headquarters of the Inquisition in New Mexico at the time" (p. 257n75).

Returning to Chavez's article, one finds a basic discrepancy between the accounts by Bandelier and Chavez. As copied by both Bandelier and Chavez from the cathedral wall, this inscription located Cuaray as the place where Father de la Llana's remains were found. In the newspaper article quoted above, as well as in the *Final Report* (Bandelier 1890–92: I, 258n5), Bandelier believed he had established Tajique as the place where Governor Marín del Valle had found Gerónimo de la Llana's remains. Chavez (1965: 114n8) wrote that Kubler (1940: 88–89), after discussing the merits of the Tajique-Quarai controversy, believed "the Tano Indian tradition may be fictitious, since other historical evidence places Quarac at its designated location." Kubler was using Twitchell (1911–17: IV, 494) as his authority that the body had been taken to Tajique. The account in Twitchell was virtually identical to the newspaper article quoted above, and Twitchell apparently accepted Bandelier's conclusion. Kubler's discussion indicated a long-standing problem relating to the identification of Quarai and Tajique. Pertinent to this note was Kubler's final paragraph in his description of San Miguel Tajique (Kubler 1940: 89). [For some reason, Kubler did not seem aware that Twitchell had credited Bandelier for these data.]

"The first question is this: did the inhabitants of Quarai really move the coffin to Tajique in 1674, or is the story an Indian fabrication made up extempore in 1759 and improved by Twitchell? Secondly, after the remains had been discovered and removed to Santa Fe, did Marin del Valle have any idea where Quarai really was? The answer to both of these questions hangs upon the authenticity of the story of the removal of the coffin from Quarai to Tajique in 1674. If the Indian's story is a fabrication, modern Quarai is correctly named, and the inscription in Santa Fe is correct. If the story, however, is true, Quarai and Tajique must be renamed. The writer inclines to question Twitchell's version, although the manuscript *'Dilixencias sobre la solizitud del venerable Pᵉ Fray Gerónimo de la Llana,'* 1759, cited by Bandelier [1890–92: II, 258–59n5], should be reviewed before this important point can be settled." Unfortunately, the translation of these documents has not solved this confusion. Varying testimony is contained in the several statements (see n 997).

185. A "free" translation of this inscription about Father Asencio de Zárate was given in the newspaper article quoted in n 184 (see n 183 for data pertaining to the discovery and history of this inscription). It is possible that when Father Burrus completes his translation of Bandelier's *Histoire*, there will be further data by Bandelier on Zárate. According to the already published table of contents for the *Histoire* (Burrus 1969b:78), Bandelier at least mentioned Fray Asencio de Zárate, among the martyrs, in Chapter V.

The inscription about Father Zárate discovered by Father Chavez on the tomb's lid (Chavez 1965: 104) with his translation (p. 106 [see n 183]), augmented Bandelier's data somewhat; it added the information that the remains had for a time been kept in the "Royal Palace [Palace of the Governors]" and then brought forth with pomp and ceremony to their resting place. Chavez added that Father Zárate came to the New World in 1600 and to New Mexico in 1621 (p. 108); he also incorporated Vetancurt's data on Father Zárate (p. 110). In addition, Father Chavez recorded and translated the inscription from the cathedral wall (p. 102).

Although Bandelier, in several instances, cited the Fleytas letter of 1706 in regard to the burial of Father de la Llana at Quarai (n 184), it is singular that, to the editors' knowledge, he never published the second paragraph of this letter which pertained to the reburial of Father Asencio de Zárate by Father Fleytas at Picuris in 1659, twenty-seven years after Father Zárate's death. Vetancurt, in his *Menologio Franciscano*, first published in 1698 (1961: 328), commented, " . . . y despues de 25. años se halló su cuerpo entero, tratable, y oloroso, en que manifestó Dios la santidad de su Siervo." If Vetancurt was referring to Fleytas's reburial of Father Zárate, he made an error of two years.

Bandelier quoted the entire Fleytas letter verbatim in a letter to García Icazbalceta on June 20, 1891 (White and Bernal 1960: 318–19). Bandelier had found this document in May 1888 at Santa Clara Pueblo (our translation of this document appears in n 997). Similarly, our translation of this Fleytas letter appears in Volume IV in association with the appropriate 1891 entry, along with editorial comments on the letter itself and also regarding White and Bernal's note.

Bandelier made no mention in his *Final Report* of Zárate. Defouri's data (1887: 146; 1893: 72) have already been cited and their discrepancies with Bandelier's data noted (n 183). Scholes (1937: 84–85) made reference to Father Asencio de Zárate, noting that Zárate had been appointed by Friar Miguel de Chavarria to act as vice-custodian of New Mexico from October 1622 to December 1625. Hodge, Hammond, and Rey (1945) made several references to Zárate. He served among the Apache (p. 89); the Xumano [Jumano] (pp. 96, 98, 312); at Santa Fe (p. 274); and sang high mass at Benavides's reception in 1626 (p. 129). In a discussion of Zárate's life, Hodge, Hammond, and Rey (p. 282n95) noted that he had died at the mission of Picuris in 1632 and was buried there, but that on May 8, 1759, his remains were removed to Santa Fe. On August 31, the remains were reinterred in the Parroquia, as a tablet indicated. [Bandelier, however, consistently used August 11 as the date of reinterment of Father Zárate in the cathedral (see journal entry of June 3, 1885, and ns 183 and 184). Salpointe (1898: 99–100) used August 31, 1759, for the date of the burial "in the old Cathedral church"; Chavez (1965: 102) and Defouri (1887: 146) also used August 31 rather than Bandelier's August 11 date of burial.] Zárate was at Picuris in 1629 but left there to go to the Jumano and then returned to Picuris prior to his death in 1632 (p. 312).

186. Sometime after 1933, Archbishop Rudolph A. Gerken assembled the Archdiocesan Archives in Santa Fe. In 1957, Fray Angelico Chavez, O. F. M., published the volume *Archives of the Archdiocese of Santa Fe, 1678–1900*.

187. This was Reverend James H. Defouri of the Church of Our Lady of Guadalupe, Santa Fe (Polk and Danser 1884a: 350). He was one of the priests brought to the United States by Bishop Lamy (Salpointe 1898: 282). Added data (Lange and Riley 1966: 409) revealed that he was born in La Palud, France, 1830; was ordained in 1854; served various missions among Plains tribes; was in Kansas in 1862; was Bishop Miege's vicar general, 1875–80; and was private secretary to Archbishop Lamy and priest at Guadalupe Church, 1881, where he rebuilt the church and built the parish house.

A publication of the Historic Santa Fe Foundation (Loomis 1966: 16) added that he had been appointed to serve as pastor for the English-speaking Roman Catholics in the area and that this church was opened as a parish in its own right on December 11, 1881.

(Guadalupe Day, or the Feast of Guadalupe, is traditionally celebrated in the Catholic Church on December 12.)

The editors have found reference to a "journal written by Father De Fouri" (Anonymous 1961: 15, 17) from which the following is quoted: "On the 15th of July, 1881, the Most Rev. J. B. Lamy, Archbishop of Santa Fe wrote to me in Denver, where I was for a year: 'If you are free and can come to Santa Fe, you will do me a favor. I appoint you the successor of Father Truchard [Lange and Riley 1966: 416]. You will be Vicar General for the English of the Diocese, my private Secretary, and you will have charge of the few English speaking people of Santa Fe, saying mass and preaching for them on Sundays.' . . . Soon after my arrival, his Grace told me, he would give the Church of Our Lady of Guadalupe, to the American congregation." Despite extensive efforts and correspondence, the editors have not been able to locate this journal of Defouri.

Defouri wrote several historical items, among them, *Historical Sketch of the Catholic Church in New Mexico,* published in 1887. It is of interest as a reflection of what the Catholic Church knew of its history and records as of the period of Bandelier's Southwestern years. Archbishop Lamy had charged Defouri with this work as a result of a request in 1884 from the *Congregation de Propaganda Fide* in Rome (Lange and Riley 1970: 413–14n465).

188. This was Lt. James Fornance of the 13th Infantry, a good friend of Bandelier; Fornance was killed in the Spanish-American War (Heitman 1903: I, 429; see also Lange and Riley 1970: 381n184).

189. Major William Francis Tucker was a member of the Paymaster's Corps (Heitman 1903: I, 973). Tucker was well acquainted with Bandelier and had been consulted at some length by him in regard to General Crook's campaign into the Apache country and northern Mexico in 1883 (see Lange and Riley 1970: 431n111; for greater detail on the Apache campaign, see Bourke 1886).

In an introduction to a reprinting of Frank H. Cushing's *My Adventures in Zuñi,* Jones (1967: vi) discussed Cushing's role in "the preservation of the pueblo's [Zuñi's] lands from encroachment." Some Indian agents disapproved of Cushing's assistance against Navajo intrusions on the Zuñi range, and next he helped the Zuñis against "encroachments of the invading Anglos."

"However, this action on his part also led directly to the termination of his activities at Zuñi. Cushing was instrumental in revealing and opposing a land scheme advanced by one Major W. F. Tucker, a plan which would have resulted in the settlement by Anglos of Zuñi lands. Although the young ethnologist, with the help of Baxter's journalistic experience, was successful in countering this scheme, he encountered the wrath of Tucker's father-in-law, General John A. Logan, then Senator from Illinois. Senator Logan advised the director of the Bureau of Ethnology that he would smash the infant agency if Cushing were not recalled. Alleging ill health, Cushing finally departed from Zuñi after many delays, in May, 1884."

190. This was the Reverend (or Doctor, as Bandelier often referred to him in the journals) Edward W. Meany, who was the Episcopal rector in Santa Fe (Polk and Danser 1884a: 352). Dr. and Mrs. Meany assisted Bandelier with his German translations from time to time (see Lange and Riley 1970: 379n171). On January 3, 1883, the *Santa Fe Daily New Mexican* commented that the University of New Mexico, Santa Fe, had been fortunate to secure the services of Reverend Professor E. W. Meany for courses in Latin, Greek, and French. The article noted that Meany held a diploma as a graduate of Oxford, England, and that prior to coming to Santa Fe "a month ago," he had held a professorship in Latin and Greek at the East Florida Seminary. Health had forced him to refuse a considerable offer after resigning in Florida.

McKenney (1888: 484) referred to Meany as Rev. E. Meany, rector of the Church of the Holy Faith, Santa Fe. Mrs. Summerhayes (1908 [1960 ed.: 206]), writing of Santa Fe in the late 1880s, mentioned "The distinguished Anglican clergyman [Rev. Meany] living there taught a small class of boys, and the 'Academy,' an excellent school established by the Presbyterian Board of Missions, afforded good advantages for the young girls of the garrison." Subsequently (p. 208), she wrote, "And many a delightful evening we had around the board, with Father de Fourri [sic], Rev. Mr. Meany (the Anglican clergyman), the officers and ladies of the Tenth [Infantry Regiment], Governor and Mrs. Prince and the brilliant lawyer folk of Santa Fé."

191. The Brothers of the Christian Schools were founded in Rheims, France, in 1681; in answer to a call from Bishop Lamy, they opened a boys' school in Santa Fe. Their history in the United States had begun with the arrival of three Brothers with Bishop Dubourq of New Orleans in 1817. In 1818, they opened a school at St. Genevieve on the Mississippi River south of St. Louis. This school flourished for a few years and was then given up. In 1846, three Brothers arrived in Baltimore and laid the foundations for the first of five provinces. In 1859, Rev. Peter Eguillon, vicar general, was sent by Bishop Lamy to France to appeal to the superior general of the Christian Schools to open a school in Santa Fe. The request was initially refused, but finally, after intercession by an old friend of Eguillon's at Clermont, four Brothers were sent. These four and a fifth from New York had an adventurous trip across the plains, arriving in Santa Fe on October 27, 1859. The Christian Brothers school was opened in mid-November of that year (Salpointe 1898: 210–22 et seq.). After an initial period of hard times, during which the school was conducted in borrowed quarters, a campus was established, with the first building completed in 1879. The school was incorporated (as St. Michael's, or San Miguel, College) in 1883 (Twitchell 1925: 363). See also n 194. (For further details of the founding and early years of St. Michael's College, see St. Michael's College 1934.)

192. William G. Ritch (1830–1904) came to New Mexico for health reasons after the Civil War. Appointed secretary for the territory in 1873, he served in that post for a number of years. In 1875, Ritch was acting governor for approximately two months following the death (June 3, 1875) of Governor Marsh Giddings (Twitchell 1911–17: II, 417, 417n343).

Ritch (1885a: 199–202), in his book *Aztlan: The History, Resources and Attractions of New Mexico,* included a brief article by Bandelier, "Ancient Pueblos in and about Santa Fe." Ritch (1885b), in *Illustrated New Mexico,* also published a letter from Bandelier relating to the prehistory of New Mexico (see Lange and Riley 1970: 215, 422n43). In 1890, these items both appeared in French translation by Beaugrand.

193. Jake Gold was one of the many German-Jewish migrants who helped shape the history of nineteenth-century New Mexico (Parish 1960). He established a curio shop at the northwest corner of Burro Alley and San Francisco Street; Twitchell (1925: 409) stated that Gold was the first curio dealer in Santa Fe, placing the founding of the shop in the early 1880s. Gold was in business at least by the late summer of 1880, as Bandelier's journal entry of August 25 revealed (Lange and Riley 1966: 72–73).

Further data on the Gold family came in the form of personal correspondence from Bruce T. Ellis (February 15, 1971): " . . . the *New Mexican Review* for May 5, 1884, carries an obit. of Moses Aaron Gold, age 40, 'one of Santa Fe's oldest citizens,' who left a large family and two brothers, Jake and Abe. And going back still further, the *Santa Fe Weekly Gazette* of Aug. 17, 1867 notes that 'Luis Gold has entered into partnership with his sons (M. A. Gold and A. Gold). . . . Their place of business is in the new rooms recently built on Main Street west of the Plaza.' Note the 'new rooms recently built'—I think that's the quarters of the present 'Original Curio Store, Established 1605'!"

194. Brother Botulph, or Botulphus, was the fifth president of St. Michael's College and is credited as the man who really made St. Michael's. He was born Peter Joseph Schneider in Germany in 1833; his family emigrated to New York in 1851. On becoming acquainted with the Christian Brothers, he joined the brotherhood and served in the East and Detroit

before going to Santa Fe, where he arrived November 2, 1870. Brother Botulph became director of St. Michael's College and Visitor of the New Mexico Province, which included the schools of Santa Fe and Mora. Under his leadership, St. Michael's grew; in 1884, its Silver Jubilee was celebrated. In 1885, Archbishop Salpointe, desiring government help for the Catholic Indian Schools of New Mexico, sent Brother Botulph to Washington, but the mission was unsuccessful. The years 1885–86 were hard for the people of New Mexico, and the number of students decreased. Brother Botulph persisted, however, and, as times improved, he planned a new building which was completed in 1887. He was often referred to in the community as Professor P. J. Schneider. He served as director and president of St. Michael's from 1870 to 1906 (St. Michael's College 1934).

195. The *Santa Fe New Mexican Review* (Vol. 22, No. 91, p. 4, c. 2) carried the following comment on Bandelier's trip to San Juan in the edition of Saturday, June 6.

> Prof. Bandelier [*sic*] and Dr. Eggert departed yesterday [actually early that same morning, the *Review* being an evening paper] on a visit to the genial Sam Eldodt at San Juan. They may take a bear hunt in the mountains before their return. By the way, Prof. Bandalier [*sic*] is no longer connected with the Archaeological Institute of America as an active member, but holds an honorary life membership. During his recent visit to Germany he displayed some scientific writings and drawings concerning the southwest which were highly complimented by all the leading scientists of the empire, and the Imperial government has decided to publish them at a cost of $100,000. The professor enjoyed a rare treat yesterday. He paid a visit to the archaeological museum of the new cathedral and assisted materially in arranging the display there. Among other things which absorbed his attention were a lot of ancient Spanish church manuscripts which were inclosed in a chest recently unearthed while tearing down the adobe walls of the old cathedral. Prof. Bandelier will remain at San Juan some weeks. Dr. Eggert will return home tomorrow.

In the above account, the term "manuscripts" must be considered an error. In entries of June 3–5, 1885, as well as in such accounts as that in the *Santa Fe Daily New Mexican* of Saturday, May 10, 1890, Vol. 27, No. 68, the term used was inscriptions rather than manuscripts.

196. The Bouquet Ranch was featured in the February 1969 *New Mexico Magazine* (Woods 1969: 32, 37). Described as an old New Mexico *placita*, sixteen miles northwest of Santa Fe on Pojoaque Creek, it once was the site of a small Indian pueblo started by people who had fled from their homes at Pecos. The Spanish came, and by 1776 the pueblo of Pojoaque had a population of only 98 people. No organized Indian settlement remains.

John Bouquet, a French pioneer, built a mansion on a mound of the old Indian site. The main part of the house was built between 1855 and 1880. With its high ceilings, corner fireplaces, and thick adobe walls, with gardens for vegetables and flowers, as well as orchards, and vineyards famous for both grapes and wines, it was a pleasant stopping place for travelers like Bandelier. In later years, Bouquet turned it into a stagecoach stop and hostelry, because it was on the Santa Fe–Taos Trail.

Bourke (Bloom 1937: 67), who sought shelter there during a storm, commented that it was a "Government Forage Agency." Bourke used the spelling "Boquet." This spelling was also used by Polk and Danser (1884a: 341), who listed John Boquet as having a general store at Pojoaque. The town's population was given as 30.

The editors had the pleasure of visiting this interesting home in July 1969, at which time it housed the New Mexico Arts and Crafts Center. However, in August of 1969 the Bouquet house was advertised for sale.

197. Father J. B. Francolon was one of the priests brought to New Mexico by Archbishop J. B. Lamy (Salpointe 1898: 282). In a letter of September 2, 1888, to Thomas Janvier, Bandelier devoted an entire paragraph to an account of their mutual friend, Father Francolon (see n 1059).

198. This was Captain James Ferdinand Simpson, at that time with the 3d Cavalry (Heitman 1903: I, 888).

199. Gerónimo was a Chiricahua Apache medicine man, born in the Upper Gila River area. In 1876, when an attempt was made to remove the Chiricahua to San Carlos, Gerónimo fled to Mexico with a band of followers. He later was persuaded to return to San Carlos but fled again in 1884 and remained hostile until persuaded by General Crook to surrender in 1886. For Bandelier's journal entry reporting the false account of his capture and murder by Gerónimo, see his April 28, 1883, entry from Fort Apache, New Mexico, and the subsequent related notes (Lange and Riley 1970: 90, 386ns239–41).

Gerónimo and his warriors were deported to Florida and, later, were finally settled in Oklahoma. Gerónimo died in 1909 (Hodge 1907–10: I, 491; see also Davis 1929).

200. These probably referred to the two "pinole affairs" associated with the early Arizona settler, King Woolsey. In January 1864, a band of Americans and Maricopa Indians under Woolsey's command lured a group of Apaches into the American camp at the "Bloody Tanks" (probably in Fish Creek Canyon) by the offer of pinole, and then slaughtered them. On another occasion, Woolsey was alleged to have given a group of Apache Indians pinole mixed with strychnine (Russell 1908: 50–51; Lockwood 1938: 148–49; Thrapp 1967: 27, 29–32; Lange and Riley 1970: 139, 388n262, 392n314).

201. This reference to "Whitlock's fight at the 'Ciénega'" is somewhat obscure. Because it was told by an army officer, Captain Simpson, it is tempting to equate the incident with the dual killing of Captain James "Paddy" Grayton and Dr. J. M. Whitlock. The two had served together in the Apache country, and Whitlock had accused Grayton of murdering some Apache men in cold blood. Meeting accidently on November 9, 1862, at Fort Stanton, the two quarreled; in an exchange of gunfire, Dr. Whitlock fatally shot Grayton. Whitlock was then in turn killed by Grayton's men, Company H of the New Mexican Volunteers. Colonel Kit Carson, commander at Fort Stanton, disarmed the company and arrested the ringleaders (Keleher 1952: 288–91). "The Ciénega" is a frequently used designation in the Spanish Southwest and, hence, is of little assistance in making a more positive identification.

202. The Eldodt Collection which Bandelier, in this entry, was arranging and, according to his July 11, 1885, entry, was also recording was purchased by Fred Harvey in 1926 (personal communication, Byron Harvey III, August 1969). Harvey, in his letter, also mentioned the existence of a Bandelier letter describing some of the Eldodt archaeological material. The ethnological material was not catalogued. The collection included a great deal of nineteenth-century pueblo pottery and some pueblo costume leather items, stoneware, etc., only bearing the label, "Eldodt Collection" with no further data. Three Spanish shields were also acquired. Part of the collection is in Albuquerque; the smaller items are at the Grand Canyon in the collection vault.

Bandelier painted a number of items from this collection while staying at San Juan Pueblo, and some of these paintings were later used as illustrations for the *Histoire*.

203. Bandelier frequently wrote articles for *Das Ausland* (see n 31). The letter that Bandelier referred to here was one of the seven which Professor Friedrich Ratzel published in *Das Ausland* in 1886. On July 6, 1885, Bandelier noted in his journal, "Painted and finished letter for Ratzel. Sent MSS. to him, 31 pp. This is the seventh letter to the Ausland." These appeared as "Briefe aus Neu-Mexico" von Adolf Bandelier [Letters from New Mexico, by Adolph Bandelier] in seven installments in *Das Ausland* (Band LIX, pp.

451–56; pp. 476–79; pp. 498–99; pp. 499–500; pp. 516–17 + ? [end page or pages missing]; pp. 535–38; and pp. 555–58). The first installment was dated Santa Fe (Neu-Mexico), 5 Juli 188⅞. The editors are not clear as to why the year was published in this manner, instead of using 1885.

In 1885, *Das Ausland* had published "Ein Brief von Adolf F. Bandelier über seine Reise im südwestlichen Nordamerika." This article had been written from Highland, Illinois, in 1883 (see Lange and Riley 1970: 149, 404n382).

204. This was Alexander Gusdorf, who was born in Germany in 1848 and who came to Santa Fe in 1864 at the request of his uncle, Zadoc Staab, a Santa Fe merchant of that day.

In 1871, Gusdorf established himself at Ranchos de Taos, where he became a successful miller, in 1880 establishing the first steam flour mill in New Mexico.

Gusdorf served as county commissioner of Taos County from 1880 to 1885 (Twitchell 1911–17: IV, 474–75).

Polk and Danser (1884a: 318, 341) also spelled this name as Gusdorf. He is listed as A. Gusdorf & Bro., general store and grist mill in Fernandez de Taos, and as postmaster of Ranches of Taos with a general store, flour and grist mill, and a dealer in livestock. Newspaper advertisements of the period support the Polk and Danser spelling.

205. There is little to identify the Mr. Campbell in this entry. The editors, however, believe it was Alejandro E. Campbell, seemingly not an Indian, who became a school-teacher at Santa Clara Pueblo. In the journal entry of May 19, 1888, Bandelier noted, "I met Alejandro." It is difficult to conclude from the wording, that this was actually their first meeting; in fact, it seems rather certain it was not. In the entry of May 21, two days later, Alejandro and the Santa Clara school were clearly associated. Bandelier must have respected his ability, as he entrusted Alejandro with copying the L'Archèvéque diligencias for him (see entry of May 31, 1888).

206. Bandelier's handwriting at this point was difficult to decipher. Benjamin Jegers, associate professor of foreign languages, Northern Illinois University, believes that Bandelier's reference was to the folktale, Goldenen Kohlen [The Golden Coals]. According to Matt T. Salo, assistant professor of anthropology, Northern Illinois University, this tale is widespread in European folklore; Salo, for example, cited versions from the Finnish literature.

207. This was probably Levi A. Hughes, whom Polk and Danser (1884a: 352) listed as deputy internal revenue collector of Santa Fe. Twitchell (1925: 469) stated Hughes was born in Minneapolis in 1858; from 1876 to 1879, he studied at the University of Indiana, Bloomington, founded by his grandfather. In 1879, he moved to Santa Fe, entering the employ of Watts and Herlow in the lumber trade; later, he engaged in the wool, sheep, and cattle trade, both in Santa Fe and in Denver. He was a leading figure in Republican circles, holding the office of chief deputy collector of Internal Revenue from 1883 to 1886. After creation of the Court of Private Land Claims, for determination of titles to Spanish and Mexican land grants in the Southwest, Hughes played a prominent role in revealing the fraudulent claim of James Addison Peralta-Reavis, which involved over half of Arizona and much of southwestern New Mexico. Upon the death of Rufus J. Palen, Hughes became president of the First National Bank of Santa Fe (*New Mexico Historical Review* 1933: 315).

208. This entry stated, "finished and sent off six letters for the *Ausland.*" There is a discrepancy here since in his entry of July 6, 1885, Bandelier noted that he had sent the MSS., 31 pp., to Ratzel. He added, "This is the seventh letter to the *Ausland.*" Perhaps Bandelier was incorrect in his use of abbreviations, making manuscripts plural, when he

intended to make it singular. However, the 31 pages, judging from the final publication (see n 203), seems unlikely for one letter and could well be correct for all seven letters.

209. There is no way of knowing if this was Eddy Huegy of Albuquerque (see ns 102 and 682), Bandelier's brother-in-law, or Eddie (Eddy) Franz of Santa Fe, son of Earhart D. Franz, businessman and friend of the Bandeliers (see ns 486 and 641). With no surname noted, it is more likely that the reference was to Eddy Huegy.

210. Miss Anna Reiss was presumably a relative of Dr. W. Reiss of Berlin; Bandelier had seen Dr. Reiss on a number of occasions when he visited Berlin earlier in 1885.

211. This was Dr. Carl Frenzel, #33 Koetheres Strasse, Berlin, Germany (see entry of June 27, 1885).

212. *Ayash-tyu-qotz* is a Keresan term commonly applied to the Tablita, or Corn, Dance. These ceremonies often occur, regularly, as a part of the celebration of major Catholic feast days among the Keresan and other pueblos (see Lange 1952; 1957; 1959: 612; Lange and Riley 1966: 258–62, 340–41).

213. The newspaper article on the Apaches was found in the Bandelier Scrapbook. Entitled "Der Indianer Ausbruch in Arizona und der Feldzug gegen die Apaches in Neu Mexiko," it was headed, "Für die Westl. Post von A. F. Bandelier." In addition to the title, Hodge (1932: 365) noted, *"Westliche Post,* St. Louis, June 21, 28, 1885" (see also n 236).

214. Personal correspondence from Dr. Alfonso Ortiz, August 19, 1969, gave this information: "Fr. Camilo Seux was a French priest, pastor at San Juan from 1868 until his death in 1922, a total of 54 years. He is buried beneath the Shrine to Our Lady of Lourdes in San Juan. He and Samuel Eldodt, the trader, were good friends and regularly refought World War I over the chess table, according to local tradition." For additional data, see Lange and Riley (1970: 412n451).

215. Chino was the nickname of José Dolores Ortiz, an Indian of San Juan Pueblo, whose native Tewa name was Te´-a-nyi (see n 253).

216. In neither the Lamy Memorial (1950) nor in Salpointe (1898) was there a mention of Father Castro, either at San Juan or elsewhere. In personal correspondence (August 19, 1969), Alfonso Ortiz provided the following information: "Fr. Juanito Castro was a pastor who preceded [Father Camilo] Seux in San Juan, who was a good friend of Seux, and who returned here [San Juan] to spend his last days after retirement. . . . He was very old when grandmother knew him."

According to Aberle, Watkins, and Pitney (1940: 184), José de Castro was a priest of the San Juan parish from July 5, 1829, to January 4, 1833, and again from November 2, 1833, to October 4, 1840. Father Seux, listed in the same source, began his service at San Juan Pueblo on July 15, 1868, serving until January 22, 1922.

217. There seem to be several misstatements in this entry. These are discussed in subsequent notes. Bandelier was beginning his work with a Tewa informant, a relative stranger, and the newness of their relationship may have been reflected in the nature of the data gathered. He was attempting a reconstruction of the history of San Juan Pueblo, a more difficult task than he possibly realized. Even today, there is not complete agreement as to San Juan history in terms of accurate historical records. Until Alfonso Ortiz's *The Tewa World* (1969) was published, no thorough and systematic study of San Juan had been made, although anthropologists had long recognized the importance of understanding the Tewas (see Parsons 1929). Ortiz (p. 3) quoted Eggan (1950: 315), "Of the Tewa specifically, he [Eggan] notes that they are 'the key group in any reconstruction of eastern Pueblo social organization.' "

After studying several varying accounts, both original sources and the secondary syntheses, in an attempt to correct any errors Bandelier might have made in his journals, we have found Schroeder (1953) and Hammond and Rey (1953) the most helpful for specific historical detail and Ortiz (1969) for ethnographic data. Unfortunately, neither the Schroeder publication nor that of Hammond and Rey seemingly used Bandelier's *Final Report* in regard to San Juan. See Schroeder (1953: 5–8) for his discussion of the history and the problems related to the history of San Juan Pueblo. See Hammond and Rey (1953: 16–36) for its introductory background on Oñate. We quote from the latter (p. 17) to give a frame of reference for the journal entries on Oj'qe, San Juan, San Juan de los Caballeros, Yunque, Yugue-Uing-ge, as well as the terms San Gabriel and San Gabriel del Yunque in the literature.

> From Santo Domingo, the Spaniards explored the nearby pueblos, and then, on July 11 [1598], at the Indian pueblo of Ohke [Bandelier's Oj-qué], they founded their first headquarters, or capital, on the east bank of the Rio Grande and named it San Juan de los Caballeros. Here they *remained for a few months* [italics added], but then they moved their camp to the Pueblo of Yunque, or Yugewinge [Bandelier's Yuge-ouinge], which they called San Gabriel, on the left bank of the Chama where it flows into the Rio Grande. This was a town of approximately four hundred houses and was more adequate for the needs of the Spanish forces. It remained the capital of New Mexico until Governor Don Pedro de Peralta, Oñate's successor, founded Santa Fé in 1610.
>
> . . . The main body of Oñate's colonists reached San Juan on August 18, 1598, having suffered from want of food on the way. The various parts of the expedition were now reunited in their new home. Immediately, after the homecoming, there was a great celebration, during which the first church in the new land was begun. Everyone helped with its construction, and on September 8th it was dedicated. . . .

Our emphasis on "remained for a few months," in the quotation above, perhaps touches on the key problem. In examining the Oñate journals, there is no sentence that actually stated when the Spaniards moved to San Gabriel. Leaving his army and carts at Caypa (Caypa is Santa Clara), which Hammond and Rey, in a note, explained was an error on the part of the person recording Oñate's itinerary (see Schroeder for comments), Oñate was gone from Oj-qué for almost a month, exploring other areas. He returned to San Juan on August 10, and on August 11 began an irrigation ditch (p. 322). The church was begun on August 23, 1598, and dedicated on September 8 of that year. It is unclear whether the ditch and church were at Oj-qué (San Juan de los Caballeros) or at Yuge-ouinge (San Gabriel).

Schroeder made much the same point, based on much more extensive research than ours. He wrote, "None of the original sources mention an actual move from one site to the other." He also found considerable disagreement as to San Gabriel's location (p. 6). Schroeder commented further, "Considering all the factors, it appears that Oñate first began to plan a separate settlement away from San Juan when the work on the irrigation ditch began in August 11, 1598. He did not establish headquarters at San Juan until the army arrived, August 19 [?]. When the padres were assigned to the various pueblos on September 9, the pueblo of San Juan as well as the city of San Francisco [de los Españoles, or San Gabriel] were listed. Thus, it appears that the main portion of the army was billeted at San Juan while the actual settlement of San Francisco [de los Españoles, or San Gabriel] was slowly being developed."

218. The "Ju-o-tyu-te" recorded in this entry is not the present-day Tewa name for San Juan. (In commenting on this statement, Ortiz wrote the editors, "He has something here! He meant Füⁿ ō chu te' which is a sacred term for any Tewa village in which the speaker

is. Thus, past Tewa and Tano villages of antiquity are referred to in this way. Usually used as a suffix to the proper name of the village in formal oratory and myth-telling.") Stubbs (1950: 39), citing Harrington (1916: 211), gave the form "Oke'onwi." While Ortiz (1969) provided numerous native terms for a variety of cultural phenomena, it is interesting that he gave no native designation for San Juan Pueblo itself. (Here, Ortiz responded, "Fair enough. This is where the native in me comes out. It never occured to me to list it or talk about it.")

In his *Final Report* (1890–92: I, 260n1), Bandelier gave the aboriginal name for San Juan as "Jyuo-tyo-te Oj-ke." In this journal entry, however, Oj-qué clearly was the initial word of the next sentence and separated from "Ju-o-tyu-te." Harrington (p. 212) stated he had not questioned the Tewa about "Jyuo-tyu-te" but felt the spelling had a "non-Tewa appearance."

Schroeder, as well as Hammond and Rey, did not cite Harrington on 'Oke. Harrington (p. 212) wrote, " . . . the present pueblo of San Juan [is] according to tradition the third to which the name has been applied." In a subsequent sentence, after giving the various forms of 'Oke from several sources, including Bandelier, he stressed that "all apply to present San Juan, no mention of the pueblo ruins to which this name is applied being there made."

It is possible that this journal entry, "Oj-qué is two miles up the river on the same bank and was abandoned probably during the time of the Spaniards," referred to one of those ruins by the same name to which Harrington made reference. For some reason, Bandelier failed to include this in the discussion in his *Final Report*. (In reference to this paragraph, Ortiz wrote as follows: "There was an O'ke:owinge a mile or so up river on the east bank, but floods and erosion have washed most of it away. It is distinguished from present-day O'ke: by words such as Se'da (old) or Pa ře (first). It is regarded as an earlier home of the community.")

Bandelier also recorded a tale at San Juan which included the founding of the pueblo of Oj-que (see entry of June 26, 1885, and the accompanying notes).

219. The San Juan Pueblo church to which Bandelier referred here is no longer in existence. Kubler (1940) depicted in Illustration 201 this church as it appeared about 1900. Regarding the accuracy of the age of the church as given to Bandelier, see Adams and Chávez (1956: 85n1). Ortiz (1969: 142) noted that a church had been in existence on the edge of the plaza "at least since 1726." The beams of the old church were acquired by the Harvey Company for its inn, El Ortiz, at Lamy (Kubler 1940: 42n18).

220. San Ildefonso is still an occupied village; it dates from pre-Spanish times. In the Tewa language, the people call their pueblo *pok-wo ghay ongwe*, "pueblo where the water cuts down through." Oñate first named it Bove, later changing it to San Ildefonso in honor of the seventh-century Archbishop of Toledo. Its mission was erected in 1617; its grant was confirmed by act of Congress, December 22, 1858, for 17,292 acres. Such writers as Parsons (1929; 1939), Harrington (1916), and Ortiz (1969) have written about aspects of San Ildefonso tribal culture. Whitman (1947) devoted an entire volume to the study of San Ildefonso culture.

221. Bandelier's wording "abandoned probably since the Conquest" appears to be either wrong or, at best, ambiguous. In his *Final Report* (1890–92: II, 63), Bandelier either corrected or clarified the statement. Placing the site of Pioge three miles north of San Juan Pueblo and noting that Pioge was smaller than Abiquiu but of similar arrangement, he continued, "Considerable pottery has been exhumed from Pio-ge, and handsome specimens are in Mr. Eldodt's possession [see n 202]. Among them are sacrificial bowls with the turreted rim that characterizes those vessels, and the symbolic paintings of the rain-clouds, of water-snakes, and of the libella. Similar fetiches of alabaster have also been unearthed. Pio-ge is claimed by the Tehuas of San Juan as one of their ancient villages,

and they assert that it was abandoned previous to Spanish times." Harrington (1916: 203) cited Bandelier verbatim and without comment, apparently expressing concurrence.

222. Schroeder and Matson (1965: 121) discussed both the pueblo of Pioge (L. A. 144) and Sajiu (L. A. 547) in reference to Gaspar Castaño de Sosa's journal of 1590–91. They believed it was possible that in the January 12, 1591, entry, Castaño was referring to these two sites on the east bank of the Rio Grande, north of San Juan Pueblo. Pioge, a large ruin, is three miles above San Juan; Sajiu, a smaller ruin almost eroded away by the river, is located about a mile north of Pioge. Both ruins exhibit Biscuit B, Sankawi Black-on-cream, and late glaze pottery, suggesting occupation into the middle and late 1500s. The Tewas claim both pueblos, and they say that Pioge was an ancestral home prior to the coming of the Spaniards. If the Indians meant abandoned before the 1598 settlement of Spaniards at San Gabriel rather than prior to the coming of Coronado in 1540, then their tradition correlates well with the ceramic evidence. Either could have been occupied at the time of Castaño (see n 221).

Regarding the name Sajiu for the one ruin, it is interesting to note that Bandelier, in the *Final Report* (1890–92: I, 305), reported that he was given this name in a rather different context. "I have lately discovered among the Tehuas the existence of another member of the cluster of 'Pato-abu' [ceremonial leaders]. Her title is 'Sa-jiu,' and she wields a great, though strictly occult power. The Tehuas are not the only Pueblo Indians among whom this office of a female chief exists. Mr. Cushing found it with the Zuñis. . . ."

223. Entries of this nature make it extremely difficult to justify any attempt at positive identification, particularly since Bandelier's informant was a San Juan Indian rather than a Taos. In his *Final Report* (1890–92: II, 32–33), Bandelier said he had never examined the ruins and garden plots that were supposed to be near Ranchos de Taos. The name, "Toma-Pooge," was not used in the *Final Report*. Harrington (1916: 185–86) used both a Taos and a Picuris term to refer to a pueblo ruin located at the modern village of Ranchos de Taos. He quoted Spinden as saying that it was quite a modern ruin, its population having been depleted by disease, with at least some of the survivors going to Taos and some to Picuris (p. 186).

Parsons (1936: 11) reported a Taos Indian tradition that the old site of Ranchos de Taos was originally Taos, but that the people there had become mixed with Mexicans and had disappeared as a cultural entity. Pearce (1965: 130) also noted a pre-Spanish settlement of Taos Indians at Ranchos de Taos and gave 1716 as the date of the Spanish settlement there. See F. H. Ellis and J. J. Brody (1964: 316–37) for their discussion of ceramic stratigraphy and tribal history at Taos Pueblo. The abstract (p. 316) and pp. 324–25 included data on the Ranchos de Taos ruins. There was no evidence for a Tewa-speaking pueblo at Ranchos de Taos. Excavations at other ruins in the Ranchos de Taos area have also been reported on by Peckham and Reed (1963). In addition to the summary data of Ellis and Brody, see Davis (1959: 73–84), G. L. Trager (1946), and Whorf and Trager (1937) for discussions of the Taos language and its affiliations.

Pearce (1965: 130) stated that Ranchos de Taos, in 1837, was called San Francisco del Rancho de Taos. The famous St. Francis of Assisi Church was built in 1772 by Franciscan missionaries. There was a post office, Ranches of Taos, in 1875.

In any case, there does not seem to have been a Tewa-speaking pueblo at the Ranchos. One must remember in such instances that Bandelier's informant, a Tewa Indian, may well have been practicing a bit of "nationalism."

224. Te-ouyi would seem to be the same pueblo ruin currently known as Te'ewi (L. A. 252). Harrington (1916: 154) actually differentiated between Te'ewi ("little cottonwood gap") and Te'ewi-onwikeji ("little cottonwood gap ruin"). Wendorf (1953: 34n2) commented that they had shortened Harrington's form for obvious reasons. Partial excava-

tions were carried out at this site during the 1950 and 1951 seasons; the report was published in 1953 (Wendorf 1953: 34–93). The site was occupied from approximately 1250 to 1500 A.D. (see also the entry of August 24, 1885, and n 390).

225. A-bé-chiu, or present-day Abiquiu, is some eighteen miles northwest of Española on U.S. highway 84. It was settled in 1747 and resettled in 1754 on the site of a Tewa ruin that was probably abandoned in the sixteenth century. In 1776, Escalante mentioned the settlement of Santa Rosa de Abiquiu (Twitchell 1911–17: III, 524). The name Abiquiu seems to be a Spanish corruption of the Tewa name, *pay shoo boo-oo* (timber-end town), for San Juan Pueblo. In turn, the Tewa-speakers took the new Spanish approximation and gave it a folk etymology, "chokecherry end," *abay,* "chokecherry" (Pearce 1965: 1).

226. Bandelier, in his *Final Report* (1890–92: II, 51–52), wrote, "about five miles from the little town [El Rito] and thirty meters above the bank of the stream, lies the very large pueblo ruin, called by the Tehuas Se-pä-ue. I consider it to be the largest in New Mexico, and it could shelter more people than Casa Grande in Arizona. I have given the plan of the ruin on Plate I (Fig. 8), and it clearly belongs to the type of the Ojo Caliente Pueblos. ...." In his *Histoire,* Bandelier included a groundplan sketch of Sapawe. Burrus (1969b: 211) listed it in his Catalogue as Item 495; in his Supplement (1969c), Burrus included a reproduction, XXII, in color, of Bandelier's sketch.
Partial excavations of this tremendous ruin were carried out for several seasons in the middle 1960s by University of New Mexico Summer Field School groups under the direction of Dr. Florence Hawley Ellis. As yet, the principal report on this work has not been published.

227. Regarding this ruin, Harrington (1916: 170) wrote, "Bandelier's 'P'o-nyi Pa-kuen' is almost certainly his spelling for Poñi-pa' ᵃ-kwajè. ...." Harrington described it as the pueblo ruin "of the plumed arroyo shrub beds height." Harrington believed the location for this ruin given by Bandelier in his *Final Report* (1890–92: II, 53) was erroneous. Large mounds lying on the mesa top mark the site of this ancient Tewa village (Harrington 1916: Map 7).

228. As other notes in the accompanying volumes (Lange and Riley 1966; 1970) amply demonstrate, the Rito de los Frijoles was a favorite place for Bandelier. The canyon and vicinity became the locale of Bandelier's novels, *Die Köshare* and *The Delight Makers,* the German and English editions both published in 1890 (see n 50). The story involved interaction and conflict between the Keresans and the Tewas, puebloan peoples who still occupy villages along the Rio Grande south and north of Frijoles, respectively, and who still claim the canyon as their former homes.
Here, Bandelier was obtaining information from Chino, a San Juan Indian, including Tewa terms and designations; earlier, he had gathered similar and even more data from the Keresan viewpoint as expressed by various Cochiti Indians (see Lange and Riley 1966: 452; see also Hendron 1946).

229. With this entry of June 14, 1885, and his notes on the lengthy conversation with Chino, a San Juan informant, Bandelier was clearly returning to his long-standing interest (see Lange and Riley 1966; 1970) in learning the puebloan designations for Southwestern ruins. This correlation of archaeological and linguistic (ethnological) distributions was a prime aspect of Bandelier's attempts at cultural reconstructions. That his overall achievement suffered from a lack of sophistication, in part attributable to the pioneering period in which he worked, there is no doubt. On the other hand, there is also no doubt that he recognized the importance of attempting such correlations.
To the careful, interested reader, it is readily apparent that Bandelier made certain

modifications of his journal field notes in the writing and publication of his *Final Report* (1890–92).

Similar early appreciation of the general problem is seen in the work of Harrington (1916). Leaning heavily on Bandelier's data, alternately confirming or modifying specific details, Harrington added many more data, including more precise linguistic designations.

With these appraisals in mind, the comments by Wendorf and Reed (1955: 159) acquire greater accuracy. In terms of sophistication, their statement, "The first general correlation of archaeology and language was by Mera in 1935 (pp. 36–39)" can be accepted as valid. At the same time, an assumption that Mera's work was the initial conceptualization of the problem would be unfortunate.

230. In the *National Zeitung* of Berlin in 1886, Bandelier published an article, "San Bernardino Chalchihuapan. Ein mexikanisches Abenteuer." This was the first journal entry referring to preparation of the manuscript. His entry of June 18, 1885, noted he was working "at the letter for Berlin" and on June 27, 1885, he noted finishing "San Bernardino Chalchihuapan" (see also ns 287 and 830).

231. This was O. W. Meysenburg of St. Louis, who in the *Santa Fe Daily New Mexican* of March 17, 1883, was listed as one of the directors of the new Santa Fe Water and Improvement Company. Also listed from St. Louis was Robert E. Carr. Other directors were: T. B. Catron, W. W. Griffin, and H. L. Warren of Santa Fe (Lange and Riley 1970: 431n109). Lange and Riley (p. 431n109) cited Polk and Danser (1884a: 354) where Robert E. Carr was given as president and O. W. Meysenberg [*sic*] as secretary and manager of the Water Improvement Co. Mr. Meysenburg was the son-in-law of General Robert Carr (Lange and Riley 1970: 434n134). Gould (1885: 805) listed Otto W. Meysenburg as a member of an iron and steel company in St. Louis but made no mention of his Santa Fe business interests.

232. More than once during this period, Bandelier wrote Joe via friends in St. Louis or Edwardsville. He seemed to have believed that letters sent directly to Highland might be intercepted, perhaps even by the postal officials.

233. According to Polk and Danser (1884a: 346), Julius Flersheim and Louis Baer operated a general merchandise store, Flersheim & Baer, on Railroad Ave., near the depot in San Marcial.

234. This was the article, "The Apache Outbreak," which was published in *The Nation* on July 2, 1885. A clipping of the article is in the Bandelier Scrapbook. Note 213 states that Bandelier had sent an article for the St. Louis newspaper, *Die Westliche Post,* dealing with similar subject matter just two days prior to this entry.

235. The novel to which Bandelier referred here was undoubtedly the unfinished manuscript of *Die Köshare,* from which he had read to several colleagues while on his visit in Germany earlier in the year (see entry of February 11, 1885, and n 50).

236. This was the second part of the Apache article cited in n 213; the article appeared in the *Westliche Post* on June 28, 1885.

237. John W. Symington was a physician in Santa Fe. Polk and Danser (1884a: 354) misspelled the name, omitting the "g." La Farge (1959: 127–28) cited an account in the *Santa Fe Daily New Mexican* of April 16, 1886, that described the unsuccessful lynch-hanging of Theodore Baker in which "Dr. Symington, the prison physician," was ultimately involved. McKenney (1888: 486) listed Symington as secretary of the Texas, Santa Fe, and Northern Railroad Co. in Santa Fe. In the *Santa Fe Daily New Mexican* of February 13, 1888, which gave an account of Archbishop John B. Lamy's death, there was an added comment that "Drs. Longwill [see n 457] and Symington" had been in attendance for the past four weeks (La Farge 1959: 132–33).

238. Don Pedro Sánchez was a relative of Antonio José Martínez, priest and stormy political figure (Grant 1934: 107–9). For a short time, 1880–84, Sánchez served as Pueblo Indian Agent; appointed by President Chester A. Arthur, he resigned when Grover Cleveland became president (Sánchez 1903: 45).

Westphall (1965: 105, 107) noted that Sánchez was indicted as the silent partner of M. Salazar, a land attorney at Las Vegas, in a case involving nineteen fraudulent homestead entries made in the interest of Sánchez. This was but one part of lengthy court proceedings (1883–86) in which Max Frost, register of the Land Office, Santa Fe, and a leading figure in the Santa Fe Ring (see Lamar 1966: 136–70), finally succeeded in having all charges against him dropped (Westphall 1965: 106–11).

239. Don Juan García was a well-to-do Spanish-American farmer and cattleman who lived in a relatively grand house where the San Juan Mercantile Co. is now located. He had two Navajo girls working for him, whom he either bought or traded for. He also had a Navajo man working for him, but apparently as a free citizen (personal communication, Alfonso Ortiz, August 19, 1969).

240. Father Seux spoke as if this had been a rather recent occurrence. We know of no case where the Pueblo Indians buried alive individuals convicted of witchcraft, or, for that matter, of any other crime.

241. This was presumably the early draft of Bandelier's *Final Report,* ultimately published by the Archaeological Institute of America in two parts, in 1890 and 1892. Bandelier had written to Mr. Parkman, April 5, 1885, from Highland, after his return from Europe and prior to the bank failure. At that time, he indicated his plans for proceeding with the report (see n 73).

242. This seems to refer to the primordial lake from which the tribal political leaders, Towa é, come (Ortiz 1969: 79–80). Bandelier's Po-qui may be Ohange Pokwinge, "The Lake of Emergence," or "Sand Lake," to which the dead go (Parsons 1929: 64, 68). Parsons (p. 64), however, did not equate this with the Keresan *shipapu,* the underworld to the north.

243. As Ortiz (1969: 4) has pointed out, dual organization is extremely important in Tewa society. Moiety structure and the associated tendency to think in dualistically contrasting sets are basic in understanding the Tewa tribes.

244. Victor Mindeleff, whose study of Pueblo architecture was written in 1886–87 and published in 1891, appears to have been one of the earliest to adopt the word *kiva* in the literature. He wrote, "Such ceremonial rooms are known usually by the Spanish term 'estufa,' meaning literally a stove and here used in the sense of 'sweat house,' but the term is misleading, as it more properly describes the small sweat houses that are used ceremonially by lodge-building Indians, such as the Navajo. At the suggestion of Major [J. W.] Powell the Tusayan [Hopi] word for this everpresent feature of pueblo architecture has been adopted, as being more appropriate. The word 'kiva,' then, will be understood to designate the ceremonial chamber of the pueblo building peoples, ancient and modern" (Mindeleff 1891: 111).

245. The summer moiety at San Juan Pueblo is *payopiiwent'owa,* or, more commonly, *kaye t'owa;* the winter moiety is called *teᵉnopiiwent'owa,* or, more commonly, *oyiket-'owa,* "ice people." The moieties are also sometimes referred to as *akompiye,* "south" (summer moiety), and *pimpiye,* "north" (winter moiety). The summer moiety is associated with femaleness, its chief being called "mother," or "old woman," and the winter moiety is male, its chief being called "father," or "old man" (Parsons 1929: 90–91; see also Parsons 1939: I, 129–30).

The ceremonial clown societies, Kossa (warm, summer) and Kwirana (cold, winter), may at one time have been associated with the two moieties, but at present, each group draws from both moieties (Ortiz 1969: 83, 144; Parsons 1929: 126). These clown societies are clearly related to the Cochiti (and other Keresan) Koshare and Kwirena societies; however, due to certain fundamental differences in the various religious organizations, the parallels are not actually as close as Bandelier's remarks would seem to suggest (see Lange 1959: 602–3; Parsons 1939: II, 1243).

246. Here, Bandelier seems again to have confused the moieties and the clown societies. Moieties are patrilineal, but recruitment from one moiety to the other is also practiced by initiation. As Ortiz (1969: 44) noted, "What is indicated is that there is no clear and unambiguous rule of recruitment into the moieties. The absence of a rule has always given a rather fuzzy quality to the Tewa data, but it is just this flexibility which has insured the survival of the system. . . ."

Women may or may not join their husband's moiety at marriage, depending on a number of circumstances (Parsons 1929: 95–96). Membership in the two clown societies is by trespass or by dedication (Parsons 1929: 125–26).

247. The cacique has been, and is, an important religious leader in most southwestern puebloan tribes, the primary exceptions being among the Hopi villages and at Zuñi where there is no cacique.

Where present, the details surrounding this official vary. In the entry of December 4, 1885, Bandelier noted that "At Acoma, they have three caciques now." Elsewhere among the Keresans, there is commonly but one cacique, the principal medicine man, the "mother" and the "father" of his "children," all the tribal members. At Cochiti, he is the headman of the Flint Medicine Society. Among the Tewas, the position is a dual one, there being a Summer Cacique and a Winter Cacique. There may also be interim, or pro tem, caciques—individuals who carry on much of the work of the office although they have not been properly installed and, hence, are not fully qualified.

In the traditional puebloan religious hierarchy, the cacique and his principal helpers, headmen of other medicine societies, annually appoint secular officers to their "elected" positions, thereby assuring the tribe of an ongoing traditionally oriented leadership (see Parsons 1939; Lange 1959; Ortiz 1969; and other monographs for further details).

248. There can be little doubt that Bandelier was quite aware of differences among the several pueblos regarding specific numbers and duties of the numerous officials. On the other hand, the conflicting or varying descriptions of these organizations were generally left unsynthesized by Bandelier, thereby producing rather confused accounts from which to extract any semblance of structural order. It may well have been that for particular periods of time, the structure remained, in fact, in flux, and improvisations were operant —a possibility occasionally overlooked by those prone to assuming a greater degree of rigid "system" than was actually the case.

For a discussion of choice of officers among the Tewa, see Parsons (1929: 102–7).

249. The *principales* of an Indian pueblo are commonly the current major officers and a council of all ex-officers, roughly speaking what Ortiz (1969: 79–103 et seq.), for the Tewa, called the "Made People." Keresan parallels were described for Cochiti by Lange (1959: 213–16).

250. In the 1880–82 journals, the editors standardized the varying forms recorded by Bandelier to "kachina" (Lange and Riley 1966: 110n89). At that time, they noted that a number of other forms had been used by various writers, some trying to write the word phonetically. Among the Keresans, such as Santo Domingo and Cochiti, the form "ka'atsina" is more common.

251. Nambé, a Tewa-speaking pueblo, still bears some resemblance to its plan as described in 1776 by Fray Francisco Atanasio Domínguez. The earliest reference to a church there was in 1613. In the 1680 Rebellion, the resident Franciscan priest was martyred and the church burned. Nambé also took part in the 1696 Rebellion. In the

nineteenth century, there was a steady decrease in population, owing in part to executions for witchcraft. This trend was reversed about the turn of the century, and the present population is about 200 (Schroeder and Matson 1965: 115–16). The reader is referred to Ellis's "Archaeological History of Nambé Pueblo, 14th Century to the Present" (1964a: 34–42). Analysis of sherds excavated in village ash piles in 1962 indicated the people of Nambé have utilized this site from 1350 to the present. Ellis also discussed ancestral Nambé pueblos.

252. Santa Clara was a pre-Spanish, Tewa-speaking pueblo. Located on the west bank of the Rio Grande two miles below Española, it was probably founded in the fourteenth century (Stubbs 1950: 43). Stubbs further noted that the double quadrangle arrangement noted by Bandelier in the 1880s existed to the present but that the older houses were falling into disrepair and that the new construction was taking place away from the plazas. The kivas are rectangular, surface structures, and free-standing, i.e., not incorporated in the house blocks.

253. Bandelier had been aware of and interested in pueblo witchcraft in general and of Nambé witchcraft specifically ever since arriving in New Mexico (Lange and Riley 1966: 96, 96n84; 1970: 173, 174).

The account of witchcraft contained in this June 18, 1885, entry was typed verbatim by Bandelier and entitled, "Relation of the Execution and preceding Manner of Discovery of the Sorcerers of the Pueblo of Nambé." This copy was found by the editors in the Catron Collection (PC 29 807). To it, Bandelier added, "This is a true copy of my Journal. But Dolores, alias CHINO, Té-a-nyi by his Tewa name, told me more about the death of the woman. I recollect it distinctly, although I did not put it down at the time. It runs as follows . . ."

Bandelier then recorded his recollections of Chino's remarks. Though the journal entry of Chino's account was made on June 18, 1885, the typewritten account was dated November 24, 1888, Santa Fe, and was signed "Ad. F. Bandelier." In the final paragraph of the typewritten account, he mentioned the reports of both Luján (see n 1017) and Chino. Bandelier stated that Luján's account was the more correct as he had been "present at least at a part of the Tragedy," while Chino "had it from hearsay."

254. For a comprehensive and relatively recent study of Navajo witchcraft, the reader is referred to Kluckhohn's study (1944) by that title, *Navaho Witchcraft*. See accompanying bibliography.

255. This was Henry Dronne of New York City. Virtually nothing has been learned of this person aside from the facts that Bandelier had corresponded with him and had visited him when he was in the East in the autumn of 1884, working at the Lenox Library and attempting to market his paintings and manuscripts (Lange and Riley 1970: 346, 348, 349).

256. Santa Cruz was founded by De Vargas as a villa, the second one in New Mexico (after Santa Fe), in 1695 on the ruins of a presumably Tewa pueblo and near an earlier seventeenth-century Spanish settlement. The city was entitled "La Villa Nueva de Santa Cruz de los Españoles Mejicanos del Rey Nuestro Señor Carlos Segundo," but was commonly referred to in official records of the eighteenth century as "La Villa Nueva de Santa Cruz de la Cañada" (Pearce 1965: 148–49; Hewett and Mauzy 1940: 60).

257. In Bandelier's *Final Report* (1890: I, 25), he wrote of "Galisteo or Ta-ge-uing-ge proper." In the companion volume (1892: II, 100, 122), he said the Spaniards called the Tano village of T'a-ge-Uing-ge "Santa Cruz de Galisteo." At one time, it was called "Ximera" by the Spaniards.

258. Here, the interregnum referred to the period between 1680 and 1692, following the Pueblo Revolt of 1680, when the Spanish Crown exercised no effective rule in New

Mexico. Interpueblo warfare was carried on, partly in terms of old enmities but probably more as a direct result of differences among the various pueblo tribes that attacked, remained neutral toward, or even were sympathetic to the Spaniards. These reactions, themselves, undoubtedly reflected to some extent the old-time interpuebloan alliances and conflicts.

259. In his *Final Report* (1890–92: II, 61–62n2), Bandelier gave another explanation for the name, "San Juan de los Caballeros." His explanation has been used frequently in the literature. Briefly stated, it was that the "de los Caballeros" honored the Indians of the pueblo of Yuge-ouinge who turned their entire village over to Oñate and his men in 1598 so the Spaniards would have a place to live while building San Gabriel. The Indians went to live with other Tewa Indians across the Rio Grande at Oj-qué, subsequently called "San Juan de los Caballeros." Bandelier noted that this disposed of the fable that the title "Caballeros" had been given to the San Juan Indians for their loyalty to Spain during the 1680 insurrection. Actually, the San Juan Indians had been among the most bitter of the rebels. Adams and Chavez, seemingly citing the identical passage in Villagrá upon which Bandelier had based his interpretation, gave quite a different explanation (1956: 89n6).

260. Los Luceros, or Lucero, is a small settlement three miles north of Alcalde in Rio Arriba County, some ten miles from Española. A post office was established at Plaza de los Luceros in 1855, and in 1877 the name was changed to Plaza del Alcalde. The post office was discontinued in 1882 (Pearce 1965: 91, 93).

Lucero was named for the famous Lucero de Godoy family whose founder, Pedro Lucero de Godoy, came to New Mexico early in the seventeenth century. In 1616–17, Lucero was one of the soldiers who escorted the wagon train bringing supplies to New Mexico from the south. At that time, he was only sixteen or seventeen years old. Pedro Lucero was married in Santa Fe by, or before, 1628. He died prior to the Pueblo Revolt of 1680, but several of his family, including his second wife, were killed by the Indians.

Pedro's eldest son, Juan Lucero de Godoy, was *alcalde mayor* of Santa Fe in 1680. Escaping south with Otermín, he returned to New Mexico in 1693. In the eighteenth century, the Lucero family became quite widespread in New Mexico, in both the Rio Arriba and Rio Abajo districts (Chavez 1954: 59–61, 209–11).

261. It is impossible to convert such vague descriptions of pottery wares to designations presently recognized by Southwestern archaeologists. The green and black suggests European, or European-influenced, wares; the cream and black sherds may well have been of the Sankewi Black-on-cream or even of the Biscuit A, Biscuit B, or Wiyo Black-on-white types. The red and black—glossy—sherds may have been, at least in part, pre-Spanish glazed wares. (For discussion of pottery types, see Hawley 1950; Mera 1935; Stubbs and Stallings 1953; for discussion of Bandelier's use of the term glossy, see n 616.)

262. Although we tend to blame outside pothunters and relic collectors for the looting of Southwestern ruins, it must be pointed out that Indians themselves have commonly mined the ruins for manos, metates, potsherds to grind as temper for new pots, and various other items, as illustrated by the collection here for a medicine bundle.

263. Maseua and Oyoyaua, or Masewe and Oyoyewe, are the Twin War Gods, common to virtually all pueblos. For discussions of variations, the reader should consult specific books and monographs on the tribes. For the Tewa, Parsons (1929: 144–45, 145n285, 145n288, 268, 272; 1939:26–1043 passim) and Ortiz (1969: 61–77, 91–97, 162n12) are particularly helpful.

264. The Lamy Memorial (1950: 52) listed Father J. B. Courbon as a priest at Abiquiu from 1882 to 1889.

265. This was Juan Picard, one of the priests added by Lamy to the Santa Fe diocese (Salpointe 1898: 283). Salpointe (1893: 10) listed Joannes Picard at Mora, N. M., in 1888.

Bandelier's use of the term "Abbé" is interesting as he tended to write Padre or Father when referring to Catholic clergymen. In spite of the many French priests brought to the Southwest by Lamy, the French "Abbé" was seldom retained.

266. In 1885, L(eBaron). Bradford Prince was a former chief justice of New Mexico, having been appointed in 1879 and having resigned in 1882. He was one of the prominent figures in New Mexico during the late nineteenth and early twentieth centuries. Born in New York, Prince came to New Mexico in 1879; he died in 1923. (See Lange and Riley 1970: 429n102; see also bibliography of the present volume for leads to Prince's considerable writings on New Mexico, both in history and anthropology [Prince 1883; 1912; 1915].)

267. This was P. L. Van der Veer, a Santa Fe attorney (Hobbs 1942b: 117).

268. This was Aaron M. Adler. Born of Jewish parents in Baltimore, Maryland, Adler had come to New Mexico in 1881 and subsequently worked as a salesman for Samuel Eldodt, Charles Ilfeld in Las Vegas, and Thomas Burns in Tierra Amarilla. In 1890, Adler purchased the mercantile establishment of T. Romero and Sons, Wagon Mound (Anonymous 1895: 272–73).

269. For comments on the famous Apache chief, Mangas Coloradas, see Lange and Riley (1970: 418n3). Keleher (1952: 293–95) provided details concerning the murder of Mangas Coloradas.

270. Fort West was a small fort at the junction of the Gila and Mangas rivers in Grant County, southwest New Mexico (Pearce 1965: 59).

271. These were probably not actual tambourines; it is more likely that they were the Plains Indian flat drum, often with single head, which was used among the northern Rio Grande Pueblo tribes with a light hoop-stick beater.

272. See Parsons (1929: Plate 34) for an illustration of the "flag." This is more akin to a decorated lance, or wand, than to the much longer, decorated pole commonly associated with Rio Grande puebloan Tablita, or Corn, Dances (see Lange 1957 for comparisons of these ceremonies).

273. A painting of *Kwitara* dancers, Tesuque Pueblo, was reproduced by Parsons (1929: Plate 34); in recent years, these ceremonies are commonly referred to as "Plains Dances," "Comanche Dances," "War Dances," etc. Parsons (Plates 31, 32, and 33) also included photographs of *Kwitara* ceremonies at San Ildefonso Pueblo.

274. In the *Final Report* (1890–92: I, 263), Bandelier stated that "The Sar-it-ye Jia-re, or dance of the French, of the Tewas was imported from the Kiowas"—Indians of the southern Plains.

Further, Parsons (1929: 169) listed a celebration at San Juan on June 24 (San Juan's Day), 1926: "Relay race or fraseshare, French (war) dance."

275. Presumably, Bandelier was talking here about the Llanos Estacados (Staked Plains) of eastern New Mexico and western Texas.

276. Montezuma legends and dances that focus on a mythological Montezuma figure have been common for many years in the greater Southwest. Bandelier's statement, then, is not surprising.

The Opata are a Taracahatian-speaking group of farming Indians, the acculturated remnants still living in northern Sonora. Presumably, after his travels in that area in 1884, Bandelier would have been able to recognize Opata words.

The real Montezuma (who bore little relationship to the latter-day mythological one) was Montezuma II, Aztec king from c. 1503 to 1520. He was taken hostage by Cortés in 1519 and killed a few months later in circumstances that, even today, remain unclear. After a short reign by Cuitlahuac, the heroic Cuauhtemoc led the Aztecs in their final days.

Bandelier had an enduring interest in Montezuma. As early as December 1873, he mentioned Montezuma in correspondence with Morgan (White 1940: I, 112). In the 1880–82 journals, there were frequent references to Montezuma (Lange and Riley 1966: 79n64, 94n82, 130, 138, 142, 155, 179, 211, 261). The topic appeared also in the 1883–84 journals (1970: 47, 158, 506). White (1940: I, 112n8) noted that Bandelier, in 1892, published in the *American Anthropologist* an article entitled, "The 'Montezuma' of the Pueblo Indians." According to Hodge (1932: 368), this article was also printed separately.

277. Parsons (1929: 217) stated that the Matachine Dance at Santa Clara was called *Poseyemu bu share* (Poseyemu his dance). The Matachine was supposed to have been also brought to Nambé by Poseyemu.

At San Juan, this folk hero was again identified with Montezuma; he was allegedly conceived when Opa'chutse (World Man) threw a piñon nut into the mouth of a girl, despised by her people. The child born to this maiden was called "No-names," but was given fine attire by his father and also the name *"Posew'e bi poseyému"* ("Dew kickball dew falls"). He became the father and ruler of all Indians (Parsons 1929: 276–77). Parsons also recognized other puebloan parallels: at Zuñi, at Jemez, and at Cochiti (p. 276n535). For additional details on the Cochiti Po' shai-añi, see Lange (1959: 267–68, 355).

Of interest here are two published stories relating to Po-Se and Po-Se-Yemo. The editors' attention was called to the latter by Dr. Theodore R. Frisbie. It appeared in Blanche C. Grant's *Taos Indians* (1925: 123–27). Entitled "Po-Se-Yemo," it was described as "an unpublished manuscript by Ad. F. Bandelier owned by Anthony Joseph of Ojo Caliente, N. M. Bandelier was one of the greatest scholars who ever came to the southwest. He worked here during the eighties." Goad's bibliography (1939) included " 'Po-Se': A tale of San Ildefonso," which was published in the *New Mexico Historical Review*, Vol. I, July 1926, pp. 335–49. Goad noted, "This ms. was left by Bandelier with Mrs. Samuel Eldodt of Chamita, N. M., probably written in 1885."

278. For further data on Yuqueyunque, see ns 392, 419, and 623.

279. Even today, the koshare, painted clowns and tricksters, play a major role in urging on stragglers and cheering the tired children or other participants in various religious dances.

280. Bandelier, in this entry, and Parsons (1939: 249–52) both recorded a San Juan origin myth which contained certain similarities, although Bandelier's informant, Chino, included parts of the Poseyemo, or Montezuma, tale with the origin myth. Bandelier's account gave some prominence to a fish taboo by "the Navajos, Apaches, and some of the Pueblos, even," while the account by Parsons made no mention of such a taboo.

In fact, Parsons (1929: 141–50), in two recorded versions of the San Juan origin myth, stated that there was no fish taboo among the Tewas (pp. 141–42n279). (See Bandelier [1890–92: I, 304–5; II, 60] for further discussion of Tewa mythology and also n 281.)

Without addressing the question of fish taboos as recorded at San Juan by Bandelier (1890–92: II, 60), Ortiz (1969: 79–80, 163–64n1) suggested the possibility of a mistranslation of the term "Patowa" from the origin myth as told at San Juan. Ortiz suggested the alternative of "Made People" for Patowa. This variance would render conceptualization of details in the origin myth rather differently from the accounts by Bandelier and Parsons. Although the editors are in agreement with Ortiz that Parsons equated "pat-'owa" with "fish people" (Parsons 1929: 141, 141–42n279), they are not convinced that Bandelier had made this correlation earlier. Also, it should be noted that Parsons's text and footnote, as well as her line of questioning, suggest that she was puzzled by this translation.

It is possible that the editors have failed to find the specific data in Bandelier (1890) to which Ortiz (1969: 79) referred, attributing the initial designation of Patowa as "Fish People" to Bandelier. The Bandelier citations from Part I of the *Final Report* given above, although containing many of the same data contained in the journals, did not translate Pato-abu (Pat'owa, Patowa) as "fish." Bandelier (1890–92: II, 60) gave nearly a verbatim recounting of this journal entry. Apparently, the "Pato-abu" (1890–92: I, 305) was Parsons's "pat'owa" and Ortiz's "Patowa." Both Bandelier and Parsons recognized this classification of important ceremonial individuals, but were not successful in learning the complete ceremonial context. Ortiz is to be credited for his analysis of these confusing data and relating them to the origin myth. The varying versions of the origin myth, the years between the studies by Bandelier and Parsons and the work of Ortiz, as well as the sophistication of different informants, have contributed to the complexity of the problem.

281. Bandelier's origin tale for the San Juan Indians differs considerably from the tales recorded by Parsons (1929) and Ortiz (1969). For a recent discussion of the Tewa origin story, see Ortiz (pp. 13–16).

282. See n 308 for Bandelier's comments on his actual visit to this ruin.

283. The site of Santa Fe seems to have been unoccupied when Governor Don Pedro de Peralta (1610–14) founded the villa of Santa Fe "at the edge of a great chain of mountains where a Tano village had been abandoned" (Pearce 1965: 149).

There were two pre-Spanish sites in the area of the city, however, one just north of Santa Fe and the other at the site of the San Miguel church. These may well have been villages of Tewa or Tano speakers; at any rate, the Santa Fe River was known by a Tewa name, 'o ghap'oo ghe (place of the olivella shell) (Reeve 1961: II, 169–71).

Chavez (1957: 194) noted a public resolution dated June 29, 1823, by the Santa Fe City Government and Clergy " 'adopting' St. Francis of Assisi as Patron of the City, and proposing means for celebrating his feast with every solemnity." Loomis (1966: 8) mentioned the same date and added that the city, earlier known as "La Villa de Santa Fé," then became known as "La Villa Real de Santa Fé de San Francisco de Assisi."

284. If by "symbols" Bandelier here meant color symbols, those of San Juan were not the same, but varied considerably from those of Zuñi. The latter had the common Pueblo pattern (excepting only the Tiwa and Tewa): north, yellow; west, blue; south, red; east, white (Riley 1963: 59).

285. A generic relationship between Tanoan and Kiowa has been suggested; for example, McKenzie and Harrington (1948: 1) wrote that Tanoan and Kiowa "speak intimately related varieties of the same language. . . ." Most linguists, however, feel that the evidence for this connection is inconclusive.

In any case, the resemblance between Tewa and Kiowa could scarcely be considered as close as Spanish and French. Dozier (1970: 37) pointed out that even within the Tanoan group, Tewa, Tiwa, and Towa are not mutually intelligible, and the eastern Tewa have considerable difficulty communicating with people of Hano on the First Hopi Mesa.

286. Julius H. Gerdes was a merchant in clothing and "gents.' goods" in Santa Fe (Polk and Danser 1884a: 350). Bandelier had made his acquaintance in Santa Fe in 1882; and in December 1882, just prior to Bandelier's departure for his extensive travels through New Mexico, Arizona, and Mexico for the Archaeological Institute of America, Gerdes had purchased a horse for him (Lange and Riley 1966: 242, 332, 372).

287. See ns 230 and 830.

288. Moiety descent rules at San Juan (and among all the Tewa) were, in fact, rather flexible (see Parsons 1929: 89–98). It is difficult to appraise this rather garbled account of Bandelier, however; alternating assignment to moieties of children has not been reported in subsequent ethnographies. However, the relative ease in changing one's moiety has frequently been commented upon—commonly, in contrast to the more complicated and demanding procedures followed in changing one's clan.

289. The pregonero, or town crier, was, and continues to be, an official found in most if not all pueblos. The function was usually one of several assigned to minor officials of the tribe; at times, the function was carried out by major officials.

290. In Hodge (1907–10: I, 298), Mooney described chunkey stones as stone disks used, along with special poles, in the well-known men's game played among the Southeastern tribes. It would seem that Bandelier was describing a somewhat atypical mortar form as far as the puebloan tribes were concerned, at least within his personal experience.

291. Father Peter Eguillon was in Santa Fe at this time as vicar general of the diocese; brought from Clermont, France, in 1854 by Bishop John B. Lamy, Eguillon succeeded Father Joseph B. Macheboeuf, the first vicar general at Santa Fe (Salpointe 1898: 207, Appendix VII). Father Eguillon earlier had served as a parish priest at Socorro and then returned to Santa Fe as priest of the cathedral; he was one of the first individuals contacted by Bandelier upon his initial arrival in Santa Fe, August 24, 1880. Father Eguillon died in 1892 (Lange and Riley 1966: 71 et seq.; 1970: 357n15).

292. This was the Frank E. Robinson of the Mimbres Mining Company of Georgetown, New Mexico, previously mentioned in the journals (Lange and Riley 1970: 420n11). In January 1884, Bandelier had written "a long letter" to Robinson at #15 Brainard Street, Detroit, Michigan.

293. Howiri, a large pueblo on the east side of Ojo Caliente Creek north of Hot Springs, has been designated L. A. 71. See Smiley, Stubbs, and Bannister (1953: 19) for further data.

294. The reader is reminded that Bandelier was recording data about Taos Pueblo from a San Juan informant. Bandelier visited Taos only twice and had little background knowledge of his own, which perhaps explains the inaccuracies of this entry. For a discussion of Te-gat-ha (Tua-tá), or Taos, and Harrington's correlation of his data with Bandelier's, see Harrington 1916: 180.

While Bandelier referred in this entry to the "former pueblo of Taos, which they abandoned since the arrival of the Spaniards," as being "Te-gat-ha," he made no mention of this association in the *Final Report* (1890–92). He did use a variant spelling, "Te-uat-ha," in referring to present-day Taos in the *Final Report* (1890–92: I, 123). Subsequently, in his *Gilded Man* (1893: 233), he made the same association, reverting to his earlier spelling, "Te-gat-ha." See entry of August 11, 1885, in which Bandelier noted the use of Te-gat-ha for present-day Taos by his Taos informants. This explains his association as stated in both the *Final Report* and *The Gilded Man*.

The "former pueblo of Taos," noted above and in the journal entry of July 3, 1885, would appear to have been the same site noted by Harrington (1916: 183), citing descriptions by both Spinden and Hewett (in French) which placed this ruin a hundred or more yards northeast of present-day Taos.

F. H. Ellis and Brody (1964: 316–27) were apparently referring to this same site, identifying it (p. 317) as Mera's L.A. 259 (1940: 34–35). Ellis and Brody referred to ancestral Taos as Taos Site I, or Cornfield Taos (due to its location in a cornfield a quarter-mile northeast of the Taos Pueblo church), in their report on excavations there (pp. 318–20). They also excavated a refuse mound, supposedly the oldest in Taos village (p. 323). They assigned dates of 1325 A.D. for ancestral Taos and placed occupation of present-day Taos possibly as early as 1400 A.D. (p. 324).

295. It should be remembered that as of this date, Bandelier had not yet visited Taos Pueblo or the immediate vicinity. The lagune referred to here was undoubtedly Blue Lake (Taos: Paw'ia, lake), the sacred lake of the Taos Indians some twenty-five miles northeast of Taos Pueblo and the point of much public controversy in recent decades. By congressional action, December 15, 1970, the lake and surrounding area were returned to the Indians of Taos Pueblo.

Subsequently, in the *Final Report* (1890–92: II, 32), Bandelier used both "Mojual-ua," and "Mojua-lu-na." Harrington (1916: 177–78) discussed this, suggesting that the term "Mojua-luna" was properly Taos Peak, rising east of the pueblo, though he also noted that the Tewa had knowledge of Bandelier's corrupted form. Although Bandelier mentioned ancestral ruins in the mountains to the east, he stated in the *Final Report* (1890–92: II, 32–33) that this was based on hearsay as he had not been able to see the area himself. Actually, there do not seem to be significant ruins in the Blue Lake area within the shelter of Taos Peak.

The Taos origin myth has the Taos people emerging from beneath a lake (cf. n 242), which some of Parsons's informants identified as Blue Lake (Parsons 1936: 11, 98, 112). Bandelier, interestingly, did not use the term "Blue Lake" either in the journals or in his *Final Report*. At this time, he may not have been sufficiently informed to distinguish between or to associate Blue Lake and the mythical lake, possibly in Colorado, or "north of New Mexico" (pp. 29–33). By 1888, as revealed in his entry of September 21, he had learned considerably more but still did not refer to the lake or mountain as anything more than a sacred area, restricted to outsiders, i.e., non–Taos Indians.

For a recent discussion of Taos and Blue Lake, see Waters's article, "Thirty Years Later: 'The Man Who Killed the Deer' " (1972: 17–23, 49–50).

296. This is the standard Tewa system of color symbolism (Riley 1963: 59). See also n 284.

297. This was apparently Bandelier's remuneration for the article cited in n 234.

298. See ns 31, 203, and 208.

299. This was probably Adolph Seligman of the important wholesale and retail merchandising house founded by the German-Jewish settler Sigmund Seligman. Adolph, with his better-known brother, Bernard, joined this firm in 1862 (Coan 1925: III, 205; Anderson 1907: II, 642; Parish 1960). In the News and Comments of the *New Mexico Historical Review* (Vol. 19, 1944, pp. 254–55), there was a list of postmasters of Santa Fé, Santa Fé County, New Mexico, which noted that Adolph Seligman was appointed on April 6, 1886.

Another possibility is that the A. Seligman mentioned was Arthur, son of Bernard Seligman. This individual was only fourteen years old at the time, but he could have been a guest of the Antonio José (Anthony Joseph; see n 387) family. Joseph, like Seligman, was a leading political figure of the time, and the two certainly knew each other well, no doubt well enough for their children to visit. Arthur Seligman became not only a successful businessman but was mayor of Santa Fe from 1910 to 1912 (Coan 1925: III, 206–7). Arthur Seligman's mother, Frances, was a leading socialite in Santa Fe and was often mentioned in the newspapers.

300. Puebloan medicine men, particularly the caciques, possess special fetishes, commonly carved of stone but also of wood, leather, perfect corn ears, feathers, or assemblages of these elements. While various animal forms are represented, the "madres," or mothers, generally have anthropomorphic features. They are among the more sacred tribal possessions, used and kept by the cacique for the well-being of his people.

301. The editors have not been successful in identifying the articles that Bandelier mentioned writing for the *Westliche Post* and mailing to Preetorius in this and subsequent 1885 journal entries. He apparently finished the complete article on September 30, mailing it October 1. While in St. Louis in early November, Bandelier saw Preetorius and again began writing for the *Westliche Post*, finishing that article on December 24. Neither the Bandelier Scrapbook nor Hodge's bibliography (1932) contained these articles or citations to them. The journal entries give no hint of their content.

302. See entry of September 7, 1885.

303. This line of demarcation fairly well fits the present distribution of Tewa and Keresan pueblos. One difficulty is that Tewa and Tano are very similar dialects of Tanoan, and the distinction between them is not always clear. There is, today, no "Tano" pueblo as such, unless Hano Pueblo (Tewa Village) on the Hopi First Mesa can be so classified.

304. Those with experience with puebloan informants generally will know that Bandelier's suspicion was well founded. There are those who flatly refuse to become involved in the divulgence of information; others will seemingly cooperate but will limit their remarks to people and activities which do not include their immediate relatives or other close associates.

305. Tyúonyi, or Tyo'onye, according to Hewett (1953: 42), is the Keres word for the principal pueblo ruin in the canyon of the Rito de los Frijoles. The word means *olla*, which is, roughly, the shape of the pueblo ruin; the word Tyúonyi has also been extended to refer to the entire valley, or canyon. However, Hendron (1946: 25, 41–42) wrote that Tyuonyi was the name for the canyon of the Rito de los Frijoles and the large ruin on the canyon floor was properly called Puwige. According to Hendron, Tyuonyi means "place of treaty," referring to the dividing line between the Keres and the Tewas; Puwige means "pueblo where the women scraped the bottoms of the pottery vessels clean."

After several remarks largely in agreement with the above statements, Hewett, in an earlier discussion (1909: 669), commented as follows: "The Tewa hold that Cañada Ancha, known to them as El Rito de los Frijoles, is the true valley of the bean fields, and they give to the Cochiti Rito the name 'Puwhige,' an obscene name which I strongly suspect to be of modern origin closely connected with a contemptuous idea which they often express touching the morals of the Cochiteños. The Tewa acknowledge the Cochiti tradition of ownership of the Rito, though my first and apparently most trustworthy informant concerning the occupants of the plateau towns, Weyima (Antonio Domingo Peña), Rain Priest at San Ildefonso, would never admit the tradition that ancestors of the Cochiteños, except certain clans, ever lived in the Rito. . . ."

These are the kinds of data conflicts that are often insolvable as available informants become convinced of the validity of a particular account, or tradition, whether on justifiable grounds or not.

306. The Piro language was only dialectically different from Tiwa; thus, the Piros were Tanoan, rather than Keresan, in linguistic terms.

307. This discussion between Juan José Montoya, a Cochiti, and Bandelier, somewhat vaguely rendered here, seemingly referred to the practice of puebloan ceremonial groups resorting to counterparts at other villages, frequently those of no linguistic affiliation, for assistance of personnel, or in paraphernalia or instruction. Such exchanges and interrelationships continue at present, and instances are also to be found in the literature if they are sought out. The data could provide the raw materials for a valuable thesis or even a dissertation.

One of the few treatments of this topic in the literature was the section entitled, "Contacts and Loans: Interpueblo," which Parsons (1939: II, 968–86) included in the chapter "Variation and Borrowing" in her monumental *Pueblo Indian Religion*.

308. Te-je is the ruin Te-je Uing-ge O-ui-ping (Harrington 1916: 337). Bandelier, in his journal entry, noted "en el medio," but in his *Final Report*, he used the San Juan "Ouiping," also meaning "centrally located." While the journal entry clearly stated "on the promontory," the *Final Report* (1890–92: II, 84) located the ruin on the "southern slope of the bleak hills on which stands the present village [Pojoaque]." Harrington (1916: 337–38) took issue with Bandelier's statement, locating the ruin "on the nearly level hilltop, which slopes slightly toward Pojoaque Creek." His map located it on the northern slope. Harrington was of the opinion that Bandelier had not seen the ruin; the journal entry, however, indicated that he had visited the site.

309. T'ham-ba, in Bandelier's *Final Report* (1890–92: II, 85), appeared as "I'ha-mba." Harrington believed that the "I" was a misprint for "T" (1916: 310). Little was known except that the site was very old and was probably occupied by ancestors of the San Ildefonso people. It was constructed of adobe.

310. "Sa-co-na," or "Ja-co-na," was the ruin of a historic pueblo, belonging to the parish of Nambé and occupied until 1696 (Bandelier 1890–92: II, 85). Harrington gave additional data (1916: 330–31); see also Schroeder and Matson 1965: 117–18.

311. In his *Final Report* (1890–92: II, 81–82), Bandelier equated "Tu-Yo" with Black Mesa. Harrington (1916: 293–95) discussed other names for Black Mesa and variants of Tu-Yo at some length.

312. Bandelier was seemingly referring to Mesa Chino (Harrington 1916: 458). For a more complete discussion of the place names used by Bandelier in this entry: "Jyuma," "Gigantes," "Oma," etc., see Harrington (pp. 323–24); "el Huerfano" (p. 294); and "Caja del Rio" (p. 102).

313. Tzi-re-ge, or Tshirege (L.A. 170), is now protected as an isolated portion of Bandelier National Monument. Sa-qué ui would seem to be Bandelier's, or his informant's distortion of Sankewi (L.A. 211), and Po-Tzu-yé, or Potsu'ui, was an earlier alternative to Otowi (L.A. 169). Both Sankewi and Otowi are now within detached portions of Bandelier National Monument (for further information, see Hewett 1953: 29–42; Harlow 1965: 27–33; and Harrington 1916: 271, 274, and 282). The citations for Harrington refer to Potzu-yc (Otowi), Tsankawi, and Tschirege, in order; all three ruins were said to be claimed by San Ildefonso as their ancestral villages rather than Tewa in general.

314. See Hewett (1906: 17–18) and Harrington (1916: 263) for more about Perage ruin. Schroeder and Matson (1965: 134) also mentioned Perage as a possible place on Castaño's route, noting that it "is the only ruin close to and on either side of the river between Santa Clara and San Ildefonso that might have been occupied in the late 1500's (Sankawi Black-on-cream pottery being present)." In his entry of July 30, 1887, Bandelier recorded being told that San Ildefonso, when the Spaniards came, stood on the west bank of the Rio Grande—on the site of Perage.

315. As indicated in this entry, Bandelier found on his return to Peña Blanca that Father Augustin(e) Navet had replaced Padre Ribera (see n 436). The Lamy Memorial (1950: 71) listed the Rev. J. R. Ribera as priest at Peña Blanca from 1873 to 1883. In the same list, Rev. Augustine Navet was given as a priest at Peña Blanca from 1844 to 1889. The editors believe this beginning date to be a typographical error and the dates for Navet at Peña Blanca should have been 1884 to 1889. Father Navet served there until January of 1889, at which time he eloped with an Indian girl, Teresa.

Navet was replaced at Peña Blanca by Rev. Agustín Baron, who was in residence as early as February 3, 1889 (see Peña Blanca *Registro* for that period). Interestingly, the Lamy Memorial does not list Rev. Baron at Peña Blanca, nor does Salpointe list Navet, indicating how difficult it is to gather accurate data on the priesthood. As later journal entries in this volume show, Navet was to assist Bandelier in his preparation of the *Histoire*, in French, for the Pope's Jubilee (see also Burrus 1969b: 12 passim).

316. Zashua was a Cochiti Indian whom Bandelier had first met in the fall of 1880 when he lived for several weeks at Cochiti Pueblo (Lange and Riley 1966). See also Lange (1959: 30) for a discussion of Zashua, also known as Santiago Quintana and later as Cyrus Dixon, a name he apparently acquired while attending Carlisle Indian School in Pennsylvania. Zashue was the name given by Bandelier to one of his leading characters in his novel, *The Delight Makers*.

Santiago, a member of the Fox Clan and Turquoise Kiva, was born March 7, 1865, and married María Cresencia Arquero, Oak Clan and Pumpkin Kiva, May 2, 1890. No death date was found for Santiago in the Peña Blanca church records. A son, Cipriano, their last child, was born to the couple March 27, 1914, and died October 1, 1916, at which time Santiago seems to have been still alive (Registro: 224–25).

317. For the next several days Bandelier was at Cochiti, Peña Blanca, Wallace, and Golden. This was a return to places and people encountered in his first trip to the Southwest in 1880–82. Consult Lange and Riley 1966: index.

318. Bandelier had been interested in the ruins of this area in 1882 (Lange and Riley 1966). In this entry, he was questioning Juan Pacheco of Santo Domingo Pueblo, a Tano, who also spoke Tewa, about the names of the ruins. In his *Final Report* (1890–92: II, 90n2), Bandelier noted that "the names in the Tehua[Tewa] language were given to me by an old Tanos [Tano] Indian living at Santo Domingo." Interestingly, Harrington took issue with every Tewa name given, saying they had no meaning or were unknown to his Tewa informants (Harrington 1916: 468–69, 486, 488, 489, 490, 508–9, 549, 550, 553, 554).

Editorial comments on the ruins in this entry will be made, as appropriate, elsewhere in the journals. For a recent discussion of linguistic affiliation of some ruins mentioned in this entry, see Schroeder and Matson 1965.

Bandelier did not revisit San Cristóbal (L.A. 80) at this time. He had been there and had made extensive notes in 1882 (Lange and Riley 1966: 335–37). Nelson (1914: 41–67) should be consulted regarding his excavations at San Cristóbal. On this trip, Bandelier did not visit Qui-pa-na, Ojana, Pueblo Colorado, or Pueblo Blanco, though all are included in his *Final Report*. Pueblo Colorado and Pueblo Blanco, within three to five miles south and southeast of the town of Galisteo, were excavated by Nelson (1914: 74–79, 85–94).

319. José Hilario Montoya was a Cochiti Indian and a good friend of Bandelier. He served as governor of the pueblo repeatedly and was an acknowledged leader among them. Samuel Ellison, first postmaster of Peña Blanca, had recommended José Hilario to Bandelier "as the best guide and informant, also as an instructor in their language" that he might secure (Lange and Riley 1966: 88). Father Noël Dumarest (1920: 200n3) praised his diplomacy and progressive attitudes.

320. This was possibly Victoriano Cordero, a Cochiti Indian. Victoriano was born March 12, 1876, making him a boy of nine at the time Bandelier took him across the Rio Grande behind him on his horse. Cordero was of the Shipewe Clan and the Turquoise Kiva; he was later in life a member of the Flint, Snake, Fire, and Koshare societies. He became cacique in December 1914, and he died in office, December 12, 1946 (Lange 1959: 457).

321. This statement was more prophetic than Bandelier could have known. In fact, the following year, 1886, the Santo Domingo church was destroyed by the flooding Rio Grande. Bandelier, himself, in his *Final Report* (1890–92: II, 187) made note of the destruction. The frontispiece used by Twitchell (1911–17: II) showed Bandelier standing by the doors of the Santo Domingo mission, "studying Coat of Arms of Spain and the Holy See in relief on the Panels."

322. It is difficult to know, here, exactly what Bandelier was told by Juan José Montoya about Cochiti caciques and medicine men. There are obvious differences between these data and those gathered by Lange (1959: 236–52) characterizing the mid-twentieth century. Seemingly, there were formerly three bona fide caciques: Ho'tshan-yi, the leading figure; Shay-qa-tze, the second; the Uisht-yagga, the third. In time, they disappeared, and their duties were taken over by the cacique, or Ho'tshan-yi, the Flint Medicine Society headman. On special occasions, he is assisted by the headmen of the Giant Medicine Society and the Shi'kame Medicine Society. However, these two helpers are not considered caciques—they are medicine men.

In his *Final Report* (1890–92: I, 275), Bandelier made these comments in discussing pueblo government in general: "We often hear of another officer whose functions are represented as being of a somewhat occult religious nature, and who is said to be really the ruling power in the pueblo. This is the Cacique, whose true position has never been clearly defined."

While Bandelier occasionally noted in his journals that he had had some contact with the cacique or simply mentioned something regarding the cacique in the pueblo where he was at the time, it is clear that he was well aware of a real importance of this individual. In this regard it is interesting to observe that it has been impossible for us to ascertain the identity of the cacique in any village at any time. The reference, or cross-reference, was always made to the "cacique," and his name was never used.

In the autumn of 1880, during his first period of residence at Cochiti Pueblo, Bandelier noted repeated visits to the cacique and a number of conversations with him. He also inquired about the office of cacique from others, learning that this was a very important official, that the person was both respected and held in affection by the people, "his children," and that nevertheless he could be brought to account by the tribe, through action of the Council of Principales, specifically charged by the war captains who were the officials who had installed him in office. After considerable concern with this topic, it is interesting that Bandelier, in his entry of November 17, concluded his discussion with, "This cacique [the office, not the person] is still an enigma to me" (Lange and Riley 1966: 212; for other citations, see p. 430).

323. In 1880, Bandelier had commented briefly on the use of guaco wood for black paint for pottery designs (Lange and Riley 1966: 110). The editors had bracketed in "beeweed stems" after guaco wood in that entry. Bandelier's interest in paints for pottery is again evidenced in this entry. James Stevenson, who was making collections of Pueblo Indian material culture at the same time as Bandelier was conducting archaeological field work in New Mexico, had also noted plant usage for paint for pottery. Stevenson wrote in his report for the Bureau of Ethnology: "It is said that among the Cochiti, Santa Clara, and some other Pueblos a vegetable matter is employed to produce some of their decorative designs; this, however, I was unable to verify, though some of the Indians assured me of the fact, and furnished a bunch of the plant, which Dr. Vasey of the Agricultural Department, found to be *Cleome integrifolia,* a plant common among the Western Territories. A few specimens of the ware, some burnt and some unburnt, said to be decorated with the oil or juice of this plant were secured" (Stevenson 1883: 331). Lange (1959: 147), in collecting ethnobotanical specimens in his study of Cochiti, identified Rocky Mountain bee weed as *Cleome serrulata* Pursh; *Peritoma serrulatum* D.C. His informants pointed this plant out as the source of *guaco,* the black paint used in decorating the characteristic black-on-cream Cochiti pottery.

324. Bandelier's entry of April 2, 1882 (Lange and Riley 1966: 247), noted that Wallace was "now called" Armville. Seemingly, that name did not last. Pearce (1965: 177) failed even to mention it among the several designations of this community, including Thornton and Domingo. Polk and Danser (1884a: 370) said Wallace contained a church, a public school, two hotels, and some stores and had a population of 1,000. It was an important mining town with deposits of gold, silver, copper, fire and potter's clay, and coal in the vicinity.

Wallace was at the end of a railroad division (A.T.&S.F.) southwest of Santa Fe. It retained some importance in the early 1900s; the town served as a railroad connection with Santo Domingo Pueblo and specially with the Cochiti mining district (Anderson 1907: II, 890). Greene (1882: 28) listed it as having a weekly paper, the *Watchman.* Pearce (p. 177) stated it had a post office from 1882 to 1887.

325. Bandelier had first known Don Jesús Sena at Peña Blanca in the autumn of 1880; at that time, Sena had a store (see Lange and Riley 1966).

Jesús Sena died September 24, 1896, at Cerrillos; he was forty-nine years old. He was listed by Father Noël Dumarest of Peña Blanca as "the legitimate son of José Antonio Sena and Soledad García de Sena" (Registro: 75).

326. Bandelier on numerous occasions noted in his journal that he had been told that the old pueblo of Santo Domingo was Pueblo Quemado (Lange and Riley 1966). This site is currently designated Pueblito, L.A. 3654. In this entry, Bandelier again expressed his belief that an old pueblo of Santo Domingo was on the potreros to the west, referring to it as "Potrero de la Cañada Quemada."

327. Francisca González may well have been the daughter of Nazario González and the wife of Manuel Baca, whom Bandelier mentioned in his entry of December 1, 1882 (Lange and Riley 1966: 369). In both entries, Bandelier was seeking information on pueblo ruins in the Bajada-Cieneguilla-Ciénega area.

328. Nelson (1916a: 42) did partial excavations at La Bajada. Walter (1915: 17, 19) noted, "Of far greater interest, however, is the large pueblo ruin across the stream on the road to Peña Blanca just after the road branches off from El Camino Real. Here, early this summer, Nels C. Nelson assisted by Earl Morris and a crew of laborers excavated for the American Museum of Natural History portions of the communal dwelling that dates from previous times." Walter noted, in addition to the usual materials, pottery and stone tools, that the excavations revealed a subterranean kiva 45 feet in diameter, and evidence of a population of five to six hundred people. This is believed to be the site now designated as L.A. 7.

Bandelier described the ruins in his *Final Report* (1890–92: II, 95–97). "Cinnecu" varies considerably from the "Tze-na-ta" of the previous day's entry and from the "Tze-nat-ay" of the *Final Report*. However, in Harrington's discussion (1916: 470–71), "Cinnecu" approximates the "Senetu" which appeared in the Merced de la Bajada, 1695, document.

329. Bandelier mentioned McIlvain in 1882 (Lange and Riley 1966: 368). Polk and Danser (1884a: 370) listed a T. W. McIlsain, owner of a saloon in Wallace. This undoubtedly was the same individual, though the spelling seems to be incorrect.

330. For a brief discussion of Valverde, see Schroeder and Matson (1965: 162–63).

331. According to Pearce (1965: 65), Golden was founded in 1879 and derived its name from the fact that it was in the center of gold mining activities. Placer gold had been discovered in 1839 on Tuerto Creek, named for a spur of the San Pedro Mountains. An earlier settlement, Real de San Francisco, had been on the same site as Golden. A post office was at Golden from 1880 to 1928.

The decrease in population mentioned by Bandelier can be attributed to the usual failures of the gold fields to match expectations. Jenkinson and Kernberger (1967: 3–14) have provided a brief sketch of mining activities in the Ortiz Mountains region—Real de Dolores, Lazarus Gulch, Real de San Francisco (Golden), Tuerto, San Pedro, and Cerrillos. Most intriguing of the numerous failures these authors reported for the area was that of Thomas A. Edison (pp. 12–13).

"Work at the field laboratory of Thomas Alva Edison, one mile southwest of the crumbling ghost of Real de Dolores, was carried on in total secrecy. It was Edison's belief that the vast deposits of gold in the Ortiz placers could be separated from their gravels by an electrostatic process. He had picked a fertile place for experimentation; the manager of his plant even found gold in the adobe bricks of his henhouse. Rumor had it that Edison was stacking gold bricks like so much cordwood. Edison's refusal to accommodate the mass-circulation magazines that wished to do stories on his gold-extraction, only heightened public belief that the gold bonanza of the century, or perhaps of all time was taking place behind the high board fence of the laboratory.

"But Edison, like those who had come before him, ultimately failed. . . ."

332. For a brief discussion of Tuerto, see Schroeder and Matson (1965: 162–63).

333. Consult Nelson (1914: 68–73) and Dutton (1952) as well as Bandelier's *Final Report* (1890–92: II, 106, 107, 107n1) for additional data on Pueblo Largo (L.A. 183).

San Lázaro (referred to as San Cristóbal by Castaño) bears the designation L.A. 91. Consult Nelson (1914: 95–102) and Schroeder and Matson (1965: 10, 121, 139–40, 154–55, 162), as well as the *Final Report* (p. 105) for further data.

334. Most commonly, Maseua, or Masewa, and Oyoyewe are the Twin War Gods, Elder and Younger Brothers, respectively, puebloan culture heroes. They are powerful deities and are undoubtedly prayed to for rain and other aspects of general well-being. In this, they could be linked with the Shiuana, or Shiwanna, a more numerous but somewhat ephemeral host of deities, the "Cloud People," the ancestors, kachinas, and bringers of good. However, the Shiuana are very distinct from the Twin War Gods (see White 1935; also Lange 1959).

335. The large ruin of Paa-ko was referred to as San Pedro by Bandelier in his earlier journal entries (Lange and Riley 1966; 1970); in his entry of July 14, 1885, Bandelier had written Pá-qa. The Tanos called San Pedro Paa-ko (Bandelier 1890–92: II, 112). Presently, the site is designated L.A. 162 and comprises one of the New Mexico state monuments. Excavations were carried out at the site during the years 1935–37; the report, *Paa-ko, Archaeological Chronicle of an Indian Village of North Central New Mexico*, was published in 1954 by Marjorie F. Lambert.

336. Bandelier had visited the ruin of Tunque (or Tonque) Pueblo in 1882 (Lange and Riley 1966: 379, 380). The site is now designated as L.A. 240. The reader is referred to two articles in *El Palacio* (Vol. 76, No. 2, Summer, 1969). One was by Helene Warren on "Tonque" (pp. 36–42), in which she analyzed the Tonque pottery and established Tonque as the site of a flourishing ceramic industry during the fifteenth and sixteenth centuries. Tonque glazed pottery dominated the economy of the neighboring Rio Grande pueblos, especially those of the Santo Domingo Valley, and was sought and traded to Zia, Zuñi, and Gran Quivira and east as far as the plains of Texas, Kansas, and Oklahoma. Warren also reviewed what data there were on Tonque culture history. The second article was a book review by Stewart L. Peckham of Franklin Barnett's "Tonque Pueblo: A Report of Partial Excavation of an Ancient Pueblo IV Indian Ruin in New Mexico" (pp. 43–44). Peckham summarized the archaeological work done at Tonque, including that of Nels C. Nelson in 1914.

337. Harrington (1916: 548) noted Chimal as a hamlet mentioned by Bandelier (1890–92: I, 125) near the pueblo ruins of Ojana and Kipana. All three were included among the "unlocated" places or features by Harrington.

338. The Tejón Grant was two miles east of Placitas, New Mexico. Pearce (1965: 164) noted that the U.S. Surveyor General had confirmed the claim of Salvador Barreras and others because they had been given possession on November 7, 1840, by the laws of Spain and Mexico.

339. Bandelier here and elsewhere in the journals was referring to the watercolor sketches that he made of various native objects, including masks and other costume items, pottery and stone objects, as well as landscapes, pueblo scenes, and groundplans. Many of these sketches were included in the *Histoire* manuscript (see also n 62).

Almost from the time Bandelier began keeping his journals in August of 1880, there were sketches and drawings in the entries and frequent reference to the fact that he was "painting." Initially, the drawings seemed to be just mnemonic devices for preparing the formal reports that were to be written from the journals. Many of these have been reproduced in the margins of the corresponding journal entries in our volumes. As noted in n 4, Bandelier had found photography cumbersome and expensive. On November 21, 1880, he wrote (Lange and Riley 1966: 216), "The painting and drawing now goes [*sic*] so well that I intend to draw and paint all implements I can get hold of. It is cheaper than buying." The following day he wrote, "The discovery that I can draw somewhat is a great relief to me, and I hope now to go ahead better and with greater results." As noted (Lange and Riley 1970: 418–19n4), Bandelier had received instruction in architectural and topographic drawing from Professor William R. Ware, who had found him a very apt student.

On April 10, 1882, Bandelier wrote Parkman (Lange and Riley 1966: 261), requesting more drawing paper, fine brush for details, and several colors. He added, "It may appear pretentious on my part to ask for such material, but I assure you, and you will see it: 'Ce n'est pas de trop. [This is not too much?]' I never put on any lights, and still have secured some dark interiors with very fair effect. It is a great help, since it makes my journal much less voluminous. In place of describing an object, I paint it." As time went on, the painting took on increased importance for Bandelier and became an integral part of his field work.

340. Here, the mesa and area around the "Cangelón" was described by Bandelier (1890–92: II, 193) as "the wild labyrinth of lava, basalt, and trap . . . north of Bernalillo." South of San Felipe Pueblo, and west of the Rio Grande, the ruin there has been claimed by Santa Ana Pueblo as an ancestral village. Bandelier, who had not visited the ruin, was not certain whether it was north or south of the mouth of the Rio Jemez. He noted that "Cangelon" meant literally prong or horn, very apt for the prominent rocky pillar rising above the volcanic mesa. Interestingly, in reference to the use of the term elsewhere, Pearce (1965: 25) suggested the term Canjilon (n 406), north of San Juan in present-day Rio Arriba County, might be related to the Spanish cangilón, earthen jar, or pitcher. He cited, however, Fray Angelico Chavez who "writes that for a long, long time, and for reasons unknown, New Mexicans have had only one meaning for *canjilón:* 'deer antler.' "

341. Parsons (1939: 898) remarked on the story of a priest at Cochiti fleeing to San Felipe where he received protection. Lange (1959: 10), citing both Bancroft (1889: 216–17) and his own informants, reported the same escape incident, with the added detail of the priest's identity—Fray Alonzo de Cisneros. Chavez (1957: 19–20) listed documents, as of 1696, pertaining to, or involving, Fray Alonso Jiménez de Cisneros of Cochiti.

In the rebellion of June 1696, the Indians of San Felipe remained loyal to the Spaniards whereas those of Cochiti, Santo Domingo, the Tewa Pueblos, Jemez, Taos, and Picuris rose again, killing priests and settlers (Twitchell 1911–17: I, 410; Reeve 1961: I, 302–3).

342. Authentic pottery made at San Felipe has continued to be a rarity, if not completely lacking, as Bandelier's comment stated. With pottery from neighboring pueblos, such as Santo Domingo, Cochiti, and Zia, it seems that the people of San Felipe simply shifted their efforts to other pursuits.

For data on this sizable Keresan pueblo, see White (1932), Parsons (1939), and Stubbs (1950); it is all too apparent that anything resembling a comprehensive study of this relatively conservative tribe has yet to be published.

343. Parsons (1939: 901) reiterated the traditional story that the ancestors of Cochiti, Santo Domingo, and San Felipe formerly lived together in the Frijoles area; perhaps the last site commonly occupied by them was Kuapa. In the course of his archaeological work of 1912–14, N. C. Nelson designated the remains as Kuapa I and Kuapa II. Both portions of the site lie south of the Cañada de Cochiti; the larger segment, Kuapa II, is to the west, separated from the smaller area by a prominent arroyo feeding into the Cañada from the southwest. In the area survey conducted by Lange, 1957–59, Kuapa I and II were designated, respectively, L.A. 3443 and L.A. 3444. Surface indications are, however, that these two sectors were occupied contemporaneously and quite probably constituted but one large community.

Long recognized as one of the largest and most important of the numerous remains on the Rancho Cañada of James Webb Young, Kuapa recently came under the ownership of the University of New Mexico, upon the gift of the ranch to the university. Still more recently, Kuapa has been named a historic site by the state of New Mexico, further insuring that it will not be disturbed until the necessary personnel and means are available to assure proper excavation of this very significant site.

344. Most of the Pueblo tribes, following their successful uprising of 1680, abandoned their villages in the more open, low areas near the streams and sought refuge in higher, more easily fortified locations. Bandelier, in his journal of March 2, 1883, made notes on his visit to the top of Thunder Mountain and the remains there, near Zuñi (Lange and Riley 1970: 47–50).

345. Potrero Viejo was the location of Old Cochiti, the site occupied between the Pueblo Revolt of 1680 and the Reconquest of DeVargas when the Spaniards and their Indian allies successfully stormed the mesa, also known as La Cieneguilla de Cochiti, April 17, 1694 (Espinosa 1940: 35; 1942: 179–81). N. C. Nelson excavated Old Cochiti, or Kotyiti, in 1912–14 for the American Museum of Natural History. The present designation of this large, block "8"-shaped ruin is L.A. 295; some outlying remains, scattered, were designated L.A. 84. All pottery recovered from both sites, or areas, was classified Group F by Mera (1940: 24–25).

346. It is difficult to assess this body of information. The clan designations given Bandelier, in English, were as follows: term applied to the former second cacique (and seemingly included here erroneously), Tobacco, Eagle, Water, Coyote, Sun, and Ivy. In Hodge (1907–10: II, 433), with data as of 1895, twenty clans were named for San Felipe; seven more were listed as having only one or two members each; and seven more were extinct but still remembered. Of these categories, the first included Tobacco, Eagle, Water, Coyote, and Sun; the second included Ivy. The 1895 data did not mention Shay-katze (Jay-shatze) at all. This appears to have been a good example of the difficulty in eliciting complete data from most informants as well as gathering misinformation.

347. Similar examples of such meddling by outsiders with puebloan political and religious structures undoubtedly have occurred over the years. However, these intrusions in tribal affairs have been rather uniformly resented, and, as at Cochiti in the early years of this century (Lange 1959: 30–32), factions and animosities have developed which take many years to eliminate.

348. These three men were among the more helpful informants that Bandelier had found among the pueblos, particularly the first two. They were, respectively: Chino, or José Dolores Ortiz, San Juan Pueblo (n 215); Juan José Montoya, Cochiti Pueblo (n 642); and Estévan, possibly the sacristan, San Felipe Pueblo, whom Bandelier had met only a few days before writing this entry.

349. Carlisle, Pennsylvania, was the site of the first nonreservation school for Indians established by the federal government. On September 6, 1879, an order was issued transferring the Carlisle Barracks and twenty-seven acres from the War Department to the Department of the Interior for Indian school purposes, pending action by Congress. A bill finally became law July 31, 1882. General R. H. Pratt was in charge from the beginning to the time of his retirement June 30, 1904 (Hodge 1907–10: I, 207–9). In 1918, the Carlisle Indian School was terminated, and the facilities were taken over by the Army War College.

350. This was a good example of the kind of social pressure that was, and continues to be, brought to bear on a deviant in Pueblo society. For a brief, general discussion, providing context for the topic, see Dozier 1970: 179–81; a more recent example of similar practices has been reported for Zia Pueblo as of 1951 (Lange 1952).

351. These are both names for mixed bloods—of which the Spaniards listed many named varieties. Cuartazo was probably the Cuarteron (Santamaria 1959: 320), which could be either a mulatto or the offspring of a mestizo and a Spaniard. We were unable

to identify Gallazo (names for mixed bloods varied from time to time and from place to place).

352. Bandelier (Lange and Riley 1966: 242) had earlier identified Antonio Tenorio as the "old governor of Santo Domingo."

Bandelier had made the acquaintance of Santiago Crispín at Santo Domingo Pueblo at the very beginning of his New Mexico fieldwork in the autumn of 1880. Crispín had been sacristan since 1848. For additional data, see Lange and Riley 1966. The Peña Blanca church records had no data on Santiago Crispín, but the Crispín name was a common one at Santo Domingo. In general, the church records for Santo Domingo are markedly less complete than for neighboring pueblos such as Cochiti. Even in the latter instance, there are innumerable gaps in the recorded information.

353. In discussing Peña Blanca, Pearce (1965: 119) noted that one of the first to establish himself in the region of this early nineteenth-century town was José Miguel de la Peña and the settlement was known as El Rancho de José Miguel de la Peña and then later was simply referred to as El Rancho de la Peña Blanca. As noted in Lange and Riley (1970: 413n463), Samuel Ellison was the first postmaster at Peña Blanca, his appointment dating from March 14, 1867. Up to 1876, Peña Blanca was a county seat, the capital of Santa Ana, one of the first seven counties of the state. At one time the main highway from Santa Fe to Fort Wingate crossed the Rio Grande at Peña Blanca and met the ancient Navajo Trail. These facts and other data on Peña Blanca and the early inhabitants of the area were given in an article by Paul A. F. Walter (1915).

354. Of this series of abandoned missions, San Pedro, Tabira, Manzano, and San Lázaro, the first named is assumed to be the large site of Paa-ko (see n 335), the excavation of which was reported by Lambert (1954). Noting that this was a Tanoan village of prehistoric and early historic times, Lambert stated that "Hewett also wished that it be determined once and for all whether an actual mission building ever existed at this site" (p. 1). In her concluding discussion, she noted, ". . . no such building, however, was located." Further, "By one interpretation (a translation of Zarate Salmeron), San Pedro de Paako existed in 1626 (Bandelier and Hewett, 1937, p. 222). Fray Angelico Chavez informed the writer that the lack of a mission structure need not exclude Paa-ko from the mission list, for a priest could have served the village along with San Cristobal and San Lazaro during the Seventeenth Century, with Galisteo, or perhaps San Marcos, as his headquarters" (p. 177).

355. Bandelier had first known Don Amado Cabeza de Baca at Peña Blanca in 1880 and 1882 (Lange and Riley 1966: 182, 183, 329). A brief biographical sketch (based on A. J. O. Anderson's notes) was given in the Register of Persons (pp. 407–8). The following data are from Otero's account, on which Anderson had based his notes.

"Early in the summer of 1872 Don Juan Maria Baca of Upper Las Vegas sent two four-mule wagons to Kit Carson [Colorado] . . . to carry home to New Mexico some boys who had been in the East to school and who were returning for the summer vacation. Four of the boys were sons of Don Juan—Eleuterio Baca, Francisco Baca y Sandoval, Domingo Baca and Antonio Baca, the last two being twins. The other boys were Amado Baca, David Baca and Valentin C. de Baca—cousins who lived at Peña Blanca, on the Upper Rio Grande—and Anastacio Ascarate, who came from Las Cruces. . . . The remaining boy was my first cousin Emanuel B. Otero, whose home was at La Constancia, in Valencia county" (Otero 1935: 57).

Chavez (1954) gave a history of the Baca family, widespread in New Mexico.

It seems quite possible that the father of Amado, David, and Valentin [Cabeza de] Baca was the Don Tomás Cabeza de Baca included in Walter's discussion of early inhabitants of the Santa Fe region (Walter 1915: 19–22). Walter quoted from U.S. Attorney W. W. H. Davis's account of his visit to Peña Blanca and the hospitality of Don Tomás Cabeza de

Baca. Otero's account further suggests that Don Tomás and Don Juan Maria Baca of
Upper Las Vegas were brothers.

356. For Bandelier's earlier associations with Don Nicolás Lucero of Peña Blanca, see
Lange and Riley (1966: 363; 1970: 23).

Don Nestor Nicolás Lucero, husband of Ana Manuela Archuleta, died August 5, 1890,
at the age of 80 years and six months. He was buried in the churchyard at Peña Blanca
(Registro: 6).

357. According to Santamaria (1959: 845), the name Pichicuata came from the Aztec
piztahuac, a straight thin thing, and *coatl,* snake. It refers to a venomous serpent from
the interior of the country; when angered, it allegedly stands erect, balanced on its tail.
From the context of the entry, it is impossible to determine the kind of snake Bandelier
saw. It may possibly have been a sidewinder rattlesnake (*Crotalus cerastes*) for which the
local, or Bandelier's own, term of reference was Pichicuata.

358. P. Cusick operated a restaurant in Wallace (Polk and Danser 1884a: 370).

359. Presumably this referred to repairs Bandelier was having made to the house
which he and Joe planned to occupy in Peña Blanca. The next entry made reference to
this, as did that of August 7, 1885. Bandelier also wrote a letter on September 10, 1885,
to Icazbalceta, which is translated in n 421, which told of their plan to live at Peña Blanca.
This plan never materialized, as the entry of November 28, 1885, indicated.

360. Bandelier had mentioned a Román Baca in 1883 (Lange and Riley 1970: 66,
381n183). He had considerable dealings with the Navajo and could easily have acquired
a Navajo name. See Twitchell (1911–17: II, 494n407) for this Román Baca's involvement
in territorial politics in the 1880s and Anderson (1907: II, 607) for Baca's loss of personal
fortune in the panic of 1893–94.

Since Bandelier was at Peña Blanca at the time of this entry, it is much more likely that
the Román Baca he referred to was the Román Baca of the following Peña Blanca burial
notice. "[On the] 29th of October, 1902, I gave Christian burial to Román Baca, husband
of Dorotea Tofolla [Tafoya], who died October 28, 1902, at age of 73 years. (signed) Padre
Teodoro Stephan, O. F. M., Peña Blanca" (Registro: 106).

A child, Román Maximo, who lived only four months, was born posthumously to Román
Baca on May 11, 1903.

361. Bandelier, throughout his Southwestern years (Lange and Riley 1966; 1970), returned from time to time to the topic of the fight at the Arroyo Seco and associated events
in the insurrection of 1837. In the rebellion, a coalition of northern settlers and Indians
from San Juan, Santo Domingo, Cochiti, and San Felipe captured Santa Fe, August 9,
1837, and executed the Mexican governor, Albino Perez. José Gonzales, reputedly a Taos
Indian, was chosen governor by the rebels. Gonzales quickly assembled a group of al-
caldes and influential citizens, mostly drawn from northern New Mexico, and on August
27, this force confirmed Gonzales's position and initiated negotiations with the authorities
in Mexico City.

A counter-rebellion was quickly organized by Manuel Armijo, who scattered the rebel
troops in a bloodless battle at Pojoaque. Aided by reinforcements from Mexico, Armijo
soon overran northern New Mexico and, by the end of January 1838, had defeated the
rebel army and executed Governor Gonzales (Bloom 1914: 3–56).

Bandelier (1881b: 124n3) credited David J. Miller with the "only printed report in
existence, except a very short one by Judge K. Benedict, on the revolt of 1837." This
appeared in an article by Miller, entitled, "Historical Sketch of Santa Fe" (pp. 22–23), in
a pamphlet on the *Centennial Celebration,* 1876. Ritch (1882) included a very brief
mention of the rebellion in his "Chronological Annals of New Mexico, etc." (p. 17).

362. In the *Final Report* (1890–92: II, 156), Bandelier gave the Keres name of Painted
Cave, or Cueva Pintada, as Tzek-iat-a-tanyi. This well-known feature of present-day

Bandelier National Monument was first visited by Bandelier on October 26, 1880 (Lange and Riley 1966: 172).

363. Pacífico Baca was a Spaniard, or Mexican, who lived at Cochiti Pueblo, as did a number of other non-Indians—a somewhat unusual feature of this village (Lange 1959: 13–20). Bandelier had a fair amount of contact with Baca during his earlier periods of residence at Cochiti (Lange and Riley 1966: 160, 161 et passim). It is interesting to note that after considerable contact in 1880 and some in 1882, there was no mention of Pacífico Baca in the 1883–84 journals. It may have been that Pacífico had more or less established residence in the Rito de los Frijoles sometime after 1880, or even 1882. Chavez (1954a) did not mention Pacífico Baca in his study of early New Mexico families; he did, however, make this comment (p. 145): "The Baca family is by far the most widespread in New Mexico. While other old names, even the more common ones, are restricted to certain family or regional groupings, the Bacas permeate all of New Mexico's people and history."

364. This site was most likely L.A. 208 which was excavated by Fred Worman. Appreciably larger than the innumerable small house sites which are scattered over the potrero tops of this region, the site was on lands of the Atomic Energy Commission, north of Bandelier National Monument and north of State Highway 4. The site was approximately a half-mile northeast of an arterial stop at the junction of a side-road with Highway 4.

365. Bandelier recorded Troomaxiaquince in his June 19, 1885, entry and Troomaxiaquino on August 2, 1885. The term does not appear in the *Final Report*. However, Hodge (1907–10: II, 819) noted, *"Troomaxiaquino.* A Tewa pueblo in N. Mex. 1598. The ruins have been located by Bandelier in Rio Arriba co.

"Pajaritos.—Bandelier in Ritch, N.M. 201, 1885 (Span. 'birds'). *Troomaxiaquino.*—Oñate (1598) in Doc. Inéd. XVI, 116, 1871. *Troomaxiaquino.*—Bandelier, op. cit. *Trovmaxiaquino.*—Bancroft, Ariz. and N.M., 136, 1889 (misprint)."

366. Bishop Lamy ordained four native priests, one of whom was Father Ramon Medina. Ordained in 1856, Father Medina served at San Juan, 1857–59 (Lamy Memorial 1950: 77); he was at Peñasco subsequently and built the first church there sometime after 1860. He was listed at Peñasco between 1866 and 1874 and again from 1892 to 1906 (p. 71). In addition, he served at Santa Cruz, 1874–75, 1885–87, and 1891–92 (p. 79). From 1876 to 1882, he was at Abiquiu (p. 52); his stations in the periods 1860–66 and 1882–85 are not known.

367. Mr. Wilborn was probably a relative of Maurice Huegy's wife, Emma, quite possibly her father.

368. The Tewa called Ojo Caliente "green spring," because the high temperature causes the growth of blue-green algae, covering the rocks with an emerald-green color. The Tewa regarded the place as the abode of tribal gods. The springs themselves were believed to be an opening between this world and the "down below world," whence their first people came. The grandmother of Poseyemo, a Tewa culture hero, was said to still live in one of the springs (Pearce 1965: 112).

369. See n 115.

370. This was one of the few times that Bandelier made a bibliographic citation for himself in the journals (other than archival materials). The reference was to Bourke's study, published the year before, "The Snake Dance of the Moquis of Arizona. . . . with an account of the Tablet Dance of the Pueblo of Santo Domingo." Bandelier thought well of Bourke and his study, as evidenced in the final remarks of his review of a subsequent publication by Bourke which Bandelier criticized for being superficial and not up to Bourke's previous standard. Referring to Bourke's *Apache Campaign* (1886), Bandelier wrote, "The subject is worthy of careful treatment, such as the 'Moqui Snake Dance' has

shown Captain Bourke capable of undertaking and accomplishing" (see n 553 for the full review by Bandelier).

371. This was Colonel Alfred Wynkoop who had been a brevet lt. col. in the Civil War (Heitman 1903: I, 1064). Wynkoop moved to Colorado after the war and settled in Santa Fe in the 1880s, living there until his death (Twitchell 1911–17: II, 382n305).

372. Henry F. Swope, A. L. Kendall, and H. D. Lewis operated the H. F. Swope & Co., a livery, feed, and sale stable on lower San Francisco Street in Santa Fe. Swope & Co. also had an Omnibus Line Co. on San Francisco Street (Polk and Danser 1884a: 354). Just a week after initial arrival in Santa Fe in 1880, Bandelier had engaged a two-horse buggy from Swope which he and two companions drove to Pecos, where Bandelier embarked on his first field work (Lange and Riley 1966: 74).

373. According to Parsons (1929: 264–65), both sun and moon among the Tewa were addressed as "Old Man." In addition, the slow moving summer sun was identified as Elder Brother, while the fast moving winter sun was called Younger Brother. At Taos, sun and moon were called Our Fathers, or Old Man (Parsons 1939: 937, 962–63), and among the Hopi, at Jemez, and at Zia, moon was also male (p. 181). At Zuñi, however, moon was sun's Younger Sister (p. 181).

The sun, as father of the twin gods, or war twins, was a common concept among the eastern Pueblos, but at Zuñi, Hopi, and among the Navajo and Apache, only one of the war gods was the son of Sun. The other was the son of Waterfall (Parsons 1939: 963).

374. For a concise history of Picurís Pueblo and a brief discussion of recent excavations there (under the direction of Herbert W. Dick), see Picurís Indians (n. d.: 1–15). Bandelier's information that there were only two kivas was erroneous. The Picurís pamphlet (p. 4) noted the excavation of three prehistoric kivas.

375. This entry is somewhat misleading, as Archbishop J. B. Lamy did not formally resign until August 26, 1885. His resignation was read in all the churches of the archdiocese on September 6, 1885. Archbishop Lamy conferred the pallium on Archbishop Salpointe on November 21, 1885, and then retired to a small country place (now called Bishop's Lodge, a resort, where the Archbishop's private chapel is maintained as it was when he lived there) north of Santa Fe, which he had purchased in 1853 (Zerwekh 1962: 149).

On August 6, 1885, Bishop Salpointe had received letters from Rome giving notice of his appointment as Archbishop of Santa Fe (p. 148) and, undoubtedly, Archbishop Lamy had requested Rome for permission to resign prior to Bishop Salpointe's notification.

Sadliers' Catholic Directory (1886: 141) gave the dates of both the resignation of Archbishop Lamy and the promotion of Salpointe to replace him as July 18, 1885. It may be that this was the date of the official actions in Rome, with subsequent dates being the actual ceremonial observances of these changes in Santa Fe. Anderson (1907: I, 483) concurred in the July 18, 1885, date and stated that Salpointe was consecrated as Archbishop on October 1, 1885. Data presented by Salpointe (1898: 272) supported Sadliers. "On the 19th of February, 1885, the Right Rev. J. B. Salpointe came to Santa Fe as coadjutor to the Most Rev. Archbishop Lamy. He was promoted to the Archiepiscopal See of Anazarba on October 11 of the same year, and succeeded to the See of Santa Fe, July 18th, 1885, by the resignation of his predecessor."

In this entry, both Father Seux and Bandelier were probably commenting upon Rome's acceptance of Archbishop Lamy's resignation. Santa Fe newspapers of this period made no reference to Lamy's approaching formal resignation nor did they give any information as to the "Denver and Mora matters" referred to here by Bandelier.

376. This picture, drawn for Bandelier by Cushing at Zuñi (Lange and Riley 1970: 51), was later included in the *Histoire* (Burrus 1969b: Illustration 106, p. 119). In the journal entry of March 2, 1883, Bandelier had recorded the name as "Matzaluna." However, the

"Mait-za-laima" of this August 13, 1885, entry appeared again in his journal of September 19, 1885, and it was also the spelling used in both the *Histoire* and the *Final Report* (Bandelier 1890–92).

Mait-za-laima, in Zuñi mythology, was the Younger War God, the twin of U'yuyewi, according to Stevenson (1904: 49–51). She named them as the first directors of the Bow Priesthood in her discussion of the origin of this society.

Bandelier, in his *Final Report* (1890–92: I, 290), referred to them as the divine and powerful twins of Zuñi mythology, equating them with the Keresan Masewa and Oyoyewa. Although Stevenson clearly indicated Mait-za-laima as the younger brother, the great majority of puebloan sources agree with Bandelier's designation of Masewa, or Mait-za-laima, as the older brother.

Bandelier's problem, in his notations following the information regarding *"Je-ro-ta,"* arose from his tendency to consider such puebloan beliefs and conceptualizations in a rather homogeneous or simplistic manner. The differences in cultural details between the western Zuñi and the eastern Keresans and Tewa tribes and also between the Keresans and the Tewa themselves were and in some instances remain quite pronounced. Striving for equivalences was accordingly naive at times, and the results were correspondingly imprecise.

377. Again, there appears to be some confusion in Bandelier's notations. The informant's identification of the masks as *"Shi-ua-na"* [Shiwanna], cloud beings, or deities was accurate; Bandelier's vague comment, "originating from the clouds in some way," would be explained in most pueblos as those kachinas, cloud people, or the departed ancestors. However, the equating of all this with *"Je-ro-ta,"* as at Santo Domingo, would appear to have been a misunderstanding. *"Je-ro-ta"* was described by White (1935: 110–11) as "Hᴇ´ruta, or Hᴇ´luta, each kiva has one; he is the chief of the katsina; only one comes at a time. He always comes out before the other dancers to ask Cacique for permission to enter the pueblo and dance . . ." He noted that among the Cochiti, Heluta was the "father of the katcinas." Information obtained for Cochiti by Lange (1959: 470–73) generally confirms the importance of this impersonation. Normally, as White noted, Hᴇ´ruta appeared as a single individual with almost every type of kachina dance. There were several forms of Hᴇ´ruta costuming, however—an interesting facet to such an important figure. The only exception to this solo performance was the so-called Hᴇ´ruta Dance, in which "an entire line of dancers dressed in identical costumes play a part in obscuring the true Hᴇ´ruta as a trick on the Ku-sha´lī (p. 470)." It may have been an awareness of this particular dance that caused Bandelier's informants to equate the line of identically dressed Shiwanna dancers with the normally unique Hᴇ´ruta, or Je-ro-ta.

378. Jade, or nephrite, was most likely used in the same way as turquoise as part of a shrine offering when a person was sick or for other purposes (see Parsons 1939: 298–300). It may simply have been, of course, that Bandelier was confusing jade with turquoise since the common Nahuatl word for jade, chalchihuitl or chalchihuites, has often been used in the Southwest to mean turquoise.

379. This appears to have been the same person identified as sheriff in the entry of May 30, 1888.

380. "The" Chinita and "the" China appear to be a form of title, extensions of "the" Chino, or simply Chino, as Bandelier referred to José Dolores Ortiz, an Indian of San Juan Pueblo (see n 215). The two individuals mentioned here were presumably members of Chino's family.

381. This article ultimately appeared in 1886; see entry of September 7, 1885, for the actual mailing of it to James Jackson, Paris. It was quite obviously prompted by receipt, two days earlier (August 15, 1885), of the information passed along by Dr. Eggert which suggested "some publications which remunerate, at Paris."

Fray Marcos de Niza was sent by Viceroy Mendoza in 1539 to investigate the new lands reported by Cabeza de Vaca and his companions. With the priest went the Black slave, Esteban. The latter reached Zuñi and was killed there; there is considerable controversy as to how far into the Southwest Fray Marcos, himself, penetrated and by what route. In any event, his report to the Viceroy led to the Coronado Expedition of 1540–42 (see ns 413 and 607).

382. According to Polk and Danser (1884a: 350), Eugene A. Fiske and Henry L. Warren were attorneys and partners in an office in the Old Government Palace.

383. This was the water serpent, or *Avanyu,* which at San Juan controls the waters of the Rio Grande. The Kossa have a ceremony to control the flow in the river by magically interceding with the *Avanyu.* Parsons (1929: 274) found at San Juan that the figures could be done either by impersonators, youths, or by images manipulated by the youths. Elsewhere (Pl. 17), Parsons reproduced a Kossa altar ceremony with a horned water snake, the Kossa chief, his assistant, and ritual paraphernalia. The two Kossa members stand on the serpent's picture.

This figure also is widely known as the horned, or plumed, serpent; as such, it is commonly portrayed in pottery designs and elsewhere among a number of the Pueblo Indian tribes.

384. Bandelier was probably describing what are presently referred to as kiva bells, bell stones, or kiva ringing stones. These objects have been recovered from numerous excavations in the upper Rio Grande Valley. Lambert (1954: 132–33) reported them from Paa-ko, calling them Pun-ku as well as the more conventional names. In her discussion, she pointed out that these archaeological objects have carried through in various pueblos into the present day among the Pueblo Indians.

385. The bullroarer, or rhombus, is a flat, often decorated, slab of wood on a string, which is used to produce the sounds of wind and thunder (thus, rainstorms) at Zuñi, Hopi, and among the Keres. At Zuñi, two stone balls are also struck together to produce a thunder-like noise. Santa Clara societies keep "two stone points" that are used to make thunder noise, also to produce rain magically (Parsons 1939: 378–79).

386. This was probably one of the two Springer brothers of Cimarron, New Mexico. Frank, who came to the territory in 1873, was an attorney for the large Maxwell Land Company of the Cimarron area, but he later moved to Las Vegas, giving up his law practice to become a palaeontologist. Charles Springer, also an attorney, arrived in New Mexico in the late 1870s and became a major lease-holder in the Maxwell Grant. In later years, Charles Springer was a leading Republican politician in the Territory (Otero 1939: 114–15; Twitchell 1911–17: II, 453).

387. This was Judge Anthony Joseph (Antonio José). Bandelier had met him briefly in March 1882 (Lange and Riley 1966: 240). The Register of Persons for that volume (p. 411) gave the following information.

> Born in Taos, 1846; early education in private school, Taos and Santa Fe; Webster College, St. Louis, Missouri. Married Elizabeth M. Foree, Clark County, Missouri, 1881. Member, Territorial Assembly; Delegate to U.S. Congress, 49th-53rd Sessions, 1880's. Lived at Ojo Caliente, Taos County, where he had a general merchandise store and served as postmaster; also ran winter resort, Los Ojos Calientes [the Hot Springs], 'sure cure for many diseases.' Vice-President, New Mexico Historical Society, for Ojo Caliente; led in building the public roads in Taos County; was instrumental in erection of capitol building, since known as Federal Building, Santa Fe (not used as capitol). Worked for admission of New Mexico as a state; succeeded in establishing Court of Private Land Claims; succeeded in obtaining annual appropriations; President,

upper branch, Territorial Assembly, 1896. Died at Ojo Caliente, 1910; buried in Santa Fe. [See also Twitchell 1911–17: II, 464n385.]

In Bandelier's *Final Report* (1890–92: II, 45n1), he commented, "The Hon. Antonio Joseph, Delegate to Congress, is my authority. He is himself the owner of the springs, and has resided there for a number of years at least part of the time." The note was in regard to the ruin of Pose-uingge (in the Ojos Calientes Valley), the remains found there, and "the supposition that Pose-uingge was destroyed by an earthquake."

388. The Codex Mendoza (or Mendocino) was a Mexican pictographic manuscript prepared by order of Don Antonio de Mendoza, first Spanish Viceroy of New Spain. It contains history and tribute lists of the Aztecs and has information on the daily life, games, etc. of central Mexican Indians. The pictographs or glyphs are glossed in Spanish by a Nahuatl-speaking priest who set down the interpretations by native Aztecs of the writings.

The original of the codex is in the Bodleian Library, Oxford, and an English translation was made by James Cooper Clark and published (Waterlow and Sons, London) in 1938 (Library of Congress 1943a: 365; Katz 1966: 1).

389. "José Ramos Ortiz was a first cousin of my paternal grandfather's (José Benavidez Ortiz) father (Antonico Ortiz). He left only two daughters, one of whom married a Maestas and the other, a Cruz, so that branch of the family ended, as such, with José Ramos. Grandmother does not recall that he was a member of one of the religious societies, but he was a good Catholic and spoke Spanish well [his name appears as a *testigo* frequently on wills and deeds until the turn of the century]." (Alfonso Ortiz, personal correspondence, August 19, 1969).

390. This comment referred to Indians fleeing from Coronado's soldiers. His army, after the Quivira fiasco in 1541, had a very hard winter among the pueblos of the central Rio Grande area and pressed the Indians for food and clothing. Actually, however, with the exception of some of the Zuñi towns, Acoma, and Pecos, the pueblos dealt with by Coronado have been only tentatively identified (see Hammond and Rey 1940; Bolton 1949; Schroeder and Matson 1965: 129–32; and Riley 1971: 295–308, for discussions of the Coronado occupation of New Mexico).

For the refugee pueblos in the San Juan Pueblo-Chama River area, Bandelier's two named villages, Te-e-ouinge and Fessere, have also been proposed, under somewhat varying designations, by Schroeder and Matson (but with no mention of Bandelier's data [1890–92: II, 58]). They used the designations Te'euinge (equated in their index with Te'ewi [see n 224]) and Pesedeuinge (see Harrington 1916: 152, citing Jeançon).

The other two sites identified by Bandelier only as "two even higher up near the Ciénega" would seemingly include one identified by Schroeder and Matson (see their map, p. 130) as Tsamauinge. Their other site, Kuuinge, would appear too distant from Tsamauinge to conform to Bandelier's "two even higher up near the Ciénega."

391. In other words, pictures of Montezuma from the Mexican codices had little meaning for Francisco—bearing no resemblance to the Tewa's Po-se-ye-mo (see entry of June 25, 1885).

392. Chamita, a quite fertile valley across the Rio Grande from San Juan Pueblo, was the site of an early capital of Oñate. A church was founded there in 1598 at or near the Indian village of Yuqueyunque with the name San Gabriel de Yunque. This settlement was on or near the present village of Chamita (Twitchell 1911–17: I, 315).

The actual capital of Oñate's New Mexico was at San Juan till 1599 or 1600 at which time it seems to have been moved to San Gabriel (Wendorf 1953: 6). See also n 419.

393. For Castañeda's comments, see Hammond and Rey (1940: 256).

394. The pottery vaguely described here was undoubtedly of the various Rio Grande glaze wares, for which a rather voluminous technical bibliography now exists. For one recent study, valuable in itself and as an example of the sophisticated scientific analyses being used, the reader is referred to Warren's report on Tonque [Tunque] Pueblo (1969).

395. Probably, a member of the Honorable Antonio Joseph family (see n 387).

396. Bandelier found these "gardenbeds" in Arizona and in Sonora and described them as rectangular spaces enclosed by upright, small stones. Some of them, at least, were probably terraces. These have subsequently been reported for numerous portions of the Puebloan, or Anasazi, area of the Southwest; they appear to have been used to catch moisture, even dew, on the upland, or mountain, slopes.

397. "From the limited description it is impossible to identify these round 'hollows' as the remains of Apache structures. However, the remains of round, semisubterranean Apache structures as much as two feet deep have been excavated. Some of the housepits were outlined by rocks" (personal communication, Dolores A. Gunnerson, April 25, 1972; for further information, see James H. Gunnerson [1969]).

398. When General Stephen Watts Kearny's forces entered Santa Fe on August 18, 1846, following the collapse of the Mexican defenses at Apache Canyon, a number of people did flee south with Governor Manuel Armijo. Kearny, however, took immediate steps to quiet the fears of the native New Mexicans, issuing a proclamation on August 22 which gave citizenship to New Mexicans and promised protection of both persons and property. A number of prominent New Mexican families welcomed the Americans, and the takeover proceeded with virtually no strife (Bloom 1915: 351–80). Bandelier's Sonoreños, having no great stake in New Mexico, probably left with, or at the same time as, Armijo (see also Lamar 1966: 56–70).

399. José Olivas had been a guide for Bandelier on a number of previous occasions (Lange and Riley 1966; 1970). In a letter of November 20, 1882, to Parkman, Bandelier wrote, "It will of course be imperative to buy a horse, which I can get for $50.–. about, & you would confer a favor by stating whether I am permitted to engage a man as companion & guide. There is much time lost in taking care of bodily wants & of the animal, whereas I have an opportunity of securing a reliable man, a former guide of Kit Carson and the Mexican boundary survey,—fee $1.– per day, who will go with me through the wastes of the S.W. in New Mexico into Chihuahua. —If you deem it right, I shall hire him, if not, I will go alone." Parkman's reply has never been found nor have the editors been able to establish that José Olivas had served either with Carson or on the boundary survey. The journal entries indicate Bandelier employed José Olivas as a guide, though because of illness (January 11, 1883), he did not accompany Bandelier on his extensive journey. Olivas was instrumental in the purchase of a horse, presumably the faithful "Chico" that carried Bandelier through much of New Mexico, Arizona, Sonora, and Chihuahua (see Lange and Riley 1966; 1970; and n 932).

400. The Cerro del Pedernal stands out as a distinctive landmark west-northwest of Abiquiu, Rio Arriba County; its elevation is 7,580 feet. Harrington (1916: 122–23) stated it was referred to by the Tewa, Cochiti, Spanish, French, and English as "flaking stone," "obsidian," or "flint" mountain. Its flints have long been recognized as valuable for the making of various implements and weapons; these finished objects, or the raw materials, have been reported from a wide area (see Bryan 1938; 1939; Dittert, Hester, and Eddy 1961; Ellis and Brody 1964; and Hibben 1937).

401. Here, Bandelier undoubtedly had reference to the lower (downstream) end of the settlement of El Rito; villages in the area are typically elongated in form, the houses strung out along the stream.

402. Polk and Danser (1884a: 317) gave El Rito as a post office in Rio Arriba Co., the community having a population of 50.

403. This was a somewhat unusual notation by Bandelier since many of the storekeepers of that period were Jewish. It may simply have been a reminder to Bandelier, since he had apparently failed to obtain the individual's name.

404. P. J. Jaramillo was the owner of a general store in El Rito (Polk and Danser 1884a: 317). He was perhaps a member of the well-known Jaramillo family of Taos County, one of whom married Governor Bent (Twitchell 1911–17: II, 234n170).

405. Bourke (Bloom 1936: 248) recorded, "The house in which I found accomodations [sic] for myself, driver and mules—the last, of course, in the stable, was one of those Establishments called in the Rio Grande country, a 'Government Station' or 'Forage Agency.' The owner was a German named Becker married to a Mexican woman, and the house and all its belongings showed the blending of two different trains of thought and breeding." Printed on a picture opposite p. 248 is "U.S. Government Forage Agency (Frank Becker) Santa Cruz, New Mexico, July 15, 1881." In 1886, Bandelier briefly visited Becker at Santa Cruz (see entry for July 20, 1886).

406. For more on this "Cangelón" of northern New Mexico, see Pearce (1965: 25) and Ortiz (1969: 19). See also n 340.

407. The Lamy Memorial (1950: 52) stated, "When Abiquiu was refounded as a town for *genízaros* [see n 408] by Governor Tomas Velez Cachupin, he designated his name-saint as titular of the church. Spanish settlers nearby named their chapel for St. Rose of Lima, and later Abiquiu wanted the same title, but officially, St. Thomas the Apostle has come down as patron."

Pearce (1965: 150) noted that St. Rose of Lima was the first canonized saint of the New World. He also commented that she was the "patronness of the eighteenth century pueblo church of Abiquiu, as well as of the Spanish settlers living close by." Presumably, Pearce referred to the chapel of the Spanish settlers, which Bandelier called Santa Rosa de Abiquiu and noted it as being "two miles farther down, or east, of here." Adams and Chavez (1956: 120–26) further clarified the history of the area, citing the Domínguez account. They located the center of the Spanish settlement of Santa Rosa as probably three miles southeast of the modern town of Abiquiu, further commenting that the ruins of the chapel, which Domínguez described, may still be seen.

More recently, about 1959, Herbert W. Dick conducted test excavations at Santa Rosa de Lima.

408. This particular pueblo of Genízaros was one of five such villages shown on the map used as the back endsheet in Chavez (1957).

For further comments on this village, see Bandelier (1890–92: II, 54–55). He stated that the village had been peopled in part by Indian captives whom the Spaniards had rescued from their captors. Some of the captives were Hopi. Prof. Eleanor Adams has informed the editors that the word Genízaros, in Colonial New Mexico, normally referred to Plains, or at least non-Puebloan, Indians (see entry of June 14, 1885, for added details about this general Abiquiu region).

409. This account referred to the rooster-pull, still popular in northern New Mexico pueblos; a rooster is buried almost to its head in an open space, field or plaza. Horsemen then attempt to pull off the head by bending from the saddle at full gallop, or, as more frequently happens, to pull the rooster from the ground and ride off, hotly pursued by other horsemen who attempt to wrest the rooster from the first rider. It is actually very difficult to seize the rooster, as the head almost disappears below ground as the pounding of the horse's hooves approaches. Once in hand, the rooster is commonly looped in the rider's reins so he can better thwart attempts of the others to seize the rooster.

An alternative form of rooster-pull was reported by Lummis (1928: 277–80) for the June 24 Feast of St. John at Acoma Pueblo. (This may well have been true for other villages and other times.) The bird was suspended from a pole by its feet while lines of dancers tried to seize it by jumping as they danced under it. Bandelier, however, was referring to the method described in the first paragraph above.

410. Don Dolores Romero was Indian Agent for the Pueblo Indian Agency with headquarters at Santa Fe (Report, Commissioner, Indian Affairs 1886: 423–24).

411. S. B. Elkins was president of the First National Bank of Santa Fe (Polk and Danser 1884a: 350). Walter, in an article on "New Mexico's Pioneer Bank and Bankers" (1946: 209–25), said that Stephen B. Elkins succeeded Lucien B. Maxwell as president of the First National Bank of Santa Fe. Walter said it was Elkins who originated the idea of a bank in the territorial capital.

Born in Ohio in 1841, Elkins accompanied his parents to Missouri as a child. He was only twenty-nine years old when he ousted Maxwell as owner and president of the bank and elected himself its president.

Elkins had graduated from the University of Missouri and was teaching school when the Civil War broke out. He enlisted in the Union Army, was captured by Confederate guerillas, and ordered shot as a Union spy. Two former pupils saved him.

Capt. Elkins came to New Mexico in 1863. He was elected to the New Mexico legislature and appointed United States attorney for the Territory when twenty-five years old. He served two terms in the United States House of Representatives from New Mexico and eighteen as United States Senator from West Virginia. He amassed great wealth and founded the town of Elkins, West Virginia.

Like Maxwell and Catron, Elkins spoke Spanish and was popular with the Spanish-speaking voters. Walter noted (p. 215), "Nevertheless, he was reputed by his political enemies to have muffed the opportunity which the Territory had to become a state in 1876 at the same time as Colorado, necessitating 34 years of additional struggle before an enabling act for New Mexico became law." Walter (p. 216) also referred to the "law office of Elkins and Catron."

412. This was Spencer F. Baird, secretary of the Smithsonian Institution and the person who had chosen Major John W. Powell to head the Bureau of Ethnology (later, the Bureau of American Ethnology) (Twitchell 1911–17: I, 6).

413. Although correspondence between Bandelier and Jackson had occurred at least as early as July 10, 1885, it seems that Bandelier had not acted until August 15, when Dr. Eggert wrote, pointing out the possibilities of selling articles to Jackson in Paris (*Revue d'Ethnographie*). The article was "La découverte du Nouveau-Mexique par le moine franciscain frère Marcos de Nice en 1539." It appeared in the *Revue* in 1886 (Vol. V, pp. 34–48, 117–34, 193–212). In 1889, the article was translated into Spanish and appeared in *El Boletín Popular.* See bibliography: Bandelier (1886j).

414. This ceremony was the Kossa initiation dance listed by Parsons (1929: 169) for September at San Juan Pueblo. Its parallel, as Bandelier himself commented, could be found elsewhere among the pueblos. See also Lange and Riley 1966: 195–200 for Bandelier's detailed account of the Koshare ceremonies at Cochiti Pueblo, November 9–10, 1880, and again, November 30, 1882 (p. 367).

415. Here again, the dualism of puebloan ceremonialism was being revealed to Bandelier. The patterns vary from village to village, even, as, for example, within the Keresans in addition to the differences between Keresans and Tanoans. Here, the "Qosare" and the "Quirana" were alternating functions from one-half of the year to the other; in other instances, alternation is from one year to the next, or at the other extreme, from one portion of a ceremony to another on the same day.

416. Torquemada (1723: I, 681) described the religious practices of the Pueblo Indians in the following words:

> They list three demons that appear to them, to these they pray for rain, to the one named Cocapo, to the other, Cacino, and to the other, Homace. The two latter appear to them in the fields in [whatever] shape they wish. Cocapo appears to them in the Pueblo and whenever the women see him they are left with severe fright. His temple is a high room, ten feet wide by twenty feet long, all painted. . . . The idol is of stone or of clay and is seated on the right hand of the temple with a gourd containing three eggs of the *gallina de la tierra* [probably turkey] and has on the other (left) hand, another gourd with green corn (or ears of corn) and in front of it is an olla filled with water. This idol [is cared for by] an old Indian woman, who is the priestess.

417. "Didn't you notice how pretty the ojua [clouds] became day before yesterday after the dance?" Candelario presumably said "despues" rather than "depuis."

418. As Ortiz (1969: 92) pointed out, the Oxua (Bandelier's Ojua) are cloud beings, a subclass of deities, differentiated because they are regularly impersonated in dances among the Tewa-speaking pueblos.

419. For a discussion of Yuge-ouinge (Castañeda's Yuque-Yunque), see ns 217, 392, and 623.

420. The Canary Islands are a volcanic group with seven main islands and several very small islets lying some 150 miles off the northwest coast of Africa. There is a tradition that they were contacted by Mediterranean peoples in Greco-Roman times, and they seem to have been visited several times by both Europeans and Arabs in medieval times. Lanzarotte Malocello touched on them in 1270, but European settlement came much later. In 1402, the Norman, Jean de Béthencourt, settled in the islands and with Castilian support became king there in 1404. In 1496, after a long war with the native Berber-speaking population, the Guanches, Spain gained effective control of the islands.

Smith's description of the agriculture suggests utilization of the rich volcanic soil, but the exact method is rather obscure. The six-fingered individuals were, interestingly enough, not mentioned by Hooton (1925) in the study of the physical anthropology of the Canaries sponsored by the Peabody Museum.

421. This letter was included by White and Bernal (1960: 281–83) in their volume; the following is our translation:

San Juan de los Caballeros, Nuevo Mexico, September 10, 1885.

My dear friend:
    There is no excuse for my delay in answering your courteous and amenable letter; nevertheless I have had serious reasons to remain, if not in hiding, at least silent until today.
    The total ruin of my father's bank brought violence to the town. It was (like) a gang of thugs whose rabidness had no decency whatsoever. After my father's escape, to a destination still unknown, his other partner [F. C. Ryhiner, Jr.], the main one, was helped by his family to leave so the only one left behind was my brother-in-law [Maurice Huegy]. Day after day, and for a month, the fury of my enemies was increasing, especially because the disappearance of my father made all the responsibilities and their suspicions to fall on me. Frightened, confined in my house, offended, threatened with death, I persisted in spite of the advice of some people who did not let the mob scare them. For four weeks we lived on charity! Finally, my brother-in-law committed suicide. Two hours later, they took me to jail. My wife was sick of shame and of fear, because the

behavior of the mob recounted the most hideous moments of the French Revolution when I left for the station. I was, finally, able to leave for New Mexico where I was received with friendship and affection; here I expect to live now on, in a poor way with the help of publications in several languages. Late in the month I will go to Peña Blanca, whose parish has offered me a place to live, humble but enough for both of us. The expenses are minimal and even when I will be making 50 or 70 dollars per month, this will be enough for me not to fall into extreme poverty.

I didn't want to annoy you with my lamentations and complaints about an ill which had no solution, and I waited to see what the future had for me. Now that I have the possibility of living honestly, I again write you with the hope that you have forgiven me for this silence and that you will help me again with your advices. I have a project to publish in English, French, and German, always in first class publications, historical and geographical essays about all the countries I have visited. So far, the articles I have submitted have been more favorably received than one could have thought even when they have produced little. I have realized $200 in three months. At the same time I keep studying, increasing the collection of drawings and plans of the ruins. This collection, according to the most important artists of Germany will have a minimum value of 30,000 pesos. I am negotiating with the Prussian government to sell them the originals, but I doubt that we will arrive at any agreement.

Even though I possess more than enough material about New Mexico, I still lack a great deal of data. There are in Mexico numerous documents printed as well as manuscript. Of course, I cannot even dream to acquire rare books, but perhaps I could save enough to acquire copies or abstracts of documents. For the time being the topics in which I am now more interested are: the epoch of the founding of Santa Fé, New Mexico, and the oldest accounts which can be found about Casas Grandes, Chihuahua. Concerning the first topic there is some information in Benavides, but this author speaks of a parish (1622) and not of the people. There is a hiatus between 1604 and 1622 which I have not been able to cover. In regards to Casas Grandes, 1667 is the oldest date which I have found. There existed a Franciscan convent which was abandoned in 1748. I would like to have, if possible, all the available data which make reference to the aforementioned regions, [and] afterward to present a scholarly and solid work that will deserve the confidence of all. To that effect I would like to solicit your advices and the help of your expertise. For the rest, I put myself in the hands of God, to give me health, goodwill, and strength to work.

I hope that my faithful companion, the only soul I have left in this world, will arrive in a few days. If you send your letter, c/o Rev. A. Navet, priest of Peña Blanca, Wallace Station, New Mexico, you will be sure that I will receive your news.

Asking you to give your family my most affectionate regards, [and] yourself receive my most endearing expressions and respect.

Affectionately yours,

Ad. F. Bandelier

422. Here, Bandelier was requesting a certain type of drawing paper. In a letter to Parkman from Cochiti, written April 10, 1882, Bandelier wrote, "The two blocks of paper which Mr. Greenleaf procured for me are nearly exhausted, and if it is the intention of the Institute to keep me at work, then I would beg instantly and with great insistency

that 2. or 3. more blocks be sent to me by mail.—It is Frost & Adams: 'Improved Sketch Book,' 9. X 11.—I am particular in regard to the size." For a discussion of Bandelier's paintings and drawings, see ns 62 and 339.

423. The Tewa Pueblos have several kinds of basket dances, sponsored and produced by the women's societies. These are fertility dances, and the one mentioned here, the *Tung-Jiare* [Parsons's T'umshare], is sometimes linked with a kachina dance performed the preceding day (Parsons 1929: 169; 1939: 675).

424. This name was given as Elias Brevoort in Polk and Danser (1884a: 348). He was a claim agent in Santa Fe, with his place of business given as the Cathedral. Huggins (1876) carried this advertisement of Brevoort. "Elias Brevoort, Resident 26 years in New Mexico, Pioneer Land Grant Agency, Santa Fe, New Mexico. Specialty, Land Grants. Has constantly on hand choice Spanish and Mexican land grants, with first-class facilities for working up grant titles and purchasing from first hands. Reliable information furnished with regards to the Territory, grants and grant titles."

Westphall (1965: 100–101), wrote, "By 1881, the incidence of fraud was such that Elias Brevoort, receiver of the Land Office at Santa Fe, on December 5, informed Commissioner N. C. McFarland, in a letter of far-reaching consequence, 'that I have quite recently become impressed with the belief there has been for some months past a system of frauds perpetrated in making entries of lands.' " In the note (100n3) accompanying this comment, Westphall gave the names of principal suspects, including José de Sena, former registrar at Santa Fé; Antonio Ortiz y Salazar, former probate judge of Santa Fé County; John Gwyn and Thomas Gwyn of Santa Fé, the latter, a former registrar; and Max Frost, especially (pp. 106ff.).

Brevoort suggested a special agent of the Interior Department be sent to the Territory at once to investigate; he also mentioned the risk to life for the investigator and those providing information.

Brevoort left office on December 8, 1881, three days after writing the Commissioner.

In the *Weekly New Mexican Review,* Santa Fe, issue of Thursday, April 22, 1888 (No. 10, p. 2), there was an article telling how Rev. H. O. Ladd had fortunately secured several hundred pounds of a new variety of corn, "100-day Lima corn," developed by a scientist at Lima, Ohio. Ladd had learned of this choice variety through a letter from Elias Brevoort who had seen it on dry and sandy wastes of western Kansas and southeastern Colorado.

Brevoort, in 1874, published a book, *New Mexico, Her Natural Resources and Attractions,* etc. (Santa Fe, 176 pp.).

425. Here was a rather typical example of the suspicion and even antagonism that even today persists between elements of the Indian and Spanish-speaking populations of New Mexico. For another example, see Lange and Riley 1966: 109–10.

426. Charles Eliot Norton (1827–1908) was born in Cambridge, Massachusetts, the son of Professor Andrew and Catherine Eliot Norton. He graduated from Harvard in 1846, subsequently going to India as supercargo in 1849. After about two years, he went to Europe for another two years, returning again to that area from 1867 to 1873. During this interval, Norton was also editor of the *North American Review* (1862–68).

From 1874 to 1898, Norton served as professor of the history of art at Harvard; he was largely instrumental in founding the Archaeological Institute of America, and he became the first president of the AIA, holding office from 1879 to 1890. Norton was also a recognized Dante scholar and served as president of the Dante Society. He translated the *Divina Commedia* and the *Vita Nuova* of Dante. He authored or edited a number of other books, including a work on Medieval church architecture; he edited the correspondence of Carlyle and Emerson, of Carlyle and Goethe, and the letters of John Ruskin and James Russell Lowell.

Norton was particularly interested in the excavation of Assos in Asia Minor and in the founding of the American School of Classical Studies of Athens. In Hodge's obituary on Norton (1908: 705), the following comment was included, "... although the important investigations by Bandelier in the Pueblo country of our Southwest were conducted during Professor Norton's presidency, his belief was that because the arts of the American aborigines are not comparable with those of the peoples of the Old World, American archaeology is not worthy of serious study." This attitude was also noted by the editors in our second volume (1970: 355–56n5). (Encyclopaedia Britannica 1967: XVI, 642; Who's Who 1908–9: 1398)

427. This somewhat enigmatic statement probably meant that the people of San Juan believed that Bandelier's pictures were in some way magic, or mana, filled, even though they were pictures of Zuñi religious personages. Inhaling, i.e., absorbing the power of something, has been a widespread puebloan ritualistic pattern. For the Tewa, see Parsons (1929: 255), and for puebloan parallels, in general, consult the index (pp. 1120–21) of Parsons's *Pueblo Indian Religion* (1939).

428. Tewa data indicate that both a winter sunwise (north-west-south-east) and a summer anti-sunwise (south-west-north-east) circuit are used ceremonially. In some Tewa villages, morning and afternoon dances on the same day may be respectively, sunwise and anti-sunwise. Ortiz (1969: 143) pointed out that the Tewa are given to reversals in color direction symbolism and in dance ritual circuits.

429. See n 284 and n 296 for comments on color symbolism.

430. See n 277.

431. The twin brothers of Zuñi mythology are the widely present Twin War Gods of the Pueblo Indians. For further data, see ns 263, 334, and 376.

432. Parsons (1929: 132–36) found the term *samayo* applied to the Hunt Chief among the Tewas. However, at San Juan, she found the term *pikœ sen^do,* instead (p. 133). This office she reported as unfamiliar at Santa Clara (p. 135), but at San Ildefonso, *samaíyo* rather than *pikœ sen^do*. At Tesuque, she was given *samayo* (p. 136), and at Nambé, she found neither term present, but remembered in terms of the office, or function (p. 136).

433. At the time Bandelier knew Captain Dougherty in 1883, he was in command of the troops sent out from Fort Apache. A native of Ireland, Captain William Edgworth Dougherty, after Civil War service, was promoted to captain, March 1, 1878, and to major in 1898. Before retirement, he had reached his full colonelcy. Most of his career was spent with the 1st Infantry (Heitman 1903: I, 380).

434. Bandelier revisited these ruins of Cieneguilla and Cienega on October 19, 1885, and noted that the church mentioned here was recent; he also noted that there was no pueblo there (see October 19 entry and n 454). He returned to these ruins again on November 1, 1887 (see n 881).

Bandelier located Cieneguilla as twelve miles southwest of Santa Fe (1890–92: II, 88n1) and on the eastern base of the high mesa of the Tetilla, nine miles to the east of La Bajada (p. 95n1).

Elsewhere in his *Final Report* (pp. 91–92), Bandelier discussed the linguistic affiliation of the historic village at the Cienega where the Santa Fe River enters the narrow defile that brings it to the Rio Grande, tentatively identifying Tziguma as a Tano settlement (see also n 318).

Nelson did partial excavations at both Cieneguilla and Cienega in 1915 (Nelson 1916a: 43; 1916b: 179).

435. See n 301.

436. Padre José Rómulo Ribera was added to the New Mexico clergy by Bishop John B. Lamy (Salpointe 1898: 283). In Chavez (1957: 136), catalogued as 1871, No. 11, is the

following entry: "Lamy to Purcell. Santa Fe, Dec. 29, 1871. Photo. Young deacon, Joseph R. Rivera [sic], with him and Loretto Sisters; free passage from St. Louis to Santa Fe. Rivera ordained, Dec. 23, 1871."

Defouri (1887: 106–18), in describing the 1867 trip of Bishop Lamy to Europe to recruit both Jesuits from Naples and additional French priests, mentioned that on May 25, Bishop Lamy left in Baltimore for a few days among others, "Romulo Richera [sic], a young Mexican who had completed his classics in Montreal (p. 108)." Defouri's implication was that Romulo Richera had joined Lamy's group in the East after their ocean crossing and prior to their trip west. The editors feel that this may well have been José Rómulo Ribera.

Padre Ribera was of considerable aid to Bandelier in his early work, as journal entries of those years indicate. However, Bandelier, in his entry of February 1, 1883, noted a report of "bad news (ill conduct)" relative to Padre Ribera, and in his entry of July 15, 1884, upon meeting Padre Ribera, with other priests, at Las Vegas, noted "a long confidential conversation [with Padre Ribera] whose contents I do not wish to put down here" (Lange and Riley 1970: 23, 337; see n 859).

437. See n 301.

438. This was probably Doña Soledad García de Sena y Sena, mother of Jesús Sena and wife of José Antonio Sena of Peña Blanca (Registro: p. 75). See also ns 325 and 863.

439. The wording, or phrasing, of this entry could lead one to assume that Romero Chavez was the cacique. However, the entry of October 8, 1885, clearly identified him as "Shquy Chayani," or Giant Society Headman. This fact leaves Bandelier consistent in his habit of referring to the cacique by title, never by name. Consequently, we have been unable to learn the identity of the cacique at any time of Bandelier's contact with, or residence in, Cochiti Pueblo. Further, no mention of Romero Chavez has been found in the Peña Blanca church records, and his name did not appear in the society rosters and family data gathered by Lange in his study of Cochiti (1959).

440. This completed Bandelier's second series of articles on Cibola, published in the autumn of 1885 in the *New Yorker Staatszeitung* (see also n 115).

441. The Cañón del Qoye, or Koye, or Colle Canyon, joins the Cañada Quemada to form the Cañada Peralta, which empties into the Rio Grande from the west just south of Cochiti. The Cañón del Qoye is a narrow chasm, undercut at the bottom so that the cliffs overhang so as to almost exclude daylight (Bandelier 1890–92: II, 182). This precipitous portion of the canyon, described by Bandelier, is limited to its uppermost section, far back from the Rio Grande.

Lange (1959: 444) was given an account of one of the last Navaho fights which took place "in Colle Canyon," where two or three Cochiti men were herding cattle.

442. Bandelier had begun his ethnographic field work at Santo Domingo Pueblo in 1880. He was finally forced to leave. For his account of this experience, see Lange and Riley (1966: 91–129). Even today the Santo Domingo Indians have a reputation of coolness to the outsider which may quickly change to outright hostility if one wishes to investigate their customs and beliefs.

443. As Bandelier noted, the governor was in error. See the discussion in n 452.

444. This entry, in conjunction with earlier entries noting work on "the novel," may best be interpreted as meaning that much of Bandelier's previous effort had been on rewriting and polishing drafts of the manuscript, *Die Köshare* (see ns 50 and 235).

445. Bandelier's notations on these details, as in a number of other instances, are interesting but frustrating. Confusion may have come from the informants' incomplete knowledge or only partially correct impressions and/or their limitations in accurately communicating their knowledge to Bandelier. It can readily be assumed also that a number of these details have undergone change between Bandelier's time and the present.

Qoshare naue and *Quirana naue* referred to the headman, or chief, of these two so-called managing societies at Cochiti (see Lange 1959: 298–309). Bandelier's accompanying remarks concerning the *chayanes,* or medicine men, are difficult to interpret; his use of the term chayanes seemed to shift between the societies, Hi-tshanyi [Flint], Shquy [Giant], and Shiqama [Shikame], and the members of these societies. For a more recent statement on these societies at Cochiti, see Lange 1959: 254–73.

446. For further insights into the complexities of puebloan caciques, the closely associated medicine men, the Koshare and Kwirena societies, kiva groups, and moieties, see Bandelier's lengthy entry of June 18, 1885, the accompanying notes and selected bibliography.

447. The members of various secret societies, not only the Qoshare (Koshare) and Quirana (Kwirena), acquire affiliations that often extend beyond their individual village and also beyond the limit of their linguistic grouping. "Chapters" acquire parent-child ceremonial relationships, stemming from the circumstances of individual or chapter initiations. This latter occurs generally where a society has lapsed in a pueblo and then is later reinstated with the aid of an outside chapter.

The "lower" and "upper" designations in this entry referred simply to the relative geographical, or terrain, features at Cochiti, where the Qoshare belong with the Turquoise Kiva, down the slope to the east from the Pumpkin Kiva with which the Quirana are affiliated.

448. This most probably referred to the Potrero of San Miguel, or Potrero del Capulin, in the southwestern corner of Bandelier National Monument. The large ruin there, San Miguel, or Ha-atze (L.A. 370), was claimed as one of the ancestral villages of the Cochiti as they moved southward from their earlier home in the Rito de los Frijoles. San Miguel lies northwest, a mile or more, from Kuapa (L.A. 3443 and L.A. 3444; see n 343).

449. A May 20, 1885, entry in the *Weekly Telephone* noted: "Gen. [W. C.] Kueffner of Belleville represents the Swiss creditors of F. Ryhiner and Co." The *Weekly Telephone* of May 27, 1885, reported, "Gen. Kueffner of Belleville, Judge Henry and Squire Henry Howard of Greenville, and Mr. Burkhardt of St. Louis, were in town concerning bank matters, last Wednesday [May 20th]."

450. James C. Pilling was the first to attempt to compile a comprehensive bibliography of North American native languages. In the Ayer Collection, Newberry Library, Chicago, there is a volume entitled, "Proof-Sheets of a Bibliography of the Languages of the North American Indians" (Distributed only to Collaborators), Washington, 1885. This work was done under the auspices of the Bureau of Ethnology, and early annual reports noted the progress of the undertaking.

Before going into the field in 1880, Bandelier had visited the Bureau of Ethnology in Washington and had received instructions on recording data, both ethnologic and linguistic. He also had received "schedules," which Major J. W. Powell had prepared (White 1940: II, 205–6). Bandelier had compiled a "Queres" [Keres] vocabulary (Lange and Riley 1966: 213, 216, 236). On October 20, 1882, when in Rochester with Lewis Henry Morgan, Bandelier had written, "My dear Mr. Pilling! I have a considerable vocabulary of the 'Queres' language of New Mexico. Shall I send it to you? It is the Cochiti dialect" (Lange and Riley 1970: 361n37).

The Smithsonian Institution files contain the receipt and a copy of this letter and a note that it was answered, but there is no indication of the nature of Pilling's reply.

Hodge (1932: 363–64), in his comprehensive bibliography of Bandelier, listed "[Vocabulary of the Keres language of Cochiti.] [16]. In Bulletin I of the Archaeological Institute of America, p. 17, Boston, 1883, Bandelier wrote: 'I have myself obtained a vocabulary (nearly one thousand one hundred words and phrases) of the Queres idiom as spoken at Cochiti, which vocabulary I have since completed, adding to it many synonyms from the Acoma dialect.' The present whereabouts of this manuscript is un-known."

In the intervening years, this manuscript has been located in the Charles F. Lummis Collection, Southwest Museum, Los Angeles. Bandelier (1890–92: I, v–vi) noted that the orthography which he had adopted for Indian names was not that adopted by the Bureau of Ethnology, recognizing that form as perhaps preferable for linguists but difficult for the general reader unacquainted with the complicated alphabet constructed for the Bureau. Bandelier adopted the continental pronunciation of the letters. The subjects of the correspondence with Pilling in this and the subsequent entries of October 21 and 26, 1885, remain unknown. Bandelier commented in his entry of October 21, "Information wanted as usual [by Pilling]."

451. These remarks on the land dispute between the pueblos of Santo Domingo and Cochiti referred to an area of overlap near the village of Zile, or Sile, west of the Rio Grande south of Cochiti and northwest of Santo Domingo. The tract in question consisted of 149.88 acres (Lange 1959: 36n1).

452. In his entry of July 24, 1885, Bandelier used for the first time the name Gui-puy for this ruin on the Galisteo River, correlating it with the old pueblo of Santo Domingo. In this entry of October 16, 1885, when he actually visited the ruin, he again used the name Gui-puy.

In December 1882, Bandelier had mentioned a ruin on the Galisteo River in two different entries (Lange and Riley 1966: 368, 371). In the second entry, the editors questioned his "east" of Wallace. The identification in the 1885 journals of this ruin as Gui-puy makes our editorial challenge an error.

Harrington (1916: 450 and Map 28) has provided a comprehensive summary, quoting from Bandelier's *Final Report* (1890–92: II, 185–87) and keying in designations of sites on his Map 28 with Bandelier's commentary.

As is clear from the quoted text, Bandelier had abandoned his idea of the thick adobe wall at Gui-puy possibly being a church wall. This site, Harrington's 28: 117, was recorded as L.A. 182, Gipuy, according to Schroeder and Matson (1965: 158). The first church at Santo Domingo, built by 1604, appears to have been erected at the newer, or historical Gi-pu-y, Harrington's 28: 106, again on the Galisteo and north of the present-day Santo Domingo Pueblo (28: 109).

For further details, see Kubler (1940: 107).

453. Presumably, this was stationery, rather than mail, as Bandelier was normally meticulous in recording sources of his mail.

454. This was Bandelier's second visit to Cienega and Cieneguilla (see n 434). Bandelier noted in this entry the great rubbish heaps of Tziguma ("Alamo Solo"), on the banks of the Arroyo Hondo. Nelson (1916a: 42) located the ruins of Cienega, as well as those of Cieneguilla, on the bank of the Rio Santa Fe (see Harrington 1916: 467–68 for his discussions of Cienega, Cieneguilla, and Arroyo Hondo).

455. Bandelier's journal entries indicated he had dreaded being summoned to return to Edwardsville and had hoped that it would not be necessary. The need for his return was in relation to the liquidation of assets of the F. Ryhiner & Co. bank, which had closed the previous May. Bradshaw, as well as his partner, Metcalf, had advised Bandelier on legal matters pertaining to the bank's holdings on several previous occasions.

456. As the *Santa Fe New Mexican Review* of October 20, 1885 (p. 4), noted: "Professor Bandalier [sic] is at Herlow's [Hotel] today. He is just in return from an extended trip to Cochiti, San Juan, and Pena Blanca."

457. This was Robert H. Longwill, M.D., who at this period advertised daily in the *Santa Fe New Mexican Review*. As of October 1885, and for years thereafter, Longwill had offices on the east end of Palace Ave., in the Rómulo Martinez house, formerly

occupied by Col. Barnes. Additional data on Dr. Longwill, often written Longwell, may be found in Lange and Riley 1970: 365–66n66.

458. General Luther P. Bradley was Commander of the Department of New Mexico, United States Army, from 1884 to 1886 (Twitchell 1911–17: II, 429n353; see also Heitman 1903: I, 239, and Lange and Riley 1970: 379n173).

459. Hubert was the son of George and Celia Hoffmann, residents of St. Louis; Celia was a cousin of Bandelier's wife, Joe. The couples were very close; following the bank failure, Hubert, in poor health, accompanied the Bandeliers west to Santa Fe. Hubert did not live with the Bandeliers but roomed and boarded with Mrs. Bush (see n 483). Thus, he was nearby and in their home often enough that they could effectively look out for him. Before the trip west, Hubert was a clerk, living with his parents at 3701 Cook Avenue, St. Louis (Gould 1885: 557). Hubert died in Denver, date unknown, of tuberculosis (Lange and Riley 1970: 399n348a).

460. The names of August and Emily Becker appear frequently in the journals. Emily, Mrs. August, Becker was a cousin of Josephine Huegy Bandelier on her mother's side (Hobbs: 1942a). The Beckers were residents of St. Louis, but as the various volumes of Gould's Directory (1880–1892) listed quite a number of August Beckers, we have been unable to identify these individuals more precisely.

461. W. F. White was general passenger and ticket agent for the AT&SF railroad at Topeka, Kansas (McKenney 1882–83: xii). Over the years, Bandelier had written White a number of times, seemingly about tickets or even passes.

462. This was William H. Krome of the law firm, Krome and Hadley, in Edwardsville (Polk and Danser 1884b: 870). The *Weekly Telephone* of May 13, 1885, said, "Messrs. Krome and Hadley of Edwardsville are engaged as attorneys by the Receivers of our bank."

463. Sister Severa was an acquaintance of some years' standing. In his account, "The Founding and Growth of St. Joseph's Hospital," Spencer (1937: 176–85) noted that the Rev. Joseph Meckel, pastor at St. Paul's, was instrumental in having sister nurses from Litchfield brought to Highland. In January 1878, the first, Sisters Severa and Silvana, came to serve in the home established as a hospital. By July, four sisters were working there; by late summer, a building committee had been organized on which Ad. F. Bandelier was one of the six members. At the dedication, August 21, 1879, "Dr. Felder was one of the speakers on the program and the fluent A. F. Bandelier was another."

464. References to the coal mine were frequent in the journals (Lange and Riley 1966; 1970), as well as in the Bandelier-Morgan correspondence (White 1940: I, II). Earlier notes (52 and 97) have already referred briefly to the mine. Up until the summer of 1971, its exact location and history remained unknown to the editors. In a *History of Madison County, Illinois* (Brink 1882: 456), however, the following was found:

> Confidence Coal and Mining Company. The mine is situated two and one-half miles north-east of Collinsville, on the line of the Vandalia railroad. The shaft was sunk in the spring of 1870, by Seybt, Bandelier & Co. In the fall of 1870, the mine was leased to the Bartlett Coal and Mining Co., and it was extensively worked by them until the spring of 1873, when they forfeited their lease and Seybt, Bandelier & Co. began operating it and have continued to the present. The depth of the shaft is 219 feet to the surface of the coal, and the vein will average seven feet. The mine is operated by machinery, run by compressed air. They employ 50 men, and the average amount of coal raised is eighteen car loads per day. The company have in all eighteen buildings including the tipple house, office, boarding houses and dwellings. Most of the dwellings are situated on the bluffs a short distance east of the mine.

This information substantiated Hobbs's statement from Elizabeth Bandelier Kaune that Seybt had been Bandelier's partner in a coal mine near Collinsville, Illinois (1940a).

Additional research in 1971 has shown that the business office of the Confidence Coal & Mining Company was, at least for a time, in St. Louis. Gould (1878: 213) listed the company at 22 S. Commercial in St. Louis, although neither Bandelier's nor Seybt's name appeared in this listing. However, Herman G. Bohn was listed by Gould (p. 134) as "com. mers. and agt. Conf. Coal & Mining Co." at the same Commercial Street address. Beyond the meager data on Bohn already presented (Lange and Riley 1970: 397n336), nothing further has been learned. Adolph F. Bandelier's name appeared in Gould in conjunction with the coal company for the first time in 1882. His St. Louis address was given as 12 S. Commercial, with his residence in Highland (Gould 1882: 112). Seybt's name also appeared for the first time in 1882 (p. 1047). In 1883, Bandelier's and Seybt's names appeared in conjuction with the Confidence Coal & Mining Co. (Gould 1883: 110), but Bohn was no longer given as an agent for the coal company, though his business address in St. Louis was the same as Bandelier's. By 1884, Seybt was listed only as a flour dealer in Highland (Gould 1884: 114); Bandelier continued to be listed with the Confidence Coal & Mining Co. (p. 114). In 1885, Gould (pp. 271, 1333) listed the company, but Bandelier's name was not included. The listing for Herman G. Bohn (Gould 1885: 171) was as "com. mers." at 12 S. Commercial, the same as the coal company. In 1886 (p. 270), the Confidence Coal & Mining Co. was listed at 314 Chamber of Commerce, and the same address was given for Bohn (p. 170). Though Bohn was listed again in 1887, the Confidence Coal & Mining Co. was not.

That the coal mine had caused Bandelier great concern over an extended period is evidenced by correspondence and also journal entries. On May 27, 1874, Bandelier wrote Morgan (White 1940: I, 164), " . . . I am at the office [the Highland Mechanical Works ?] from 7 A.M. to 5 P.M., have to attend to a coal mine in the spare hours, & only what is left of the night hours can I devote to study." On September 24, 1874, he wrote Morgan (p. 174), "I have been passing some very hard times. My coal mine has given me much trouble but it is now in shape, & working, as it was intended, the best mine in the west." In November 1874, he wrote Morgan (p. 179), "I *have just* returned from an exciting trip, meeting 500–600 more or less armed & more or less sober coal miners, who had come up to my mine to stop my men forcibly." On January 15, 1875, Bandelier wrote Morgan (p. 203), "A few words in much hurry, as you can see by the style of paper to which I am 'reduced.' " [White noted here that "This letter, as well as many that follow, is written on stationary of the 'Confidence Coal & Mining Company, D. W. Fox, Superintendent.' In the upper left-hand corner is the name 'C. H. Seybt, Highland, Ills.' and in the upper right-hand corner, that of 'A. F. Bandelier, Highland, Ills.' "

On April 23, 1875, Bandelier wrote Morgan (p. 271), "In business, there is again before me one of those periods of suspense which are so very disagreeable. I have been improving the hard times to increase my real estate connected with the coal mine, and shall soon have 500 acres of coal in one body, within 14 miles of St. Louis. This has greatly engrossed my attention, & diverted me from other matters. I hope the time will come now to derive some benefit from these operations."

In a reproduction of a letter of September 28, 1875 (fac. p. 244), Fox's name no longer appeared on the letterhead, and C. H. Seybt with A. F. Bandelier beneath it were bracketed together in the upper left-hand corner.

Burrus (1969b: 21) cited a letter from Bandelier to F. W. Putnam, June 8, 1877, in which he wrote, "This afternoon may, perhaps, decide upon a sudden departure for Boston, on my part. Nearly four years ago, I became the victim of one of those coal-bubbles, whose stock was held at Boston. My property was brought to the verge of utter destruction and ruin, while the leasees, going pleasantly into bankruptcy, paid nothing and remained as before: 'high-toned gentlemen,' of unblemished character, Christians, etc. There may be a chance, however, now to recover something; and, should it prove thus, I may come to see you one fine morning. Today's meeting at St. Louis will enable me to judge of the prospects."

On April 26, 1878, Bandelier (White 1940: II, 97) apologized to Morgan for not having written for some time and explained,

> The main reason is business matters. You know, & I informed you of it sometime ago, that the great impediment in my way was a certain coal mine. Now this obstacle has become unbearable, and I have, lately, taken steps to remove it—almost at any cost. Not being made of light stuff, I could not keep up the concern without putting all my heart into it, and thus have succeeded in becoming almost everybody's slave. Now I have taken steps to get rid of that burthen in a very decided manner,—it is for sale, or rather for exchange, against any other kind of real estate. It is not money that I need, only mental & bodily relief, & this I cannot find unless that inf . . . hole is disposed of. If there is, down east, anyone owning respectable or only decent real estate, who of his own free will & accord will step into my shoes and desires to own one-half of the largest coal mine west of the Alleghanies, he will find me very ready to change places with him. He will, I am sure, make money out of it, but for my part I value my intellectual happiness more than anything else, and as I have other paying branches on hand, I want to get rid of this mental scourge. Excuse my frank exposure, but 'there the beauty lies'—I want rest, freedom of action, the possibility of again quietly enjoying scientific labor, and the obstacle in my way is that ill-starred coal enterprise.

The extent to which Bohn had been involved in the mine is suggested by Bandelier's entry of August 14, 1883. Bandelier indicated that Bohn had surrendered his interest in the mine, and "We promised to surrender his bond upon return of notes. Thank God for it; that much is over at last. The mine will be sold now" (Lange and Riley 1970: 145).

However, following the bank failure, the *Weekly Telephone* of June 17, 1885, had the following account: "In last week's *Union* one note of $1,000 and four of $500 each, by H. G. Bohn to Ad. F. Bandelier, Oct. 1st, 1878, were also added to the above account, making it higher by $3,000. This was an error. The notes were payable to Bandelier, who transferred them to the bank and received credit for the amount." Presumably, these were the notes to which Bandelier had reference in his August 14, 1883, entry. That something had happened to prevent the sale of the mine was further substantiated by the October 11, 1883, entry, "Were it not for the coal mine, I might leave with comparatively easy mind" (Lange and Riley 1970: 149).

The next reference to the coal mine was in the July 25, 1884, entry, "In the afternoon was called to Seybt's about coal (Krapp's deed and brick machine)" (p. 399). Then, in the entry of August 18, 1884, Bandelier noted, "I went to the mine and found everything in very good condition. But it would be imprudent to sell land now. Reported to Seybt" (p. 341). On November 8, 1884 (p. 347), "I went to St. Louis . . . Coal meeting very satisfactory . . . Everything about the mine is promising." The final mention of the mine by Bandelier was in the entry of October 31, 1885, following his legal summons to Edwardsville from New Mexico in regard to the bank failure. This is the statement from which this particular note stemmed, "Made an arrangement with Bradshaw and Krome to transfer the coal mine to the assignees and the house [in Highland ?] to Mr. Bradshaw. Mudge assents to it."

465. Ida Becker's marriage to Rudolph Streiff was reported in the *Weekly Telephone* of Highland on March 27, 1884 (Lange and Riley 1970: 403n373). C. Rudolph Streiff was

listed in Gould (1885: 1124, 1239) as a partner in the St. Louis firm of Wild and Streiff (Henry Wild, C. Rudolph Streiff, and Albert J. Wild), diamond setters.

466. Gould (1885: 289) listed Eugene B. Cronin as a justice of the peace in St. Louis.

467. This was George Julius Engelmann, surgeon, gynecologist, and member of the American Anthropological Association. He was born in St. Louis, July 2, 1847, the only son of the physician and well-known botanist, George Engelmann, and his wife, Dora Horstmann, a cousin, who were married at Kreuznach, Germany, June 11, 1840.

George J. Engelmann graduated from Washington University in 1867 and took an A.M. degree there in 1870; he studied medicine at the Universities of Tübingen, Berlin, and Vienna, serving as a surgeon during the Franco-Prussian War. Subsequently, he practiced in St. Louis and later in Boston. Dr. Engelmann traveled extensively and pursued both ethnological and archaeological research; his collections were in the Peabody Museum, Cambridge, and the National Museum, Washington, as well as in museums in Berlin and Vienna.

Engelmann belonged to various medical and other learned societies and published numerous works bearing chiefly on gynecology, for example, *Labor Among Primitive Peoples,* St. Louis, 1882 (German transl., Vienna, 1884; French transl., 1886).

G. J. Engelmann died suddenly at Nashua, N.H., November 16, 1903 (Dixon 1903: 739).

At this point, the editors would like to clarify their earlier confusion regarding the above Dr. George J. Engelmann, physician and anthropologist, and his father, Dr. George Engelmann, physician and botanist, with both of whom Bandelier corresponded and otherwise interacted.

In the October 16, 1883, entry (Lange and Riley 1970: 150), the editors incorrectly placed n 385 after the name of George Engelmann; n 385 should have been placed after "old Dr. G. Engelmann" of the October 20, 1883, entry (p. 150). The Engelmann of the October 19, 1883, entry was also a reference to the son.

The elder Engelmann died on February 4, 1884, but Bandelier did not learn of this until May 5, 1884, as he was in the field in northern Mexico. The index items of the second volume (p. 493), on reexamination, with one exception, all pertain to the father, George, and not to the son, George J. George J., the son, was taken into corresponding membership of the Anthropological Society of Washington (a group of twenty-one, including Bandelier) on March 15, 1884 (Lange and Riley 1970: 243, 424n59).

In our first volume (1966: 433), the confusion between the two Engelmanns also occurred. While some entries cannot be precisely designated (pp. 87, 373), it is our belief that those on pp. 253, 267, 271, 277, 296, 298, and 357 did, in fact, concern the father while those on pp. 127 and 375 were to the son. The first of those to the son, at the end of the entry for October 4, 1880, is of interest in light of the bibliographic example cited earlier in this note, "George [J.] Engelmann, however, asks a little too much. I cannot photograph women in childbirth."

The confusion between the two Engelmanns appears elsewhere in the literature, justifying our extended treatment here. For example, White (1940: II, 101n5) referred to "George J. [*sic*] Engleman [*sic*] (1809–84), a physician who practised medicine in St. Louis; achieved considerable distinction as a botanist; was first president of the St. Louis Academy of Science."

During the summer of 1971, the editors visited the Missouri Botanical Garden, St. Louis, examined the few Bandelier contributions to the Engelmann collections, and obtained copies of the existing Bandelier-Engelmann (Sr.) correspondence there.

The three items were written in German, dated as follows: 27 Juni 1879 from Highland, Illinois, from Adolph F. Bandelier; 12 März 1881 from Adolphe Eugene Bandelier. Since these contained references to cacti, they had been translated by Mrs. Carla Lange, assistant librarian, who was working on the Engelmann correspondence. A third letter, dated 23 Dez., corrected to 23 Nov., 1882, from Santa Fe, N.M., described Bandelier's purchases for the Berlin Museum (see also n 60) and had not been translated. This letter appears to have been a direct result of the meeting Bandelier had with George J. Engelmann just before his departure from St. Louis for the Southwest, as related in the journal entry of November 1, 1882. " . . . then took dinner at Engelmann's. His ethnological collections are very fine. He wants me to buy things for him and for the Berlin Museum."

Our initial surprise at the very limited Bandelier-Engelmann correspondence has, in retrospect, become understandable when it is noted that a number of Bandelier's writings were directed, not to the father, Dr. George, but to the son, Dr. George J.

468. Bandelier had been summoned to Edwardsville from New Mexico in regard to the liquidation of assets of the F. Ryhiner & Co. bank. It is interesting that Bandelier made no comment on F. C. Ryhiner, Jr., at this point. The latter had also probably been summoned to appear. The November 6, 1885, entry noted that Ryhiner "wanted to turn State's evidence" against Bandelier but had not been accepted. Biographical data and the role of F. C. Ryhiner, Jr., in the bank are further discussed in ns 68, 146, 148, and 169.

469. Gould (1888: 1432) carried the following listing:

> Blanke & Bro. Candy Co.,
> 608, 610, and 612 Market St.
> We Manufacture the Largest and Best
> Line of Fine and Strictly Pure Candies
> in the West and Especially Adapted
> to the Fine Retail Trade. Send for Price List.

George Hoffmann (n 124) and Gustave Bandelier (n 142) were both employed there.

470. Polk and Danser (1884b: 2157, 2307) gave Dr. J. S. B. Alleyne, M.D., as Dean of the St. Louis Medical College, Corner of 7th and Clark, with an office at 3132 Washington Avenue. A faculty of ten members was listed, with an additional thirteen lecturers.

471. Timothy Gruaz was born in Lyons, France, June 8, 1831, of Swiss parents; the family came to America in 1849. Having attended the University of Bern, Timothy was initially a private tutor in area households. Since two accounts (Brink 1882: 436 and Biographical Publishing Co. 1894: 162–63) stated that Bandelier had been privately tutored by Timothy Gruaz and since documentation of this fact, as far as the editors know, has not previously appeared in biographies of Bandelier, it seemed important to incorporate these data. Throughout the literature, the statement has run that Bandelier never attended public schools in Highland but was privately tutored at home.

The account of the Biographical Publishing Co. noted that, in 1853, Mr. Gruaz was employed as a private teacher in the home of Adolph [Adolphe Eugene] Bandelier of Highland. He was twenty-one at the time, and Adolph F. Bandelier was thirteen. The Senior Bandelier was then consul of the Mississippi Valley for the Swiss government. How long Gruaz tutored Bandelier is not known. The account indicated a much closer business relationship between Gruaz and the Bandeliers and the F. Ryhiner & Co. bank than the editors previously suspected. In addition to Gruaz's tutoring the young Bandelier, he also kept the books for the consul and aided him in the office. Upon establishment of the F. Ryhiner & Co. bank, July 1, 1854, he was chosen cashier, and remained in that position for five years, using his leisure time to teach in a singing school.

Upon resigning from the bank, Gruaz formed a partnership with Messrs. Huegy and Bandelier, and under the firm name of T. Gruaz & Co. opened a general mercantile store, platting the town of Sebastopol, five miles southeast of Highland. He continued as head of this firm until 1862, when he disposed of his interest in the store and became publisher of the Highland *Bote*. The Brink account, cited above, reversed certain of the details above in sequence, but Gruaz's roles as tutor and cashier in the bank were both mentioned.

Earlier journal entries (Lange and Riley 1966) revealed Gruaz as one of the colleagues with whom Bandelier enjoyed discussing literature and politics. The citations above provide additional insights, and an additional sentence (Biographical Publishing Co. 1894: 162), indicating that in 1881, Gruaz had been sent to Mexico by a mining company to examine titles, would suggest that an interest in Mexico would have been an additional bond between Gruaz and Bandelier.

However, the July 22, 1883, entry (Lange and Riley 1970: 142) indicated that their former relationship had deteriorated, which explains Bandelier's surprise at Gruaz's gestures of friendship noted in this entry. Gruaz, in 1884, was in real estate and had been elected city attorney in April of that year (Polk and Danser 1884b: 1003). Hobbs (1940a) noted Mrs. Kaune's statement that Gruaz had followed Bandelier to Santa Fe in a clandestine way to see "how he lived." At the time of the bank failure, rumors persisted that Adolph F. Bandelier had drawn heavily on monies not rightfully his and that much of his Southwestern and Mexican research had thus been financed. There is no evidence to support this, however; the journal entries of this volume, as Bandelier grasped at every straw that would bring him a little income, suggest that Gruaz did not find him living at all lavishly in Santa Fe. In fact, he had to ask close friends for small loans, at times, and to purchase necessities on credit.

472. Ad. Suppiger was Adolph Anthony Suppiger, the son of Anthony and Monica (Wickenhauser) Suppiger. Anthony Suppiger came from Switzerland in 1831 and with his brothers, Joseph, Bernard, Godfrey M., and David, established the first flouring mill in Madison County. Adolph Suppiger attended the State Normal University and taught for two years at Marine, Illinois, after which he served as principal of the Highland schools for six years, conducting a book and music store as well. In 1870, he married Miss Leah P. Baer and in 1873 was elected Madison County Superintendent of Schools. In 1877 he moved to Pierron, where he engaged in mercantile pursuits. He returned to Edwardsville and continued in business until 1886, when he again was elected County Superintendent which position he held to 1890 (Biographical Publishing Co. 1894: 172–73).

473. Sir Clements R. Markham had edited and made notes for Edward Grimston's 1604 English translation of José de Acosta's "The Natural and Moral History of the Indies," which was printed for the Hakluyt Society in London in 1880. In 1892, Markham published a *History of Peru*. Because of similar scholarly interests, the editors feel that the Mr. Markham referred to in this entry may well have been Sir Clements R. Markham.

474. Gould's 1885 Directory for St. Louis contained no reference to a "Dr. Taussig." However, Hyde and Conard (1899: IV, 2218–19) listed Dr. William Taussig who was born in Prague, February 28, 1826, and studied classics and medicine at the University of Prague. He came to the United States in 1847, to New York, and in 1848 to St. Louis as a chemist in a drug company. He married, in 1857, Adele Wuerpel of St. Louis. He held various public offices, serving as one of the St. Louis County judges in the 1860s. President Lincoln appointed him examining surgeon of the 1st Military District in 1865. He also served as an internal revenue collector. For thirty years, 1866–96, Taussig was chairman of the executive committee of the Illinois and St. Louis Bridge & Tunnel Company. In 1889, Dr. Taussig was president of the Terminal R.R. Association of St. Louis. Bandelier was seemingly contacting him as an influential person in railroading for assistance in securing railroad passes.

475. Lizzie Hagnauer was Elisa Felder Hagnauer, wife of Robert Hagnauer (Biographical Publishing Co. 1894: 228; see also n 163).

476. Polk and Danser (1884b: 1004) listed Lorenz Winter as owner of a general store in Highland.

477. John Bardill was a member of the Madison County Board of Commissioners, serving from December 1, 1875, to April 1, 1876. He ran a store in Saline and was instrumental in getting a post office established at Saline (Brink 1882: 113, 176, 537).

478. As of this time, November 10, 1885, Bandelier's direct involvement with matters surrounding the bank failure was essentially terminated. The following summary of the affair, written some twenty-five years after the bank failure, is helpful for its overall evaluation and perspective.

> In 1854 A. E. Bandelier, Dr. F. Ryhiner and M. Huegy opened a private bank under the firm name of F. Ryhiner & Co., the first and only bank in Highland up to April 30, 1885, when it failed with liabilities of about $800,000. The principal reason of their failure was the very high rate of interest paid in time deposits. This brought large sums from Switzerland, amounting to about $375,-000 at the time of their failure. In order to place this large amount of money they employed agents in some of the counties in the southern part of the state. These agents, in order to make their commission, loaned large sums on any kind of poor land, and finally the bank would have to take the land for the debt. Then poor crops and hard times came along, so that the bank was unable to dispose of the lands to meet its obligations, and consequently causing its failure. After seven years the affairs of the bank were finally wound up, the creditors receiving in all 28.65% on their claims. The assignees were Joseph C. Ammann, Fred B. Suppiger, John H. Hermann and Adolph Ruegger. Though this failure was a hard blow to many of the poorer class of our people, yet it caused no perceptible suffering, the people simply continuing to work and saving up as before (Norton 1912: 534-35).

479. The Mercantile Library of St. Louis, established in 1846, is one of the few subscription libraries extant in the United States. With St. Louis an important departure point for the West during the nineteenth century, it is not surprising to find valuable collections of Western Americana among the holdings. The Reverend John Mason Peck, an untiring collector of works on frontier America, bequeathed his book and manuscript collection to the Mercantile Library in 1858. In 1876, Mr. John N. Dyer, librarian at the Mercantile since at least 1865 (Edwards 1865: 149), made valuable purchases at the sale of three libraries, all rich in Americana: Samuel Gardener Drake, a Boston bookseller for more than a half century; E. G. Squier, a former United States diplomat in Central America and a collector of materials on that region; and William Menzies, New York, also a well-known collector of Americana.

Yearly additions to these materials have resulted in the present outstanding holdings. In August 1971, the editors enjoyed the opportunity to work in this library briefly and regret that circumstances did not permit more extensive use of the sources available there. We are indebted to Mrs. Elizabeth Kirchner, Head Librarian, for her generous assistance and for the historical background data included here. Though our interest centered on Western Americana, the library has broad holdings including St. Louis area newspaper files and many rare volumes in other fields. In addition to manuscripts, books, and papers, there are collections of drawings, paintings, and sculpture.

Bandelier, returning in November to St. Louis in response to a legal summons, availed himself of the opportunity to check sources pertaining to his research.

This entry regarding the Mercantile Library was not Bandelier's first in his journals, but it does constitute the first reference in our published portion of the journals. On January 19 and 21, 1882, Bandelier had consulted two volumes of Lord Kingsborough. These entries were omitted from Volume I of the published journals, 1880-82, but the editors did note that Bandelier had done library research in St. Louis (Lange and Riley 1966: 237). In these January entries, he was checking material on Cholula and his Mexican fieldwork of 1881.

The only prior reference the editors have made to the Mercantile Library was when General Robert E. Carr was identified as president of the St. Louis Mercantile Library

Association (Lange and Riley 1970: 434n134). Carr's son-in-law, O. W. Meysenburg, had visited Bandelier in Santa Fe.

Examination of the Bandelier-Morgan letters shows that on May 27, 1874, Bandelier had written Morgan (White 1940: I, 164).

> My good fortune has placed at my disposal a perfect copy of Lord Kingsborough's "Antiquities of Mexico," 9 vols., great-folio. I do not, of course, place any reliance upon anything in this work which his Lordship has written but the 9th volume contains prints of several MSS which I have sought for in vain, & which are of the utmost importance for the history of Mexico.

He went on to ask Morgan how to arrange for printing of translations of these MSS, etc. He added (pp. 164–65),

> I have made formal application to the Mercantile Library of St. Louis for the 9th volume of Lord Kingsborough's "Antiquities of Mexico." If the work is obtainable, then I shall at once go to work on the "Crónica Mexicana." [This was by Hernando Alvarado Tezozomoc.] With your permission, I will send you the MSS translation to make use of it for your purposes. What I have yet seen leads me to the conclusion that it will prove to be the most valuable document published on the aboriginal institutions of Mexico.

That he was able to borrow the volume so he could work on it at home in Highland is evident by his letter, December 12, 1874, to Morgan (p. 201), "Am here at St. Louis, having ret'd the book to the Library, released my Bondsman, & found a *Spanish-Mexican Dictionary* (A. de Molina, 1571)."

It is of interest that Bandelier's first letter to García Icazbalceta was in regard to Tezozomoc's *Crónica Mexicana* and Icazbalceta's reply has also been preserved (White and Bernal 1960: 101–2, 103–4). The reply noted that Bandelier was translating this work into English (p. 103); it is important to note that Bandelier's translation has never been found (see White 1940: I, 71, 74n25). As White (p. 74n25) pointed out, Bandelier wrote Putnam, April 20, 1877, "Translation of the *Crónica Mexicana* [is] now approaching completion. What shall become of that elephant? It is a perfect megalosaurus at my hands, being nearly 800 pages qto, with the introduction and the (very copious) footnotes." White commented, "Every effort should be made to rescue this important work—if, indeed, it is still extant."

Concluding this note on the Mercantile Library, it should be emphasized that the very existence of this library with its rare holdings which were of particular interest to Bandelier makes it possible to understand how Bandelier acquired at least some of his familiarity with early sources. That he knew and used them is clear from reading the correspondence between Bandelier and both Morgan and García Icazbalceta. Time and time again, he wrote Morgan, "These are at St. Louis." We still lack information explaining his initial interest in Mexico and the early Spanish records, but the proximity of Highland to St. Louis and the Mercantile Library, with the borrowing privileges which were extended to him, even with rare books, helps us to appreciate how well equipped he was to work in the archives of the Southwest and Mexico. The years of this volume, 1885–88, found Bandelier deeply involved in documentary research. The reader who is particularly interested in an evaluation of this aspect of Bandelier's work is referred to such publications as Waterman (1917), White (1940), and Burrus (1969a), in addition to Bandelier's own publications which stemmed from these years of research.

480. This was Dr. Hugo Kinner, a St. Louis physician (Gould 1885: 644). He had practiced medicine in St. Louis since 1864. He was a member of the American Anthropological Association and the Archaeological Institute of America and had traveled exten-

sively among American Indian tribes. In September 1883, Dr. Kinner had visited Bandelier in Highland (Lange and Riley 1970: 148, 403n375).

481. Mr. and Mrs. Henry Hesse, of St. Louis, had attended the wedding in Highland of Elizabeth Bandelier and Henry S. Kaune in September 1883 (Lange and Riley 1970: 201). Mrs. Hesse was Elizabeth Donne, a daughter of Robert and Gertrude Donne, Breese, Illinois pioneers, and a sister of Sarah A. Donne, who had married Henry S. Kaune's brother, William G. Kaune (Casey et al. 1956: 27; see also ns 110 and 111).

482. Alvar Nuñez Cabeza de Vaca and three companions, sole survivors of the Narváez Expedition to Florida (1528–29), eventually made their way across Texas and northern Mexico to Culiacán, arriving in this settlement in 1536 (Bolton 1907: 1–126).

483. Mrs. Bush has been identified only as the landlady with whom Hubert Hoffmann found room and board. Other entries mentioning her, sometimes mention the "Dr." also. It seems most likely that this was Dr. William Eggert (see n 12) who moved to Mrs. Bush's home December 19, 1885, when he became ill with pneumonia. How long he remained there has not been determined (see n 507).

484. These were Abraham and Julie Schuster Staab, married December 25, 1865. Z. Staab & Co., according to an advertisement on Huggins' Map (1876), were "Wholesale Dealers in General Merchandise." Z. Staab's address was New York City, while A. Staab's was in Santa Fe. Polk and Danser (1884a: 353, 354) listed A. Staab as a partner in the Z. Staab & Bro. general store at the northwest corner of the Santa Fe Plaza and President of the Santa Fe Gas Co. Bloom (1943: 261n20) noted that Zadoc Staab was born in Westphalia, Germany, and arrived with his brother Abraham in 1857 in Santa Fe. From 1858, "Zadoc Staab and Brother" were engaged in general merchandise and became one of the most important firms. Zadoc Staab died in 1883. Abraham and Julie Staab had eight children, one of whom died in infancy. Others were: Mrs. Louis Ilfeld of Albuquerque, Mrs. Louis Baer of Boston, Mrs. Max Nordhaus of Albuquerque, Julius, Paul, Arthur, and Edward. Mrs. Staab died in 1896; Abraham, in 1913 (Twitchell 1925: 479–80). The Staab home on East Palace Avenue, Santa Fe, has been incorporated into the office, dining areas, and rooms of La Posada de Santa Fe (Gregg 1968: 99).

Bond (1946: 344) commented that "Mr. A. Staab . . . was the leading wholesale dealer of General Merchandise in Santa Fe and, I believe, the whole Territory. He was very shrewd and keen. I always considered him the brightest business man in the state. He carried general stock and did a large business."

485. McKenney (1888: 482) listed an A. Grunsfeld and an E. A. Grunsfeld with H. Lindheim as partners in Grunsfeld & Co., a general merchandise store on the southwest corner of the plaza in Santa Fe. An advertisement on the Huggins' Map (1876) listed a Grunsfelt as a director of the Second National Bank of New Mexico in Santa Fe.

486. Eddie Franz, or Edward W. Franz was the son of Earhart D. Franz. Eddie was born in Los Lunas, New Mexico, September 10, 1867, and at the age of sixteen joined the White Hardware Company of St. Louis, remaining with that firm for a year and a half. Following his business experience with the St. Louis concern, Eddie rejoined his father in Santa Fe (sometime in 1885) and worked with him until 1888 or 1889 (Anonymous 1895: 618–19).

E. D. Franz sold hardware and house furnishing goods in Santa Fe. His store was located on San Francisco Street (McKenney 1888: 482; Polk and Danser 1884a: 350).

487. On this date, November 19, 1885, the *Santa Fe Daily New Mexican* (p. 4) reported, "Prof. A. F. Bandalier [sic] came in from the mountains yesterday and joined his wife who is just out from Highland, Ill. Prof. Bandalier will henceforth make his home at Peña Blanca. It is said that the gentleman is engaged in preparing a scientific history of both old and New Mexico for the Smithsonian Institute."

This was a somewhat erroneous account as the Bandeliers had arrived in Santa Fe together the day before, November 18, coming from St. Louis via El Paso and Albuquerque. As the entry of November 24–28 revealed, Bandelier reassessed his original intention of setting up their home at Peña Blanca and concluded, "I cannot get Joe to such a place under no circumstances whatever. . . . But another delay [in research and writing] is inevitable, for I must move to Santa Fe at once. Peña Blanca is no place for us."

488. Polk and Danser (1884b) carried an advertisement (p. 391) for: "*The Illinois Staats Zeitung,* Sunday Edition: *Der Westen;* Chicago, Illinois, The Leading German Newspaper, Having the largest circulation of any German Paper Published in the West; Daily, Sunday, Weekly." Elsewhere (p. 585), A. C. Hesing was given as President, and C. F. Pietsch as Secretary, with offices at 89 and 91 Fifth Avenue.

489. Padre John B. Brun was of French ancestry. He was a brother of Mrs. Dumas Provencher and was ordained by Bishop John B. Lamy on August 15, 1868. After serving briefly at Taos and Pecos, he was given charge of the churches of Cebolleta, Cubero, San Rafael, San Mateo, Laguna, Acoma, and Zuñi (Jenkins: personal communication). Defouri (1887: 112) quoted from a journal of Father Brun. The editors have found no other reference to this journal, and Father Angelico Chavez (personal correspondence) said that he was unaware of it.

490. See n 301.

491. This is an interesting sidelight on a shift in observance of a Catholic holiday for "weather" reasons. It may well have been that in New Mexico, the Feast of Guadalupe did not have the deep significance that it did in many parts of Mexico where the celebration extends for several days clustering around December 12, regardless of weather. One can only wonder, also, if weather were the actual, or only, reason for the shift; Cañada, Cochiti, and several other communities, at some distance from one another, were served by the priest(s) at Peña Blanca where Guadalupe was the Patroness. Difficulties in travel would have often precluded observances at each church on a particular date. Churches in other communities had other patrons, although at Cañada de Cochiti, as at Peña Blanca, the mission was dedicated to N. S. de Guadalupe.

492. This house, rented by the Bandeliers, belonged to John G. Schumann, a Santa Fe dealer in shoes and boots.

Schumann had acquired the house in 1878 and on December 10, 1919, sold it to Henry S. and Elizabeth Bandelier Kaune (Register of Deeds, Records, Santa Fe County Court House). Located at 352 East De Vargas Street, the house has remained in the Kaune family since then, presently the residence of the youngest of the Kaune children, Anna, Mrs. R. L. Ormsbee.

The Historic Santa Fe Foundation (Loomis 1966: 25) has placed a plaque on the home, marking it as the Adolph Bandelier House. While the Bandeliers lived there from 1885 until April 1891 (more than a year before they departed for South America in the spring of 1892), they never owned the home. The move was prompted by an arm injury suffered by Joe, making it difficult for her to maintain the larger Schumann house. (In the description of the Bandelier House [p. 25], there a number of errors, such as the Bandeliers living there beginning in 1882; other details can be checked against information contained in the various journal entries.)

As the journals reveal, Mr. Schumann was a frequent visitor at the Bandeliers' home.

493. This was Captain George H. Pradt, surveyor and veteran of the Civil War. He married a Laguna woman and later served as governor of this pueblo. For more complete biographical data, see Lange and Riley 1970: 358n23.

494. This was probably Dumas Provencher of the Acoma and San Rafael area. Biographical data on Provencher were given in Lange and Riley 1970: 380n180.

495. The Spanish phrase *jornada del muerto* is "journey of the dead man." This celebrated topographic feature lay on the caravan routes from Chihuahua to Santa Fe, and
was chosen for travel because it shortened the route by at least a day. It was a waterless
stretch of nearly 90 miles from Rincon to San Marcial. In addition, many miles were
sandy, and Indians made their attacks from hiding places in the mountains or arroyos.
Since hundreds perished in this crossing, women and children as well as men, "journey
of death" seems a much more fitting translation (Pearce 1965: 77).

496. At present, in those pueblos which adhere to traditional forms of government and
have not yet changed over to some form of constitutional structure, the war captains carry
out the decisions of the principales. The war captains are responsible for safe-guarding
the tribe against all enemies, whether these are seen as witches, intruders from the
outside, or deviants on the inside. While it is extremely difficult for outsiders to learn
about such matters, for obvious reasons, there is reason to believe that an occasional
execution is still carried out in a number of pueblos for serious offenses against the tribe.

497. Adelaido Montoya, Cochiti, was born December 25, 1860, the son of Trinidad
Pancho, of the Cottonwood Clan, and Juan José Montoya (see n 642). Adelaido married
Lucia Romero, September 25, 1887; Lucia died January 29, 1906. Adelaido subsequently
married Victoria Quintana. Four children were born of the first marriage; two of the
second.

498. Bandelier had visited with several members of the Lucero family at the Cañada
de Cochiti in 1880 and 1882 as he searched for ruins in the Cochiti area. However, he
made no specific reference to a Luciano Lucero (Lange and Riley 1966).

499. Adams and Chavez (1956: 356) gave this definition of *luminarias* (always femi-
nine; usually plural in N. M.): "Small firewood bonfires to outline flat rooftops and procession routes on festive occasions. The term is now often misapplied to improvised
lanterns made of candles in sand-filled paper bags, a relatively recent innovation, which
are properly called *farolitos* (little lanterns)."

Farolitos placed along flat-topped building walls give the effect of outlining each
building with dots of light; they are used extensively in New Mexico communities for a
variety of celebrations. On the basis of the remarks by Adams and Chavez, one wonders
if Bandelier in this entry was not commenting on the earlier true *luminarias.*

500. Colonel Max Frost was a prominent figure in the territorial life of New Mexico.
He was a member of the notorious Santa Fe Ring. An ardent Republican, he used his
newspaper, the *New Mexican Review,* for political purposes (see Stratton 1969: 27, 202–
4). He was secretary and treasurer of the San Mateo Cattle Co. and also a register in the
U.S. Land Office in Santa Fe (Polk and Danser 1884a: 353, 354).

Westphall (1965: 106) wrote that Frost had come to New Mexico as a sergeant in charge
of the military telegraph line built into Santa Fe. His title of "colonel" derived from his
serving as adjutant general of New Mexico from 1881 to 1883. He was associated with
four newspapers. In 1884, with others, he formed the New Mexico and Kentucky Land
and Stock Company. Westphall discussed at length the charges brought against Frost for
his actions as register in the U.S. Land Office in Santa Fe (pp. 106–11). All charges were
ultimately dismissed, in some cases because the files were missing, which Westphall
considered was more than coincidence. Frost was permitted to resign in 1885 as register
of the Land Office (for further data on the Santa Fe Ring, see Lamar 1966: 136–70).

Regardless of Frost's involvement in questionable land grant practices, he has been
recognized for his ceaseless efforts in working for New Mexico statehood, primarily
through the use of the Santa Fe *New Mexican* of which he became both publisher and
editor in 1889 (Stratton 1969: 86, 203). Stratton (p. 203) commented, "The conclusion
seems warranted that Frost and the *New Mexican* despite their record in politics made
a significant contribution to the development of New Mexico."

501. This article could not be located in *The Nation.* Subsequent entries of December 16 and 18, 1885, and of January 15, 1886, noted that Bandelier sent a second land grant article to *The Nation,* as well as a third "prefacing the two on landgrants." On May 5, 1886, he wrote to Garrison "again about land grants." Whether the land grant manuscript referred to in the June 5, 1886, entry was the one submitted to Garrison is not clear. The editors have been unable to find, in *The Nation* or elsewhere, an article by Bandelier on land grants.

502. Antonio Ortiz y Salazar, former probate judge of Santa Fe County, had been named among the principal suspected parties in land frauds by Elias Brevoort, receiver of the Land Office in Santa Fe, in a letter of December 5, 1881 (Westphall 1965: 100–101; see n 424).

503. Don Diego de Vargas Zapata Luján Ponce de Leon was made governor of New Mexico in 1692 as part of a reconquest plan (the Pueblo Indians having revolted and driven the Spaniards south to El Paso in 1680). Over an eight-year period, 1692–1700, De Vargas succeeded in reoccupying New Mexico (Twitchell 1911–17: I, 380 et seq.).

Several fragments of the original De Vargas journal seem to be extant. In addition to the one noted in this entry, Governor Ritch also had a section (Lange and Riley 1966: 246–47). Espinosa (1942: xvii) commented, "Pile was not the only territorial governor of New Mexico who contributed to the diminution of the local archives. A section of Vargas' original journal, formerly a part of the Santa Fe Archives and translations of other documents from the same source (made by Samuel Ellison), were recently acquired from the estate of William G. Ritch, governor of New Mexico in 1875, by the Huntington Library, San Marino, California, where they now constitute a part of the Ritch Collection."

While in Santa Fe in July 1884, Bandelier made abstracts at the archives, Ellison assisting him. In his journal entry he gave the complete title of the Diego de Vargas journal, noting that it "began in 1692 and continued at least until 1696" (Lange and Riley 1970: 334, 431n110). Defouri (1887: 161–62), in notes at the end of his book, included a copy of Vargas's journal of December 18, 1692, which Ellison had made and certified to him as being authentic. The original was at that time in the Santa Fe Archives (see Twitchell 1914: II, 78–111 for his data regarding the De Vargas journal).

504. That the Territory of New Mexico lost many important historical documents due to Governor William A. Pile (1869–71) is a statement found frequently in the literature. Twitchell (1914: I, viii–xv) traced the history of the Santa Fe Archives and the provisions made for their care after New Mexico became a United States Territory in 1851. He noted that during successive administrations, recommendations were made to the territorial legislature for appropriations for the care of these documents. Twitchell commented, "Meanwhile many of them disappeared, and during the administration of Governor Pyle, it is said, many were carried off. In a measure this is true, but they were not destroyed, as nearly all of them found their way into private collections in Santa Fe and elsewhere" (see n 503).

Whether Bandelier was correct in stating that the De Vargas journal fragment had been sold at auction by Governor Pile, the editors do not know. Within days of his arrival in Santa Fe in 1880, Bandelier had been regaled with stories of Pile's "wanton destruction of the archives" (Lange and Riley 1966: 73, 74). In the biographical sketch of Ellison, Territorial Librarian, 1881–89, the editors quoted from notes of Dr. A.J.O. Anderson on Governor Pile written by Ellison for Bancroft for his *History of New Mexico and Arizona* (p. 410). Bandelier's journal entries obviously reflected Ellison, who held Governor Pile's actions to have been irresponsible. Here one finds the statement so often seen in the literature—that Pile had sold the archives to the merchants for wrapping paper and at great expense to the Territory, the citizens forced him to recover them. Even after recovering them, they were not properly cared for.

505. Reverend Anthony, or Antonio, Jouvenceau was mentioned in Salpointe (1898: 273) as Superintendent of Indian Schools of the Santa Fe diocese.

506. The *Santa Fe Daily New Mexican* for December 19, 1885, carried this item on "This Morning's Rain." "The extent of the heavy rain this morning was the subject of much comment throughout the city to-day. To ascertain how this rain compared with other December rainfalls, a NEW MEXICAN reporter called on Observer Twadell this morning: 'No,' he said, in response to our scrib's [*sic*] question, 'I don't know as this was an unusual precipitation to-day for this time of year. We will go and see how the rain gauge stands.' " [A chart was presented, giving the December total precipitation for the years 1872 through 1882; the rainfall of December 19, 1885 was 35/100th inch.] The concluding paragraph stated, "It will be seen, therefore, that the rainfall this morning was thirty-five times greater than the total rainfall for December, 1872, and that it was equal to more than one-half of the average for the entire month of December for the eleven years given above."

507. The *Santa Fe New Mexican Review* for December 19, 1885 (p. 4), reported on Dr. Eggert's illness as follows: "Owing to a slight illness, Dr. Eggert has moved to Mrs. Bush's residence where he will be found at all hours." Mrs. Bush ran a small boarding house in Santa Fe (see n 483).

508. This was the infamous incident at Camp Grant, Arizona, in 1870. A well-known Tucson attorney, William Sanders Oury, led a group of Americans, Mexicans, and Papago Indians in a slaughter of perhaps a hundred Apache women and old men. Some twenty-five or thirty children were taken captive and seem to have been sold into slavery in Mexico, en masse or nearly so. Oury was tried for this outrage, but in spite of pressures from President U.S. Grant, a local jury in Tucson refused to convict him. For further details, see Smith (1967: 186–203); Paré (1965: 121–23); Lange and Riley (1970: 428n96).

509. This elaborate ceremony reflects the Pima belief in and fear of ghosts of the enemy dead. It also points up the strong feelings about the ritual uncleanliness involved in any death, common to all the Pima and Papago. According to Russell (1908: 200–5), capture of Apache children was not unusual, and some of these grew to adulthood among the Pima. Adult captives of either sex seem to have been killed as a part of the ceremonial victory observances.

510. In the Bandelier Scrapbook, there was an article entitled "The Progressive Indian." Its subtitle was "What Advanced Civilization and the Winchester Have Done for the Red Man." The article was headed "Special Correspondence of the Globe-Democrat, Santa Fe, N.M., December 21, [n. d.]" The article was signed "Espejo." This item was not included in the Hodge Bibliography (1932), but there can be little doubt that the author was Bandelier. (The entry of December 29, 1885, notes that this article had appeared in print, December 26.)

511. This was Albert Samuel Gatschet (1832–1907), an American ethnologist and linguist associated for many years with the Bureau of Ethnology in Washington, D.C. Bandelier had corresponded with him in 1880 and 1882 (Lange and Riley 1966). In 1876, he had published, "Zwölf Sprachen aus dem südwesten Nord-Amerikas" (Weimar), one of the earliest publications on American Southwest languages.

512. In 1880, Bandelier had made a surprise return from New Mexico to Highland to be with the family and Joe at Christmas time; in 1881, he had returned from his Mexican year, again to Highland. However, in 1882, Bandelier was camping in the field in the Salinas area during the Christmas season. In 1883, he was in southern New Mexico, and in 1884, he had been in Switzerland (see entries in Lange and Riley 1966; 1970).

In the period surrounding the bank failure and during the remainder of 1885, the journal entries contain more numerous and more overt expressions of affection for Joe than do the entries prior to this time.

513. Present throwing is another form of gallo (see n 409) at various pueblos. It is a common aspect of several saint's day celebrations, and there are parallels in portions of certain native religious celebrations, as at Cochiti where certain Koshare and Kwirena dances have present throwing (Lange 1959: 597). The celebrant and his family accumulate items of a considerable variety, tobacco, soap, bread, dishes, cloth, ribbons, fruit, etc., which they throw from their roof to the crowd which gathers around the house. Bandelier's observation of presents being thrown to the celebrant is a reversal which has been neither observed nor reported in recent times.

514. See Goldfrank (1927: 110–11) for a brief description of the Cochiti scalp dance. In her time of fieldwork, 1921–22, the dance had not been performed for a number of years so that her data came from informants. Lange (1959: 273–81) provided additional descriptive and comparative data.

515. This seems to have been the article "The Progressive Indian," by "Espejo," one-and-three-quarters columns (*St. Louis Globe Democrat*, December 26, 1885, p. 12).

516. This was Dr. Norton B. Strong, United States Army; in his Preface to *The Delight Makers* (1890c), Bandelier acknowledged those who had assisted him, naming in particular Reverend E. W. Meany and Dr. Strong.

517. This was a time of financial hardship in Bandelier's life, and he was continually looking for ways to increase his meager income. From various journal entries of that period, we know he gave lessons in foreign languages to a number of people. Teaching Dr. Meany Spanish may have been Bandelier's method of repaying him for his assistance in the German translations (see n 190); similarly, Dr. Strong had helped Bandelier (see n 516). Lt. Fornance may have been paying for his lessons as no evidence of his assistance to Bandelier has come to light.

NOTES

1886

518. Bandelier, in the company of Julius H. Gerdes, was participating in the traditional New Year's Day calls. Whether this was the L. E. Theo Fischer family or the C. F. A. Fischer family (or even a joint call) was not indicated. It is quite possible that this was the "old Mr. Fischer" of the February 12, 1886, entry, that we have suggested was L. E. Theo Fischer, returning this particular call.

In any event, this was the first mention of any Santa Fe Fischer in his journals. As subsequent entries reveal, the relationship between the families grew from this time on, and members of the Bandelier and Fischer families frequently visited one another (see n 566).

519. This was Willi Spiegelberg, one of several brothers who were merchants and freighters on the Santa Fe Trail. According to Twitchell (1911–17: II, pl. facing 284), the brothers were Willi, Lehman, Jacob S., Levi, and Emanuel. Parish (1960: 11) listed six Spiegelberg brothers, Willi, Lehman, Levi, Emanuel, Bernard, and Elias, as well as a nephew, Abraham Spiegelberg, and a cousin, Aaron Zeckendorf (who, with his brother, or brothers, later started a rival store in Santa Fe). However, in an *errata* section of the publication cited above, Parish (p. 150) stated, "There was no known brother named Bernard Spiegelberg."

520. Colonel William W. Griffin was cashier of the First National Bank of Santa Fe, a director of the Santa Fe Water and Improvement Company, vice-president of the Santa Fe Academy, and generally prominent in the life of the city at the time of Bandelier (see Lange and Riley 1970: 497). Lamar (1966: 142–43, 145) described the involvement, about 1869–77, of Griffin, U.S. Deputy Surveyor of New Mexico, with the Santa Fe Ring.

Born in West Virginia, Griffin came to Santa Fe in 1860. He surveyed the famous Maxwell Land Grant. At the time of his death in 1889, he was president of the First National Bank, Santa Fe (Anderson 1907: I, 413–14).

521. Charles M. Creamer, born in Ohio, November 15, 1855, came to New Mexico, September 17, 1880, just a month after Bandelier's first arrival. He was listed as a druggist (with Fischer & Co.) on the southwest corner of the plaza in Santa Fe (McKenney 1888: 481). Creamer was first a clerk in the firm established by L.E. Theo. Fischer in 1865; by 1884, Creamer had become full owner of the company (Anonymous 1895: 590). Here, Bandelier was perpetuating a very common German custom of calling on one's friends on New Year's Day.

522. This was most probably Dr. E. T. Hamy, Curator at the Musée d'ethnographie, Paris, who was listed among the members of the 7th International Congress of Americanists which met in Berlin in 1888. Hamy served on the Council of the Congress as the representative of France; he was named president of the succeeding congress which was to be held in Paris in 1892 (Cong. Internat. Amer. 1890: 15, 30, 790–92).

523. This letter, dated January 3, 1886, was among those published by White and Bernal (1960: 284–86); our translation follows:

Very dear sir:

Just a few words to wish you the greatest happiness for this year that has now begun. May God protect you, shelter you, and keep you for yours. I also wish the same for your family and for my Mexican friends who still remember me. I, for my part, have not forgotten anything, nor anyone. And although I do not see before me even a remote possibility of again enjoying the most generous and beautiful land in the world, I still keep missing the happy moments I spent there.

I returned a month ago, accompanied by my wife, with whom I was reunited last November. I was unable to resist the temptation of showing her a little of Mexico, small as it was. In order to do this, we took the southern line and from El Paso we stopped to watch the tri-colored flag waving over the fields of El Paso del Norte. This was the first chance she had to see the Republic, as we say here, and I am afraid this time is the last.

Although in some poverty, we live more contented than before. We are short of money even though I work day and night. Literature pays little; but living is not expensive and our friends have not yet abandoned us. However, if the literary works keep paying so little, I will have to change my future and become a schoolteacher. Perhaps I will go as preceptor to the Apache. The government is interested in creating schools for the Indians, and the Church helps them in this pursuit. The relationship between the present administration and Catholicism is better than ever; there exists a cordiality for the Catholic clergy that has never existed in the past and almost all teaching of the natives is gradually placed in the hands of the Church. If I cannot earn a living with my pen, I will try to obtain a job even when it may be among these mere savages. We shall see. Meanwhile, I keep working as before, and if the economic results cannot be compared to those in the past, we are neither hungry nor cold, even when the snow here covers the ground with a layer twelve or more inches deep.

I am very sorry to hear that you have entirely abandoned the scientific field. It is a calamity, and I hope that sooner or later you change your mind and decide to return to the exercise of your old profession. We are not able to excuse you for taking this decision; you are necessary in everything, and, in particular, to me. Your work and advice are essential to me; what could I do without you? I lack the information about New Mexico contained in the work of Father [Antonio] Daza, as well as that in the work of Father [José de] Arlegui, about the missions in Chihuahua, and I need a copy of the important letter of Don Antonio de Oca Sarmiento in Volume III of the *Documentos para la Historia de Méjico*, 4th series, pp. 231–34. Without this information, my most important work on the History of New Mexico will not be completed.

Not long ago, I sent you a somewhat revolutionary pamphlet written against the school of writers who are still having harmful effects on the history of America. I am now writing on behalf of the Spanish policy in the colonies and, in particular, the effects of this policy on the natives.

We have been experiencing penetratingly cold weather, but the air is dry, and the elevation of this place (7,047') together with the blue sky help us forget the inclemency of the temperature, and with peace and tranquility, we quietly wait for the future, one which it will probably be best not to speak about. It will surprise me to find good luck now.

Please extend my warmest regards to your children and with the best regard and salutations to you, I remain as always your faithful servant and affectionate godchild.

Ad. F. Bandelier

P.S. I suffer from rheumatism in the right arm, the reason why I am scribbling.

524. Actually, the Bandeliers had been married in 1862, making January 5, 1886, the twenty-fourth anniversary and not, properly speaking, "our Silver Wedding." While Bandelier may have simply miscounted, it appears, instead, that he was using this unusual method of counting. This interpretation is supported by the subsequent entry of 1888. In 1887, there was no mention of the January 5 anniversary, while in 1888, he observed, "Quietly at home, for it is our 27th anniversary of marriage."

525. Richard H. Tompkins, clerk of the Circuit Court at the time of the Nambé witch episode (1850s), was listed by Polk and Danser (1884a: 354) as "lawyer, Palace." Earlier, in 1878, the well-liked Henry L. Waldo had resigned as chief justice of the Supreme Court of New Mexico; replacing him, according to the *Santa Fe Daily New Mexican* of July 13, 1878, was difficult because for "integrity, ability, and perfect fairness," Waldo was "the peer of any man who ever sat upon the bench in New Mexico." Poldervaart (1947: 36) stated that the territorial legislature in 1878 had "memorialized the President of the United States directing his attention to the qualifications of R. H. Tompkins of Santa Fe, a resident of the territory for some thirty years." Tompkins had served as a justice of the peace. President Grant, however, named Charles McCandless, a member of the bar of Pennsylvania. Tittman (1929: 144–45) mentioned Tompkins as an attorney for the defense in a trial of October 1867 in which accusations of treason during the invasion of New Mexico by Confederate troops were being heard.

526. The capital of New Mexico was assigned to Santa Fe by the first legislative assembly, and in 1850 Congress appropriated $20,000 for the construction of public buildings, including the first capitol. An additional $50,000 was appropriated in 1854, and the structure was raised to one-and-a-half stories. The fire referred to by Bandelier was probably the reason why still another appropriation of $60,000 was made in 1860. The building was, in fact, not completed till the late 1880s and was then used to house other territorial offices (Twitchell 1911–17: II, 326).

A bill passed by the 26th legislative assembly in 1884 called for the building of a new capitol and for a penitentiary. There was vigorous opposition from various parts of the territory, especially from the Albuquerque area (pp. 494, 494n407).

On May 12, 1892, this capitol building also burned with a loss of many public documents. The fire was suspected of being of incendiary origin (p. 515).

527. Presumably, this was the same Vigil that Bandelier had reference to in his October 11, 1882, entry when he wrote, "Spent several hours with Mr. Ellison and Señor Vigil at the archives" (Lange and Riley 1966: 143).

528. The Bandelier Scrapbook contained an article, in very poor state of preservation and with no date, from the *Belletristisches Journal*, entitled, "Ein Hexenprozess in Neu-Mexiko vor vierunddreissig Jahren" von Ad. F. Bandelier. Hodge's Bibliography (1932: 367) cited the publication date for this article as 1889(?). His title of the newspaper was misspelled, omitting the final "s" in *Belletristisches*.

The editors believe that the manuscript of this January 12, 1886, entry was an earlier manuscript concerning Nambé witchcraft, partly because of the discrepancy in the title of the manuscript and that of the article and partly, and more significantly, when the thirty-four years of the published title are added to the 1855 date of the witchcraft trial (see ns 253 and 1017), they total 1889, clearly establishing 1889 as the publication year (for additional data on the *Belletristisches Journal,* see n 50).

529. Udo Brachvogel of Missouri and New York was an editor of the *Belletristisches Journal,* New York City, as well as a poet and translator. His papers are now in the Manuscript Division of the New York Public Library (Hamer 1961: 428). Bandelier's novel, *Die Kö-Sha-Re,* first appeared in this weekly paper in serial form, beginning January 1, 1890.

530. No article about a tour of Virginia in 1856 has been found by the editors.

531. This was Mrs. Thomas B. Catron, nee Julia A. Walz. She was born in Springfield, Ohio, March 28, 1857, and died in Santa Fe on November 13, 1909 (New Mexico State Archives n.d.: Catron File). Mrs. Catron was one of several people to whom Bandelier gave foreign language lessons.

532. Here, as in entries both earlier and later, Bandelier made rather frequent references to the "Doctor." Invariably, the reference was quite obviously to Dr. Eggert, the family physician and also a close friend and frequent helper with translations.

Dr. Norton B. Strong appears to have been specifically identified in each case. Dr. Edward W. Meany, at this period in the journals, was most commonly referred to simply as "Meany," or "Mr.," rather than "Dr." or "Reverend." However, it is occasionally not clear which of these individuals Bandelier had in mind in a given entry.

533. This was Mrs. George Cuyler Preston; see n 567.

534. This is one of the few instances in which Bandelier recorded an explicit expression of pleasure or satisfaction in his work. It may well have been prompted by the relief from the recent discouraging and unhappy events of this period in his life. It is interesting that the comment was in relation to his novel—quite in contrast to the "hard work" (entry of February 11, 1886) noted in regard to his Report which was being worked on intermittently at this time.

535. In December 1882, while examining ruins in the Manzano area, Bandelier had stayed at the curacy as a guest of Father Louis Bourdier (Lange and Riley 1966: 386, 388). Bandelier also made reference to him in his January 1883 journals, but by July 2, 1884, Bandelier noted meeting Father Bourdier and commenting that he was "at Belen now" (Lange and Riley 1970: 14–20 passim, 332). Salpointe (1898: 282) listed Father Bourdier as one of the priests added by Bishop Lamy to the New Mexico clergy. He had been ordained in 1868 (Chavez 1957: 134).

536. In all probability, this was the wife of H. Hartmann, the Santa Fe cartographer (see Lange and Riley 1970: 430–31n108 for data on Hartmann). Hobbs (1940a) identified Mrs. Hartmann as an "aunt of Mrs. [Gerard D.] Koch."

537. Despite several references to the *Boston Advertiser,* including this notation on the sending of "eight pages" to J. C. Chamberlain, the editor, no record was found of anything having been published for Bandelier.

538. This letter, dated February 3, 1886, from Mexico City, was one of those published by White and Bernal (1960: 287–88); our translation follows:

> My esteemed godchild:
> I have received with pleasure your valuable letter of last January third. I sincerely thank you for your greetings for the New Year. The past one was not so good for me. After a long illness we lost a child, the only son of my daughter, who was the joy of the household. This caused me terrible sorrow.
> I am happy to know that you are tranquil and happy in your private life. According to the information at hand from everywhere, this winter has been a rigorous one and for many days we have experienced temperatures below 4° C., which for us is very cold. I have been unable to go to the "tierra caliente" as is my custom because of the condition of my daughter who eight days ago had a baby girl; but as soon as this obligation ends next week, I will go to see my sugar cane plantations and to enjoy a more agreeable climate.
> The news you have given me concerning the advances made by the Catholic clergy in that country have much interested me; that is the only thing which could help civilize the Indians. Here we look at things differently, with different results.
> I received and read the pamphlet, and in truth it is quite revolutionary. I shall note with great pleasure what you write about the Spanish policy.
> You have indicated to me that you need some materials. I am ready to make available to you those which I possess. Please inform me which ones, more precisely than in your last letter.
> Very slowly I keep compiling the *Bibliografía* of the sixteenth century. The article on *Sahagún* has given me a great deal of trouble. I shall not be able to really finish it, but there will be something new in it about the author and his works. I do not think that you would be interested in the *Bibliografía;* to me it is the worst and most costly book of those which I have published. It does not offer anything new, nor of any interest except to the bibliographers. Science will not profit from it.
> In order not to waste time, I have begun to edit a small volume entitled *Cartas de Religiosos, 1562–1588,* almost all unpublished. These letters deal with many things such as administrative affairs, conversions, creation of the *Comisario General de Indias* and many other points. I expect this to be of some interest to you, and as soon as the little volume is finished I will send it to you.
> Now you see that I can't devote myself to idleness, but all I will do is to publish documents. I plan to do no original work. The only original work I did (*La Vida de Zumárraga*) left me so unsatisfied that I do not plan to walk along the same road again. I now belong to a past generation; I cannot match the present level of American studies, and I wish to retire, before they begin booing me.
> How are we coming along in the most important thing of all? How have you gotten along in your beliefs and practices? Remember that I was your godparent and became your guarantor.

A thousand regards, my godchild; keep yourself well, live quietly, and receive the affection of your godparent.

Joaquín García Icazbalceta

Postal Box No. 366

539. See n 459.

540. This was Bandelier's groundplan of Sapawe Pueblo ruins on the Rito Colorado, northern New Mexico (see Bandelier [1890–92] and Burrus [1969b: 211]). This sketch, indexed in Burrus as "Cepaué (El Rito Colorado)," has been reproduced in color by Burrus (1969c) as Sketch XXII. See also n 226.

541. As the Bibliography of this volume and subsequent entries show, Bandelier was successful in having at least two articles published in the *Magazine of Western History* by Mr. Williams (see n 607). For the first article, on Alvar Nuñez Cabeza de Vaca, the date of actual submission remains obscure; numerous mentions of correspondence between Bandelier and the editor, Mr. Williams, were made, but none specified mailing this manuscript (see Bibliography, Bandelier [1886g]).

542. In this letter, Bandelier acknowledged the $100 Parkman had sent him. In Lange and Riley (1970: 366n72), the editors, following Jacobs, had considered that this money might have been a personal gift from Parkman. There is, however, rather stronger evidence from the reply to Parkman quoted below that this was actually money from the Archaeological Institute of America. Bandelier's letter to García Icazbalceta (see n 543) supports this interpretation.

Bandelier wrote to Parkman:

> A thousand thanks—to you first, to Mr. Brimmer [who was on the AIA Council in 1886–87] and to whoever [*sic*] has taken such kind interest in my future. I go to work at once, & divide my time as follows:
> The day for the Institute.
> Evenings & night for my novel, which will be a valuable auxiliary to the scientific writings and which has progressed to Cap. XI. (All night work.)— Besides, reading to my wife.—
> Sundays at painting, which I do not give up, although since December, I have only painted two heads of dancers. I did that work in sheer despair, not having anything else to do, and not knowing what to do. Since the beginning of December, I had received in all twenty-Dollars only, of which $13.– for Spanish lessons (at –.50¢ a "head").

Bandelier then presented a detailed outline for his *Final Report,* which he owed the Institute on his New Mexico fieldwork. The terse notation, dated February 26 [1886], "Tell him to conform to plan of report in his letter of August last," the editors presume was written by Charles Eliot Norton, president of the Archaeological Institute of America. The August letter was not among those received by the editors from the Massachusetts Historical Society.

Bandelier concluded his letter to Parkman with, "Now another query!—Would the Boston Library let me consult Vol. XIV or XV of the 'Colección de Documentos Inéditos sacados del Archivo de Indias.'?—I am afraid not, still if I can have them one month, I could copy the whole of Oñate's Report & annexed Documents. Were I able to spend one month at the City of Mexico I could finish everything at once, as far as Documents are concerned."

543. This letter, dated February 9, 1886, was among those published by White and Bernal (1960: 289–91); our translation follows:

Very dear sir and dear godparent:

The quick arrival of your most welcome letter of the third of the month is something of a surprise; since we are not used to have mail service delivered so fast. As I told you, your letter left Mexico on the 3rd, and I received it the morning of the 7th. On my way to mass I had the pleasure of opening it, and without any delay I went to Church to thank God for all the good feeling that is still held for me in foreign lands.

I warmly thank you for your friendship and love, although on thinking back I can't see any cause because I have given few proofs that I deserve them. On the contrary, I deserve to be forgotten. But God has decided otherwise, and to him I give thanks for all the benefits he has provided me with.

Almost simultaneously with your letter a letter from the Institute arrived, informing me that the necessary means were available to continue with my scientific work, or better said, to help me finish the conclusions of my findings. This decision of the Society—for which reputation I had, at times, exposed my own life, has given me tremendous relief, in addition to the fact that it arrived at a time when our resources were almost gone, because for the last two months our income did not exceed twenty *pesos.*

I saw myself with my convalescent wife at the edge of misery (even though we did not spend more than twenty-five *pesos* a month) when this help came down from heaven. From now on, I will feel at ease; the numerous articles that I had written for various newspapers will bring remuneration, small as it is, but with economy and the practical sense of my wife we will be able to live cheaply.

You have allowed me to impose myself on your kindness to request information from you pertaining to the history of New Mexico and about the *Provincias Internas* in general. I am afraid that this request is too heavy, and because you have asked that I should "specify," I immediately begin with some requests:

(1) The *"Libro de Oro"* contains an account of V. P. Motolinia regarding the discovery of New Mexico. Could I obtain a copy?

(2) I do not know the work of Father Daza except for what Betancurt writes about it. I suppose, consequently, that this work will contain the report which determines the date of the foundation of the *Villa de Santa Fé,* as well as the major part of old missions in the country. In this case, abstracts about this matter will have a very great value for the work I am preparing.

In case that Daza doesn't contain any information, perhaps the *Historia de la Conquista del Nuevo México* by Captain Pedro Villagrán (1611) would contain something, or series three of the documents for the history of Mexico. In my possession I have an abstract of Benavides.

This is a lot, and I fear that it is too much. However, any information I could obtain, will be an important step forward.

You have communicated to me the sad news of the death of a child in your household. On the part of my wife, as well as on my part, please accept our very sincere condolences.

I add with pleasure my sincere felicitation for the birth of the other daughter —whose presence, without any doubt, will help to dissipate the sorrow caused by the loss of her predecessor. We have never experienced what it is to lose a child, and that is the only pain that God has not yet given us. Now it is too late for the two of us to experience it together.

I am writing in the middle of a horrible winter, even in this climate ordinarily amenable, and so even. Not since 1854 has such a snowfall been seen; for eight, even twelve days, the mail was interrupted–railroad trains were stopped–buried under snow in the plains.

Another snowstorm started yesterday; however, the clouds went over the Santa Fe plains without releasing their cargo this time, while to the north and south, and of course, in the plains, we had again considerable snowfall.

This is good luck for the farmer of our so dry land—but: Oh my God! the floods that will follow in the Spring. The Rio Grande will not lack in deserving its old name: "El Rio Bravo del Norte."

Good-bye, my dear sir and friend. May God protect you and keep you. Happiness and prosperity to yours and best regards to those who still remember your turbulent but affectionate godchild and faithful servant.

Ad. F. Bandelier

544. This was quite probably the same Fischer upon whom Bandelier had called with Julius Gerdes on New Year's Day. Subsequent entries which mentioned various members of the Fischer family would suggest that "old Mr. Fischer" was L. E. Theo. Fischer, Santa Fe business man of some prominence (see ns 521 and 566).

545. W. P. Garrison, editor of *The Nation*, sent Bandelier a copy of John G. Bourke's *An Apache Campaign in the Sierra Madre* for review. The work had first been published serially in *Outing Magazine* in 1885; it was issued as a book the following year by Charles Scribner's Sons. Bandelier sent in his review February 24 (see n 553).

546. In the Bandelier Scrapbook, there is at least a part of the article "Die neu-mexikanischen 'Pueblos,' " which appeared in serial form in the *New Yorker Staatszeitung*, January 10, 17, 24, 31, 1886. Presumably, the $24.00 was Bandelier's remuneration.

Mention is also made at this time of additional publications by Bandelier in the *New Yorker Staatszeitung* of which the editors are aware, but for which there was no corresponding journal mention.

According to Hodge (1932: 362), Bandelier continued to publish during 1885–86 in this newspaper additional episodes of "Über die Saga des 'Dorado' im nördlichen Süd Amerika," which he had begun in April 1876, and published serially until July 1877.

Bandelier also published an article on "Quivira," which appeared in the February 21, 28, March 7 and March 14, 1886, issues of the *New Yorker Staatszeitung*. Bandelier did not make journal entries from March 3 to March 21, 1886, which may explain the lack of a journal reference to this article. It is quite possible that the $26.25 Bandelier recorded "from the 'Staats-Zeitung' " on March 23, 1886, was his payment for the Quivira article.

547. As early as March 1882, Ellison had told Bandelier there were pueblo ruins five miles south of Santa Fe on the Arroyo Hondo. David J. Miller confirmed this (Lange and Riley 1966: 245, 246). In November 1882, in company with Mr. Evans, Bandelier visited the Arroyo Hondo ruins; he made two photographs and a sketch which he labeled "Upper Ruins on the Arroyo Hondo" (p. 361). The journal entries included some descriptive notes (pp. 359–60). After making the photographs, a Mexican told them that the main Arroyo Hondo ruins were one-and-one-half miles west, or lower down the arroyo. Sundown overtook them before they could reach the ruins and apparently Bandelier did not have the opportunity to examine the principal Arroyo Hondo ruins until the time of this entry, February 18, 1886. In passing through Santa Fe in 1884, he had been told of two sites on the Arroyo Hondo (Lange and Riley 1970: 332–33, 334).

Nelson conducted excavations in 1914 at the Arroyo Hondo ruin he called Kuakaa (1916b: 162). This site was subsequently designated L.A. 76 (Smiley, Stubbs, and Bannister 1953: 19–20). Elsewhere in Nelson's report (1916b: 179), he listed two Arroyo Hondo ruins, No. 1 and No. 2, at which excavations had been carried out, 12 rooms at the first and 108+ at the second. However, neither of these was given as Kuakaa and that designation was not on the list although Peñas Negras was included.

Bandelier's discussion in the *Final Report* (1890–92: II, 90) is helpful; he referred to Kua-kaa, or Kuakay, as two Tano ancestral villages on the Arroyo Hondo. The larger unit, on the south bank, was included as Fig. 21 in his Plate I; the smaller unit was a mile to the east, at the upper end of a rocky gorge through which the stream had cut its canyon.

Another site, or the same as Bandelier's larger unit(?), on the south bank of the Arroyo Hondo, with Glaze A potsherds, has been designated L.A. 12 (Mera 1940: 29). Peñas Negras, or Peña Negra (Nelson 1916b: 179), eight miles southeast of Sante Fe, has been designated L.A. 235 (Smiley, Stubbs, and Bannister 1953: 5, 27). (See also Lange and Riley 1970: 332–34.)

548. This was the wife of Colonel Ed. A. Haren (n 557).

549. This was Mrs. Louis Foellinger. See entries of March 27, 1886, and April 6 and 7, 1886. Bandelier, not yet well acquainted with some of these people, simply noted their names as he thought he heard them. Hence, it was Vollinger, as rendered here on February 18, and Foulinger, as in the entry of March 27. Whether there was any relationship or not is unknown, but the wife of C. F. A. Fischer (see n 566) was Margaret Foellinger Fischer.

550. Anita was Ana A. Staab, daughter of Abraham and Julia Schuster Staab (n 484). Ana was about sixteen years old at this time; she later married Louis Ilfeld, of Albuquerque, a member of another prominent German-Jewish family of New Mexico (Anonymous 1895: 634–35).

551. See n 507.

552. Judge and Mrs. L. Bradford Prince (see n 266) had a curio collection. In entries of February 20, 21, 22, and 27, 1886, Bandelier referred to borrowing, painting, and returning idols belonging to the Princes. On March 2, he had these sketches identified by a Cochiti Indian. In subsequent entries of March 21, 27, and 28, 1886, Bandelier sketched additional idols from the Prince collection, and on March 21, a second Cochiti verified their earlier identification as medicine gods.

In "notes on the Bandelier atlas and 4 vols. of illustrations (Rome, Bib. Vaticana)" and dated May 19, 1938, in Rome and signed by L. B. Bloom (from the file of the Museum of New Mexico, Bloom-Hewett correspondence), Bloom noted, "0-VIII, 238 . . . and the last four water-color sketches are of 7 stone idols from Potrero de las Vacas, n. of Cochiti, one with turquoise necklace and 5 with id. eyes. (I recognize these as idols belonging now to Hist. Society.)" See also Bloom-Hewett correspondence referred to in n 602.

Bloom's letter of May 18, 1938, also cited a Historical Society paper No. 2, on "The Stone Idols of Cochiti." The published catalogue of *Histoire* illustrations (Burrus 1969b: 142–43) also listed Bandelier's sketches of the seven idols; two were dated and correspond to the journal entries of February 22 and February 27–28, 1886, noted here.

Bloom had black-and-white film made of all of Bandelier's illustrations (Bloom-Hewett correspondence, MNM; note in *El Palacio*, Vol. XLIV, Nos. 25–26, pp. 165–66). More recently, colored slides of these illustrations have become available (see n 62), and Burrus (1969c) in a supplement to Volume I (1969b) has reproduced, in color, thirty sketches and ten maps from the original Bandelier volume.

553. Bandelier's review of Bourke's book on the *Apache Campaign in the Sierra Madre . . . 1883* appeared in *The Nation* of March 11, 1886; it was unsigned. In the review, elaborating on the comment, "a mighty poor affair," in his February 15, 1886, entry, Bandelier was for the most part negative, repeatedly criticizing the volume's shortcomings and lamenting the fact that Bourke had not maintained the high standards he had shown in his *Snake Dance of the Moquis.*

The review is reproduced here in its entirety; the reader is urged to compare it with the journal passages covering Bandelier's trip in the Sierra Madre area in the late winter and early spring of 1884, shortly after General George Crook's campaign there (Lange and Riley 1970: 482, 521).

> *An Apache Campaign in the Sierra Madre:* An Account of the expedition in pursuit of the hostile Chiricahua Apaches in the spring of 1883. By John G. Bourke, Captain Third Cavalry, U. S. Army, author of "The Snake Dance of the Moquis." Illustrated. Charles Scribner's Sons. 1886. 112 pp.

This little volume is handsomely bound, the print is good and large, but the illustrations are insignificant. Whoever has read Captain Bourke's excellent book on the Snake Dance must regret that he has not done better by his present highly interesting subject—General Crook's Sonora expedition, of which he was the acting Adjutant-General. His failure, however, is mostly ascribable to the fact that the text is composed of magazine articles, which originally appeared in *Outing*.

Captain Bourke always writes well and pleasantly for the general and superficial reader, but in this instance the public had a right to ask for positive geographical information, for an historical introduction explaining the real causes of the Chiricahua troubles, and, above all, for much greater impartiality. Our author says truly: "Within the compass of this volume it is impossible to furnish a complete dissertation upon the Apache Indians or the causes which led up to the expedition about to be described." But there was absolutely no need for a volume of such limited compass, and as to the geographical data, we insist on them, first, because nobody in the present century has described the regions traversed, and because geography is, according to Count Moltke, one-half of military science, and to pretend explaining Indian warfare without resorting to it is futile. Capt. Bourke has many clever descriptions of local scenery, and scattered allusions to vegetation and rock-formations, but what we miss is a clear and comprehensive topographical statement. A single page would have sufficed for that purpose, but the book has not even names of mountain chains in it; that of "Sierra Madre" excepted.

The Chiricahuas are not at all to be confounded with the rest of the Apaches, and Captain Bourke ought to have dispelled a common error which imputes to the whole tribe the acts of only a small fraction of desperadoes, with whom that tribe disclaims, and disclaimed in 1883, any communion. The history of the Chiricahuas can be gathered from *printed* sources; it goes as far back as 1684, but might have been summed up in half a page. Captain Bourke does well to shield the Apaches from numberless distorted and slanderous statements. His excellent description of their physical appearance and of their character stands in happy contrast with Mr. H. H. Bancroft's incorrect appreciation. It is, however, in bad taste for an officer of the United States army to lean so strongly to the Apache side at the expense of the Mexican people and army. Mexicans, more particularly in the mountain districts of Sonora and Chihuahua, were always at a great disadvantage. Fire-arms, until lately, were scarce and of very old patterns. The Apache was far better provided. Regular troops hardly came into play, being needed to head off "revolutions" and unable to protect the Sierra Madre; and yet the Mexicans have not done so very badly after all. Of course, the affair at Tres Castillos, when Victorio, after outgeneralling and whipping everybody in New Mexico, was wiped out by the Chihuahua militia, does not count. But the Alisos fight on the 30th of April, 1882, is sadly misrepresented by Captain Bourke, following Apache statements. It is true that a great majority of Indians killed were women and children, but as to the Chiricahuas' claim "that when the main body of their warriors reached the scene of the engagement, the Mexicans evinced no anxiety to come out from the rifle pits they hastily dug," just the opposite occurred. A number of Apaches hid in a sinkhole and were exterminated there at the point of the bayonet. Mexicans have been surprised time and again; so have our troops, even during the last campaign. As to killing the Mexicans with rocks only, Captain Bourke should have known that it was an Indian boast in allusion to an affair at Taraysitos in the Sierra Madre. There they did indeed hurl rocks upon the troops and wounded some; but when the "cowardly" Mexicans scaled the almost vertical cliffs, the "brave" Apaches vanished.

The book contains a number of covert slurs and flings at the army and people of our neighbor republic. As far as the army is concerned they are mostly concealed behind Apache utterances; still, their tendency is to bias and prejudice the reader's mind. In regard to the people he is more outspoken, so much so that even buildings do not escape his wrath. He speaks of churches as "in the last stages of dilapidation," and includes the temple at Babispe, a noble structure, built after the plan of San Javier del Bac, only much larger, of masonry and not with an "adobe exterior." Careless statements abound. The "Estancia" is called a "hamlet" like Huachinera, whereas it is only a *hacienda* belonging to Don Antonio Samaniego. No clue is given to the locality where General Crook met the Apache camp, no names of mountain chains surrounding it. For the benefit of the acting adjutant-general we will state that it is called Los Metates, and lies between the Sierra de Huachinera and the Sierra de los Parapetos, almost north of Nacori. The cañon which they moved up "in an easterly direction" is called Cajon de Bamochi, and the Apaches had camped in its upper parts for some time previous, as every child at Huachinera well knew. The Opata-Indian name for the range at whose feet the *rancheria* was surprised, is Quéva-ué-richi. Of the Opatas, who still form the bulk of population along the upper Yaqui (called Babispe) River, not a word is said, yet they are a most interesting people.

Like carelessness is evinced even in matters pertaining to the so-called "campaign" proper. In the first place, it was no "campaign"—rather an armed peace mission, and General Crook was actuated by motives which forever commend him to sincere admiration. He would have carried it out exclusively on that plan had it not been for the cowardly rashness of his own scouts. At Los Metates they fired prematurely, against the positive orders of Captain Emmet Crawford, and it is very doubtful if more than two of the renegades were killed (Captain Bourke says nine). The fourteen or fifteen Apaches who were in the rancheria afterwards defied all of the scouts boldly and openly from the tops of the cliffs, but the others did not dare to attack; they were and always have been mortally afraid of the Chiricahuas. These scouts were the weak element in General Crook's force; they came very near upsetting all his plans and bringing him and his troops to the verge of utter ruin. It was in the negotiations which followed, and in the fact that General Crook remained quietly where he was without pursuing or retreating, that he showed his genius and ability. Thus he secured the women and children, and saved himself from a surprise at daybreak that Gerónimo had planned. There is much more romance about this Sonora dash than Captain Bourke has intimated, and its commander has claims upon more respect, admiration, and gratitude than this book would entitle him to. The subject is worthy of careful treatment, such as the "Moqui Snake Dance" has shown Captain Bourke capable of undertaking and accomplishing.

554. Bandelier had corresponded with Frank P. Smith, Rochester, New York, on other occasions (see Lange and Riley 1966; 1970). In a letter to Pilling (1966: 361n37), Bandelier requested publications be sent to his friend, Frank P. Smith, *Democrat and Chronicle* office. The April 4, 1886, journal entry noted his receiving "letter from Frank P. Smith with $40.— in it from Rochester friends." Subsequent entries, such as April 14, suggest he was sending articles to Smith for publication.

555. This was presumably Mrs. L. E. Theo Fischer, seemingly the mother of C. F. A. Fischer who had called on the Bandeliers February 25, 1886, with his daughter, Louisa.

556. Lt. Thomas Staniford Mumford, a West Point graduate, was assigned to the 9th Cavalry as a 2d lt., June 12, 1871. He was transferred to the 13th Infantry, June 13, 1872, and was promoted to 1st lt., January 8, 1873. Lt. Mumford served as regimental quartermaster from March 1, 1882, to September 1, 1886. He retired with the rank of captain February 24, 1891 (Heitman 1903: I, 735).

557. Colonel Ed. A. Haren was the passenger agent for the AT&SF Railroad in Santa Fe (Lange and Riley 1966: 411).

558. The Historic Santa Fe Association (Loomis 1966: 13) gave a history and picture of the Boyle House. Its present address is 327 East De Vargas while the Adolph Bandelier House is at 352 East De Vargas. Arthur Boyle, having purchased the western portion of the house in 1881, would have been a close neighbor of the Bandeliers as of the date of this entry. For Arthur Boyle's role in the Tertio-Millenial Celebration, see p. 44; see also Lange and Riley 1970: 393n321 for more on these topics.

559. As noted earlier (see n 544), this was most likely L. E. Theo Fischer; entries of the next few days suggest that the older Fischers were leaving Santa Fe.

560. There is a possibility that this could have been Emma Huegy, the widow of Maurice Huegy, Josephine Bandelier's brother. However, it is more probable that this was Emma Bandelier, a cousin of Adolph F. Bandelier, daughter of Emil and Rosalie Bandelier, and sister of Elizabeth Bandelier Kaune and Gustave A. Bandelier (see ns 127 and 142). Emma Bandelier's name appeared infrequently in the journals, and little biographical material has been found for her. She married Willie Schnepple of Santa Fe (personal conversation, Mrs. R. L. Ormsbee, August 1969).

Regarding Bandelier's comment in this entry, it must be recognized, in fairness to either Emma, but particularly Emma Bandelier, that it must have been rather difficult for anyone with the name of Bandelier, and possibly Huegy, to live in Highland in the months following the bank failure.

561. This man was most likely C. B. Hayward, who had recently been editor of the *Santa Fe Daily New Mexican* and who in 1883 had served as an editor of the *New Mexican Review* in Santa Fe. Hayward had also been a postmaster at Santa Fe in the early 1880s (Stratton 1969: 34, 287). As of this date, Hayward was still postmaster, according to newspaper reports of the time.

562. Bandelier noted that Padre Acorsini had assisted in the Feast of Nuestra Señora de Guadalupe at Peña Blanca on December 12, 1882 (Lange and Riley 1966: 232). Father J. A. Acorsini, that same month, had been appointed to a new church at Springer, N.M. (p. 407). Sadliers (1886: 144) still listed him at Springer. He apparently was visiting Santa Fe at the time of this entry, when he administered Communion to Bandelier.

563. Gerónimo was a famous chief of the Chiricahua Apaches. For details of his life, see Davis 1929. In Lange and Riley (1970: 385n235), it was noted that Lt. Charles B. Gatewood (n 690) was the officer that persuaded Gerónimo to surrender. The comment was also made that Lt. Gatewood was never given proper credit for this achievement. See Davis (1929) for added data on Gatewood's role in the surrender of Gerónimo.

564. John Dawson Gilmary Shea (1824–92) was an American historical writer and philologist. He was admitted to the bar, but abandoned his law practice to write. He was

the author of: *Discovery and Exploration of the Mississippi Valley* (1853); *History of the Catholic Missions among the Indian Tribes of the United States* (1854); and also, grammars and dictionaries of various American Indian languages (White 1940: I, 259).

Of particular interest to Bandelier was Shea's volume, published in 1882, on *The Expedition of Don Diego Dionisio de Peñalosa, Governor of New Mexico, from Santa Fe to the River Mischipi and Quivira in 1662, as described by Father Nicholas de Freytas, O. S. F.* (For further data on Peñalosa and the alleged authorship of Freytas, see ns 184 and 727. See also Burrus 1967: 69–70, 69n8, 70n9.)

Burrus (1967: 80–83) published letters from Shea to Oscar W. Collet which were written both before and after Shea published his book on the Peñalosa expedition. Of special interest here is Shea's letter of March 27, 1883 (pp. 80–81), written after he had learned of Duro's work on Peñalosa, published also in 1882. Shea wrote:

> As to Peñalosa's expedition he [Duro] believes the relation to have been written not by Freytas but by Peñalosa himself and concocted simply to impose on the French, using Coronado or Oñate.
>
> It is some satisfaction to have induced a learned society [Royal Academy of Madrid] to examine a subject carefully and by the light of authorities. As the result is only a conjecture, it leaves us all free to agree or disagree.

On April 4, 1883, Shea wrote (p. 82), "Captain Duro makes out a strong case against Peñalosa, and I purpose giving his documents and arguments to complete my Peñalosa." [Burrus (1967: 70) noted that Shea's intention to publish a complete account of the traitorous Peñalosa was never realized. Other tasks intervened, and Shea died in 1892 (p. 70).]

Continuing, Shea (p. 82) commented,

> The Spanish government obtained the Freytas narrative almost immediately, for interrogatives were sent out to New Mexico, and there are two documents, evidently replies which cover all the exploring expeditions the writers knew, and they are silent as to Peñalosa's.
>
> Spanish archives give data as to his [Peñalosa's] career in London and Paris, his assumption of titles, etc. From all the evidence Duro concludes that he [Peñalosa] wrote the account himself in the name of Fray Freytas in order to impose upon the French government.
>
> . . .
>
> The *Informe* [Duro's work] is the result of a pretty thorough examination of the manuscript matter accessible to the members of the Real Academia, and is important from that point of view.

565. Fort Marcy was the first U.S. Army post in New Mexico, being founded in August 1846, shortly after the American occupation of Santa Fe. The fort, an elaborate system of earthworks, was named for Captain R. B. Marcy, discoverer of the Canadian River headwaters and author, in 1861, of *The Prairie Traveller.* The fort was abandoned in 1897 (Pearce 1965: 58; American Guide Series 1940: 200).

566. This was Bandelier's first journal entry noting his going "out to Fischer's." As evidenced by entries before and after this one, the relationship between the Bandeliers and the Fischers had steadily grown since the New Year's Day call that Bandelier had made in the company of Gerdes.

Aside from the social relations between members of the two families was the fact that the Fischers, in addition to other business interests, were proprietors of the principal, if not the only, brewery in Santa Fe.

Beginning in the mid-1860s, the brewery passed through several changes in ownership before its acquisition in 1881 by the Fischers. At a meeting of the board of directors of the Fischer Brewing Co., December 20, 1881, the following officers were elected: E. D. Franz, president; L. E. Theo Fischer, treasurer; and C. F. A. Fischer, secretary and general manager (*Santa Fe Daily New Mexican,* December 22, 1881).

In a subsequent article in the same newspaper (May 2, 1882), it was noted that "Mr. Fischer is one of Santa Fe's most enterprising citizens. He came here from St. Louis where he was for a long time in business." The article continued, noting that the brewery was at the eastern extremity of Palace Avenue and that, while the avenue stopped short, the river road—to be improved—did link the two.

> The brewery building stands upon a bluff overlooking the river. It is a pleasant spot naturally, and has been made still more attractive by the enterprise of its owners. It is a long building ranging east and west. At the western end is a suit of rooms, which are now nicely furnished and occupied by Mr. Fischer. Next comes a long hall, and at the eastern end is the brewery proper. The building faces towards the south, and in front of it is a terrace which has been beautified considerably during the present spring. It has also a verandah, and from this an admirable view of the city may be had. Upon this porch are tables, and [also] upon the terrace where the newly-leafed trees afford a pleasant shade. The beer drinkers here find Elyseum, and as they quaff the cooling beverage may look down upon the world and feel themselves exalted above its sordid cases. Every day such happy mortals avail themselves of the luxury, and upon all holidays the place is thronged.

Twitchell (1911–17: IV, 69) in a sketch of Adolph [Adolf] Jacob Fischer stated that he was deputy state auditor under William G. Sargent and had compiled an excellent record of public service in a variety of positions. He was born in St. Louis, 1867, the son of C. F. A. and Margaret Foellinger Fischer, both of whom were natives of Germany. They had come to America in early life, had married in Indiana, and had lived in St. Louis prior to coming to New Mexico.

567. George Cuyler Preston and his wife were friends of the Bandeliers. The *Santa Fe Daily New Mexican* of December 26, 1887 (No. 261, p. 4) carried the item that Lt. and Mrs. James Fornance "and pretty baby daughter" from Fort Wingate were spending the holidays in Santa Fe as guests of the Prestons. Fornances were also close friends of the Bandeliers, Lt. Fornance also being among those taking foreign language lessons from Bandelier when he was stationed in Santa Fe (see entry of December 23, 1887).

568. Batonapa was a "Trincheras," or fortified hill, a short distance south of Banamichi in Sonora (see Bandelier 1890–92: II, 491–92; Lange and Riley 1970: 234–36). Burrus (1969c) reproduced this sketch, XXVIII, in color. It was listed in his Catalogue (1969b: 212) as Item 501.

569. See entry of April 7, 1886, for explanation of this development.

570. Marcos Eldodt was one of three brothers, Samuel, Nathan, and Marcos, German-Jewish settlers in the United States. Samuel Eldodt was a good friend of Bandelier and was host to Bandelier a number of times when the latter was in San Juan Pueblo. Originally, the Eldodts formed one company with merchandising stores in Santa Fe, San Juan, and Abiquiu, but, in 1882, the firm split, leaving Marcus to handle the Santa Fe business (Anonymous 1895: 420–21).

In the summer of 1969, the editors visited San Juan Pueblo and found displayed on the wall in the San Juan Mercantile Co. the following letter from the U.S. Indian Service, Pueblo Indian Agency, Santa Fe, dated March 23, 1880.

"Eldodt Bros., U. S. Indian Traders, San Juan, N. M. Gentlemen: I enclose herewith a renewal of your license to trade with the Pueblo Indians at San Juan for the term of one year from the 30th day of the present month, granted by the Hon. Commissioner of Indian Affairs, the 18th inst."

This was signed by Ben M. Thomas, U.S. Indian Agent, and another person whose signature was unclear but which we recorded as Rev. [?] E. M. Finck, or Finch. On display with the letter was the actual license:

> License to Trade with Indians—
> Marcos Eldodt and Samuel Eldodt
> March 18, 1880
>   R. E. Trowbridge, Comm.

571. This letter from Mexico City, dated April 6, 1886, was one of those included by White and Bernal (1960: 294–97); our translation follows:

> Dear friend and godchild:
>
> I received your estimable letter of 9 February, opportunely, but was unable to answer it soon because around that time a new sorrow fell on me. The birth of the baby girl that I announced to you had mitigated the sorrow for the death of the boy, and because everything went well, I decided to go on February 10 to the haciendas, where there were some disturbances which demanded my presence there; that had already been delayed too long. I had only been there five days when I received a telegram with the announcement that the girl was gravely ill with pneumonia. I took the first train, and in twenty-four hours, I entered my house. But four hours prior to my arrival, the child had died, and the only thing I found was her dead body. This second blow renewed and aggravated the first, and, overwhelmed with sorrow, I did not want to leave my daughter who was inconsolable. I decided against returning to the plantations and sent my son in my place. Since then misfortunes have rained on me and have left me spiritless. Even today I have too many sorrows, but I want to take a moment to say that I have received your letter and I thank you for the regards you sent me. I take comfort in knowing that your position has improved relatively.
>
> With great pleasure I would send you all the information you requested for the progress of your works, but I lack time and spirit. For the time being I enclose a copy which I made from the *Libro de Oro*, regarding Cibola. In Father Daza's I have not found anything that would seem to be useful; nevertheless, when I have time I will copy what there is, although it is long; there is no date either. *The Historia de la Conquista de Mexico* by Villagrá, is a dull poem, one which I need to study slowly in order to see if something could be drawn out of it. In the third series of the *Documentos para la Historia de Mexico* there is, as you know, enough about the *Provincias Internas* so that it is impossible even to think about copying it and I do not know what we could do, because it is a very rare volume. I do not have any hope of finding it to give you, and that would be the only way I could make it available to you. Try to see if you could indicate to me something on this matter, because nothing occurs to me, and I want to help you.
>
> Dr. Brühl, of Cincinnati, came to pay me a visit and asked me about you. I have received other visits from mercantile and literary agents. Here, Americans are everywhere!

May God protect you and all yours and relieve you from your sorrows, as I wish and hope. Do not forget your affectionate godfather who now has little time in this world.

Goodbye,

García Icazbalceta

572. On February 9, 1886, Bandelier had written García Icazbalceta requesting the *Libro de Oro,* because it contained an account of V. P. Motolinia regarding the discovery of New Mexico (see n 543). On April 6, 1886, García Icazbalceta replied, enclosing a copy which he had made from the *Libro de Oro* regarding Cibola (see n 571). This document, entitled "Esta es la Relación postrera de Sivola: y de mas de quatro cientas leguas adelante.—(Sacada a la letra de la obra manuscrita de Fray Toribio de Paredes, ó 'Motolinia,' intitulada: 'Libro de Oro o'Thesoro indio,' en poder de Don Joaquín García-Ycazbalceta, México.)," was among the copied documents in the Catron Collection (PC 29 807). Signed by Bandelier in Santa Fe, on December 3, 1889, the document was in a hand other than Bandelier's.

Wagner (1937: I, 106, 108, 113) referred to the *Relación postrera de Sívola.* Of particular interest is the reference on p. 108: "This document is contained in a book of manuscripts which formerly belonged to Motolinía, now in the possession of the García Pimentel family. My opinion is that this is a copy of a piece that had been printed, very likely in Mexico City, when received there some time in 1541." Luis García Pimentel was the son of García Icazbalceta (see n 782). By Wagner's time, this book of manuscripts would undoubtedly have passed from father to son. Winship included a translation of the *Relación postrera de Sívola* in his account of the Coronado Expedition (1896: 113). Fewkes (1895: 307) listed this as "l. Last Account of Sivola. Fray Toribio Motolinia, 1541."

The question of possible lost works of Motolinia has been raised again by Riley (1973). Riley noted that the curious "South Sea" section of the Benavides Memorial of 1630 actually reproduced material also found in the *Apologética Historia Sumaria* of Bartolomé de Las Casas. It is possible that Benavides borrowed from one of the manuscripts of the *Apologética Historia* known to have been extant in the late sixteenth and early seventeenth centuries. It is also possible, however, that Benavides and Las Casas utilized a common source. If so, this source may have been a manuscript of Motolinia now lost, perhaps an early expanded version of the *Libro de Oro.* For further discussion, see Riley (1973) and O'Gorman (1971: xxi, xlix, l, et seq.).

573. There were storms all over central New Mexico from the 18th to the 20th of April, 1886. According to the *Santa Fe Daily New Mexican* of April 20 (p. 4), one bridge across the Santa Fe River had been washed out and another was expected momentarily to go.

The house where the Bandeliers lived was not far from the Santa Fe River and the San Miguel Mission. This mission, still one of the historic landmarks in Santa Fe, is often referred to as "the oldest church in the United States." Adams and Chavez (1956: 37n1) denied this claim, stating that it is eighteenth century while Laguna is seventeenth century. This statement was based on the archaeological work done by Stubbs and Ellis in 1955 at San Miguel. While they found older and distinct foundations within the present chapel, all four walls dated 1709–10. The present reredos, cleaned and restored by E. Boyd, disclosed a date of 1798.

See Lange and Riley (1966: 144) for Bandelier's recording of an inscription on a beam of 1710 at San Miguel and Kubler (1939: 5–6) for his comments on translations in the literature of this particular inscription.

574. These callers were probably Louise (Louisa, or Luisa) and Julia Fischer, daughters of C. F. A. and Margaret Foellinger Fischer; the Fischers also had a son, Adolf Jacob, born in St. Louis in 1867 (see n 566).

575. Though Bandelier's journals do not record his sending this article on Cabeza de Vaca for publication, Lange and Riley (1970: 378n157) cited an article by Bandelier in the *Magazine of Western History,* Cleveland, July 1886, entitled, "Alvar Nuñez Cabeza de Vaca, the First Overland Traveler of European Descent, and His Journey from Florida to the Pacific Coast—1528–1536." Hodge (1932) gave the same citation. However, Wagner (1937: I, 40), in listing several historians who had written on Cabeza de Vaca, cited Bandelier in the *Magazine of American History,* July 1886. Unfortunately, Wagner did not cite either title or place of publication. Bandelier noted in his June 11, 1886, entry that he had received, corrected, and returned proof sheets to Cleveland, and on July 27, 1886, he noted a letter "from Cleveland with $14.25." There were no journal entries to suggest that he was simultaneously working on two separate articles on Cabeza de Vaca. Presumably, the entries all referred to the *Magazine of Western History,* and Wagner's citation of "American History" rather than "Western History" was incorrect (see Bandelier 1886g).

576. These were two of the daughters (perhaps Cyrillia and Eugenia) of William H. and Josefita Salazar Manderfield (see n 596). At the time of her marriage to Manderfield, Josefita already had two children, Cyrilia, or Cyrillia, and Enrique. Cyrilia took her stepfather's name, but Enrique retained his mother's maiden name, Salazar. Three children, all girls, were born to the Manderfields; they were Eugenia, Florentina, and Josefita (Manderfield file in New Mexico State Archives; see also n 1131). Twitchell (1925: 472) referred to "Judge" Manderfield. The journal entry of November 22, 1886, mentioned Cyrilia and Eugenia by name.

577. This letter, dated May 3, 1886, was among those published by White and Bernal (1960: 294–97); our translation follows:

My very dear sir and friend:

Because of my right arm that only permits me to write the most urgent things, the answer to your letter of April 6, has been disproportionately delayed. Even now, at the moment of writing these lines, I still wonder if I will be able to finish them today. I have my hand almost paralyzed, or as we say here, "stiff," without strength nor dexterity, the fingers opposing my will; in short, I suffer from that infirmity the French call *"crampe des ècrivains,"* which for me is a real calamity. But by writing slowly, making the letters one after another like a small child perhaps I will be able to reach the end of the page. For years I have been free of this disease, but now it returns with increased strength.

With great pain and sadness, we were informed of the new sorrow God inflicted on you. It must have been a terrible shock to your children, and we sympathize as much with them as with you. Each one of us in our own way has prayed to God to give relief and repose to our friends from Mexico.

I thank you very much for the copy of the *Relación Postrera,* which is of great value to me. But I thank you even more for offering me your invaluable help. For the moment, what interests me most is information about the ruins of Casas Grandes, Chihuahua. In 1884, I spent an entire month there measuring the said ruins, but still I have not been able to find traces of the Indians who inhabited the valley at the time of first Spanish contact. I would like to know:

(1) Which is the earliest information available about Casas Grandes, its content, its date, and what information it provides concerning its occupants. Not about the occupants of the buildings, but rather the inhabitants of the region at the moment of the Spanish arrival.

(2) Date of the foundation of the convent and of the church (now abandoned) of San Antonio de Casas Grandes. [Matias de la] Mota Padilla (p. 357) [*Historia*

de la Conquista de la Provincia de la Nueva Galicia, Mexico, 1870] mentions
this mission without indicating the date.

The fourth series of the *Documentos,* Vol. III, p. 234, mentions the place, but
I do not have the details the document provides. In Arlegui's *Cronica* there
must exist information about this mission and indications about the Indians and
their language.

What I know I found in Ternaux's book *Recueil de piéces relatives á la
Conquete du Mexique,* by Cabrera which says, speaking about Juan de Oñate:
"They arrived in the last town of the new Kingdom of Vizcaya, from where it
is believed the Indians came who inhabited ancient Mexico . . ." It mentions an
enormous piece of meteoric iron. I suspect that this might be the first mention
made about Casas Grandes (pp. 436–37). I imagine that Cabrera freely drew
from the poetic work of Villagrán.

(3) Volumes XII, XIII, XIV, XV of the *Documentos Inéditos . . . del Archivo
de Indias . . .* encompass a great amount of valuable information. I know, for
sure, that the Spanish government has made available these books at no cost.
I do not ask anything from the crown, or from the government of Spain,
although it is rather sad for a friend of the Spanish race like myself, because I
am and I have demonstrated it, to see how the "Cartas de Indias" are being
distributed with no result among Americans, and even among people who do
not understand them, while a supporter of the Spanish people and their religion
is overlooked. I would like to know if these four volumes are sold separately and
at a reasonable price. Eventually, I hope to be able to save some *pesetas* and
earmark them to buy books. For the time being, I cannot, but if God still
protects me I will.

I am still more disconcerted by the ignorance of the public about the Spanish
administration in the New World. There is not a writer who tells the truth
concerning this matter. From the moment they are confronted with anything
Spanish, even the most impartial gets confused. Not until I have gathered the
necessary data will I be able to raise my voice on your behalf, but I plan to do
it.

There is not anything here worth mentioning in a letter, unless I speak to you
about floods, disasters caused by storms and a preposterous desire by the "gringos" to implant here their language, their feverish behavior, and their lack of
faith. The stolid conservatism of the Indians opposes the first and last points, and
the second point is defeated by nature itself which stops all the efforts that are
made to transform this land into a rich land like Quito.

Despite the poverty of the land we are satisfied and half-happy. A poor land
goes alongside with people without resources, and as long as we have beans we
will not be hungry. Regarding the Church, I still fulfill and observe my obligations, and I have never regretted the important step I took in Cholula. On the
contrary, my last confession was a great relief to me.

If the work that I am about to finish turns out as I expect, I believe that it will
not be long before I could spend some days of leisure under the Mexican sky
and introduce you to my wife.

Now, my dear sir, I have sore fingers and my wrist is stiff. For this reason, and
solely for this reason, I close this letter.

We pray to God for you, and for those in your household, for your well-being
and your complete happiness.

I beg you to excuse the insistence with which I return to literary and scientific
problems. I apologize with a phrase you wrote me some time ago: "Qui a bu,
boira!" [He who has drunk, will drink!]

Many salutations and affectionate regards for all.
Your faithful servant and affectionate godchild.

Ad. F. Bandelier

578. This article on Santa Fe was entitled, "Das Alter der Stadt Santa Fé, Neu-Mexiko." It appeared in the *New Yorker Staatszeitung*, Sonntagsblatt, Juni 20, 1886. In the Bandelier Scrapbook, presented to the editors by Prof. Fred Eggan, a clipping of this article was included; an inked marginal note stated, "This is the beginning of what will be the last article in the book."

579. Hartmann, a cartographer, undoubtedly found the sketches (Lange and Riley 1966: 173, 175) and accompanying pages of description (pp. 164–76) from Bandelier's 1880 journal of considerable help in drawing the Map of the Western Rio Grande Shores, north of Cochiti, referred to in this entry. These sketches and description had resulted from Bandelier's first trip from Cochiti north to the Rito de los Frijoles, returning via the Stone Lions and Painted Cave, which he had made in the latter half of October of that year.

580. This entry of May 12, 1886, in Bandelier's original journals was reproduced in its entirety on the cover of *El Palacio*, Vol. XLIX, No. 6, June 1942. Underneath was the caption, "ONE DAY'S ENTRY FROM BANDELIER'S JOURNALS, TELLING OF THE COMPLETION OF 'THE DELIGHT MAKERS.'" This issue included Hobbs's article, "The Story of the Delight Makers from Bandelier's Own Journals" (Hobbs 1942b).

Though Hobbs was aware that the original novel was in German (pp. 116–17; see also Hobbs 1942c), the caption on the *El Palacio* cover is misleading because the novel that Bandelier had completed in May 1886 was *Die Köshare* and not *The Delight Makers*. Hobbs (1942c) did not cite *Die Köshare* per se, though she did comment that Bandelier, on March 23, 1890, noted receiving a copy of the *Evening Post* of New York "containing the first notice of my 'Koshare.'" She also commented that this was the only instance in which Bandelier referred in his journals to the work as anything other than "the novel" or "my novel" (p. 123).

Hodge (1932: 368), in his bibliography of Bandelier, included this citation: Die Köshare. Eine Erzählung aus dem Leben der Pueblo-Indianer von Neu-Mexiko. *Belletristische [sic] Journal*, New York, Jan. 1–May 14, 1890.

581. Rev. George Kelly Dunlop was elected Bishop of the Episcopal missionary district of New Mexico and Arizona in 1880 and was consecrated on November 21 of that year.

Dunlop was born in northern Ireland on November 10, 1830, and came to the United States in 1852, following his graduation from Queens University, Galway. Bishop Dunlop died on March 12, 1888 (Anderson 1907: II, 488–89).

582. On April 28, 1882, Bandelier had noted in his journal (Lange and Riley 1966: 271) his preparations for "my lecture." He also noted "revising the proof afterwards at the *New Mexican* office" (p. 272). The lecture, entitled "Kin and Clan," was delivered before the New Mexico Historical Society in "The Palace" in Santa Fe. It appeared in its entirety in the *Santa Fe Daily New Mexican*, April 29, 1882. It was reprinted as a pamphlet of eight pages from the newspaper article by the Historical Society in 1882. The *New Mexico Historical Review*, Vol. VIII, No. 3, July 1933, pp. 165–75, reprinted its earlier paper as an article in the regular issue, noting that some changes in spelling and format had been made.

583. Apparently, Clotilde was employed by the *New Yorker Staatszeitung*. Several entries suggest this. On May 23, 1886, after Bandelier had noted, "Letter from Papa" (n 585), he wrote to Clotilde in addition to Bertha [Huegy Lambelet, a relative of Joe's] and to Mr. Balsiger [a very close friend of the senior Bandelier]. On October 19, 1886,

Bandelier made a journal entry, "Cashed a check for $25.-which Clotilde sent us for Papa." Apparently, this was payment for a series of articles which the senior Bandelier, Adolphe Eugene Bandelier, had published on Venezuela in the *New Yorker Staatszeitung* (n 809).

584. The Francisca Hinojos House, 355 East Palace Avenue, Santa Fe, has been designated as "worthy of preservation" by the Historic Santa Fe Foundation, and a bronze plaque has been placed on it. The house was designed and constructed by itinerant French artisans who were brought to Santa Fe from Louisiana by Bishop Lamy to build the Cathedral. Although made of adobe, the exterior design is more like that of the French period of Louisiana. Don Alfredo Hinojos's mother, Francisca, acquired the property between 1856 and 1870, and in 1887, she bequeathed it to her son.

Don Alfredo Hinojos was a prominent political figure and also organist at the Cathedral for nearly fifty years (Loomis 1966: 38).

585. Bandelier had seemingly not heard from "Papa" since May 8, 1885. After Adolphe E. Bandelier's departure from Highland, April 27, 1885, just prior to the bank failure, Bandelier had received, according to the journal entries, only two letters from his father —on May 4 and May 8 of that year. Whether Bandelier learned from this letter received on May 23, 1886, that his father was and had been in Venezuela is not made clear (see ns 117 and 809).

586. This was undoubtedly the same Mr. Gaertner who was mentioned in an article in the *Weekly New Mexican Review* of Santa Fe in the issue of April 5, 1888 (p. 3). The article was "About the Brewery" and mentioned that under its Manager, C. F. A. Fischer, the brewery had undergone a number of great improvements including an appreciably increased production capacity. The article continued, "But the most ingeneous part of the improvements consists in the innumerable labor-saving devices which have been put in by Superintendent Robert Gaertner. Machinery does it all. Where a dozen men had to be employed a year ago but two are now required" (see n 566).

587. Bandelier had left his illustrative plates in Berlin with Dr. Hermann Gerlich of the German Consulate with the hope that he could sell them. See entry of March 12, 1885, and n 62.

588. Defouri (1887: 159) spoke of "the uncompromising Father Stephan in the Bureau of Indian Affairs." Salpointe (1898: 274) wrote, "Before leaving the subject of the New Mexico Pueblo Indian schools, we must acknowledge the services we received from the members of the Bureau of Catholic Indian Missions and especially from its director, Monseigneur J. A. Stephan, for their support during our administration of the Archdiocese of Santa Fe. To the Venerable Stephan we are indebted for the encouragement he gave to the pupils and teachers of these schools by visiting them several times and, when needed, by procuring the means of enlarging or repairing the school buildings." (A photograph of the Rt. Rev. Monsignor J. A. Stephan faces page 281.)

589. This was probably Vaillant's Ixtaccíhuatl (White Lady), one of Mexico's great volcanoes (1944: 275). Whether this paper was ever published is unknown. In May 1881, Bandelier had climbed Iztaccihuatl (Ixtaccihuatl Mountain) and reported this adventure in a letter to *Die Union,* a Highland German-language newspaper. See Hammond and Goad (1949: 100–110) for a translation of this letter, which appeared under the chapter heading, "Exploring Iztaccihuatl."

590. This was General Henry M. Atkinson, Surveyor General of New Mexico, 1876–82, and U.S. Surveyor General, 1882–83. He was "capable, honest, and popular." He resigned in 1883. About 1880, he had helped reorganize the New Mexico Historical Society. He died in 1886 (Lange and Riley 1966: 407).

Presumably, Bandelier had asked Atkinson to read and criticize his manuscript on land grants, taking advantage of Atkinson's familiarity with the subject.

591. Harrington (1916: 227), in discussing etymology, noted that San Juan, "Yuge-ouinge," clearly meant "down at the mockingbird place." His Tewa informants agreed with this meaning, but they claimed they never thought of a mockingbird or any other etymology when using this term.

Presumably, Bandelier's "Spottvogel" article had to do with Yuge-ouinge, perhaps as related to Oñate's colonization (see n 217).

592. This paper appeared under the title, "Southwestern Pine Timber," in *The Nation*, No. 1096, July 1, 1886.

593. See n 193.

594. There were numerous entries in the journals referring to this manta of the malinche, beginning with the November 23, 1880, entry, when Bandelier received permission from the cacique to paint it (Lange and Riley 1966: 218). Burrus (1969c) reproduced this sketch, in color, as number XXI. It was listed in his Catalogue (1969b) as Item 494. In his December 26, 1885, entry, Bandelier recorded a description of the performance of the Matalotes and Malinches at Cochiti.

Lange (1959: 280), interestingly, obtained quite a different sketch of the malinche's manta seventy years later at Cochiti. This manta, highly sacred to the Cochiti, is an example of on-going modification—even in the more esoteric aspects of culture, supposedly the most stable elements in culture.

Burrus (1969b) also cited in his Catalogue additional drawings related to the Cochiti malinche dancer, Items 81 and 96. Item 81, in color, comprised four sketches: A. the scarf with embroidered fringe; B. the headdress; C. Bracelet; and D. Shell brooch. Item 96 was one sketch, in color, of the bust of the Malinche. Though Burrus added San Juan, his additional data noted that in the corners of the sheet Bandelier had written: "Rio Grande; Cochiti; Tzumal a Canyi (Malinche of A-ca-canyi); Santa Fe, N. M. 1/1/86." Bandelier made no journal entry that he worked on the malinche figure on that date. He was undoubtedly recording details he had observed at the dance on December 26, 1885. In this entry of June 11, 1886, he was continuing to refine his painting of the malinche manta. Probably, it was one of the drawings that had been returned to him from Berlin shortly before that by Consul Gerlich.

595. See entry of September 3, 1886; "Noodles" was almost assuredly Bandelier's uninformed phonetic rendition of Christian Noetel's surname.

596. William Henry Manderfield was born in Pennsylvania in 1841. He learned the printer's trade as a youth and in the late 1850s moved to Illinois and later to Missouri, in both states editing country newspapers. In 1863, in the employ of the government, he "whacked bulls," freighting supplies for New Mexico military posts, arriving in Santa Fe in 1863. He found employment on the *Santa Fe Republican*, where Thomas Tucker was foreman. A close friendship between the two men and astute money management resulted in their partnership and ownership of the plant and the weekly paper, the name of which they changed to the *New Mexican*. In 1868, they also began the publication of the *Daily New Mexican*, the first daily newspaper published in the Southwest. The newspaper was influential in the early political life of the Territory. In 1881, Manderfield sold his interest in the paper to the Atchison, Topeka and Santa Fe Railroad, which controlled policies of the paper until 1883 when the railroad company retired from the area of Southwestern journalism.

Manderfield was elected county commissioner and later judge of the probate court, after which he retired to private life.

A few years after his arrival in Santa Fe, he married Josefita Salazar, the ceremony having been performed by Archbishop Lamy. Born in Santa Fe, her parents traced their ancestry to the descendants of soldiers of de Vargas in the Reconquest of New Mexico.

In 1885, Judge Manderfield's health became impaired and though he lived until early

December of 1888, his condition gradually weakened and he rarely appeared in public (Twitchell 1925: 471–72).

597. Presumably, this was a reference to the ruins of Chaco Canyon in northwestern New Mexico, perhaps the most impressive in the Southwest and at present the object of a fifteen-year multidisciplinary research effort by the United States National Park Service. Strangely, Bandelier in all his Southwestern years never visited the Chaco Canyon area.

White (1940: II, 217n9) commented that Morgan, in his "The Seven Cities of Cibola," *North American Review,* Vol. 108, pp. 457–98, April 1869, cited evidence to support the hypothesis that the Seven Cities were the pueblos of Chaco Canyon. In his letter of October 22, 1880 (p. 217), Bandelier had written Morgan, "As for those Chaco houses being the towers of Cibola, it is *utterly out of the question.* The Cibola of Coronado was *Zuñi, . . .*"

This conclusion, reached by Bandelier within weeks of his initial arrival in New Mexico, may well have served to relegate the area to such a low priority that he never found time to make a Chaco trip. Bandelier did, however, include blueprints of four Chaco Canyon ruins (Pueblo Pintado, Pueblo Bonito, Pueblo del Arroyo, and Pueblo Peñasco Blanco) among the *Histoire* illustrations (Burrus 1969b: 144–45).

598. Father J. B. Mariller had been brought to the Santa Fe area by Bishop Lamy (Salpointe 1898: 283). The Lamy Memorial (1950: 63) listed Rev. B.A. [?] Mariller as pastor at Jemez from 1881 to 1894. Sadliers (1886: 142) gave J.B. as the initials but spelled the last name as "Marilles." The editors believe Salpointe's J.B. Mariller is the proper form and that the other forms refer to this individual.

599. Otero (1939: 149–50) recounted this episode but gave it as occurring June 17. Joseph W. Stinson was a saloon owner on the east side of the Santa Fe Plaza. In a drunken quarrel, Stinson shot William W. McCann. Fortunately, McCann recovered but on July 19, 1886, a grand jury indicted Stinson; he was fined $100.00. Not long before, Stinson had been tried and acquitted (self-defense) of killing one Walter Henderson. The *Santa Fe Daily New Mexican* of June 17, 1886 (Vol. 23, No. 75, p. 4) gave the story of the McCann shooting in considerable detail under the heading, "A Brutal Act."

Seemingly an unrelated affair, the incident between Cross and Hill must stand without elaboration.

600. In his entry of May 13, 1886, Bandelier noted, "Wrote at 'Peru' for Rochester." He mailed the article to Frank P. Smith on May 14, and on June 13, 1886, he mentioned the return of the article from Smith. Bandelier added, "Will have to rewrite it." Entries on June 14 and 16 indicated he was working "on Peru." Presumably, his "Finished and mailed 'Ancient Peruvians' " was the rewritten article on Peru for Frank P. Smith.

601. Bandelier presumably mailed this article, another the next day, a third and fourth on June 24 and 25, and a fifth and sixth on July 1 and 2 before leaving Santa Fe on a two-week trip. The articles, or installments, were sent to Preetorius in St. Louis for publication in the *Westliche Post.* Upon his return on July 22 from the trip to San Juan, Santa Clara, etc., he finished parts VII and VIII of the "Nahr- und Nutzpflanzen" paper and mailed them, two days later, on July 24. To date, citations for this article, or series, on "Food and Useful Plants," if published, have not been found.

602. This entry concerning idols and the cacique's using them for curing and simultaneously manufacturing them for sale at Cochiti is of interest in light of the Bloom-Hewett correspondence which questioned the authenticity of the Cochiti idols in the Prince collection (see n 552). (For an earlier account of manufacturing idols for sale at Cochiti by the cacique through Bandelier to Col. James Stevenson who was collecting for the Bureau of Ethnology, see Lange and Riley 1966: 191.)

Bloom, writing May 18, 1938, after finding the illustrations in Rome, commented, ". . . at least his last illustrations are of seven of those identical idols. I think you once told me you considered them fakes picked up by Gov. Prince? Well, here they are, vouched for by Bandelier and perhaps acquired by him."

Hewett's reply, dated June 3, 1938, stated that,

> Up to Bandelier's time there had been no one to question the authenticity of the "stone idols" in the Prince collection. I was convinced of their spurious character when I first came to New Mexico in the late nineties, and I discovered that Professor Starr had arrived at the same conclusion, probably long before I did. We compared notes on the matter about the year 1899. The complete exposé of the "stone idols" was made by John P. Harrington after he came on our staff and is contained in a manuscript which I have on file, but which I never thought best to publish, especially as the collection practically disappeared many years ago, and no contention has been made as to its authenticity. I personally knew Cleto Yulino [Urina?] and his son, who between them manufactured practically all of the idols of the Prince collection, and I knew their workshop under the big cottonwood tree down the arroyo a few minutes' walk from the pueblo.

603. For a discussion of Cochiti medicine societies, see Lange (1959: 254–73).

604. On July 8, 1520, the Battle of Otumba, or Otumpan, was fought in the valley of that name, east of the Lake of Mexico. The Spanish and Tlascalan forces, badly mauled in the escape from Mexico City on July 1 (the *Noche Triste*), nevertheless engaged the forces of the Aztecs and their confederates. The fighting was indecisive for a time, but then the Spaniards managed to kill one of the Aztec leaders, whereupon the Aztec forces retreated (Prescott 1893: II, 336–39; see also Vaillant 1944: 253–64).

605. Data on the precise relationships between medicine men and medicine societies of one pueblo and another, as between Jemez and Cochiti, are very difficult to learn. On the basis of tradition and past precedent, however, it is reasonable to assume that joint and reciprocal activities still are carried on. For a limited discussion of these matters, see Lange (1959: 236–68).

606. This was Eugene Allen Fiske who came to Santa Fe in 1876 to practice law. From 1889 to 1893, Mr. Fiske was United States Attorney for New Mexico (Anonymous 1895: 305–6).

607. This paper, entitled "The Discovery of New Mexico by Fray Marcos de Nizza," appeared in the *Magazine of Western History,* Cleveland, Vol. 5, pp. 659–70, in September of 1886. Hodge (1932: 366) noted that the article had been reprinted in *New Mexico Historical Review,* Vol. IV, No. 1, pp. 28–44, in 1929 and also that a condensed reprint appeared in *The Masterkey,* Vol. II, No. 8, pp. 5–15, in 1929.

Bandelier had written an earlier French version, which was also published in 1886 (see n 413). Wagner (1937: I, 95), in referring to this article, spoke of "Adolph Bandelier, who took up the cudgel in favor of the friar [Niza]."

608. Mrs. Henry Huning was apparently visiting in Santa Fe at the time of this entry. Bandelier had known both Henry and Franz Huning. In 1883, Bandelier had seen Henry while looking for ruins in the Showlow, Arizona, area (Lange and Riley 1970: 81–82, 384n215, n216, n221). In regard to this last note, correspondence with Mrs. Spencer C. (Lina F.) Browne, a granddaughter of Franz Huning, and to whom we are indebted for assistance, suggested that the flour mill of L. H. Huning of Los Lunas "perhaps should have been L. & H. Huning" (personal correspondence, April 11, 1971). Further clarification was furnished by a cousin of Mrs. Browne's, Louis H. Connell, who wrote, "I can clear

up the confusion of identity of the Huning mentioned as living at Showlow, Arizona, and that of Louis Huning of Los Lunas. Louis Huning and his brother Henry were business partners at Los Lunas. The partnership was dissolved, to the best of my knowledge, in the latter 1870s. Henry Huning moved to Showlow, while Louis Huning remained in Los Lunas, where he had a mill, general store and various ranching enterprises" (personal correspondence, April 26, 1971). Louis H. Connell's mother was Emma Huning, daughter of Louis.

609. The editors are inclined to believe that this reference was to General Eugene Asa Carr although it may well have been General Robert E. Carr.

Gould (1886: 237) listed Eugene A. Carr as a major general in the United States Army, with a residence in St. Louis. In the October 7, 1887, entry, Bandelier noted that he met General Carr of the 6th Cavalry [Eugene Asa] "by a mere accident" in Santa Fe (see Heitman 1903: I, 285). In the entry of October 9, 1888, Bandelier also noted that General and Mrs. Carr and Clark Carr were in Santa Fe from [Fort] Wingate. The *Santa Fe Daily New Mexican* for March 6, 1883, had reported that "General Robert Carr, the owner of Santa Fe's waterworks, who had been so-journing among us for several days, leaves for his home in St. Louis . . ." (Lange and Riley 1970: 434n134). This same newspaper account also stated that "General Carr is president of the St. Louis Mercantile Library Association" (see n 479). Conard (1901: 495–96) wrote of Robert E. Carr as follows: "A man of the highest administrative ability and fine social qualities, he was one of the most popular as well as one of the most widely known business men of St. Louis during the years of his active life."

Bandelier knew both Eugene Asa Carr and Robert E. Carr; each had St. Louis connections as well as Southwestern involvements. Accordingly, it is impossible to establish positively the identity of the General Carr in this entry.

610. In the Catholic calendar, June 29th is St. Peter and St. Paul's Day. Father Eguillon's given name was Peter, and Bandelier was conforming to the Catholic pattern of giving a gift on the person's Saint's Day rather than on his actual birthday.

611. These articles on Gerónimo, noted as being mailed in the entries of June 29 and 30, 1886, appeared in the *New Yorker Staatszeitung* on July 5, 12, and 17, 1886. They were among the items included in the Bandelier Scrapbook.

612. The following item appeared in the *Santa Fe Daily New Mexican* of July 8, 1886 (Vol. 23, No. 118, p. 4):

"Professor and Mrs. Bandelier, Lieutenant Fornance and Dr. Wm. Eggert in company with Dr. Bernard of the Baltimore and Ohio Railroad, and Judge Cross of Baltimore left this morning on a fishing and hunting trip to San Juan and Santa Clara, thence intending to cross the mountains and return via the Pecos valley."

As revealed in the journal entries, Bandelier failed to note any intention of returning via the Pecos valley, or the Jemez (which would have been closer); actually, he returned alone and on foot, via the Rio Grande valley, by way of Cuyamungue and Tesuque.

613. Much of this area which Bandelier described in this entry has been developed by the Santa Clara Indians as a recreation area for the general public. Camping, fishing, and picnicking are available for a modest entrance fee.

614. Shu-finné, or Shupinna, which means "narrow point" in Tewa, is a small ruin on the high mesa which rises above the plateau on the north side of Santa Clara Canyon, some ten miles west of Santa Clara Pueblo (Hewett 1953: 28–29).

615. On October 14, 1880, Bandelier had met Mr. Stevenson (Colonel James), "who told me about his remarkable discoveries in the Santa Clara Canyon" (Lange and Riley 1966: 145). However, Bandelier had not visited the Puye area until this trip. In his *Final Report* (1890–92: II, 67–78), he discussed both Shufinné and Puye extensively, as well as

including a sketch (p. 68) which showed their position relative to Santa Clara Canyon. In two notes (p. 67n1 and p. 69n1), Bandelier quoted from Mr. Stevenson in his descriptions of the ruins in 1880 and his interpretation of how the cave rooms had been formed.

616. Bandelier's use of the terms "glazed" and "glossy" was discussed previously (Lange and Riley 1970: 357n13). To summarize, he had used the term "glazed" in his 1880 journals. Putnam had criticized the use of the term "glazed" in Bandelier's Pecos Report manuscript, and Bandelier consequently (1881b: 131) changed to "varnished." Apparently dissatisfied with this term, he substituted "glossy" in his subsequent journal entries.

This entry again indicated that Bandelier equated "glossy" with "glazed." In his *Final Report* (1890–92), Bandelier returned to using the term "glazed." Bandelier (1881b: 131n1) cited Holmes (1876: 404 [*sic*] 1878: 404), who had written, "Most, if not all, of the painted pottery has received a thin coating of some mineral solution that gives a beautiful enamel like surface, not greatly inferior in hardness to the vitreous glazing of our potters."

Bandelier (1881b: 105, 105n2) also cited De Sosa, "Some of the pottery was glazed." In 1904, Bandelier reminded Holmes that a quarter of a century previously, he had suggested that an analysis of the coarse glaze on Pueblo pottery from the so-called Conquest period be made (letter from Bandelier to Holmes, dated July 13, 1904, National Anthropological Archives, Smithsonian Institution, Letters Received: #560.4).

617. For a discussion of the excavations at Puye, see Hewett (1953: 60–85). Schroeder and Matson (1965: 134) named Puye as a Tewa village possibly still occupied at the time of Castaño de Sosa.

618. Bandelier's persistence in inquiring about old documents proved in this case to be of great value to him. He did not return to Santa Clara Pueblo to work on these documents, however, until May 20, 1888, and gave no indication meanwhile in his journals that he knew of the extent and value of the documents there.

Except for Bandelier's own publications (1890a: 187; 1890d: 457; 1890–92: II, 62n1, 65n1), the editors have found little in the literature about these documents. Twitchell (1914: I, 13) and Chavez (1954a: 129) both referred briefly to Bandelier's use of Santa Clara documents concerning Juan de Archeveque, the betrayer of La Salle (see entry of May 30, 1888).

Puzzled that various discussions of pueblo church history made no reference to an archive at Santa Clara, the editors continued their research until finding Bandelier's own statements about the documents there. A condensation of his data appeared anonymously in the American Guide Series volume on New Mexico in the discussion of Santa Clara Pueblo (1940: 352). Bandelier's discussion is quoted in its entirety (pp. 291–94) from his chapter on Jean L'Archévèque in *The Gilded Man* (1893: 289–302).

> In this homely Indian village has lain concealed for many years a treasure of historical knowledge, an archive rich for America, so poor in archives, of the history of New Mexico. The Indians preserve and guard the treasure with superstitious care. It was entrusted to them years ago; and although their care for it has been limited to a superstitious guardianship and a cautious preservation, and no catalogue exists and no thought is taken of the greedy mice, the papers are still tolerably well preserved, and might safely lie there for yet many a year, suspiciously watched by men to whom the text is still a puzzle—for to them reading is a mystery, and the art of writing seems a kind of magic.
>
> The collection is the remains of the archives of the Franciscan order in New Mexico, the *"Custodia de la conversion de San Pablo de la Nueva-Mexico,"* which have lain here for more than thirty years, or since the time when the old military chapel (called *Castruenza*) of Santa Fé was condemned as unsafe. Such

of the documents and church-books stored there as were not immediately needed were securely deposited in Santa Clara; for a priest then lived in the pueblo, and Santa Clara formed a parish by itself. When the parish was discontinued and the seat of the pastorate was removed to Santa Cruz, the archives were left. No one having any use for them, they remained in an old cupboard of the ruined convent till an Indian, who could neither read nor write, but had a clear head and respect for the old and venerable, proposed to commit the care of the papers to private hands. It took long and solemn meetings for consultation before the *Principales* of the pueblo would agree to such an innovation. They would keep the documents, indeed, as something having an incomprehensible sanctity, but to remove them from the ruins, where they were given up to mold and decay, seemed at first a doubtful step. Those above, the "Shiuana," might be displeased at it. The spiritual powers were finally consulted, and their decision was in favor of the innovation. The Franciscan archives were thus carried into the dark back-room of an Indian house, where a blind man was their first guardian; but they are now in charge of an intelligent, tolerably clear-seeing citizen of the village.

I tried in 1886 to obtain access to these old manuscripts, but was at once refused. It is of no use to importune an Indian. If he denies a request he is fixed in it, and one must wait. I waited two years, provided myself with a most urgent letter of introduction from the archbishop and an order from the priest of Santa Cruz, and went again. At last the prohibition was withdrawn, and after three protracted visits to Santa Clara, the last of which lasted twenty days, I was able to say that I had exhausted all the material and had accurate and complete copies of all the documents which had any important bearing on the history of New Mexico. It was no easy work, for the hand-writing was often nearly illegible, and the ink had faded and the paper grown yellow, and become almost rotten.

The contents of the archives of Santa Clara may be divided into three classes. The first class consists of documents not strictly ecclesiastical, among which I found much that was valuable; the second, of the special church books, including registers of baptism, marriage, and death, many of the last of which begin with the date of 1694. Many valuable facts were also found in these. The papers called *Diligencias Matrimoniales,* or *Informaciones,* official inquiries to determine the civil standing of the contracting parties, which preceded every marriage, were the most numerous. Many of these were very long; some of them are of the seventeenth century, and they unfold an extremely instructive picture of the customs of those times. There are hardly any documents left in New Mexico of the period before the great insurrection of 1680, and I have the few that have been saved. But I found in Santa Clara a large number of details concerning the years preceding the insurrection, although contained in manuscripts that were composed one or two years after the troubles broke out. There have come to light little "court histories" of the governor of the time, scenes from the private life of long-vanished families which were then playing an important part in the troubled world called the Spanish Colony of New Mexico; notices of many an event which is never mentioned in the printed annals, and which was still of great importance. The real life of the people has taken shape out of these obscure writings of the monks, and many a striking revelation has been obtained from them. One of the discoveries made in them has given occasion to the present paper. [A detailed discussion of the identity of L'Archévèque followed.]

In his "Documentary History of the Rio Grande Pueblos of New Mexico" (1910a: 23–24), Bandelier spoke of these documents as "formerly at the Pueblo of Santa Clara and now preserved in Santa Fé through the efforts of the late Archbishop J. B. Salpointe." Chavez (1957: 3–4) did not indicate any archival collection from Santa Clara Pueblo, though his index included scattered Santa Clara documents in the Archives of the Archdiocese of Santa Fe.

The editors, while aware that the Catalogue of the Hemenway Expedition (Fewkes 1895) listed Santa Clara manuscripts, came upon a sheaf of documents quite by accident in the summer of 1969 while doing research on the Catron Collection, Coronado Library, University of New Mexico. These had been copied by Bandelier, and realizing their value to the editing of the last two volumes of the journals, the editors obtained photocopies of them. Many of the items proved to have been copied from the Santa Clara books referred to in this entry. One is a copy of a pre-Rebellion (April–June 1680) *diligencia*. These documents appear to be little known, despite the fact that Bandelier's transcriptions for the Hemenway Expedition were deposited in the Peabody Museum of Harvard University (Hodge 1914: 353). Because of the consequent unavailability of these materials, Bandelier, himself, could make little subsequent use of them. Similarly, one cannot look for information about the Santa Clara materials in Burrus's translation of the *Histoire*, as Bandelier made his transcriptions after the *Histoire* had been completed for the Pope's Jubilee. At appropriate places in the journals, these documents are discussed in relation to Bandelier's position as historiographer of the Hemenway Southwestern Archaeological Expedition.

619. See n 623.

620. Details of this affair did not reach Santa Fe until July 20. (La Joya is some ten miles above Española and not far from San Juan.) The *Santa Fe Daily New Mexican* (Vol. 23, No. 128, p. 4) of that date reported the incident. A Swedish tramp (name not given) stole a horse from a La Joya citizen named Martinez. The latter, with a friend named McGill, caught up with the thief, and in the shooting that followed, the Swede and McGill were both killed.

While Bandelier's notes on the incident varied in detail from the account given in the newspaper, his reactions to the events as he had understood them are of interest.

621. When Bandelier published his *Final Report* (1890–92: I, 308–9), he made a distinction between the Tewa war gods and another pair of Tewa gods, the To-a-yah. In this July 19, 1886, entry, Bandelier had equated the "twin idols, *To-a'* " with the Keresan and Zuñi twins. The twin idols, stone representations of the To-a-yah, were also described (p. 309).

Because Bandelier had attempted to find exact parallels to the Cochiti and Zuñi twin war gods (see n 376) at San Juan, he had come to this erroneous distinction.

At San Juan there are six *Towa é* (Ortiz 1969: 72). Ortiz has maintained that "the *Towa é* are just the Tewa manifestation of the pan-Pueblo ideology of the 'Twin War Gods.' " See his discussion (p. 162n12) which emphasized that the number of war gods may vary from pueblo to pueblo. This complexity would have contributed to the seemingly contradictory data Bandelier obtained from various Indian informants.

In summary, it appears that Bandelier, in giving four names for the Tewa twin war gods, two of which he considered synonyms, and in recognizing the pair of To-a-yah, had in essence the six *Towa é* of Ortiz without realizing it. His inexperience prevented him from comprehending the actual situation.

622. The habits of the Franciscan monks are discussed in n 44. Bandelier's remarks about the twin idols of stone at San Juan looking like coarse pictures of Franciscan monks and being suggestive of Catholic origin are interesting. Bandelier's surprise at the acculturative forces at work is in itself surprising in view of his years of travel, observation, and

research in the Southwest and Mexico. There have been innumerable examples of such cultural borrowing pointed out and more continue to be "discovered."

In his *Final Report* (1890–92: I, 309), Bandelier described these stone idols in much the same way as he did in this entry. However, he placed less emphasis on their being Catholic in origin. He wrote, "There is another pair of Tehua gods which is called To-a-yah, and they are active twice a year, in spring and in fall. Their fetiches are clumsy human forms, made of stone, and painted brown and white, with black faces. At first glance, one might be tempted to take them for rude pictures of Franciscan monks" (see n 621).

623. Just what meaning "When whites first came" would have had to Candelario is not clear. Castañeda's history of the Coronado Expedition of 1540 (Hammond and Rey 1940: 259) listed "Yuque-Yunque, in the sierra, six pueblos."

Schroeder and Matson (1965: 129) noted that in 1591 Castaño's party visited the pueblo of Yuqueyunque, directly across the river from San Juan. Seven years later, the people of this pueblo were to turn over their entire pueblo to Don Juan de Oñate and his colonists, and they were to join their relatives at San Juan. On the basis of ceramic evidence, Schroeder and Matson (p. 134) postulated that three other Tewa villages on the Rio Grande—Puyé, Tsankawi, and Tsirege—were possibly also occupied at that time.

624. Bandelier wrote "Harry S. Budd" in this entry of July 19, 1886, but on February 24, 1888, wrote "Henry S. Budd." Harrington's bibliography (1916: 585) listed him as H. S. Budd and credited him with two manuscripts: (1) Taos vocabulary [Tanoan stock], from Taos, 1885–1886, MS. No. 1028, Bureau of American Ethnology, and (2) Picuries [Picuris] vocabulary [Tanoan stock], from Taos, July 29, 1886, MS. No. 1023, Bureau of American Ethnology.

625. Bandelier's wording, "station opposite Española," referred to the stagecoach station on the east bank of the Rio Grande. The railroad spur from Española to Santa Fe, the "Chili Line Branch," was not to become operational until some six months later. See n 844.

626. Salpointe (1898: 283) listed Father Manuel Ribera as one of the priests added by Archbishop Lamy. In the Lamy Memorial (1950: 65), Rev. Manuel A. D. Ribera was noted as being at the second Las Vegas parish, the Immaculate Conception, from 1890 to 1892; later, he served at Sapello—in 1899 and again in 1909 (p. 80). However, this same source did not list him among those who served at Santa Cruz.

627. Schroeder and Matson (1965: 114–15), in discussing Castaño's route among the Tewas, noted that on January 8, 1591, he had arrived at Cuyamungué Pueblo, "evidently several stories high." They also commented that little is known concerning the history of this pueblo on the west bank of Tesuque Creek. About 1641, it was a *visita* of Nambé, holding the same status in 1680, when its inhabitants took part in the Pueblo Rebellion. In 1694, Cuyamungué became a *visita* of Tesuque, and in 1696, in the course of another rebellion, the village was abandoned, its people joining other Tewas. Bandelier had commented briefly on the ruins of this pueblo in 1883 (Lange and Riley 1970: 170, 173). Schroeder and Matson (p. 115) concluded their remarks with the following statement: "The results of the excavations undertaken at this site by the Museum of New Mexico have not yet been published."

628. Although Bandelier consistently and clearly wrote A. G. Henry in the entries of July 23 and 29, 1886, the editors believe this was the same person referred to in Lange and Riley 1970: 149 as Judge Henry and noted (p. 404n379) as Andrew J. Henry, a county judge of Greenville, Illinois. It is, of course, possible that Polk and Danser (1884b: 978) were in error in printing J. for G.

629. From the *Santa Fe Daily New Mexican* (Vol. 23, No. 132, p. 4) of July 24, 1886, came this item: General Vicente Riva Palacios, the Mexican minister to the Royal court

of Spain, and a party arrived in Santa Fe on the morning of July 24. A reception of prominent citizens was organized for them. Palacios left on July 25 for New York."

630. The "Mr. Wolff" mentioned here was quite possibly Bandelier's misspelling of the name of the Mr. A. J. Wolf who was taken into membership in the Historical Society at its meeting about two weeks later. See entry of August 12 and the accompanying notes. (It is also possible that the newspaper was in error on the name.)

631. The Bandelier Scrapbook contained an article entitled "Archaeological Chronology," which appeared in *The Nation* on August 21, 1886. It was signed "Ad. T.[*sic*] Bandelier." This may have been the article referred to in this entry.

632. According to the July 30 issue of the *Santa Fe Daily New Mexican* (Vol. 23, No. 137, p. 4), "Something of a political sensation prevailed in the city last evening when it was announced that Hon. Dolores Romano [*sic*], agent for all the Pueblo Indians, had been removed from office and Mesmoth C. Williams of North Carolina appointed to the position."

The newspaper went on to say that Romero had been a long-time leading Democrat of Mora County and a friend of Delegate [Anthony] Joseph but was opposed by the Ross faction "whose efforts to 'down' him have been especially vigorous during the last two months."

633. The *Santa Fe Daily New Mexican* of August 5 (Vol. 23, No. 142, p. 4), in a story headlined, "A Lecherous Old Lout," described the incident. Rev. Dr. Wm. E. Jones was deposed as pastor of the First Presbyterian Church of Santa Fe. Rev. Jones, who had been at this post for about a year, was rather unpopular because of what the newspaper called "crochety" mannerisms. On July 25, Rev. Jones announced that he was resigning his post as of October 1, 1886. However, on Monday, July 26, Rev. Jones left for the G.A.R. convention in San Francisco, taking with him a female member of the congregation (unnamed by the newspaper). The actions of the two on the sleeping car to San Francisco were such that the church requested that Jones not return.

634. This was possibly a reference to a mass meeting of citizens to protest the incorporation of the city of Santa Fe (*Santa Fe Daily New Mexican*, Vol. 23, No. 142, p. 4, August 5, 1886).

635. In an item from the London "Academy" of October 5, 1878, in the Bandelier Scrapbook, Lucien Carr was listed as an assistant to F. W. Putnam. White (1940: II, 96n1), in a footnote to Bandelier's letter of March 21, 1878, to Morgan, stated, "Lucien Carr (1829–1915), Assistant curator of the Peabody Museum at Cambridge, 1877–94; wrote *The Mounds of the Mississippi Valley Historically Considered* (1883)." Bandelier had written, "L. Carr, Esq., is at St. Louis, where I met him yesterday, & had much pleasure. Expect him out here on Sunday, that is, if he can get loose" (p. 96).

636. This brief entry recorded the beginning of Bandelier's translation into English of his German novel, *Die Köshare,* which he had already completed (see entry of May 12, 1886). The English edition was to be published in 1890 as *The Delight Makers.* Although it was to receive little acclaim in Bandelier's time, it has become a classic in Southwest literature, having been reprinted in several editions, and most recently (1971) in paperback. It is regrettable that with the resurgence of interest in Bandelier's works the new introduction to the paperback edition perpetuates many of the factual errors found in various biographies of Bandelier. More accurate and corrected information was readily available in published form (see Riley 1972 for a review of the paperback edition). For added data on both the German and English novels, see ns 50, 73, 89, 228, 235, 444, and 580.

637. On December 11, 1882, Bandelier had noted meeting Mr. Mahler in Santa Fe. "I was overjoyed." The two men had dinner together, both on December 11th and 12th

(Lange and Riley 1966: 373). The *Santa Fe Daily New Mexican* (Vol. 23, No. 148, p. 4), on the date of this entry, August 12, 1886, mentioned, "S. Mahler of St. Louis, half brother to Col. Mahler." The suspicion registered by Bandelier may well have been the result of the 1885 bank failure in Highland and related business affairs in St. Louis.

638. This was the Post Hall at Fort Marcy. The lecture was on the significance of decoration of Pueblo Indian pottery.

The *Santa Fe Daily New Mexican* of August 14 (Vol. 23, No. 150, p. 4) had the following story:

> In introducing Prof. Bandelier last evening, President Prince of the Historical Society stated that an effort would be made to have similar pleasant entertainments semi-occasionally throughout the fall and winter. The following name[d] committee was appointed to take the enterprise in hand: Prof. H. O. Ladd, Major J. C. Dickey, Mr. Arthur Boyle, Rev. E. W. Meany, Mr. William M. Berger, Dr. Wm. Eggert, Mr. J. C. Pearce. The society last evening announced as new members Rev. E. W. Meany, Mr. Marcus Eldodt, Mr. A. J. Wolf, Mr. Arthur Boyle, and Mr. Geo. C. Preston.

639. The *Santa Fe Daily New Mexican* (Vol. 23, No. 149, p. 4) of August 13 noted that "Prof. H. O. Ladd returned to the city from the east . . . He expressed satisfaction at the status of Indian School affairs." This was the Reverend Horatio Oliver Ladd who James said "was sent to Santa Fe by one of the Protestant denominations to aid in planting educational institutions. He traveled extensively over the then Territory of New Mexico, became enamoured with it, was privileged to read the unpublished, as well as the published, writings of Bandelier, and was thus rendered well qualified to write *A Story of New Mexico* when the D. Lothrop Company of Boston—who were publishing a series dealing with all the States—asked him to do so. It is a fairly-well considered volume of nearly five hundred pages and gave to many thousands their first idea of this fascinating land" (James 1920: 356).

Reeve (1933: 201–10) wrote that Rev. Horatio O. Ladd, a Congregational Minister, was asked to teach in the Santa Fe Academy, which had been founded in 1878. Ladd and his family arrived in Santa Fe in September 1880. Disappointed in the frontier aspects of life in Santa Fe and also with the physical plant of the Academy, coupled with problems with members of his local board in regard to student discipline and religious instruction, Ladd soon involved himself with the planning of a separate school. William Berger of Santa Fe backed Ladd, and the University of New Mexico, in Santa Fe, was incorporated on May 11, 1881, positively stating its goal of providing Protestant Christian education. The university opened in September 1881, with classes meeting in President Ladd's home. The university's growth and Ladd's raising of funds for it are related in Reeve. For unknown reasons, Ladd was removed from the presidency in 1887 and forced from the ministry, an action which some believed was unduly harsh (p. 208n31).

Coan (1925: I, 484) gave a rather different account, stating that Ladd continued his school until 1888, when it was permanently closed. Coan also noted that this was the second school to bear the University of New Mexico name. The first University of New Mexico had been incorporated in 1862, but it had never opened.

640. This was quite probably the owner of Tamony's restaurant in Santa Fe. The *Santa Fe Daily New Mexican* (Vol. 23, No. 269, p. 4) of January 5, 1887, carried the following advertisement: "Tamony's Delmonico Restaurant, 1st class in every particular. Open day and night. All game and fruits in season. Special inducements to day boarders and families. Regular meals 50¢. Boarders $6. per week."

641. See ns 209 and 486 for further data on Mr. E. D. Franz and his son, Eddie.

642. Juan José Montoya was one of Bandelier's first and best friends at Cochiti Pueblo; the two shared a number of trips into the mountains and canyons in the Cochiti-Frijoles region. Detailed and lengthy conversations occurred between the two, and Bandelier learned much from Juan José. According to the records of the Franciscan Fathers at Peña Blanca, Juan José was born about 1836; his grave was blessed August 12, 1886.

Elsewhere in the church records, it was noted that Juan José Montoya, "age about 50," had died on August 11, 1886. He was buried in "la capilla" at the church of San Buenaventura in Cochiti. Father Agustin Navet conducted the ceremonies. See Registro, Peña Blanca, for that date.

643. The Bandelier Scrapbook contains an article entitled, "Das 'Gemetzel' von Cholula (1519)," von Ad. F. Bandelier. In the margin of this page, there has been written "N.Y. Staatszeitung, Sonntagsblatt, 5, 12, 19 Sep. 1886."

644. Monsignore Straniero's identity has not been established. On the basis of the next day's entry (August 24, 1886), he seemed to have been in the Santa Fe Archdiocese to make preliminary arrangements for Pope Leo XIII's Golden Jubilee, of his priesthood, to be celebrated on December 31, 1887, and of his first Mass, to be celebrated on January 1, 1888 (Burrus 1969b: 9). See n 645 regarding the drawings Monsignore Straniero and Bandelier discussed.

645. For data on Bandelier's drawings, see n 62. On May 27, 1886, Bandelier was informed that his plates were at St. Louis (see also n 587). In the entry of May 29, 1886, Archbishop Salpointe called Bandelier "down [to town]" and his drawings were examined by Father Stephan, who promised to do what he could for their publication. Obviously, these were not the drawings from Berlin that had arrived in St. Louis, but others on which he had been working since his arrival in New Mexico in June 1885. The drawings from Berlin did not reach Santa Fe, forwarded from St. Louis, until June 4, 1886. This entry is the first intimation that they were to be presented to Pope Leo XIII. The editors have no knowledge of Bandelier's having received a monetary payment as a result of the "sale" of the drawings. As noted in n 62, many of these drawings did become a part of the Golden Jubilee presentation to Pope Leo XIII.

646. This very brief entry referred to the *Histoire de la Colonisation et des Missions de Sonora, Chihuahua, Nouveau-Mexique, et Arizona jusqu'à l'année 1700 [History of the Colonization and of the Missions of Sonora, Chihuahua, New Mexico, and Arizona, to the Year 1700]*. Bandelier was commissioned by Archbishop Salpointe to write this for the Golden Jubilee of Pope Leo XIII. The search for this manuscript became a story in itself; it can only be briefly told here.

Seen in the Vatican in late 1907 or early 1908 by Edgar L. Hewett, Lansing B. Bloom was granted funds in 1938 by the Bandelier Centennial Committee for archival research in Italy; one of his major goals was the finding of Bandelier's *Histoire*. He did not find the 1,100 or 1,400 page foolscap manuscript, but he did find the several volumes of drawings and maps. Bloom had black and white pictures made as well as color photographs. These latter, suspected of being none too accurate, were to be supplemented by extensive color notations by Mrs. Bloom so that the drawings could be accurately reproduced by a Santa Fe artist (files, Museum of New Mexico).

Through the years, others have tried in vain to locate the manuscript of the *Histoire*, well aware of its great value. In 1956, the present editors initiated their search. This was prompted by the founding at St. Louis University, St. Louis, Missouri, of the Pope Pius XII Memorial Library, including the Knights of Columbus Vatican Film Library. For many years, Father Ernest J. Burrus, S.J., had also been searching for the missing Bandelier *Histoire* manuscript. The successful outcome of his efforts has been well told in the first of several volumes he is currently editing (Burrus 1969b: 9–13). Since its location in June 1964, the manuscript is being translated from the original French into English. It consists of 1393 pages, foolscap, plus seven title pages, totaling the 1,400 pages described for it by Hodge (1932: 366) in his bibliography.

To date, Burrus has published Volume I, *A Catalogue of the Bandelier Collection in the Vatican Library*, Jesuit Historical Institute (1969b). Subsequently, Burrus has completed a Supplement to Volume I, *Reproduction in Color of Thirty Sketches and of Ten Maps*, Jesuit Historical Institute (1969c).

Because these specific works by Burrus are still little known in the United States and are not readily available in numerous libraries, the editors, at appropriate journal entries, will cite Burrus and also incorporate pertinent data from his several publications.

647. Bandelier had been concerned about flood damage by the Rio Grande at Santo Domingo almost since his first fieldwork there (Lange and Riley 1966: 105). See also Lange and Riley 1970: 332, 429n106, and the entry of July 18, 1885, and accompanying note in the present volume for comments on the precarious location of the Santo Domingo church. It is interesting that Bandelier, despite being only thirty miles away in Santa Fe, at the time of the flood in early June, did not comment upon the flood or the destruction until August 27.

The journal entries of 1880–82 (Lange and Riley 1966) regarding Santo Domingo Pueblo take on increased importance for the data therein. The *Histoire* contained a number of photographs and groundplans of Santo Domingo made before 1886, and the journals included sketches and measurements of architectural features, as well as descriptions of church furnishings. Adams and Chavez (1956: 131n1, 137n6, 221n1) gave added information regarding the flood damage at Santo Domingo, particularly in relation to the loss of the library, which Domínguez had carefully recorded in 1776. Adams and Chavez wrote, "This library has disappeared and may have been lost when the church and convent were swept away by the Rio Grande in 1886" (p. 221n1). Chavez (1957:4) noted it was "anybody's guess" as to how much was lost in the 1886 flood at Santo Domingo.

With the passing of time and further research, the editors must call attention to a comment by Bandelier in the journal of September 24, 1880. In reference to the Santo Domingo church, he observed, "Fine library of Dominicans." While no comment was added in our first volume, it would appear that Bandelier either slipped or was guilty of an outright error—the archival materials and/or library at the Santo Domingo church were in no way associated with the Dominican Order insofar as we have been able to learn. According to data presented in the Lamy Memorial (1950:94), the Order of St. Dominic and the Franciscans have been closely allied since their founding, but the Dominicans were seemingly not in New Mexico until 1950.

648. See entry of October 17, 1886, which would suggest that F. Coste was on the staff of the *Westliche Post*, a German-language newspaper of St. Louis.

649. An unsigned article with the title, "Removal of the Apaches from Arizona," was found in the Bandelier Scrapbook. It had been published in *The Nation*, No. 1106, September 9, 1886, pp. 208–9.

650. In McKenney's Business Directory (1882–83), Varden was cited as a member of the Santa Fe firm of Varden & Varney, mining engineers.

651. Like Christian Noetel, Edward Miller was a rancher in the Tesuque area. We have relatively little information on him. He did reach the attention of the *Santa Fe Daily New Mexican* (Vol. 22, No. 272, p. 4) of January 8, 1886: "Edward Miller has stocked his Tesuque Valley pond with fifty German carp which he was fortunate in securing from the U.S. Fish commissioner."

652. Prince was in error in referring to the large ruin on the Potrero de las Vacas as Pueblo Quemado. Bandelier used this name to refer to both Pindi Pueblo (Lange and Riley 1966: 90, 143, 217, 247; see also Stubbs and Stallings 1953) and Pueblito, the ruin

on Potrero de la Cañada Quemada (see n 326). Yapashi (L.A. 250) and the Pueblo of the Stone Lions are the common names for the large site on the Potrero de las Vacas (Lange and Riley 1966: 171n110). The latter designation comes from the famous Shrine of the Stone Lions which is nearby on the Potrero de las Vacas. Hendron (1946: 13) stated that Yapashi means "sacred enclosure," referring to the shrine.

653. See his *Final Report* (1890–92: II, 166) for Bandelier's remarks concerning the Pinini story which was told by the Cochiti about the village on the Potrero de las Vacas. In a footnote (166n2), Bandelier added these comments. "The name Pinini is a corruption of the Spanish Pygméos. The Spanish-speaking inhabitants of New Mexico usually pronounce it Pininéos, whence the Indians have derived Pinini. The tale about these dwarfish tribes, described as 'small but very strong,' looks to me quite suspicious. I incline to the simpler but more probable story that the Tewas were the aggressors."

654. Bandelier's mention here of General Bartlett was probably to Edward L. Bartlett of Santa Fe. In the *Official Reports* (1884) of the Territory of New Mexico, there was a listing (p. 66) which included "Capt. E. L. Bartlett, A. G. [Adjutant General], Santa Fe." Elsewhere (p. 77), there was a reference to Col. E. L. Bartlett, A. G., Santa Fe, June 30, 1883. Obviously, several promotions would have been required in a very short period to reach the rank of general, and the post-Civil War period was a slow time for military promotions. It is possible that the "general" may have referred to a former brevet rank (Civil War period) although Heitman (1903) included no E. L. Bartlett in his directory. It is more likely that the rank of either captain or colonel was simply bypassed by people such as Bandelier who preferred the "General" from the position of adjutant general.

655. Hayoua, or Hayoue, or Ha-io-ua, had been a friend of Bandelier during Bandelier's residence at Cochiti Pueblo in 1880. In Lange and Riley (1966), he was indexed as "Dixon, John. See Pancho, Juan de Jesús." The many entries reflect the degree of their friendship. Like Zashue (see n 316), Hayoue was one of the leading characters in Bandelier's novel, *The Delight Makers.* In the novel setting, the two were brothers, while in actual life, they were not closely related (see Lange 1959: 30).

656. In Bandelier's entry of November 21, 1880 (Lange and Riley 1966: 216), Gervasio was identified as a brother-in-law of Hayoua.

657. The rather detailed vocabulary and ceremonial data obtained by Bandelier from Hayoua may well have been gathered for potential utilization in the rewriting and expansion of *The Delight Makers* on which Bandelier was then working. According to Lange (1959: 236), the cacique (Hishtanyi Chayan) was originally the official in charge of the pueblo during times of peace, as contrasted with the naht'ya, or war chief, who assumed leadership of the pueblo in periods of hostilities. However, the loss of this latter official appears to have caused a blending of functions in the person of the cacique, a change which had occurred even by Bandelier's time.

658. This quotation from Goethe's *Faust* did appear in Chapter V of *The Delight Makers,* "part of the power that still Produceth good, whilst ever scheming ill" (Bandelier 1890c [1946 ed.]: 119).

659. Bandelier apparently decided not to use this second quotation from Goethe's *Faust.* This entry corroborates the editors' comment in n 50 that Bandelier, in translating *Die Köshare* into English, also expanded it.

660. The editors believe that although Bandelier had already started work on the *Histoire* (see entry of August 26, 1886, and n 646), there was still some question concerning it. The arrangements were not finalized until October 1, 1886.

661. Professor O. C. Marsh was a paleontologist at Yale University; he was a nephew of George Peabody, founder of the Peabody Museum at both Harvard and Yale Universi-

ties. According to the *Santa Fe Daily New Mexican* (Vol. 23, No. 176, p. 4) of September 14, Marsh was staying at the Palace Hotel during his visit in Santa Fe.

662. The term "Po-jyu-uinge" approximated several terms given by Harrington (1916: 334–35) and Bandelier (1890–92: I, 124, 160; II, 83, 84) for the inhabited pueblo of Pojoaque. In their discussions, however, a ruin was not mentioned. Harrington (1916: 337) gave "Po-su-e-we-ge-oe-wi-ke-ge" as "drink water place pueblo ruin in the vicinity of Posue-we-ge [Pojoaque]." His informants said that this name was descriptive, and that the name "Te-je-Uinge-ge-Oui-ping" was the "real old name" of the pueblo. Harrington further pointed out that Bandelier, Hewett, and Hodge had incorrectly located the pueblo ruin. See ns 282 and 308 on "Te-je-Uinge-Ouiping," which also reflect the confusion concerning the location of this ruin.

663. This was probably Waterman Thomas Hewett (1846–1921), professor of German philology at Cornell University from 1883 to 1910 (Johnson and Malone 1946: VII, 603).

664. "Madlle," or Mademoiselle, Rousse was probably of the Rousse family of Pecos. In the entry of July 13, 1884 (Lange and Riley 1970: 335), Bandelier had noted, on his arrival at Pecos, that he had been "most cordially and handsomely received by Father Mailluchet and by Mr. Rousse." In this entry, Father Mailluchet was again accompanied by one of the Rousse family.

665. A fanega is both a measure of land and a measure of grain; in this entry, it was probably a measure of land, from which a yield of wheat had been expected. Lange (1959: 39, 39n) discussed the usage of this word at Cochiti Pueblo.

666. This was E. W. Dietrich, the father of Mrs. H. Hartmann. It is interesting to note that Bandelier continued to misspell this name in a number of entries up to the time of Mr. Dietrich's death, February 10, 1888, despite the friendly relations between the Hartmann and Bandelier families (see also n 934).

667. Miss Amalia Nehber was listed as an Instructor in German and French and as Teacher of the Primary Department of the University of New Mexico, Santa Fe, when it opened September 5, 1887 (*Santa Fe Daily New Mexican*, Oct. 22, 1887, No. 208, p. 3).

668. The Bandelier Scrapbook contained an article entitled, "Das 'Gemetzel' von Cholula (1519)," which appeared in the *New Yorker Staatszeitung*, Sonntagsblatt, on September 5, 12, and 19 of 1886. Undoubtedly, the $18 of this entry was his payment for this article (see entry of August 23, 1886, and n 643).

669. The *Santa Fe Daily New Mexican* (Vol. 23, No. 187, p. 4) of September 27, 1886, noted that "Hon. Lionel A. Sheldon, receiver of the Texas Pacific railroad, arrived in the city on a special car this morning, accompanied by Mrs. Sheldon and her sister, Mrs. Kelley, of Cleveland, Ohio."

670. Twitchell (1911–17: IV, 99) provided a biographical sketch of Camilo Padilla. Born in Santa Fe in 1865 to Rafael and Rita (Domínguez) Padilla, he was educated in Santa Fe schools and also attended St. Michael's College, Santa Fe, and the Jesuit College at Las Vegas, N.M. Returning to Santa Fe, he learned the printer's trade. For ten years, he served as compositor for the daily paper in Santa Fe, the *New Mexican*.

From 1890–98, he served as Congressman Antonio Joseph's private secretary in Washington, D.C. Later, he was a translator for the State Department. In 1898, Padilla married Luisa Romero in Las Vegas.

In 1901, he returned briefly to Santa Fe, but then established a weekly paper in Mora. Subsequently, he taught in the public schools in Santa Fe. In 1907, in El Paso, Padilla began publication of a monthly magazine in Spanish. In 1912, he again returned to Santa

Fe and continued publishing his magazine, achieving recognition in the literary circles of the state.

As of 1917, Padilla was serving as Chief Deputy Game Warden of the State of New Mexico.

671. In the Catron Collection was a typed copy, five pages in length, at the top of which Bandelier had written, "From the Life of St. Brandan. (Edited by Thomas Wright.) Copied from Longfellow: 'The Divine Comedy of Dante Alighieri,' 1871. Vol. I. 'Illustrations,' pages 406, 407, 408, 409, & 410."

672. From the Catron Collection (PC 29), the editors obtained a copy of a Carta Pastoral [Pastoral Letter] issued by Archbishop J. B. Salpointe on January 28, 1886, announcing plans for the celebration of the Jubilee of Pope Leo XIII. This announcement followed receipt of a Carta Encíclica [Papal Letter], dated December 22, 1885.

After a number of preliminary conferences between Bandelier and the Archbishop and also between one or both of these individuals and other church authorities, the commissioning of Bandelier to produce his *Histoire*, text and illustrations, as a gift from the diocese was finalized, much to Bandelier's satisfaction. Subsequent entries of 1886 and 1887 reveal Bandelier's extended involvement in this mammoth project.

It is interesting that it was not until almost a year later, September 4, 1887, that Archbishop Salpointe issued his call to churches of the diocese for general support of Bandelier's task (see n 838).

673. Cushing (1886: 481n1) described Bandelier as "one of the most indefatigable explorers and careful students of early Spanish history in America." Undoubtedly, Cushing based his remarks not only on personal association with Bandelier in 1883 (Lange and Riley 1970) but also on his knowledge of Bandelier's publications, in which there was extensive use of Spanish documentary sources (consult the Bibliography for Bandelier's publications prior to 1886). Outstanding among these were his three Mexican monographs, his *Historical Introduction to Studies Among the Sedentary Indians of New Mexico* (which had been written at Professor Norton's request prior to Bandelier's first trip to New Mexico in 1880). (See White 1940: II, 204–8; see also Bandelier 1881a and 1881b.) In 1879, Bandelier had also published a report on Spanish documents he had examined in the Lenox Library (*The Nation*, Vol. 29, July–Dec. 1879, pp. 347–48; this was in the Bandelier Scrapbook). With these qualifications and with their mutual interest in Southwestern anthropology, it is not surprising that Cushing asked Bandelier to serve as historiographer of the Hemenway Southwestern Archaeological Expedition, which, apparently, was the request in Cushing's letter to Bandelier referred to in this entry.

The "almost too much for me at once" had reference to Bandelier's having lived on no fixed income since May 1885. The little money available came for the most part from the sale of articles he had written or in return for instruction in foreign languages from a few Santa Fe friends. Now, he found himself with two important assignments, the *Histoire* for the Pope's Jubilee and the opportunity to be historiographer for the Hemenway Expedition. Certainly, a regular salary for the Hemenway work was most welcome news to Bandelier. The financial arrangements about the *Histoire* are less clear. The "sale" of drawings has been mentioned elsewhere (n 645). From time to time, Bandelier received amounts of cash from the Archbishop, but there were no journal entries which stated explicitly that these were in the nature of payment for his work on the *Histoire*. White (1940: I, 97, 99n10) wrote, "Bandelier received $1500.00 for this work and at a time when he was in dire straits financially." This information was contained in a letter to Norton from Santa Fe, May 27, 1887. In addition to easing his financial situation, Bandelier must have experienced a general satisfaction for the recognition his work was receiving.

For background on the Hemenway Expedition, see Congrès International des Améri-canistes, 1889. Cushing's paper (pp. 151–94) was entitled, "Preliminary Notes on the Origin, Working Hypothesis and Primary Researches of the Hemenway Southwestern Archaeological Expedition." Bandelier's paper (1890d: 450–59) was on "The Historical Archives of the Hemenway Southwestern Archaeological Expedition."

Mrs. Fanny R. Bandelier had at one time intended to publish the journals of these years, 1886–89, when Bandelier was historiographer for the Hemenway Expedition (see the Preface and n 1 for these details).

A catalogue of "The Bandelier Collection of Copies of Documents Relative to the History of New Mexico and Arizona [From the archives of the Hemenway expedition.]" was prepared by Dr. J. Walter Fewkes in connection with the Columbian Historical Exposition held at Madrid, Spain, in 1892–93, where at least some of these copies were on exhibit. The catalogue was subsequently published as a part of the official Report (Fewkes 1895: 305–26).

More recently, Burrus (1969a) published a discussion and appraisal of Bandelier's manu-script sources for the study of the American Southwest. It is interesting to note, however, that he made no mention of Fewkes's published catalogue (1895). Burrus (p. 37) cited a catalogue published in Madrid, 1892, which contained an index and at the end indicated the place and date that Bandelier had made his transcriptions. Where possible, the editors have correlated journal entries which referred to Bandelier's copying of documents to the catalogue of Fewkes. The reader further interested in this collection of documents should also consult Burrus (1969a) and the original Hemenway collection in the Peabody Mu-seum, Harvard. Hodge (1914: 353) wrote, "On the termination of the work of the Hemen-way Expedition in July, 1889, Bandelier's collection of copies of documents, together with a few originals, comprising in all about 350 titles, was deposited in the Peabody Museum of Harvard University." As noted elsewhere, at least some of these copied documents are present in the Catron Collection, Special Collections, University of New Mexico Li-brary.

674. Father Julius Deraches was chaplain of St. Vincent's Hospital, Santa Fe, in the 1880s (Salpointe 1898: 273).

675. This letter from Bandelier to García Icazbalceta has never been recovered. White and Bernal (1960: 88), in publishing the Bandelier-García correspondence, commented that, ". . . 66 letters of Bandelier have been preserved; not all have been saved for one or two lacunae have been noted, but certainly letter number 1 [of the text] is the one that initiated the correspondence. In it Bandelier presents himself to García Icazbalceta . . ."

It seems likely that a considerable number of the letters have in fact been lost. There are other indications in the journals of letters to García Icazbalceta that did not appear in the White and Bernal collection (see, for example, n 718).

676. Bandelier had met Captain Louis Felsenthal soon after his arrival in Santa Fe in 1880 (Lange and Riley 1966: 73). Felsenthal (p. 410) had come to New Mexico in 1855, became clerk in the legislative House, and was active in the Historical Society, helping to reorganize it following the Civil War. Bandelier had examined the document of 1643 which Felsenthal had, December 8, 1883, and Bandelier made notations regarding it (Lange and Riley 1970: 174–75).

The editors have been unable to determine what became of this document. Bandelier cited it in his *Final Report* (1890–92: II, 261n2, 281n1). In Xerox copies of Bandelier's indices for the Hemenway Expedition in the Peabody Museum Library, Harvard, which were sent to the editors by Miss Margaret Currier, Librarian, this document was listed as Vol. III, No. 23, with the title, "Autos de Proceso. (Original)." Alonso Pacheco de Heredia was given as the author with the date of 1643. Bandelier had drawn a line through the entry and written, "Mine," preceding No. 23 and "Taken out" after the title.

Fewkes (1895: 23) listed the same document and noted that it was mentioned in the table of contents but was not in the volume.

Burrus (see n 743) thought Bandelier had copied this document in Mexico City. In his examination of Bandelier's indices to the Hemenway, he also learned that this was a personal document of Bandelier. Burrus (1969b: 78), in his catalog of the contents of the *Histoire,* indicated that Chapter VI included events of 1643 and data on Governor Alonso Pacheco de Heredia.

677. An unsigned review of John Fergusen McLennan's *Studies in Ancient History,* comprising a reprint of *Primitive Marriage: an Inquiry into the Origin of the Form of Capture in Marriage Ceremonies* [1865] (Macmillan and Co., London, 1886, 387 pp.) appeared in *The Nation,* Vol. 43, No. 1119, December 9, 1886, p. 483.

This review contained a vigorous defense of Lewis H. Morgan's position, especially in his interpretation of American Indian kinship relationships. There seems little doubt that this was, in fact, Bandelier's review. (See Lowie [1937: 43–44] for an appraisal of McLennan's overall contributions to early anthropology.)

678. This was Mr. J. B. Dow of St. Paul, Minnesota, who had been visiting Santa Fe with Reverend P. B. Champagne of Duluth (*Santa Fe Daily New Mexican,* October 16, 1886, Vol. 23, No. 204, p. 4).

A wool factory in Highland had been among the unsuccessful involvements of the F. Ryhiner & Co. bank; in entries of the 1883 and 1884 journals (Lange and Riley 1970: 498), Bandelier was still concerned with disposing of the Highland enterprise and seemingly exploring possibilities of some such venture in Santa Fe. Hence, Mr. Dow's visit may have been of more than casual interest although there is no evidence in the journals that anything came of it as far as Bandelier was concerned.

679. Salpointe (1898: 273) noted that the Archbishop [Salpointe] had a large building erected near the chapel of Our Lady of the Rosary, a short distance north of Santa Fe. The cost was paid by the Rev. Mother Catherine Drexel, and for this reason, the school was called St. Catherine's School. The cornerstone was blessed June 17, 1886, and the building was dedicated on April 11, 1887. A boarding school for boys had been started at about the same time in a rented house in Bernalillo. No suitable permanent location could be found, and after seven months, the boys were brought back to Santa Fe, temporarily to the Guadalupe Church and, after the completion of St. Catherine's, to that building. (See Salpointe [pp. 273–74] for additional moves of both Indian girls and boys from St. Catherine's after 1887.)

680. Plenary councils of the Roman Catholic Church took place from time to time in Baltimore, Maryland. Salpointe (1898: 157) referred to the Third Plenary Council of Baltimore in 1885.

681. "Replied." tends to be somewhat misleading. Without prior mention in the journal, at least, the reply proved to be a rather lengthy response concerning the "Seven Cities of Cibola," which Bandelier addressed to Cushing. The letter was actually more of a report, totaling fifteen handwritten pages, interspersed with additional pages of extensive bibliographic and other notations. The editors obtained a Xerox copy of this item from the Archives, Peabody Museum, Harvard.

682. In our second volume (Lange and Riley 1970: 393n320), we noted that Bandelier's reference, at rather widely spaced intervals, to Eddy Huegy, his brother-in-law, was "he is always the same." Here, Bandelier seemingly completed the thought—"he is always the same fool and presumptuous fellow." The Highland *Weekly Telephone* of March 18, 1885, citing a story from the Albuquerque, New Mexico, *Morning Journal,* identified Huegy as "the carpet man."

683. Examination of the October 1886 issues of the Edwardsville *Intelligencer* gave no clue to this comment of Bandelier's.

684. While there was an Adolf Jacob Fischer, son of C. F. A. Fischer, it is much more likely that Bandelier had reference to the father. At this point in time, Adolf would have been only nineteen years old; it is reasonable to assume that it was the father, in company with Mr. Hartmann and Mr. Schumann, who was calling on Bandelier (see n 566).

685. In his entry of October 30, 1886, Bandelier had noted seeing José B. Ortiz about manuscripts from the seventeenth century. It has not been possible to identify the documents of 1695–98 and 1755 cited here.

686. This may have been J. B. Dow, mentioned in the entry of October 17, 1886, as considering the establishment of a wool factory in Santa Fe.

Tajique, on the eastern slope of the Manzano Mountains and at the western fringe of the Estancia Basin, would have been a likely spot for sheep-raising and wool.

687. This entry referred to the birth, November 10, 1886, of Alfred William Kaune, second child of Henry S. and Elizabeth Bandelier Kaune, of Breese, Illinois (from the Kaune Family Bible).

688. The *Santa Fe Daily New Mexican* (November 15, 1886, Vol. 23, No. 229, p. 4) gave prominent place to this ball, under the heading, "Right Royally Done." The reception for Brig. Gen. Nelson A. Miles at the Palace Hotel was attended by many of the leading citizens. The Bandeliers, however, were not listed among the invited guests. General Miles had had a distinguished record during the Civil War, and he was an important figure in the western Indian campaigns following the war (Heitman 1903: I, 708–9).

689. Bandelier's letter to Cushing, from this period, was dated November 11, but there was no mention of this in the journal entry of that date or any other near the 11th. Bandelier often began a letter but did not complete and mail it until some days later. Since this entry of the 14th noted his finishing "work for Cushing," it is plausible that the letter may have more or less accompanied the material being mailed (Hemenway Files, Peabody Museum, Harvard University).

Santa Fé, N.M., 11. Nov: 1886.

F. H. Cushing, Esq'r.
Director,
Manchester, Mass:
Dear Sir!
An attempt to present the History of the Zuni-tribe from the stand-point of spanish documents alone is not without its peculiar difficulties.—However impartial one may desire to be, he cannot possibly remain without bias, as the material at his command represents mostly but one side of the question under treatment. Still the method of simple: "documentary History," that is: the publication of a series of documents in more or less chronological order, would hardly be adequate.—The gaps intervening between paper and paper must be filled and can be filled in part. But if it would be in the form of insertion of other "vouchers" relating thereto, the work would become such an unwieldy mass as might require a still more voluminous commentary yet. I prefer therefore to submit to you the material in the shape of a historical discussion, every date and fact of which is substantiated by reference to the corresponding documents. How far the version thus attained may correspond to Indian recollections, will be determined by your own researches.

The work divides naturally into the following sections.
I. First Discovery of Zuni. 1538 and 1539.
II. Spanish expeditions into New Mexico up to 1597.
III. The Conquest of 1598 and Establishment of the Missions.

IV. Zuni between 1630 and 1680.
V. The General uprising of the Pueblos and the reconquest. 1680.–1704.
VI. 1705 to 1846.

I have the honor to remain, Sir!

Very Respectfully Your obed't serv't

Ad. F. Bandelier

690. At this time, Lt. Charles B. Gatewood was aide-de-camp to General Nelson A. Miles (see n 688). For further information, see Heitman 1903: I, 450; Lange and Riley 1970: 385n235.

691. This was Jesse Clifton Chance, of Ohio. He entered service in the Civil War as a private, and was commissioned 2nd lt., March 17, 1895. Chance reenlisted after the war, and following other duty, was assigned to the 13th Infantry, March 4, 1870. He became 1st lt., October 18, 1871, and captain, October 16, 1884. Subsequently, he was a major in the 5th Infantry, as of September 28, 1898; lt. col., 26th Infantry, February 2, 1901; and colonel, 4th Infantry, as of May 28, 1902 (Heitman 1903: I, 294).

692. Sporadic journal entries prior to this November 19, 1886, entry have indicated that Bandelier suffered periods of intense pain in his right hand and arm, aggravated by his extended note-taking and writing. At such times, he found he could still paint or draw, which he did, until he was able to resume his writing. Apparently, with the dual tasks which he had undertaken in October 1886 (the writing of the *Histoire* and the duties of historiographer for the Hemenway Expedition, both of which involved extensive writing), Bandelier had decided to purchase a typewriter.

In Hodge's paper, "Personal Recollections," given at the Bandelier Memorial Conference in 1940 (unpublished manuscript, Bandelier Collection, Museum of New Mexico Files), he wrote, "Bandelier continued to use his facile pen until scrivener's paralysis necessitated the use of a typewriter. It was known as a 'Hammond,' and looked like a miniature monitor warship. But even this did not always serve our scholar's needs, for it got out of order and a Santa Fe blacksmith did not help matters. The Hammond was succeeded by the Blickensderfer which may be seen among the Bandelieriana now exhibited in the Palacio here."

693. W. S. Woodside was a notary public in Santa Fe (McKenney 1882–83: 341). He had been mentioned in the 1883 journals (Lange and Riley 1970: 63).

694. Sylvester Baxter was secretary of the Hemenway Expedition, as reported in *Science,* January 11, 1889: 29–30. Earlier, he had been a correspondent for the *Boston Herald* and had also been associated with the Archaeological Institute of America (Lange and Riley 1970: 374n131). In the May 8, 1886, issue of *The American Architect and Building News,* he had reviewed Bandelier's *Report of an Archaeological Tour in Mexico in 1881,* in which he wrote, "It strikes us that Mr. Bandelier may be in error in looking too closely for evidences of the communal theory to which he is devoted; in seeking a savage origin for everything, he may be led somewhat to depreciate the real achievements of the various sedentary races which inhabited this continent." This review was among the clippings pasted in the Bandelier Scrapbook, as was the *Science* article cited above. See also n 1057 in which Baxter's attendance at the Congrès International des Américanistes is noted. The $116.00 was the monthly payment by the Hemenway Southwestern Archaeological Expedition to Bandelier for his work as historiographer.

695. The editors are aware of two Bandelier Scrapbooks. One was made available to them through the courtesy of Professor Fred Eggan of the University of Chicago whence it had gone with a number of other items following the death of Mrs. Fanny R. Bandelier.

It is interesting to note, however, that items in this scrapbook extend well beyond this time when Bandelier wrote he had finished it—possibly meaning only that he had brought it up to date. A second Bandelier Scrapbook was found in the Bandelier Collection of the Museum of New Mexico. While we have used this one also, we do not have the beginning or terminal dates of the items contained in it.

696. The *Santa Fe Daily New Mexican* (Vol. 23, No. 247, p. 4) of December 7, 1886, remarked that "Mr. O. W. Meysenburg's many Santa Fe friends are pleased to see him out from St. Louis once more" (see n 231).

697. This was Christian Barthelmess, principal musician in the 13th Infantry's regimental band at Fort Wingate in 1883. Bandelier had talked with him while at Fort Wingate with Dr. Washington Matthews. Barthelmess became very much interested in the Navajo and their music, publishing two papers in *Der Westen*, a Chicago German newspaper (see Lange and Riley 1970: 374–75n135; also Frink and Barthelmess 1965).

698. Fort Bayard, 10 miles east of Silver City, had its first garrison in August 1866; the post was established later that year. It was named for General G. D. Bayard; in 1884, there was a population of 400, mostly soldiers (Polk and Danser 1884a: 318). See also Pearce (1965: 58).

699. See n 1007 for information on Will M. Tipton.

700. A Mr. Holton, identified only as "of Lancaster," had driven Bandelier, Willie Borchert, and Mr. Peter Weber to Cañón del Oso in the Sandias on June 4, 1882 (Lange and Riley 1966: 309). Whether or not this had been Henry Holton is unknown.

701. This was the first journal entry to indicate that Father Augustine Navet, the resident priest at Peña Blanca, was to copy the *Histoire* for Bandelier, at the same time editing the French text. Earlier, Bandelier had noted in the entry of October 9 to 14, that Father Julius Deraches would "copy my manuscript for the Pope." (As subsequent entries indicate, Father Deraches rather promptly changed his mind, for some unknown reason, and never actually participated in the work.)

702. Father J. M. Garnier had been brought to New Mexico by Bishop J. B. Lamy (Salpointe 1898: 282). In the Lamy Memorial (1950: 84), Father Garnier was listed in 1899–1900 as stationed at Trujillo in San Miguel County. The same source (p. 59) listed him at Costilla in 1912; other than these mentions, no further data were found.

703. Eugene Boban had presented a book entitled *Cuadro arqueologico y etnografico de la república Mexicana* (New York, Clinton Place, 1885) to the VII Congrès International des Américanistes in Berlin in 1888 (Congrès International des Américanistes 1890: 798). There were obviously books in his library that were of interest to Bandelier.

704. This fragment concerning the Presidio has not been identified. In Mexico City in 1887, Bandelier copied a document of Rivera's on a general inspection of presidios or forts in the interior provinces of New Spain (see n 785). Gerald (1968) has recently published on the "Spanish Presidios of the Late Eighteenth Century in Northern New Spain."

705. In the *St. Louis Daily Globe-Democrat*, Tuesday morning, December 14, 1886, there was the following brief death notice:

Hoffman[n] Sunday, December 12.
Cecilie N., nee Horn, beloved wife of George Hoffman[n], after a lingering illness, at the age of 41 years. Funeral Tuesday, December 14, at 1 o'clock p.m., from 3701 Cook Avenue. No flowers, the request of the deceased.

The following day's issue of the same newspaper carried notice of the burial permit, repeating the name [Cecilia], age, and address, but adding cancer as the cause of death. Also on December 15, 1886, the Edwardsville *Intelligencer* (Vol. 25, No. 1259, p. 18) contained this item: "Mrs. Cecilia Hoffmann died at her home in St. Louis Sunday. Mrs.

Hoffmann had quite a large number of relatives who sincerely regret her untimely demise."

706. Presumably, the "two ladies" in company with Cushing were his wife, Emily T. Magill Cushing, and her sister, Miss Margaret W. Magill. Bandelier had made their acquaintance at Zuñi Pueblo in 1883. For added data on Mrs. Cushing, see Lange and Riley 1970: 45, 54, 69, 147, 357n136; see pp. 46, 69, 383n201 for information about Miss Magill. This latter note, citing Haury (1945: 6), indicated that in 1886, Miss Magill was to serve as an artist on the Hemenway Expedition of which Cushing was in charge (see n 673).

Later, Margaret W. Magill became Mrs. Frederick Webb Hodge (Fuller 1943: 86n76); Hodge also served on the Hemenway Expedition as general secretary and assistant to Cushing.

707. Frederick Webb Hodge's recollections of this meeting, his first with Bandelier, have been preserved in a paper he presented at the Bandelier Memorial Conference held in Santa Fe in August 1940. The paper is in the Files of the Museum of New Mexico. Hodge wrote:

> In the fall of 1886, Cushing, who had spent the summer at the home of Mrs. Mary Hemenway at Manchester, Massachusetts, with three Zuñi Indians (when Cushing's "Zuñi Folk Tales" were recorded), perfected plans for the organization of the Hemenway Southwestern Archaeological Expedition, with Cushing as director and Bandelier as historiographer, the details of which were to be revealed when the two met in New Mexico in December. Bandelier went to Lamy, where he joined Cushing on the train and rode as far as Albuquerque. In this way, being secretary of the Expedition, I met Bandelier for the first time. A convention of some kind caused Albuquerque accomodations [sic] to be scarce, but Bandelier and I finally found lodgment in the second story of an adobe bunk-house, and as we shared the only bed, we became well acquainted in a trice, for Bandelier immediately and literally kicked me out of bed, calling me a "damned scrub," which was my pet name forever after.

Announcement of the establishment of the Frederick Webb Hodge Anniversary Publication Fund, to be administered by the Southwest Museum, Los Angeles, was made in the *New Mexico Historical Review* (Vol. X, No. 4, 1935, pp. 346–47). The article began as follows: "In December of 1886, Dr. Frederick Webb Hodge joined the Hemenway Southwestern Archaeological expedition to Arizona, and began a career in anthropology which will reach its fiftieth year in 1936."

The article continued, pointing out that Hodge was one of the pioneers of American anthropology. A founder of the American Anthropological Association, he edited the *American Anthropologist* during its first fifteen years, meeting much of the initial expense from his own pocket. The *Handbook of American Indians North of Mexico* (1907–10) was but one of Hodge's many editorial and original contributions to the study of aboriginal America. He headed the Bureau of American Ethnology for eight years; he was director of the Southwest Museum, Los Angeles, from 1932 to 1956, at which time he became director emeritus.

Hodge was born in Plymouth, England, in 1864, coming to this country and the Washington, D.C. area as a small boy. In his obituary of Hodge, Cole (1957: 518) stated that Hodge's experience with the Hemenway Expedition "determined his life interest." Hodge died September 29, 1956. Cole (p. 517) wrote, "In the passing of Frederick Webb Hodge, American anthropology lost a leader whose scientific career was intimately interwoven with the origin and development of the American Anthropological Association and its journal—the *American Anthropologist.* No man of this generation 'served longer or more faithfully.' "

As a long-time colleague of Bandelier, Hodge wrote the obituary of Bandelier for the *American Anthropologist* (1914: 349–58) and a biographical sketch of Bandelier for the *New Mexico Historical Review* (1932: 353–70). As mentioned, he was a participant in and contributor to the 1940 Bandelier Memorial Conference held in Santa Fe in conjunction with Bandelier's birthday, August 6.

708. On Fanny Bandelier's typescript of the 1886–89 journals, there was an addition to the entry of December 16, 1886, which was at the bottom of the page and initialed, "F. W. H. [F. W. Hodge]." The addition read: "*These two Zuñis were Waihusiwa and Héluta."

709. This was the Girard Hotel, or House, of Albuquerque; J. F. Girard, the proprietor, advertised in leading New Mexican papers almost daily at this period, claiming to have "the best table board west of the Missouri River."

710. Bandelier had also called on Mr. Altheimer in Albuquerque on January 2, 1883 (Lange and Riley 1970: 23).

711. This was Franz, or Frank, Huning, a prominent Albuquerque business man (see Lange and Riley 1970: 23, 365n63). In regard to this note, Lina F. Browne (Mrs. Spencer C. Browne), a granddaughter of Franz Huning, wrote, "Fierman is in error on one small point. Franz Huning did not go to California but stopped in Santa Fe, later moving to Albuquerque in the early 1850's" (personal correspondence, April 27, 1971).

712. On February 1, 1883, Bandelier had gone to Candelaria's (Lange and Riley 1970: 23, 364n56). He had made another call on July 1, 1884 (p. 332). In this entry, Bandelier was apparently saying good-bye to a number of Albuquerque friends prior to his departure for Mexico City.

713. Sadliers' Catholic Directory for 1885 (p. 141) listed the Very Reverend A. M. Gentile, S. J., as a member of the Council of the Archbishop in Santa Fe. In the 1886 Directory (pp. 141–42), Father Gentile was again among the members of the Council of the Archbishop but he was also serving as Superior of the Jesuit Mission in Albuquerque.

714. Sadliers' Catholic Directory for 1885 (p. 141) and again for 1886 (p. 142) listed the Rev. F. Durante, S. J., as one of several Jesuits stationed at the church in Albuquerque.

715. Bandelier (1890–92: I, 120n1) wrote that Fray Marcos had reports about "Marata." As he did in this entry, Bandelier credited Cushing with supporting evidence that Zuñi tradition confirmed these reports. Bandelier correlated the term with the ruins of "Ma-tya-ta," or "Ma-kya-ta," along the trail from Hawikuh to Acoma and said their descendants were among the Zuñi population. On another occasion, Bandelier spoke of them as a "branch of the Zuñis" (II, 327). Elsewhere (1892b: 6, 6n2), Bandelier wrote in greater detail about the circumstances under which Fray Marcos de Niza first learned of the Marata.

716. A short biography of Professor N. A. Bibikov appeared in the *Santa Fe Herald* of November 26, 1888 (Vol. 1, No. 45, p. 4). Bibikov was born in Russia where he studied geology. He immigrated to the United States and became an expert on coal outcroppings and oil fields. He was also one of the first discoverers of tin deposits in New Mexico.

717. Twitchell (1914: I, 29, 30, 66, 68) cited documents in the Office of the Surveyor General in Santa Fe that pertained to Albuquerque. From the context of the journal, it is impossible to identify the document mentioned in this entry. See n 920 for a brief history of the United States Surveyor General's Office in New Mexico.

718. This letter of December 26, 1886, to García Icazbalceta was not among the collection published by White and Bernal (1960) and was seemingly lost (see also n 675).

719. Mr. Wedeles was of the firm of Wedeles & Eldodt in Santa Fe (see n 837).

720. Money had been appropriated in 1884 for the building of a new capitol (see n 526).

721. In the Eighth Annual Report, 1886–87, of the Archaeological Institute of America (1887: 47–48), the following paragraph appeared:

> The Council greatly regret not to have received from Mr. Bandelier the final Report which they had reason to expect from him, but the delay in regard to it has not been without good reason. In October last Mr. Bandelier was commissioned by the Archbishop of Santa Fé to write a History of the Colonization and Missions of New Mexico, Arizona, Sonora, and Chihuahua, from the Spanish Conquest and Settlement of these regions to A.D. 1700. The work is to be offered to His Holiness Leo XIII., on occasion of the Pontiff's Jubilee. The preparation of it involved a residence in the City of Mexico for the purpose of studying the unpublished documentary material preserved in the archives there; and Mr. Bandelier rightly assumed that acquaintance with this material would be of great assistance in the preparation of his Final Report to the Institute. In December last [1886] he accordingly went to Mexico, whence he has lately returned, having made a thorough study on the contents of the civil and ecclesiastical records bearing on his subject, and having secured a vast mass of hitherto unprinted and unused documents, which supply him with original resources of the highest value for his work. He now expects to have the Report for the Institute ready before next May; and there can be no doubt that it will form a very important addition to knowledge of the archaeology and history of the southwestern regions of the United States.

722. There are numerous hot mineral springs, many of them large, along the eastern flanks of the Sierra Madre Occidental. Today, there are local "spas" in various towns in this area where people bathe for health reasons or simply for pleasure.

723. These rather crude sandals are made from the leaves of *Yucca decipirus*. A detailed description of Tarahumar footware and other material aspects of Tarahumar life can be found in Pennington (1963: 201–14).

724. The Bandeliers traveled from El Paso del Norte to Mexico City on the Mexican Central Railroad. Silao was a division point where the trains coming from Guanajuato joined the main line. Even today, it is customary for some Mexican trains to have meal stops, and the Bandeliers probably ate at the railway restaurant or at a small nearby French restaurant, both of which Janvier (1888: 415) considered to have "tolerably good food." On arriving in Mexico City, the Bandelier party detrained at the Buena Vista Station, on the west side of Mexico City north of the Paséo de la Reforma (p. 112).

725. The Hotel del Bazar, located at #8 Calle de Espiritu Santo (three blocks west of the Plaza Mayor), had "a few good rooms and a fair restaurant" (Janvier 1888: xvii). The Hotel Central where the Bandeliers moved on January 2, 1887, was not mentioned in Janvier's guide and was presumably even smaller—and perhaps less expensive—than the Bazar. It seems to have been located still farther west.

NOTES

1887

726. The Zócalo was, and is, the large open area in central Mexico City flanked by the National Palace and the Metropolitan Cathedral which dates from the 1520s. The plaza of the Zócalo was called in Bandelier's time, as today, the Plaza Mayor de la Constitución (see Janvier 1888 for additional details).

727. For a general discussion of Don Diego de Peñalosa, governor of the Province of New Mexico, 1661–64, see Twitchell 1914: II, 2–3, and Wagner 1937: II, 281–83. Captain Cesáreo Fernández Duro in 1882 published in Madrid an *informe* on Peñalosa and his discoveries. Among these documents were a number which indicated Spain's early knowledge of Peñalosa's intrigues at the French court. Fernández Duro (1830–1908) was a Spanish historian whose works were widely read in Bandelier's day. Copies of two documents (1685, 1686) from Duro's work on Peñalosa were found in the Catron Collection (PC 29 807). Fewkes (1895: 306) listed these as: "2. Royal decree, 1685; 3. Report to the King on the lands of New Mexico, Quivira, and Teguayo. Fr. Alonso de Posados [*sic*], 1686" (for related material, see ns 184 and 564).

Burrus (1969a: 39n22) provided a detailed discussion of Bandelier's use of Fernández Duro's work.

728. This was probably the Paséo de la Reforma, in Bandelier's time the most fashionable drive in Mexico City. The Paséo was two miles wide and ran from the small plaza in which stood the equestrian statue of Charles IV southwestward to Chapultepec Park. A second Paséo, that of Bucareli, also started from the statue of Charles IV and ran to the south (Janvier 1888: 279).

In present-day Mexico City, the Paséo de la Reforma has been extended a considerable distance to the north and east, cutting through an area that in Bandelier's day was filled with narrow streets and crowded houses.

729. San Lázaro Station was the same as the Interoceanic (Morelos) Station, located several blocks east of the Plaza Mayor (Janvier 1888: end map).

730. The Museo Nacional was in the National Palace, fronting on the Calle de Moneda (now Calle Zapata). At the time of Bandelier's visit, the museum was divided into two sections, Natural History and Antiquities, of which the latter was the more impressive (Janvier 1888: 155–56).

731. The Calendar Stone was described in some detail by Janvier (1888: 156). It is a millstone-shaped block of stone twelve feet in diameter and weighing over twenty tons. At the center of the stone is the carved face of the sun god, Tonatiuh, flanked by cartouches giving the dates of the four ages of the world and the twenty day names. These in turn are flanked by a band of glyphs representing jade and also glyphs of star signs. The stone was used in sacrifice, with a center depression used to burn hearts. According to Aztec accounts, the stone was carved in 1479. It was quarried on the mainland and then dragged across the causeway to the Aztec capitol of Tenochtitlan, now central Mexico City (see Vaillant 1944: 101, 162–64). Of further interest here is the two-part article, "Comment on Ph. Valentini and his The Mexican Calendar Stone," which Bandelier had published almost ten years earlier in *The Nation* (1878d and e).

732. There is no way of knowing whether Bandelier was making quotations in dollars or pesos. In 1887, however, this was not important for the silver dollar and the silver peso

were approximately at par (see Whitaker 1886: 377 for quotations against British currency). The dollar was quoted at d 49.3, and the peso, at d 48.5, a difference of less than 2%.

733. This was the Mexican historian, Alfredo Chavero (1841–1906), author of many studies of Mexican antiquities and perhaps best known for the work *México a través de los siglos*. Chavero also wrote plays, novels, and short stories (Enciclopedia de México 1967: II, 1214).

734. José María Vigil was the librarian of the Biblioteca Nacional (National Library) (Janvier 1888: 147). Burrus (1969b: 13n18) wrote of Vigil (1829–1909) as the director of the Biblioteca Nacional in Mexico City as of the time of Bandelier's visits (see n 741).

735. More than one series referred to as *Documentos Inéditos* had been printed at the time of Bandelier's trip. This was probably the series edited by Joaquín F. Pacheco and Francisco de Cárdenas: *Colección de Documentos Inéditos, Relativos al Descubrimiento, Conquista y Organización de las Antiguas Posesiones Españoles de América y Oceania, Sacados de los Archivos del Reino, y Muy Especialmente del de Indias* (42 vols. Madrid, 1864–84).

On February 9, 1886 (see n 542), Bandelier had written to Parkman asking if he could arrange with the Boston Library to let Bandelier borrow "Vol. XIV or XV of the 'Colección de Documentos Inéditos sacados del Archivo de Indias.' " Now, he was copying from Volume XV, and, as noted in the entry of January 28, 1887, he had purchased Volumes III and IV, presumably of the same series.

736. This "presentation" may have been a copy of *Manual compendio de el Regio Patronato Indiano*, by Antonio Joaquín de Ribadeneyra y Barrientes, printed in Madrid, 1755.

737. Bandelier (1890–92: I, 193n1) cited Vasco de Puga's *Cedulario* (1878, 2d ed.). A more complete citation was given in Fuller (1950); Vasco de Puga, Provisiones, cédulas, instrucciones de su Majestad (2 vols., Madrid, 1878), II.

738. In Berlin, March 2, 1885, Bandelier had made notes on Francisco Javier Alegre's "Historia de la Compañia de Jesus en Nueva España," published by C. M. de Bustamante, Mexico, 1841 (see ns 59 and 61). Undoubtedly, this was the book Bandelier purchased in this entry of June 8, 1887.

739. Here, Bandelier in all probability meant the Biblioteca Nacional, which was in fact quite splendid. Janvier (1888: 144–45) described it in considerable detail. It would seem that in Bandelier's day the San Agustín Church which housed the library had been recently renovated and considerably redecorated.

740. Chapultepec Hill was originally on the outskirts of Tenochtitlan. In Bandelier's time, the President's residence and the National Military Academy were located there, though the former was in the process of renovation, the work not being completed until 1888. The hill was stormed by General Gideon Johnson Pillow during the Mexican-American War, and it was here that the cadets of the military college made their brave stand. The monument to these courageous youths was erected in 1880 at the eastern base of the hill (Janvier 1888: xix, 300–303).

Today, Chapultepec is a major park and is the site of the magnificent Museum of Anthropology.

741. The Biblioteca Nacional in Mexico City was housed in the old San Agustín Church on San Agustín Street a few blocks south and west of the Plaza Mayor. In Bandelier's time, there were holdings of some 150,000 volumes, and it was especially rich in theology and church history. The library included collections taken from several major monasteries (Janvier 1888: 145–47).

742. The National Palace occupied the entire east frontage of the Plaza Mayor (695 feet). In Bandelier's day, it housed the presidency, treasury, army headquarters, archives, post office, and other bureaus plus the National Senate. The Mexican Chamber of Deputies was also housed there until a fire on August 22, 1872, destroyed the meeting rooms of this chamber. In 1887, the Chamber of Deputies was meeting in the nearby Iturbide Theatre (Janvier 1888: 140–42).

743. The National Archives, in Bandelier's day, filled fourteen rooms in the National Palace on the Plaza Mayor de la Constitución (Janvier 1888: 147). In the next few months, until his departure in mid-May 1887, Bandelier was to do a considerable amount of work in the archives.

From Burrus (1969a), the editors learned that with the Hemenway Expedition collection of Bandelier's copied documents were indices made by Bandelier to many of the volumes. The data given on these documents were seemingly more complete (p. 38n19) than the notations made by Bandelier on his own copies, many of which ultimately became part of the Catron Collection of which the editors obtained Xerox copies.

On the basis of Burrus's discussion, the editors also obtained Xerox copies of the indices to Volumes I–III of the Hemenway Collection documents. Margaret Currier, Librarian, Peabody Museum, Harvard University, thoughtfully added volume numbers and total pages, according to Burrus, to the Fewkes Catalogue to assist us further. The editors have appreciated this confirmation of the correlation between Fewkes and Burrus as Burrus's paper was based on the "Catálogo de los objetos etnológicos y arqueológicos exhibidos por la Expedición Hemenway (Madrid, 1892)" (see also n 673). The editors had been hesitant in assuming this correlation without an opportunity to actually compare the two catalogues. With the indices to these three volumes, written in Bandelier's hand, and adding supplemental data not in the indices, it has been possible to gain an overall picture of the extent of Bandelier's work in the Archivo General de la Nación (see also n 799).

Because Burrus's commentary was helpful in understanding the extent and nature of Bandelier's archival work in Mexico City, the paragraphs pertaining to the three volumes of documents copied there have been quoted verbatim.

> The first volume, entitled "Sonora," contains 19 documents totaling 80 pages. Bandelier signed each document, compiled an index, and at the end indicated the place and date where he made the transcription: Mexico City, March–April, 1887. He copied the documents not from the originals in the Archivo General de la Nación but from the one printed volume constituting the third series of the *Documentos para la historia de México*, although he notes that the originals are in the AGN, and in one instance adds that he has compared the transcript with the manuscript. [Burrus noted that this was the case in the 1697 account of Kino's expedition to the Gila River, the tenth document in the volume of transcripts (p. 38n21).] Seventeen of the nineteen documents transcribed deal with the Jesuit missions in Sonora, and furnished abundant material for his chapters on them in the *Histoire*. The years covered are from 1659 to 1772.

> The second volume is entitled "Nuevo Méjico, 1595–1778." It contains the typed manuscripts of 12 documents for a total of 149 pages. The index is in ink. Both text and index are the work of Bandelier. After the seventh manuscript, he notes: "Copies finished, Mexico (Mexico City), 7 January, 1887, Ad. F. Bandelier." Again, the transcripts were made not from the originals in the AGN but from the printed volume cited in the preceding paragraph without any mention of checking them against the corresponding manuscripts. [Burrus commented that Bandelier in his index listed separately an item disregarded by the *Catálogo: Apuntamientos* by Padre Juan Amando Niel, S. J., designating it as No. 8a, following Zárate Salmerón's Relaciones, which was No. 8. In turn, Cur-

rier added to the "8a. Apuntamientos—que sobre el terreno hizo el Padre Juan Armand Niel de la Campañia de Jesús. 1729. Extractos Archivo General. Historia, Tomo II," the full citation. See Burrus (1969a: 39n22) for his discussion of the Niel document as a forgery, and for Burrus's comments on the extensive notes added by Bandelier to his transcription of February 17, 1887.]

The third volume, entitled "Nuevo Méjico, 1541–1793," lists in its index 51 documents, of which the text of one is missing. [In his manuscript index, Bandelier had drawn a line through the title "Autos de Proceso, Alonso Pacheco de Heredia, 1643" and written in front of Item 23, "mine."] Bandelier signs his transcripts in the AGN in the months of February, April and May of 1887. Presumably all except one document were transcribed directly from the originals in the archive. He indicates the source of each: Reales cédulas, Provincias internas, Historia, vols. 1, 25–26. The transcripts total 331 pages, and found their way into several of Bandelier's works (Burrus 1969a: 38–40).

744. This was probably Mary Hagnauer Suppiger, the widow of Robert Suppiger (see Lange and Riley 1970: 146, 401n364). She was the sister of Robert Hagnauer (see n 163).

745. Burrus (1969b: 13, 13n19) wrote that Don Justino Rubio was director of the Archivo General de la Nación, of Mexico City, at the time of Bandelier's research there.

746. Fewkes (1895: 317) listed the following item: "29. Letter to the Governor of New Mexico, Count of Revillagigedo, 1751."

747. Fray Antonio (1657–1726) was a Franciscan missionary who, in the early eighteenth century, was active on the Texas frontier of New Spain (Bannon 1970: 114, 116, 119–21).

Wagner (1937), in his index, listed "Margil de Jesús, Antonio: life of, by Espinosa, 370–74 [1737]; by Vilaplana, 439–40 [1763]." From Bandelier's entry, it is impossible to tell whose "Life of Father Antonio Margil de Jesús" he had purchased.

748. The complete citation for this work is: Gerónimo de Zarate Salmeron, *Relaciones de todas las cosas que en Nuevo México* se han visto y sabido . . . desde el año 1538 hasta el de 1626 (in the Third Series, Documentos para la Historia de México, 20 volumes, México, 1853–57).

A copy of this document, 66 foolscap pages in length, was in the Catron Collection (PC 29 807). Sixty-four pages and a portion of p. 65 were in a handwriting other than Bandelier's. Bandelier had typed the remainder of p. 65 and all of p. 66; he noted omitting certain paragraphs by number. In addition, he noted that it was a copy of a copy made for him in Mexico in 1887.

The editors had some difficulty identifying the transcription as it had no heading. Bandelier's added notation that Padre Niel's *Apuntamientos* and some critical notes concerning it were on the following pages aided in making positive identification (see n 743). Fewkes (1895: 306) listed this as "8. Accounts of all things which have been seen and known in New Mexico both by sea and land, from the year 1538 to the year 1626. Fray Jerónimo de Zarate Salmeron, 1626." Data from Burrus (1967: 78n62) and comparison of the translation by Bolton (1916: 268–80) of paragraphs 44 to 57 of Zárate Salmerón with the corresponding paragraphs of Bandelier's copy of the Spanish document, confirmed this.

749. This was the epic poem, written by Gaspar Pérez de Villagrá, one of Oñate's captains. Hodge, in his Foreword to Espinosa's volume (1933: 19) on Villagrá's *Historia de la Nueva México* in the Quivira Society series, commented that the history has little poetic merit, but is extremely valuable to the student of the colonization of New Mexico and of the tragedy at Acoma. The poetic account had been printed in Alcalá, Spain, in 1610 (p. 40).

For the use and appraisal of this work by historians, the reader is referred to the Foreword, by Hodge (pp. 19–26). Hodge was in error, however, in postulating that Bandelier had transcribed the work by hand in 1881 in Mexico City (p. 20). Had Bandelier done so, it is unlikely that he would have been copying passages in this entry. More to the point, Bandelier noted in his entry of June 1, 1889, "A letter in the afternoon from Justin Winsor, informing me that the book of Villagrán [Villagrá] had been sent to me with permission to copy it." Fewkes (1895: 326) listed this work under "Other volumes." See Burrus (1969a: 45, 45n37) for additional comments upon this labor of love by Bandelier. In his scholarly writings, Bandelier made extensive use of Villagrá.

Bandelier continued to copy from Villagrá in the entry of January 27. Portions appear to have been complete cantos, while others were only parts of cantos. Some he labeled: "At Socorro," "At Acoma," "Defense of Acoma," etc. Alongside the last, the account in Canto XXVII, Bandelier had drawn a line and then in the margin had written, "Qöshare!!"

750. Burrus (1969a: 45–46), in his article on the documents in the Hemenway Collection, wrote: "The fifteenth and last volume, a large ledger, contains in its 470 pages two items: Manje, *Luz de tierra incógnita*, from the manuscript in the Biblioteca Nacional (Mexico City), and Kino, *Relación diaria*, from the AGN. [Here, Burrus added a footnote, "Recorded in the *Catálogo*, p. 116. On Manje and his *Luz de tierra incógnita*, see Wagner, op. cit., pp. 409, 515. The Spanish text of Kino's *Relación diaria* was edited in *Las misiones de Sonora y Arizona* (Mexico City, 1913–1922), pp. 397–413, and the English version with a detailed commentary by Fay Jackson Smith, in *Father Kino in Arizona* (Phoenix, 1966), pp. 1–34."] Pages 1–419 take up the first item, pages 420–426 list in a general index its 37 chapters; pages 427–470 transcribe the second item. The transcript in ink is calligraphic, not in Bandelier's hand. On page 472 is the following important observation [our translation of the Spanish follows]: 'The manuscript lacks orthography, accentuation and punctuation; because of that there will be observed some confusion in the ordering of the sentences. It is copied with all possible exactness and, on comparing it with an example of a manuscript that exists in the private library of Sr. Don José María de Agreda, the omissions are corrected between the lines and [also corrected are] the large number of mistakes found in the manuscript from which it was copied, the one that exists in the National Library of Mexico.' " This was undoubtedly the Señor Agreda to whom Bandelier made reference in this entry.

Fewkes (1895: 326) included the Manje item (spelled Mange by Fewkes), but he failed to catalog the Kino item, although Burrus, as indicated above, noted both were present in the Hemenway Collection of documents, Volume XV, at Peabody.

751. The mailing to Archbishop Salpointe was the chapter, XIV, in the *Histoire*, written in French by Bandelier, which Burrus (1969b: 75), in his English translation, listed as "The definitive establishment of the missions. Submission of the Pueblos. The revolt of Acoma. The beginning of the missionaries' difficulties."

Undoubtedly, the work with Villagrá, mentioned on January 13, was for background on this chapter.

752. In 1881, Bandelier had made the acquaintance of Don Antonio Miera in Puebla (Hammond and Goad 1949: 69).

753. The complete citation for this work by Ribas is: Pérez de Ribas, P. Andrés. *Historia de los Triumphos de nuestra Santa Fe entre gentes las mas Barbaras y Tieras del Nuevo Orbe*, etc. Madrid, 1645, 763 numbered pages (Wagner 1937: I, 249). This book is a history of the Jesuit missions in Sinaloa from their founding in 1590 up to the year 1644. Fray Pérez de Ribas, himself, had gone to Sinaloa in 1604 and been engaged in missionary activities. In 1617, with Tomás Basilio, he undertook a mission to the Yaquis. He was ordered to write a general history of the Mexican province, which he completed before his death in 1655, entitled *Crónica y Historia Religiosa de la Compañia de Jesús de México*

en Nueva España ... hasta el año de 1654. This remained in manuscript until a very limited two-volume private edition was published in 1896 (pp. 249–51). Bandelier's reference was obviously to the 1645 work, *Historia de los Triumphos.* A glance at the index to his *Final Report* (1890–92) and at the bibliographic citations in his other works, indicates how extensively Bandelier relied on this work (see Quirk, Tafoya, and Redmond 1942).

754. Wagner (1937: II, 278–79) listed this work by Padre Francisco de Florencia as "Professo de la Compañia de Jesus en la Provincia de Nueva-España." This was published in Mexico in 1689.

755. Fray José de Arlegui was a Franciscan who had been selected by his province in 1734 to write a provincial history. This resulted in the book *Chronica de la Provincia de N. S. P. S. Francisco,* Mexico, 1737. The book was reprinted in Mexico in 1851 (Wagner 1937: II, 365–69). Bandelier had referred to this work in his January 3, 1886, letter to García Icazbalceta (White and Bernal 1960: 285; see n 523).

756. The Paséo Nuevo was also known as the Paséo de Bucareli which had been opened November 4, 1778, and named for the then-viceroy Don Antonio María de Bucareli. In Bandelier's time, this Paséo was very little used (Janvier 1888: 279; see also n 728).

757. This was cited in Steck (1943: 64) as A. Prieto, *Historia, geografía y estadística del estado de Tamaulipas,* México 1873, 361 pp.

758. White and Bernal (1960: 316n4) gave this citation: "Aguiar, Rodrigo de, Sumarios de la Recopilación General de las Leyes, Ordenanzas, Provisiones ... que se han promulgado ... para las Indias Occidentales ... Madrid, 1628 y México 1677. Hay Ediciones posteriores: México, 1913 y Paris, 1921."

759. This was Dr. Gustav Brühl, M. D., of Cincinnati, Ohio, former editor of *Das Deutsche Pionier* (1869–71); Brühl was an early acquaintance and professional colleague of Bandelier, having common interests in the prehistory of the Americas (Lange and Riley 1970: 396n326). Bandelier's comments may reflect the fact that relations between the two men had seemingly lapsed for some length of time. As subsequent entries reveal, however, a considerable correspondence followed over the ensuing months of 1887–88.

White and Bernal (1960: 282n1) added excerpts from two letters from Brühl to García Icazbalceta, in a footnote relating to Bandelier's letter, dated September 10, 1885, to Icazbalceta. From a September 7, 1885, letter, ". . . Sr. Bandelier to whom unfortunately a sad calamity has befallen ..."; and from a letter of November 4, 1885, ". . . I am extremely sorry of his [Bandelier's] fate, but being a man of great activity and enterprise, he will, I hope, come out all right. I have a high opinion of his genius and consider him one of the most diligent, rational and critical students of American Ethnology, Whose judgement is never whirled away by imagination."

760. This day celebrated the extremely progressive and enlightened constitution of Mexico, adopted on February 5, 1857, which established the Federal system.

761. José de la Cruz Porfirio Diaz (1830–1915) began his career as an army officer under Juarez. After the latter's death, Diaz became president (in 1877) and then, either in or out of the presidency, ruled Mexico for more than thirty years. Diaz, who was part Indian, began as a reformer, but his governments became increasingly tyrannical. In 1910, Diaz was forced to flee from Mexico (Meine 1940: 466).

In the Bandelier Scrapbook was a loose newspaper clipping from a Madrid, Spain, newspaper, with a Paris release on the death of Porfirio Diaz. Penciled at the top was "Sábado, 3 de Julio, 1915."

762. The entry of February 14, 1887, in an uncomplimentary manner, indicated that Antonio Gutierrez assisted Bandelier in copying documents.

763. Father Agustín Fischer was at one time the confessor of the Emperor Maximilian. He was a friend of both Bandelier and García Icazbalceta. For a mention of Father Fischer's death, see the journal entry of December 23, 1887. Bandelier, in 1890, purchased the Fischer library for Thomas B. Catron, Santa Fe (Radin 1942: 27).

White and Bernal (1960: 305n1) gave these additional details. Father Agustín Fisher [sic] was born in Germany in 1825 and was ordained as a priest in Durango in 1852. Later, he was the parish priest at the church at San Cosme, to which Icazbalceta belonged. Father Fischer's death was given as December 18, 1887.

764. Fewkes (1895: 307–8) listed this item as "21. Report to the Count de Salvatierra. Don Juan de Palafoa [sic] y Mendoza. Bishop, etc. 1642."

765. Fewkes (1895: 308) listed this item as "43. 'Historical Notes on New Mexico. Antonio Bonilla, 1776.'" This report was cited by Adams and Chavez (1956: 42, 42n73) and by Twitchell (1914: II, 309); both gave the date of Bonilla's report as 1776, seemingly making Bandelier's 1774 an error.

766. Father José Vicente Campos was the priest who, on July 31, 1881, had received Bandelier into the Catholic Church at the Parroquia de San Pedro, Cholula, Puebla, Mexico (White and Bernal 1960: 248; Lange and Riley 1970: 4).

Bandelier had written to Highland from Cholula, March 8, 1881 (Hammond and Goad 1949: 71), "The priest of the place, Padre Campos, has placed at my disposal the church records, which go back to 1531. He himself, an old man of 75 years, has been priest in the place since 1830, speaks Mexican [Nahuatl], and will introduce me to the Indians."

Father Campos's name was also attached to the Códice de Cuauhtlantzinco (White and Bernal 1960: 233n2, 236n2).

767. An obsolete definition of "bobo," according to Velásquez (1946: I, 90), is a "stage buffoon." In common usage, it means, "dunce, dolt, fool, or one who is easily cheated." Considering the context of this entry, it would appear that Bandelier was referring to someone who had acted in this manner rather than to an actual person named Mr. Bobo.

768. This reference to Celia is puzzling to the editors. Celia (Cecile, Cecilia) Hoffmann, a relative of Joe Bandelier, had died in December 1886, as noted in the journal of December 16 (see n 705).

769. Bandelier's physical disability at this time caused him to cease journal notations on the documents he was then examining and even to suspend making entries in the journal itself. However, a number of items copied or extracted during this period appeared subsequently in the Hemenway Collection (Fewkes 1895) and/or the Catron Collection (PC 29 807). Bandelier also made extensive use of these materials in compiling his *Histoire*. See Burrus (1969b) for his Table of Contents for the seven parts of the *Histoire*, particularly pp. 73–81. More precise correlations can be made when the main text of the *Histoire* has been translated and published by Burrus, an event which is eagerly awaited.

A number of items in the Catron Collection were in a hand other than Bandelier's although some were signed by Bandelier in a form of postscript or in conjunction with a brief summary he added. Among items in the Catron Collection were the following:

Descripción Geográfica del Nuevo México, escrita por el R. P. fr. Juan Agustín de Morfi, Lector Jubilado, é hijo de esta Provincia del Sto. Evangélio de México, Anno de 1782 (Archivo general, México. "Historia." Tomo 25. fol. 92–116). This is a handwritten copy, twenty-eight and one-half pages, foolscap, in another hand than Bandelier's, copied February 19, 1887; Bandelier did sign his name at the end. Fewkes (1895: 308) listed this as "44. Geographical description of New Mexico. Fray Juan Agustín Morfi, 1782." A limited edition of one hundred volumes of this brief treatise (48 pp.) was printed in 1947 in Mexico City by the Biblioteca Aportación Histórica, Editor Vargas Rea.

Carta [to Father Morfi] del Fray Silvestre Vélez de Escalante, April 2, 1778, a document of fourteen pages, foolscap. All but the final half page were in another hand than Bandelier's; however, his signature appeared at the end with "Copia. México, 20 de Februro a D. 1887." The transcriber noted that the document was from the "Archivo General–Historia–Tomo II. Impresa en la tercera série de los Documentos para la Historia de México," f. 127. Fewkes (1895: 307) listed this as "11. Letter to Father Fray Agustín Morfi. Fray Silvestre Vélez de Escalante. 1778."

Real Cédula al Virey Marques de Guadalcazar. Sobre Asuntos Publicos del Nuevo México. [Archivo General de la Nación. Ciudad de México. Ramo de "Historia." Carta del Padre Fray Francisco de Ayeta, Fecha 1676. Tomo 25. Copia.] Ayeta had copied a statement of May 20, 1620, which pertained to Santa Fe, as of October 3, 1617. This document, one-half page foolscap, had been copied in Mexico City, March 24, 1887. Bandelier made a copy on the typewriter December 7, 1889, in Santa Fe, adding almost another page of notations. These two pages were found among the documents in the Catron Collection (PC 29 807). Fewkes (1895: 308) listed this as item "31. Letter to the Viceroy. Fray Francisco de Ayeta, 1676."

770. This was Joseph Antonio Villa-Señor y Sánchez. His work, *Theatro Americano, Descripción General De Los Reynos y Provincias De La Nueva-España y Sus Jurisdicciones* was printed in two volumes in Mexico in 1746. See Wagner (1937: II, 381–82, 393–95) for greater detail.

771. The *Rudo Ensayo* was one of a number of works selected by Bandelier for extensive annotation at the Royal Library in Berlin (see ns 56 and 58, as well as the entry of February 27, 1885, in regard to Bandelier's knowledge of the author of this work). Fewkes (1895: 316) listed this as "10. Geographical descriptions, natural and curious, of the province of Sonora, by a friend of the province of Sonora, by a friend of the service of God and of our Lord the King. 1764 (103 pp.)."

Bolton's Bibliography (1936: 622) listed: "Nentuig, Juan (?). Rudo Ensayo. Tentativo de una prebencional Descripción Geographica de la Provincia de Sonora, sus terminos y confines; ... Edited by Buckingham Smith. Internal evidence makes it appear that the author was Father Juan Nentuig, missionary of Guasavas, Sonora. *Cf.* an original MS. in A.G.P.M., Historia, 393."

Burrus (1969a: 41–42) provided additional comments, pertinent to the copying of the *Rudo Ensayo* noted in this entry. "The seventh volume, the title of which reads 'Descripción geográfica, natural y curiosa de la provincia de Sonora, por un amigo del servicio de Dios y del Rey nuestro señor, año de 1764,' transcribes the well-known account of Sonora by the Jesuit missionary Juan Nentwig. It had already been published twice: first, by Buckingham Smith, who gave it the title of *Rudo ensayo;* a second time in *Documentos para la historia de México.* The folios are marked 1 to 103, to which the '205 páginas' of the Catálogo correspond. The writing is not Bandelier's. A note by Bandelier points out that the transcript was made from the published *Documentos.*" (See Burrus [p. 41n27] for his comments and additional citations regarding the authorship of this document.)

772. Louis Huning was born in Hannover, Germany, on April 6, 1834, and came to New Mexico in 1861. He joined two brothers, Franz and Charles, who had mercantile interests in Albuquerque and Los Lunas. In 1865, Louis became a member of the firm, and somewhat later he joined with E. D. Franz as co-owners of a store in Los Lunas. Louis Huning became sole owner of the Los Lunas store, but in 1866 became a partner in the firm of L. and H. Huning which continued until 1871. After this partnership was dissolved, Louis Huning continued to invest in property, livestock, and land.

On October 28, 1876, Louis Huning married Miss Henny Bush of Bremen, Germany, his second marriage. His children were named Emma, Frederick, Lewis, and Lolita, all born in Los Lunas (Anonymous 1895: 350–51).

773. Amecameca is a town south and east of Mexico City. Vaillant (1944: 275) described a trip southeast of Mexico City as follows: "Leaving the lakes, one climbs high into the mountains, approaching the great volcanoes of Popocatépetl (Smoking Mountain) and Ixtaccíhuatl (White Lady) by the nearest route. Tlalmanalco is the first stop, and here a fine open chapel combines pure elements of Indian and European sculpture—a church built from the stones of a destroyed temple. The road ascends past the shrine of Amecameca, . . ."

774. Henry Augustus Ward (1834–1906) was born near Rochester, New York, the son of Henry M. and Elizabeth Chapin Ward. The serious poverty of his farm family caused Henry to be apprenticed to a farm neighbor at the age of 12. In 1849, young Ward was sent to Middlebury Academy (Wyoming, N.Y.) and then attended Williams College. Returning to Rochester, Ward entered the Temple Hill Academy.

In 1854, Henry Ward met the Harvard geologist, Agassiz, who took the young man to Cambridge to work in his museum collections. Later in the 1850s, Ward studied in Paris and began his famous geological collecting trips. In 1861, Ward returned to Rochester and was given the professorship of natural sciences at the University of Rochester where he remained for some fifteen years.

During his later years, Ward became greatly interested in meteorites, and his specimens now form part of the Field Museum Collection. Ward traveled extensively in both the New and Old World (see n 1058). At the time of his death (in an automobile accident), Ward was preparing a massive work on the subject of meteorites (Dictionary of American Biography 1936: X, 421–22).

775. The Bandelier and Huning families had known each other for some time, and it is not surprising that Joe went back to the Territory of New Mexico with Louis Huning and his wife.

776. Bandelier cited this work of Antonio de León y Pinelo in his *Final Report* (1890–92: I, 224n2). Wagner (1937: II, 514) referred to León y Pinelo's better known *Epitomé de la Biblioteca*, 1629. León y Pinela died in 1660.

777. Bandelier, in his *Final Report* (1890–92: I, 193n1), cited "Francisco de Montemayor, *Sumarios de las Cédulas, Ordenes, y Provisiones Reales*, 1678." Fewkes (1895: 309) listed "51. Royal directions and decrees concerning the treatment of the Indians and their protection. Juan Francisco de Montemayor, 1530–1677." Bandelier made extensive notes in his journals, but only one cédula was among the copied documents in the Catron Collection (PC 29 807). It was titled "Sumario de Real Cédula Tocante a los Carros del Nuevo México y de la Limosna a los Misioneros."

778. The Tonkawa, an archaic Indian group of central Texas, have been commonly characterized as having practiced cannibalism. At the time of which Father Fischer spoke (1853), there were probably fewer than 300 Tonkawa left. In 1887, less than 100 of these Indians remained; they were settled at Fort Griffin, Texas, to protect them from their enemies (Hodge 1907–10: II, 781–82).

For more recent discussion of this tribe, see Newcomb 1961: 133–53, and Sjoberg 1953.

779. Will C. Barnes was the telegrapher at Fort Apache, Arizona, when Bandelier arrived there in 1883, and the two were together when the false report of Bandelier's death was telegraphed to that post. According to Barnes, reminiscing long after the event, he did not meet Bandelier again until 1907. As this entry indicates, however, the two men had corresponded in the meantime.

Barnes (1915: 302–8) gave a rather inaccurate account of the false report on Bandelier's death at the hands of the Apaches. For Bandelier's own comments on the incident and its ramifications, see Lange and Riley 1970: 90, 93, 386n239, 386n240, 399n345, 432–33n122.

Burrus (1969b: 42–43, 42n84) credited Barnes with the naming of Bandelier National Monument. ". . . as Assistant Forester, Barnes was instructed to lay out and map Frijoles

Canyon and select a name for the area as a national monument, [and] he appropriately chose that of Bandelier."

780. These documents on Otermín's retreat to El Paso in August of 1680 comprised pp. 7–33 in a typewritten copy of 34 foolscap pages, consecutively numbered, which Bandelier noted (in Spanish) was "a copy of the copy made in Mexico on April 6, 1887." He had completed the typewritten copy in Santa Fe on January 23, 1890 (Catron Collection, PC 29 807). Fewkes (1895: 308) gave "36. Journal of the Departure from New Mexico. Antonio de Otermín. 1680." Bandelier's caption was *Diario de la Retirada de Don Antonio de Otermín para El Paso del Rio Norte.* Hackett (1942) translated many of the same documents. His two volumes should be consulted concerning Otermín and the Pueblo Indian Revolt of 1680. Page 34 of the typewritten copy contained extracts from *Carta al Virrey de los Difinidores de la Custodia del Nuevo Mexico.* [Octubre 15 de 1680. El Paso del Norte.—Extractos.] Included were data Bandelier considered pertinent to Otermín's retreat and Fray Francisco de Ayeta.

Pages 1–7 of the typewritten copy contained the *Diario del Sitio de Santa Fé: Nuevo México: por los Indios Sublevados.* Fewkes (1895: 308) gave this as "35. Journal of the Siege of Santa Fe. Antonio de Otermín. 1680." See also Hackett (1942).

For the heading of the typewritten copy, Bandelier gave *Documentos que sobre el Levantamiento del Año de Mil-Seiscientos y Ochenta forno Don Antonio de Otermín, Gobernador y Capitan General del Reyno del Nuevo México* [Sacados del Archivo General de México, *Historia,* —Tomo veinte y seis].

781. Juan Martinez del Cerro was married to María García Pimentel, the only daughter of Don Joaquín García Icazbalceta (White and Bernal 1960: 298n2).

782. Luis García Pimentel was the son of Don Joaquín García Icazbalceta (White and Bernal 1960: 299n2). Wagner (1937: II, 511) noted, in his bibliography under "García Icazbalceta, Joaquín. *Documentos historicos de México manuscritos de la collección del Señor don Joaquín García Icazbalceta.* Mexico. 1903–07. 5 vols., " that this series had been published by Luis García Pimentel after his father's death.

783. This was the *Memorial de Fray Francisco de Ayeta, en nombre del Gobernador, Cabildo, Justicia y Regimiento de la Villa de Santa Fé,* Nuevo México.—al Virrey (1676). [Archivo General. México.—Historia.—Tomo 25—Folio 158 á Folio 161.]

Father Francisco de Ayeta was the custodio and procurador general of New Mexico at the time of the 1680 Pueblo Revolt. He provided invaluable assistance to Otermín throughout this period (Hackett 1942).

A copy of this document, made on January 12, 1890, by Bandelier on a typewriter, is in the Catron Collection (PC 29 807).

The annexed documents were extracts of two Reales Cédulas, of 1570 and 1600, respectively. These were from the Archivo General. Historia—Tomo 25 — Folio 161 and Folio 160. These items, copied on the same date by Bandelier, are also in the Catron Collection.

784. "Ramo de Tierras" appeared frequently on the typewritten copies of Bandelier's Mexico City documents. It referred to a classificatory subdivision of manuscripts within the Archivo General de la Nación, Mexico.

785. According to Bandelier's index (see Burrus 1969a) to Volume I of the Hemenway documents, he copied General D. Pedro de Rivera's *Informe al Virey, del Estado de las misiones de la Compañia en Sinaloa y Sonora.* 1727. Fewkes (1895: 305) listed this as "3. Report to the Viceroy of the State of the Company's Missions in Sinaloa and Sonora. General Don Pedro Rivera, 1727."

Bandelier's index to Volume II of the Hemenway documents indicated that he also copied Don Pedro de Rivera's *Diario y derrotero de lo caminado, visto, y observado en el discurso de la visita general de presidios situados en las provincias Ynternas de Nueva*

España, 1736. This was listed by Fewkes (1895: 307) as "10. Diary and itinerary of the traveling, seeing, and observing in the account of the general inspection of forts situated in the interior provinces of New Spain. Don Pedro de Rivera, 1736." See Wagner (1937: II, 362–64) for additional data on this diary.

This second document was the subject of correspondence between Fred Eggan and Bruce Ellis, July 25–28, 1960. In the material which came to the University of Chicago from Fisk University following the death of Fanny R. Bandelier, Eggan wrote, "I have a manuscript copy by Bandelier of a *Diario y Derrotero . . .* by D. Pedro de Rivera covering 1729 & following— including a trip to Santa Fe, N.M. He had an engineer along who prepared maps, etc. The report was apparently printed in Guatemala for Sebastian Arebelo in 1736, with or without the maps . . ." Ellis promptly expressed an interest in the Museum of New Mexico's "inheriting" the manuscript, adding it to its collection (Bandelier Collection, Museum of New Mexico).

786. This was probably one of the works of José Mariano Beristain de Souza (1756–1817), perhaps his *Biblioteca Hispano Americano Septentrional* (A. Valdes, México, 1816–21, 3 vols.). This was reprinted in seven volumes in Mexico in 1883.

787. Bandelier referred here to Antonio José Alvarez de Abreu's *Victima legal real.* 2d. ed. Madrid, 1769.

788. This was probably Luis Velarde (fl 1692), one of the Jesuit missionaries in Sonora and Arizona; a citation for the particular volume or document mentioned here has not been found.

789. On the basis of Bandelier's index to Volume III, Hemenway Collection, coupled with Burrus's commentary (see n 743), all of the "very important documents, from 1604 on" of this entry have been identified. All but four, which are cited in this note, have been noted at the appropriate journal entries (see ns 791, 793, 795, and 796). These documents comprise Items 6–20 in Bandelier's index and correspond to Fewkes's (1895: 307) Items 6–20. Copies of all these documents are in the Catron Collection (PC 29 807).

The 1604 document was listed by Fewkes as "6. Petition against Juan Lopez Holguin. Settlers of San Gabriel 1604." Bandelier noted, "I copied, paleographing." On the typed copy in the Catron Collection, he had attempted to reproduce the signatures in the style of the original document. All of the signatures are handwritten and in ink. The complete title of this document is "Petición de los Pobladores de la Villa de San Gabriel de la Nueva Mexico, a Don Cristobal de Oñate. Tocante al Destierro de Juan Lopez Holguin." [Archivo General de la Nación. México. Ramo de Tierras. Original. 1604.]

The other three documents are: "Mandamiento del Apostolico y Real Tribunal de la Santa Cruzada. Sobre Asuntos del Nuevo México." [Archivo General. México. "Provincias Internas." Tomo 35. Legajo 7. P. 16] which was listed by Fewkes (1895: 307) as "10. Order of the Court of the Holy Crusade. Don Lopez Altamirano y Castilla, 1633."; "Mandamiento del Virey de la Nueva España. Marqués de Cerralvo." [Archivo General. México. "Provincias Internas." Tomo 35. Leg: 7. Fol: 19.], listed by Fewkes as "11. Order of the Viceroy of New Spain. Marquis of Cerralbo, 1634."; and "Carta al Virrey. Del Sargento Mayor Francisco Gomez en Nombre de los Soldados del Nuevo México." [Archivo General. México. "Provincias Internas" Tierras. Tomo 34. Fol: 28] listed by Fewkes as "19. Letter to the Viceroy, Francisco Gómez, Soto Mayor, 1638."

790. This was probably the *Instrucción Politica y practica judicial, conforme al estilo de los consejos, audiencias, y tribunales de corte, y corregidores . . .* by Alonso de Villadiego Vascuñana y Montoya (fl 1615), first published in Madrid in 1617, with later editions in 1766 and 1788.

791. These documents referred to *Autos del Proceso Contra El Soldado Juan de Escarramad.* [Archivo General, Ciudad de México. Ramo de "Tierras." Original. 1617. 6] On

December 7, 1889, in Santa Fe, Bandelier made a typewritten copy (now in the Catron Collection: PC 29 807) from a copy made of these originals in Mexico City. In addition to the locale given after the title of the document, he added in the closing notation that the autos were in "El Tomo 34. de 'Provincias Internas.' Archivo General de México." Fewkes (1895: 307) listed "7. Proceedings in the suit against Juan de Escañamad [sic]. 1617." See Scholes (1937: 29, 34, 35, 43–50) for the charges made against Escarramad, who had served under Oñate in the conquest and occupation of the province, and in 1617 was a citizen of Santa Fe.

792. As indicated in the journal entries, Father Fischer from time to time provided Bandelier with rare books from his personal library to aid him in his Hemenway research. The library of Father Fischer will be discussed in greater detail in the 1890 journals, when Bandelier purchased the collection for Catron (see n 763). A preliminary search among the Bandelier papers of the Catron Collection in the summer of 1969 did not uncover the catalogue to which Bandelier made reference here (see also entries of April 30, May 1, and May 5, 1887).

793. In the Catron Collection (PC 29 807) were a number of typewritten copies of documents bearing a date of 1636. Those that are not specifically cited elsewhere have been included in this note.

Autos sobre Restablecer las Misiones en los Pueblos de los Zuñis. [Archivo General. México. "Provincias Internas." Tierras. Tomo 34. No. 1.] Scholes (1937: 113n14) had cited this identical document in its entirety as a footnote to the following statement (p. 108): "Finally on September 24, 1636, Friar de Cristóbal de Quiros, the Custodian, addressed the governor in a formal *auto* in which he reviewed the situation at Zuñi, stated his desire to re-establish missions there, and called upon Baeza to furnish sufficient military escort for the friars that were to be sent. His request was stated in the following language: 'therefore I beg and beseech, and, if necessary require it, in behalf of His Majesty, that you appoint and send . . . military escort.'"

Bandelier, in his typewritten copy, included this as page 1, together with pages 2, 3, and 4 which contained other *autos* of Baeza and Fray Cristóbal de Quiros. Bandelier did paleographing of the signatures in some cases. He also added a note and above his own signature, wrote, "Es copia, catejada y corregida, y valen los interpolaciónes. Santa Fé, N.° México, Diciembre 16. de 1889." Fewkes (1895: 307) listed this as "12. Documents Concerning the Zuñi Missions, 1636."

Carta del Pᵉ Frai Xpoual [Cristóbal] de Quiros, Custodio del Nuevo México, escrita al dho Gou'or y Cap'an Gen'l Franc'o M'rn'z de Baeza, en Respuesta de una suya en que le Remitio la Carta Arriva Contenida. [Archivo General. México.—"Provincias Internas" Tierras.—Tomo 34. No. 1.] In his typewritten copy of this letter, made in Santa Fe, December 14, 1889, Bandelier noted, in Spanish, that this was a copy of a copy made by him in Mexico; he added, "El documento es un traslado de la mano del secretario de Francisco Martinez de Baeza, y queda anexo al Documento que sigue, en el mismo Legajo." The document to which this was attached is the next listed document.

Carta al Virey, del Custodio y de los Definidores del Nuevo México. [Archivo Generales de México. "Provincias Internas." Tomo 35. Leg. 7.] This letter was signed by Fray Cristóbal de Quiros and four other friars, Bandelier paleographing their signatures. He noted, in Spanish, that annexed to this document was the certification by Padre Custodio Fray Cristóbal de Quiros, which Bandelier copied. A typewritten copy of the letter and certification was made by Bandelier in Santa Fe, January 4, 1890 (Catron Collection PC 29 807). Fewkes (1895: 307) listed these as: "17. Letter to the Viceroy. Custody and defence [sic] of New Mexico, 1636." and "18. Certification. Fray Cristóbal de Quiros."

Carta al Virey de la Nueva España. Escrita por el Padre Fray Pedro Zambrano. [Archivo General. México. "Provincias Internas." Tierras. Tomo 35. Leg. 30.] A typewritten copy made by Bandelier on December 23, 1889, in Santa Fe was in the Catron Collection (PC 29 807). Fewkes (1895: 307) listed it as "15. Letter to the Viceroy. Fray Pedro Zambrano, 1636."

Carta al Virey: Escrita por el ministro de Pecos, Fray Antonio de Ybargaray. [Archivo General. México. "Provincias Internas." Tierras. Tomo 35. Leg. 30.] Bandelier made a typewritten copy of his Mexico City copy on January 10, 1890, in Santa Fe (Catron Collection PC 29 807). Fewkes (1895: 307) listed it as "16. Letter to the Viceroy. Fray Antonio de Ybaragay [*sic*], 1636."

See Scholes (1937) for a discussion of church and state relations in New Mexico in 1636. The *auto* and letters cited above, which Bandelier had recognized as significant, reflect this struggle.

794. This document was entitled *Autos sobre Quexas contra los religiosos del Nuevo Mexico.* [Archivo General. México. "Provincias Internas," Tierras. T. 34. F. 20 á 26.] A typewritten copy of four pages was made by Bandelier in Santa Fe, December 22, 1889; this was among the items in the Catron Collection (PC 29 807). Bandelier had concluded with the remark, in Spanish, that this was "a copy of my proper [accurate] copy."

Literally, "Proceedings on Complaints against the Clergy of New Mexico," this document seems to have been the same as that listed by Fewkes as "13. Decrees concerning excommunications. 1636." Included in the four-page copy was the item listed separately by Fewkes as "14. Letter to Fray Cristóbal de Quiros. Fray Jerónimo de la Llana. 1636" (see n 184).

The seeming discrepancy in the titles may be explained by the following remarks concerning excommunications in the early seventeenth century; according to Scholes (1937: 114n19), "In the autumn and early winter of 1636, Baeza compiled evidence concerning the practice of Father Quiros and his associates of excommunicating persons for failure to attend mass on feast days, and the alleged inconvenience that was involved in seeking out the prelate in order to obtain absolution." Bandelier cited this manuscript in his *Final Report* (1890–92: II, 189n1).

795. This was the *Real Cédula al Virey de la Nueva España que Informe sobre que Fray Francisco de Sossa Comissario de Corte y Secreto Gen'l. del Orden de San Francisco Fide se Haga Erección y Nombramiento de Obispo en el Rey[n]o y Provincias del Nuevo México.* [Archivo General de México. Reales Cédulas. Tomo 10. 1609 hasta 1642. No. 73.] Bandelier noted, in Spanish, done in Madrid, May 19, 1631.

A typewritten copy of this document was made by Bandelier in Santa Fe, December 7, 1889. This was among the items in the Catron Collection (PC 29 807).

The *Real Cédula* of 1631 concerned the question of establishing an episcopate in New Mexico. Bandelier noted that it seemed to draw heavily on the Report of Father Alonso de Benavides made the previous year, especially for information on the numbers of converts. Fewkes (1895: 307) listed "8. Royal Decree, 1631." Presumably, it was the one cited above as this was the only one given with a 1631 date.

The *Real Cédula* of 1636 was entitled *Real Cédula, al Virrey de la Nueba España Vea la Cédula aqui Inserta y Tome Relaciones muy Puntuales y Ajustados del Estado que Tienen las Cossas de la Conversión de los Naturales del Nuebo Méx[i]co y de Aviso dello y de lo Demas que contiene Dha Cédula y se le Ofreciere en la Materia.* [Archivo General. México. "Reales Cédulas." Tomo 10. 1609 a 1642. No. 171.] Done in Madrid, June 26, 1636. Bandelier made a typewritten copy of this document in Santa Fe, December 14, 1889, and noted, in Spanish, it was a copy of a copy made by him in Mexico (Catron Collection PC 29 807). Presumably, Fewkes (1895: 307) referred to this document in his listing, "9. Royal Decree, 1636."

The episcopacy was, in fact, never established in New Mexico during the Colonial Period (Reeve 1961: I, 134).

796. A typewritten document, six foolscap pages, entitled *Carta del Cabildo de la Villa de Santa Fé al Virey contra los Religiosos de Nueva México* (1639), which contained the complaint of the New Mexican civil government against the Franciscans was copied by Bandelier in Santa Fe, January 9, 1890, from the copy which he was working on in this entry of 1887. Bandelier added the following note in Spanish.

"[This document] is important, not so much for the accusations against the religious ... but for the general picture of the condition of the poverty of the Territory [of New Mexico]." Also of interest was the statement that in 1639 Santa Fe did not contain more than thirty Spanish families (Catron Collection PC 29 807).

Bandelier had made his first copy from a document in the Archivo General, Mexico, "Provincias Internas" Tierras. Tomo 35. Leg. 7. Fewkes (1895: 307) listed this as "20. Letter to the Viceroy. Corporation of Santa Fé. 1639." See Scholes (1937: 120–24) for his discussion of church and state relations at this time, though this specific document was not cited.

797. This was the *Real Cédula al Virrey de la Nueva España en Raçon de las Cosas Tocantes al lebantamiento del Nuevo México.* [Archivo General. México.—"Reales Cédulas."—Tomo 20. 1643 á 1647. No. 11.] Bandelier made a typewritten copy of his copy in Santa Fe, January 10, 1890 (Catron Collection PC 29 807). Fewkes (1895) listed only one Real Cédula, 1643 (p. 308, Item #22). Presumably, it was the one cited here.

Scholes (1937: 172) mentioned this July 14, 1643, Cédula. The administration of Luis de Rosas, who was Governor of New Mexico from 1637 to 1641, is fully discussed (pp. 115–51). The actual murder of Rosas occurred on January 25, 1642 (p. 158).

798. The following typewritten copies of *Reales cédulas* were in the Catron Collection (PC 29 807):

"Real Cédula al Virrey de Nueba España. Remitiendole Una Copia de Carta. Sobre las Vexaciones, que se ha entendido hazen. Los Governadores de Nuebo México, a los Yndios, para que siendo cierto, Procure Ympedir las, y los Ampare, y Hauise de lo que Executare." [Archivo General. México. Reales Cédulas. Tomo 3d. 1648 á 1650. No. 103.—], listed by Fewkes (1895: 308) as "25. Royal Decree. 1650."

"Real Cédula al Virrey de la Nueva España, sobre el Alivio de los Naturales Yndios del Nuevo México." [Archivo General. México. Reales Cédulas. T: 50? 1654 á 1657.—No. 9.], listed by Fewkes as "26. Royal Decree. 1654."

"Real Cédula al Virrey Marques de Mancera. Informe sobre el Asiento de los Carros del Nuevo México." [Archivo General de México. Reales Cédulas. Tomo 8—1665. No. 74.—], listed by Fewkes "28. Royal Decree. 1665."

"Real Cédula al Virrey de la Nueva España. Remitiendole la Execución de lo que Pareciere Combenient Tocante á los Carros del Nuevo México." [Archivo General México. Reales Cédulas.— Tomo 10º 1668–1669.—No. 69.], listed by Fewkes as "29. Royal Decree. 1668."

"Real Cédula al Virrey de la Na Espª Aprovandole el Socorro qe embio álas Provᵃˢ del Nº Mexᶜᵒ y Dandole Graˢ por ello y qᵉ Ota de lo que Con el se ofre." [Archivo General. Reales Cédulas. Tomo 16º—1678.—No. 126.], listed by Fewkes as "34. Royal Decree. 1678."

799. This comment suggests that Bandelier had arranged to pay copyists to continue the work he had begun in Mexico City, a plan he had earlier discussed with Don Joaquín García Icazbalceta, according to his January 11, 1887, entry. From neither Fewkes's catalogue (1895) nor Bandelier's indices to the three volumes of documents copied in Mexico City in 1887 can it be determined which were done by Bandelier and which by copyists; Burrus (1969a) did not comment on this. It would be necessary to examine the original copies at the Library, Peabody Museum, Harvard, to determine this (see n 743). According to Burrus, however, Bandelier in the months from January to May 1887 copied (or arranged to have copied) 82 documents, totaling 560 pages of transcription.

800. The May 5 celebration commemorated the victory over the French at Puebla in 1862 (Janvier 1888: 19).

801. Joe had returned to New Mexico with Louis Huning and wife on March 14. She obviously had been asked to discuss Bandelier's work with Archbishop Salpointe—possibly work on the *Histoire*.

802. In the Catron Collection (PC 29 807) was a typewritten copy of a document which had first been copied in Mexico during the preceding months, January–May 1887, and for which there was no mention in the journals of that period. It was entitled "Copia de la Carta a su Magestad, que escribio Fray Andres Suarez desde el Nuevo México. [Archivo General. México.—Reales Cédulas—Tomo 3º. 1648 á 1650. No. 103.]" It was listed by Fewkes (1895: 308) as "24. Letter to the King. Fray Andrés Suarez, 1647."

803. Bandelier commented on this ruin of San Clemente in his *Final Report* (1890–92: II, 219n2). He wrote, "Be-Jui Tu-ay, or the ruin of San Clemente, near Las [*sic*] Lunas, was a pueblo of the Tiguas, but in all probability not the extreme southerly settlement. On the other side, the Piros villages must have been quite near. Espejo (*Relación del Viage*, p. 112) says that only half a league (1⅓ miles) separated the Tigua from the Piros country . . . In 1680, Isleta was the most southerly Tigua pueblo, and Sevilleta, to-day La Joya, the most northerly of the Piros. The distance by rail is about thirty miles" (see Lange and Riley 1970: 154, 406n406).

804. This letter, dated May 25, 1887, was among those published by White and Bernal (1960: 298); our translation follows:

> Very dear sir:
> On returning from a barely tolerable trip, with some delay and no little procrastination, I wish to dedicate this first free hour to writing, thanking you and notifying my friends of my arrival and putting myself at their disposal for whatever I can offer them. It is natural for you to have headed the list of persons who in Mexico provided me with guidance and shelter, and the sole reason for these lines is to express my immense gratitude for the reasons stated above. The letter will be brief because I want it to arrive as soon as possible; later, when I have been able to recover my calm and the necessary equilibrium for daily work, I shall write you, giving details. For the time being I only say: I am here, contented and happy, and Thanks!
> The "expedition" to Mexico appears to have notably improved my wife's health. I have just seen her happy and now almost totally cured. She asks me to present to you her deepest respects, a thing which because of her ignorance of the language prevented her doing in the proper manner.
> Hoping that time will allow me to write you a longer letter and asking you to give my regards to Don Lorenzo, Don Juan [Juan Martínez del Cerro, married to María García Pimentel, only daughter of Joaquín García Icazbalceta] and to your wife, and to Don Luis [Luis García Pimentel, García Icazbalceta's son], keeping for yourself the most affection and gratitude.
>
> Your affectionate servant and godchild,
>
> Ad. F. Bandelier

805. For possibilities on the identity of this Schuster, see n 1035.

806. Bandelier's good friend, Thomas A. Janvier, was probably in Mexico at this time. Later, Janvier helped Bandelier in making arrangements for publication of *The Delight Makers* (see Radin 1942).

807. See n 33.

808. The May 28, 1887, issue of the *Santa Fe Daily New Mexican* gave the following account of this event.

> May 28, 1887: A UNIQUE PROCESSION. The Jicarilla Apaches Pass through the City To-day.
>
> The Jicarilla Apache tribe that passed the plaza this forenoon en route to their new reserve in Rio Arriba county, found the streets crowded with people, all anxious to see the unique and motley out-fit. The ladies and children especially enjoyed the scene. The tribe numbered 502, mostly women and children, and travelled in true Apache fashion, most of the women being mounted on ponies or burros with a child in front of her and a little one either hanging on behind or bound to her back in a blanket. Of loose ponies, burros and dogs, pack animals, raw-hide bundles, tepee-poles, etc., there seemed to be no end. Capt. Welton led the procession and three U.S. cavalrymen brought up the rear, while the direction of the band, the route of march, etc., was in the hands of ten stalwart bucks who "marshalled" the tribe through town and obeyed Agent Welton's orders to the letter.
>
> In front of the district headquarters building forty-one Jicarilla boys and girls from Ramona Indian School were drawn up in line and exchanged grins of recognition with the members of the tribe as they passed. Many of the women checked their horses for a moment and called out to a son or daughter who walked solemnly forward to the street curb and shook hands with them, and there were tears in the eyes of the smaller girls when they shook hands for the good-bye and resumed their place among the pupils. The bucks in the party wore an expression of general satisfaction, as in fact, did the women also, for they are delighted at the idea of once more getting back to their former home in northern New Mexico (La Farge 1959: 131).

809. On May 23, 1886, Bandelier noted receiving a letter from "Papa." In the meantime, the whereabouts of Adolphe E. Bandelier had been unknown following his disappearance just prior to the bank failure. There was only the vague item in the *Weekly Telephone* of April 29, 1885, indicating that he was going to New Orleans and possibly then to Cuba (see ns 117 and 585).

With this entry, noting Bandelier's receipt of "Papers from Papa—his articles on Venezuela in the *New Yorker Staatszeitung*," the editors are certain that a series of articles on Venezuela included in the Bandelier Scrapbook, though unsigned, are the articles referred to here. Interestingly, the first was written on July 1, 1885, in Caracas and published (in German) on July 27, 1885. If he did go to Cuba, he could not have stayed long as in his first article he wrote of the steamer's being alongside of Curacao on the 14th of May. In the Bandelier Scrapbook are six articles, including the one of July 1, cited above. The others were written and published, respectively, August 10 and September 21, 1885; October 28 and November 23, 1885; February 9 and March 15, 1886; April 19 and May 29, 1886; and August ? and September 17, 1886. All except the sixth were written at Caracas; the last was written at La Victoria.

810. As noted in n 62, many of Bandelier's drawings and plates were ultimately incorporated in the *Histoire*. In the catalogue of illustrations prepared by Burrus (1969b: 95–212), he repeatedly noted, "All writing in the corners was erased," or "All writing was scraped off." Apparently, Bandelier was removing extraneous notes and data and then writing titles to make the plates and drawings more appropriate for the Pope's Jubilee.

811. Bandelier had met Charles Longuemare in Socorro in 1882 and had examined his collections (Lange and Riley 1966: 320, 322, 324, 412). Bandelier also saw him in 1883 (Lange and Riley 1970: 176, 409n428, 415n472). That Bandelier meant Gran Quivira is

verified by the June 27, 1887, *Santa Fe Daily New Mexican* (Vol. 24, No. 108, p. 4): "Prof. Charles Longuemare of the Socorro Bullion is chatting with Santa Fe friends today. He has not been in good health of late and was forced to take a trip to the ruins of the Gran Quivira from whence he has just returned much improved in health and with a fund of archaeological information."

Unfortunately, Bandelier and the editors (Lange and Riley 1966; 1970 [see Tabira corrections]) have contributed to the perpetuation of errors in the literature regarding Quivira, Gran Quivira, Las Humanas, and Tabira. See Hayes (1968: 35–40) for recent archaeological work done at these sites and for clarification and identification of these places.

812. This was Henry S. Kaune of Breese, Illinois, who had married Bandelier's cousin, Elizabeth Bandelier. Henry had decided to move to Santa Fe permanently and had come to look for employment prior to Lizzie and their two small children joining him (see n 110).

813. This was probably the basic map by Hartmann which Bandelier used in the *Histoire*. See Burrus (1969b: 11, 27n50, and 198, under item 436) for the title, description, and use of this map. See also Burrus 1969c for other reproductions of these maps.

The reader's attention is also directed to Burrus's "Foreword" (pp. v–vi) for his discussion of technical difficulties in reproducing Hartmann's hectographed maps after a lapse of so many years. Burrus noted that Bandelier's data, which Bandelier had added to these maps, were "the result of long research, and constitute an important contribution to the history of the Southwest and a helpful aid in following his text." The text, to which Burrus referred, was, of course, Bandelier's *Histoire*. Though drawn to accompany the *Histoire*, the maps are also valuable in supplementing Bandelier's journal entries, many of which pertained to his writing of the *Histoire*. Expedition routes of Coronado, Chamuscado, Espejo, Castaño de Sosa and Leyva, Oñate, Kino, and others, as well as locations of missions, pueblos, tribes, ruins, etc., were given on these maps. Burrus (1969b: 198–208) described the maps and the data contained on them in his catalogue of the Bandelier Collection in the Vatican Library.

For additional data on Hartmann, see ns 112 and 579.

814. Burrus (1969b: 17n32) noted Bandelier's entry of May 16, 1888, in which Bandelier had mailed Peñafiel his Pima vocabulary. Antonio Peñafiel (1839–1922) was a Mexican doctor, historian, and authority on Indian languages.

In a list of books, presumably from Bandelier's library, in the Files of the Museum of New Mexico and stamped "Bandelier Collection," are two books by Antonio Peñafiel, both printed in 1885. One was titled *Nombres Geográficos de México* and the other *Arte Mexicana compuesta por el padre Antonio del Rincón de la Compañia de Jesús*. 1595 (Reimpreso bajo dirección del Dr. Peñafiel).

815. Journal entries indicate that Bandelier's father became acquainted with Dr. A. Ernst in Venezuela. Dr. Ernst was director of the Museum of Natural Sciences and a professor at the University of Caracas, Venezuela. In 1888, he presented a paper in Berlin at the Seventh International Congress. It was entitled "De l'Emploi de la Coca dans les Pays Septentrionaux de l'Amérique du Sud" (Congrès des Américanistes 1890: 230–43).

816. This was the journalist and miner, S. B. Evans, postmaster of Ottumwa, Iowa, who at that time owned property in Santa Fe (*Santa Fe Daily New Mexican,* July 20, 1887, Vol. 24, No. 127, p. 4). In the first volume (Lange and Riley 1966), Bandelier was with Mr. Evans (no further identification) as they visited the Arroyo Hondo ruins (pp. 358–59), and Evans, alone with a Cochiti Indian, had visited the Frijoles area (p. 247).

In the second volume (1970), Evans (p. 358n25) was further identified, as given above, although there appeared to have been still others by the name of Evans noted in the journals. Bourke (1884: 5) made the following comments regarding this person, differing in detail but not necessarily erroneous: "I had also comtemplated inviting Mr. S. B. Evans of Illinois, an experienced archaeologist, then in New Mexico, but he did not return in time from his visit to the interesting ruins near Cochiti, so I was compelled to go without him."

In 1888, in Berlin, at the Seventh Meeting of the Congrès International des Américanistes, S. B. Evans, postmaster of Ottumwa, Iowa, was listed among the members; he presented a paper entitled "Observations on the Aztecs and their probable relations to the Pueblo Indians of New Mexico" (Congrès International des Américanistes 1890: 226–30). While the paper may have been presented by Evans, it would appear that this was not the case. Elsewhere, Bastian (p. 194) had singled out Sylvester Baxter and Edward S. Morse for being the first from the United States to have attended the Congrès; presumably, they were the only persons in attendance from this country.

Bandelier had written S. B. Evans a letter regarding Gran Quivira after visiting that ruin in January 1883 (see Lange and Riley 1970: 358n25). Extracts from this letter were ultimately published in the *Saturday Evening Post,* Burlington, Iowa, December 1, 1888. The clipping was found in the Bandelier Scrapbook.

817. Both James Vautier and "Aunt Sauvant" appear to have been relatives of the Bandelier family; as yet, their precise relationship has not been determined.

818. This was a stunning loss for Rafael Lopez; he had no insurance and the damage was reported to be in the neighborhood of $60,000.

Lopez, a leading Santa Fe merchant, had his home and store together. He, his wife, and family narrowly escaped the fire (*Santa Fe Daily New Mexican,* July 25, 1887, Vol. 24, No. 131, p. 4).

819. Yerba del Pueblo may have been *Haplophyton* sp., also called Yerba de la Cucaracha, the dried leaves of which are mixed with molasses or sugar and used as an insecticide.

820. This was Allan W. Hauck, age twenty-two, and originally of Lebanon, Penn., who was killed at 5:03 P.M. when a Tufts type soda water generator at C. M. Creamer's Drug Store exploded. Three physicians, Drs. Symington, Strong, and Sloan, were nearby but were unable to save him (*Santa Fe Daily New Mexican,* July 28, 1887, Vol. 24, No. 134, p. 4).

821. Bandelier answered García Icazbalceta's letter the same day he received it, August 3, 1887, although there was no mention of this in the journal. White and Bernal (1960: 299–300) included Bandelier's letter in their volume; our translation follows:

Very dear sir and esteemed friend:

Although the typewriter is out of order I feel obliged to use it to write these lines. My hand now cannot hold and guide the pen; it doesn't obey me now and I scarcely can sign my name. I thank you very much for your amiable letter that I received today, a moment ago; and because I have a free moment to spare, I am going to use it to chat with you. I am very happy to know that all enjoy perfect health, as much in San Cosme #4 as in San José #13 [the home of García's son, Luis García Pimentel] and I beg you to transmit to both houses our most affectionate regards.

Perhaps before the year ends, I will have the pleasure of again saying hello to my friends there, even if it may be only for a moment. I have hope (still remote) of going to Veracruz to receive my father, whom we are determined to bring here, if God gives us life and the resources to do so. Here we are in a little earthly paradise; small and modest in truth, but a paradise, for the peace and relief we enjoy. The work goes forward, although thirty chapters remain.

If you would remember me regarding the recently acquired documents, I would be very thankful. The section of the history of this territory where I talk about the seventeenth century I have left for the last month, and his lordship [Archbishop Salpointe] has understood that there is no point doing otherwise.

According to the last news that I have recieved from Rome, they lack space for the display of gifts there, and because the work will go to the Vatican Library, we will comply by sending the atlas and the five folio volumes of pictures, maps, and plans, sending what is missing later on. I have been able, in several chapters, to make comparisons between the Spanish Indian policy and that of the United States. I have not been able to much praise the latter. In general terms, the tone of the work is more or less a defense. I defend Spain when she deserved it, and I see many reasons and occasions to act this way.

Please excuse the composition of this "little letter." If you can take care of the manuscripts you have mentioned, the good father has at his disposal a copyist who also works for me, and who is an intelligent and conscientious person, who will do the work with punctuality, running the expenses to my account.

Your affectionate servant and godchild, "Comme Toujours [As always]."

Ad. F. Bandelier

822. The St. Louis earthquake to which Bandelier referred in this entry had occurred at 12:36 A.M. on August 2, 1887, in the Compton Hill area. The St. Louis *Globe-Democrat* of that date (Vol. 13, No. 69) gave front page coverage and devoted three columns to the story, under the heading, "The Earth Trembled." The Market Street Mounted Police Station reported the quake to have been of 15 to 20 seconds duration. Shocks were recorded from a number of other communities, including Nashville, Tennessee; Evansville, Indiana; Louisville, Kentucky; and Murphysboro and Anna, Illinois. The event was of sufficient significance to warrant front page coverage again on August 3 (Vol. 13, No. 70), under the heading, "An Exciting Night."

823. Salpointe (1898: 283) listed Father Francisco Lestra as one of the clergy added by Archbishop Lamy. In the Lamy Memorial (1950: 81), he was listed as Reverend F. M. Lestra, parish priest at Socorro from 1888 to 1890. The journal entry, however, seems to indicate that Father Lestra was serving in Socorro in 1887.

824. Clara Huning was the daughter of Franz Huning of Albuquerque; she married H. B. Fergusson. Before her marriage, she had visited the Bandeliers when they were in Albuquerque and had also accompanied them on short trips (Lange and Riley 1970: 142, 154). H. B. Fergusson was a Territorial Delegate to Congress, 1877–99, and he served as Representative for the State of New Mexico from 1912 to 1915 (Fierman 1961: 242n28).

825. Alois Widmer was most probably a member of the Widmer family of Highland, Illinois (see n 100).

826. Bandelier had corresponded with Professor Eben Norton Horsford in 1883 (Lange and Riley 1970: 70, 383n202). A chemist and a native of New York (1818–93), Horsford had been nominated for honorary and corresponding membership in the Historical Society of New Mexico. He was voted into membership in 1860. Horsford was also a life member of the Archaeological Institute of America.

827. This may have been the Johanna Franz of the entry of November 18, 1887.

828. The meteor of August 20th received considerable notice. The *Santa Fe Daily New Mexican*, on August 22, 1887 (Vol. 24, No. 155, p. 1), reported it and remarked that it had been visible for at least 10 seconds.

829. The book from Dr. Brühl was probably the final portion of *Die Culturvölker Alt-Amerikas.* This publication consisted of four parts comprised of twenty Abtheilungen, or chapters. They were printed by Benziger Bros., of New York, Cincinnati, and St. Louis; the first appeared in 1875 and the final, just received by Bandelier, in 1887. The final volume consisted of Abtheilungen x-xx, pages 243–516. The surprise registered by Bandelier in his entry of February 2, 1887, seven months earlier (see n 759), may well have stemmed from the fact that Bandelier had reviewed Brühl's earlier volume (*Cincinnati Volksfreund,* 11 February 1878) rather harshly, criticizing Brühl's inclination toward superficial and uncritical use of source materials and his willingness to accept unproven statements. Bandelier's comments may also explain, in part, why there was a lapse of almost a decade between the appearances of the portions of Brühl's volume. At the same time, it is noteworthy that the volume of 1887 was dedicated by Brühl to "Ad. F. Bandelier, Prof. Dr. Ph. J. J. Valentini, and Prof. Alb. S. Gatschet." While Bandelier's initial reaction appeared to be more favorable to this second volume, the editors have as yet found no published review of it.

830. According to marginal notations accompanying the clippings of this article in the Bandelier Scrapbook, the original appeared in four installments in the *National Zeitung,* Berlin, in 1886, seemingly in volumes, or issues, numbered 581, 593, and 595. The title was "San Bernardino Chalchihuapan. Ein mexikanisches Abenteuer" (Bandelier 1886c). (This was listed in the bibliography compiled by Hodge [1932: 365] although there was a typographical error, "Chalschihuapan." It should also be noted that Bandelier himself in this journal entry of August 24, 1887, omitted the third "h," rendering the name as "Chalchiuapan.") (See also ns 230 and 287; Bandelier had written this article in June 1885, finishing and mailing it on June 27. There was some delay in both the publication and the remuneration.)

831. In both the Bandelier Collection in the Museum of New Mexico Files and in the Coronado Room Special Collections, University of New Mexico Library, are manuscripts, as well as articles, by Flora Spiegelberg (Mrs. Willi Spiegelberg). She had come to Santa Fe as a young bride in March 1875, having traveled by stagecoach from Las Animas, Colorado, on the Santa Fe Trail. The Bandeliers knew the Spiegelbergs in Santa Fe. Later, Bandelier and his second wife, Fanny Ritter Bandelier, were to know the Spiegelbergs in New York City. Mrs. Spiegelberg and Fanny became close friends, which would explain the presence of Mrs. Spiegelberg's writings among the Bandelier papers.

832. Bandelier had mentioned this book in 1885 (see n 98). His purpose in writing Garrison in this entry is unclear.

833. H. G. Bartsch was a tobacconist in Santa Fe who advertised regularly in the Santa Fe papers of this period.

834. See n 88.

835. The *Santa Fe New Mexican* was founded in 1849 but published only intermittently until 1863 when W. H. Manderfield became publisher. In 1864 Manderfield took in Thomas Tucker as co-publisher, and the two put out the paper until 1880. In 1868, the paper became the *Daily New Mexican* (see also n 596).

In the 1880s, the *Daily New Mexican* was deeply involved in state and local politics, and its very existence was, at one time or the other, seriously threatened. In 1880 the paper was purchased by a group of officials of the Santa Fe Railroad, and Charles W. Greene was placed in charge. In 1889 Max Frost became editor and publisher, having earlier purchased large portions of the *New Mexican* stock. Under Frost's control the *Daily New Mexican* not only survived but became extremely influential.

Editors and publishers of the *New Mexican* include: W. H. Manderfield and Thomas Tucker until 1880; Charles W. Greene, February 1881; E. B. Purcell, December 1881; C. B. Hayward, July 1885; T. W. Collier, November 1885; James A. Spradling, February 1887; and Max Frost, October 1889 (Stratton 1969: 3, 26–27, 286).

836. This was brevet Major General Benjamin Henry Grierson, of the 10th Cavalry. After his Civil War career, Grierson returned to the service as colonel in the 10th Cavalry, a position in which he served from July 28, 1866, to April 15, 1890. Shortly before his retirement in July 1890, he was promoted to the rank of brigadier general (Heitman 1903: I, 478).

837. Henry Kaune's employment was at Wedeles and Eldodt, dealers in groceries, drygoods, and general merchandise. S. Wedeles and Marcos Eldodt advertised daily in the *New Mexican* at this period.

838. While Bandelier carried on with the writing of his *Histoire* manuscript, Archbishop J. B. Salpointe issued a Circular, dated September 4, 1887, which was sent to the churches of the Santa Fe Archdiocese. The following portion has been extracted from the Circular; our translation follows:

> In regard to the method of honoring the Sainted Father on this occasion [his Golden Jubilee], there is, according to what we see in the newspapers, a competition among the various Catholic dioceses as to which will be able to give the richest and finest present. In the matter of material riches, we have felt that the diocese of Santa Fe cannot enter into the competition, and for that reason we have judged that it is better not to ask for a general contribution in order to make a money present to His Holiness. What we have decided, with our limited resources, [is to send] . . . a donation to the Holy Father for the benefit of the Vatican Library of an artistic and literary work by Professor Adolph F. Bandelier on the colonization of this land and the establishment of missions among its various Indian tribes. . . . We hope that the work of Señor Bandelier, because of the historical richness of the text, maps, plans, and accurately painted works of a large number of ancient objects that accompany and adorn it, may not lack in being appreciated for its true value.
>
> With the end of making the cost of this work less weighty . . . we hope that it will be possible for all the churches, from the peoples as well as the priests, to give us something extra. Thus, we shall at least be able to mention with pleasure in our letter of presentation to the Holy Father that the gift, humble as it may be, is offered by all the missions of the diocese (from the Catron Collection [PC 29]).

839. Bandelier's suspicion was correct. This grant and others of 1689 allegedly made to the Pueblo Indians by Governor and Captain-General Don Domingo Jironza Cruzate, at El Paso, were spurious. See Twitchell (1914: I, 477, 481–82) and Jenkins (1961: 51, 51n14, 51n15, 52n17).

Interestingly, it was Tipton, a close friend of Bandelier, who was credited with detecting the forgeries in this Laguna Grant of 1689.

840. See n 647 for the flood destruction of the church, convent, and library at Santo Domingo Pueblo. Bandelier, in his letter to Don Joaquín (translation in n 841), elaborated on his "find" in the archdiocese papers in Santa Fe. White and Bernal (1960: 301n1) gave the following citation: "García Icazbalceta, 'El Sermonario en lengua mexicana,' *Bibliografía Mexicana del siglo XVI*. México, 1886, p. 241 [*sic?*], 215." They noted that Bandelier's letter implied that there were two books, and commented that the *Catecismo* was actually a continuation of the Sermonario.

841. This letter noted in the entry of September 8, 1887, but dated September 9, was among those included by White and Bernal (1960: 301); our translation follows:

> Dear sir:
>   What a find! I have just seen an example of *Sermones en mexicano* by Father Juan de la Anunciación, 1577, and the *Catecismo* by the same author (Antonio

Ricardo, 1577). *Sermones* do not have a title page, and they begin on page three. On page 124, the engraving of the saint does not exist and never was part of the book because the page is intact and the lines and paragraphs do not show any interruption. Otherwise the book has been badly mistreated, and the last thirty or forty pages of the *Catecismo* are worm-eaten. The binding, although broken, seems to have been a deluxe one. At present, the book belongs to the Archbishop, but before, it was the property of the old convent (now in ruins) of Santo Domingo Pueblo which is located some ten leagues from here. Do you wish more details? I do have them at my disposal, and you can have them as well as a photograph of the title page of the *Catecismo*.

I am looking for a missal which I suspect may be that of 1561. Soon I shall know whether it is or not.

I send these lines right away in case they could be useful to you. Much and many affectionate regards.

Yours as always

Ad. F. Bandelier

842. In fact, heavy rains throughout the territory caused serious damage, and various trains were delayed (*Santa Fe Daily New Mexican*, September 10, 1887, Vol. 24, No. 172, p. 4).

843. This comment referred to the baseball game between Las Vegas and Santa Fe in which Santa Fe retained the New Mexican championship. Two thousand people saw the game in spite of rainy weather. As the *Santa Fe Daily New Mexican* (September 12, 1887, Vol. 24, No. 178, p. 4) said, "Everybody is talking baseball now." Quite obviously Bandelier's views on baseball paralleled his feelings regarding politics, as noted elsewhere.

844. Since Bandelier had already made several trips between Santa Fe and the Tewa Basin, it may reasonably be inferred that this was his first trip via the Texas, Santa Fe & Northern Railroad Company's thirty-five mile, narrow-gauge spur, linking up with the Denver & Rio Grande's system at Española. The spur, known as the "Chili Line Branch," had been completed the previous winter, while the Bandeliers were in Mexico (see Gjevre 1969: 3–7). The first passenger run from Santa Fe to Española occurred January 9, 1887; La Farge (1959: 129–30) included comments from the *Santa Fe Daily New Mexican* of the following day.

> . . . The train consisted of the passenger engine, "Gen. Meily," a baggage and mail car and two passenger coaches. . . . About halfway out the wheels on the rear trucks of the baggage car slipped the tracks and caused a short delay, but this was soon adjusted and the crowd went on its way rejoicing. The track, its easy grade and solidity, elicited very general comment. The line strikes the river about twenty miles out and thence hugs the mountain side for five miles, crossing the Rio Grande on a 700 foot bridge at the southern entrance of the Santa Clara valley. Thence an easy grade leads on to the village of Espanola. Arriving here at 4 o'clock a splendid dinner was served at the railroad hotel, and after an hour spent in sight seeing, the visitors boarded the train on the return trip. . . . The run from Espanola to Santa Fe was made in two hours, which is a rate of speed seldom made on even the older mountain roads. The trip throughout was most enoyable.

Harrington (1916: Map 20) showed the train route described in this entry. By Harrington's time, the Denver & Rio Grande Railroad operated the spur to Santa Fe.

845. It is difficult to know the precise nature of the "usual cavalcade" which went out to meet, or receive, the Archbishop and Father Garnier. At other times and places, even among the rather pedestrian-oriented Pueblo Indians, festive gatherings were prone to attract numerous horsemen—frequently in sufficient quantity and with trappings which would have done credit to the more equestrian-minded Plains tribes to the east and north of the Rio Grande pueblos.

One of the more dramatic incidents of this kind was described by Lt. Col. W. H. Emory when the Indians of Santo Domingo rode out to greet the U.S. Army troops September 3, 1846 (Emory 1848: 37–38). This account has subsequently been reprinted in White (1935: 18–19), Lange (1953: 219–20), and elsewhere.

846. Burrus (1969b: 128) listed as item #145, "One sketch in color . . . showing a large vase . . . Río Chama; Abiquiu; . . ."

847. Bandelier was apparently referring to his early publications on the Ancient Mexicans (see Bibliography: 1877a, 1878c, and 1880a). As far as the editors are aware, these monographs were never reprinted.

848. Frederick Ward Putnam (1839–1915) became Curator of the Peabody Museum of Archaeology in 1875. In 1886, he was given the Peabody Professorship and subsequently (1891–94) was chief of the Department of Ethnology, World Columbian Exposition. From 1894–1903, he was Curator of Anthropology for the American Museum of Natural History. Finally, he became the first professor of anthropology at the University of California and was also the director of the Anthropological Museum. Putnam achieved prominence and recognition in a variety of scientific organizations. Putnam had supported sending Bandelier to the Southwest at the time of his first fieldwork in 1880 (Lange and Riley 1966: 16–17).

849. Radin (1942) did not include this letter, either because it was no longer extant or because it had nothing to do with Bandelier's novel.

850. At this time, Dr. Benjamin M. Thomas was a dentist in Santa Fe. In 1889, he was to become Territorial Secretary. When Bandelier first knew him in 1880, he was Pueblo Agent and General Agent for United States Indian Affairs in New Mexico. A more detailed biographic sketch is given in Lange and Riley 1970: 380–81n182.

851. This was Yom Kippur, the day of atonement, that takes place on Tishri 10 (ten days after New Year). In 1887, the Jewish New Year began at sundown, Saturday, September 17.

852. This letter of September 29, 1887, was among those published by White and Bernal (1960: 302–3); our translation follows:

> Very dear sir and friend:
> I thank you much for your last letter. At present, I am expecting an answer from our parish priest regarding the missal from Tezuque. Within a few days, I shall be able to hear something about it, and if there is anything important, I shall communicate it to you immediately.
> From the hands of the Tezuque (Te-Tzo-qué) Indians, I have received three old books. These Indians do not know how to read; however, they do not allow anyone touching these volumes. In order to obtain the missal, we shall consider the possibility of substituting for the real one, another book of the same size and similar binding. My Indian brothers care little about which book is in their archival box as long as there are three volumes there.
> There is another missal in the pueblo of Cía; it is also very old, but I still have not been able to find out anything about its date of publication. The Indians hide it. During the next smallpox epidemic, it being a pueblo with few people, we

shall hope that God, etc., etc . . . This missal was given to the Galisteo convent (today in ruins) by the Countess of Albuquerque.

I am looking for other bibliographic and linguistic items at the same time.

Any piece of material which makes mention of New Mexico is precious to me, as long as it is before 1800 or 1825. I beg you, then, to inform me about the price of the manuscripts you obtained. Later, I will send you the money, asking you to have a copy made for me. The Papal work is about done and before November, I hope to be able to send you a copy of an interesting document in relation to the history of New Mexico.

Many warm regards for all, and very especially for you, in behalf of my wife and your affectionate and faithful servant.

Ad. F. Bandelier

853. A biographical sketch of Thomas Benton Catron, based on the notes of Dr. A. J. O. Anderson, was included in the Register of Persons (Lange and Riley 1966: 408). For additional data on his role in the life of Territorial New Mexico, see Lamar (1966). See n 531 for Mrs. Catron.

Catron's extensive library and legal papers were given to the University of New Mexico and form the Catron Collection (PC 29, with various subdivisions) in the Coronado Room of the Library. The editors found copies of a number of documents copied by Bandelier in Mexico City in 1887 in this collection. Many notes to entries in this volume refer to the Catron Collection.

854. This was probably the wife of S. Spitz, jeweler in Santa Fe (see n 958).

855. See n 609.

856. This was Charles A. Kaune of Breese, Illinois, a brother of Henry S. Kaune (see n 111).

857. Major Charles Pessels was a popular person in Santa Fe. On Oct. 15, 1887, the *Santa Fe Daily New Mexican* (Vol. 24, No. 202, p. 4) had a detailed obituary about the Major, of which we give an abridgement.

Major Charles Pessels died at 5:00 A.M. at St. Vincent's Sanitorium. On the evening of October 14, Pessels had been out riding his horse when it became frightened and threw him on the main Santa Fe River bridge.

Pessels was a native of Bavaria and was 52 at death. In 1868, the late Z. Staab had invited him to come to Santa Fe. He was with that firm, Zadoc Staab and Brother, for the full period of his stay in Santa Fe; for the eight months prior to his death, he had been in charge of the house of Staab and Brother during Abraham Staab's stay in Europe. Pessels was single and was a cousin of S. Wedeles of Wedeles and Eldodt.

858. An anonymous review of Daniel G. Brinton's *Ancient Nahuatl Poetry* (1887) appeared in *The Nation*, February 2, 1888 (Vol. 46, No. 1179, pp. 102–3).

859. On retiring from the priesthood, perhaps as a result of breaking the vow of chastity (see the journal entry of September 29, 1885), Father Ribera settled at La Bajada, his place being taken at Peña Blanca by Father Agustín Navet.

860. Bandelier had met David Vaca [Baca] in Peña Blanca in 1882 (Lange and Riley 1966: 371, 376). See also n 355.

861. This was the second time that Bandelier had copied this "Nota." On October 4, 1880, he had copied it into his journal (Lange and Riley 1966: 126). Chavez (1957: 244) stated that Fray Juan Caballero Toril was at Cochiti from September 1816, to January 1820. Chavez made reference to this "Nota" in his section on Books of Marriages. "Note by Fray Juan Caballero Toril, that on November 19, 1819, he found the Indians of this pueblo adoring an altarful of idols; he confiscated them, broke them, and burned them

in the middle of the plaza; advises successors to watch for such things and do likewise. 'Toril' surname not always used by Padre" (p. 221, M-8, Cochiti (Box 6) 1776–1827).

Bandelier had made his copies at Peña Blanca; by Chavez's time, however, Fray Caballero's "note" was among the Archives of the Archdiocese of Santa Fe. Lange (1959: 11) mentioned that " ... [in] 1817 and 1818, reports showed Cochití as a mission; in both years, Father Fray Juan Caballero Foril was listed as the resident friar (Biblioteca Nacional, *Legajo X:* Documents 79, 80)." In both instances, the "Toril" was misread in the originals as "Foril."

862. In this entry of October 24, 1887, Bandelier noted he had copied at Peña Blanca the lists of Franciscans of Santo Domingo, Cochiti, and Santa Ana from 1770 to 1830. Among the copied documents in the Catron Collection (PC 29 807) were the Santo Domingo and Cochiti lists. They were entitled "Lista de los Curas Párrocos de la Misión del Pueblo de Santo Domingo. (sacada del 'Libro de Entierros,' desde el año de 1770 hasta el de 1826. M.S.S.)" and "Lista de los Curas Párrocos de la Misión de San Buenaventura Cochiti. (sacada del 'Libro de Bautismos,' desde el año de 1776, hasta el de 1826.)" At the end of this last item was a brief extract from the "Libro de Entierros" from Cochiti, with a brief roster of priests from 1779 to 1825. These lists, in Bandelier's handwriting, were dated October 24, 1887, Peñablanca, N.M. No comparable list for Santa Ana Pueblo was found in the Catron Collection. (See n 890 for reference to a document pertaining to Santa Ana priests from 1712 to 1746, and, in part, to 1753. However, this document had been copied in Santa Fe, November 22, 1887.)

863. José Sena was perhaps José Antonio Sena, the father of Don Jesús Sena of Peña Blanca (see n 325).

864. Antonio Baca and his wife, Maria de los Angeles Gutierrez, were important citizens of Zile. Baca died on the 25th of November, 1891, and was buried in Peña Blanca the following day (Registro: 30).

865. Pearce (1965: 105) stated that the old Spanish name for Mount Taylor was Cebolleta Mountain, but he also gave Sierra de San Mateo for it (p. 147). Anglo-Americans named the peak for Zachary Taylor, twelfth president of the United States.

866. Although Bandelier had been interested in Jemez Pueblo ever since his initial fieldwork at Pecos Pueblo in 1880 at which time he had made frequent journal entries regarding the move of the Pecos survivors to Jemez (Lange and Riley 1966), this was his first visit to Jemez. For a recent treatment of Jemez social organization, see F. H. Ellis (1964b); a much earlier and more comprehensive study of Jemez was done by Parsons (1925).

867. Cotton was grown in pre-Spanish times in the Southwest. In the Coronado Expedition's reports, use of cotton cloth was noted for a number of areas, but it was identified as growing only from "Totonteac," probably the Hopi area (Hammond and Rey 1940: 159). In the reconquest period, Luxán also noted cotton for the Hopi (Hammond and Rey 1966: 191–92), and Gallegos, for the Tiwa area. The "Brief and True Account" of 1582 also mentioned cotton fields on the Middle Rio Grande (p. 142).

The fertility of the Jemez area was noted by Domínguez in 1776, though grapes were not specifically mentioned. Domínguez did comment on vineyards in other parts of the middle Rio Grande area, however (Adams and Chavez 1956: 176–82, et seq.).

868. Jemez Pueblo is the one remaining Towa-speaking village. Bandelier used the term "dialect" in reference to the Jemez language. He undoubtedly considered Jemez Towa as one of the three components of the Tanoan language, the others being Tewa and Tiwa. Pecos had also been a Towa-speaking pueblo.

The reader is referred to Reiter's two-part monograph on excavations at *The Jemez Pueblo of Unshagi, New Mexico* (1938) for detailed discussions of Jemez, Unshagi, and other sites of the Jemez area . Included are remarks appraising and correlating material, published and/or verbal, from Bandelier, Bloom, Harrington, Hewett, Kubler, Scholes, and others.

For more recent discussions, both of the antiquities and the ethnography of present-day Jemez Pueblo, see Florence Hawley Ellis (1952, 1953, 1964b). For Jemez ethnography, as well as notes on the Pecos people at Jemez, see Parsons (1925; 1939).

869. The Winter and Summer people Bandelier noted for Jemez reveal the existence of a moiety, or dual, social structure which is common among the eastern, or Rio Grande, puebloan tribes.

However, the terms Winter and Summer are more typical of the Tewa tribes; at Jemez, as among the Eastern Keresans, the common reference is to the Turquoise and Squash, or Pumpkin, peoples and the corresponding kivas and kiva memberships.

Within these gross similarities, there are innumberable variations, distinctions, and contrasts. Many of these appear to have been the result of deaths of members and other changes which have forced either accommodation or abandonment among the survivors, depending upon the appraisals of necessity and propriety at a given time. (See F. H. Ellis [1964b] for a discussion of Jemez social organization.)

Parsons (1929: 89) did comment that at Jemez the association of the Turquoise Kiva and the Squash Kiva with ideas of summer and winter was stronger than among the Keresans, thereby substantiating Bandelier's notations to some degree. Parsons went on to point out that among the Tewa, the Summer people associate with Turquoise and the Winter people, with Squash in a number of instances, a reversal that she stated Harrington had also found (pp. 89–98).

870. As noted elsewhere (n 306), the Piros spoke a language only dialectically different from Tiwa. This places them within the broader Tanoan grouping, but does not give any close affiliation with the Towa spoken at Jemez Pueblo.

871. This was the general Towa association of colors with directions except that west is blue rather than green in the Towa system. Green is a very uncommon color to associate with a direction among the Pueblo Indians (Riley 1963: 59).

It may be worth noting a tendency among Southwestern tribes to merge blue and green under a more or less inclusive designation such as turquoise. This type of association may have been involved in the gathering of this information by Bandelier.

872. Zia (Sia, Tsia) is a Keresan-speaking pueblo on the north bank of the Jemez River, about sixteen miles northwest of Bernalillo. Stubbs (1950: 79) thought it had been occupied since about 1300 A.D. F. H. Ellis conducted both ethnographic and archaeological fieldwork at Zia. See F. H. Ellis (1966: 806–11) for her "Immediate History of Zia Pueblo as derived from Excavation in Refuse Deposits." A test pit was dug at Punamesh Zia, one of the original sites of the Jemez Valley Zias, according to tribal tradition. From analysis of the evidence gained, two occupation periods were determined: one from between 1200 and 1300 A.D. and the second, from 1300 to perhaps 1350 or 1375. From the three excavations at Zia Pueblo itself, Ellis concluded that the top of Zia Mesa definitely was occupied during the 14th century and from then on to the present. This occupation, according to Ellis, was broken only by a short period in the late seventeenth century when, from tradition, historical references, and data from sherds at the site, the Zia people were living in their refugee site on the top of Red Mesa near the present pueblo of Jemez, some ten miles to the north. Ancestral Punamesh and early Zia were occupied contemporaneously, although Ellis thought Punamesh might be somewhat older (p. 810).

873. Father Stephen (or Etienne) Parisis, ordained in 1869, was pastor of Bernalillo; he had been brought to New Mexico by Bishop Lamy (Defouri 1887: 54; Salpointe 1898: 283; Chavez 1957: 134).

874. Adams and Chavez (1956: 172n2) gave a detailed history of the Zia church. A convent of Nuestra Señora de la Ascensión existed at Zia as early as 1613. By 1706, Father Alvarez said the church was "now at a good height." Domínguez (1776) stated that Fray Davila built the church during the five years he resided at Zia [in the 1750s]. Adams and Chavez questioned that he had built an entirely new church and were more of the opinion that he had made extensive repairs to an existing church.

An article in *El Palacio* (Halseth and Boyd 1971: 19–22) reported on the 1923 church restoration at Zia Pueblo by Odd Halseth, and a postscript by E. Boyd to the Zia Mission Report described an earlier altar screen that was exposed when the existing altar screen was partially removed in 1923. Closer study has shown this Zia retable to have been the work of a major santero, the same one who had done the retable at Laguna, Santa Ana, and elsewhere, according to Boyd.

Early in the article (p. 19), it was stated that "The mission at Zia Pueblo, which dates from the 1740s if not earlier, . . ."

875. Santa Ana is a Keresan-speaking pueblo on the north bank of the Jemez River, about eight miles northwest of Bernalillo. It was probably founded about 1700. It occupies a barren site, with sand dunes, volcanic mesas, and alkaline water combining to cause a scarcity of farm land and good water. Accordingly, most of the families have moved to reservation land along the Rio Grande, living at Ranchitos, or the Ranchos de Santa Ana, much of the year. Stubbs (1950: 75–78) considered the town pattern European in its layout. Families return to the pueblo for ceremonial observances, and a few people are left in the pueblo to protect against unwanted intruders. It is noteworthy that even in Bandelier's time, the fields were at some distance from the pueblo.

Kubler (1940: 109) reported a small church recorded by Father Alvarez in 1706. In 1734, the church was rebuilt under Friar Diego Arias de Espinosa. In 1927, a new roof and windows were added with funds raised by the Indians; the work was done under the direction of the same committee that had done the Zia restoration (see n 874).

876. See Schroeder and Matson (1965: 167–72) for a thorough discussion of historic contacts with Puaray Pueblo and also for the confusion that has existed concerning the location of Puaray in various conflicting accounts. Schroeder and Matson (p. 171), on the basis of Castaño de Sosa's journal, associate Puaray with L.A. 677. Bandelier's Puaray was identified by them as L.A. 325. See Map 15 (p. 169) for Schroeder and Matson's location of these two sites.

877. Sandia Pueblo is located on the east side of the Rio Grande, fourteen miles north of Albuquerque. Its people speak Tiwa, one of the components of the Tanoan family. Dozier (1970: 121) indicated that for Sandia and three other Tiwa villages "each . . . speaks a variant virtually unintelligible to the others."

Potsherds indicate that Sandia has been occupied continuously since about 1300 A.D. Coronado is thought to have visited Sandia in 1540. Although most of its inhabitants are reported to have fled to the Hopi towns at the time of the 1680 Pueblo Rebellion and remained there until 1742, the sherd evidence indicates no significant gap in occupancy of the village site (Stubbs 1950: 31–34).

878. Professor Edward Seler and his wife, Berlin, Germany, were noted in the *Santa Fe Daily New Mexican* of October 24, 1887 (No. 209, p. 4), as guests at the Palace. Presumably, Seler's letter which Bandelier received October 29, in Bernalillo, announced their presence in the Santa Fe area. From Bandelier's comment in his entry of October 31, his meeting the Selers while at Peña Blanca was not anything he had looked forward to with pleasure. Whether the displeasure was a personal matter or whether the visit was simply viewed as an intrusion on Bandelier's fieldwork is not clear although the implication was rather in favor of the former. Again, however, as it so often happened, the meeting proved to be less painful than Bandelier had anticipated it would be.

879. Father Stephan was Director of the Bureau of Catholic Indian Missions (see n 588). In the entry of November 14, 1887, Bandelier noted that this agreement was definite. He began work for Father Stephan on December 1, 1887 (see n 1003).

880. See ns 436 and 859.

881. It is interesting that in this entry, Bandelier referred to the ruin at Cieneguilla as "Tshiguma." In earlier entries (July 14, July 25, September 26, and October 19, 1885), conflicting locations had been gathered by him for Tziguma. In the *Final Report* (1890–92: II, 91–92), Bandelier correlated Tziguma and Ciénega.

882. Alice Amalia Kaune had been born on July 22, 1884, and Alfred William Kaune, on November 12, 1886. Both children were born in Breese, Illinois, to Henry S. and Elizabeth Bandelier Kaune. Alfred was educated in Santa Fe's public schools and at St. Michael's College and the New Mexico Military Institute at Roswell. He served as book-keeper in his father's mercantile business, and for a short period as a State Bank Examiner. He was later a teller at the First National Bank in Santa Fe, a position from which he resigned after eight years to become auditor for the New Mexico Power Company. Concurrently, he was president of the Kaune Grocery Company but was not active in its management. Two brothers, Richard, as manager, and Charles H., as buyer, operated the company.

Alfred Kaune married Miss Ruth Thompson, January 8, 1933. They had one son, Eugene (Davis 1945: I, 716).

883. Bandelier, in a letter of November 28, 1889, to Mrs. Hemenway (Peabody Museum Archives, Harvard University) summarizing his work for the Hemenway Expedition, wrote, "By your orders, the rare Memorial of Benavides (1630) was copied from the Original at Harvard and sent to me."

This entry was apparently Bandelier's notation of the receipt of this copy. In his publications, Bandelier made extensive use of the Benavides 1630 Memorial (see also ns 37 and 38). For Bandelier's own evaluation of Benavides, see Bandelier 1910: 17–18.

884. This letter of November 2, 1887, was included in the volume edited by White and Bernal (1960: 304); our translation follows:

> My dear sir:
> Although with a certain reticence, [I must give] a certain Dr. Eduard Seler of the Berlin Museum a card of introduction. I gave it to him after convincing myself that he is a person who will not give you any trouble because he is not nosey nor pretentious. Although he is a northern German, he is modest and prudent. I have never dared to introduce you to an American, because I know them. If Dr. Seler comes to you, he will do nothing more than ask you for advice. I have told him that your library is not public and furthermore it doesn't have the materials he is looking for, which are the paintings and manuscripts in Maya. Also I have provided him with letters of introduction to other persons, but in that which refers to you, I have told him that I would never bother you with strangers.
> I have just returned from a very hard field trip to a pueblo whose lands border those infested by Apaches. I walked all the way alone and without weapons. I accomplished a lot.
> I have now finished with the work for the Pope, but on the horizon I begin to perceive a mountain of work.
> With most affectionate regards for everyone and in particular for you, I remain your grateful and faithful servant.
>
> Ad. F. Bandelier

885. Bandelier's *An Outline of the Documentary History of the Zuñi Tribe* was published by Fewkes in 1892 in *A Journal of American Ethnology and Archaeology.* Hodge (1932: 368) noted that the paper was also published separately. The research for this publication was done as part of Bandelier's work for the Hemenway Expedition (Congrès International des Américanistes: 458–59). Part I, Chapter II, referred to in this entry, dealt with the history of the Zuñi tribe from 1539 to 1600, as reconstructed from early Spanish documents.

886. Herman Frederik Carel ten Kate was born in Amsterdam, Holland, July 21, 1858. He abandoned the field of art, where his father was an eminent figure and in 1877 studied medicine and natural science at the University of Leiden. Later, he studied at Paris with leaders of the French anthropological school. In 1880, he went to Germany, studying at Berlin, Göttingen, and Heidelberg. After graduating in 1882, ten Kate traveled in the United States and northern Mexico, at which time he most probably visited Frank Hamilton Cushing at Zuñi. Publications and other travel followed. " . . . in October, 1887, he sailed for the third time to America, to join the Hemenway Archaeological Expedition as physical anthropologist at the invitation of Cushing, its director, then conducting excavations in the Salt River valley of Arizona" (Heÿink and Hodge 1931: 416).

Undoubtedly, Dr. ten Kate was on his way to Arizona via Santa Fe at the time he stopped for a visit with Bandelier and his wife. He stayed with the Hemenway Expedition for about a year before moving on to Mexico and then back to Holland. He traveled extensively and he published widely in several languages and countries. His bibliography comprised perhaps 150 titles. He died in Carthage, northern Africa, on February 5, 1931.

887. For many years now, this "ranchito" has been The Bishop's Lodge, resort hotel north of Santa Fe. Archbishop Lamy's residence and chapel are still maintained and may be visited; it is indeed "a lovely place."

888. This employment was with the Bureau of Catholic Indian Missions. The nature of Bandelier's duties has remained somewhat obscure. However, he appears to have visited various pueblos for Father Stephan (see n 588), most frequently to participate in juntas, or meetings, with local officials in regard to educational programs and other school matters (see n 1003).

889. Johanna Franz was probably one of several children of E. D. Franz who at that time owned a large hardware store in Santa Fe (Anonymous 1895: 619).

890. This list of priests from Santa Ana Pueblo, copied by Bandelier in Santa Fe on November 22, 1887, was among the Catron Collection papers (PC 29 807). The document, entitled "Lista de los Padres Ministros de la Misión de Santa Ana, sacada del 'Libro de disposición del convento de la mission [*sic*] de Santa Ana,' se puso año de 1712.— 1712–1746. (and in part to 1753.)," was in Bandelier's handwriting.

891. Two documents concerning San Felipe Pueblo, which were copied by Bandelier on the date of this entry, were in the Catron Collection (PC 29 807). One was entitled, "Estado de la Misión de San Felipe de los Queres, en el año de 1712. (Cura - Párroco: Fray Miguel Muñiz de Luna.)" A second was "Lista de los Curas Párrocos de la Mission [*sic*] de San Felipe de los Queres, desde el año de 1712, hasta el de 1746. (Sacada de un fragmento de 'Libro de Fábrica y Visitas.')"

Two additional documents copied on this date, November 23, 1887, but unmentioned in the journal entry, were: "Lista de los Padres Ministros de la Misión de Nª Sª de los Angeles de Pecos.—desde el año de 1716, hasta el año de 1757.—(sacada del 'Libro de Fábrica' de la dicha Misión. M: S: S:)" and "Inventario de las Pinturas sobre Lienzo y Cueros de Anta, que se hallaban en la Iglesia de Nuestra Señora de los Angeles de Pecos, —el año de 1717—Cura Ministro: Fray Carlos Delgado. Not: del Sº Oficio. (Libro de fabrica de Pecos.)" These two documents were also in the Catron Collection (PC 29 807).

All four copies were made in Santa Fe and were in Bandelier's handwriting.

892. This was J. C. Dougherty who was listed in an advertisement in the *Daily New Mexican* of January 8, 1890 (p. 3), as "Contractor and Builder," with a shop on lower San Francisco Street.

893. Bandelier's pleasure at working with an original document shows in his use of the exclamation point. A handwritten copy by Bandelier of this document, which he signed November 24, 1887, in Santa Fe, was in the Catron Collection (PC 29 807). It was entitled *Lista de los Curas Párrocos de la Misión de Santa Clara.* (Sacada de un "Libro de Fabríca" - de 1717 á 1736.) The second page appeared to consist of notations by Bandelier, which included a list of "Pinturas en el Convento de Santa Clara. 1712." Chavez (1957: 251) gave Fray Juan Mingues at Albuquerque, July–August, 1706; . . . at Santa Clara, July 1712– October 1713 and from September 1714 to July 1719. The document copied by Bandelier listed Father Minguez at Santa Clara from 1717 to 1720.

894. Interestingly, Bandelier's review of Brooks's book, *The Story of the American Indian,* did not appear in *The Nation.* It may have been rejected by Garrison or passed on by him to another publication.

895. This article, entitled, "Irrigation in the Southwest," appeared in *The Nation* (Vol. 45, July–December 1887, p. 474).

896. Although Bandelier did not mention it in his entry of December 1, 1887, he had copied, on the typewriter, one page from the *Libro de Visitas y de Entregas, de Laguna, San Agustín de la Isleta, y de Zuñi.* He listed the priests at Laguna in 1743–44 and also listed the paintings at the Laguna church in 1743 and 1744. The copy was signed in Bandelier's hand and dated December 1, 1887, in Santa Fe. The editors obtained their copy from the Catron Collection (PC 29 807).

897. Burrus (1969a) referred to indices made by Bandelier which appeared with the volumes of copied documents compiled by Bandelier for the Hemenway Expedition. These fifteen volumes are in the library of the Peabody Museum, Harvard University. Presumably, Bandelier was working on a portion of this index at the time of this entry.

898. Bandelier made no journal entry for December 15, 1887. In the Catron Collection (PC 29 807), however, there was a manuscript in Bandelier's hand, dated December 15, 1887, Santa Fe. It was entitled "Inventarios del Convento de la Misión del Pueblo de Santa Ana (sacados del 'Libro de Disposición' — año de 1712)."

The article Bandelier noted in this entry as sent to the *New Yorker Staatszeitung* appeared in the January 1 and January 8 issues, 1888. It was entitled "Die Kirchen und Kirchen-Ornamente aus der spanischen Zeit." A clipping of this article was found in the Bandelier Scrapbook.

899. This December 16, 1887, letter from Bandelier to Parkman was missing from the correspondence the editors obtained from the Massachusetts Historical Society. On November 29, 1887, Bandelier noted, "Began to write for the Institute." The intervening entries indicate that he continued writing for the Institute (see n 542). It is reasonable to assume that Bandelier was at work on his *Final Report,* the report he owed the Archaeological Institute of America for the fieldwork which the Institute had asked him to undertake in the Southwest and had financed in 1880, 1882, 1883, and 1884. The Institute had granted his request to delay the writing of this report in order to work in the archives of Mexico City for the Pope's Golden Jubilee *Histoire* from late December 1886 to May 1887, recognizing that this same material would undoubtedly enrich his *Final Report* (see n 721).

900. Apparently, it was not unusual for Bandelier to be permitted to take home certain rare and valuable books and documents for copying.

901. In the *Final Report* (1890–92: I, 80n1), Bandelier cited *"El Diario del Viaje de Juan Domínguez de Mendoza á la Junta de los Rios y hasta el Rio Nueces,* MS. copy in my possession." He noted that there were documents annexed to it. This document was among those gathered for the Hemenway Expedition. Fewkes (1895: 310) listed it as "28. Diary of the journey to the confluence of the rivers, and to the Pecos and Nueces Rivers (fragment). Juan Dominguez Mendoza, 1684."

902. These pamphlets referred to Bandelier's article, in French, on Fray Marcos de Niza (see ns 413 and 607).

903. Amado Cháves (not Chávez) was born in Santa Fe on April 16, 1851, a descendant of a family that came to New Mexico with De Vargas. Cháves was a successful politician, serving at one time as speaker of the house of the legislative assembly. Cháves became the first Superintendent of Public Education in New Mexico (Twitchell 1911–17: II, 508n425).

904. Twitchell (1914: I, 81, No. 230) cited Manuel Vaca to Fernándo Duran y Chaves. Bernalillo, May 5, 1701. This document dealt with the original grant of the lands at Bernalillo. The grant had been made by De Vargas to Felipe Gutierrez; it had previously [?] been granted to Gutierrez by Governor Cubero, December 3, 1701. According to Twitchell, De Vargas, in 1704, had revalidated the grant.

Bandelier, in 1880 (Lange and Riley 1966: 181), noted that the Merced of Bernalillo of 1701 had been found and laid aside for him, but there was no indication he had copied it. Earlier, he had copied a Bernalillo manuscript owned by Gold (p. 144).

Pearce (1965: 16) noted that there were several petitions to the U.S. Land Court and Court of Private Claims in 1893–94 by petitioners claiming to be descendants of Gutierrez, to whom a land grant had been made by Governor Cubero on January 21, 1704. Because boundaries were ill-defined and documentation inadequate, the courts made adverse rulings.

A copy of this grant was listed by Fewkes (1895: 313) as "14. Grant of Bernalillo. Pedro Rodrígucz Cubero, 1701."

905. Although there was no journal entry for December 28, 1887, the Catron Collection (PC 29 807) contained a copy made on this date from the "Archivos de Santa Fé" of a "Fragmento y muy mutilado." It was not in Bandelier's hand, but it bore his signature at the end; its title was *Petición del Capitán Francisco de Anaya al Gobernador D^n Domingo Gironza Petris de Cruzate.* It was dated 1684. Fewkes (1895: 310) listed this item as "22. Petition to Governor Petriz de Cruzate. Francisco de Anaya. 1684."

906. Burrus (1969b: 12n17) wrote that "Bandelier kept in his Journal a copy of the printed notice of Fischer's death and burial. Ayer a las siete y tres cuartos de la noche / falleció en esta Capital / El Sr. Pbro. D. Agustín Fischer / Cura Párroco de San Antonio de las Huertas, antiguo Secretario / privado de Su Majestad El emperador Maximiliano / Sus amigos lo participan a Vd., esperando eleve / al Cielo una plegaria / México, Diciembre 19 de 1887 / El duelo se recibe en la Yglesia de San Cosme, a las ocho de la / mañana del día 20, y se despide en el Panteón Francés de la Piedad."

907. This letter of December 28, 1887, was among those included by White and Bernal (1960: 305–6); our translation follows:

> My dear sir and godfather:
>
> I scarcely can handle the pen so much do I suffer from writer's cramp. This obliges me to limit myself to some few lines although I would have to fill many pages to express how much I feel, and have felt, the death of our illustrious Father [Augustín Fischer]. I received the news two days ago, and if I have not

replied before today, it is only that it was impossible for me to do so. It is the same as if I had been maimed. The obituary, together with a very warm letter from Don Justino Rubio, arrived at the same time as some lines from the same person announcing that the aforementioned priest had become very sick. However, that letter did not mention the possibility of such a sad conclusion.

It is not necessary that we repeat how much we have felt the death of our dear Father. You knew him, treated with him, and understood him better than any other person in Mexico. You, better than anyone, were able to appreciate his merits, and your appreciation will allow you to fill the vacuum left by his death. I wish I could write his obituary in German to bring out his many and great virtues, but I lack the most elementary facts.

The Father, despite the monumental erudition that he possessed, left not a single written work, and to evaluate the importance of what he did, it is necessary to judge the facts "honoris causa," taking into consideration the circumstances which surrounded him and especially judging the ideas that influenced him in his path. I do not consider myself capable of undertaking such a task although I would have loved to do so.

I shall not speak about studies on this occasion. Because the typewriter broke down, I am making the letters with painstaking work like a shield-bearer who has begun to write for the first time. I can hardly copy more than three or four pages a day. I had been able, despite my trouble, to obtain copies of beautiful documents which I pulled from the tomb of oblivion and mud that the gringos had made in the archives of Santa Fe. Among them, there is one which without doubt would be of interest to your friend Capt. [Cesáreo] Fernández Duro. It is the official journal with attached documents of the expedition made by the Maestro de Campo, Domínguez Mendoza, to the interior of Texas in 1683–4.

With nothing more for the moment and repeating my sorrow for the loss that has befallen you, as much for an old friend as a parishioner, I wish that next year will be for you and yours, one of happiness.

Your affectionate and faithful servant and godchild

Ad. F. Bandelier

NOTES
1888

908. The San Francisco band was mentioned in an article in the *Santa Fe Daily New Mexican* of December 13, 1890 (Vol. 27, No. 250, p. 1).

" 'Guadalupe Day' was kept this year with more than ordinary ceremony. At 6 P.M. on the evening of the 11th, the sweet chimes of Guadalupe Tower and the well timed music of the San Francisco band announced to the assembled multitude the beginning of solemn vespers."

909. Mrs. Gerard D. Koch normally received from 1 till 7 P.M. on New Year's (in 1888 on January 2, because New Year's Day was on a Sunday), according to Santa Fe papers of the time. The *Santa Fe Daily New Mexican* of Jan.3, 1888 (Vol. 24, No. 268, p. 4), had this comment: "The New Years callers were not as numerous yesterday as usual. The ladies who kept open house entertained right royally and many private parties took place last evening."

910. Lt. James Fornance and wife were at that time visiting the George Cuyler Preston family in Santa Fe. On Jan. 8, the Fornances returned to Fort Wingate (*Santa Fe Daily New Mexican,* Jan. 6, 1888, Vol. 24, No. 271, p. 4). (See also ns 533 and 567.) The Fornance family had also come from Fort Wingate for a Christmas visit with the Prestons in 1887 (see entry of December 23, 1887).

911. For an explanation of Bandelier's calculation of anniversaries, see n 524.

912. Bandelier was probably referring to the great smallpox epidemic of 1780–82. In the *Final Report* (1890-92: II, 23), he reported that at Santa Clara and San Juan, alone, 500 people died within two months time in 1782. White (1942: 28) stated that the whole pueblo country was ravaged in the period 1780–81, Santa Ana Pueblo being decimated to the point that it was reduced from mission to visita status by the church.

A discussion of the attacks on Tewa-Tano and other eastern puebloan peoples by nomadic Plains Indians during this same period may be found in Bandelier's *Final Report* (1890–92: II, 102, et seq.).

913. In this entry, Bandelier was referring to his *Final Report* (1890–92). (See n 542.)

914. For this entry and the remainder of the year 1888, the editors have been unable to find any of the letters Bandelier wrote to Parkman.

915. Presumably, Bandelier was consulting Dr. Strong about his ailing hand. The entries of this period reveal a rather pronounced change and deterioration of his handwriting.

916. Father Joseph P. Macheboeuf was born in Riom, France, August 11, 1812, and was ordained on Christmas, 1836. Macheboeuf was a close friend of Archbishop John B. Lamy, coming from the same French department and diocese as Lamy. After Pope Pius IX created the Vicariate Apostolic of New Mexico, July 19, 1850, Lamy became its first bishop. Macheboeuf accompanied Bishop Lamy there, arriving in Santa Fe in the summer of 1851 as Lamy's Vicar-General. Macheboeuf was consecrated Bishop, August 16, 1868, in Cincinnati, Ohio. He became the first Bishop of Denver, where he died August 10, 1889 (Lamy Memorial 1950: 27; Salpointe 1898: 229).

917. This was Monsignor Denis J. O'Connell. Bloom had written E. L. Hewett from Rome on June 22, 1938, in his search for the *Histoire* at the Vatican, ". . . I called again at the American College and had a good talk with him [Bishop Hayes]. He says however, that they clear out their routine correspondence every five years; and that Mgr. Denis J. O'Connell (1884–1895) kept no journal while he was rector" (Museum of New Mexico: Bloom File). The letter to Dr. O'Connell referred to in this entry was undoubtedly to inform him that the manuscript of the *Histoire* had been completed and was being sent to Rome by express.

918. Bandelier was to go to Arizona to visit the excavations of the Hemenway Expedition.

919. McKenney (1888: 486) gave Samuel Ellison as librarian of the Territorial Law Library; he served until his death in 1889. Ellison, first postmaster at Peña Blanca, was an early and valuable contact for Bandelier (see Lange and Riley 1966: 433; 1970: 493).

920. The office of surveyor-general of New Mexico was created by act of Congress on July 22, 1854. William Pelham was the first appointee. Twitchell (1914: I, ix-xxi) discussed the work of the surveyor-general in New Mexico and the archives associated with his work. Twitchell's two volumes (1914: I, II) were devoted to the Spanish Archives of New Mexico. At the time Twitchell compiled his listings, the documents were in the Library of Congress. It is the editors' understanding that these were subsequently returned to the State of New Mexico. Westphall (1965: 1–36) gave two chapters to the establishment of the surveying system in New Mexico and to the public surveys.

921. In McKenney's Southern Coast Directory for 1888–9, Otto Dieckmann was listed (p.439) as secretary-treasurer of the Albuquerque Hardware Company, of which Franz Huning was given as president. The Dieckmanns and Bandeliers were acquaintances of some years standing (see Lange and Riley 1970: 364n59). Twitchell (1911–17: III, 42–43) noted that Dieckmann had been born in Germany in 1847, coming to this country at the age of 16 or 17, first to St. Louis and then to Albuquerque. He had a variety of business interests and experiences. He died November 3, 1913.

922. See n 933 for an account of the severity of this May 1887 earthquake in Bavispe, Sonora, and a comparable increased flow of springs in Chihuahua.

923. For probable identification of Mr. Conway, see Lange and Riley 1970: 429n 103.

924. Cushing (1890: 160–61) referred to Mr. Charles A. Garlick as the topographer and general field manager for the Hemenway Expedition. Cushing spoke of Garlick's "long experience in the service of the United States Geological Survey."

925. In his *Final Report* (1890–92: II, 446), Bandelier wrote, "The plain between the Salado and Gila south of Tempe also contains numerous ruins. Here the Hemenway Expedition made its first researches, and the forthcoming report relieves me from the need of detailed allusion to the remains disseminated over that section." For Bandelier's reconnaisance in the Gila-Salado area in 1883, see Lange and Riley 1970. Some data from the excavations of the Hemenway Expedition were not published until Haury's 1945 monograph on "The Excavation of Los Muertos and Neighboring Ruins in the Salt River Valley, Southern Arizona."

926. This was Father Francis X. Jouvenceau, who had been brought to New Mexico in 1859 by Bishop J. B. Lamy. Jouvenceau served for a time as priest at Sapello but in 1866 was sent to Arizona. The same year, a Father Patrick Birmingham was assigned to Gila City (present-day Yuma) but after a few months left for reasons of health to go to California. Father Jouvenceau then seems to have been assigned the Gila City post. In 1869, Jouvenceau was replaced by a Reverend Francis Lestra, and Jouvenceau was put in charge of the Tucson parish. By the time of Bandelier's comment, Jouvenceau seems to have been shifted to Phoenix. He died at St. Mary's Hospital in Tucson in July 1900 (Salpointe 1898: 222, 252, 259, App. VII added in 1900 [September]).

927. This was John D. Walker, born in Nauvoo, Illinois, in 1840, who settled among the Pima and, in 1865–66, served in the Arizona Volunteers, commanding Pima Indian troops. Walker, at one time, was the probate judge of Pinal County (Thrapp 1967: 33–36).

Bandelier, in his *Final Report* (1890–92: I, 254) cited J. D. Walker as the "best living authority on the subject of this tribe [the Pima]."

928. Dr. Joseph B. Girard was post surgeon at Fort Lowell, Arizona Territory. Bandelier had become well acquainted with him in 1883 (see Lange and Riley [1970: 141, passim and 393n319] for additional reference and biographical data).

929. Bandelier had visited Fort Lowell in late January of 1884, before going to Mexico, and again in June when he made a quick trip over to Tucson from Deming while waiting for the storm damage in the Rio Grande Valley to be repaired so he could return home to Santa Fe (see Lange and Riley 1970: 494 for data pertaining to Fort Lowell).

930. This was Captain Stanton Augustus Mason (Heitman 1903: I, 695) whom Bandelier had known in December 1883 at Fort Cummings (Lange and Riley 1970: 180).

931. Bandelier had mentioned Henry Holgate on his brief visit in southwestern New Mexico and southern Arizona in the summer of 1884. McKenney (1882–83: 941) noted him as in Holgate & Raithel, a meat market. Polk and Danser (1884a: 315) mentioned him as active in livestock in the Deming area.

932. Chico was the horse that Bandelier had ridden many miles in New Mexico, Arizona, and northern Mexico. On June 13, 1884, the journal entry noted "Chico rather poor too." Seemingly, Bandelier had left Chico in the care of Henry Holgate as he traveled by train on June 20 from Deming to Tucson. Soon after, having returned from the southwest to Highland and having had a letter from Holgate, on July 12 just before leaving Santa Fe, Bandelier wrote Holgate July 28, with the comment in his journal, "My saddle, blankets, etc., etc. came [to Highland]. Poor Chico, I will have to sell him at last" (Lange and Riley 1970: 327, 330, 339). Bandelier had bought Chico for $50.00 in Santa Fe with the help of Mr. Gerdes on December 6, 1882, in preparation for his trip into the Galisteo-Salinas area, and on into Arizona and Mexico, on which he left December 18 with his guide, José Olivas (1966: 372, 376). "Started almost at a gallop. Horse splendid, fierce, lively, and still tame. It was almost a gallop to the Arroyo Hondo." From Laguna, February 20, 1883 (1970: 36), Bandelier traveled by rail and foot to Zuñi; not until March 25, after his return to Laguna and some trying experiences afoot and astride a mule, did Bandelier mention Chico by name—and then within a period of several days with rather consistent enthusiasm and praise (1970: 64). Apparently, Holgate had sold Chico to someone who had taken the horse to Mexico.

933. The earthquake of May 1887 was widespread in northern Mexico. According to Lister and Lister (1966: 195): "In Bavispe, Sonora, every house crashed to the ground in a heap of dirty rubble. Arizpe, Apunto, Bocachi, and Fronteras were damaged badly. Casas Grandes, Galeana, and El Carman knew destruction and death."
Increased flow of springs seems to have been a characteristic of several areas. The Listers also noted that the Mormon settlement at Colonia Juárez in Chihuahua, established a short time before, in a rocky, barren area, received from the earthquake a series of new springs and generally better water conditions.

934. Mr. E. W. Dietrich died at 11:00 A.M., February 10, 1888. He was the father of Mrs. H. Hartmann (see n 666); Dietrich was 75 years old and had come to Santa Fe from Marshalltown, Iowa (*Santa Fe Daily New Mexican*, February 10, 1888, Vol. 24, No. 300, p. 4).
It is probable that Mr. Dietrich (corrected from Bandelier's "Dittrich") was the same person who had done some home repair work for the Bandeliers and Mr. Schumann as noted in the entries of November 30, December 1, and December 9, 1887.

935. In personal correspondence of August 19, 1969, Dr. Alfonso Ortiz wrote, in regard to San Juan Pueblo, "First, the San Juan church has good records going back to 1726, and the priests and Indians, at least, could be identified through these. Second, Sophie D. Aberle mined these records through about 1940, and she could probably shed some light on Fr. Padilla and a few others. Her article in *Human Biology* (1940), entitled 'Vital History of San Juan Pueblo,' lists all of the priests in residence here since 1726, and their periods of tenure" (see Aberle et al. 1940).

936. Bandelier stayed at the Dibble House which stood on the northwest corner of the plaza in Taos and was owned by Thomas Dibble and his Indian wife, Tomasita Dibble (Grant 1934: 181).

937. Father Joseph Valezy, one of the priests brought to New Mexico by Lamy (Salpointe 1898: 283), was listed by Sadliers (1885–86) at Taos. The Lamy Memorial (1950: 82) added that he was a Franciscan at Taos who served the mission church at Fernandez de Taos from 1866 to 1896.

938. Taos Pueblo (Braba or Valladolid) was visited by two of Coronado's captains, Hernando de Alvarado in 1540 and Francisco de Barrionuevo in 1541 (Hammond and Rey 1940: 244).

"The two big houses" mentioned in this entry refer to the two large house blocks, North House and South House, which have long dominated the Taos landscape. The somewhat pyramidal North House has become one of the more familiar scenes of New Mexico with its multitiered cluster of homes and rooms.

939. Salpointe (1898: 272) in 1886 had gone to Washington, D.C., in the hope of obtaining contracts from the U.S. Commissioner of Indian Affairs, Oberly, for four day schools to be established in four pueblos with the promise of four more as soon as the Commissioner had money enough to issue contracts for them. Shortly after, Commissioner Oberly, through the Bureau of Catholic Indian Missions (see n 588), issued contracts for seven day schools and one industrial boys' boarding school. The day schools were established at the pueblos of Acoma, Pahuate, the village of Laguna, Santo Domingo, Jemez, San Juan, and Taos. Bandelier's comment in the journal that "The school is going on well." had reference to one of these Catholic day schools. Bandelier was visiting the Taos school in his official capacity for Father Stephan (see n 1003).

940. Here, Bandelier was trying to elicit some comment on the age of Taos Pueblo and the old wall under discussion. In essence, he was asking if it dated back to the time of Popé and Chato and the Pueblo Indian Revolt, 1680. The final conspiracy, which resulted in the outbreak, started from Taos, although it had been instigated by the San Juan Indian, Popé (Bandelier 1890–92: I, 139n1). See Hackett (1942: I, II) for a detailed discussion of the events of the Revolt of 1680, including mention of [El] Popé, [El] Chato, Alonso Catití, [El] Saca, and others from the pueblos of San Juan, Taos, Picurís, and various collaborating Keresan villages. On the basis of archaeological evidence, Taos at the time of the Revolt was at its present location (see n 294).

It is difficult to know the specific feature to which Bandelier was referring here. Domínguez in 1776 described a number of defensive walls at Taos, some with fortified towers. A number of these were undoubtedly erected as protection against Apache and Comanche raids in the eighteenth century (Adams and Chavez 1956: 110–12).

941. This, possibly, was Alois Scheurich, a Taos trader who in 1865 had married Teresina Bent, daughter of Governor Charles Bent. At any rate, Scheurich and Alexander Gusdorf were friends (Grant 1934: 161, 169; see also n 204).

942. In her study of Taos, which began in 1922, Parsons (1936: 17) wrote: "Most of the houses are two storied, several consist of three stories, a few of four stories, and in the north side cluster there is one house of five stories. With very few exceptions the upper stories are used merely as store rooms."

943. For a convenient translation of the *Relación del Suceso*, see Hammond and Rey (1940: 284–94) and for the *History* of Pedro de Castañeda de Najera, see pp. 191–283.

944. The traditional explanation of Braba is that it is a variant of *bravo*, or *brava*, meaning "brave" or "fearless." Hammond and Rey (1940: 244) suggested that this term may have been applied to the pueblo because of the "abrupt scenic background."

945. Cordoba, or Cordova, is a small town 14 miles east of Española. Once named El Pueblo Quemado, Cordoba dates from the mid-eighteenth century. A post office was established in 1900, and the name was changed to Cordoba honoring Don Miguel Peralta de Cordoba who settled in Santa Cruz in 1692 and whose children or grandchildren moved on to Cordoba (Pearce 1965: 40).

946. The plates and drawings, sent as part of Bandelier's *Histoire* manuscript, were, in fact, not lost and are still in the Vatican Library. Father Ernest J. Burrus, S. J., has published a complete catalogue and a limited selection of them (Burrus 1969b and 1969c).

947. These two sources on Peru were probably:

Ephriam George Squier, Peru: incidents of travel and exploration in the land of the Incas, Harper and Bros., N. Y., 1877, 509 pp.

Johann Jakob von Tschudi, Travels in Peru, during the years 1838–1842, Trans. from the German by Thomasina Ross, Barnes, N. Y., 1865, 354 pp.

948. The novel referred to here was Bandelier's *The Delight Makers*. Cushing was one of several to whom he sent his English translation and expanded version of the novel for reaction and criticism (see n 50).

949. Radin (1942) did not include this letter, actually mailed to Janvier the following day, the 28th, probably because it no longer existed or possibly because it had no significant bearing on the writing and publication of Bandelier's novel. Radin also made no mention of the "few lines" which Bandelier mailed to Janvier on February 29, along with the first five chapters of the novel.

950. In 1884, Arthur L. Frothingham, Jr., of Baltimore became Secretary of the Executive Committee of the Archaeological Institute of America (Lange and Riley 1970: 398n338). He continued to serve on the Council of the Institute until at least 1892, as his name appeared with those of other council members at the front of Bandelier's *Final Report* (1892: II). (In the first volume [1890: I], Frothingham's name had appeared in a similar list, but without the "Jr.")

951. This was probably H. Crampton, mentioned in the *Santa Fe Weekly New Mexican* of Feb. 2, 1888 (No. 50, p. 1) as "The old reliable furniture dealer, . . ." In the March 8, 1888, issue of the same paper (p. 4), H. Crampton was mentioned as "Commander, Carleton Post, G.A.R." McKenney (1888: 480) listed H. Crampton, Furniture and Crockery, on San Francisco Street.

952. Polk and Danser (1884b: 391, 585) did not mention Mr. Boeninghoven in the data on the *Illinois Staats Zeitung*. No further information on him came to light (see also n 488).

953. Fewkes (1895: 312) listed this item as "44. Sentence against the captive Indians of the pueblo of Santa Ana. Pedro Reneros de Posada. 1687." See Fewkes (p. 312: Items 43 and 45) for two other proclamations of 1686 and 1687 of Reneros de Posada and also Twitchell (1914: I, 2; II, 75–76) for data on Pedro Reneros de Posada, the spurious nature of the documents in the Surveyor General's office in Santa Fe regarding Reneros de Posada, and a list of proclamations from the El Paso del Norte archives, comparable in their listing but not identical with the items included by Fewkes.

Pedro Reneros de Posada, Governor at El Paso del Norte, 1686–88, made a raid into New Mexico, reaching Santa Ana Pueblo during the summer of 1687. The Santa Ana people refused to surrender, and after an assault the town was captured and burned. A number of Indians were killed in the fighting and in the burning of the pueblo that followed the Spanish victory (Bandelier 1890–92: II, 194–95). Twitchell (1914: II, 76#44) noted a proclamation "sentencing ten Queres captives to be sold into slavery in Nueva Vizcaya for ten years," dated October 6, 1687.

954. We were unable to identify this particular agent, but Hubert Howe Bancroft, himself, had some influence (albeit largely negative) on Bandelier. Bancroft (1832–1918) was born in Granville, Ohio, of Puritan, abolitionist parents. After some secondary school education, Bancroft, at sixteen, went to work for his sister's husband who owned a bookstore in Buffalo, New York. In 1852, Bancroft went to California, intending to open a branch of the bookstore on the west coast but instead he became a merchant. In 1858, the firm of H. H. Bancroft and Co., a publishing as well as a mercantile enterprise, was founded. Bancroft soon became an avid collector of books on the Pacific Coast area. From about the mid-1860s, Bancroft and an assistant, Henry L. Oak, were engaged in a vast editorial project on history and on native peoples of Mexico and the western United States. These multiauthored works still remain valuable sources today (Dictionary of American Biography 1957: 570–71).

955. Felicitas Garcia was a neighbor with whom bonds of friendship grew in the course of time with the Bandelier and Kaune families. When Henry S. and Elizabeth Bandelier Kaune had a daughter, July 23, 1890, she was named Felicitas Ernestina Kaune, reflecting this warm friendship. At a later date, the child went by the name of Elizabeth.

956. This was the first letter included in Radin's book (1942: 1); it was a brief note and is included here in its entirety.

Santa Fé, New Mexico, 12 March 1888.

My Dear Tom:
Your kind favor is just in and I will not let it go unanswered—even if the reply must be short—thanks, many thanks. Now do not be too much prejudiced against that poor "romance" of mine, but read it first. I shall have three more chapters ready soon, and will send them to you. After the whole is complete and in your hands, then I must copy the first five chapters again, annotate the whole, write glossary and introduction. Shall I put the English of each Indian word in the text, in notes, or only in the glossary?
Touching "Davis"—impossible to get him, except by chance and the merest chance only. I had a copy, and that copy was stolen at Santa Fé. It is one of the hardest books to get. [This was probably *El Gringo*, by W. W. H. Davis, published in New York in 1857.] And it is not worth much, utterly unreliable in its appreciation of Spanish times and totally unreliable in regard to the earliest expeditions. Davis could not read Spanish, and had to have all his documents translated for him. Our best regards to both. More shortly.

Yours como siempre,

Ad. F. Bandelier

957. Two of these letters written for Sam Eldodt were preserved in the Bandelier Collection of the Museum of New Mexico Library. One, written in English, was to Janvier; the other, in German, was to be presented to Dr. Julius Simonsfeld, Königl. Hülfs-bibliotheka, München. This Royal Branch, or Auxiliary, Library, was apparently distinct from the Hof-und Staats-Bibliothek mentioned in n 36. The editors have been unsuccessful in finding further information on this library, but Bandelier's handwriting on the letter envelope was very clear.

958. S. Spitz was listed by McKenney (1888: 486) as dealing in Mexican filigree jewelry in Santa Fe. His place of business was on the Plaza next to the post office. The *Santa Fe Daily New Mexican*, Jan. 4, 1887, mentioned Solomon Spitz, manufacturer of gold and silver filigree jewelry (p. 4).

959. A typewritten copy of this testimony of Sebastian de Herrera was in the Catron Collection (PC 29 807). It was entitled "Fragmentos del Testimonio del Sargento Mayor Sebastian de Herrera. [44 años de edad. Fecha del Testimonio: Octubre de 1681.]" It constituted parts of pages 7 and 8 of a twelve-page, foolscap typewritten document, listed by Fewkes (1895: 309) as "9. Decrees and proceedings on depositions of some persons. Antonio de Otermín, 1681." Although Bandelier, in the entry, noted that he had obtained a copy of this testimony from the [Christian] Brothers in Santa Fe, the provenience of the typewritten composite document was given as "Archivos territoriales, Santa Fé, México Nuevo, *Original,* Extractos."

960. A typewritten copy, five foolscap pages long, of this document, entitled *Historia de Montezuma,* was in the Catron Collection (PC 29 807). At the end of the document,

Bandelier noted that this was a corrected copy of a copy he had first made on January 16, 1886 [from the original in the archives of the Historical Society in Santa Fe]. The transcription referred to here was dated March 20, 1888. Although Bandelier had made frequent inquiries about Montezuma since starting his fieldwork in 1880, it was not until 1892 that he published on Montezuma specifically (Bandelier 1892a).

961. Antonio Ortiz y Salazar, born December 19, 1831, was from an old New Mexican family. Ortiz was born in Española but moved to Santa Fe at the age of six after his father was accidentally killed. Ortiz became politically active in the American period, becoming treasurer of Santa Fe County in 1859, sheriff in 1861, and chief clerk of the council in 1864. He was made probate judge in 1865 and in 1872 was appointed by Governor Giddings as treasurer of the territory, serving in that office (except for two years) until 1891. Ortiz was married in 1854 to Refugia Duran, also from an important family in New Mexico (Anonymous 1895: 341).

962. This was Samuel Ellison, Territorial Librarian of New Mexico (see n 919).

963. As subsequent entries of 1888 reveal, the breaking off of all relations with Henry Kaune was but another example of Bandelier's emotional outbursts which were invariably reversed or forgotten with the passage of time.

964. Among the Bandelier papers in the Catron Collection (PC 29 807) was a typewritten copy which Bandelier had made on March 18, 1890, from a copy he had first made on March 23, 1888. This was the 1681 document he referred to in this entry. It had come from the Territorial Archives in Santa Fe. It was entitled, "Extracto del Libro Real de Asientos y Pagas de Pobladores y Soldados Aviados con el Rl Sueldo de su Mag^d para la Reducción de los Yndios Alzados de la Nueva México."

Fewkes (1895: 309) listed this as "6. Extracts from the Royal Book of Entries and Payments of Settlers and Soldiers, etc. Antonio de Otermín. 1681."

965. This was W. Henry Brown of the photographic firm of Bennett and Brown who worked with Bandelier from 1880 to 1883. For additional information see Lange and Riley 1970: 355n4 and n 4 in the Preface of the present volume.

966. It seems quite probable that this was the same Dr. Hamy to whom Bandelier had written in 1886 (see n 522).

967. El Paso del Norte is present-day Juarez. It is across the Rio Grande from El Paso, Texas. For details on the history of this city and the State of Chihuahua, see Lister and Lister (1966).

968. Bandelier had visited El Paso del Norte in November 1883. Although his journal entries of that period did not include mention of Emile Duchene, it is evident from this present entry that Bandelier had met him earlier—presumably at El Paso del Norte. Bandelier had called on Cura Ramón Ortiz and had copied church books at El Paso del Norte (Lange and Riley 1970: 160, 161, 162, 163, 165, 166, 408n420). Considerable biographical material on Father Ortiz may be found in Puckett, edited by Fray Angelico Chavez (1950: 265–95).

969. Bandelier had made the acquaintance of Nicomedes Lara or [y?] Leyva in El Paso del Norte in November 1883 (Lange and Riley 1970: 160). Manu Huero was probably the same person as the Manuel Guero of the entry of November 13, 1883 (p. 165). However, Bandelier did not refer to him as the cacique at that time but rather as being with the cacique. There may have been confusion in the 1883 entry, or it may have been a case of a change in caciques during the interval between the two entries.

970. This may have been the Mr. Wilandy, presumably of Highland, Illinois, who had sent Bandelier "a poisonous letter" through Mr. Balsiger, evoking the response in that entry of May 7, 1885, of "Poor old man, I pity him."

971. On this date, Bandelier copied from the "Libbro [sic] Primero de Casamientos. El Paso del Norte. Fojas 74 y 75. 1659," which Father Ortiz had shown him. He copied the Act of Foundation (1659) and the blessing of the cornerstone (1662) of the 1888 church. A typewritten copy of the copy which Bandelier made was included in the Catron Collection (PC 29 807). It was entitled "Auto de Fundación de la Misión de Nuestra Señora de Guadalupe de los Mansos del Paso del Norte." On the second page was a copy of the 1662 document, entitled "Certificación de la Bendición de la Piedra Fundamental de la Yglesia de Nuestra Señora de Guadalupe del Paso del Norte."

Fewkes (1895: 309) listed these as "3. Decree of the establishment of the Mission of Our Lady of Guadalupe of the Mansos of Paso del Norte, Fray García de San Francisco, 1659." and "4. Certificate of benediction of the corner stone of the church of Our Lady of Guadalupe of the Pass. Fray García de San Francisco, 1662."

Bandelier also made random notes from the *First Book of Marriages.*

972. This list, entitled "Lista de los Párrocos de la Misión de N^ra S^ra de Guadalupe del Paso del Norte.—desde 3^d de Febrero 1662, hasta 13. de Marzo 1707. (Libro primero de Casamientos.—Paso del Norte.—Año de 1662.)," and consisting of four foolscap pages, was found in the Catron Collection (PC 29 807). It was in Bandelier's hand, and he noted that he had made the copy and extracts in El Paso del Norte, Mexico, on April 5, 1888. Father Ortiz had shown him the book on April 3, and on April 4, he had copied a part of it (see n 971).

973. This happy reaction to the return of Papa Bandelier to the family circle must be contrasted with the bitter statements in the journal entries of May 1885 (on the 4th of May, for example), as well as with the sentiments expressed in a letter of May 6, 1885, to García Icazbalceta (White and Bernal 1960: 280, a translation of which appears in n 136).

974. Bandelier was still annoyed at what he considered immature behavior on the part of Henry Kaune.

975. In 1856, Bishop Lamy sent his Vicar General, Reverend Joseph Machebeuf, to France to recruit additional missionaries. Among the six procured was Joseph M. Coudert, also known as José María Coudert, who had been ordained on December 12, 1856. In 1859, he was parish priest at Albuquerque. Coudert accompanied Bishop Lamy on an arduous trip from Santa Fe to visit the missionaries in Arizona and to see the principal settlements of that Territory in the autumn of 1863. As secretary to Bishop Lamy, he went to Rome with him in 1866 (Salpointe 1898: 208, 223, 240, 257, 282). Chávez (1957: 259) listed Coudert at Sandia Pueblo in February 1857. In 1880, Bandelier made the acquaintance of Father Coudert in Las Vegas, New Mexico, and they visited a number of ruins near Las Vegas (Lange and Riley 1966: 342). In 1899, he became pastor at Bernalillo (Salpointe 1898: App. VII).

976. A typewritten copy of this document was in the Catron Collection (PC 29 807). Fewkes (1895: 309) listed this as "1. Royal decree in favor of Don Juan de Oñate and his descendants. Don Philip III, 1602."

977. After this date in the journals, May 2, 1888, there were sporadic references to the fact that the Senior Bandelier was copying documents for Bandelier. Burrus (1969a: 43) noted that the handwriting of Bandelier's father appeared for the first time in the ninth volume of the Hemenway documents (see October 1, 1888, entry).

978. Hodge (1932: 366) listed, "42. Letter of Ad. F. Bandelier [on the progress of archaeological and ethnological research in America, especially in the United States]. Santa Fe, N. M., May 4, 1888. *Ninth Annual Report of the Archaeological Institute of America,* 55–61, Cambridge, 1888."

The entries of May 4 and May 5, 1888, referred to this letter.

979. This was probably the same person listed by McKenney (1888: 481) as Francisco Delgardo [*sic?*], a stenographer in Santa Fe.

980. See entry of February 23, 1888.

981. This was Mrs. Julius H. Gerdes (see n 286).

982. Burrus (1969b: 17), in referring to this journal entry, wrote, "I have not come across any data to explain his compilation of Pima vocabularies for Peñafiel." The editors are unaware of any extensive Pima vocabulary compiled by Bandelier. He had been among the Pima in June 1883, and the journal entries of that period contained a number of Pima words with their English equivalents (Lange and Riley 1970: 121–41). Part of that time, Judge J. D. Walker, whom Bandelier considered the greatest living authority on the Pima, was with him (see n 927).

983. Aside from the scattered references in the journals, nothing further has been learned about Alejandro E. Campbell. Quite obviously, Bandelier had considerable interaction with him at Santa Clara and the vicinity and valued Campbell as a source of information as well as for his friendship.

984. This may have been H. I. Bartsch who was listed in McKenney's Directory for 1888–9 as a partner with Henry F. Wulff in Bartsch & Wulff, wholesale liquors, west side of the plaza, Santa Fe.

It might also have been the H. G. Bartsch, tobacconist in Santa Fe, mentioned in n 833.

985. The dispute between the two factions at Santa Clara had longlasting ramifications, permeating to many facets of the tribal culture (see Parsons [1929: 9, 105–6, 113–4; 1939: 15] for later appraisals of this controversy).

986. Apparently, several successive Santa Clara pueblos have been called by the name Kapo. See Harrington (1916: 247) for his discussion of the site referred to in this entry and for his unsuccessful attempts to obtain the etymology of this term (pp. 240–41).

987. Here, Bandelier was adding to his knowledge about the Rito de los Frijoles, a standing interest; the Santa Clara term augmented the Tewa data which he had gathered at San Juan earlier (see n 228). All of this research contributed to the authenticity of his novels, *Die Köshare* and *The Delight Makers*, on which he was then working, revising, expanding, and translating (see n 50).

988. Archbishop Salpointe had established day schools at the pueblos of Cochiti, San Felipe, Santa Clara, and Zia in 1888 with money he had received from collections in the Catholic churches throughout the United States for the education of Indians and Negroes. These schools lasted three years at the first three pueblos mentioned, but for only one year at Zia (Salpointe 1898: 274). Bandelier's comments were in relation to his official assignment from Father Stephan (see n 1003).

989. The specific "diligencia" of this entry has not been identified. Stressing the importance of this kind of document, Bandelier (1893: 293) wrote, "The papers called *Diligencias Matrimoniales, or Informaciones,* official inquiries to determine the civil standing of the contracting parties, which preceded every marriage, were the most numerous. Many of these are very long; some of them are of the seventeenth century and they unfold an extremely instructive picture of the customs of those times."

990. For a general discussion of the Santa Clara archives, see n 618. Presumably, Felix Valverde [Velarde] was the "intelligent, tolerably clear-seeing, citizen of the village," of that note, although Bandelier did not actually name the archive-keeper in his discussion.

In his April 6, 1889, entry, Bandelier wrote the name as "Felix Velarde"; this remark was in connection with a letter he wrote to Velarde. On April 10, 1889, he noted receiving a letter from "Felix Velarde," and in subsequent entries, the reference was consistently to Felix, or to Don Felix, Velarde wherever the surname appeared.

As in other instances, Bandelier's early renditions of a new acquaintance's name were verbal or phonetic and sometimes erroneous. Subsequently, as correspondence was exchanged, or for some other reason, the correct rendition usually emerged. Hence, Velarde would appear to be the proper form for Don Felix of Santa Clara Pueblo.

In this regard, it must be acknowledged that Bandelier, over the years and despite considerable familiarity, persisted in misspelling the surnames of such individuals as Washington Matthews and Emil Preetorius, omitting one of the "t's" and one of the "e's" from these names, respectively.

991. Bandelier (1890–92: I, 267) dated the Santa Clara church of his day from 1761. According to Adams and Chavez (1956: 115n1), the nineteenth century church was actually begun in 1756. The earlier Franciscan church in Santa Clara had been founded by Fray Alonzo de Benavides. Presumably, it had been destroyed during the Pueblo Revolt, for another church was built around 1706. From the Domínguez account (pp. 114–16), it would seem that the 1756 church was on or near the site of the 1706 church. Further data may be found in the discussions of Kubler (1940), Walter (1916), and others.

992. The exclamation mark after the date of 1680 in this entry suggests Bandelier's elation at finding a pre-Revolt document at Santa Clara. It was entitled, "Informaciones y Diligencias matrimoniales de Diego Lucero de Godoy. (Archivos del Pueblo de Santa Clara, N° Mex°.—Avril y Juni 1680.)" In the Catron Collection (PC 29 807) was a twelve-page transcription of this document, ten pages of which were in a hand other than Bandelier's, the final two pages having been typewritten.

Above his signature, Bandelier had typed, "Es copia sacada de la copia que hize en Santa Clara, Nuevo México. A 23 May de 1888." The transcription of the document he had copied in Santa Clara was made on January 10, 1890, in Santa Fe. Fewkes (1895: 312) listed this as "2. Marriage notice and proceedings of Diego Lucero de Godoy, 1680." This was one of a very limited number of pre-Revolt documents to have survived in New Mexico.

993. This must have meant a Mr. Wallace [unidentified] rather than the settlement of Wallace, just east of Peña Blanca, which would have been too far away to fit the circumstances of this entry.

994. See n 811.

995. In the Catron Collection (PC 29 807) were two transcriptions in Bandelier's handwriting, both marked "Extracto—San Juan, N° México," and dated on the date of this entry, May 26, 1888. One was entitled "Lista de los Padres franciscanos que administraron el Pueblo de San Juan de los Caballeros, Nuevo México, desde el año de 1726, hasta el de 1776." (Libro de Casamientos de San Juan, Año de 1726.—1776.) The other was entitled, "Lista de los Padres franciscanos que administraron en Santa Clara." (Libro de Entierros—1726 á 1833) Below his signature at the end of this transcription, Bandelier had written, "Fray Ramon Gonzalez hizo edificar, en 1782, los dos retablos actuales de la Iglesia de Santa Clara; segun las inscripciones en los mismos Retablos" (see entry of May 29, 1888).

996. In a partial catalogue by Bandelier of the Hemenway documents (Catron Collection [PC 29 807]), he noted that he had copied from an authorized copy in possession of Don Juan García of San Juan. Fewkes (1895: 318) listed this item as "53. Order to the chief alcalde of Santa Cruz. Fernando de la Concha. 1793."

997. This document, copied by Bandelier, was entitled *Diligencias practicadas sobre la solicitud de el cuerpo del Venerable Padre Fray Gerónimo de la Llana* (Para el Archivo de la Custᵃ) (Archivos del Pueblo de Santa Clara, N. México.—Año de 1759).

A handwritten copy, made by Bandelier at Santa Clara, May 29, 1888, was found in the Catron Collection (PC 29 807). At the end of the document, Bandelier had noted, "Autos originales." Fewkes (1895: 317) listed this among the papers of the Hemenway Expedition as "31. Documents concerning the anxiety about the body of Fray Jerónimo de la Llana."

Francisco María [*sic*] del Valle, 1759." Another copy is now in the Peabody Museum Library, Harvard University. Miss Margaret Currier, Librarian, kindly made a comparison of the two copies for us and stated that the texts were the same but noted that there were differences in handwriting, capitalization, spelling, and the use of abbreviations and numerals.

Bandelier made considerable use of this document (see ns 183, 184, and 185). The original document has seemingly disappeared, and Bandelier's copies appear to be the only ones remaining.

At the end of his copy of this document, Bandelier included above his signature a qualifying statement that he had omitted some "formulas and repetitions" in the transcript text, and "the quotations from the work of Vetancurt."

Because of its significance, a complete translation of Bandelier's copy found in the Catron Collection is presented here. The translation is primarily the work of Jan Faust, undergraduate anthropology major, Northern Illinois University, and Luz Maria Pelaez, Secretary, Latin American Institute, Southern Illinois University—Carbondale.

Measures Taken for the Finding of the Body of the
Venerable Father Fray Gerónimo de la Llana

(For the Archives of the Custodia)

(Archives of the Pueblo of Santa Clara, New Mexico, 1759.)

Don Francisco Anttonio Marín del Valle, Governor and Captain General of this Kingdom of New Mexico and Warden of his Royal Forces and Garrisons for His Majesty, etc:—

Sr. Bachiller Don Santiago de Roybal, Vicar and Ecclesiastical Judge of this Kingdom: you are informed that having had repeated reports on the burial place in one of the ancient and deserted pueblos of the Province of las Salinas of a religious man named the Venerable Father Fray Gerónimo de la Llana whose virtue is well-known in this Kingdom, one and all verify the declaration made on October 26, 1706, in Mexico City by Rev. Fr. Fray Nicolás de Fleytas whose testimony is in my possession. I desire to see if I can find the venerable body, I am determined to leave personally on Tuesday of next week, the 27th of this month, in search [of his body], and if I am successful, it will be necessary in order to give testimony of the finding that someone from the Ecclesiastical Court go [with me]; therefore, I request and exhort you on behalf of his Majesty (God keep him), and on my part I beg you and recommend that if you cannot go in person, you send your Notary to carry this out and be ready for the day of the 27th, so he can testify to everything that occurs; that, if not done in this manner, I myself shall be obliged to do the same [as if you had done it].

Villa of Santa Fe, March 24, 1759

Francisco Anttonio Marín de Valle. (S/.)

In the town of Santa Fe on the 24th day of March, 1759, Sr. B. D. Santiago de Roibal, Vicar and Ecclesiastical Judge of this kingdom of New Mexico, its jurisdiction and districts, etc., having seen the preceding exhortation of Sr. Don

Francisco Anttonio Marín del Valle, Governor and Captain General of the
Kingdom, and finally the Honorable Vicar having been so kind as to facilitate
the most convenient means for the success of the finding of the bones of the
Venerable Rev. Fr. Gerónimo de la Llana of the Order of the Seraphic Fr. St.
Francis as contained in the exhortation; His Lordship having been injured, it
was painful for him to ride a horse for such a long distance to the Missions; His
Lordship ordered Phelipe Tafoya, the Ecclesiastical Notary Public of the town,
to be ready on the 27th day of the present month and to continue to accompany
the Governor in order to witness and give true testimony of all that should take
place during the journey, so that the petition [for the search] desired for so
many years [would be granted] and thus his Lordship the vicar resolved and
signed before me the present Certificate to which I attest.—

B: Santiago de Roibal (S/.)

Before me: Phelipe Tafoya, Notary Public (S/.)

Santa Fe, March 24, 1759

In view of the preceding reply from the Vicar and seeing in it that his
Lordship, because of his injury, could not go, he should order and did order the
message to the Vice Custodian, Manuel Zambrano, so that his superiors name
Rev. Fr. Thomas Mariano de la Cruz to accompany me as Chaplain, who on
Wednesday 28 should be at San Pedro, on which day I should be there to
continue my journey on foot, whereas I did decree, ordered and signed, I, Don
Francisco Anttonio Marín del Valle, Governor and Captain General of this
Kingdom, acting with attending witnesses to which I attest.

Marín (S/.)

Witnesses: Joseph Maldonado (S/.)—Juan Francisco de Arroniz (S/.)

In the deserted and ruined Pueblo and mission commonly called Quarac,
Province of las Salinas, on the 30th day of March, 1759, I, Don Francisco
Anttonio Marín del Valle, Governor and Captain General of this Kingdom of
New Mexico, having departed from the capital town of Santa Fe, on the 27th
day of the current month, with two squadrons of soldiers, a second lieutenant,
Don Bartholomé Fernandez, a Sergeant Bartholomé Maese, the Notary Phelipe
Tafoya, and 35 Indians, bringing all the equipment necessary for excavating
and, en route on the 28th day, at a place called Tunque we found Rev. Fr.
Ex-Vice-Custodian Thomas Murziano de la Cruz; in the company of all, I arrived at this town today, a feast day; and found here Captain Don Antonio Baca,
and the Rev. Fathers Pasqual Sospedra and Francisco Campo Redondo, with 10
neighbors and 20 Indians; and being late, I ordered nothing be done until the
following day, Saturday 31 of the current month, on which, after celebrating
Mass, the Rev. Fr. Thomas Murziano de la Cruz began to excavate, examining

the presbytery and table of the main altar, whereas I resolved, ordered, and signed, acting with attending witnesses to which I attest.—

Francisco Anttonio Marín del Valle S/.

Witnesses: Joseph Maldonado S/. Juan Francisco de Arroniz S/.

In this town of Quarac on the 31st day of the same month and year, having celebrated Mass and started excavating and separating the ruins, the Presbytery plan was found, more than two *estados* [approximately 14 feet] deep without having discovered a trace of a body in the excavations in all that area nor around the altar table. The second lieutenant Bartholomé Fernandez then informed me that the town which he had known as Quarac is now called Taxique, and that he would see Santiago Coris, an Indian from the pueblo of Santo Domingo, who had information that in the pueblo of Taxique there had appeared to some Indians on two occasions, an ecclesiastic. With this information and that of Juan el Sé, the Indian from the pueblo of Galisteo, that he had heard the Indian Tempano, now deceased, tell that when first the pueblo of Quarac was [deserted], the body of a religious man was removed, but he did not know where it had been taken. Because of that, I should order and do order that being late as it is, all work should be suspended, and tomorrow, Sunday, 1st of April, after Mass, we return to the town of Taxique to perform similar work, thus I resolve, etc., etc.—

(Signatures as above)

In this ruined and deserted pueblo and mission called Taxique, on the 1st of April, 1759 (F:3.R:), having arrived here at ten o'clock, while at church I remembered having read the Mexican collection of plays and menology [*Teatro Mexicano*] written by R. F. Fray Agustín de Vetancurt, and according to it along the mountain range which continues from the eastern pueblos on this border of the North River close to las Salinas, I believe that we are in the pueblo of Quarac and not Taxique as it is now called; it being an error easily made in names of pueblos deserted for so many years. Therefore, I ordered for the excavations to start to see if the body of the Venerable Father Gerónimo de la Llana could be found, and having commenced work in my presence and that of Rev. Fathers Thomas Murziano de la Cruz, Pasqual Sospedra, and Francisco Camporredondo, and the Ecclesiastical Notary Public, and the other soldiers, neighbors, and Spaniards; having excavated everywhere known [as] the presbytery and main altar, to the rear, seven feet [approximately] from the terreplein there about four o'clock in the afternoon on the Gospel side under a wall which was attached to the main altar table (which it is believed was done to hide the body underneath), a skeleton of an emaciated cadaver was found. The skeleton appeared to be intact and undisjointed, at the same time some fragments were found which clearly were from a box or casket; this occurred in the presence of the aforementioned Rev. Fathers, the Notary, [to whom] I said to take note so that he could attest to all that he should see. Having ordered to carefully separate the dirt from the skeleton of the cadaver, the feet, legs, and arms were disjointed, leaving the backbone complete. The ribs which form the chest and the thorax were disjointed as well as the skull which still had the teeth intact. The dirt around the bones was the color of the habit, having found some fragments of the (F:3.V:) cord, pieces of the habit, and of a silk cord, which seems to be from the Rosary, on the neck and the hair on the moist parts was still incorrupt, and on the thorax, a sort of wax from the nuspero [Néspero?=Medlar tree] already corrupt and changed to dirt, and having pulled out the skeleton and excavated another seven feet further, not a bone was found in all the presbytery nor any vestige of another body; whereas I ordered work to cease and told the Notary to attest to all that he had seen and ordered that the testimony drawn from the declaration made by Rev. Fr. Fray Nicolás de Fleytas be added to these writings, and to clarify whether the Pueblo called Taxique is in reality Quarac. I ordered that upon arrival at the Capital the book titled "Teatro Mexicano" written by the Rev. Fr. Fray Agustín de Betancurt be requested and reviewed for the part related to establishing the true identity of Quarac or Taxique and, whatever the date, it should be put on these writings. If it should turn out to be Quarac, the material that this "Teatro" has on the Venerable Fr. Fray Gerónimo de la Llana, should be abstracted and the attestation given by the Notary be added to these writings, thus I resolve.

(Signature as above)

(F:4.R:) Corrected—:

On October 26, 1706, the Rev. Fr. Fray Nicolás de Fleytas declared that in the Convent of Quarac, Province of Las Salinas, when he went to visit the Shrine, he removed the body of the Venerable Father Fray Gerónimo de la Llana, whom he had buried in a very humid spot and, after ten years, had found him intact and incorrupt in his habit and put him in a pine wooden casket and placed it on the table of the main altar and between his hands he placed a parchment with the inscription that the Father was an apostolic man.—

In like manner in the Convent of San Lorenzo de las Pecuries [Picurís] he found in mid-church the body, buried there, of the Venerable Father Fray Asensio de Sarate and who in that vicinity was considered a man of great virtues, and he put him in another casket, placing him on the main altar, and he signed on the day, month, and year in this our Convent of San Francisco of Mexico.—

Fray Nicolás de Fleytas (S/.)

This testimony agrees with the original (to which I refer) from which I, Don Francisco Anttonio Marín del Valle, Governor and Captain General of this Kingdom of New Mexico, had it copied and it is certain and true, corrected, and amended and to witness the writing, correcting, and amending were present Dr. Juan Joseph Moreno, Don Carlos Franz, and Don Francisco Guerrero, neighbors and residents of this town of Santa Fe, and so it may be on record for convenient purposes, I sign it on the tenth day of the month of September of 1758, acting with attending witnesses, I attest.—

In testimony of the truth I set my signature:

Francisco Anttonio Marín del Valle (S/.)

Witnesses attending: Joseph Maldonado (S/.)—Juan Francisco de

Arroniz (S/.)

(F:5.R:)

In the ruined pueblo called Taxique of the Province named Salinas of the Kingdom of New Mexico on the first day of April, 1759, I, Phelipe Tafoya, ecclesiastical Notary Public of the Capital City of Santa Fe, having been sent for that purpose by the Vicar and Ecclesiastical Judge of the Kingdom, Bachiller Don Santiago Roybal, at the request of Don Francisco Anttonio Marín del Valle, political Governor, Captain General and Warden of the Royal Forces and Garrisons of the mentioned Kingdom: I certify, attest, and give true testimony of how the Governor proceeded in search of the body, deceased and buried, of the Venerable Fr. Fray Gerónimo de la Llana of the Order of the Seraphic Fr. St. Francis by virtue of a declaration made of the location of the body by Rev. Fr. Nicolás Freitas which was *on the main altar of the pueblo Quara* [*Quarac*], *Province of las Salinas,* as revealed in the declaration included herein, an exact copy of the original which remains filed in the convent of the City of Santa Fe. His Lordship decided to depart personally from the City in search of the body on the 27th day of March of said year taking as his chaplain, the Rev. Fr. ex-Vice-Custodian Fray Thomas Murziano de la Cruz, and having arrived at the Province of Salinas and pueblo which was called Quara on the 30th day of the month of March, he found there Don Antonio Baca, mayor and military captain of the town of Albuquerque, to whom his Lordship had sent a message to meet him there for that purpose, and the Rev. Fathers Pasqual Sospedra and Francisco Campo Redondo, who had offered to accompany the mayor, and because nightfall was near his Lordship suspended all work. On the following day, the 31st of March, it being Saturday, his Lordship ordered the aforementioned chaplain to celebrate Mass to Our Lady of Light. After his Lordship and all his people had heard it, [they began] separating the ruins, to excavate all the area recognized as and being well-known as having served as a chapel and main altar, which was done all that day. His Lordship, having seen that more than 14 feet had been excavated and that the sun was beginning to go down and not a vestige or sign of the body, again called and asked those considered to have the most accurate information on the Pueblo, Spaniards as well as Indians, in order to see if by chance an error had been made. Could it be that some other of the neighboring pueblos was the Quara mentioned in the declaration? To which the Second Lieutenant of the Royal Garrison, Don Bartholomé Fernandez, said that he had always known as Quara the nearby ruined town they had passed and which his Lordship had seen when they passed it the previous day, and that this had been his understanding all his life. The most Hispanicized Indian, named Santiago Coris, said that in the last town which they called and had for Taxique, he knew and had heard truthful Indians say that there had appeared a religious man on two occasions to two Indians and that the final one died on the third day. The Tano Indian of the pueblo of Gallisteo called el Che, also very Hispanicized, said that he knew and had heard several times, that a very old Indian called Tempano (F:5.V:) who had come from these old ruined pueblos had told that the town called Quara was deserted first, and that the remaining people from there had joined the Indians of the nearest town called Taxique, and that when Quara was deserted the body of a deceased religious man had been removed but that he didn't know where it had been taken; that it was thus that the old Indian, Tempano, told it. With this information, his lordship decided to return the following day to the town called Taxique to perform the same work in search of the body and on the first day of April he ordered his chaplain to celebrate Mass, and his lordship and his people having heard it, they departed and arrived about ten o'clock that day at the town called Taxique. [The Governor] immediately ordered and went personally to the ruined church of the pueblo to see the clearing and excavating of all the area on the site which was definitely recognized as having served as a chapel and main altar. About four in the afternoon, after having excavated approximately seven feet on the Gospel side, at the same level of what was known as the main altar, separated by a small adobe wall, they supposed, some pieces of wood were found, which because of the lace they had, appeared to be from the casket. On separating the dirt with their hands, the whole skeleton of an emaciated body was discovered with some fragments of a habit still incorrupt and on the neck some fragments of a silk string, the kind used for stringing a small rosary, with the brains of the skull not completely corrupt but clinging to the skull. The entire skeleton appeared to have measured seven cuartas [approximately 63 inches]. This was seen and recorded in my presence by the Governor and the aforementioned Rev. Father Alferez, Chief Mayor, and other soldiers, Spaniards, and Indians who were present. His Lordship ordered that a chest be brought and that in it be arranged the bones and the other fragments which were found pertaining to the religious man, in order to transfer it to the Church of the Convent of the City of Santa Fe. After this was done in his presence, his Lordship ordered me, the Notary, to give testimony and attest to all that has been referred and to excavate another seven feet deeper from where the bones had been found which was done and seeing that no vestiges of a grave appeared he ordered a halt, and decided to return on the following day to the Capital City of Santa Fe. All of which I certify, attest, and give true testimony of having taken place in my presence, as I have referred. And so that it shall be available where and as it shall be most suitable, I give the present certification, attestation, and testimony at the request of the aforementioned Governor in the mentioned pueblo called Taxique on said day, month, and year, and sign with my own hand and customary flourish.—

Phelipe Tafoya, Notary Public (S/.)

(F:6.R:)

In the Capital City of Santa Fe on the 7th day of the month of April, 1759, I, Don Francisco Anttonio Marín del Valle, Governor, having arrived here about five o'clock in the afternoon, I quickly requested the "Teatro Mexicano" written by the Rev. Fr. Agustín de Betancurt, and recognized from the 3rd chapter, which begins on 94th page, [material] which deals with the Custodia of the Conversion of St. Paul of New Mexico; page 103 on the pueblo of Chilili: which is the first one in the valley of las Salinas. The following one [Betancurt] names Concepción de Quarac, being the second pueblo where the body was removed, as expressed in the preceding certification, known in this Kingdom by the Spaniards by the name of Taxique. I should declare, and I do declare, that the one called Taxique is (in reality) Concepción de Quarac. After this pueblo follows San Miguel Taxique, according to the aforementioned history, and then San Gregorio Abbo, which are the pueblos on the mountain chain east of the Sandía mountain range. According to the description, there is absolutely no doubt that [the mission] where the body was removed is Quarac, and not Taxique, and there is also no doubt that the bones removed are those of the Rev. Fr. Gerónimo de la Llana, and so it will be on record, etc. etc.—

Francisco Anttonio Marín del Valle (S/.)

Witnesses: Joseph Maldonado (S/.)—Juan Francisco de Arroniz (S/.)

(Following are the Extracts of the works of Fr. Agustín de Vetancurt: *"Crónica de la Provincia de Santo Evangelio de México,"* p. 103. Par. 59. *"Menologio Franciscano,"* p. 75, with certification and witnesses. [Bandelier's (?) notations.])

Santa Fe, April 10, 1759

Having prepared the preceding writings, I should order and (F:7.R:) I do order that the originals by request and commission be given to Rev. Fr. Manuel Zambrano, Vice Custodian of the Holy Custody and President Minister of this Mission of the City of Santa Fe, so that the Principal orders the Rev. Fathers Thomas Murziano de la Cruz; Pasqual Sospedra, and Francisco Camporredondo, who were present at the finding of the bones of the Rev. Fr. Gerónimo de la Llana, to reveal right after what they saw and that these writings be returned to me. Thus I decree, etc., etc.—

(Signatures as above)

In this Mission of St. Francis of the City of Santa Fe, on April 16, 1759, Fray Manuel Zambrano of the religious community of St. Francis, retired Notary, etc. of the Holy Office, Ex-Inspector, Ex-Vice Custodian, several times, and present Vice-Custodian of this Holy Shrine of the Conversion of St. Paul of New Mexico, orders the Rev. Missionary Fathers Thomas Murziano de la Cruz, Francisco Campo Redondo, and Fray Pasqual Sospedra, to express and declare what they saw in the discovery and finding of the bones of the above mentioned Venerable Fr. Gerónimo de la Llana, in the manner requested by the Governor and Captain General of this Kingdom, Don Francisco Anttonio Marín del Valle, in the preceding [writing], for which we recommend the above mentioned Fathers to declare at the foot of this writing [what they saw] as expressed in the Governor's request. These, our letters, having been given in an envelope of the

Convent of the City of Santa Fe, on the same day, month, and year, and signed by our undersigned Provisional Secretary.—

Fr. Manuel Zambrano (S/.)
Vice Custodian

Fr. Joseph de Urgijo (S/.)
Provisional Secretary

In this Mission of San Felipe de Jesús on the 17th day of April, 1759, I, Fray Thomas Murciano de la Cruz, General and Provincial Superior of this Mission, immediately upon receiving the order from a higher authority regarding that expressed by the Rev. Father Vice Custodian Manuel Zambrano, and the request and recommendation made by the Governor Captain General of this Kingdom, Don Francisco Anttonio Marín del Valle, I set forth, declare, and certify in the best manner I can and should: that I saw with my eyes, recognized, touched everything in the finding of the preceding and truly esteemed bones of the Venerable Fr. Fray Gerónimo de la Llana, set forth and declare in these writings the said Governor, etc. etc. on page three; and the envelope from the Notary Public, Ecclesiastical Don Phelipe Tafoya, in his reliable testimony on page five, to which I refer, for it being the same declaration and testimony and complete and exact expression of all that I saw, recognized, touched, and in my presence took place. And so that it may be on record wherever or however it may be more fitting by my own hand, I sign—etc., etc., etc.—

Fr: Thomas Murciano de la Cruz (S/.)

(F:7.V:)—(The same declarations in the same tenor follow by the other Fathers, Fray Francisco Campo Redondo, in S<u>ta</u>. Ana, April 18, 1759, and Fray Pasqual Sospedra, in Isleta, April 26, 1759. [Bandelier's (?) notations.])

(F:8.R:)—City of Santa Fe, April 25, 1759.—

Regarding the following writings on the finding of the cadaver of the Venerable Father Fray Gerónimo de la Llana, having heard that in this Kingdom there were widespread reports on the great virtue of this religious man, and that God, Our Lord, by intercession of the Venerable Father, had worked some miracles: I said that these writings be given to Sr. Don Santiago de Roybal, Vicar and Ecclesiastical Judge of this kingdom, so that his lordship by request and recommendation investigate the reports on said Venerable Fr. Fray Gerónimo de la Llana, and having completed them, to return them to me. Whereas I resolved, ordered, and signed, etc., etc., etc.—

Marín (S/.)

Witnesses: Juan Francisco de Arroniz (S/.)—Miguel de Aliri (S/.)

In the Capital City of Santa Fe, etc., etc., on the 14th day of May, 1759, the Señor Bachiller Don Santiago de Roybal, Vicar, etc., etc., having seen the preceding decree, dated April 25, of the current year, issued by Don Francisco Marín del Valle, Governor, etc., etc., in which by request and recommendation he asks his Lordship to investigate the reports made by some persons of this Kingdom regarding the great virtue and high opinion in which the Venerable Father Fray Gerónimo de la Llana died; and that the Governor with his great zeal and effectiveness succeeded in finding the cadaver of the above mentioned Father in the pueblo of Quaraa [Quarac] as recorded in the testimony and certification of the Notary Public and of the Rev. Fathers appearing in these writings. His Lordship said that he had no jurisdiction in such affairs as these, as evaluations of the fame, sanctity, virtues, wonders, prodigies or miracles of servants of God are bestowed by office and apostolic constitutions on the Diocesan Bishops or to whom they should designate for which reason his Lordship could not possibly take over juridically said investigations, that he could only participate as a witness of exception, and certify to what he had heard said on the subject of the Venerable Fr. Fray Gerónimo. I ordered and your Lordship ordered that these original writings remain in the archive of this Ecclesiastical Court, and that the Notary Public draw the testimony to the letter and return it to the Governor for the purposes he may deem convenient.—Whereas his Lordship the Vicar resolved, ordered, and signed, etc., etc.—

Br. Santiago de Roibal (S/.)

Before me: Phelipe Tafoya (S/.)
Notary Public

I, Bachiller Don Santiago de Roibal, a native of this Kingdom of New Mexico, a presbytery cleric residing at the Bishopric of Durango, Vicar, etc., etc., say that I certify as much as I can and should (due to the great distance to the Bishopric and so that no delay occur in these matters) that since the year 1728 when I was ordained a priest, I have been hearing and seeing the desire, and the longing of the governors, missionaries, and settlers to remove the body of the Venerable Fray Gerónimo de la Llana from the ruined missions of the Province of las Salinas of this jurisdiction, in the pueblo called Quaraa. The great virtue and piety in which he—being the Benjamin, or youngest, of the custodia —lived and died, has been, and still is being, discussed. These measures have continued to the current year of 1759 in which the present Governor Don Francisco Anttonio Marín del Valle, with great care, and effectiveness, clarity, and zeal, decided to personally go in the company of the Rev. Missionary Fathers and my Notary Public for the purpose of seeing if he could obtain what so many others had longed for. Taking with him the declaration made by Rev. Fr. Fray Nicolás de Fleytas in the Convent of San Francisco of Mexico on the 26th day of October, 1706, who buried him, and having returned ten years later found him intact and incorrupt, and placed him within the table of the main altar, [the Governor] succeeded as shown in the certification of my notary, and the Rev. Fathers. The cadaver was brought by him to this Capital City of Santa Fe for burial; this having been of singular joy for all the inhabitants of this Kingdom, as upon arrival at the door of the church, the order was given to toll three or four times, and the Sacristans instead of tolling gave out solemn peals without being able to control themselves.

I have known and heard tell that in the recent year of 1753, an Indian from the pueblo of Cochiti while hunting in those missions in the same pueblo of Quaraa had appeared to him a Father saying that he was buried there and asked him to deliver the message that he be removed from there and be buried in the Sanctuary, having warned him that after delivering the message he would die and would go and accompany him, which happened as said. And from the descendants of the people who participated in the [Reconquest of New Mexico] I have heard several tell special things about the life of the Venerable Father. The discovery of the body produced more stories, the first one being Pasquala Vasquez, mestiza more than a hundred years old, who told me that while her parents were living at the Post of el Alamo an Indian called Don Esteban arrived at the mission from Quaraa who told her parents that Fr. Fray Gerónimo, not having a kitchen, a cook, not even fire in the convent, at regular meal times would order the table be set and, without knowing from where the food came, he would eat tasty food and dine. He also heard him talk and laugh sometimes, which caused him admiration, and he attested to this with two Sacristans that were with him from the Pueblo; that his bed was the floor and his pillow an adobe. Don María Marquez, a reliable person, told me that he always heard his greatgrandmother Juana say that Doña Catharina de Zalazar had told her that when she lived in her ranch, in the jurisdiction of the Pueblo of Quaraa, the Venerable Fr. Fray Gerónimo de la Llana arrived there. At that time, the daughter-in-law of Doña Catharina was having a problem pregnancy because of a strong craving for a lettuce and trout salad—this was in the month of January—to which the Father said that he didn't owe them anything [whereupon] he asked them for some trifle [Literally, "a pin," *un alfiler,* but perhaps a miscopying of *alfileres,* "trifles," or "small change."] and went out and found in a room an Indian woman who had been a cripple for seven years. He ordered her to get up and go out to the vegetable garden with a shovel, remove the snow, and search for lettuces. When she showed reluctance, he took her by the hand and sent her in good health to the vegetable garden, and she brought the lettuces which had headed under the snow, and after a while the Venerable Father came with a trout in his hands which he caught in a spring near the house, and having made the salad the problem pregnancy stopped. This being over, the Venerable Father said to the aforementioned Catharina that his arrival there had been to see if they would lend him a mount to go to his Mission to say Mass, that it was Saturday and the woman answered, lamenting that there were nothing but just some wild mares in the corral, and that he accepted and went and got one with his cord and saddled her and found her gentle to the reins as he left.

In like manner, Salvador Gonzales, a resident of this town, told me that in the year 1739 he had gone to the post of Temochi, Mission of Sonora. Present were a Jesuit, Father Juan Anttonio, and Fr. Landor, the head of this Mission, [who] said: you poor souls, you have come from so great a distance with so much danger and hardships in search of livelihood, have hope in God that in removing the body of the Venerable Fr. Fray Gerónimo who is buried in Quaraa and reburying him in the Parish of New Mexico, it will become the new Mexico. Sr. Gonzales up to then had never heard of such a Father. These and other things are what I have heard tell now and before in this Kingdom, of the Venerable Fr. Fray Gerónimo de la Llana, of his many and exemplary virtues, being considered as a just and saintly man to all of which I certify having thus heard, and in case your most illustrious Lordship should order an investigation and some having died, as shown in my certification, making the necessary attestation for whatever may arise where this may be presented, on the present I sign my name with the customary flourish before my Notary Public on the 16th day of the month of May of the year 1759, I attest.—

Br. Santiago de Roibal—(S/.)

Before me:

Phelipe Tafoya (S/.)
Notary Public

[This] is a copy, minus some formulas and repetitions indicated in the text of the same copy, and the quotations from the work of Vetancurt. Pueblo of Santa Clara, New Mexico, May 20, 1888.—

Ad F. Bandelier (S/.)

Original decrees.

998. According to a list Bandelier copied at San Juan Pueblo (see n 995), Fray Ramón Gonzalez was a priest at Santa Clara from 1782 to 1784.

999. Many of these documents were listed in the Fewkes Catalogue of the Hemenway Expedition documents (1895). Fewkes identified some as having come from the Santa Clara Archives, but many known to have come from the same collection were not so identified. Examination of Bandelier's copies in the Peabody Museum Library, Harvard, would undoubtedly enable one to determine this, as it is the editors' understanding that this information was included by Bandelier for each document. As mentioned in n 618, the editors do not know the location of the original documents copied at Santa Clara by Bandelier in May 1888.

1000. Bandelier considered these items to have been among his most important documentary discoveries. The significant data were contained in two documents at Santa Clara, prompting his entry, "wrote to Mr. Parkman about l'Archévèque." As noted earlier, the Massachusetts Historical Society had no letters of Bandelier to Parkman written in 1888, and so we have relied on information in Bandelier's *The Gilded Man* (1893) to reconstruct the sequence of events.

The first document Bandelier cited (p. 294) was "Information'of Pedro Meusnier—a Frenchman—1699." Fewkes (1895: 313) listed this as "12. Marriage notice and proceedings of Pedro Meusnier and Lucia Madrid. 1699." In the Xerox copy of a partial catalog by Bandelier of the Hemenway documents (Catron Collection [PC 29 807]), this was listed as, "1699. Ynformación y diligencias matrimoniales de Pedro Meusnier y Lucia Madrid. (Santa Clara.)" Bandelier had typed in the adjoining column, "Vease Archeveque. El casamiento tuso lugar en El Paso Diciembre 28 1699."

The second document Bandelier cited (p. 295) was an *Información* about Santiago Grolee. In Fewkes (1895: 316), Grolee was incorrectly given as Geollet and Giollet, in the Spanish and English listings, respectively. It was listed as "8. Marriage notice of Santiago Giollet [*sic*]. 1699." Bandelier's partial catalog curiously gave no date, but he wrote, "Informaciones matrim^les de Santiago Grolee (Grollet) y de Elena Gallegos. (Santa Clara.)"

In the column adjoining, Bandelier had written, "De la Rochela 'vide: libro de Bautismos de Bernalillo, 2 Abril, 1703. Baut² del hijo Antonio." Bandelier (1893: 294–95) commented, "The supposition seems at least well founded that Juan de Archeueque was the traitor L'Archévèque, and Santiago Grolee was his accessory in a lesser degree, the sailor Grollet."

Bandelier wasted no time in publishing on his findings. "The Betrayer of La Salle," appeared in *The Nation*, August 30, 1888 (Hodge 1932: 366[#40]). Hodge added, "Dated 'Santa Fé, August 13, 1888.' " Hodge [#43] also listed an article in German, "Jean L'Archévèque, *New-Yorker Staats-zeitung*, Mär 24, 1889." Bandelier utilized many of these data in Part V of his *Contributions* (1890a: 179–206) and in *The Gilded Man* (1893: 289–302) devoted a chapter to Jean L'Archévèque.

Twitchell (1914: I, 13–14) quoted extensively from Bandelier's article in *The Nation*. He commented that Bandelier had been the first writer in English to identify the writer of a specific document (pp. 12–13) as the Jean L'Archévèque of the ill-fated La Salle expedition although an account of L'Archévèque's purchase from the Texas Indians by Governor Alonzo Leon by Palacio Rivas in his *A Través de Los Siglos,* which had been published several years prior to Bandelier's article had already made this identification. Bandelier noted the fact that he had not seen Leon's original report in Washington but cited two accounts, one by Fray Isidro Felis Espinosa [1746] and one by P. Andres Cavo, S. J. [n. d.]. [Bandelier had made notes on Cavo while in Munich; see n 40.] Both Espinosa and Cavo gave full details of the event (Bandelier 1890a: 180n2). Bandelier also cited Cavo in *The Gilded Man* (p. 295). These accounts were not mentioned by Twitchell, but they do show that Bandelier was aware of pertinent earlier Spanish sources. He considered his work with the Santa Clara archives served to confirm Cavo's statements. Bandelier continued to search at Santa Clara and in Santa Fe for documents which reinforced his identification of L'Archévèque and rounded out his biography.

1001. For discussion of the several Santa Clara churches, see n 991.

1002. Bandelier had noted church books at Santa Cruz de la Cañada when he visited there on December 1, 1883 (Lange and Riley 1970: 172–73). He had found books from San Diego de Xemes [Jemez] there, and this entry indicates that some of the Santa Clara archives had also been taken to Santa Cruz. It is interesting that on this date, Bandelier's copying was from a Jemez book at Santa Cruz. It was entitled "Lista de los Padres Franciscanos, Curas de la Mission [*sic*] de San Diego de Jemez, desde el año de 1720, hasta el año de 1769" (Libro de Défuntos de Jemez,—Parroquia de Santa Cruz, 4 de Agusto 1720). This copy, in Bandelier's hand, was in the Catron Collection (PC 29 807). Bandelier noted "Extracto—fecho en Santa Cruz de la Cañada, N° México a 1ª de Junio de 1888."

1003. Bandelier had been working for some time with the Bureau of Indian Affairs, or, more properly, the Bureau of Catholic Indian Missions. He had been engaged on November 14, 1887, by Father Stephan (see n 588) for one year, beginning December 1, 1887, at $25.00 per month and travel expenses.

1004. The *Santa Fe Daily New Mexican,* October 22, 1887 (p. 3), described the opening of the University of New Mexico, Santa Fe, "The first Protestant college of New Mexico," September 5, 1887. Among the staff members was listed E. L. Cole, A. M., Instructor in Mathematics and English Literature. In our second volume (1970: 490), "Mr. Cole" was indexed as of Santa Fe with several citations regarding his excavations on the Arroyo Hondo, Peñas Negras, and Fort Marcy. He was also noted several times in our first volume (1966: 431).

1005. This letter to Parkman was not included among those of which copies were obtained from the Massachusetts Historical Society.

1006. Many of the letters from Bandelier to Parkman in the collection of the Massachusetts Historical Society end, "With best regards to Miss Parkman." Francis Parkman lived with his sister. The editors believe the "letter from Mrs. Parkman" in this entry was simply a mistake and Bandelier actually meant Miss Parkman.

1007. Will M. Tipton was a native of Nebraska, moving to Santa Fe in the late 1870s. There, he became a translator in the office of the surveyor-general, Henry M. Atkinson. Largely through the efforts of Levi A. Hughes and Tipton, the fraudulent claim of James Addison Perálta-Reavis and wife to 12,467,456 acres, covering "all of the best portion of Arizona and about half of New Mexico," was rejected in June 1895, by the Court of Private Land Claims which had been created by Congress in 1891. Familiarity with and interest in the documents in the surveyor-general's office obviously gave Bandelier and Tipton much that was of common interest (Twitchell 1925: 419–27).

1008. Although there was no mention in the journal entry, Bandelier, on July 2, 1888, copied a document entitled "Testimonio de Real Cédula, dirigida al Comandante General de las Provincias Internas de Nueva España" (Archivos territoriales, Santa-Fé, N° México, Año de 1815). A copy of this document in Bandelier's writing was in the Catron Collection (PC 29 807). Bandelier noted that he compared and corrected the copy.

1009. The papers were some of the possessions of David J. Miller, who had died in St. Louis, Missouri, December 22, 1887 (see n 174).

B. Ellis (1968: 5–9) reported on five original manuscript documents from the Spanish and Mexican periods of New Mexico history. They had been found among the papers of Paul A. F. Walter in an envelope with a notation that they had "Belonged to D. J. Miller, long-time Chief Clerk and Translator in the U. S. Surveyor General's Office in Santa Fe, and in 1888 had been loaned to Adolph F. A. Bandelier, then in Santa Fe engaged in Southwestern research" (p. 5). Ellis went on to say that, judging from the Catalogue of the Hemenway Expedition, Bandelier had made copies of at least three of them.

These remarks are interesting in light of Bandelier's attempt in this entry to give a receipt to someone for the documents he was borrowing from the David J. Miller estate. A translation of one of these documents, with editorial comments, followed Ellis's introductory page.

This was a proclamation by Don Ygnacio María Sanchez Vergara, Alcalde Mayor of Jemez in the Province of New Mexico. The document was dated Jemez, April 25, 1813, and was designated as Document 1092c in the Spanish Archives of New Mexico. Fewkes (1895: 326) listed this as "8. Order of the Chief Alcalde Mayor de la Jurisdición de Jemez. Papers of David J. Miller, Santa Fe, 1813." Fewkes (p. 314) listed also "26. Copy of a document concerning the foundation of Albuquerque, Santa María de Orado and San Diego de Pojuaque. Ignacio Flores Mogollón, 1713." An additional listing in Fewkes (p. 326) was "14. Promulgation of the decree of the Provincial Assembly of New Mexico, ordering a loan of 12,000 pesos. 1845." [A partial catalogue of documents in the Catron Collection (PC 29 807) by Bandelier noted that both of these were from the David J. Miller papers.]

1010. This was Frank W. Clancy, born in New Hampshire in 1852. Clancy came to New Mexico in 1874 and was admitted to the bar of the Territory the same year. In 1879 Clancy was appointed Clerk of the Supreme Court for a period of three and half years. Clancy practiced in Santa Fe from 1883 to 1891 (Anonymous 1895: 330).

1011. Bandelier made no mention of it in his journal entry, but on this date, July 5, 1888, he copied, in Santa Fe, a document entitled, "Ayuntamiento de Cochiti: cuenta q^e manifiesta el fondo q^e reconose este Ayuntam^{to} con explicación de la entrada Salida y existencia q^e a havido hasta la presente" (papers belonging to the firm of Catron, Clancy

& Knaebel, Santa Fé, N. M.—No. 85). Fewkes (1895: 326) listed this as "10. City Council of Cochiti: account showing the capital which this Council recognizes, with a statement of the receipts, disbursements, and stock up to the present time." The document was dated 1826 and was in Bandelier's handwriting.

1012. See n 639.

1013. See also n 712.

1014. By the time Bandelier wrote his Final Report (1890–92: II, 84), these site names had been slightly altered: T'o B'hi-päng-ge, Ke-gua-yo, A-ga Uo-no, and Ka-ä-yu, respectively. The recent study by Ellis (1964a: 38–42) has brought the identification of ancestral Nambé sites more up to date. Utilizing the interest of Antonio Trujillo, First Councilman of Nambé, Ellis recorded the following designations for the four sites, in order: Nambe bugge, Kekwaiye ouinge, Ago'wano ouinge, and Agá wi ouinge. For the first site, she was able to add the designation, L.A. 254.

1015. Harrington (1916: 357) noted, "It is said Mr. Fritz Müller of Santa Fe owns a mineral spring situated in the hills south of Nambé and east of Tesuque."

1016. As noted in n 251, Nambé Pueblo had experienced a gradual decline in population during the nineteenth century. Undoubtedly, part of the decrease was due to various epidemics which were very common among the pueblos at that period, but many Nambé were said to have left because of the rash of executions for witchcraft (see n 1017).

1017. The details of this witch trial and execution of 1855 were given Bandelier by Don Juan Luján who lived near Nambé Pueblo. Bandelier took down the account on July 12, 1888, and the following morning it was verified in all important details by the cacique of Nambé. The executioner was Juan Diego Trujillo who had died in 1887. Luján's account was recorded in Spanish and entitled, "Relación del Descubrimiento y Castigo de los Brujos de Nambé." It was written in longhand and was a part of the Catron Collection (PC 29 807). The July 12 date is at variance with the journal entries.

Nambé seems to have had something of a reputation for witch executions. Parsons (1929: 304–6) received information on the execution of a witch from a somewhat later period than that of Bandelier, probably from around the turn of the century.

1018. This was Captain John G. Bourke. Although Bourke's name has appeared from time to time in the journals, this was the first entry to record an actual meeting. Like Bandelier, Bourke visited most of the pueblos and made notes on his observations. Bourke's diaries on the Southwest were edited by Lansing B. Bloom (1936; 1937; 1938) and published serially in the New Mexico Historical Review (see n 98).

1019. Salpointe (1898: 283) listed this priest as Luciano Remuson, one of those brought to New Mexico by Lamy. The Lamy Memorial (1950: 71) listed Reverend L. Remuzon as having served at Peñasco from 1876–78 and at Santa Cruz de la Cañada, 1875–80.

1020. This was Bandelier's first visit to the spectacular Valle Grande (Big Valley), an enormous depression formed by a series of Pleistocene volcanic explosions that rained volcanic debris on much of north-central New Mexico. The connected calderas left by these eruptions form the Valle Grande, an essentially open range surrounded by timbered slopes.

1021. It is of interest here that Bandelier noted and discussed a number of pueblo ruins in the vicinity of Jemez Pueblo and then added a brief discussion on the now famous Soda Dam on the Jemez River. However, just above Soda Dam, on the western canyon wall and hence with an eastern exposure is the site of the well-known Jemez Cave. It is clearly visible from the dam below. Nonetheless, Bandelier was quite obviously not at all interested in it, either as a geological feature or as a possible site of human habitation.

In fact, excavations at the cave in 1934 and 1935 were carried on with the results published also in 1935 (Alexander and Reiter 1935). More recently, Richard I. Ford carried on excavations at the cave in search of additional data; the results of this work have not yet been published. The cave is an important site in Southwestern culture history, but it failed to arouse the interest of Bandelier.

1022. W. S. Harroun was listed in McKenney (1888: 483) as a physician and surgeon with an office on Palace Ave. in Santa Fe. It was popular at this time to seek out thermal springs for their therapeutic value. The springs at Jemez and those near Las Vegas, N. M., were both used by Santa Fe and Albuquerque residents (note Bandelier's spelling, Haroun).

1023. Mariano S. Otero (1844–1904), of Bernalillo, was a cousin of Miguel A. Otero, territorial governor of New Mexico (1897–1906) (Otero 1939: 82).

Mariano Otero was a stockman, landowner, and coal-mine operator. In 1893, he moved to Albuquerque and became a leading banker (Anderson 1907: II, 544).

1024. See Reiter 1938: Fig. 2 and Ch. II for a detailed discussion of Jemez area ruins.

1025. For comprehensive survey and appraisal of the antiquities of the Jemez area, see Reiter (1938). Harrington (1916: 390–408) and Hewett (1906: 44–51) were earlier sources utilized by Reiter; however, both merit examination for additional data not included by Reiter.

1026. Manuel Chavez was listed by Salpointe (1898: 282) as a priest added by Lamy to the New Mexico clergy. The Lamy Memorial (1950: 63) listed Reverend Manuel José Chaves at Jemez, 1876–81.

1027. It seems likely that the man and wife killed for witchcraft were the same couple mentioned by Stevenson (1894: 19) in her study of Zia Pueblo; however, she made no mention of private revenge.

Wizards and witches have been tried and punished by the war captains; capital punishment has been carried out for such offenses within the relatively recent past.

1028. This is the present-day Jemez State Monument, containing the excavated ruins of the pueblo of Giusewa and the mission, earlier identified as San Diego de los Jemez but now recognized as San José de los Jemez. See Reiter for a summary discussion of the ruins of this vicinity (1938: Fig. 2 and Ch. II).

1029. For data on Zia ceremonialism and other facets of culture, see Stevenson (1894) and White (1962).

1030. It is of interest to compare these data on the Pecos survivors with those published by Parsons (1925: 130–35) as a portion of her Jemez monograph. Reconciling the differences and working out correlations in identifications would constitute an interesting and rewarding research project in data retention and retrieval.

1031. Bandelier's data in this entry, both in regard to the age of the church and an earlier site for the pueblo, were in error. See n 874 for the history of the Zia church, and n 872 for recent archaeological dating of Zia Pueblo.

1032. A brief history of Santa Ana Pueblo was given in n 875, placing the occupation of the present location as 1700. White (1942: 23) placed Santa Ana on the Mesa de Santa Ana up to 1687 at which time it was destroyed by the Spanish. He doubted Bandelier's statement (1890–92: II, 194) that ruins on the Mesa del Cangelón were prehistoric Santa Ana. Bandelier's statement in this entry that the first Santa Ana pueblo was in the caja southwest of the present village site was not included in his *Final Report* nor was it mentioned by White.

In addition to White's monograph on Santa Ana Pueblo (1942), the reader is referred to Fox (1967) for an interpretation of Keresan culture history. In fashioning his "Keresan Bridge" within Puebloan culture, Fox grouped Santa Ana with Zia under the designation Central Keresans, as contrasted with the Western Keresans, Acoma and Laguna, and the

Eastern, Cochiti, Santo Domingo, and San Felipe. Also of interest in this regard are White's study of "Keresan Medicine Societies" (1930) and Lange's discussion of "The Keresan Component in Southwestern Pueblo Culture" (1958).

1033. Vespers were noted at a number of Rio Grande pueblos on the evening prior to a major feast day, including the Feast of Santa Ana, July 26, 1969, by M. Kathleen Daly and Nanciellen Davis, graduate students in anthropology, Southern Illinois University, Carbondale. Bandelier's entry indicates that this was a long-standing practice at Santa Ana Pueblo.

1034. Bandelier's description of the Santa Ana Pueblo Feast Day ceremonies provides considerable detail which has great value in time depth and also comparative studies. The ceremonies at Santa Ana have numerous parallels with other eastern Puebloan observances of this type. However, there are also a number of significant differences unique to Santa Ana; a number of these have persisted to the present time. For a comparative study of Rio Grande Pueblo *Tablita,* or Corn, Dances, see Lange 1957.

1035. This may have been B. P. Schuster, listed as a general merchant in Bernalillo in McKenney's Directory of 1888–89 (p. 450). There was also a Max Schuster, in the general merchandise business, Old Town (Albuquerque) (p. 446), and in El Paso, the same source (p. 424) gave Ben Schuster as a partner in Berrott & Schuster, wholesale liquors, 222 El Paso.

1036. This may have been I. B. Block, listed in McKenney's Directory for 1888–89 as a merchant in the Jemez area (p. 459). Dike (1958: 327) listed John B. Block as the first postmaster at Archuleta, near Jemez; the post office at Archuleta was established March 19, 1888, and was continued to January 31, 1894, when the name was changed to Perea.

Rather than two individuals, it may well be that McKenney's "I. B." should have read "J. B." since a number of similar errors have been detected in McKenney's data.

1037. Father Joseph Fialon seems to have replaced Reverend Thomas A. Hayes at Bernalillo sometime after 1859. At the time Bandelier wrote this journal entry, the resident priest was Father Etienne Parisis (Salpointe 1898: 223, 283–84).

1038. Matilda Coxe Stevenson who studied Zia Pueblo in the 1880s described the ceremonies of the Zia Snake Society in some detail (1894: 76, 88–91). In the rain and fertility ceremonies, occurring in the spring after corn planting time, snakes were handled and "fed" corn pollen. During the ceremonial period, the snakes were kept in pottery vessels, and the actual ceremonies took place in a conical structure of corn stalks some six or seven miles from the pueblo. At the close of the feeding ceremony, the snakes were exhorted to beg the cloud people for rain; then they were taken in the vessels to a shallow cave a mile or more from the ceremonial structure. The snakes were released, and the vessels were stored in the cave which was closed with a close-fitting slab to disguise the opening.

The practice of using snakes as messengers to the gods was and is widespread in the Pueblo world. Bandelier's account would seem somewhat garbled, however, since an integral part of such practices was to release the snakes for their messenger duties.

1039. Such superstitions surrounding the practice of witchcraft and countermeasures were often derived from European culture; however, it is virtually certain that a considerable body of such practices was of native Pueblo Indian culture (see Parsons 1929: 109, 128).

1040. Bandelier mentioned this Spanish settlement of Bajada, or La Bajada, frequently as it lay on his route from Santa Fe to Peña Blanca, Cochiti, and Santo Domingo. He had searched for ruins in this area and had noted them in his journal. The community lay at the base of the volcanic escarpment, several hundred feet high, commonly called La

Bajada Hill. In Spanish colonial days, it was a *visita* of Peña Blanca and later a stage station and overnight stopping place on the road to Santa Fe (American Guide Series 1940: 243). From 1870 to 1872, there was a post office there (Pearce 1965: 80). In the 1940s, there were still a few Spanish-American families living at La Bajada. Today, the village is deserted, except for a cluster of ranch buildings near the Santa Fe River.

1041. At this point in the journals, Bandelier's handwriting became almost illegible.

1042. Bandelier here was again functioning in his assignment from Father Stephan. Cochiti was one of the pueblos in which a day school had been established by the Bureau of Catholic Indian Missions in 1888 (see n 988). The Cochiti early recognized the value of education for their children (see Lange 1959: 27).

1043. Danckengny was a partner in a Belen, New Mexico, wine growing operation (see Lange and Riley 1970: 366n70).

1044. Although Bandelier made no comment, this entry of August 12, 1888, was his first typewritten journal entry. The limitations of the typewriter made it necessary for him to continue to write the last several lines by hand in the bottom inch of each page.

1045. On the basis of Hodge's Bandelier Bibliography (1932: 366#40), one of these articles was: "The Betrayer of La Salle," *The Nation,* XLVII, August 30, 1888, pp. 166–67. Hodge appended to the citation a note: "Dated 'Santa Fé, August 13, 1888' " (see also n 1000). The second article for *The Nation* noted in this entry has not been identified.

1046. On September 2, 1888, Bandelier wrote to Janvier (Radin 1942: 1–5), acknowledging the letter he had received from Janvier August 16. The second and third paragraphs of his rather lengthy response (see n 1059) are pertinent to this entry of the journals.

1047. William H. Goebel was manager of the E. D. Franz store in Santa Fe (McKenney 1888: 482). See also n 486.

1048. For purposes of comparison and evaluation, the reader is referred to Lange's study of Cochiti (1959). In an effort to provide explicit time depth, many of Bandelier's data were presented to Lange's informants for comment and appraisal. All in all, most details were found to be acceptable or discrepancies could be explained in terms of culture change in the interval since Bandelier's time. Informants found outright errors to be rather few in number; in some instances, culture loss prevented informants from making an appraisal of any kind.

1049. The *Ko-ton-a,* or corn fetish (Ï'arīko, "mother," or yaya), has traditionally been among the most sacred objects at Cochiti Pueblo (Lange 1959: 101, 247, et passim). Variously decorated in different ritual contexts, this object, basically a perfect ear of blue corn in most instances, is essentially a puebloan universal. An interesting comparison, or contrast, to Cochiti is found in the Zuñi material gathered by Stevenson (1904).

In Plate CI, Stevenson pictured a single, decorated Mili, or perfect ear of corn, a beautiful object reproduced in color; Plate CIV showed, again in color, an altar with an array of ceremonial items, including some twenty or more Milis. In her discussion of the preparation of a Mili, Stevenson (p. 418) noted that the required perfect ear could be improvised by straightening with heat, water, and splints or by gluing other kernels in the place of missing ones. This is hardly the conventional image of rather rigid exactitude expected in puebloan ceremonialism!

1050. On September 3, 1886, Bandelier had noted Judge Prince's reference to the name of the pueblo ruin on the Potrero de las Vacas as Yapashi, because of the number of stone idols found there (see also n 652).

Bandelier's informant's laughter could be interpreted as meaning that Bandelier had learned the true name and that Hayoua, for purposes of tribal secrecy or personal reasons, did not wish to deny or confirm Bandelier's statement. Actually, much of what Hayoua disclosed to Bandelier, as noted in the lengthy entry of August 20, 1888, seems to have been incorporated in passages of *The Delight Makers,* on which Bandelier was then working.

1051. *Kan-At-Ya Na-Ua* literally means witches, or bad people, chief. See Lange (1959: 252–54) for more recent discussion of the general topic of witchcraft and superstition and also the following section (pp. 254–73) concerning medicine societies, traditionally and collectively the tribe's principal bulwark against witches and their evil activities.

1052. Bandelier used this belief in talking corn with considerable dramatic effect in *The Delight Makers* (1890c: 47–51). In the German version of this novel, *Die Kö-sha-re,* he used the word schwarz, or black, rather than the violet he had stressed in this journal entry. In the English edition, he used either dark-colored or black rather than violet in reference to the talking corn of the sorcerers.

1053. Bandelier's comment on death among the Pueblo Indians being a "final atone-ment" is strongly suggestive of ethnocentrism on his part, although the acculturative impact of Christian teachings must be recognized. Traditionally, the Pueblos have not thought in terms of retribution in the Christian sense. There has been a firm belief in a world of the dead, however, and the intimate contact between this world and that of the dead has held a prominent place in their conceptualization of such matters. For an excellent popular survey of Pueblo religion, see Underhill 1965 (especially pp. 203–24); a classic study in this field is Parsons's monumental *Pueblo Indian Religion* (1939).

Bandelier's treatment of this topic in *Die Kö-sha-re* is of interest here. He wrote: "Der Indianer glaubt nicht an ein Vergeltung nach dem Tode. Alles rächt sich hienieden. Gute und Böse gehen an einer Ort ewiger Freude. [The Indian does not believe in reward, or reprisal, after death. Everything is balanced here on earth, in this world. Good and bad go to a place of eternal joy.]" (1890b: January 15, p. 1.)

1054. Ritual songs and visual forms of trickery have been widely reported for the puebloan tribes. In other areas of North America, such effects as disappearing, dancing, or moving objects have been, for the most part, associated with individual shamanistic performances, even more than among the Puebloans. Here, as Bandelier was noting for Cochiti, the efficacy of the song was held in great respect.

1055. Juan Bautisto Fayet was the first pastor of the Anton Chico parish of Santa Fe, having been appointed to this parish in 1857. In 1889, he was at the San Miguel parish (Chavez 1957: 124, 143).

1056. The Lamy Memorial (1950: 83) listed Father J. B. Ralliere as a priest at Tomé from 1858–1913. He had been brought to New Mexico by Bishop Lamy (Salpointe 1898: 283). Some of Father Ralliere's wooden handtools, letters, and notes have been preserved in the museum at Tomé (Holben 1969: 16). Ellis (1955) has provided an extended discus-sion of Father Ralliere and the parish of Tomé.

1057. The paper for Cushing referred to here was one Bandelier had written for presentation at the Seventh Session, Congrès International des Américanistes in Berlin in October 1888. Neither Bandelier's nor Cushing's paper (see n 1088) arrived in time to be read; however, Sylvester Baxter and Professor Edward Morse, representing the He-menway Expedition at the Congress, made oral summaries, respectively, of Bandelier's and Cushing's work. Their papers later appeared in the published proceedings (see n 673). Mr. Bastian thanked both Baxter and Morse for attending, commenting that they were the first members from the United States ever to have attended.

In the Catron Collection (PC 29 807) was found a typewritten manuscript, dated the same as this entry (August 28, 1888) which appears to have been the original of Bandelier's published paper.

1058. This was Professor H. A. Ward, of Rochester, New York, who was reported as staying one night at the Palace Hotel (*Santa Fe Daily New Mexican*, Aug. 31, 1888, Vol. 25, No. 142, p. 4).

1059. This letter was among those included by Radin (1942: 1–5); since this small volume is rarely available, the letter is reproduced here in its entirety.

> Santa Fé, New Mexico, 2d Sept. 1888.
>
> My Dear Tomasito [Thomas Janvier]:
>
> Your very kind letter reached me late, for I was absent when it came, and returned home only at the beginning of August—to leave again TWICE for the country. For this reason I have not answered it sooner. You have utterly misapprehended Baxter or he has misunderstood my intentions. I did not want him to pull your ears, it was your raven locks I told him to get, with a strip of the basis to which [they] are fastened over the cranium. We western savages do things right. We are not content with small revenges, but take it out in blood and thunder. Now that you have repented and become a good little boy again, I will take your photograph in atonement and leave the scalp in your possession for a while yet. In the course of the week I shall be able to send you our own portentous countenances on condition however always, etc., etc.
>
> Many thanks for your very valuable letter. Until I got it, I was groping in the dark in regard to one of the most important points namely, the style in which a manuscript should be presented to an editor. What had been published for me heretofore were strictly scientific papers only and these do not require such care in getting up. I readily see the point and shall act accordingly. Only I must ask another, perhaps foolish, question. It will be impossible for me to prepare an absolutely CLEAN manuscript. While copying (which I do with the typewriter) changes, erasures, and corrections are inevitable. Still the appearance is of course clearer than if it were done with the pen. Will those corrections impair the chances of the work? I have now copied the English part of it THREE times and still—I am far from satisfied. There is always something to improve.
>
> Again let me ask you: Can I put in a few short, explanatory foot-notes? It seems as if many passages must remain unsatisfactory unless annotated. Of course there will not be any quotations, neither will the notes assume such formidable proportions as in my other lucubrations. Finally, what would you think of a short vocabulary? I do not hold it to be absolutely necessary, still, it might be useful. As the matter stands, I have gone to work after your directions and when the WHOLE is done including an introductory preface, I will send it to you, not before. I conceive that fragments are of no consequence, only reading of the whole can decide.
>
> Don't be angry at me on account of my failure in regard to the Mexican work. That will come also, and be so much the better for the delay. At present the undertaking would have taken me out of the field where I am in duty bound to work. To bring the various essays up to the present standard of knowledge requires fresh study, application in a line that I have partly or at least temporarily abandoned since 1882. Never mind the delay, it will come, and I consider

the "novel" of much greater importance in regard to Mexico even. We have, Mr. Morgan, and I under his directions, unsettled the Romantic School in Science, now the same thing must be in literature on the American aborigine. Prescott's Aztec is a myth, it remains to show that Fennimore Cooper's Indian is a fraud. Understand me: I have nothing personal in view. Cooper has no more sincere admirer than I am, but the cigar-store red man and the statuesque Pocahontas of the "vuelta abajo" trade as they are paraded in literature and thus pervert the public conceptions about our Indians, THEY-I want to destroy first if possible. Afterwards the time will come for a republication of the scientific tracts. I am now devoting, every day, a part of my time to the translation and copying of the so-called novel. I have here a circle of kind friends who assist me materially by revising the King's English; a very necessary task, for more and more I see how lamentably deficient I am in knowledge of the language. It is a matter to be ashamed of, but it is never too late to mend. Within six months I hope to get through.

During my various excursions in the country I spent a few days with our esteemed mutual friend Father Francolon at Santa Cruz de la Cañada. If I could repeat to you all that has been said of you and of Mrs. Janvier during that time it would make you come double-quick. The kindest, most affectionate memories and earnest hopes for a speedy visit from both of you were expressed time and again. That Virgin occupies the place of honor in the house. Our friend (I don't recollect if I told you) has been singularly unfortunate in one sense. Three years ago he was poisoned in the chalice by some unknown FIEND! His mother's practical sense saved his life, but he was obliged to go to France where the waters of Vichy restored his health after three years of intense suffering. When he returned last winter, he was still very weak, now his face has become fuller and he has recovered at least a large part of his former vitality. Madame Francolon (Madame Mère as we call her) is always the same charming lady. When you come, you will be expected at Santa Cruz and here.

Nothing new under the sun besides. Our rainy season is very poor. We had, in all, one week's rain. It threatens every day but never comes. Thousands and thousands of sheep and cattle have already perished from the drouth, and if it continues the loss will be irreparable. Crops are good on account of irrigation. That saves us at all times. Still, the Rio Grande dried up completely south of Albuquerque for nearly three months; between Socorro and Isleta and near Mesilla. Our little river has been dry nearly all summer.

I direct this to your last address, hoping, that it may reach both of you and find you in the enjoyment of everything enjoyable. Whenever you change your address please drop me a line, so that I can keep track of you at all times. I may have to go to Zuñi shortly, but only for a few weeks.

Our best and kindest regards. Write soon again and let me know how you get along. I shall write to Baxter tomorrow or soon after.

Yours affectionately, Adolphe.

1060. This statement undoubtedly referred to the writing of *The Delight Makers*. As work on the novel progressed, Bandelier had been sending chapters of it to innumerable friends to read, as well as asking for help and advice from Santa Fe friends. He had apparently come to realize that he could not integrate or reconcile the suggestions he had received and was now deciding to go ahead on his own.

1061. Fewkes (1895: 319) listed these two items as: "18. First volume of war documents concerning the rising of 1696. Diego de Vargas, 1696" and "19. Second volume (incomplete). Diego de Vargas, 1696."

1062. The Embudo is a small settlement some 20 miles northeast of Española on present-day U.S. Highway 64. It was named in the seventeenth century by Spanish settlers, because Embudo Creek flows through a narrow pass resembling a funnel (embudo). It is not clear from Bandelier's entry if he was referring to the creek or to the settlement (Pearce 1965: 53).

1063. It is not clear why a shower in Abiquiu should have affected the rivers in the Embudo and Taos areas. Perhaps Bandelier simply meant that he noted a shower in the direction of Abiquiu which had either moved to or from the east or was part of a more general storm.

1064. See n 295 for a discussion of Bandelier, Taos, and the sacred Blue Lake.

1065. Larkin Gregory Read was a native of New Mexico, born in Santa Fe, May 26, 1856, the son of Capt. Benjamin Franklin Read and Ygnacia Cano. Read had been for some years a teacher in Taos. He also served as interpreter and, in 1884, with his brother Benjamin M. Read, was a translator for the revision of the New Mexican laws. In 1886 Read was admitted to the New Mexico bar. He was for a time, in the 1890s, president of the Board of Education of Santa Fe (Anonymous 1895: 335–36).

1066. According to Francis (1956: 273), Santiago Valdez [or Valdes] was "indeed mentioned with some emphasis in Don Antonio's testament of June 27, 1867, as 'of his family,' a phrase used by others, clergymen and laymen, for servants and orphans aggregated to their household. Referring to Valdez, the Padre here makes the following statement: 'I have from his infancy taken care of him and adopted him with all the privileges and educated him . . . he has not recognized any other father and mother but me, and besides he has been obedient to me; for this reason I depose and it is my will that his sons take and carry my surname in the future.' Valdez was also one of the executors of his will and inherited his books and papers."

Don Antonio was also known as Don Antonio José Martínez and as Padre Martínez, parish priest at Taos for over forty years, beginning in 1826. Francis disputed Grant's statement that Santiago was a natural son of the priest who was often at odds with Archbishop J. B. Lamy (Grant 1934: 325). Francis maintained that Martínez had been married, had lost his wife after a year, had entered the priesthood, and subsequently had lost a twelve-year old daughter of this earlier marriage. His ultimate departure from the Catholic Church was on grounds of ecclesiastical disagreements over church laws and policies rather than on moral grounds. Francis, in advancing this claim, added that "Fray Angelico Chavez informs me that Padre Martínez was never openly attacked by even his bitterest enemies on grounds of immorality, something that Latins will use first if they can lay hands on it and which they sometimes fabricate. But not with Martínez." (See Francis [1956] for a more complete discussion.)

1067. Fewkes (1895: 326) listed as "13. Grant of the Colorado River. Archives of Taos County, 1842." It is likely that this was the document Bandelier copied at the courthouse.

1068. Because of geographical location, Taos traditionally served as a contact point between the Puebloan and the Plains tribes. (The same was true for Pecos Pueblo.) Plains tribes in contact included the Comanches, Kiowas, and numerous Apachean groups, among which were the Jicarillas. For details on these relationships, see the several works by Thomas (1932; 1935; 1940a; and 1940b); see also more recent studies by Forbes (1960); Kenner (1969); Dolores A. Gunnerson (1974); James H. Gunnerson (1969); and James H. and Dolores A. Gunnerson (1970).

1069. Elizabethtown, named for the daughter of John W. Moore, after the discovery of gold in 1866, was five miles northeast of Eagle Nest in the north end of Moreno Valley. It is now deserted (Pearce 1965: 51–52; see also Jenkinson 1967: 15–27).

1070. According to Grant (1934: 28), the Lucero and Godoy families in Taos were linked.

1071. This was possibly William L. McClure who came to Taos in 1877 and was a merchant and rancher. McClure also served as postmaster in the 1880s. He died in 1929 (Grant 1934: 16, 326).

However, it could easily have been the Indian Agent McClure whose death "last night" was noted by Bandelier in his journal entry of December 16, 1889, when Bandelier was in Santa Fe.

The relationship, if any, between these two men has not been established.

1072. Although Bandelier made no mention of them in his journal entry, there were copies of two documents in the Catron Collection (PC 29 807) in Bandelier's handwriting dated September 24, 1888, Taos. One was entitled "Carta Cordillera tocante al Arancel." (Libro de Cordilleras, E. Taos.—Papeles del Padre Martinez.) Bandelier had written the date of 1730 in the upper righthand corner of the first page. The second was "Lista de los curas Párrocos de la orden de San Francisco del Pueblo de San Gerónimo de Taos, desde el año de 1789, hasta 1826." (Libro de Bautismo de Taos, B.: fragmento.) Bandelier made extracts from this book.

1073. Dr. William A. Kittrege was the only physician in Taos in the 1880s (Grant 1934: 151).

1074. In his *Final Report* (1890–92: II, 334), Bandelier mentioned "Mr. S. I. Bigelow, C. E. of San Francisco" who had drawn a plan for Cushing of the arrangement of the Zuñi ruins. In a footnote, he cited the reproduction of this map with Cushing's 1888 Berlin paper (see n 1088). The legend on this map, however, had "Geo. T. Bigelow," rather than "S. I." The editors have been unable to identify Husher but believe that, like Bigelow, he was at Taos and in Santa Fe for Cushing on matters related to the Hemenway Expedition.

1075. The Rio Abajo is the middle course of the Rio Grande, south of La Bajada Mesa, 19 miles southwest of Santa Fe. North of this point is the Rio Arriba (Pearce 1965: 133). Construction would vary, and continues to vary, between the two regions because of such differences as the greater availability of timber and logs and the greater amounts of rain and snow in the Rio Arriba area. (For a study of "Pueblo Indian Land Grants of the 'Rio Abajo,' New Mexico," see Brayer 1938.)

1076. In the Lamy Memorial (1950: 71), the following comments were made in reference to the St. Anthony Parish. "The little settlements of the Peñasco area in Taos County were originally dependent on the Indian Mission of Picuris. The oldest known of these was called Santa Barbara. The village of Peñasco developed from a cluster of homes nearby, as did other hamlets, once known together as 'Rincones.' Sometime after 1860 the parish seat was transferred from Picuris to Peñasco. The first church was built by Father Ramon Medina, and the present one by Father Delaville around 1916." Reverend F. Guyot was listed as pastor from 1878 to 1892.

1077. Although the journal entry indicates that Bandelier copied from the church books at Peñasco on September 26, 1888, copies of these records in the Catron Collection (PC 29 807) bore the date of September 27, 1888. One transcription was entitled "Lista de los Curas Párrocos de la Orden de San Francisco, de San Lorenzo de los Picuries, desde el año de 1776 hasta 1829." (Archivo de la Parroquia de San Antonio del Peñasco.) His data were taken from *Libro de Bautísmos de Picuries* and on the second page, before his signature, Bandelier had added, "Extracto, Peñasco, N.° M.°, Setiembre 27 de 1888." After his signature, he had copied data about two additional priests from the *Libro de Casamiento: 1776, á 1837. Picuries.* He again added his signature following these notations.

The second item in the Catron Collection, also dated September 27, 1888, at Peñasco, with the notation, "Extracto y copías," was entitled "Lista de los Curas Párrocos, de la

Orden de San Francisco en el Pueblo de San Ildefonso, de 1725 hasta 1833." (Archivos de la Parroquia de San Antonio del Peñasco.) *Libro de Entierras de San Ildefonso.* Both transcriptions were in Bandelier's handwriting.

1078. The Penitentes organization of northern New Mexico consisted of folk Catholic groups that concentrated on a realistic re-enactment of the crucifixion of Christ with the person acting the role of Jesus sometimes actually dying from the treatment. In addition, flagellation and other harsh measures were practiced by the Penitentes. (See Weigle 1970, Chavez 1954b, and Horka-Follick 1969; this last source was sharply criticized in a review by Boyd [1970].)

The excesses of this group were finally suppressed by the Catholic Church, but modified Penitente practices continue to this day (see Hedrick, Kelley, and Riley 1971).

1079. A certain amount of confusion exists as to the number of church edifices that have been built at Picurís Pueblo. See Kubler (1940: 108–9) and Adams and Chavez (1956: 92–101) for their accounts of the history of the Picurís church, or churches. Bandelier's statement that the old church was burned by the Comanches did not seem to have support from the account by Adams and Chavez (p. 93n1). "This means that Father Zárate's remains (see n 185) must have been found in the ruins of the seventeenth-century church, which had been replaced by a post-Reconquest structure, perhaps the one mentioned by Father Alvarez in 1706. In 1769 this latter church was deliberately razed and a new church in a safer location begun, as we learn from Domínguez."

In the summer of 1969, in the course of leveling an area southeast of the present church for a parking lot for the newly erected community house and museum, the foundations of an old church were found by Herbert W. Dick.

1080. See ns 217 and 278.

1081. In n 977, Burrus (1969a: 43) was cited for his comment on the appearance of transcripts copied by Bandelier's father in the ninth volume of the Hemenway documents. Although Bandelier made no mention that his father had copied the manuscript he was returning to Sam Ellison in this entry of October 1, Burrus (p. 43) noted that the transcripts made by the senior Bandelier were dated October 1, 1888, in Santa Fe, adding that they were three petitions sent to the Governor of New Mexico, Diego de Vargas.

Fewkes (1895: 319) listed these as: "12. Petition to Diego de Vargas. Chapter of New Mexico, 1696"; "14. Petition to Diego de Vargas concerning the impending rising of the towns. Chapter of New Mexico, 1696"; and "15. Petition to Diego de Vargas. Fray Francisco de Vargas, 1696." Item 13 in the above sequence in Fewkes was a "Letter to Diego de Vargas concerning the conspiracy of the Indian towns. Chapter of New Mexico, 1696."

1082. This was probably the archaeological museum of the new cathedral mentioned in n 195 (see also n 180). This museum actually was more comprehensive than the term "archaeological" would imply.

The American Guide Series (1940: 202) volume on New Mexico stated that in the cathedral "back of the high altar, through the sacristy and behind a locked door which will be opened upon request, is the Museum where one of the finest pieces of ecclesiastical art in America was formerly kept." This reference was to the stone *reredos* (n 183), which in 1940 was moved to Cristo Rey Church. At that time the Museum also contained a collection of primitive paintings and carvings in wood from old churches. Chavez (1965: 104) wrote of it as a " 'Cathedral Museum' poorly featuring the stone reredos and a welter of old images, paintings, vestments, and candlesticks." Bandelier mentioned a few of the items in his June 5, 1885, entry.

1083. Willie (William) Borchert's name appeared frequently in the 1883–84 journals (Lange and Riley 1970). Since then, additional data have been found through the extensive research by Mary Jean and Ernst Blumenthal, Jr. (Mrs. Blumenthal is Librarian, Clinton P. Anderson Room, University of New Mexico Library), and by further research in St. Louis by the editors. To the information already published (1970: 364n57), the following data have been added.

Several sources listed, or mentioned, William Borchert: 1880, Territorial Census, forty-nine years old, clerk in store, boarder; 1882, Jr. partner in firm of E. S. Codington & Co. (*Albuquerque Evening Review,* April 15, 1882); Firm of E. S. Codington & Co., furniture dealers and undertakers dissolved, Mr. Codington retiring, and Mr. Wm. Borchert and Mrs. Mary Scott continuing the business under name of Borchert & Scott (*Albuquerque Evening Review,* May 24, 1882); name of Scott & Borchert, 1883 Albuquerque and Las Vegas City Directory; going out of business sale, Albuquerque papers, 1883; Salesman, 1896 Albuquerque City Directory; clerk with E. Monfert, undertakers and embalmers, 1897 Albuquerque City Directory; justice of the peace, New Mexico Business Directory, 1903–04, as well as coroner of precinct; justice of the peace, 1904 Albuquerque City Directory; not listed in 1907.

Directories were not available for the years not cited, and the resulting time gaps do not necessarily mean that Borchert was away from Albuquerque. In an unpublished thesis, Rebord (1947: 115n27) gave William as one of the first officers of Masonic Lodge No. 6 in Albuquerque and also as an officer of the Germania Club. (The preceding data have come from the Blumenthals, personal correspondence, August 1971; February 1972.)

The St. Louis supplementary data were added in n 65 together with data on Annie Borchert, wife of William. The added Albuquerque details clearly conflict with the reference in Gould that Anna J. Borchert of St. Louis was the widow of Wm. Borchert (Gould 1888: 182). As suggested in n 65, it is possible that there were two William Borcherts, each with a wife Anna, or Annie, and the Bandeliers interacted with both families, in St. Louis and in Albuquerque, during the journal years. At any rate, the Borcherts appear to have been close friends, if not, in fact, relatives of the Bandeliers.

1084. Manuelito (McKinley County) is a settlement on U.S. Highway 66, sixteen miles southwest of Gallup, New Mexico. Also on the Santa Fe Railroad, Manuelito was named for a famous Navajo leader. The area around Manuelito, today, contains several hundred Navajo Indians. A post office was established at Manuelito in 1880 (Pearce 1965: 96).

1085. Daniel Dubois was mentioned several times in the 1883 journals (Lange and Riley 1970: 51, 73, 74, 75, 76). His identity has not been further established.

1086. Douglas D. Graham was postmaster at Zuñi Pueblo when the post office was reestablished there on October 10, 1882. It was discontinued on May 23, 1883, mail thereafter being distributed from Fort Wingate. A Zuñi post office was reestablished in 1892, but Graham was not the postmaster. After March 29, 1894, Zuñi was serviced from the Gallup post office. On February 18, 1898, with the return of a post office to Zuñi, Graham again served as postmaster (Dike 1958).

1087. Bandelier had met one of these Zuñi Indians, Pala-ua-tiua, in 1886 on the train with the Cushings and F. W. Hodge. See entry of December 16, 1886.

1088. Bandelier in this entry was hearing Cushing's paper that was later published with the other papers of the Seventh Session of the Congrès International des Américanistes. Actually, this entry postdated the Berlin meeting of the Congress, which occurred October 2–5, 1888. As noted in n 1057, Cushing's paper did not arrive in time to be read, but Professor Edward Morse gave a verbal synopsis of Cushing's research for the Hemenway Expedition. See n 673 for a complete citation of Cushing's paper.

1089. Hawikuh was the westernmost of the historic Zuñi Pueblos, situated just east of the present New Mexico–Arizona boundary. It is about five miles south of New Mexico State Highway 53 and some fifteen miles southwest of present-day Zuñi Pueblo (see also n 1094).

1090. According to Spier (1917: 225), "A mile and a half west of Zuñi, a spur of hills projecting into the valley from its southern border terminates at the south bank of the river in a low knoll. On this lies the ruin of Pinnawa, now almost entirely destroyed" (see also Lange and Riley 1970: 40–41).

While at Zuñi in February 1883, Bandelier was told the story of the "Poor Boy of Pinawa" (p. 41), a tale he repeated to listeners in Highland, on shipboard, and elsewhere (pp. 144, 145, 348, 372n113).

1091. For general discussions of Zuñi church history, see Kubler (1940: 95–97) and Adams and Chavez (1956: 195–202). Under the circumstances, the existence of church books at Zuñi Pueblo in 1888 is of interest. Actually, in this entry, Bandelier noted he was copying and making extracts from the church books; on his copy, however, he noted that the *Libro de Bautismos* was in Cushing's possession (see complete citation below). The documents which Bandelier also copied at Zuñi on October 9 and 11, 1888 (see ns 1095 and 1098), lacked this particular notation.

On October 7, 1888, Bandelier copied "Lista de los Ministros de la Orden de San Francisco de la Misión de N^{a}S^a de Guadalupe de Zuñi. (Álona.) desde el año de 1775, hasta el de 1834." (*Libro de Bautismos, en manos del Sr Cushing, à Zuñi.*) A copy of this four-page document in Bandelier's hand was in the Catron Collection (PC 29 807). The fourth page contained two notations from the *Libro de Casamientos: 1776.* Above his signature, Bandelier had noted, "Copias y Extractos: Zuñi, N^o México, Octubre 7 de 1888."

1092. We could find no specific data on a snakebite antidote used in association with the famous Hopi Snake Dance. According to Hodge (1907–10: II, 605), participants in the dance were rarely bitten because of careful handling of the reptiles, rattlesnakes and others. Parsons (1933: 12) discussed the ordinary treatment of snakebite by the Hopi Snake societies, but these were essentially magical in nature.

1093. See the discussion in n 1097.

1094. The identification of Hawikuh with the Cibola of Coronado has been generally accepted for some time. (See Hodge [1937] for a discussion of this problem.) Hawikuh continued to be occupied and in fact was a mission station with a permanent priest. Hawikuh, however, was quite exposed to Apache raids, and in 1673, the pueblo was largely destroyed; many of its people were killed or enslaved in an Apache raid. The resident priest, Fray Pedro de Ayala, was among those killed, and the mission church was burned (Adams and Chavez 1956: 197). The church was apparently reestablished by the time of the Pueblo Revolt of 1680 as Fray Agustín de Vetancurt, writing shortly after the Revolt, cited a tradition of the Hawikuh missionary escaping the uprising (p. 197). According to Hodge (1937: 102), however, the Zuñi have had a tradition that the Hawikuh priest was accepted into their tribe.

In any case, Hawikuh was deserted by or around the beginning of the eighteenth century.

1095. On October 9, 1888, although he made no journal mention of it, Bandelier copied a document at Zuñi Pueblo. A copy of this was in the Catron Collection (PC 29 807). It was entitled "Carta Cordillera á los Religiosos del Nuevo México." *Libro de Patentes, Pueblo de Zuñi—1743—Fojas 6. & 7.* This was in Bandelier's handwriting; below his signature and to the left, he had written and underlined "Traslado."

1096. This idea of Bandelier seems rather unlikely. Father Juan de Bal, or Val, was in fact killed at Halona (approximately the site of modern Zuñi), and his body was never recovered. Father Juan was originally from Castile and was transferred to the Mexican Franciscan Province in 1668. He appears to have replaced Father Juan Galdo at the Halona mission at some time after 1673 (Adams and Chavez 1956: 196–97).

1097. Kubler (1940: 96–97) briefly discussed the small stone church at Kechipauan, to which Bandelier was referring in this entry of October 11, 1888. Kubler believed the church had been built about 1630 and finally abandoned in 1680.

Kubler's identification agreed with the notes and appraisal on Kettcippawa made by Spier (1917: 222); also, his estimation of a brief occupancy period coincided with Spier's interpretation, citing Mindeleff's earlier survey and adding that the church appeared to have been built, at least in part, on an ash heap.

However, the observations by Bandelier in this entry of October 11th, clear in themselves, become confusing when considered alongside of his remarks in the entry of October 8, only three days earlier. It would seem that, in the earlier entry, Bandelier's "Chyana-ué (Canabi!)" was actually Ketship-a-uan, or as Spier termed it, Kettcippawa.

The confusion apparently arose from Bandelier's failure to realize that the site Cushing was telling him about, Ketship-a-uan, was the same site that he had visited three days earlier, at which time he was given the name of "Chyana-ué" for the ruins, missing the fact that Ketship-a-uan was a part of the same cluster. (It seems probable that Chyana-ué actually embraced both Ky'atcekwa and Kettcippawa, only a short distance apart [Spier 1917: 222].) There appears to be no question that there was but one church in the vicinity, aside from the ones at Hawikuh and Halona on which there was no confusion.

1098. On October 11, 1888, at Zuñi, Bandelier copied three documents; transcriptions of these were in the Catron Collection (PC 29 807). These were:

"Carta Patente, del Obispo de Durango, estableciendor el Vicariato Toránio de Albuquerque." *Libro de Patentes del Pueblo de Zuñi, Año de 1801. Testimonio.*

"Nota, sobre Casamientos el Pueblo de Zuñi." *Libro de Casamientos—Zuñi—Año de 1847—Fojas 60 & 61.* [This was noted at the end, "Original."]

"Nota del Padre Custodio Fray Mariano de Jesús Lopez." *Libro de Cordilleras: Pueblo de Zuñi,—Año de 1847.*

At the end of this third document, Bandelier had written: (De lo que antecede se puede deducir que la Custodia del N? México no fué abolida sino hasta despues de 1847).

All three were in Bandelier's handwriting.

1099. The taking of scalps as a part of the ceremonial complex was common to all the Pueblo tribes. For a discussion of Hopi (Bandelier's Moqui) and Zuñi customs regarding scalps and scalping, see Parsons 1933.

1100. Heshota Tzina could not be correlated with any of the published works of Spier (1917) or of others, such as Frank H. H. Roberts, Jr., who have worked in the Zuñi area. However, in Bandelier's *Final Report* (1890–92: II, 333), the ruin was included with the name of Heshota Tzinan.

Bandelier gave its location as at the western edge of a waterless plain between Inscription Rock and Pescado. There, in the western hills, were the "sources of the Zuñi River, and in the very gateway where these abundant springs come to the surface stand the two circular, or rather polygonal ruins, called by the Zuñis Heshota Tzinan. Both are prehistoric, and they yield peculiar and handsome pottery."

1101. El Morro, a majestic sandstone bluff, or headland, now a National Monument in New Mexico, catches the imagination of the viewer with its numerous early Spanish and other inscriptions. This visit of October 1888 was Bandelier's first and only visit there. Lt. J. H. Simpson has been credited with naming it "Inscription Rock." He and R. H. Kern visited El Morro in 1849 and copied the inscriptions (see also n 1104).

Bandelier's statement in this entry, "There is no water at the Morro," is of interest as one of the commonly accepted explanations for the many inscriptions was that it was a watering hole for man and animal as well as a shaded resting place. (Though no longer used for drinking purposes, there is still a pool of water, from run-off rather than springs, at the base of the cliff.)

It is beyond the scope of this note to annotate in detail the inscriptions which Bandelier wasted no time in copying. MacGregor (1970: 25–31) gave a popular but accurate account of the history recorded in the inscriptions on El Morro. Lummis (1892: 176–78) and Hodge (in Ayer 1916), among others, have also provided data on El Morro. In 1912, an expedition of the Bureau of American Ethnology, in charge of F. W. Hodge, visited El Morro and made photographs and paper squeezes of all inscriptions of historical importance. Casts were made in plaster from these, and with the original paper negatives, they were preserved in the National Museum.

1102. This was the same Tinaja referred to by Pearce (1965: 166). Pearce located it in Valencia County, northeast of El Morro, and noted that the Spanish word refers to a large earthen jar for holding water or other liquids. He stated that Tinaja received its name because it was close to an Indian ruin in a circular depression or sink in the lava, which gave it a bowl-like appearance. A walk-in well was the source of drinking water.

1103. At present, the National Park Service maintains a loop trail to the top of El Morro so that the two ruins there may be observed at close range. According to the Guidebook, the larger ruin, some 200 by 300 feet in size, has been called "Atsinna, a Zuñi word referring to the 'writing on rock.' " It may have been, in part, as much as three stories high; it was occupied during the twelfth and thirteenth centuries. Upon abandonment, its survivors supposedly moved to the west, merging with the Zuñis (Anonymous, n.d.: 15–17).

1104. After a visit to El Morro and an examination of the actual Oñate inscription and also the literature which gave Don Juan de Oñate's inscription of 1605 as the oldest and most famous of the inscriptions, the editors were surprised to find a plate in Espinosa's edition of Villagrá's Historia (1933: Pl. X [credited to the U. S. National Museum (see also n 1101)]) in which the date 1606 was clearly discernible. In this entry, Bandelier had copied "1604." In Appendix U of Espinosa's volume (pp. 291–92), was the following comment by F. W. Hodge:

> The inscription shown in Plate X reads, *"Paso por aqui el adelantado Don Juan de Oñate del descubrimiento de la mar del Sur a 16 de Abril 1606."* With respect to the date, Bandelier in an unpublished "Preliminary Report on the most valuable Inscriptions still visible on the 'Rock of El Morro'," dated October 30, 1888, and addressed to Frank Hamilton Cushing (original in possession of F. W. Hodge), comments as follows: "The inscription is genuine, only the year, which has been reconstructed as 1606, is erroneous. Oñate left San Gabriel on the 7th of October, 1604, and returned thither on the 25th of April, 1605. The date must therefore be the 16th of April 1605. Not as I myself suggested 1604. But of the genuineness of the inscription there is not the least possible doubt."

> If the date has been altered and is not an error on the part of the petrographer, then the change was made before September 17–18, 1849, when "Lt. J. H. Simpson USA. & R. H. Kern Artist, visited and copied these inscriptions," for in Simpson's *Journal of a Military Reconnaissance from Santa Fé, New Mexico, to the Navajo Country* (Washington, 1850, pl. 69), the date is plainly given as 1606.

The inscription, it will be observed, was carved across an ancient Indian pictograph.—F. W. Hodge.

A Xerox copy of Bandelier's unpublished manuscript was obtained from the Archives of the Peabody Museum, Harvard. The last sentence of Hodge's quotation from Bandelier's statement reversed the words "possible" and "doubt." The last sentence should have read, "But of the genuineness of the inscription there is not the least doubt possible."

1105. In his unpublished preliminary report on the El Morro inscriptions (see n 1119), Bandelier wrote: "The Inscription, which apparently is of oldest date reads as follows: PeDRo RoMeRo i 1580. This seems to indicate the year 1580. While at the Morro, I was under the impression that Francisco Sanchez Chamuscado at the head of eight soldiers and escorting three Franciscans, had visited Zuñi with his men [the Priests remained among the Tiguas at Bernalillo—A.F.B.] in the fall of 1580. Upon referring to the original documents however, I found it was in 1581. The date of the inscription therefore still remains in doubt."

Espejo, in March 1583, according to Luxán's narrative (Hammond and Rey 1929: 88) noted: "We set out from this place on the eleventh of the month and marched three leagues and stopped at a water hole at the foot of a rock. This place we named El Estanque del Peñol." In a footnote (p. 88n85), Hammond and Rey stated that El Estanque del Peñol was evidently El Morro, or Inscription Rock, but there was no indication that any of the Spanish explorers had inscribed their names there before Oñate did so on April 16, 1605.

1106. In his unpublished manuscript on the El Morro inscriptions (see n 1119), Bandelier wrote: "Diego Luzero Godoy. One of the most able and valiant officers under Otermin and his immediate successors. He lived at TAOS previous to the outbreak of 1680." In May 1888, Bandelier had found a pre-Revolt document concerning Diego Lucero de Godoy in the Santa Clara church archives (see n 992). See also n 1070 for New Mexico descendants of this man.

1107. This was presumably Sheriff Francisco Chavez of Santa Fe. Twitchell (1911–17: II, 510–11, 511–12n429) noted him as Sheriff of Santa Fe County in 1885. He was murdered in 1892 as a result of a feud involving a number of Santa Fe families. At the time, he was a promising Democratic politician (Lamar 1966: 193).

1108. Grants, in Valencia County, New Mexico, was named for the Grant Brothers, Angus A., Lewis A., and John R., who were contractors in the construction of the AT&SF Railroad and who maintained a workers' camp called "Grants Camp." A post office was founded in 1882 under the name Grant; it was changed to Grants in 1936 (Pearce 1965: 66).

1109. Emil Bibo was a member of the extensive Bibo family, some of whom came to New Mexico in the 1860s. The Bibos had merchandising and ranching interests in the Grants and Laguna-Acoma area (Anderson 1907: II, 610).

1110. Although not entirely accurate, Lummis, in his introduction to *The Delight Makers* (Bandelier 1890c [1918 edition: xiii]), gave this account of his first meeting with Bandelier.

"One day of August, 1888, in the teeth of a particular New Mexico sandstorm that whipped pebbles the size of a bean straight to your face, a ruddy, bronzed, middle-aged man, dusty but unweary with his sixty-mile tramp from Zuñi, walked into my solitary camp at Los Alamitos. Within the afternoon I knew that here was the most extraordinary mind I had met. There and then began the uncommon friendship which lasted until his death, a quarter of a century later; and a love and admiration which will be of my dearest memories so long as I shall live."

Bandelier was not out of the Santa Fe–Cochiti–Peña Blanca area in August of 1888. However, this October 18, 1888, entry was the first journal entry referring to Lummis.

Lummis was correct in his recollection of a sandstorm; but in addition to the date, he also erred in stating that Bandelier had made this trip on foot, as the previous day's entry clearly indicated that he had ridden in a wagon at least a part of the distance.

1111. The Mesa Encantada (Acoma Katsimo) is a sandstone mesa rising some 430 feet above the Acoma Basin. It is some 2500 feet long and varies in width from 100 to 350 feet (Hewett and Mauzy 1940: 140).

1112. According to Hewett and Mauzy (1940: 140), the Acoma believe that a number of people on the Mesa Encantada were cut off by the legendary storm. The Acoma therefore moved to their present village. Their name for the Mesa, Katsimo, means haunted or accursed.

Actually, several people have reached the top of Enchanted Mesa and no house remains have been found there, though it does seem to be an Acoma ceremonial site.

1113. Although Bandelier noted spending the day at San Rafael with the padre, he neglected to note that he had also copied church records. In the Catron Collection (PC 29 807), there were two transcriptions made at San Rafael on October 19, 1888. Both were in Bandelier's handwriting.

One was entitled "Lista de los Ministros de la Orden de N: S: P: San Francisco del Pueblo de San José de la Laguna, de 1777, hasta 1837." *Libro de Entierros de Laguna. Archivos del Curato de San Rafael.* He noted "Extractos" with the place and date at the end of his transcription. The second was entitled "Acurdo con los indios de Laguna sobre Derechos de Partidos." *Libro de Casamientos, del Pueblo de Laguna, Arch. de San Rafael.* At the top of the page, he had written, "A.D. 1846."

1114. See Lange and Riley 1970: 381n183 for probable identification of Don Manuel Chavez, credited by some with the founding of the settlement of San Mateo, New Mexico.

1115. This was probably Louis Baer, a son-in-law of Abraham Staab (see n 484). Twitchell (1925: 479–80), in listing the Staab children, gave "Mrs. Louis Baer of Boston."

1116. It is an interesting commentary on New Mexico society of the late nineteenth century that a few weeks after Bandelier's visit, Reverend Gentile was charged by a Mrs. Cutonoli (an Albuquerque rooming house proprietor) with embezzling $1800.00! (*Santa Fe Herald,* Dec. 10, 1888, Vol. 1, No. 47, p. 4). Nothing seems to have come of the charges, however.

1117. A transcription, dated October 24, 1888, of extracts from Albuquerque by Bandelier was in the Catron Collection (PC 29 807). It was entitled "Lista de los Curas Ministros de la Parroquia de San Felipe de Albuquerque, desde el año de 1776 hasta el de 1841." *Libro de Entierros; Libro de Casamientos.*

1118. See Lange and Riley 1970: 432n121 for possible identification of Rupe, or Ruppe.

1119. This typewritten report by Bandelier was entitled "Preliminary Report on the most valuable INSCRIPTIONS still visible at the Rock of 'EL MORRO.'" It was signed by Bandelier in Santa Fe, October 30, 1888 (the date of this entry) and submitted to Cushing as Director of the Hemenway Southwestern Archaeological Expedition. After his usual signature, "Ad. F. Bandelier," he had added, "Cust: Hist. Archives." A Xerox copy of this report was obtained from the Archives of the Peabody Museum, Harvard, and has been cited for a number of notes.

1120. This was probably Judge W. C. Hazeldine of Albuquerque, upon whom Bandelier had called in 1882 (Lange and Riley 1966: 276, 325).

1121. Bandelier was never enthusiastic about political democracy as practiced in the United States (see entry of April 21, 1885, for another example).

The ticket of Benjamin Harrison and Levi P. Morton defeated President Grover Cleveland and Vice President Allen G. Thurman in the national elections of 1888.

1122. The *Santa Fe Daily New Mexican* (November 8, 1888, Vol. 25, No. 201, p. 4) reported the death of D[umas] Provencher who was murdered at San Rafael in Valencia County while poll watching. Provencher was a brother-in-law to Father John B. Brun (see n 494).

1123. Theodore Fischer was listed as President of the Fischer & Co. Ice business in Santa Fe. In the same listing, L. E. Theo Fischer was given as treasurer of the Fischer Brewing Co. and also with the Fischer & Co. Drug Store on the plaza in Santa Fe (Polk and Danser 1884a: 350). The relationship between these two Fischers has not been established.

1124. Carl F. Huegy, son of Maurice and Emma Wilborn Huegy, was an important source of information for Goad's biographical appraisal of Bandelier (1939) and contributed a number of items to the Museum of New Mexico's collection of Bandelieriana which was made as part of the preparations for the Bandelier Centennial in Santa Fe in August of 1940 (see also ns 66 and 143).

1125. In the partial catalogue of the Hemenway documents (Catron Collection [PC 29 807]), Bandelier listed "1713. Causa criminal contra Gerónimo Dirucaca, Indio del pueblo de Picuries." This corresponds to the item listed by Fewkes (1895: 324) as "2. Criminal prosecution against Jerónimo Dirucaca, an Indian of the town of Picuries. Territorial Archives, Santa Fe, New Mexico (original), 1713. Writ of accusation and charge."

1126. Two typewritten transcriptions made on November 16, 1888, were in the Catron Collection (PC 29 807). They apparently were made from the books of Father Deraches referred to in this journal entry. The first was entitled "Lista de los Padres Custodios de la Custodia de la Conversión de San Pablo del Nuevo-México, desde el año de 1697 hasta el de 1790, incluso." [*Libros de Patentes de la Parroquia de la Villa de Santa-Fé.* -- B: y G:] Bandelier noted, "La Lista de arriba está incompleta, pero se puede completar en tanto que toca á los años entre 1680 y 1697." He added six additional names from 1680 through 1696.

The second document was "Lista de los Visitadores, desde 1697 hasta 1790. Segun los Libros de la otra pagina." Bandelier noted that this list was also incomplete. Following his signature, Bandelier made the following notation: "Hay, en los mismos dos Libros, varias Cartas Patentes y un Mandamiento del Tribunal de la Inquisición. No propongo sacar copias de esos documentos con tiempo. Hasta 1790 no parece ni una sola Visita episcopal, aunque segun las Inscripciones del 'morro,' el Opispo del Durango, Don Martin de Elizaecoechea visitó el Territorio en 1737."

1127. In Bandelier's partial catalogue of the Hemenway documents (Catron Collection [PC 29 807]), he listed "1703. Autos justificando, del Cabildo de Sta Fé, al Gob^r Diego de Vargas. (Testimonio.) (Arch. terr., Santa Fé.) This corresponds to Fewkes (1895: 320): "28. Documents of justification to Diego de Vargas. Corporation of Santa Fe, 1703."

1128. Teresa and Ophelia were apparently local girls, more likely from Peña Blanca, less likely from Cochiti Pueblo. In January 1889, Father Navet eloped with Teresa, a fact that Bandelier noted with great disgust in his journal entry of January 23, 1889. Navet's action seems to have greatly shocked church authorities also. Archbishop Salpointe, when writing his *Soldiers of the Cross* (1898) a few years later, actually omitted Navet's name from the list of priests who had served in New Mexico. However, in the Lamy Memorial (1950), Father Navet was listed as having served at Peña Blanca from 1844 [*sic;* 1884] to 1889 (p. 71).

1129. This was the Right Reverend N. C. Matz, D. D., who was still head of the Denver diocese as late as 1899 (Salpointe 1898: App. VII).

1130. The *Santa Fe Daily New Mexican* (December 5, 1888, Vol. 25, No. 223, p. 4) reported the arrival of Frank C. Hunter of Nebraska City who stayed at the Palace Hotel. The wedding, however, escaped the notice of the newspaper.

1131. Judge William H. Manderfield died on December 3, 1888 (Haines 1891: 581–82; see also n 596). The *Santa Fe Daily New Mexican,* in its December 7, 1888, edition (Vol. 25, No. 225, p. 4) gave a detailed description of the funeral of Manderfield. The long procession of friends was led by four priests: "Vicar General Rev. Father Eguillon, Rev. James H. DeFouri, Rev. Father Deracht [Deraches?] and Rev. Father Rolli." Pallbearers included Col. V. S. Shelby, Judge Henry L. Waldo, Gov. Samuel B. Axtell, Gen. Edward L. Bartlett, Hon. T. Alarid, Hon. Antonio Ortiz y Salazar, Hon. W. W. Griffin, and Mr. Julius H. Gerdes.

1132. The church to which Bandelier referred in this entry was Nuestra Señora de Guadalupe. See Kubler (1940: 101–2) and Historic Santa Fe Foundation (Loomis 1966: 16) for the history of this church.

In 1881, Father Defouri had been appointed priest for the English-speaking Catholics in Santa Fe, and this church, after a long period of disuse, was assigned to them, following some renovation and remodelling (see n 187). Bandelier, in deciding to attend the Guadalupe church because it was heated, "instead of the cathedral," made one of his very few journal references to the cathedral. Although he had been in almost daily contact with church personnel since his arrival in Santa Fe in 1880, he almost ignored the cathedral per se. He had attempted an interior photograph in 1882, and early in this volume (see ns 183, 184, and 185) had aided in the deciphering of two inscriptions on a sarcophagus that was unearthed as the cathedral was being built. With the extensive rebuilding from the earlier adobe Parroquia to Lamy's French-inspired stone cathedral, much of which occurred during Bandelier's residence in Santa Fe, it is surprising that he commented so rarely on it.

The reader is referred to both Kubler (1940: 100–101) and Historic Santa Fe Foundation (Loomis 1966: 39) for brief histories of the cathedral. Gregg (1968: 100–101) included several illustrations showing the cathedral, as Lamy had planned it, an interior, and a view during construction. On June 23, 1823, the local Mexican government and secular clergy adopted St. Francis of Assisi as Santa Fe's patron saint. The cathedral is the Cathedral of St. Francis.

1133. Bandelier was presumably referring to his *Final Report,* Part I (1890), and specifically to the second portion: "II. Ethnographic Condition of the Southwest in the Sixteenth Century," ultimately pages 44–187 of the first part.

1134. Dr. L. Zabala was credited in Hodge's Bandelier Bibliography (1932: 365 [#34]) with the translation from the French to the Spanish of Bandelier's "La découverte du Nouveau-Mexique par le moine franciscain frère Marco de Nice en 1539." Dr. Zabala was also credited with writing an introduction to the Spanish translation of this article.

1135. A typewritten copy of this transcription made by Bandelier December 26, 1888, in Santa Fe, was in the Catron Collection (PC 29 807). It was entitled "Testimonio de una Carta escrita por el Padre Fray Juan Bermejo tocante a la Misión de Zuni." [Archivos Territoriales. Santa-Fe. Nuevo-México. Miscelaneos—Año D 1783]

Bandelier made a note in Spanish after his transcription, pointing out an irregularity in the books and lists of the mission at Zuñi. The reader with particular interest in the Zuñi mission from 1782 to 1785 should consult this transcription for Bandelier's detailed comment.

His terminal note read as follows: "Copia á la Letra. Expica á la iregularidad en los libros y listas de la Misión de Zuñi. Segun la lista sacada del Libro de Bautismos, abia, hasta entónces, dos Ministros en Zuñi; á lo Menos lo mas del Tiempo. Pero en 1782 y hasta el Año de '84, no parece sino uno solo, el Padre Fray Tomas Salvador Fernandez. En 1785 consiguió como compañero al P: Fr: Ambrosio Guerra."

GLOSSARY

abuelo—grandfather

acequia—irrigation canal or ditch

acostar (se)—to lie down, to go to bed

adobe—sun-dried brick for house, wall, or other construction

afanes—workers, toils

agua dulce—literally, sweet water; potable water

aguardiente—a distilled beverage, perhaps mezcal or sotol, brandy, etc. ("firewater")

agua sedativa—an herbal headache medicine, varying in composition

aguja—needle or spine

alameda—public walk (also a grove of poplar trees)

álamo—poplar tree, cottonwood tree

albañales—dikes

alberjones (albejones)—peas (Spanish *arveja, arvejón*)

alguacil—constable or other minor official (see also *topil*); sheriff

almacén—storehouse

almagre—Indian red; ochre

almirez—mortar

amarillo—yellow

amole—soaproot

amugereado (amujerado)—effiminate person, transvestite

ancón—in Bandelier, a recess or canyon in a hill

angostura—narrow pass

apachita (apacheta)—ceremonial stone heap made by travelers

aparijo (aparejo)—travel gear; pack saddle

apellido—family name or surname

arboleda—a woodland or wooded area; usually *arbolera* in New Mexico

arroyo—stream bed with deep-cut sides, common in semidesert and desert countries

atajo—short cut; in Bandelier, lead animal of a pack train. This is possibly a misspelling of *hatajo* (herd or group of animals).

atole—a watery mush made of maize; corn mush

ayudante—assistant or adjutant

azoteas—rooftops

azul—blue

babosa—silly or dirty; at one point, Bandelier seems to have meant an Indian group

baile—dance

bajada—descent; the *bajada* referred to by Bandelier, however, may have been originally *majada*—sheepfold

barranca—canyon; ravine

barrial—muddy place

barro—pottery clay; mud; in Bandelier, also a place name

barro blanco—white clay

bellotas (vellotas)—acorns, or juniper berries

blanco—white

bolas—balls; in Bandelier also large boulders

boquilla—literally "little mouth"; sometimes used to refer to the opening of a canyon, valley, or ditch

bordo—bank (of a stream)

bosque—forest or woodland near the water (*monte,* woods on hillside or on mountain, scrub vegetation)

brazo—arm, also used for a channel of a river

brujo—witch

"buena gente"—literally, "Good people"; in Bandelier, "friends," a form of greeting

caballito—a native dance

cabildo—a town government, also the building used to house it

cabra—goat

cacica—cacique's wife or female assistant

cacique—chief or headman in the pueblo, the religious leader

cactli—sandals (from Nahautl)

cadenas—"chains" of ten meters

caja—literally, box; in Bandelier, drum

cajeta—in Mexico, jelly or a container of jelly; New Mexico preserve (jelly in New Mexico is *jalea* or "jelly")

cajón—a large box or in America a narrow (box) canyon. Bandelier used the term in the latter sense and also for large boxlike chunks of adobe used in house construction.

calentura—fever

calle—street

campo santo—cemetery

canoa—canoe or boat; in New Mexico, trough

cañada—canyon or glen

cañón—canyon

cañutilla—wreath made of rushes

capellán—chaplain

capitán de la guerra—war captain

carretero—wagon (road) master (*carretera,* highway)

carrizal—land filled with reed grass

carrizo—reed grass, bamboo

castruenza (probably *castrensa*)—in standard Spanish, *la castrense*—a military chapel

cavador—wooden hoe

caxete (*cajete*)—large bowl; or more often, tub

cedro—cedar

ceja—summit; ridge

cerrito—small hill or mountain

cerro—hill or highland

ciénaga—a marshland or swamp

cienaguilla—a small marsh often used as a place name

ciénega—alternative spelling of *ciénaga;* Bandelier preferred the form *ciénega,* instead of Spanish, *ciénaga,* the latter not used in New Mexican Spanish

cimarrón—mountain or wild sheep; from Spanish, *cima* (mountain) top

cofradía—association of persons, especially confraternity, brotherhood, or sisterhood

colorado—red or colored; but usually the color red (Spanish *rojo*)

comal—a flat earthenware pan for cooking tortillas

como jurados—like juries

compañero—companion

común—tribe; also, in the Southwest, toilet

conducto—normally, channel through which business is conducted; Bandelier used the word to mean a pack train or *cordón*

convento—convent

coralillo—normally, coral snake; Bandelier, however, used the term to mean a bush or shrub (red bearberry used as a substitute for tobacco)

corcho—corkwood

cordón—ridge; string (shoestrings = *cordones*), cord

corona—crown; Bandelier also used this word to mean ceremonial headdress in native dances = *tablita?*

corral—a yard or enclosure; corral

cosa acabada—something old or worn out

cosecha—harvest

cotón—printed cotton for Spain; cotton or wool jacket

crestón—outcropping

cuartazos—*cuarterón?* Mulatto or offspring of a mestizo and a Spaniard

cuartel—a district or ward of a town, sometimes a single dwelling

cuarto—room

cuate—double or twin, chum, friend; in southern New Mexico, double-barrelled shotgun

cuerno—horn

cuesta—cliff; ridge; hill

cúmaro—perhaps a variant of *comino* (*cumin*)

cumbre—summit or top

cura—priest; parish priest

chalchihuitl (*chalchihuite*)—turquoise (this and several other words in the glossary are borrowed from Nahuatl, the language of the Aztecs)

chamizo—literally, burned wood; in Bandelier, one of the various shrubs of the eastern New Mexico area, normally sagebrush

chaparro—the evergreen oak; scrub oak or scrub vegetation

chiquihuite—basket

chiquita—small girl

chiquito—small or tiny as a small child

choyo—*cholla* cactus

chongo—bun hair style, worn, among Southwestern Indians, by both men and women

dátil—date; fruit of the date palm or fan palm

desagüe—drainage ditch
diligencias matrimoniales—marriage documents
Dios—God
enagua (see also *nagua*)—petticoat; originally a piece of cloth wrapped around a woman's waist and legs and worn under the *huipil;* usually plural, i.e., *enaguas,* "petticoats"
encina—oak
encinal—oakwood; grove of oak trees
encino—oak
encino colorado—red oak
enojar (se)—to vex; to become angry
enseñar—to show or teach
equipota—pack train
escalera—family or household (literally ladder)
escaramuza—contest, skirmish; mock skirmish
escondida—hidden place (e.g., Rio Escondido, "hidden" river)
escudilla—porringer
espiga—ear or head of corn
estaca—stake; in Bandelier, probably a loom fixed in the ground
estancia—a farm or cattle ranch; also a hill or room
estanque—reservoir
estufa—stove, also used to refer to the underground ceremonial rooms or kivas of the Pueblo Indians
falda—slope
fandango—a Spanish dance or the music for this type of dance. In New Mexico *fandango* means any dance.
fanega—measure of land; measure of grain
fariseo—literally, pharisee; clown in a Spanish-Indian ceremony; heretic
fecha—date
fiebre—influenza
fieros—terrible; in New Mexico, ugly
fiesta—a celebration often on a saint's day or other religious holiday
fiscal—one of the Pueblo Indian village officers
flecha (baile de la)—arrow dance
fósforos—matches
frijoles—beans
gallazo—a caste designation
gamuza—antelope skin

garbanzos—chickpeas
gavilán—sparrow hawk
genízaro—Indians, normally nonpueblo, rescued or ransomed by
    the Spanish and resettled in Spanish territory
gente—people; in Bandelier, occasionally "clan"
gobernador—governor
governador—governor
grama—couch grass
guacamayo—macaw (male)
guaco wood—bee-weed stems
guaje—gourd; gourd rattle
guante—gloves?
guaraches (huaraches)—sandals
guerra—war
guerra de los Gachupines—war of the Spaniards
hacienda—large ranch
hava (haba)—mange; also horse bean
hermano—brother
higuera—fig tree
hombre—man
hombres de armas—warriors
hondo—deep
horcón—forked branch, also roof, or roof support
huero—blonde person
huerta—orchard or garden
huipil—a sleeveless blouse worn by Mesoamerican women
Indios bárbaros—unacculturated Indians
Indios genízaros—Hispanicized Indians
jacal—adobe house or hut, brush and pole structure
jarra—jug or pitcher; jar
jaspe—material used as whitewash (literally jasper)
jefe político—chief officer
jícara (sometimes *xícara*)—basket; cup or other container
juego de gallo—rooster pull
junto—together, united
kiho—a Piman word for a special kind of carrying basket
labores—in Bandelier, a cultivated field (*milpa*)
lagarto—lizard
laguna—lake
lagune (laguna)—lake or marsh

lechuza—barn owl

legua—league; this is of varying lengths, a common one being some 3 miles; Bandelier seems to have used a 5-mile league

libela (*libélula*)—dragonfly

librado—clerk, exempt

loma—hill

los antiguos—the ancient ones

loza—pottery

llanito—small plain

llano—a plain or flat basin

llorona—ghost or weeping woman legend

macana—war club

macho—stallion; male. In New Mexico *garañón* is the more common word for stallion.

madroño—strawberry tree (madrone, *Arbutus unedo*)

maíz—corn; in New Mexico = *maiz* (no accent)

malacate—in America a spindle or spindle-whorl; windlass

malpais—bad lands, usually lava extrusions

mano—hand, hand stone for grinding corn

manta—a blanket or overgarment

mantel—altar cloth

manzanilla—camomile, one of several plants of the aster family, the dried leaves sometimes used medicinally

máquina—literally engine; sawmill

más bonita—prettier

matalote—saddle horse, often meaning an old or worn-out animal; also male dancer, as in war and matachina dances

maxtatl—kilt; breechcloth from the Nahuatl

médano(s)—dune(s)

médico—medical doctor

medio—half or middle; in Bandelier, a small coin (*medio real*)

merced—land grant

mesita—small mesa or flat-topped hill

metate—grinding stone for making maize meal

mezcal—mescal agave, or an alcoholic drink distilled from this plant

mezcla—lime mortar

milla—mile

milpa—cornfield

mimbral—osier, willow or willow grove

mogote—flat-topped cliff or hill

mole—chocolate-based sauce

molote(s)—men's hair style (see *chongo*)

monarca—king

muchacha—little girl

muerto—corpse

mula—a she-mule; Bandelier also uses the term to mean macaw

muy colorado—very decorated

muy curiosa—careful; painstaking, curious

muy malo—very bad

mygah—gila monster

nagua—see *enagua*

negro—black

nopal—nopal cactus

Nuestra Señora—The Virgin

ocote—pitch-pine

ocoteas (*ocotillo*)—coachwhip plant

oficial—official

ojo—spring

ojos colorados—"Red Eyes"; Indian ceremonial group at Isleta
    Pueblo

ojos negros—"Black Eyes"; Indian ceremonial group at Isleta
    Pueblo

olla—pottery vessel used to carry or store water; jar

olote—corncob

padre—Catholic priest

paeso—peso (the Mexican coin) alternate pronunciation

palo blanco—hackberry tree; probably *Celtis sp.* (also can mean
    pimp or whoremonger)

palo de fierro—testota tree; *Olneya sp.*

palo verde—palo verde tree; *Cercidium sp.*

panocha—wheat sprout pudding

paraje—place, campground; resting place, stop

para platicar—to talk

pariente—relative

partido—party, group division

peñascosa—rocky

peñol—large rock

peón—sharecropper or other rural laborer

petate—woven sleeping mat

picacho(s)—sharp-pointed hill(s)

picota—in Bandelier, post or pillar

pinabete—spruce tree. In standard Spanish *pino abeto, pinabete,* spruce fir tree

pinito (baile del)—Little Pine Dance

pinole—a drink made of parched corn and water, usually with sugar

pinta—painted or marked

piñón—pinyon tree; the nut or fruit of this tree

pita—agave fiber

plato—plate

plaza—open area in town center; fortified town; town or village; downtown, shopping center

poniente—west

por contento—satisfactory

portal—porch or entryway

potrero—pastureland; in New Mexico, a tongue of high ground

pozo—waterhole or pond

pozole—a boiled mixture of beans and barley, or sometimes maize with pork

pregón—public announcement

pregonero—town crier

presa—dam

presidio—fort or army post

primicias—first fruits

primo—cousin

principales—headmen of a town

pueblito—small village or town

pueblo—village, also a group of village Indians in the Southwest

puerta—door

puertecita—small gate

punche—homegrown or native tobacco

¡Quién sabe!—perhaps

¿Quién sabe?—"Who knows?"

quince—15; also another name for the gambling game, *patol,* or *patolli*

ramos (baile de los)—Bough Dance, possibly Evergreen Dance

ranchería—hamlet

rancho—ranch or ranchhouse

real—Spanish colonial coin of varying values and sizes, a common variety containing one ounce of silver; a 19th century real = 12 1/2 ¢; 4 reales = 50¢

rebosa—shawl or stole; usually *rebozo*

rechicero (*hechicero*)—medicine man

relámpago—lightning

represas de agua—water catchment areas; Bandelier uses the phrase to mean agricultural terraces which retain ground water

rezar—to pray

rillito—small stream; in Bandelier the name of such a stream in the Tucson area, from Spanish *riito* (*ri[o]* + *ito* = *rito*)

rincón—corner (or a room, cliff indentation, forming miniature box canyon)

rio—river

ristra—a string of green or red chile hung out to dry

rito—rite or ceremony; also a stream

rosa de Castilla—Spanish rose; in Bandelier an unidentified rose

sabino—juniper

sacristán—sacristan or sexton

sahuaro—*saguaro* cactus

St. Iago—Santiago

salvado—bran

sandía—watermelon

sangrantado (perhaps *sangrentado*)—in Bandelier, some kind of wood

sangría—bleeding or blood-letting; bleeder (used by Bandelier, however, to denote a small irrigation canal)

sepultura—grave

serape (*sarape*)—a blanket worn across the shoulder; a narrow blanket worn by men over the shoulders

sernícola (*cernícola*)—sparrow hawk

shaparro—see *chaparro*

sierra—mountain range

sopa—soup; bread pudding (in New Mexico soup is *caldo*)

sotol—the sotol cactus or a drink distilled from it

tablas (sometimes *tablitas*)—headboards used in ceremonial dances among Southwestern pueblos

tambor—drum; in Bandelier, also a war drum

taparico—gate
tapeste—*tapeiste, tapesto* (from Nahuatl, *tlapechtli*), a kind of
  roof or shelter supported by poles
tasajo—strips of dried pumpkin
tecolote—owl; from Nahuatl *tecolotl*
teguas—boots
tembladas—chills
tendejón—store (or perhaps commissary tent)
tepalcate—potsherd
tequío—in Mexican usage, a tax
tienda—store; tent
tilma—blanket; cloak
tilmita—a small blanket or cloak
tinaja—an earthenware jar; a natural basin
tío—uncle
ti-suin (or *tiswin*)—maize beer
tomado—drunk
tombé—drum
topil—sometimes used interchangeably with *alguacil;* a low-
  grade political office, the kind normally held by young men in
  Spanish-Indian communities
torito—little bull
torrejón—tower
tortilla—flat corn or wheat cake
tortuga (baile de la)—Turtle Dance
trigo—wheat
tulas (tul or *tules)*—reeds
tuna—fruit of the Opuntia cactus
túndita—in Bandelier, a towerlike rock
tusa—prairie dog
uña de gato—cat's claw plant
vadito—ford of a small stream
vara—a rod or pole, also a cane of office given to Latin American
  town officials; measure (3 ft. +)
vega—field
vellotas—see *bellotas,* acorns or juniper berries
venado (baile de)—Deer Dance
venado alazán—elk
verde—green
verdolaga—purslane

vereda—trail or path
viga—rafter
visita—inspection by civil or church government official
vívora—snake
xícara (*jicara*)—basket or container, cup
yeso—gypsum
zacate—grass or hay
zahuarro—*saguaro* cactus

BIBLIOGRAPHY

Aberle, S. D., J. H. Watkins, E. H. Pitney
    1940. The Vital History of San Juan Pueblo. (Human Biology,
        Vol. 12, No. 2, pp. 141–87)
Adams, Eleanor B., and Fray Angelico Chavez
    1956. The Missions of New Mexico, 1776: A Description by
        Fray Francisco Atanasio Domínguez, with other Contem-
        porary Documents. (University of New Mexico Press, Al-
        buquerque, 387 pp.)
Alexander, Hubert Griggs, and Paul Reiter
    1935. Report on the Excavation of Jemez Cave, New Mexico.
        (Monograph, University of New Mexico, School of Ameri-
        can Research, Vol. 1, No. 4, Albuquerque, 67 pp.)
American Guide Series
    1940. New Mexico: A Guide to the Colorful State. (Coronado
        Cuarto Centennial Commission and the University of
        New Mexico. Hastings House, New York, 458 pp.)
Anderson, George B.
    1907. History of New Mexico, Its Resources and People. (Pa-
        cific States Publishing Company, Los Angeles. Two vol-
        umes, pp. i-xxvii+1-522 and pp. 523-1047)
Anonymous
    1895. An Illustrated History of New Mexico. (The Lewis Pub-
        lishing Co., Chicago, 671 pp.)
    1937. Bandelier Material Enriches School Library. (El
        Palacio, Vol. XLIII, Nos. 7-8-9, pp. 49–50)
    1938. Bandelier Drawings Found. (El Palacio, Vol. XLIV,
        Nos. 25–26, pp. 165–66)

1961. Our Lady of Guadalupe Church: Dedication Program, December 17, 1961. (Ortiz Printing Co., Santa Fe, New Mexico, 52 pp.)

1972. Old Santa Fe Today. (Published for The Historic Santa Fe Foundation, University of New Mexico Press, Albuquerque, 79 pp.)

n.d. El Morro Trails. (National Park Service, Globe, Arizona, 17 pp.)

Archaeological Institute of America

1888. Eighth Annual Report, 1886–87. (Archaeological Institute of America, Cambridge, pp. 1–48)

Ayer, Mrs. Edward E., translator

1916. The Memorial of Fray Alonso de Benavides, 1630. (Annotated by Frederick Webb Hodge and Charles Fletcher Lummis. Privately printed, Chicago, 309 pp.)

Baedeker, Karl

1909. Süddeutschland: Oberrhein, Baden, Württemberg, Bayern und die Angrenzenden Teile von Österreich. (Handbuch für Reisende, Leipzig, 470 pp.)

Baldick, Robert

1965. The Duel. (Clarkson N. Potter, Inc., New York, 212 pp.)

Bancrcft, Herbert H.

1889. Arizona and New Mexico, 1530–1889. (History of the Pacific States of North America XII. History Company, San Francisco, 829 pp.)

Bandelier, Adolph F.

1873. Letter to Lewis Henry Morgan in regard to the dependability of the statements of authors of early works on Spanish America, dated Highland, Ill., Dec. 20, 1873. (In Stern, Bernhard J., Lewis Henry Morgan, Social Evolutionist, Chicago, 1931, pp. 112–15)

1874–78. Highland, Illinois. (Article in Johnson's New Universal Cyclopedia)

1876. Über einige Spuren von Verbindungen zwischen Amerika und den östlichen Erdtheilen vor der Zeit des Columbus. (New Yorker Staatszeitung, Sonntagsblatt, Mai 1–Aug. 15, 1876)

1876–77. Über die Sage des "Dorado" im nördlichen Süd-
Amerika. (New Yorker Staatszeitung, Sonntagsblatt, Apr.
16, 23, 30, 1876, to Juli 1877)

1877a. On the Art of War and Mode of Warfare of the Ancient Mexicans. (Tenth Annual Report, Peabody Museum
of American Archaeology and Ethnology, Cambridge,
pp. 95–161)

1877b. Review (unsigned) of E. G. Squier's Peru: Incidents of
Travel and Exploration in the Land of the Incas. (The
Nation, Vol. 24, June 21, pp. 367–69, and June 28, pp.
383–84)

1877c. Review of Morgan's Ancient Society. (The Nation,
Vol. 25, July, pp. 92–93, and Dec., pp. 107–108)

1877d. Letter to Lewis Henry Morgan on the probable reception of Morgan's Ancient Society by Anthropologists,
dated Highland, Ill., Aug. 8, 1877. (In Stern, Bernhard J.,
Lewis Henry Morgan, Social Evolutionist, Chicago, 1931,
p. 196)

1878a. Comment on the work of Aug. Le Plongeon. (The
Nation, Vol. 26, p. 135)

1878b. Comment on Dr. Gustav Brühl: Die Culturvölkes Alt-
Amerikas. (Cincinnati Volksfreund, Feb. 11, 1878)

1878c. On the Distribution and Tenure of Lands, and the
Customs with Respect to Inheritance, among the Ancient
Mexicans. (Eleventh Annual Report, Peabody Museum of
American Archaeology and Ethnology, Cambridge, pp.
385–448)

1878d. Comment on Ph. Valentini and his The Mexican Calendar Stone. (The Nation, Vol. 27, No. 684, p. 84)

1878e. Comment by Ph. Valentini on The Mexican Calendar
Stone, with rebuttal. (The Nation, Vol. 27, No. 690, pp.
176–77)

1879a. The National Museum of Mexico and the Sacrificial
Stone. (The American Antiquarian and Oriental Journal,
Vol. II, No. 1, pp. 15–29)

1879b. Des Calpullis mexicains; de leur administration de
leur origine et du principe communiste qu'ils impliquent.
(International Congress of Americanists, 3rd Session, Vol.
I, Brussels, pp. 58–60)

1879c. On the Sources for Aboriginal History of Spanish America. (Proceedings, American Association for the Advancement of Science. St. Louis Meeting, 1878. Salem, Massachusetts, pp. 315–37)

1879d. Review (unsigned) of E. B. Tylor's Researches into the Early History of Mankind (1878 edition). (The Nation, Vol. 28, p. 170)

1879e. Sources of Spanish American History, signed "A. D." (The Nation, Vol. 28, p. 265)

1879f. Review (unsigned) of Ad. Bastian's Die Culturländer des Alten Amerika. (The Nation, Vol. 28, pp. 357–58)

1879g. An Important Discovery for Mexican Antiquities. (The Nation, Vol. 29, pp. 347–48)

1880a. On the Social Organization and Mode of Government of the Ancient Mexicans. (Twelfth Annual Report, Peabody Museum of American Archaeology and Ethnology [1879], Cambridge, pp. 557–699)

1880b. Review of Primitive Manners and Customs, by J. A. Farrer. (The Nation, Vol. 30, pp. 33–34)

1880c. Review (unsigned) of Charles Rau's The Palenque Tablet in the U.S. National Museum, etc. (The Nation, Vol. 30, pp. 423–25)

1880–92. Original Bandelier Journals. (Library, Museum of New Mexico, Santa Fe, New Mexico)

1881a. Historical Introduction to Studies among the Sedentary Indians of New Mexico. (Papers of the Archaeological Institute of America, American Series, Vol. I, No. 1, Boston, pp. 1–33. 2nd Edition, 1883)

1881b. A Visit to the Aboriginal Ruins in the Valley of the Rio Pecos. (Papers of the Archaeological Institute of America, American Series, Vol. I, No. 2, Boston, pp. 34–133) A second "edition" of the entire volume, items 1881a and 1881b, was issued. (Boston: published by Cupples, Upham, & Co., London: N. Trübner and Co. 1883)

1881c. Bandelier's Researches in the Southwest. (The Nation, Vol. 32, p. 94)

1881d. Letter regarding Cochití. (Second Annual Report of the Executive Committee of the Archaeological Institute of America, Cambridge, 1881, pp. 19–20)

1882a. Kin and Clan. (Address delivered before the Historical Society of New Mexico in "The Palace," Santa Fe, N.
M., April 28, 1882. 8 pp. Reprinted from Santa Fe New
Mexican, April 29, 1882; reprinted again in the New Mexico Historical Review, Vol. VIII, No. 3, July 1933, pp.
165–75)

1882b. Notes on the Bibliography of Yucatan and Central
America. (Proceedings of the American Antiquarian Society, New Series, Vol. I, 1880–81, Worcester, pp. 82–118)

1883a. Vocabulary of the Keres Language of Cochití. (Mentioned by Bandelier in Bulletin I, Archaeological Institute
of America, Boston, 1883, p. 17. Now in Charles F. Lummis Collection, Southwest Museum, Los Angeles)

1883b. Report by A. F. Bandelier on His Investigations in
New Mexico in the Spring and Summer of 1882. (Bulletin
of the Archaeological Institute of America, I, Boston, pp.
13–33)

1883c. Letter dated Fort Apache, Arizona, 29 April, 1883.
(Addressed "Lieber Herr Pretorius," in which various
pueblos and pueblo remains are mentioned. Westliche
Post, St. Louis)

1883d. Die indianischen Ruinen des Westens. (Anzeiger des
Westens, Mittwoch [St. Louis], 26 Sept.)

1884a. Report of an Archaeological Tour in Mexico, in 1881.
(Papers of the Archaeological Institute of America,
American Series II, University Press, Boston, 326 pp.
Identical second edition printed as An Archaeological
Reconnoissance into Mexico. Boston: Cupples & Hurd,
publishers. The Algonquin Press)

1884b. Reports by A. F. Bandelier on his Investigations in
New Mexico during the Years 1883–1884. (Fifth Annual
Report of the Executive Committee, Archaeological In-
stitute of America, Cambridge, pp. 55–98. Reprint of
Casa Grande account in Fewkes, J. W., Casa Grande,
Arizona, Twenty-eighth Report of the Bureau of Ameri-
can Ethnology, pp. 71–72, Washington, 1912)

1884c. Reisebriefe aus dem südwestlichen Nordamerika,
April 22, San Buenaventura de Kochiti, Bernalillo
County, Neu-Mexico. (Das Ausland, nos. 31–32, pp.
601–7, 625–33, München, Aug. 3–10, 1884)

1884d. Ein Brief über Akoma von Adolf F. Bandelier, Mai 20, (1882) Pueblo of San Estévan of Acoma. (Das Ausland, Band LVIII: 241–43)

1885a. The Romantic School in American Archaeology. (Read before the New York Historical Society, Feb. 3, 1885. New York, 14 pp. Reprinted by Trow's Printing and Book Binding Co., 14 pp., 1885)

1885b. Cibola I [I-VII]. (New Yorker Staatszeitung, Sonntagsblatt, Mai 24, 31; Juni 7, 14, 21, 28; Juli 5.) Cibola II (Zweite Serie.) [I-IV]. (New Yorker Staatszeitung, Sonntagsblatt, Okt. 25; Nov. 1, 8, 15, 1885)

1885c. Ancient Pueblos in and about Santa Fe. (Ritch, W. G., Aztlan, 6th ed., 199–202, Boston. French translation in H. Beaugrand. Six mois dans les Montagnes-rocheuses, pp. 146–53, Montréal, 1890)

1885d. Letter to W. G. Ritch, Secretary of the Territory of New Mexico, at Santa Fe, dated Fort Huachuca, Arizona, February 15, 1884, relating to the prehistory of Santa Fe. (Ritch, Illustrated New Mexico, Santa Fe, 1885. French translation in H. Beaugrand. Six mois dans les Montagnes-rocheuses, 146–153, Montréal, 1890)

1885e. Ein Brief von Adolf F. Bandelier über seine Reise im südwestlichen Nordamerika, Highland, Okt. 12, 1883. (Das Ausland, Band LVIII: 974–75)

1885f. Der Indianer Ausbruch in Arizona und der Feldzug gegen die Apaches in Neu-Mexiko. (Westliche Post, St. Louis, Juni 21, 28)

1885g. The Apache Outbreak. (The Nation, Vol. 41, No. 1044, pp. 8–9)

1885(?)h. "Po-Se" (A Tale of San Ildefonso). (New Mexico Historical Review, Vol. I, July 1926, pp. 335–49. Goad noted, "This ms. was left by Bandelier with Mrs. Samuel Eldodt of Chamita, N. M., probably written in 1885.")

1885i. "The Progressive Indian: What Advanced Civilization and the Winchester Have Done for the Red Man." (St. Louis Globe Democrat, St. Louis, December 26, p. 12)

1885–86. Über die Sage des "Dorado" im nördlichen Süd-Amerika. (New Yorker Staatszeitung, Sonntagsblatt, continued from 1876–77. According to Hodge [1932: 362], this was the German original of The Gilded Man [1893].)

1886a. Why New Mexico Does Not Flourish. (The Nation, Vol. 42, pp. 70–71)

1886b. Must We Have Another Indian War? (The Nation, Vol. 42, pp. 397–98)

1886c. San Bernardino Chalchihuapan. Ein mexikanisches Abenteuer. (National Zeitung, Berlin, Vols. 581, 593, 595)

1886d. Die neu-mexikanischen "Pueblos." (New Yorker Staatszeitung, Sonntagsblatt, Jan. 10, 17, 24, 31)

1886e. Quivira, I-IV. (New Yorker Staatszeitung, Sonntagsblatt, Feb. 21, 28; März 7, 14)

1886f. Review of John G. Bourke's "An Apache Campaign in the Sierra Madre . . . 1883." (The Nation, March 11, 1886, No. 1080, p. 222)

1886g. Alvar Nuñez Cabeza de Vaca, the first overland traveler of European descent, and his journey from Florida to the Pacific Coast—1528–1536. (Magazine of Western History, Vol. V, July, Cleveland, pp. 327–36)

1886h. Das Alter der Stadt Santa Fé, Neu-Mexiko. (New Yorker Staatszeitung, Sonntagsblatt, Juni 20)

1886i. Southwestern Pine Timber. (The Nation, Vol. 43, No. 1096, p. 8)

1886j. La découverte du Nouvcau-Mexique par le moine franciscain frére Marcos de Nice en 1539. (Revue d'Ethnographie, Vol. V, Paris, pp. 34–48, 117–34, 193–212. Spanish translation in El Boletin Popular, Jan. 17–Mar. 7, 1889, Historia del descubrimiento de Nuevo Mexico por el Monjé Franciscano Fray Marcos de Niza en 1539. Por el Prof. Ad. F. Bandelier. Traducida del frances por el Dr. L. Zabala)

1886k. The Discovery of New Mexico by Fray Marcos de Nizza. (Magazine of Western History, Vol. V, Sept., Cleveland, pp. 659–70. Reprinted in New Mexico Historical Review, Vol. IV, No. 1, Santa Fe, Jan. 1929, pp. 28–44; condensed reprint in The Masterkey, Vol. II, No. 8, Los Angeles, April 1929, pp. 5–15)

1886l. Geronimo. (New Yorker Staatszeitung, Sonntagsblatt, Juli 5, 12, 17. Three letters written at Santa Fe in June, July 1886)

1886m. Archaeological Chronology. (The Nation, Vol. 43, pp. 132–33)

1886n. Das "Gemetzel" von Cholula (1519). (New Yorker Staatszeitung, Sept. 5, 12, 19)

1886o. Removal of the Apaches from Arizona. (The Nation, Vol. 43, No. 1106, Sept. 9, pp. 208–9)

1886p. Review (unsigned) of John F. McLennan's Studies in Ancient History. (The Nation, Vol. 43, No. 1119, p. 483)

1887. Irrigation in the Southwest. (The Nation, Vol. 45, No. 1172, p. 474)

1887–88. Histoire de la Colonisation et des Missions de Sonora, Chihuahua, Nouveau Mexique, et Arizona: Jusqu'à l'année 1700. (Manuscript, 1,400 foolscap pages, 400 watercolor drawings by the author, in four volumes, with an atlas; in Vatican Library, manuscripts, Vat. Lat. 14111–14116)

1888a. Letter on Gran Quivira, addressed to S. B. Evans, dated Belen, New Mexico, Jan. 21, 1883. (Saturday Evening Post, Burlington, Iowa, Dec. 1)

1888b. Review of Daniel G. Brinton's Ancient Nahuatl Poetry. (The Nation, Vol. 46, No. 1179, pp. 102–3)

1888c. Die Kirchen und Kirchen-Ornamente von Neu-Mexiko aus der spanischen Zeit. (New Yorker Staatszeitung, Jan. 1, 8)

1888d. Letter on the progress of archaeological and ethnological research in America, especially in the United States, by Ad. F. Bandelier, Santa Fe, New Mexico, May 4, 1888. (Ninth Annual Report of the Archaeological Institute of America, pp. 55–61, Cambridge)

1888e. The Betrayer of La Salle. (The Nation, Vol. 47, pp. 166–67)

1888f. Preliminary Report on the most valuable INSCRIPTIONS still visible at the Rock of "EL MORRO." October 30, 1888, unpublished report to F. H. Cushing, Archives of the Peabody Museum, Harvard.

1889a. Archaeological Work in Arizona and New Mexico During 1888–89. (Tenth Annual Report of the Archaeological Institute of America, Cambridge, App. III, pp. 106–8)

1889b. New Mexican Spanish Antiquities. (The Nation, Vol. 48, pp. 265–66)

1889c. Jean L'Archévèque. (New Yorker Staatszeitung, Mar. 24)

1889d. Winsor's Aboriginal America. (The Nation, Vol. 49, pp. 134–35)

1889e. Quivira. (The Nation, Vol. 49, pp. 348–49, 365–66)

1889f. Datos historicos sobre Paso del Norte. (El Centinela. Ciudad Juarez [Paso del Norte], Oct. 20–27)

1889(?)g: Ein Hexenprozess in Neu-Mexiko vor vierund-dreissig Jahren. (Belletristisches Journal, New York)

1890a. Contributions to the History of the Southwestern Portion of the United States. (Papers of the Archaeological Institute of America, American Series, V, Cambridge)

    I. Sketch of the Knowledge which the Spaniards in Mexico possessed of the Countries north of the Province of New Galicia, previous to the return of Cabeza de Vaca, in the Year 1536, pp. 3–23

    II. Alvar Nuñez Cabeza de Vaca, and the Importance of his Wanderings from the Mexican Gulf to the Slope of the Pacific for Spanish Explorations towards New Mexico and Arizona, pp. 24–67

    III. Spanish Efforts to penetrate to the North of Sinaloa, between the Years 1536 and 1539, pp. 68–105

    IV. Fray Marcos of Nizza, pp. 106–78

    V. The Expedition of Pedro de Villazur, from Santa Fé, New Mexico, to the Banks of the Platte River, in search of the French and the Pawnees, in the Year 1720, pp. 179–206

1890b. Die Köshare. Eine Erzählung aus dem Leben der Pueblo-Indianer von Neu-Mexiko. (Belletristisches Journal, New York, Jan. 1–Mai 14)

1890c. The Delight Makers. (Dodd, Mead & Co., New York, 490 pp.;

    Reprinted, 1916, Dodd, Mead & Co.;

    Reprinted, 1918, Mrs. Fanny R. Bandelier;

    Reprinted, 1946, Dodd, Mead & Co.;

    Reprinted, 1971, Harcourt Brace Jovanovich, Inc.)

1890d. The Historical Archives of the Hemenway South-western Archaeological Expedition. (Congrès International des Américanistes, Septième Session, 1888, Berlin, pp. 450–59)

1890e. The Unification of Mexico. (The Nation, Vol. 50, pp. 409–10)

1890f. The Industrial Condition of Mexico. (The Nation, Vol. 50, pp. 427–29)

1890g. The Ruins of Casas Grandes. (The Nation, Vol. 51, pp. 166–68, 185–87)

1890h. The Siege of La Paz . . . I. (Reprinted from U.S. Catholic Historical Society Record, pp. 243–64)

1890i. Fray Juan de Padilla, the First Catholic Missionary Martyr in Eastern Kansas. 1542. (American Catholic Quarterly Review, Vol. XV, No. 59, Philadelphia, pp. 551–65)

1890–92. Final Report of Investigations among the Indians of the Southwestern United States, carried on mainly in the years from 1880 to 1885, Parts I and II. (Papers of the Archaeological Institute of America, American Series, III and IV, Cambridge, pp. 1–319 and pp. 1–591)

1891a. The Southwestern Land Court. (The Nation, Vol. 52, p. 437)

1891b. Existing Cave-Dwellers. (The Nation, Vol. 53, pp. 408–9)

1892a. The "Montezuma" of the Pueblo Indians. (American Anthropologist, Vol. V., Washington, Oct., pp. 319–26)

1892b. An Outline of the Documentary History of the Zuñi Tribe. (Journal of American Ethnology and Archaeology, Vol. III, No. iv, Cambridge, 115 pp.)

1892c. Review of The Story of New Mexico, by H. O. Ladd. (The Nation, Vol. 54, p. 237)

1893. The Gilded Man (El Dorado) and Other Pictures of the Spanish Occupancy of America. (D. Appleton and Company, New York, 302 pp. Reprinted by The Rio Grande Press, Chicago, Ill., 1962)

1897. Bandelier's Researches in Peru and Bolivia. (American Anthropologist, Vol. X, Washington, Sept., pp. 303–11, by F. W. Hodge based on report written to him by Bandelier. Issued also separately)

1903a. Review of Around the Caribbean and across Panama, by F. C. Nicholas. (The Nation, Vol. 77, p. 411)

1903b. Review of Pioneer Spaniards in America, by W. H. Johnson. (The Nation, Vol. 77, p. 473)

1904a. Aboriginal Myths and Traditions Concerning the Island of Titicaca, Bolivia. (American Anthropologist, n. s., VI, pp. 197–239. Issued also separately)

1904b. Aboriginal Trephining in Bolivia. (American Anthropologist, n. s., VI, pp. 440–46. Issued also separately)

1904c. Review of The Indians of the Painted Desert Region, by G. W. James. (The Nation, Vol. 78, pp. 156–57)

1904d. Review of William Hickling Prescott, by Rollo Ogden. (The Nation, Vol. 78, p. 357)

1904e. Review of A. J. Burdick's The Mystic Mid-region. (The Nation, Vol. 78, p. 391)

1904f. Review of Mary Austin's The Land of Little Rain. (The Nation, Vol. 78, pp. 391–92)

1904g. Review of The Journey of Coronado, by G. P. Winship. (The Nation, Vol. 78, pp. 439–40)

1904h. Review of G. A. Dorsey's The Arapahoe Sun Dance. (The Nation, Vol. 78, p. 497)

1904i. Boundary Readjustments in South America. (The Nation, Vol. 79, pp. 155–56)

1904j. Review of E. H. Thompson's account of Yucatan ruins. (The Nation, Vol. 79, p. 357)

1904k. Review of The League of the Ho-De-No-Sau-Ne or Iroquois, by L. H. Morgan (a new edition by H. M. Lloyd). (The Nation, Vol. 79, pp. 362–63)

1904l. On the Relative Antiquity of Ancient Peruvian Burials. (Bulletin XX, American Museum of Natural History, New York, pp. 217–26)

1904m. The Cross of Carabuco in Bolivia. (American Anthropologist, n.s. VI, pp. 599–628. Issued also separately)

1905a. The Aboriginal Ruins at Sillustani, Peru. (American Anthropologist, n. s. VII, pp. 49–68, map, pls. Issued also separately)

1905b. The Basin of Lake Titicaca. (Bulletin, American Geographical Society, XXXVII, pp. 449–60)

1905c. Narratives of the career of Hernando de Soto. (The Nation, Vol. 80, p. 197)

1905d. Introduction to The Journey of Alvar Nuñez Cabeza de Vaca, translated by Fanny R. Bandelier. (New York, pp. v–xxii)

1905e. Letter of Mendoza and report of Father Marcos of Nizza.—Introductory note. (*In* The Journey of Alvar Nuñez Cabeza de Vaca, translated by Fanny R. Bandelier, New York, p. 195)

1905f. Review of Indian Basketry, by O. T. Mason. (The Nation, Vol. 80, p. 219)

1905g. Father De Smet. (The Nation, Vol. 80, pp. 274–75)

1905h. Review of California and Its Missions, by B. J. Clinch. (The Nation, Vol. 80, p. 404)

1905i. Traditions of Pre-columbian Landings on the Western Coast of South America. (American Anthropologist, n. s. VII, pp. 250–70. Issued also separately)

1905j. The Truth about Inca Civilization. (Harper's Monthly Magazine, CX, no. 658, pp. 632–40)

1906a. La danse des "Sicuri," des Indiens Aymará de la Bolivie. (Boas Anniversary Volume, New York, pp. 272–82)

1906b. Review of Lowery's Spanish Settlements in the United States. (The Nation, Vol. 82, pp. 225–26)

1906c. Traditions of Pre-columbian Earthquakes and Volcanic Eruptions in Western South America. (American Anthropologist, n.s. VIII, pp. 47–81. Issued also separately)

1906d. Über Trepanieren unter den heutigen Indianern Bolivias. (XIV Internationaler Amerikanisten-Kongress, Stuttgart, 1904, 1er Hälfte, pp. 81–89, Berlin, Stuttgart, Leipzig, 1906)

1907. The Indians and Aboriginal Ruins near Chachapoyas in Northern Peru. (Historical Records and Studies of the United States Catholic Historical Society, V, pt. 1, New York)

1910a. Documentary History of the Rio Grande Pueblos of New Mexico. I. Bibliographic introduction. (Archaeological Institute of America, Papers of the School of American Archaeology, No. 13, Lancaster, Pa., pp. 1–28)

1910b. The Islands of Titicaca and Koati. (The Hispanic Society of America, New York, xviii, 358 pp.)

1911. The Ruins at Tiahuanaco. (Proceedings, American Antiquarian Society, XXI, Worcester, Mass., pp. 218–65)

1913. Letter to Dr. E. L. Hewett on the age of Santa Fe. (El Palacio, I, No. 1, Nov., p. 7)

1914. Extracts from two letters addressed to Charles Eliot Norton, one of which was written at Cochití in 1880. (El Palacio, I, Nos. 6–7, Apr.–May, p. 8)

1923–26–37. Historical Documents relating to New Mexico, Nueva Vizcaya, and Approaches thereto, to 1773. (Collected by Adolph F. A. Bandelier and Fanny R. Bandelier. Spanish text and English translations. Edited with introductions and annotations by Charles Wilson Hackett. Three volumes. Washington, D. C. Published by the Carnegie Institution of Washington, 502 pp., 497 pp., and 532 pp.)

1926. Po-sé, a Tale of San Ildefonso Pueblo. (New Mexico Historical Review, I, July, pp. 335–49)

1927. Certification regarding facsimiles of two war-god idols of San Juan Pueblo, New Mexico, in the handwriting of Bandelier, who signs as one of the witnesses. Dated San Juan de los Caballeros, March 1, 1889. (Indian Notes, IV, No. 4, New York, Oct., p. 397)

1929–30. Documentary History of the Rio Grande Pueblos, New Mexico. Part I—1536 to 1542, New Mexico Historical Review, IV, Oct. 1929, pp. 303–34; V, Jan. 1930, pp. 38–66; Apr. 1930, pp. 154–85. Part II—1542 to 1581, ibid., July 1930, pp. 240–62. Part III—1581 to 1584, ibid., Oct. 1930, map, pp. 333–85)

n.d. Unpublished manuscript on various inscriptions. (Catron Collection [PC 29 807], Archives, University of New Mexico Library)

Bandelier, Adolph F., Memorial Conference

1940. Memorial Conference Program, In Commemoration of the One Hundredth Anniversary of the Birth of Adolph F. Bandelier, August 6th to 8th, 1940, Santa Fe, New Mexico. 7 pp. (From Louis Latzer Memorial Public Library—Highland, Illinois)

Bandelier, Fanny Ritter

n.d. Recollections regarding the early years of Adolph F. Bandelier. (Archives, Museum of New Mexico, Santa Fe)

Bandelier Scrapbook
    n.d. Sent to the editors by Dr. Fred Eggan, University of Chicago. Clipped to first page: "A Book of Newspaper Clippings Prepared for Adolf Bandelier."
    n.d. Scrapbook, with no date or other identifying data. (In Bandelier Collection, Museum of New Mexico, Santa Fe)

Bandelier, Adolph F., and Edgar L. Hewett
    1937. Indians of the Rio Grande Valley. (Publications, University of New Mexico, School of American Research, Albuquerque, 274 pp.)

Bandelier, Adolph F.—Francis Parkman letters
    v.d. (Massachusetts Historical Society)

Bannon, John Francis
    1970. The Spanish Borderlands Frontier, 1513–1821. (Holt, Rinehart and Winston, New York, 308 pp.)

Barnes, Will C.
    1915. Adolph F. A. Bandelier. A Tribute and Reminiscence. (Old Santa Fe, Vol. II, No. 3 [Jan. 1915], Old Santa Fe Press, Santa Fe, pp. 302–8)

Baxter, Sylvester
    1886. Review of Adolph F. Bandelier's Report of an Archaeological Tour in Mexico in 1881. (The American Architect and Building News, May 8, pp. 219–20)

Beaglehole, John Cawte
    1966. The Exploration of the Pacific. (3rd edition, Stanford U. Press, Stanford, California, 346 pp.)

Bernays, Thekla
    1912. Augustus Charles Bernays, A Memoir. (C. V. Mosby Company, St. Louis, 309 pp.)

Biographical Publishing Company
    1894. Portrait and Biographical Record of Madison County, Illinois. (Biographical Publishing Company, Chicago, 549 pp.)

Bloom, Lansing B.
    1914. New Mexico under Mexican Administration: V. (Old Santa Fe, Vol. II, No. 1, July, pp. 3–56)
    1915. New Mexico under Mexican Administration: VIII. (Old Santa Fe, Vol. II, No. 4, April, pp. 351–80)
    1933. Bourke on the Southwest. (New Mexico Historical Review, Vol. VIII, No. 1, pp. 1–30)

1936. Bourke on the Southwest. (New Mexico Historical Review, Vol. XI, pp. 77–122, 188–207, 217–82)

1937. Bourke on the Southwest. (New Mexico Historical Review, Vol. XII, pp. 41–77, 337–79)

1938. Bourke on the Southwest. (New Mexico Historical Review, Vol. XIII, pp. 192–238)

1943. Historical Society Minutes, 1859–1863. (New Mexico Historical Review, Vol. XVIII, Santa Fe, pp. 247–311)

Bloom-Hewett Correspondence

v.d. Museum of New Mexico Files (Santa Fe): 1938, etc.

Bolton, Herbert E., ed.

1907. Spanish Explorers in the Southern United States, 1528–1543. (Original Narratives of Early American History, Charles Scribner's Sons, New York, 411 pp.)

1916. Spanish Exploration in the Southwest, 1542–1706. (Original Narratives of Early American History, Charles Scribner's Sons, New York, 487 pp.)

1936. Rise of Christendom, A Biography of Eusebio Francisco Kino, Pacific Coast Pioneer. (The Macmillan Company, New York, 644 pp.)

1949. Coronado, Knight of Pueblos and Plains. (University of New Mexico Press, Albuquerque, 491 pp.)

Bond, Frank

1946. Memoirs of Forty Years in New Mexico. (New Mexico Historical Review, Vol. XXI, pp. 340–49)

Bourke, John G.

1884. The Snake Dance of the Moquis of Arizona . . . with an account of the Tablet Dance of the Pueblo of Santo Domingo. (Charles Scribner's Sons, New York, 371 pp.)

1886. An Apache Campaign in the Sierra Madre: An Account of the Expedition in Pursuit of the Hostile Chiricahua Apaches in the Spring of 1883. (Charles Scribner's Sons, New York, 128 pp. 1958 reprint of the 1886 edition. Introduction by J. Frank Dobie)

Boyd, E.

1970. Review of Los Hermanos Penitentes . . . [by] Lorayne Horka-Follick. (El Palacio, Vol. 76, No. 3, pp. 33–34)

Brayer, Herbert O.

1938. Pueblo Indian Land Grants of the "Rio Abajo," New

Mexico. (University of New Mexico Press, Albuquerque, 135 pp.)

Brevoort, Elias
1874. New Mexico. Her Natural Resources and Attractions, etc. (Santa Fe, 176 pp.)

Brink, W. R., and Co.
1882. History of Madison County, Illinois. (W. R. Brink & Co., Edwardsville, Illinois, 603 pp.)

British Museum
1959–66. General Catalogue of Printed Books ... to 1955. (Pub. by Trustees of the British Museum, London, 263 vols.)
1964a. Volume 250, 857 pp.
1964b. Volume 251, 1038 pp.

Brühl, Gustav, ed.
1869–71. Das Deutsche Pionier: Eine Monatsschrift für Erinnerungen aus dem Deutschen Pionier-Leben in der Vereinigten Staaten. (Cincinnati, 1869–1884)

Bryan, Kirk
1938. Prehistoric Quarries and Implements of Pre-Amerindian Aspect in New Mexico. (Science, n.s., Vol. 87, No. 2259, pp. 343–46)
1939. Stone Cultures near Cerro Pedernal and their geological antiquity. (Bulletin, Texas Archaeological and Paleontological Society, Vol. 2, pp. 9–43)

Burrus, Ernest J., S. J.
1967. Quivira and Teguayo in the Correspondence of Bandelier and Shea with Collet (1882–1889). (Manuscripta, Vol. XI, published by St. Louis University Library, Lowrie J. Daly, S. J., ed., pp. 67–83)
1969a. Bandelier's Manuscript Sources for the Study of the American Southwest. (Homenaje a José Maria de la Peña y Camara. Ediciones José Porrua Turanzas, Madrid, pp. 29–48)
1969b. A History of the Southwest: A Study of the Civilization and Conversion of the Indians in Southwestern United States and Northwestern Mexico from the Earliest Times to 1700, by Adolph F. Bandelier. Volume I: A Catalogue of the Bandelier Collection in the Vatican Library. (Jesuit Historical Institute, Sources and Studies for the

History of the Americas: Vol. VII. Rome, St. Louis, 233 pp. See Bandelier 1887–88)

1969c. A History of the Southwest: A Study of the Civilization and Conversion of the Indians in Southwestern United States and Northwestern Mexico from the Earliest Times to 1700, by Adolph F. Bandelier. Supplement to Volume I: Reproduction in Color of Thirty Sketches and of Ten Maps. (Jesuit Historical Institute, Sources and Studies for the History of the Americas: Vol. VIII. Rome, St. Louis, 8 pp., 30 sketches, 10 maps. See Bandelier 1887–88)

Carr, Lucien
1883. The Mounds of the Mississippi Valley Historically Considered. (Smithsonian Institution, Annual Report, 1891. Washington, 1893, pp. 503–99; reprint of the original which appeared in 1883, 107 pp.)

Carter, Clarence E., ed.
1950. The Territorial Papers of the United States: Vol. XVII, The Territory of Illinois, 1814–1818. (U.S. Government Printing Office, Parts 5–7, 750 pp.)

Casey, Mrs. Charles T. et al.
1956. Breese Centennial Celebration: Souvenir Program and History of Breese. (Breese Journal, Breese, Ill., 82 pp.)

Cather, Willa
1927. Death Comes for the Archbishop. (Alfred A. Knopf, New York, 303 pp.)

Catron, Thomas Benton
n.d. Archival Collection in University of New Mexico Library. Bandelier material is coded PC 29 (with various subdivisions) and is filed in nine manila folders

Chavez, Fray Angelico, O.F.M.
1950. See Puckett, Fidelia Miller
1952. A Sequel to "The Mystery of Father Padilla." (El Palacio, Vol. 59, No. 12, pp. 386–89)
1954a. Origins of New Mexico Families in the Spanish Colonial Period. (Historical Society of New Mexico, Santa Fe, 339 pp.)
1954b. The Penitentes of New Mexico. (New Mexico Historical Review, Vol. 29, No. 2, pp. 97–123)

1957. Archives of the Archdiocese of Santa Fe. (Academy of American Franciscan History, Bibliographic Series, Vol. III, 283 pp.)

1965. The Unique Tomb of Fathers Zarate and de la Llana in Santa Fe. (New Mexico Historical Review, Vol. 40, No. 2, pp. 101–15)

Coan, Charles F.

1925. A History of New Mexico. (The American Historical Society, Inc., Chicago and New York. Three volumes, 586 pp., 523 pp., 506 pp.)

Cole, Fay-Cooper

1957. Frederick Webb Hodge, 1864–1956. (American Anthropologist, Vol. 59, No. 3, pp. 517–20)

Conard, Howard L., ed.

1901. Encyclopedia of the History of Missouri. (The Southern History Company, New York, Louisville and St. Louis, Vol. 1, 632 pp.)

Congrès International des Américanistes

1890. Congrès International des Américanistes, Compte Rendu de la Septième Session. (Berlin 1888, 806 pp.)

Cushing, Frank Hamilton

1886. A Study of Pueblo Pottery as Illustrative of Zuñi Culture Growth. (Bureau of [American] Ethnology, 4th Annual Report, 1882–83, Washington, pp. 473–521)

1890. Preliminary Notes on the Origin, Working Hypothesis and Primary Researches of the Hemenway Southwestern Archaeological Expedition. (Congrès International des Américanistes, Septième Session, 1888, Berlin, pp. 151–94)

Davis, Britton

1929. The Truth about Geronimo. (Yale University Press, New Haven, 253 pp.)

Davis, Ellis Arthur, ed.

1945. The Historical Encyclopedia of New Mexico. (New Mexico Historical Association, Albuquerque. Two volumes, pp. 1–1032, 1037–2079)

Davis, Irvine

1959. Linguistic Clues to Northern Rio Grande Prehistory. (El Palacio, Vol. 66, No. 3, pp. 73–84)

Davis, W. W. H.
1857. El Gringo; or, New Mexico and Her People. (New York, 432 pp.)

Defouri, Very Rev. James H.
1887. Historical Sketch of the Catholic Church in New Mexico. (McCormick Bros., Printers, 410 Sansome Street, San Francisco, Calif., 164 pp.)
1893. The Martyrs of New Mexico. A Brief Account of the Lives and Deaths of the Earliest Missionaries in the Territory. (The "Revista Católica" Printing Office, Las Vegas, N. M., 78 pp.)

Dictionary of American Biography
1936. Dictionary of American Biography, Dumas Malone, ed. (Vol. X, Charles Scribner's Sons, New York, 662 pp.)
1957. Dictionary of American Biography, Allen Johnson, ed. (Vol. I, Charles Scribner's Sons, New York, 613 pp.)

Dike, Sheldon H.
1958. The Territorial Post Offices of New Mexico. (Published by Dr. S. H. Dike, 1611 Bayita Lane, NW, Albuquerque, N.M., 56 pp. This monograph was also published in several numbers of the New Mexico Historical Review: Vol. 33, 1958, pp. 322–27, and Vol. 34, 1959, pp. 55–69, 145–52, 203–26, 308–9)

Dittert, Alfred E., Jr., Jim J. Hester, and Frank W. Eddy
1961. An Archaeological Survey of the Navajo Reservoir District, Northwestern New Mexico. (Monographs of the School of American Research and the Museum of New Mexico, Santa Fe, 277 pp.)

Dixon, Roland B.
1903. George Julius Engelmann [Obituary]. (American Anthropologist, Vol. 5, No. 4, p. 739)

Dozier, Edward P.
1970. The Pueblo Indians of North America. (Case Studies in Cultural Anthropology, Holt, Rinehart and Winston, Inc., New York, 224 pp.)

Dumarest, Father Nöel
1919. Notes on Cochiti, New Mexico. (Memoirs of the American Anthropological Association, Vol. VI, No. 3, pp. 137–236)

Dutton, Bertha P.
   1952. Senior Girl Scout-Museum Archaeological Program of
      1952. (El Palacio, Vol. 59, No. 11, pp. 342–52)
Edwards, Richard
   1865. Directory of St. Louis, 1865. (Edwards & Co., Publish-
      ers, St. Louis and New York, 865 pp.)
Eggan, Fred
   1950. Social Organization of the Western Pueblos. (Univer-
      sity of Chicago Press, Chicago, 373 pp.)
Eggan, Jacob
   1933. History of Highland. (Originally written in German in
      1887; trans., Rev. C. E. Miche; ed., A. P. Spencer. Two
      scrapbooks. Louis Latzer Memorial Public Library, High-
      land, Ill., pp. 1–44 and pp. 45–105)
Ellis, Bruce [T.]
   1968. An Alcalde's Proclamation: A Rare New Mexico Docu-
      ment, Marc Simmons, trans. and ed. (El Palacio, Vol. 75,
      No. 2, pp. 5–9)
Ellis, Florence Hawley
   1952. Jemez Kiva Magic and its Relation to Features of Pre-
      historic Kivas. (Southwestern Journal of Anthropology,
      Vol. 8, No. 1, pp. 147–63)
   1953. Authoritative Control and the Society System in Jemez
      Pueblo. (Southwestern Journal of Anthropology, Vol. 9,
      No. 4, pp. 385–94)
   1955. Tomé and Father J. B. R. (New Mexico Historical Re-
      view, Vol. 30, Nos. 2–3, pp. 89–114, 195–220)
   1964a. Archaeological History of Nambé Pueblo, 14th Cen-
      tury to the Present. (American Antiquity, Vol. 30, No. 1,
      pp. 34–42)
   1964b. A Reconstruction of the Basic Jemez Pattern of Social
      Organization, with Comparisons to Other Tanoan Social
      Structures. (University of New Mexico Publications in An-
      thropology, No. 11, Albuquerque, 69 pp.)
   1966. The Immediate History of Zia Pueblo as Derived from
      Excavation in Refuse Deposits. (American Antiquity, Vol.
      31, No. 6, pp. 806–11)
Ellis, Florence Hawley, and J. J. Brody
   1964. Ceramic Stratigraphy and Tribal History at Taos Pue-
      blo. (American Antiquity, Vol. 29, No. 3, pp. 316–27)

Emory, W. H.
  1848. Notes of a Military Reconnaissance from Fort Leaven-
    worth, in Missouri, to San Diego, in California, including
    part of the Arkansas, Del Norte, and Gila Rivers. (Thir-
    tieth Congress, 1st Session, Ex. Doc. No. 41, Washington,
    pp. 7–126)
Enciclopedia de México
  1967. Enciclopedia de México. (Institute de la Enciclopedia
    de México, 10 vols. Vol. II, 1232 pp.)
Encyclopaedia Britannica
  1967. Encyclopaedia Britannica, Volumes 16 and 17. (Ency-
    clopaedia Britannica, Inc., William Benton, Publisher,
    1199 pp., 1223 pp.)
Espinosa, Gilberto
  1933. History of New Mexico by Gaspar Pérez de Villagrá,
    Alcalá, 1610. (Introduction and Notes by F. W. Hodge,
    Quivira Society Publications, IV, 308 pp.)
Espinosa, J. Manuel
  1940. First Expedition of Vargas into New Mexico, 1692.
    (University of New Mexico Press, Albuquerque, 319 pp.)
  1942. Crusaders of the Rio Grande: The Story of Don Diego
    de Vargas and the Reconquest and Refounding of New
    Mexico. (Institute of Jesuit History Publications, Chicago,
    410 pp.)
Evans, S. B.
  1890. Observations on the Aztecs and their Probable Rela-
    tions to the Pueblo Indians of New Mexico. (Congrès In-
    ternational des Américanistes, Septième Session, 1888,
    Berlin, pp. 226–30)
Fernández Duro, Cesáreo
  1882. Don Diego de Peñalosa y su descubrimiento del reino
    de Quivira. (Informe presentado a la Real Academia de
    la Historia. Madrid. This report also appeared in the
    Memorias de la Real Academia de la Historia, tomo X,
    Madrid, pp. 1–160, in 1885)
Fewkes, J. Walter
  1895. The Bandelier Collection of Copies of Documents Rel-
    ative to the History of New Mexico and Arizona [From
    the archives of the Hemenway expedition]. (Report of the
    United States Commission to the Columbian Historical

Exposition at Madrid, 1892–93, with Special Papers. Washington, pp. 305–26)

Fierman, Floyd S.
1961. Nathan Bibo's Reminiscences of Early New Mexico. (El Palacio, Vol. 68, No. 4, pp. 231–57)

Forbes, Jack D.
1960. Apache, Navaho and Spaniard. (University of Oklahoma Press, Norman, 304 pp.)

Ford, Thomas
1945. A History of Illinois from Its Commencement As a State in 1818 to 1847. (Edited by Milo M. Quaife, The Lakeside Press, Chicago, Vol. I, 374 pp.)

Fox, Robin
1967. The Keresan Bridge: A Problem in Pueblo Ethnology. (London School of Economics, Monographs on Social Anthropology, No. 35, The Humanities Press, Inc., New York, 216 pp.)

Francis, E. K.
1956. Padre Martínez: A New Mexican Myth. (New Mexico Historical Review, Vol. XXXI, No. 4, pp. 265–89)

Frink, Maurice, with Casey E. Barthelmess
1965. Photographer on an Army Mule. (University of Oklahoma Press, Norman, 151 pp.)

Fuller, Clarissa Parsons
1943. Frank Hamilton Cushing's Relations to Zuñi and the Hemenway Southwestern Expedition, 1879–1889. (Unpublished M.S. thesis in history, Library, University of New Mexico, 104 pp.)
1950. A Reexamination of Bandelier's Studies of Ancient Mexico. (Unpublished doctoral dissertation in history, Library, University of New Mexico, Albuquerque, 107 pp.)

Galvin, John, ed.
1966. Western America in 1846–1847. The Original Travel Diary of Lieutenant J. W. Abert, who Mapped New Mexico for the United States Army, with illustrations in color from his sketchbook. (John Howell-Books, San Francisco, 116 pp.)

Gerald, Rex E.
1968. Spanish Presidios of the Late Eighteenth Century in

Northern New Spain. (Museum of New Mexico Research Records, No. 7, Santa Fe, 60 pp.)

Gjevre, John A.
  1969. Chili Line: the Narrow Rail Trail to Santa Fe: the Story of the Narrow Gauge Denver and Rio Grande Western's Santa Fe Branch, 1880–1941. (Rio Grande Sun Press, Española, New Mexico, 82 pp.)

Goad, Edgar F.
  1938. Bandelier's Early Life. (The Historian, pp. 75–82)
  1939. A Study of the Life of Adolph Francis Alphonse Bandelier, with an Appraisal of His Contributions to American Anthropology and Related Sciences. (Unpublished Ph.D. dissertation, University of Southern California, Los Angeles, 229 pp.)

Goldfrank, Esther S.
  1927. The Social and Ceremonial Organization of Cochiti. (Memoir No. 33, American Anthropological Association, 129 pp.)

Gould, David B., ed.
  1873–92. Gould's St. Louis Directory. (David Edwards & Co., Printers, St. Louis, through 1883; Gould Directory Co., St. Louis, thereafter: 1873, 1146 pp.; 1874, 1231 pp.; 1875, 1255 pp.; 1876, 1254 pp.; 1877, 1279 pp.; 1878, 1242 pp.; 1879, 1298 pp.; 1880, 1394 pp.; 1881, 1474 pp.; 1882, 1538 pp.; 1883, 1486 pp.; 1884, 1488 pp.; 1885, 1564 pp.; 1886, 1590 pp.; 1887, 1603 pp.; 1888, 1693 pp.; 1889, 1712 pp.; 1890, 1774 pp.; 1891, 1859 pp.; and 1892, 2055 pp.)

Grant, Blanche C.
  1925. Taos Indians. (Taos, New Mexico, 127 pp.)
  1934. When Old Trails were New. (Press of the Pioneers, New York, 344 pp.)

Greene, Chas. W.
  1882. A Complete Business Directory of New Mexico and Gazeteer of the Territory for 1882. (New Mexico Publishing and Printing Company, 256 pp.)

Gregg, Andrew K.
  1968. New Mexico in the Nineteenth Century: A Pictorial History. (University of New Mexico Press, Albuquerque. 196 pp.)

Gunnerson, Dolores A.
1974. The Jicarilla Apaches: A Study in Survival. (Northern Illinois University Press, DeKalb, xv + 326 pp.)

Gunnerson, James H.
1969. Apache Archaeology in Northeastern New Mexico. (American Antiquity, Vol. 34, No. 1, pp. 23–39)

Gunnerson, James H., and Dolores A. Gunnerson
1970. Evidence of Apaches at Pecos. (El Palacio, Vol. 76, No. 3, pp. 1–6)

Hackett, Charles W., ed.
1923–26–37. Historical Documents Relating to New Mexico, Nueva Vizcaya, and Approaches Thereto, to 1773. (Collected by Adolph F. A. Bandelier and Fanny R. Bandelier. Spanish text and English translations. Edited with Introductions and annotations by Charles Wilson Hackett. Three volumes. Washington, D.C. Published by the Carnegie Institution of Washington; 502 pp., 497 pp., 532 pp.)
1942. Revolt of the Pueblo Indians of New Mexico and Otermin's Attempted Reconquest, 1680–1682. Parts I and II. (University of New Mexico Press, Albuquerque, ccx + 262 pp. and 430 pp.)

Haines, Helen
1891. History of New Mexico. (New Mexico Historical Publishing Co., New York, 631 pp.)

Halseth, Odd S., and E. Boyd
1971. The Laguna Santero. (El Palacio, Vol. 77, No. 3, pp. 19–22. Halseth portion of article reprinted from El Palacio, Vol. 16, No. 1, 1924)

Hamer, Philip May, ed.
1961. A Guide to Archives and Manuscripts in the United States. (Yale University Press, New Haven, 775 pp.)

Hammond, George P., and Edgar F. Goad
1949. A Scientist on the Trail: Travel Letters of A. F. Bandelier, 1880–1881. (The Quivira Society, Vol. X, Los Angeles, 142 pp.; reprinted by Arno Press, New York, 1967)

Hammond, George P., and Agapito Rey
1929. Expedition into New Mexico made by Antonio de Espejo, 1582–1583, as Revealed in the Journal of Diego Pérez de Luxán, a Member of the Party. (The Quivira

Society, Vol. I, Los Angeles, 143 pp.; reprinted by Arno
Press, New York, 1967)

1940. Narratives of the Coronado Expedition 1540–1542.
(University of New Mexico Press, Albuquerque,
Coronado Cuarto Centennial Publications, 1540–1940,
Vol. II, 413 pp.)

1953. Don Juan de Oñate, Colonizer of New Mexico, 1595–
1628. (The University of New Mexico Press, Albuquerque, New Mexico. Two volumes, pp. 1–584 and
585–1187)

1966. The Rediscovery of New Mexico. 1580–1594.
(Coronado Cuarto Centennial Publications, 1540–1940,
Vol. III, University of New Mexico Press, Albuquerque,
341 pp.)

Harlow, Francis H.

1965. Recent Finds of Pajaritan Pottery. (El Palacio, Vol. 72,
No. 2, pp. 27–33)

Harrington, John P.

1916. The Ethnography of the Tewa Indians. (Bureau of
American Ethnology, 29th Annual Report, 1907–1908,
Washington, pp. 29–636)

Haury, Emil W.

1945. The Excavation of Los Muertos and Neighboring Ruins
in the Salt River Valley, Southern Arizona. (Papers of the
Peabody Museum of American Archaeology and Ethnology, Harvard University, Vol. XXIV, No. 1, Cambridge, Mass., 223 pp. and 90 plates)

Hawley, Florence M. (See also Florence H. Ellis)

1936. Field Manual of Prehistoric Southwestern Pottery
Types. (University of New Mexico Bulletin, Anthropological Series, Vol. 1, No. 4; revised, 1950, 126 pp.)

Hayes, Alden

1968. The Missing Convento of San Isidro. (El Palacio, Vol.
75, No. 4, pp. 35–40)

Hedrick, Basil C., J. Charles Kelley, and Carroll L. Riley

1971. The North Mexican Frontier: Readings in Archaeology, Ethnohistory and Ethnography. (Southern Illinois
University Press, Carbondale, 255 pp.)

Heitman, Francis B.

1903. Historical Register and Dictionary of the United States

Army from its Organization, September 29, 1789, to March 2, 1903. (Two volumes. Washington, D.C., pp. 1–1069 and pp. 1–626)

Helvetia Schützen-Gesellschaft
1883. Fest-Kalendar. (Mai-Juni. Highland. 129 pp.)

Hendron, J. W.
1946. Frijoles: A Hidden Valley in the New World. (Edited by Dorothy Thomas, Rydal Press, Inc., Santa Fe, 89 pp.)

Hewett, Edgar L.
1906. Antiquities of the Jemez Plateau, New Mexico. (Bureau of American Ethnology, Bulletin 32, 55 pp.)
1909. The Excavations at El Rito de los Frijoles in 1909. (Archaeological Institute of America; School of American Archaeology, Papers, No. 10; reprinted from the American Anthropologist, Vol. 11, No. 4, pp. 651–73)
1953. Pajarito Plateau and its Ancient People. (The University of New Mexico Press and The School of American Research, revised by Bertha Dutton, 174 pp.)

Hewett, Edgar L, and Wayne L. Mauzy
1940. Landmarks of New Mexico. (University of New Mexico Press, 200 pp.)

Heÿink, Jac., and F. W. Hodge
1931. Herman Frederik Carel ten Kate. (American Anthropologist, Vol. 33, No. 3, pp. 415–18)

Hibben, Frank C.
1937. Excavations of the Riana Ruin and Chama Valley Survey. (University of New Mexico Press, Anth. Ser., No. 300, Vol. 2, No. 1, Albuquerque, 60 pp.)

Hobbs, Hulda R.
1940a. Notes on interview with Mrs. Elizabeth Bandelier Kaune, Santa Fe, New Mexico. (Files, Library, Museum of New Mexico, Santa Fe)
1940b. Bandelier in the Southwest. (El Palacio, Vol. 47, No. 6, pp. 121–36)
1942a. Notes on interview with Mrs. Elizabeth Bandelier Kaune, Santa Fe, New Mexico. (Files, Library, Museum of New Mexico, Santa Fe)
1942b. The Story of the Delight Makers from Bandelier's Own Journals. (El Palacio, Vol. 49, No. 6, pp. 109–24)

1942c. Addenda to "The Delight Makers." (El Palacio, Vol. 49, No. 8, pp. 163–66)

Hodge, F. W.

1896. John Gregory Bourke. (American Anthropologist, Vol. IX, o.s., July, pp. 245–48)

1907–10. Handbook of American Indians North of Mexico, Parts I and II. (Bureau of American Ethnology, Bulletin 30, pp. 1–972 and pp. 1–1,221)

1908. Norton Obituary. (American Anthropologist, n.s., Vol. 10, No. 4, pp. 704–5)

1914. Bandelier Obituary. (American Anthropologist, Vol. 16, No. 2, pp. 349–58)

1932. Biographical Sketch and Bibliography of Adolphe Francis Alphonse Bandelier. (New Mexico Historical Review, Vol. VII, No. 4, pp. 353–70)

1937. History of Háwikuh, New Mexico: One of the So-called Cities of Cíbola. (Southwest Museum, Los Angeles, 155 pp.)

1940. Unpublished paper presented at a Memorial Conference, August 6–8, 1940, in Santa Fe, as a part of centennial celebration of Bandelier's birth. (Archives, Museum of New Mexico)

Hodge, Fredcrick W., George P. Hammond, and Agapito Rey

1945. Fray Alonzo de Benavides' Revised Memorial of 1634. (Coronado Cuarto Centennial Publications 4, University of New Mexico Press, Albuquerque, 368 pp.)

Holben, Richard E.

1969. The Treasures of Tomé. (New Mexico Magazine, Vol. 47, No. 1, January, pp. 16–17, 39–40)

Holmes, William H.

1878. Report on the Ancient Ruins of Southwestern Colorado, Examined during the Summers of 1875 and 1876. (Tenth Annual Report of the United States Geological and Geographical Survey of the Territories, 1876, Washington, pp. 383–408)

Hooton, Earnest A.

1925. The Ancient Inhabitants of the Canary Islands. (Harvard African Studies, Vol. VII, Peabody Museum, Harvard University Press, Cambridge, 401 pp.)

Horka-Follick, Lorayne Ann
  1969. Los Hermanos Penitentes: A Vestige of Medievalism in Southwestern United States. (Westernlore Press, Los Angeles, 226 pp.)

Huggins
  1876. Huggins' Map of New Mexico. (Compiled from Official Records, in Surveyor General's Office; published by New Mexico Stock & Agricultural Association, Chicago, Ill.)

Hyde, William
  1896. Newspapers and Newspaper People of Three Decades. (Missouri Historical Society, Vol. 1, No. 12, St. Louis, pp. 5–24)

Hyde, William, and Howard L. Conard
  1899. Encyclopedia of the History of St. Louis. (The Southern History Company, New York, Louisville and St. Louis. Four volumes: pp. 1–622, 623–1,226, 1,227–1,912, and 1,913–2,572)

Jacobs, Wilbur R.
  1960. Letters of Francis Parkman: edited and with an Introduction by Wilbur R. Jacobs. (Two volumes. University of Oklahoma Press, Norman, pp. 1–204 and pp. 1–286)

James, George Wharton
  1920. New Mexico: The Land of the Delight Makers. (The Page Company, Boston, 469 pp.)

Janvier, Thomas A.
  1888. The Mexican Guide. (3rd Edition. C. Scribner's Sons, New York, 523 pp.) 1st—1886—310 pp. C. Scribner's Sons; 4th—1890—531 pp. C. Scribner's Sons; 6th—1895 —531 pp. C. Scribner's Sons

Jenkins, Myra Ellen
  1961. The Baltasar Baca "Grant": History of an Encroachment. (El Palacio, Vol. 68, Nos. 1 and 2, pp. 47–64, 87–105)

Jenkinson, Michael, with Karl Kernberger
  1967. Ghost Towns of New Mexico: Playthings of the Wind. (University of New Mexico Press, Albuquerque, 156 pp.)

Johnson, Allen, and Dumas Malone
  1946. Dictionary of American Biography. (Charles Scribner's Sons, N.Y. Vol. VII, 612 pp.)

Jones, Oakah L., Jr.
1967. Introduction to Frank H. Cushing, My Adventures in Zuñi. (Filter Press, Palmer Lake, Colorado, pp. iii–viii)

Kaeser, Jennie Latzer, trans.
1970. The Story of the Settling of Highland, by Solomon Koepfli. (Translated from Die Geschichte der Ansiedlung von Highland, published by the Highland Bote, 1859. Edited and annotated by Raymond J. Spahn, with an Introduction by John C. Abbott. Privately printed, Lovejoy Library, Southern Illinois University at Edwardsville, 2nd printing, 1971, xi + 139 pp.)

Kargau, E. D.
n.d. Mercantile, Industrial, and Professional St. Louis. (St. Louis, 674 pp.)

Katz, Friedrich
1966. Situacíon social y económica de los Aztecas durante los siglos XV y XVI. (Universidad Nacional Autónoma de México, Instituto de Investigaciones Históricas, Dirección General de Publicaciones, México, 208 pp.)

Keleher, William A.
1952. Turmoil in New Mexico: 1846–68. (The Rydal Press, Santa Fe, 534 pp.)

Kenner, Charles L.
1969. A History of New Mexican-Plains Indian Relations. (University of Oklahoma Press, Norman, x + 250 pp.)

Kluckhohn, Clyde
1944. Navaho Witchcraft. (Papers of the Peabody Museum of American Archaeology and Ethnology, Harvard University, Vol. XXII, No. 2, Cambridge, Mass., 149 pp.)

Köpfli, Kaspar
1833. Die Licht- & Schattenseite von New-Switzerland in Nordamerika. (Sursee, 61 pp.)

Köpfli, Salomon
1842. Neu Schweizerland in den Jahren 1831 und 1841. (Verlag von Xaver Meyer, Luzern, 82 pp.)

Kubler, George
1939. The Rebuilding of San Miguel at Santa Fe in 1710. (Contributions of the Taylor Museum of the Colorado Springs Fine Arts Center, Colorado Springs, 27 pp.)
1940. The Religious Architecture of New Mexico in the Colo-

nial Period and Since the American Occupation. (Contributions of the Taylor Museum, Colorado Springs, Colo., 232 pp.) (Revised and reprinted, University of New Mexico Press, Albuquerque, 1973, 264 pp.)

Ladd, Horatio O.
    1891. The Story of New Mexico. (D. Lothrop Company, Boston, 465 pp.)

La Farge, Oliver
    1959. Santa Fe: The Autobiography of a Southwestern Town. (University of Oklahoma Press, Norman, 436 pp.)

Lamar, Howard Roberts
    1966. The Far Southwest, 1846–1912: A Territorial History. (Yale University Press, New Haven and London, 560 pp.)

Lambert, Marjorie F.
    1954. Paa-ko, Archaeological Chronicle of an Indian Village in North Central New Mexico, Parts I–V. (Part VI, by Spencer L. Rogers, The Physical Type of the Paa-ko Population. The School of American Research, Santa Fe, Monograph 19, Parts I-V, 183 pp.)

Lamy Memorial
    1950. Archdiocese of Santa Fe, 1850–1950. (Santa Fe, 98 pp.)

Lange, Charles H.
    1952. The Feast Day Dance at Zia Pueblo, August 15, 1951. (Texas Journal of Science, Vol. IV, No. 1, pp. 19–26)
    1953. A Reappraisal of Evidence of Plains Influences among the Rio Grande Pueblos. (Southwestern Journal of Anthropology, Vol. 9, No. 2, pp. 212–30)
    1957. Tablita, or Corn, Dances of the Rio Grande Pueblo Indians. (The Texas Journal of Science, Vol. IX, No. 1, pp. 59–74)
    1958. The Keresan Component of Southwestern Pueblo Culture. (Southwestern Journal of Anthropology, Vol. 14, No. 1, pp. 34–50)
    1959. Cochiti: A New Mexico Pueblo, Past and Present. (University of Texas Press, Austin, 618 pp. Reprinted by Arcturus Books, Southern Illinois University Press, 1968)

Lange, Charles H., and Carroll L. Riley, eds.
    1966. The Southwestern Journals of Adolph F. Bandelier,

1880–1882. (University of New Mexico Press, Albuquerque, 462 pp.)

1970. The Southwestern Journals of Adolph F. Bandelier, 1883–1884. (With the assistance of Elizabeth M. Lange. University of New Mexico Press, Albuquerque, 528 pp.)

Library of Congress

1942–46. A Catalog of Books . . . issued to July 31, 1942. (Edwards Brothers, Inc., Ann Arbor, Mich., 167 Vols.) 1942 Volume 6, 640 pp.; 1943 Volume 30, 640 pp. (1943a); 1943 Volume 57, 787 pp. (1943b); 1946 Volume 158, 640 pp.

Lister, Florence C., and Robert H. Lister

1966. Chihuahua: Storehouse of Storms. (University of New Mexico Press, Albuquerque, 360 pp.)

Lockwood, Frank C.

1938. The Apache Indians. (The Macmillan Company, New York, 348 pp.)

Loomis, Sylvia Glidden, ed.

1966. Old Santa Fe Today. (Prepared by The Historic Santa Fe Foundation; published by The School of American Research, Santa Fe, 48 pp.)

Lowie, Robert H.

1937. The History of Ethnological Theory. (Farrar & Rinehart, Inc., New York, 296 pp.)

Lummis, Charles F.

1892. Some Strange Corners of Our Country. (The Century Co., New York. xi + 270 pp. Reprinted 1903, 1911)

1928. The Land of Poco Tiempo. (Charles Scribner's Sons, New York, 310 pp.)

MacGregor, John

1970. El Morro, America's First Guest Book. (New Mexico Magazine, Vol. 48, Nos. 3–4, pp. 24–33)

Markham, Clements R.

1892. A History of Peru. (C. H. Sergel & Co., Chicago, xvi + 11–556 pp.)

McKenny Directory Company

1888. Southern Pacific Coast Directory for 1888–89, being a Business Directory of San Francisco, Central and Southern California, Arizona, New Mexico, and Southern Colorado. (Pacific Coast Publishing Co., Oakland, California, pp. 5–1260)

McKenney, L. M., and Co.

1882–83. McKenney's Business Directory of the Principal Towns of Central and Southern California, Arizona, New Mexico, Southern Colorado, and Kansas, 1882–1883. (Pacific Press Publishers, San Francisco, 941 pp.)

McKenzie, Parker, and John P. Harrington

1948. Popular Account of the Kiowa Indian Language. (School of American Research, Monograph No. 12, Albuquerque, 21 pp.)

McLennan, John F.

1886. Studies in Ancient History. (Macmillan and Co., London, 387 pp.; a reprint of : Primitive Marriage: an Inquiry into the Origin of the Form of Capture in Marriage Ceremonies, Edinburgh, Adam and Charles Black, 1865, xii + 326 pp.)

Meine, Franklin J. et al., ed.

1940. Webster's Encyclopedia Dictionary: Dictionary of Biography. (Columbia Educational Books, Inc., Chicago, pp. 435–538)

Mera, H. P.

1935. Ceramic Clues to the Prehistory of North Central New Mexico. (Technical Series, Bulletin No. 8, Laboratory of Anthropology, Santa Fe, 43 pp.)

1940. Population Changes in the Rio Grande Glaze-Paint Area. (Technical Series, Bulletin No. 9, Laboratory of Anthropology, Santa Fe, 41 pp.)

Mindeleff, Victor

1891. A Study of Pueblo Architecture: Tusayan and Cibola. (Bureau of Ethnology, Eighth Annual Report, 1886–87, Washington, pp. 13–228)

Morgan, Lewis Henry

1869. The Seven Cities of Cibola. (North American Review, Vol. 108, No. 223, April, pp. 457–98)

The Nation

1885. The Week. (The Nation, Vol. 40, No. 1035, New York Evening Post Publishing Company, New York, pp. 351–55)

National Academy of Science
1902. Biographical Memoir of George Engelmann. (Biographical Memoirs of the National Academy of Science, Vol. IV, Washington, D.C., pp. 3–21)

Nelson, Nels C.
1914. Pueblo Ruins of the Galisteo Basin, New Mexico. (American Museum of Natural History, Anthropological Papers, Vol. XV, Pt. I, New York, pp. 1–124)
1916a. New Mexico Field Work in 1915. (El Palacio, Vol. III, No. 2, pp. 42–55)
1916b. Chronology of the Tano Ruins, New Mexico. (American Anthropologist, Vol. 18, No. 2, pp. 159–80)

Newcomb, William W., Jr.
1961. The Indians of Texas, from Prehistoric to Modern Times. (The University of Texas Press, Austin, 404 pp.)

New Mexico Historical Review
1933. Necrology: Arthur Seligman. (New Mexico Historical Review, Vol. VIII, No. 4, pp. 306–16)
1944. News and Comments. (New Mexico Historical Review, Vol. 19, No. 3, pp. 254–55)

New Mexico State Archives
n.d. Catron File
n.d. Manderfield File.

Newspapers
Albuquerque Evening Review: 1882
Albuquerque Morning Journal: 1882, 1884, 1885
Belletristisches Journal (New York City): 1886, 1889, 1890
Daily New Mexican (Santa Fe): 1890
Das Ausland (Stuttgart and München): 1882–86 (Wochenschrift für Länder und Völkerkunde unter Mitwirkung von Professor Dr. Friedrich Ratzel und anderen Fachmännern herausgegeben von der J. G. Cotta'schen Buch=handlung in Stuttgart und München. Bande I–LXVII, 1828–1894.)
Die Highland Union—Reisebriefe: 1881
Die Union (Highland, Illinois): 1869
Evening Post (New York): March 17, 1890
Highland News Leader: 1927, 1937
Intelligencer, The (Edwardsville, Ill.): 1885–86

National Zeitung (Berlin): 1886
New Mexican, The (Santa Fe, N.M.): 1968
New Yorker Staatszeitung (New York): 1885, 1886, 1888
Santa Fe Daily New Mexican: 1878, 1881–83, 1885–88, 1890
Santa Fe Herald: 1886, 1888
Santa Fe New Mexican: 1954
Santa Fé New Mexican Review: 1883–85
Santa Fe Weekly Gazette: 1867
St. Louis Globe Democrat: 1885–86
Saturday Evening Post (Burlington, Ia.): 1888
Weekly New Mexican Review (Santa Fe): 1888–89
Weekly Telephone, The (Highland, Ill.): 1884–85
Westliche Post (St. Louis): 1883, 1885

Norton, W. T.
  1912. Centennial History of Madison County, Illinois, and Its People, 1812 to 1912. (The Lewis Publishing Company, Chicago and New York. Two volumes, pp. 1–618, 623–1208)

Official Reports
  1884. Official Reports of the Territory of New Mexico for the Years 1882 and 1883. (Published by authority. New Mexican Review Company, Santa Fe, 140 pp.)

O'Gorman, Edmundo, ed.
  1971. Fray Toribio de Benavente o Motolinía, Memoriales ... con inserción de las porciones de la Historia de los Indios de la Nueva España que completan el texto de los Memoriales. (México Universidad Nacional Autónoma, 591 pp.)

Ortiz, Alfonso
  1969. The Tewa World. (The University of Chicago Press, Chicago and London, 197 pp.)

Otero, Miguel Antonio
  1935. My Life on the Frontier 1864–1882. (The Press of the Pioneers, Inc., New York, Vol. I, 293 pp.)
  1939. My Life on the Frontier, 1882–1897. (University of New Mexico Press, Albuquerque, Vol. II, 306 pp.)

Pacheco, Joaquín, and Francisco de Cárdenas
  1864–84. Colección de Documentos Inéditos, Relativos al Descubrimiento, Conquista y Organización de las An-

tiguas Posesiones Españolas en América y Oceania, Sacados de los Archivos del Reino, y Muy Especialmente del
de Indias. (Madrid. 42 vols.)

Paré, Madeline F., with the collaboration of Bert M. Fireman
1965. Arizona Pageant. (Arizona Historical Foundation,
Phoenix, 336 pp.)

Parish, William J.
1960. The German Jew and the Commercial Revolution in
Territorial New Mexico, 1850–1900. (New Mexico Historical Review, Vol. XXXV, Nos. 1 and 2, Parts I and II, pp.
1–29 and pp. 129–50)

Parsons, Elsie Clews
1925. The Pueblo of Jemez. (Published for the Department
of Archaeology, Phillips Academy, Andover, Mass., by
Yale University Press, 144 pp.)
1929. The Social Organization of the Tewa of New Mexico.
(Memoir No. 36, American Anthropological Association,
306 pp.)
1933. Hopi and Zuñi Ceremonialism. (Memoir No. 39,
American Anthropological Association, 108 pp.)
1936. Taos Pueblo. (General Series in Anthropology, No. 2,
George Banta, Menasha, Wisconsin, 121 pp.)
1939. Pueblo Indian Religion. (University of Chicago Press,
Chicago. Two volumes, pp. 1–549 and pp. 551–1275)

Pearce, T.M.
1965. New Mexico Place Names, A Geographical Dictionary.
(University of New Mexico Press, 187 pp.)

Peckham, Stewart L.
1969. Review of Franklin Barnett's Tonque Pueblo: A Report of Partial Excavation of an Ancient Pueblo IV Indian
Ruin in New Mexico. (El Palacio, Vol. 76, No. 2, pp. 43–
44)

Peckham, Stewart [L.], and Erik K. Reed
1963. Three Sites Near Ranchos de Taos, New Mexico.
(Highway Salvage Archaeology, The New Mexico State
Highway Department and the Museum of New Mexico,
IV: 1–28)

Penniman, T. K.
1952. A Hundred Years of Anthropology. (Gerald Duck-
worth & Co., Ltd., London, revised edition, 512 pp.)

Pennington, Campbell W.
   1963. The Tarahumar of Mexico. (University of Utah Press,
      Salt Lake City, 267 pp.)
Picurís Indians
   1941. People of the Hidden Valley: Guidebook to Picurís
      Pueblo, Taos County, New Mexico. (Picuris, New Mexico,
      15 pp.)
Pilling, James Constantine
   1885. Proof-Sheets of a Bibliography of the Languages of the
      North American Indians. (Distributed only to Collabora-
      tors. Washington, xl+1135 pp., 29 pls.)
Poldervaart, Arie
   1947. Black-Robed Justice in New Mexico, 1846–1912. (New
      Mexico Historical Review, Vol. 22, Nos. 1–4, pp. 18–50,
      109–39, 286–314, 351–88)
Polk, R. L., & Co., and A. C. Danser
   1884a. Colorado, New Mexico, Utah, Nevada, Wyoming, and
      Arizona Gazeteer and Business Directory, 1884–1885.
      (891 pp.)
   1884b. Illinois State Gazeteer and Business Directory, 1884.
      (2,323 pp.)
Prescott, William H.
   1893. History of the Conquest of Mexico. (David McKay,
      Philadelphia. Vol. II, 402 pp.)
Prince, LeBaron Bradford
   1883. Historical Sketches of New Mexico, from the Earliest
      Records to the American Occupation. (Leggat Brothers,
      New York; Ramsey, Millet & Hudson, Kansas City, 327
      pp.)
   1912. Old Fort Marcy, Santa Fe, New Mexico. (Santa Fe, 16
      pp.)
   1915. Spanish Mission Churches of New Mexico. (The Torch
      Press, Cedar Rapids, Iowa, 373 pp.)
Puckett, Fidelia Miller
   1950. Ramon Ortiz: Priest and Patriot. (Fray Angélico
      Chávez, ed. New Mexico Historical Review, Vol. XXV,
      No. 4, pp. 265–95)
Quirk, Martin H., Adolfo Tafoya, and Mary F. Redmond
   1942. Index to Final Report of Investigations among the In-
      dians of the Southwestern United States by A. F. Bande-

lier. (The Historical Society of New Mexico, The New Mexico Historical Records Survey, Santa Fe, 86 pp.)

Radin, Paul
1942. The Unpublished Letters of Adolphe F. Bandelier concerning the writing and publication of The Delight Makers. (Southwestern Archaeologica, Charles P. Everitt, New York, 33 pp.)

Rebord, Bernice Ann
1947. A Social History of Albuquerque, 1880–1885. (Unpublished thesis in partial fulfillment of the requirements for the Degree of Master of Arts in History, University of New Mexico, Albuquerque, 115 leaves)

Reeve, Frank Driver
1933. The Old University of New Mexico at Santa Fé. (New Mexico Historical Review, Vol. 8, No. 3, pp. 201–10)
1961. History of New Mexico. (Lewis Historical Publishing Co., Inc., New York. Two volumes, 485 pp. and 449 pp., including index for both volumes)

Registro para los Entierros para Peña Blanca, etc. 1890–1926

Reiter, Paul
1938. The Jemez Pueblo of Unshagi, New Mexico, with notes on the Earlier Excavations at "Amoxiumqua" and Giusewa. (The University of New Mexico, Bulletin, Monograph Series, Vol. 1, Nos. 4–5, Parts I and II, pp. 7–92, 97–211)

Report of the Commissioner of Indian Affairs
1886. Report of the Commissioner of Indian Affairs, Report of the Secretary of the Interior, Vol. 1, No. 1. (The Executive Documents of the House of Representatives, 49th Congress, 2nd Session, 1886–87, Doc. 1, Pt. 5, Vol. 1, pp. 79–1163)

Riley, Carroll L.
1963. Color-Direction Symbolism. An Example of Mexican-Southwestern Contacts. (América Indígena, Vol. 23, No. 1, pp. 49–60)
1971. Early Spanish-Indian Communications in the Greater Southwest. (New Mexico Historical Review, Vol. XLVI, No. 4, pp. 285–314)
1972. Review of the Delight Makers, by Adolf F. Bandelier. New York: Harcourt Brace Jovanovich, 1971. Pp. xxxii,

490. (New Mexico Historical Review, Vol. XLVII, No. 1, pp. 67–68)

1973. Las Casas and the Benavides Memorial. (New Mexico Historical Review, Vol. XLVIII, No. 3, pp. 209–22)

Ritch, W. G.

1882. The New Mexico Blue Book 1882: The Legislative Blue Book of the Territory of New Mexico. (Charles W. Greene, Public Printer, Santa Fe, New Mexico, 154 + 46 pp.) (Reprinted by the University of New Mexico Press, Albuquerque, 1968)

1885a. Aztlan: The History, Resources and Attractions of New Mexico. (D. Lothrop & Co., Boston, 253 pp.)

1885b. Illustrated New Mexico. (New Mexico Bureau of Immigration, Santa Fe, 5th ed., xvii + 140 pp.)

Russell, Frank

1908. The Pima Indians. (Bureau of American Ethnology, 26th Annual Report, 1904–05, Washington, 389 pp.)

Sadlier, D. and J., & Co.

1885. Sadliers' Catholic Directory, Almanac and Ordo for the Year of Our Lord 1885. (D. and J. Sadlier & Co., New York, Part I, 400 pp.)

1886. Sadliers' Catholic Directory, Almanac and Ordo for the Year of Our Lord 1886. (D. and J. Sadlier & Co., New York, Part I, 412 pp.)

Salpointe, J. B.

1893. Constitutiones Synodoriem Dioecesanarum Sanctae Fidei Novi Mexici Primae, Secundae et Tertiae. (Revista Catolica, Las Vegas, New Mexico, 64 pp.)

Salpointe, Most Rev. J. B., D.D.

1898. Soldiers of the Cross. Notes on the Ecclesiastical History of New Mexico, Arizona, and Colorado. (St. Boniface's Industrial School, Banning, California, 299 pp. Reprinted by Calvin Horn, Publisher, Inc., Albuquerque, N.M., 1967)

Sanchez, Pedro

1903. Memorias sobre la vida del Presbitero Don Antonio José Martínez. (Compania Impresora del Nuevo Mexicano, Santa Fe, 54 pp.)

Santamaria, Francisco J.

1959. Diccionario de Mejicanismos. (Editorial Porrua, S. A. Av. Rep. Argentina, 15, Mexico, 1st edition, 1197 pp.)

Scholes, France V.
1937. Church and State in New Mexico, 1610–1650. (Historical Society of New Mexico, Publications in History, VII, 206 pp.)

Schroeder, Albert H.
1953. Brief History of the Chama Basin. (Archaeological Institute of America, School of American Research, Santa Fe, Monographs, No. 17, pp. 5–8)

Schroeder, Albert H., and Dan S. Matson
1965. A Colony on the Move: Gaspar Castaño de Sosa's Journal: 1590–1591. (The School of American Research, Santa Fe, New Mexico, 196 pp.)

Science
1889. Two Discoveries in Human Osteology by the Hemenway Expedition. (Science, Vol. XIII, No. 310, pp. 29–30)

Shea, John Gilmary, trans. and ed.
1882. The Expedition of Don Diego Dionisio de Peñalosa, Governor of New Mexico, from Santa Fe to the River Mischipi and Quivira in 1662, as described by Father Nicholas de Freytas, O. S. F. (New York. Reprinted by the Rio Grande Press, Inc., Chicago, vii + 101 pp., 1964)

Simpson, James H.
1850. Journal of a Military Reconnaissance from Santa Fe, New Mexico, to the Navajo Country. (Reports of the Secretary of War, Senate Executive Document 64, 31st Congress, 1st Session, Washington, D.C., pp. 56–168)

Sjoberg, Andrée F.
1953. The Culture of the Tonkawa, a Texas Indian Tribe. (Texas Journal of Science, Vol. 5, pp. 280–304)

Smiley, Terah Leroy, Stanley A. Stubbs, and Bryant Bannister
1953. A Foundation for the Dating of Some Late Archaeological Sites in the Rio Grande Area, New Mexico: Based on Studies in Tree-Ring Methods and Pottery Analyses. (University of Arizona, Tucson, 66 pp.)

Smith, Cornelius C., Jr.
1967. William Sanders Oury. (University of Arizona Press, Tucson, 298 pp.)

Smithsonian Institution
1864. List of Meteorological Stations and Observations of the Smithsonian Institution for the Year 1863. (Annual Report of the Board of Regents of the Smithsonian Institu-

tion for the Year 1863, Government Printing Office, Washington, 419 pp.)

1874. Annual Report of the Board of Regents for the Year 1873. (Government Printing Office, Washington, 452 pp.)

1904. Letter from Adolph F. Bandelier to William H. Holmes, dated July 13, 1904. (National Anthropological Archives, Letters received: #560.4)

Spencer, A. P., ed.

1937. Centennial History of Highland, Illinois, 1837–1937. (Centennial Commission, Highland, 273 pp.)

Spier, Leslie

1917. An Outline for A Chronology of Zuñi Ruins. (Anthropological Papers of the American Museum of Natural History, Vol. XVIII, Part III, New York, pp. 207–331)

Squier, Ephriam George

1877. Peru: Incidents of Travel and Exploration in the Land of the Incas. (Harper and Bros., New York, 509 pp.)

Steck, Francis Borgia, O.F.M.

1943. A Tentative Guide to Historical Materials on the Spanish Borderlands. (The Catholic Historical Society of Philadelphia. Philadelphia, Pa., 106 pp.)

Stevenson, J.

1883. Illustrated Catalogue of the Collections Obtained from the Indians of New Mexico and Arizona in 1879. (Bureau of [American] Ethnology, 2nd Annual Report, 1880–81, Washington, pp. 307–422)

Stevenson, Matilda Coxe

1894. The Sia. (Bureau of [American] Ethnology, 11th Annual Report, 1889–1890, Washington, 157 pp.)

1904. The Zuñi Indians: Their Mythology, Esoteric Societies, and Ceremonies. (Bureau of American Ethnology, 23rd Annual Report, 1901–02, Washington, pp. 1–608)

Stirling-Maxwell, Sir William

1910. Stories of the Spanish Artists until Goya. (Duffield and Company, New York, xxiv + 309 pp.)

St. Michael's College

1934. Seventy-five Years of Service, 1859–1934: An Historical Sketch of St. Michael's College. (Santa Fe, N.M., 130 pp.; Appendices, pp. 132–39)

Stratton, Porter A.
1969. The Territorial Press of New Mexico 1834–1912. (University of New Mexico Press, Albuquerque, 306 pp.)
Stubbs, Stanley A.
1950. Bird's-Eye View of the Pueblos. (University of Oklahoma Press, Norman, 122 pp.)
Stubbs, Stanley A., and W. S. Stallings, Jr.
1953. The Excavation of Pindi Pueblo, New Mexico. (Monographs of the School of American Research and the Laboratory of Anthropology, No. 18, Santa Fe, 165 pp.)
Summerhayes, Martha
1908. Vanished Arizona: Recollections of the Army Life of a New England Woman. (2nd Edition, 1911, The Salem Press Co., Salem, Mass., 319 pp.; 4th Edition, 1960, Arizona Silhouettes, Tucson, 273 pp.)
Thomas, Alfred B.
1932. Forgotten Frontiers: A Study of the Spanish Indian Policy of Don Juan Bautista de Anza, Governor of New Mexico, 1777–1787. (University of Oklahoma Press, Norman, 420 pp.)
1935. After Coronado. (University of Oklahoma Press, Norman, xii + 307 pp.)
1940. The Plains Indians and New Mexico, 1751–1778. (University of New Mexico Press, Albuquerque, 232 pp.)
1941. Teodoro de Croix and the Northern Frontier of New Spain, 1776–1780. (University of Oklahoma Press, Norman, xiii + 273 pp.)
Thrapp, Dan L.
1967. The Conquest of Apacheria. (University of Oklahoma Press, Norman, 405 pp.)
Tittman, Edward
1929. The Exploitation of Treason. (New Mexico Historical Review, Vol. IV, No. 2, pp. 128–45)
Torquemada, Fr. Juan de
1723. La Monarquia Indiana, Part I. (Nicolas Rodriguez Franco, Madrid, 768 pp.)
Trager, George L.
1946. An Outline of Taos Grammar. (In Harry Hoijer and others, Linguistic Structures of Native America. Viking

Fund Publications in Anthropology, No. 6, New York, pp. 184–221)

Twitchell, Ralph Emerson

1911–17. The Leading Facts of New Mexican History. (Torch Press, Cedar Rapids, Iowa, five volumes, 506 pp., 631 pp., 571 pp., 567 pp., 505 pp.)

1914. The Spanish Archives of New Mexico. (The Torch Press, Cedar Rapids, Iowa, two volumes, 525 pp., 683 pp.)

1923. The Story of the Conquest of Santa Fe, New Mexico, and the Building of Old Fort Marcy, A. D. 1846. (Historical Society of New Mexico, Publication No. 24, Santa Fe, 63 pp.)

1925. Old Santa Fe: The Story of New Mexico's Ancient Capital. (Santa Fe New Mexican Publishing Company, 488 pp. Reproduction of 1925 edition by Rio Grande Press, Chicago, 1963)

Underhill, Ruth M.

1965. Red Man's Religion. (University of Chicago Press, Chicago and London, 301 pp.)

Vaillant, George C.

1944. Aztecs of Mexico: Origin, Rise and Fall of the Aztec Nation. (Doubleday, Doran & Company, Inc., Garden City, New York, 340 pp.)

Valentini, Ph.

1878. See Bandelier, Adolph F., 1878d

Velázquez de la Cadena, Mariano et al.

1946. A New Pronouncing Dictionary of the Spanish and English Languages. (Wilcox & Follett Company, Chicago and New York. Two parts, 681 pp., 766 pp.)

Vetancurt, Fray Agustín de

1961. Teatro Mexicano: Chronica de la Provincia del Santo Evangelio, III; Menologio Franciscano, etc., IV. (Colección Chimalistac de Libros y Documentos Acerca de la Nueva España, José Porrua Turanzas, editor, Madrid, 372 pp., 526 pp. Reprint of 1697–98 edition)

von Tschudi, Johann Jakob

1865. Travels in Peru, During the Years 1838–1842. (Translated from the German by Thomasina Ross, Barnes, New York, 354 pp.)

Von Wuthenau, A.
  1935. The Spanish Military Chapels in Santa Fe and the
    Reredos of Our Lady of Light. (New Mexico Historical
    Review, Vol. X, No. 3, 175–94)
Wadleigh, H. R.
  1910. Munich: History, Monuments, and Art. (T. Fisher Un-
    win, London and Leipsic, 312 pp.)
Wagner, Henry
  1937. The Spanish Southwest, 1542–1794. (The Quivira Soci-
    ety, Vol. VII, Parts I and II, Los Angeles, pp. 13–274 and
    pp. 275–552. Reprinted by Arno Press, New York, 1967)
Walter, Paul A. F.
  1915. Peña Blanca and the Early Inhabitants of the Santa Fe
    Valley. (El Palacio, Vol. III, No. 1, pp. 17–41)
  1916. A New Mexico Lourdes. (El Palacio, Vol. III, No. 2, pp.
    2–27)
  1931. The Cities that Died of Fear: The Story of the Saline
    Pueblos. (School of American Research, Santa Fe. Re-
    printed by El Palacio Press, 46 pp.)
  1946. New Mexico's Pioneer Bank and Bankers. (New Mex-
    ico Historical Review, Vol. XXI, No. 3, pp. 209–25)
Warren, Helene
  1969. Tonque. (El Palacio, Vol. 76, No. 2, pp. 36–42)
Waterman, T. T.
  1917. Bandelier's Contribution to the Study of Ancient Mexi-
    can Social Organization. (University of California Publi-
    cations in American Archaeology and Ethnology, Vol. 12,
    No. 7, Berkeley, pp. 249–82)
Waters, Frank
  1972. Thirty Years Later: The Man who Killed the Deer.
    (New Mexico Magazine, Vol. 50, Nos. 1–2, pp. 17–23,
    49–50)
Weigle, Marta
  1970. The Penitentes of the Southwest. (Ancient City Press,
    Santa Fe, 46 pp.)
Wendorf, Fred
  1953. Salvage Archaeology in the Chama Valley, New Mex-
    ico. (Monographs of the School of American Research,
    No. 17, Santa Fe, 124 pp.)

Wendorf, Fred, and Erik K. Reed
1955. An Alternative Reconstruction of Northern Rio
    Grande Prehistory. (El Palacio, Vol. 62, Nos. 5–6, pp. 131–
    73)
Westphall, Victor
1965. The Public Domain in New Mexico, 1854–1891. (The
    University of New Mexico Press, Albuquerque, 212 pp.)
Whitaker, Joseph
1886. An Almanack for the Year of Our Lord 1886. (London,
    J. Whitaker, 488 pp.)
White, Leslie A.
1930. A Comparative Study of Keresan Medicine Societies.
    (Twenty-third International Congress of Americanists,
    Proceedings, 1928. New York, pp. 604–19)
1932. The Pueblo of San Felipe. (Memoir No. 38, American
    Anthropological Association, 69 pp.)
1935. The Pueblo of Santo Domingo, New Mexico. (Memoir
    No. 43, American Anthropological Association, 210 pp.)
1940. Pioneers in American Anthropology: The Bandelier-
    Morgan Letters, 1873–1883. (University of New Mexico
    Press, Albuquerque, two volumes, pp. xv + 272, and vii
    + 266)
1942. The Pueblo of Santa Ana, New Mexico. (Memoir No.
    60, American Anthropological Association, 360 pp.)
1962. The Pueblo of Sia, New Mexico. (Bureau of American
    Ethnology, Bulletin 184, Washington, xii + 358 pp.)
White, Leslie A., and Ignacio Bernal
1960. Correspondencia de Adolfo F. Bandelier. (Instituto
    Nacional de Antropologiá e Historia, Seria Historia, VI,
    México, 322 pp.)
Whitman, William
1947. The Pueblo Indians of San Ildefonso. (Contributions to
    Anthropology, No. 34, Columbia University, New York,
    164 pp.)
Whorf, B. L., and G. L. Trager
1937. The Relationship of Uto-Aztecan and Tanoan. (Ameri-
    can Anthropologist, Vol. 39, No. 4, pp. 609–24)
Who's Who in America
1908-9. Volume 5. (Albert N. Marquis, ed., A. N. Marquis
    and Co., Chicago, 2,400 pp.)

Who Was Who in America
  1963. Historical Volume, 1607–1896, A Component Volume
    of Who's Who in American History. (A. N. Marquis Co.,
    Chicago, 670 pp.)
Wilson, John P.
  1973. Quarai. (El Palacio, Vol. 78, No. 4, pp. 14–28)
Winship, George P.
  1896. The Coronado Expedition, 1540–1542. (Bureau of
    [American] Ethnology, 14th Annual Report, 1892–93,
    Washington, pp. 329–613)
Woods, Betty
  1968. The Mimbres. (Chamber of Commerce, #41, Silver
    City, Grant County, N.M., 2 pp.)
  1969. Trip of the Month: Bouquet Ranch. (New Mexico Mag-
    azine, Vol. 47, No. 2, pp. 32, 37)
Zerwekh, Sister Edward Mary, C. S. J.
  1962. John Baptist Salpointe, 1825–1894. (New Mexico His-
    torical Review, Vol. XXXVII, No. 1, pp. 1–19; No. 2, pp.
    132–54; No. 3, pp. 214–29)

The following designations and special abbreviations are used:

AEB   Adolphe E. Bandelier ("Papa")

AIA   Archaeological Institute of America

B.   Adolph F. Bandelier

Bs.   Adolph F. and Josephine H. Bandelier

Cat. Coll. "in Cat. Coll." refers to docs. and mss., mostly copies, made by B. in various archives. Many are copies of the copies made by B. for the HSAE. The Catron Collection is in Special Collections, Zimmerman Library, University of New Mexico, Albuquerque.

doc(s).   document(s)

Fewkes   "in Fewkes" refers to the catalogue prepared by J. W. Fewkes to accompany an exhibit in Madrid, 1892, of the collection of docs. and mss., mostly copies, made by B. from various archives for the HSAE. The catalogue by Fewkes was published in 1895; B.'s collection is in the Peabody Museum Library, Harvard University.

HSAE   Hemenway Southwestern Archaeological Expedition

ICA   Seventh Congrès International des Américanistes, Berlin, 1888

Joe   Josephine Huegy Bandelier (Mrs. Adolph F.)

L. A.   New Mexico state survey numbers for archaeological sites

MNM   Museum of New Mexico

ms(s).   manuscript(s)

SAR   School of American Research

UNM   University of New Mexico

INDEX

Abadiano's (Mexico City), 191, 192
Abbé, B.'s use of term, 50, 386–87n265
A-bé-chiu. *See* Abiquiu
Aberto (Mexico City), 201
Abiquiu, N.M., 90, 92, 290, 402n366, 535n1063; ancient Tewa Pueblo, 42, 381n225; B. located old pueblo of, near the "Puente," 79; jar from, in Eldodt Collection, 85; B. at area ruins, 92–95; surface remains noted, 93–95; old pueblo of Genízaros at, 93, 408n407, 408n408; patron saint of, 93, 408n407; round tower noted, 94; ruin called Fe-jui, 97; in ruins by Oñate's time, 164; B. painted vase from, 219, 495n846. *See also* "Puente," the
Abiquiu Peak, N.M., 92, 93, 127
Abiquiu Range, N.M., 293, 294. *See also* Sierra de Abiquiu
Abiquiu River, N.M., 95
Abó, N.M.: rock painting near, depicts Ko-share handling snake, 79; seventeenth-century Piro pueblo, 364–70n184
Academy (Sante Fe), 372–73n190. *See also* Santa Fe Academy
Acequia(s): at San Felipe, 68; two, noted at Rito de los Frijoles, 76; in El Rito area, 91; at Phoenix, 244; at Santa Clara, 261, 268; at Santa Fe, 279
Acoma Pueblo, N.M.: B. at, 6; rock paintings of masks near, identified as "Shiuana," 79, 81; San Juan burial rites compared to, 101; three caciques at, 123; Father A. Jouvenceau went to, for children, 179; population of, 216; trail from Hawikuh to, 297, 308; tradition of Mesa Encantada, 308, 543n1111, 543n1112; Feast of St. John, rooster pull, 408–9n409; B. added Acoma dialect to Cochiti vocabulary, 415–16n450; Villagrá account of attack on, 476–77n749, 477n751; Indian day school at, 508n939

Acorsini, Father A. J. (Springer), 141, 441n562
Acosta, José de: Markham's notes for English translation of, 422n473
Adams, Reverend: B. sent photographs to, 320–22n4
Adler, Aaron (Abiquiu area), 50, 82, 94, 387n268
Adolph Bandelier House (Santa Fe), 426n492, 441n558. *See also* Kaune, Henry S.; Ormsbee, Mrs. R. L.; Schumann, John G.
Aebi, Mr. (Bern, Switzerland), 12, 15
Aebi, Rudolph (Bern, Switzerland), 324n17
African Colonization Society (Berlin), 20
Agaaono (Nambé site), 267, 528n1014. *See also* Ago'wano ouinge
Agá wi ouinge (Nambé site), 528n1014
Ago'wano ouinge (Nambé site), 528n1014
Agreda, Señor Don José María (Mexico City), 192, 197, 477n750
Agua Caliente (San Juan area): ruin of Pose-o-uinge at the baths of, 97. *See also* Ojo Caliente, N.M.; Pose-uingge
Agua Fria (Santa Fe area), 114, 122, 125
Agua Fria (Zuñi area), 308
Aguas Calientes (near Zacatecas, Mexico), 189, 472n722
Aguiar, Rodrigo de: *Recopilación General . . .* Madrid, 1628, Mexico, 1677, bought by B., 194, 478n758
Aguilar, Alonzo (San Ildefonso), 56, 57, 107, 262, 514n994
A. Gusdorf & Bro. (Fernandez de Taos), 376n204
Ahuiuta: younger brother of Zuñi War Gods, 102, 281. *See also* Twin Brothers; Twin War Gods
AIA. *See* Archaeological Institute of America
Alameda, N.M.: Sandia Pueblo Indians located Puaray at, 229, 499n876

BANDELIER'S SOUTHWESTERN JOURNALS

ico City): B. worked with docs. of, 191–
203 passim, 475–76n743, 476n745,
479n764, 479n765, 479n769, 480n771,
481n776, 481n777, 482n780, 482n783,
482n784, 483n789, 483–84n791, 484–
85n793, 485n794, 485n795, 486n796,
486n797, 486n798, 487n802; extent of
B.'s work in, 475–76n743; Burrus's commentary on B.'s work quoted, 475–
76n743; B. often failed to use originals
even if available, 475–76n743. See also
National Archives; Rubio, Don Justino
Archuleta, N.M., 530n1036
Archuleta, Ana Manuela (Peña Blanca),
401n356. See also Lucero, Ana Manuela
Archuleta
Archuleta, Juan de: El Morro inscription,
301
Arebelo, Sebastian, 482–83n785
Arivaypa Massacre, Ariz., 127, 429n508
Arizona: B.'s 1883 reconnaissance in, 6,
506n925; gardenbeds, 87, 407n396;
drouth in, 126; B. to visit HSAE in, 241,
505n918; HSAE excavations in Gila-
Salado area, 506n925. See also Hemen-
way Southwestern Archaeological
Expedition
Arkansas, 119
Arlegui, Fray José de: B. made journal
notes on "Crónica . . ." in Mexico City,
193, 478n755; B. wrote García Icazbal-
ceta about work of, 431–32n523, 446-
48n577
Armijo, Gov. Manuel: 1837 counterrebel-
lion, 401n361; at Apache Canyon,
407n398
Armville, N.M., 395n324
Arquero, María Cresencia (Cochiti), 393–
94n316. See also Quintana, María Cre-
sencia Arquero
Arrasain, Don Ygnacio de: El Morro in-
scription, 301
Arricivita, Juan Domingo: B. examined
"Crónica . . ." in Berlin, 21, 333n61
Arroniz (Aroniz), Juan Francisco de: witness for Gov. Marín del Valle, 514–
25n997
Arroyo de Abiquiu, N.M., 95
Arroyo de la Cañada, N.M., 75
Arroyo de la Cieneguilla, N.M., 107
Arroyo de la Yuta, N.M.: glossy pottery
noted, 63; small house ruins and watch
houses at, 63, 64
Arroyo del Caja del Rio, N.M., 57
Arroyo de Santa Clara, N.M., 158
Arroyo Hondo, N.M.: ruin on, called Cua-
qaa, 73, 75, 437–38n547; B. placed Tzi-

guma on, 114, 416n454; B. revisited
ruins at, 136–38, 437–38n547; Nelson's
excavations at, 437–38n547; L.A. desig-
nations for, 437–38n547; Cole's excava-
tions at, 526n1004. See also Cua-qaa;
Kuakaa [L.A. 76]
Arroyo of Galistéo, N.M., 110, 113. See also
Gui-puy
Arroyo of Tunque (San Felipe area), 63, 68;
San Felipe ancestral ruins on, 68
Arroyo of Valverde, N.M., 62
Arroyo San Pedro, N.M., 63
Arroyo Seco, N.M., 268; engagement of
1837 at, 75, 401n361
Arroyo (del) Tuerto, N.M., 61, 62, 63. See
also Tuerto
Arroyuelo de los Vasquez (near Santo
Domingo): B. placed old pueblo of Santo
Domingo on, 72–73
Arthur, Pres. Chester A., 383n238
Ascarate, Anastacio (Las Cruces, N.M.),
400–401n355
Aschersohn, Dr. Paul F. A. (Berlin), 20, 21,
332n57
Asher & Co. (Europe), 21
Asplund, Christ., and wife, 27
Atanasio (Santa Fe): worked at B.'s house,
232, 233, 234, 235, 249
Atchison, Topeka and Santa Fe Railroad,
358n172, 417n461, 441n557, 450–
51n596, 492n835
Atencio, Martin (San Juan), 43, 47
Atkinson, Gen. Henry M. (Santa Fe), 150,
166, 171, 449n590, 527n1007
Atlantic and Pacific Railroad, 145
Atotonilco, Chih., 194
Atsinna (El Morro ruin), 541n1103
Ausland. See Das Ausland
Austin, Mrs. Mary, ix, 320n1
"Autos de Guerra," 1696: B. obtained from
Ellison and copied, 289, in Fewkes,
534n1061. See also Vargas, Diego de
Avanyu, 405n383. See also Poo-va-nyu;
Water serpent
Axtell, Gov. Samuel B., 545n1131
Ayala, Fray Pedro de (Hawikuh), 539n1094
Ayash-tyu-qotz (Tablita, or Corn, Dance):
San Juan dance compared to Cochiti, 41,
377n212; B. saw, at Santo Domingo, 279.
See also Santo Domingo Pueblo; Tablita,
or Corn, Dance
Ayer, Mrs. Edward E.: 1630 Memorial of
Benavides translated by, 327n37
Ayer Collection, Newberry Library
(Chicago), 1, 326n33, 415–16n450
Ayeta, Fray Francisco de: B. finished copy-
ing Otermín's retreat and extracted data

García Icazbalceta, Don Joaquín: correspondence
—Hewett Correspondence. *See* Hewett, Dr. Edgar Lee: correspondence with Bandelier, Adolph F.
—Hodge Correspondence. *See* Hodge, Frederick Webb
—Janvier Correspondence. *See* Janvier, Thomas A.
—Morgan letters. *See* Morgan, Lewis Henry: correspondence, Bandelier-Morgan letters
—Parkman letters. *See* Parkman, Francis: correspondence with B.
—documentary research: during 1885–88, deeply involved in, 423–24n479; had already used Spanish sources for publication base, 464–65n673; arranged to pay copyists to continue Mexico City work in, 486n799, 490–91n821; permitted to copy rare items at home, 423–24n479, 502n900. *See also* Catron Collection; Hemenway Southwestern Archaeological Expedition: Documents
—drawings and paintings of, 7, 11, 16, 18, 20, 21, 22, 66, 149, 150, 169, 240, 333–35n62, 397–98n339, 411–12n422, 435n542, 450n594, 460n644, 460n645, 460–61n646; B. hoped to sell, 23, 333–35n62, 410–11n421, 449n587, 460n645, 464–65n673. See also *Histoire:* illustrations
—emotional outbursts of, 511n963
—English language, shortcomings of, in using, x–xi
—ethnographic data: striving for equivalencies in comparative details at times naive and led to errors, 383–84n245, 403–4n376, 456n621
—European trip, 1884–85: B. in Switzerland and Germany, 11–23; B.'s account of return, 23–26; passengers on return named, 23–26 passim; multiple purposes of trip, 333–35n62, 339–40n84
—evaluated by Moorehead, ix–x
—financial problems of: hoped to have income from writing, 7, 28, 131–32, 410–11n421, 431–32n523, 436–37n543, 464–65n673; hoped to sell drawings, 23, 333–35n62, 410–11n421, 449n587, 460n645, 464–65n673; undertook study of law temporarily, 156–57; B. wrote García Icazbalceta about, 350–51n136, 410–11n421, 431–32n523, 436–37n543
—foreign language lessons given by, for added income, 130–75 passim, 430n517, 433n531, 435n542, 443n567, 464–

65n673. *See also* Catron, Mrs. Thomas B.; Edsdell, Mrs.; Fornance, Lt. James; Meany, Dr. Edward W.; Preston, Mrs. George C.; Strong, Dr. Norton B.; Van der Veer, P. L.
—F. Ryhiner & Co. bank: relation to, 3, 6–7, 30, 333–35n62, 339–40n84, 342n97, 344n109, 350n134, 350–51n136, 352–53n148, 353–54n151, 354n153, 410–11n421; Gruaz wrote, was "free," 179, 466n683; alleged to have used bank funds for research, 347–48n123, 421–22n471; accusations of fund misuse not supported by journals, 347–48n123; direct involvement ended, 423n478. *See also* Edwardsville, Ill.; F. Ryhiner & Co. bank; Highland, Ill.
—Highland: treatment of, by community, 7, 29–37, 347n123, 349n126, 350n134, 410–11n421; B. decided to leave, 30; B. advised to leave permanently, 37; B. left, for N.M., 38; B.'s property to creditors, 82. *See also* Highland, Ill.; Highland *Weekly Telephone*
—irritation over business matters, 29, 108, 112, 114, 339–40n84, 341n92, 341n93
—Mercantile Library: B. copied at, 117, 118, 119; significance for career of, noted, 423–24n479
—Mexican monographs of: to be reprinted, 219, 495n847; B. mailed to Peñafiel, 241; three significant publications by, 464–65n673
—New Mexico: B. left Highland for, 7, 38; did field work at San Juan, 40–107 passim; planned to live at Peña Blanca, with Joe, 75, 78, 108, 401n359, 410–11n421; Joe returned to, with B. from St. Louis, 119–20, 425–26n487; reassessed Peña Blanca as impractical, 121–22, 425–26n487; rented Schumann's house and with Joe made home in Santa Fe, 122, 426n492
—novels by. See *Delight Makers, The; Die Köshare; "Fray Luis the Lay Brother..."*
—photography, use of, by, 320–22n4, 397–98n339
—physical disability of, in writing: complaints about in journals, 145, 146, 157, 210, 237, 238, 239, 240, 241, 248, 254, 255, 256–57, 279, 290, 431–32n523, 446–48n577, 468n692, 490–91n821, 503–4n907, 531n1041; suspended journals in Mexico City because of, 197, 479–80n769; consulted Dr. Strong about, 240, 505n915. *See also* Bandelier, Adolph F.: typewriter purchased by

—medicine societies, 140, 153, 282, 284–85, 452n603, 452n605, 532n1051. *See also* specific societies elsewhere in this entry
—mining district of, 395n324
—Moon, "mother" at, 283
—mythology, 67–68, 70, 111, 153–54, 154–55, 283, 388n277, 398n341
—Nahī'ya (war chief): had ceased to exist by B.'s time, 462n657; alternated with cacique (peace chief), 462n657
—Na-Ua: chief, or head, of societies, 282
—novels by B. reflected Keresan values as expressed at, 381n228
—Oyoyewa, one of twin brothers at, 153; war captain, earthly representative of, 281; corresponded to Zuñi Ahuiuta, 281
—paisano (roadrunner): symbolic use of track of, in death rites, 283
—population of, 216
—Pó shai-añi, 388n277. *See also* Pose-Yemo
—Potrero Viejo, 227, 399n345
—pottery, 395n323
—*Principales*, Council of, 384n249, 394–95n322
—Qannat-Yaya: witches, 155. *See also* Kan-At-ya (this entry)
—Rebellion of 1696, participated in, by, 398n341
—Revolt of 1680: retreated to Potrero Viejo, 399n345
—Rito de los Frijoles, ancestral home of, 398–99n343
—San Buenaventura Church: B. copied Fray Juan Toril's "Nota" at, 224, 496–97n861; B. copied priest lists of, at Peña Blanca, 224, 497n862, in Cat. Coll., 497n862; records of, at Peña Blanca, 400n352, 460n642; served by Peña Blanca priests, 426n451; mission with resident friar (1817–18), 497n862. *See also* Feast Day (this entry)
—Sandals, yucca, used as snowshoes by, 111
—scalps, 109, 140, 531n1048. *See also* Dances: Scalp (this entry)
—Sen-quit-ye. *See* Cenquitye
—Shay-qa-tze (hunters), 56–57, 59, 282. *See also* Shyay-yaq (this entry)
—Shikame Medicine Society: head is Shyay-yak, hunter, 59; Shikama Chayan, or head, closely associated with hunting, 172; head, assistant to cacique, 282, 394–95n322
—Shipap, Shi-pap-u, 124
—Shipewe Clan at, 394n320

—Shiwanna (Shiuana), 283; kachina masks called, 110, 111. *See also* Kachinas (this entry)
—Shkuy-Chayani and Shkuy-Naua. *See* Giant Medicine Society (this entry)
—Shyay-yaq, 57, 59, 153, 155, 172, 281. *See also* Shay-qa-tze (this entry)
—Snake Medicine Society, 153, 394n320
—songs: contain tribal origin tale, 283; magical powers of, 285, 532n1054
—stone idols, 138, 139–40, 141, 153, 168, 438n552, 451–52n602
—Sun, "father" at: was also Kopishtai and Shiwanna, 283
—Tanos, called by, 56
—Tewa name for, 57
—T'shay-qa-tze. *See* Shay-qa-tze (this entry)
—Twin Brothers, Twin War Gods, 111, 153; war captains, earthly representatives of, 281
—Twin Sisters, 153–54
—Uisht-yaqqa: third [assistant] cacique, 57, 59
—visual trickery. *See* Magic (this entry)
—War: Nahī'ya, head of Pueblo during time of, 462n657
—War Captain(s), 59, 281, 282, 394–95n322, 427n496
—War Medicine Society, 153
—warfare: ceremonial aspects of, 282, 531n1048
—Warriors Society, 57, 153, 172, 282; Jemez cacique blessed weapons of, 154
—watercolors of, by B., 333–35n62, 438n552, 450n594. *See also* Bandelier, Adolph F.: drawings and paintings of
—water serpent (Tzitz Shruuwi), 111
—witchcraft at, 123–24, 155, 282–83, 283–84, 427n496, 532n1051, 432n1052; talking corn used in, 284, 532n1052; B. used corn color symbolism associated with, in novels, 532n1052
—"yaya(s)" ("Madre[s]," or "Mother[s]"): used by medicine men, 56–57, 59, 123–24, 154–55, 282, 531n1049. *See also* Kotona (this entry)
—*See also* Keres, Keresan; Peña Blanca
Cocoyes: possibly extinct branch of Zuñi, 296; dressed in cotton robes, 296
Codex Mendoza, 83, 406n388, 406n391. *See also* Mendoza, Antonio de
Codex of 1607, 83, 406n391
Códice de Cuauhtlantzinco: Father Campos's name attached to, 479n766
Cole, E. L. (Santa Fe), 264, 267, 526n1004
Colección de Documentos Inéditos . . . ,

washed away, 71, 113, 416n452; B. gave location, 110, 113; B. at, 113; surface remains, 113; church wall, 113; B. abandoned idea of church, 416n452; Vol. 1 data clarified, 416n452. *See also* Gipuy [L. A. 182]

Gusdorf, Alexander (Ranchos de Taos), 40, 41, 247, 291, 376n204, 508n941

Gutierrez, Don Antonio (Mexico City), 195, 196, 197, 199, 200, 203, 478n762

Gutierrez, Felipe: B. copied 1701 Bernalillo Grant of, 236, 503n904; in Fewkes, 503n904

Gutierrez, Don José (Bernalillo), 277; B. met at Sandia Pueblo, 229

Gutierrez, José María (Mexico): helped B. catalogue Father Fischer's library, 202

Gutierrez, María de los Angeles (Sile): married Antonio Baca, 497n864

Gutiérrez de la Chica, Fray Juan (Quarai), 364–70n184

Gutzdorf. *See* Gusdorf, Alexander

Guyot, Father F. (Peñasco), 292, 293, 311, 314, 536n1076

Guys, Armand (Boston), 12, 323n10

Gwyn, John (Santa Fe), 412n424

Gwyn, Thomas (Santa Fe), 412n424

Ha-atze. *See* San Miguel [L.A. 370]

Hacha and Hachita (Mts.), N. M., 186

Hackluyt Society: B. made notes on 1851 reprint of, "Gentleman of Elvas," 118–19; copy made at Mercantile Library, 119, 423–24n479

Hagnauer, Elisa (Lizzie) Felder (Mrs. Robert) (Edwardsville), 118, 422n475

Hagnauer, Robert (Edwardsville), 37, 117, 356n163, 422n475, 476n744

Hagnauer, William and Johanna Suppiger (Highland), 356n163

Hagner, Maj. J. R.: El Morro inscription, 300

Ha-ka-nyi Chayani. *See* Cochiti Pueblo: Fire medicine men

Ha-ka-nyi Na-ua. *See* Cochiti Pueblo: cacique

Halevy, León: French translations of Tacitus and Horace, 60

Haller, Berchthold (Switzerland), 12

Haller, Mr. and Mrs. (Switzerland), 14

Halona (Zuñi area): church at, 540n1096, 540n1097

Hamburg, Germany, 23

Hammond Typewriter: B. purchased, 182, 468n692

Hamy, Dr. [E. T.?], 131, 254, 255, 431n522, 511n966

Hano Pueblo: Tewa village on First Hopi Mesa, 389n285; classified as Tano-speaking, 392n303

Haren, Col. Ed. A. (Santa Fe), 141, 213, 215, 220, 242, 267, 273, 441n557; B. obtained railroad passes from, 242, 251, 252, 289

Haren, Mrs. Ed. A. (Santa Fe), 138, 438n548

Harlow, Mrs. (Santa Fe), 311

Haroun, Dr. *See* Harroun, Dr. W. S. (Santa Fe)

Harrington, John P.: added Tewa material to B.'s data, 381–82n229; attempted to correlate archaeology and languages, 381–82n229; exposed spurious nature of idols in Prince collection, 451–52n602

Harrison, Benjamin: 1888 presidential election, 313, 543n1121

Harroun, Dr. W. S. (Santa Fe), 272, 529n1022

Hartmann, Mr. (Alsace), 15, 139[?]

Hartmann, H. (Santa Fe), 31, 39, 41, 139[?], 141, 166, 168, 180, 203, 206, 208, 216, 217, 233, 245, 248, 256, 265, 287, 289; B. got map from, 31, 345n112; B. gave 1880 journal pages of map data to, 146, 448n579; B. deposited 256 groundplans and 16 photographs (for *Histoire*) with, 205; B. worked on map with, 207, 489n813; brought maps to B., 210

Hartmann, Mr. and Mrs. H. (Santa Fe), 146, 149, 151, 155, 174, 175, 180, 223, 242, 278, 289, 314

Hartmann, Mrs. H. (Santa Fe), 134, 138, 143, 145, 147, 148, 175, 176, 178, 180, 185, 234, 242, 249, 259, 267, 279, 434n536, 463n666, 507n934; among those B. read novel to, 136, 148

Hartmann, Mrs., Sr. (Santa Fe), 175

Harvey Company, 379n219

Harvey, Byron, III (Phoenix): personal correspondence, 375n202

Harvey, Fred: purchased Eldodt Collection, 375n202

Hassaurck, Mr. (Switzerland), 13, 14

Hauck, Mr. (Philadelphia), 56

Hauck, Allan W. (Santa Fe), 209, 490n820

Hauicu. *See* Hawikuh

Hawikuh, N. M.: B. with Cushings, Husher, and Hubert Hoffmann to, 296, 539n1089; identified with Coronado's Cibola, 297, 539n1094; B. noted trail to Acoma and Rio Grande with Zia trail branching off, 297; ruins on trail noted, 297; church at, 540n1097

INDEX

—guaco, source of Cochiti black paint for, 395n323
—classification of Kotyiti types of, 399n345
Powell, Maj. John Wesley (Bureau of [American] Ethnology), 338n76, 383n244, 409n412, 415–16n450
Prada, Father José de la (Cochiti mission): San Felipe archive doc. about 1804 campaign against Navajos, 73
Prado, Feliciano (Santa Fe): worked at B.'s home, 144
Pradt, Capt. George H. (Laguna Pueblo), 122, 296, 310(?), 426n493
Pradt, William, 310(?); B. met at Zuñi, 296
Pratt, Gen. R. H.: head of Carlisle Indian School, 399n349
Preetorius, Dr. Emil (St. Louis): B. saw in St. Louis, 37, 116; AEB's article rejected by, 288; editor, *Westliche Post*, 357n167. *See also Westliche Post*
—B. submitted articles to: on Apache(s), 41, 377n213; unidentified ms., 56, 108, 117, 391n301, 413n435, 414n437; on useful plants of Southwest, 152–53, 156, 157, 165, 169, 451n601; Mockingbird ["Spottvogel"], 168; Chapters I and II, *Die Köshare*, 172; B. received negative letter from, 174; B. requested chapters be sent to Brühl, 215
—B. wrote to, 100, 108, 126, 132, 134, 168, 171, 175, 177, 178, 230, 278; B. letter from, 108, 166, 171, 176, 177, 288
"Preliminary Report on the most valuable INSCRIPTIONS still visible at the Rock of 'EL MORRO' ": ms. by B., 311, 541–42n1104, 542n1105, 542n1106, 543n1119
Presbyterian Board of Missions: established Academy, Santa Fe, 372–73n190
Present throwing: at Cochiti dance, 129; among Pueblos, 430n513
Presidio [Santa Fe?]: Vigil owned book fragment about, 186; Rivera's doc. on presidios cited, 469n704, 482–83n785. *See also* Rivera, Gen. Don Pedro de
Press of the Pioneers, Inc., The: prospectus of Fanny R. Bandelier's publication of B.'s 1886–89 journals for Hemenway years issued by, ix; plan to publish abandoned following Fanny R. Bandelier's death, 320n1
Preston, George Cuyler (Santa Fe), 142, 150, 443n567, 459n638
Preston, Mrs. George Cuyler (Santa Fe), 142, 155, 433n533, 443n567; B. gave foreign language lessons to, 133, 139, 140, 141, 143, 144, 146, 147, 149, 150
Preston, Mr. and Mrs. George Cuyler

(Santa Fe), 188, 236, 443n567, 505n910
Pretorius. *See* Preetorius, Dr. Emil
Prieto, A.: B. bought book on Tamaulipas by, 194, 478n757
Prince, Judge (Gov.) Le Baron Bradford (Santa Fe), 50, 53, 131, 387n266; B. got idol from, for painting, 138; B. returned idol and borrowed #2 from, 139; B. showed paintings of idols of, to Cochiti for identification, 139–40, 153, 438n552; B. painted two more idols of, 140; lectured on Potrero de las Vacas, 170–71, 461–62n652, 531n1050; B. introduced by, at N. M. Historical Society lecture, 459n638. *See also* Prince, Judge (Gov.) and Mrs. Le Baron Bradford
Prince, Mrs. Le Baron Bradford (Santa Fe), 141, 142, 147, 148, 156
Prince, Judge (Gov.) and Mrs. Le Baron Bradford (Santa Fe), 372–73n190; curio collection of, 438n552; B. sketched idols in Prince Collection, 438n552, 451–52n602
Prince Collection. *See* Prince, Judge (Gov.) and Mrs. Le Baron Bradford
Principales: at San Juan, 45, 54; at San Felipe, 72; defined, 384n249; Tewa, 384n249; at Cochiti, 384n249, 394–95n322; decisions of, carried out by war captains, 394–95n322, 427n496
Principals. *See Principales*
"Progressive Indian, The": article by B., signed "Espejo," in *St. Louis Globe Democrat*, 127, 130, 429n510, 430n515. *See also* "Espejo"; *St. Louis Globe Democrat*
"Progress of Archaeological and Ethnological Research in America . . .": letter by B., published by AIA, 258, 512n978. *See also* Archaeological Institute of America
Provencher, Mr.: called on B., 122; probably Dumas Provencher, 426n494. *See also* Provencher, Dumas
Provencher, Dumas (Acoma–San Rafael area), 426n494; murder of, reported, 313, 544n1122
Provencher, Mrs. Dumas (Acoma–San Rafael area): sister of Father Brun, 426n489
Pu-a-ge: Tano name for Santo Domingo Pueblo, 73
Puaray Pueblo, N. M.: B. noted soil discoloration at Tunque, similar to what he saw at, 64; Sandia Indians located, near Alameda, 229; confusion regarding location of, 499n876; B.'s Puaray, a different ruin, 499n876
Puebla, Mex., 5, 487n800

paint used at Cochiti by male dancers of, 59; vermillion paint used by Cochiti female dancers, 59; location of, at San Felipe, 68; location of, at Cochiti, 111, 415n447; at Jemez, 498n869. *See also* Tanyi [Pumpkin] Kiva

Punamesh Zia (Jemez Valley): Zia ancestral site, excavations at, 498n872

Pun-ku: kiva bells, found at Paa-ko, 405n384

Purcell, E. B. (Santa Fe): editor, publisher, *Daily New Mexican,* 492n835

Purdy, Mr. (Santa Fe): B. called on, 143

Putnam, Frederick Ward (Cambridge, Mass.), 219, 417–19n464, 454n616, 458n635, 495n848

Puwige (Puwhige): Hendron's name for large ruin in Rito de los Frijoles Canyon, 392n305; Hewett gave, as Tewa name for El Rito de los Frijoles, 392n305

Pu-yé (Santa Clara Canyon): San Juan name for northern branch of Santa Clara Canyon, 42; caves inhabited by Tewa, 42, 163–64, 261, 454n617; Pojoaque denied caves inhabited by Tewa, 56; B. described area, measured ruins, gathered pottery, 159–62, 453–54n615, 454n616, 454n617, pueblo at, ancestral Santa Clara, 162; drouth, Navajo hostilities forced abandonment of, 164. *See also* Santa Clara Canyon

Pu-y-ie. *See* Pu-yé

Pygmies: in Keres tale, 70, 462n653

Pyle, Gov. William A. *See* Pile, Gov. William A.

Qannat-Yaya (witches), 155. *See also* Witchcraft

Q'a-tish-tye: Keres name for San Felipe Pueblo, 68; name derived from "Qa-tish-tyam," an earlier pueblo near Cubero, 71

Qo-o Jyare (San Juan Pueblo): dance in which two small buffalo horns at times replaced buffalo head, 107

Q'o-Q'a-Tyumishe, maseua: Cochiti war captains as earthly representatives of, 281; correspond to Mait-za-laima and Ahuiuta of Zuñi, 281. *See also* Zuñi Pueblo, N. M.: Twin Brothers

Qö-sare, Qosare, Qö-share, Qo-share. *See* Koshare Societies

Quarac. *See* Quarai

Quarai (Saline area), 39, 359–63n183, 364–70n184, 364–70n184[*6], [*8], [*19], 514–25n997. *See also* Llana, Fray

Gerónimo de la; Parroquia de la Villa Santa Fe; Inscriptions; Tajique

Quarai-Tajique confusion in de la Llana account, 364–70n184, 514–25n997

Que-guayo (Nambé site), 267, 528n1014. *See also* Kekwaiye ouinge

Queres. *See* Keres, Keresan

Quintana, Cipriano (Cochiti), 393–94n316

Quintana, Epimenio (Puente): ruins on property of, 94–95

Quintana, José de la Cruz (Santa Fe), 123

Quintana, María Cresencia Arquero (Cochiti), 393–94n316

Quintana, Santiago. *See* Zashua

Quintana, Victoria (Cochiti): married Adelaido Montoya, 94–95

Quio-Tráco: ruin east of Tesuque, 47

Quirana. *See* Kwirena Societies

Qui-pa-na (Tejón area): B. told of Tano ruin at, 58, 394n318. *See also* Kipana

Quiros, Father Cristóbal de: B. copied 1636 docs. related to, 201, 364–70n184, 484–85n793, 485n794; in Cat. Coll. and in Fewkes, 484–85n793, 485n794

Qui-tara-jyare: French dance at San Juan, 50–51, 387n273; also called "Sa-ri-tyé," 51, 387n274. *See also* Kwitara ceremonies; Kwitara dancers

Quito, Tex., 120

Quivira: B. referred to Great Plains and to Gran Quivira ruin as, 206, 364–70n184[*14]; B. told, was Tabira, 262, 364–70n184, 364–70n184[*14]; B. told, was "La Gran Quivira," 262, 514n994; confusion in literature regarding, 488–89n811

"Quivira": articles by B., published in *New Yorker Staatszeitung,* 437n546

Raab, Director (Munich), 18, 19

Ralliere, Father J. B. (Tomé): at Peña Blanca, 286, 532n1056

Ramo de Tierras (Archivo General de la Nación, Mexico City), 199, 482n784

Rancho Cañada (Cochiti area), 398–99n343

Ranches of Taos. *See* Ranchos de Taos

Ranchitos, Ranchos de Santa Ana Pueblo, 228, 499n875

Rancho del Dado (San Mateo area), 310

Ranchos de Taos, N. M.: B. recorded name of Tewa ruin near, 42, 380n223; B. at, 246, 291. *See also* Toma-Pooge

Raton, N. M., 38

Rattermann, Mr., 220; B. mailed pamphlet to, 148

Rattlesnake(s): B. noted killing one on road from Sile to Jemez, 224; accounts of

—birth, 41, 45
—bullroarer: in Eldodt's collection, 83, 405n385
—cacique(s) (winter and/or summer), 44, 45, 56, 84, 103, 104, 164, 384n247, 391n300; official manta of, 47. *See also* Po-a-toyo (this entry); Tzi-ojque (this entry)
—Cai-yi: altar, or stations, for prayer, 43
—census: ruin names given as personal names in, 96
—ceremonial directions, 102, 413n428
—ceremonial organization at, 83, 104–5; B. recorded "leading chiefs of superstition," 104
—ceremonies: ritual smoking, 53; ritual inhaling, 101, 413n427; strewing of sacred meal, 102, 413n428; to bring rain, 162–63, 164; by Kossa to control river waters, 405n383. *See also* Dances, Kachina (this entry); Dances, Public (this entry)
—charms, medicinal: B. obtained, for Eldodt, 105; listed with B.'s identifications, 105–6; gathered by medicine men, 106
· –church: building to which B. referred, no longer extant, 42, 379n219; organ, 82; choir members noted, 82; B. painted skull and crossbones for, 102; Father Seux showed B. books of, from 1726 on, 246, 507n935; Seux, priest at, 377n214, 377n216; Castro, priest at, 377n216; Medina, priest at, 402n366; B. copied priest list of San Juan de los Caballeros from book at, 514n995; in Cat. Coll., 514n995; B. copied Santa Clara priest list from book at, 514n995; in Cat. Coll., 514n995; further Santa Clara data found by B. at, 525n998
—clans, 45, 80–81; gens, gentes terminology used by B., 45, 54
—clothing: official manta of cacique, 47; manta, girdles of tule, 47; yucca sandals, 47
—clusters. *See* moieties (this entry)
—color-direction symbolism at, 53, 55, 391n296; B. in error in likening to Zuñi, 53, 389n284; of stars, 102, 413n429; regular Tewa color system at, 55, 391n296
—corn, 97, 98, 103, 104, 106, 163; as sacred meal, 43, 83, 102, 106
—curing: fetishes for, 163, 164
—Dances, Kachina: Deer, Antler, Pipe, Fruit, 45–46, 384n250
—Dances, Public: Go-he-ye (brazo de baylar), Go-he-ye-jiare (Baile de las Tabletas), 41, 46; B. compared Go-he-ye with Cochiti's Ayash-tyu-qotz, 41,

377n212; Deer, public form of, 45–46; Baile de los Franceses [?], 46; Quitarajyare, dance of the French, 50–51, 387n273; Sa-rit-yé Jiare, 51, 100, 101, 387n274, 387n275; Snake, evidence for former, seen by B., 79; Kossa, 97–98, 98, 99, 409n414; Basket (Baile de la Jícara, Tung-Jiare), 101, 102, 412n423; Te-inbe Jiare, 101–2, 103–4, 104–5
—death, 47, 101, 102
—document(s): B. copied copy of Concha doc. of Don Juan García at, 262, 514n996; in Fewkes, 514n996. *See also* church (this entry)
—dual organization, 99, 409n415; important in understanding of Tewa society, 383n243
—day school: established (1886), 508n939
—fasting, 44, 54, 81, 83, 84
—fetishes, 40, 43, 56, 83, 102, 106, 127, 163, 164, 379–80n221, 391n300. *See also* "Madre(s)" (this entry); To-a (this entry)
—fishing: river trap for, described, 96–97
—fish taboo: in origin tale, 52, 388n280
—gens, gentes. *See* clans (this entry)
—governor, 44, 45, 54, 98
—Hunters Society: medicine men, 83; no longer extant in B.'s time, 83
—hunting: Francisco Chavez in charge of, 84; Ojuas of deer, bear petitioned for success in, 99, 101; rabbit hunt at, 102; Sa-mayo, chief of, 105, 413n432. *See also* Sa-mayo (this entry)
—Indians of: at Santa Clara Feast Day, 80; name for Americans, 83; name for Mexicans, 83; at Santa Rosa Feast Day, Abiquiu, 94; B. met trading party of, going to Utes, 95; cautioned B. against showing mask paintings to Mexicans, 101, 412n425; inhaled from B.'s Zuñi mask paintings, 101, 413n427
—Insurrection of 1837: participated in, 401n361
—Interregnum: attacked by other Pueblos during period of, 47, 385–86n258
—jade, ritual use of, 81, 83, 404n378, 405n384
—Kachinas, 45–46, 99, 101, 384n250, 412n425
—kiva bells, kiva ringing stones: use of, 83, 405n384
—kivas: two at, 44; dance rehearsal in, 48, 103
—Kossa, 44, 48, 52, 54, 79, 97–98, 99–100, 103–4, 104–5, 383–84n245, 384n246, 388n279, 405n383, 409n414, 409n415; B. painted, 98, 100

villa, 385n256; settled by Cordoba, 508n945; B. copied 1793 doc. of Concha to chief alcalde of, 514n996; in Fewkes, 514n996; Remuzón, priest at, 528n1019. *See also* La Villa Nueva de Santa Cruz de la Cañada
Santa Fe, N.M.: B.'s 1880 arrival in, 320–22n4; B. left Highland for, 7, 30, 38, 350–51n136; B.'s decision to stay and to go on to San Juan, 38, 358–59n176, 410–11n421; B. left for extensive fieldwork at San Juan, 40–107 passim; B. to Peña Blanca and Cochiti for added data and to Peña Blanca for possible housing for the Bs., 107–13 passim; B. returned to, 114, 416n656; B. left, for St. Louis and Edwardsville, 115; Bs. moved to, permanently, abandoning plan to settle in Peña Blanca, and Cochiti for added data and to Peña Blanca 120–25, 324n16, 410–11n421, 425–26n487, 426n492, 431–32n523; Bs. in Santa Fe, 120–319 passim, except for occasional trips together or individually to Pueblos, ruins, archives, HSAE field camps, and their more extensive Mexico City trip of 1886–87, 188–203; financial situation of the Bs. difficult, 421–22n471. *See also* Bandelier, Adolph F.: financial problems of, Highland, New Mexico; Bandelier, Josephine (Joe) Huegy (Mrs. Adolph F.): Hemenway Southwestern Archaeological Expedition: documents copied by B. as historiographer . . . : Santa Fe
—acequias, 279
—Archives: de Vargas, original journal of, at, 428n503; history of, as traced by Twitchell and others, 428n504; B. copied fragment of Anaya's 1684 petition to Cruzate from, 503n905; in Cat. Coll. and in Fewkes, 503n905; B. described condition of, to García Icazbalceta, noting the finding of Mendoza journal in, 503–4n907. *See also* New Mexico: Territorial Archives
—baseball excitement in, 218, 494n843
—capitol, B. walked out to new, 188, 432–33n526, 472n720
—Cathedral. *See* Cathedral of Saint Francis
—elections in, 180, 311, 312, 543n1121
—historical data concerning: B. noted church books began with 1698, 39, 371n186; site of Tano pueblo, 53, 58, 389n283; Insurrection of 1837, 75, 401n367; witchcraft trial at, in 1850s, remembered, 133, 385n253, 528n1017;

book fragment on Presidio of, 186, 469n704; "Carta" of the Cabildo of, 1639, copied by B. in Mexico City, 202, 486n796; in Cat. Coll. and in Fewkes, 486n796; "Carta" contained complaint of civil government against Franciscans, 202, 486n796; Apache name for, 260; early stereoscopic and photographic views of, 320–22n4; Lamy became Bishop, then, later Archbishop, of Diocese of, 359n177; Villa of, founded 1610, 377–78n217, 389n283; Juan Lucero de Godoy, 1680, alcalde mayor of, 386n260; two pre-Spanish sites in area of, 389n283; St. Francis of Assisi adopted as patron saint by, 389n283, 542n1132; B. interested in epoch of founding of, 410–11n421; hiatus, 1604–1622, in data, 410–11n421; capital of Territory assigned to, 432–33n526; history of capitol buildings of, 432–33n526, 472n720; American occupation of, in 1846, and founding of Fort Marcy, 422n565; incorporation of, 458n634; 1680 siege of, 482n780; Escarramad, 1617 citizen of, 483–84n791; 1639 population of, 486n796; Kearny's 1846 entrance into, 494n844
—newspapers of: *Daily New Mexican,* 216, 450–51n596, 492n835; *Weekly New Mexican Review,* 412n424, 449n586; *New Mexican Review,* 427n500, 441n561; *New Mexican* (earlier, *Santa Fe Republican*), 450–51n596
—Parroquia. *See* Parroquia de la Villa de Santa Fe
—publications about, by B.: article mailed to *New Yorker Staatszeitung,* 146, 448n578; B. received newspaper with article in, 155–56 [*See also* "Das Alter der Stadt Santa Fé, Neu-Mexiko"]; "Franciscan Sepulchres in the Cathedral at Santa Fe, The": B.'s 1890 *Santa Fe Daily New Mexican* article quoted in entirety, 364–70n184; letter from B., pertaining to prehistory of, published by Ritch, 373n192
—rainfall, 126, 429n506
Santa Fe Academy, 431n520, 459n639. *See also* Academy
Santa Fe Cañón, 182
Santa Fe Range: B. subdivided into groups: Santa Fé and Nambé group, 86, Truchas, 86, 90; Jicarrita, 86, 90; Sierra de Nambé, with "Baldy," 90
Santa Fe Ring, 383n238, 427n500, 431n520

Sidler, Mr. (Switzerland), 14
Sierra Blanca, Ariz.: visible from Zuñi area, 296
Sierra Blanca, N.M.: tale concerning, 101; "two days north," lake of San Juan origin in, 102
Sierra de Abiquiu, N.M., 246. *See also* Abiquiu Range
Sierra de Chusca, Ariz. *See* Chuska Mountains
Sierra de Gallegos, N.M.: above Chililí, 62
Sierra de la Gruya (Grulla), Colo.–N.M.: source of Rio Grande, 73
Sierra de la Hacha, N.M., 185–86
Sierra de (las) Truchas, N.M., 51, 86, 90, 98, 294; Tewa name for, 261. *See also* Truchas Mountains
Sierra del Dátil, N.M., 296
Sierra del Manzano, N.M., 224
Sierra de los Ladrones, N.M., 58, 69, 224, 229
Sierra de los Nuevos Placeres, N.M. *See* Ortiz Mountains
Sierra del Oso, N.M., 58
Sierra de Magdalena, N.M., 229
Sierra de Maricopa, Ariz., 244
Sierra de Nambé, N.M., 78, 90, 98
Sierra de Picurís, N.M., 92, 93, 246, 291, 292, 293
Sierra de San Andres, N.M.: B. told of old Pueblo west of, 176
Sierra de San Antonio, N.M., 246. *See also* San Antonio Mountains
Sierra de Sandía, N.M., 69, 87, 224, 229. *See also* Sandia Mountains
Sierra de San Francisco (Golden area), 61, 63
Sierra de San Mateo, N.M., 224, 308, 497n865. *See also* Cebolleta Mountain; Mount Taylor
Sierra de San Miguel, N.M., 76
Sierra de San Pedro, N.M., 63. *See also* San Pedro Mountains
Sierra de Santa Fé, N.M., 63; "laguna" [lake] in, property of all Pueblos, 124. *See also* Santa Fe Range
Sierra de Socorro, N.M., 229
Sierra de Taos, N.M., 246, 292. *See also* Taos Range
Sierra de Zuñi, N.M., 58, 302
Sierra Ladrona, N.M. *See* Sierra de los Ladrones
Sierra Madre Occidental (Chih.), 6, 76, 472n722; B.'s 1884 trip to, 438–40n553
Sierra of Jicarrita, N.M., 51, 86, 90, 98, 246, 261, 292, 294; mountain sheep seen in, 270

Sierra Sangre de Cristo, Colo.: Taos place of origin in, 80; also called Culebra, 86
Sierra Sangre de Cristo, Colo.–N.M., 86. *See also* Culebra Mountain
Sierra San Martín, Tex., 120
Siguenza y Gongora, Carlos de: B. made notes on, at Royal Library, Berlin, 19, 332n55
Silao, Chih., 189, 472n724
Sile, N.M., 59, 224–25, 416n451
Silvana, Sister (Highland), 417n463
Silver City–Gila Cliff Dwellings: B. in area of, 6
Simancas, Spain: archival work of B. and Fanny in, 10
Simonsfeld, Dr. Julius (Munich), 18, 19, 39, 252, 330n49, 510n957
Simpson, Mr.: visited B. at San Juan, 82, 95
Simpson, Capt. James Ferdinand, 40, 375n198, 375n201
Simpson, Lt. J. H.: El Morro inscription, 302; in 1849, copied El Morro inscriptions, 540–41n1101, 541–42n1104; credited with name, "Inscription Rock," 540–41n1101
Sinaloa, Mexico: Jesuit missions in, 477–78n753. *See also* Peréz de Ribas, P. Andrés, S. J.
Sioux Indians: Sun Dance, one of two papers read by Fornance on, 147
Sisters of Loretto (Santa Fe): induced by Lamy to found Santa Fe settlement, 359n177
Sitgreave, L. [Lt.]: El Morro inscription, 302
Skinner, Harry (Santa Fe): called on Bs., 233, 236; B. to, 235
Sloan, Dr. (Santa Fe), 490n820
Smallpox: epidemic of 1780–82. 239, 505n912
Smith, Mr.: at San Juan, 95, 100; data on Canary Islanders questioned, 100, 410n420; in Santa Fe, 120, 121; noted by B. as "Smith," in Santa Fe, 143
Smith, Buckingham: conjectured as to who author of *Rudo Ensayo* was, 20; published *Rudo Ensayo*, 332n56. *See also* *Rudo Ensayo*
Smith, Frank: B. sent photographs to, 320–22n4. *See also* Smith, Frank P.
Smith, Frank P. (Rochester, N.Y.): B. wrote to, 140, 146, 157, 165, 166, 169, 180, 186, 208, 441n554; B. letter from, 140, 142, 146, 147, 151, 157, 165, 169, 183, 209; B. wrote to, enclosing Popocatepetl views, 143; B. finished and sent article "for Rochester," 144; B. mailed "Peru" arti-

Tuerto: Tano pueblo ruin, 58, 61–62, 396n332

Tuerto Creek, N.M., 396n331

Tunque Pueblo: Tano Pueblo, 58, 71; B. at, 63; ruins described, 63–64; surface remains noted, 66; B. painted plat of, 95; also called Tonque [L. A. 240], 397n336; flourishing ceramic industry of fifteenth and sixteenth centuries at, 397n336; sophisticated scientific analyses of pottery of, 407n394; Marín del Valle met Murziano de la Cruz at, 514–25n997

Tu-po-ge: San Juan name for Rito de los Frijoles, 42, 381n228. See also Rito de los Frijoles

Turkheim, Alsace: B. at, 15

Turners, Turnverein. See Highland Turners Hall

Turquoise Kiva: at Cochiti, 59; brown body paint used at Cochiti by male dancers of, 59; vermillion paint used by Cochiti female dancers, 59; location of, at San Felipe, 68; location of, at Cochiti, 111, 415n447; at Jemez, 498n869. See also Shyuamo [Turquoise] Kiva

Tusayan. See Hopi Pueblos

Tu-siu-ba: Taos ancestral ruin, on Rio Colorado headwaters, 79–80

Tu-Yo (San Ildefonso area): post-1680 house ruins on, 57; permanent water tanks on, 57; B. equated with Black Mesa, 393n311. See also Black Mesa

Twin Brothers, Twin War Gods: Tewa names for, 48, 386n263; at Taos, 79, 403n373; at San Juan, 81, 102, 163, 403–4n376, 413n431, 456n621; at Cochiti, 153, 281, 403–4n376; at Zuñi, 81, 102, 163, 281, 403–4n376, 413n431, 456n621; distinct from Shiwanna, 397n344. See also Ahiuta; individual Pueblos; Mait-za-laima; Masewa; Oyoyewa

Twin War Gods. See Twin Brothers, Twin War Gods

Twitchell, Ralph E.: used B.'s account of "Franciscan Sepulchres . . . ," 364–70n184

Tylor, J. J. (N.Y.C.): B.'s correspondence with, 114, 115

Typewriter: B. used, 468n692, 531n1044

Tyúonyi, or Tyo'onye (Bandelier Nat. Mon.), 57, 70, 392n305. See also Puwige

Tzé-na-ta, Tze-nat-ay. See La Bajada

Tzigo-umo Ojua (San Juan): B. began to paint at picture of, 162

Tzi-gu-mo. See Tziguma

Tziguma: confusion in identity and location of pueblo ruin of, 73, 107, 114, 230, 413n434, 416n454, 500n881. See also

"Alamo," or "Alamo Solo"; Ciénega; Cieneguilla; Tzi-muc-o

Tzi-muc-o [Tziguma?]: Tano pueblo ruin, 58

Tzi-mu-o. See Tzi-muc-o

Tzi-ojqui (San Juan): tribal officer, "parent" of the Pueblo, 104

Tzi-o-ueno Ojua: name of stone idol in Eldodt's collection, 127

Tzipia-Kué. See Zipias

Tzi-quiat-a-tanye. See Painted Cave

Tzi-quit-e: Towa name for Pecos Pueblo, 275, 529n1030

Tzi-re-ge. See Tshirege

Tzi'ui (San Juan): Candelario Ortiz's office called, 104; one of tribal hierarchy, 104

Tzu-yu-na: ruin at mouth of Rio de Santa Fé, opposite Cochiti, 73

Ua-la-na: Jemez name for own pueblo, 73

Ui-la-na: Tewa name for Picurís Pueblo, 55

Uilat-ha: Taos name for Picurís Pueblo, 79

"Über die Saga des 'Dorado' im nördlichen Süd-Amerika": article by B. in New Yorker Staatszeitung, 437n546

Uisht-yaqqa: third [assistant] cacique, at Cochiti, 57, 59

Umpa (Cochiti): Ompi, or Warriors, 128–29; also known as Matadores and Matalotes, 128–29. See also Cochiti Pueblo: Dances; Cochiti Pueblo: Warriors Society

Uña de Gato, N.M., 63

Union. See Die Union

United States: B. citizen of, 4, 343n101; B. expressed dislike for, on occasion, 30, 343n101; B. unenthusiastic about political democracy in, 543n1121

United States Army: troops in N.M. (1846), 89, 133, 407n398, 495n845; B. copied Mexican campaign doc., 133; Bradley, Gen. Luther P., Commander of Dept. of N.M., 417n458. See also Tenth Infantry Regiment

United States Commissioner of Indian Affairs: contracts for schools with Bureau of Catholic Indian Missions, 508n939. See also Bureau of Catholic Indian Missions

United States Government Forage Agency: at Bouquet's Ranch (Pojoaque), 374n196; at Becker's (Santa Cruz de la Cañada), 408n405

United States Indian Service, Pueblo Indian Agency (Santa Fe): B. at, 114; "Agency" matters, 166; B. obtained population data on N.M. Pueblo Indians from, 216

—Agents: Don Dolores Romero, 166,